PARTICIPATION IN CRIME

This book provides an impressively comprehensive analysis of the key concepts related to participation in crime. From a local perspective, it will be very useful to many Arab Spring countries which are currently endeavouring to reform and modernize their national criminal justice systems to address new forms of criminal liability. The volume could provide valuable solutions to cases pending in the region.

Judge Adel Maged, Vice President at the Court of Cassation (Criminal Chamber), Egypt

Substantive Issues In Criminal Law

Series Editors:
Alan Reed and Michael Bohlander

Substantive Issues in Criminal Law presents a series of volumes that systematically address areas of the criminal law that are in need of reform or which belong to the core areas of law where doctrinal abstraction or greater analysis is required. One part of each book is dedicated to an in-depth look at the situation in the UK, with individual chapters analysing points of current interest. A second feature of each volume is a major comparative section of other domestic jurisdictions. These international contributions are written to a uniform research grid provided by the editors in order to ensure a maximum degree of ease of comparison. The key purpose of the series is to produce a major library of reference works to which all actors in the wider criminal justice and policy community in the UK and elsewhere will have recourse for academic, judicial and policy purposes.

Participation in Crime
Domestic and Comparative Perspectives

Edited by

ALAN REED
Northumbria University, UK

MICHAEL BOHLANDER
Durham University, UK

ASHGATE

Published by
Ashgate Publishing Limited
Wey Court East
Union Road
Farnham
Surrey, GU9 7PT
England

Ashgate Publishing Company
110 Cherry Street
Suite 3-1
Burlington, VT 05401-4405
USA

www.ashgate.com

British Library Cataloguing in Publication Data
Participation in crime : domestic, comparative and
    international perspectives. -- (Substantive issues in
    criminal law)
    1. Criminal liability. 2. Criminal liability--Great
    Britain. 3. Criminal liability (International law)
    I. Series II. Reed, Alan (Matthew Alan) III. Bohlander,
    Michael, 1962-
    345'.04-dc23

Library of Congress Cataloging-in-Publication Data
Participation in crime : domestic, comparative and international
perspectives / By Alan Reed and Michael Bohlander [editors].
    p. cm. -- (Substantive issues in criminal law)
  Includes bibliographical references and index.
  ISBN 978-1-4094-5345-1 (hardback) -- ISBN 978-1-4094-5346-8
(ebook) -- ISBN 978-1-4724-0406-0 (epub) 1. Accomplices. 2.
Accomplices--Great Britain. I. Reed, Alan (Matthew Alan), editor of
compilation. II. Bohlander, Michael, 1962- editor of compilation.
  K5093.P37 2013
  345'.03--dc23

2012044460

ISBN 9781409453451 (hbk)
ISBN 9781409453468 (ebk – PDF)
ISBN 9781472404060 (ebk – ePUB)

Printed and bound in Great Britain
by MPG PRINTGROUP

Contents

Notes on Contributors

Kai Ambos – Legal education at the universities of Freiburg, Oxford and Munich 1984-1990. First State Exam in Bavaria, 1990; Second State Exam in Baden-Wuerttemberg, 1994. LL.D. 1992 and Habilitation (Post-Doc) at the Ludwig-Maximilians University of Munich, 2001 (*venia legendi* in Criminal Law, Criminal Procedure, Criminology, Comparative Law and Public International Law). Former Senior Research Fellow at the Max-Planck Institute for Foreign and International Criminal Law and Senior Research Assistant at the University of Freiburg im Breisgau, Germany. Acting Professor in Freiburg, summer term 2002 and winter term 2002/2003, calls to chairs from the universities of Göttingen and Graz. Since May 2003 Chair of Criminal Law, Criminal Procedure, Comparative Law and International Criminal Law at the Georg-August University of Göttingen, Germany. Head of the Department of Foreign and International Criminal Law, Institute of Criminal Law and Justice at the University of Göttingen. Responsible for the Master's programmes since April 2006. Judge at the District Court (Landgericht) of Lower Saxony in Göttingen since 24 March 2006. Dean of Students of the Faculty of Law at the University of Göttingen between April 2008 and 2010.

Petter Asp is Professor of Criminal Law at Stockholm University and the present holder of the Torsten and Ragnar Söderberg Chair in Legal Science.

Mirko Bagaric is a Professor at the Deakin Law School, Australia. He is the author or co-author of over 25 books and 100 refereed articles. He is the editor or co-editor of several law journals, including Australia's leading criminal law journal: *The Criminal Law Journal*. His main research areas are sentencing, evidence, substantive criminal law, and moral and legal philosophy. He is also a practising lawyer.

Stefanie Bock is a Senior Research Assistant of Professor Dr Kai Ambos, Department for Foreign and International Criminal Law, University of Göttingen and an Assistant Professor in the same department. She has studied law at the University of Hamburg and holds a PhD in Criminal Law from the same university. Prior to taking up her current position, she worked as a research assistant at the universities of Hamburg and Göttingen and as an intern at the International Criminal Court. Her main fields of research are international criminal law, European criminal law and comparative criminal law.

Michael Bohlander is the Chair in Comparative and International Criminal Law at Durham Law School and the Visiting Chair in Criminal Law at the Rijksuniversiteit Groningen in the Netherlands.

Manuel Cancio Meliá – México, D.F., 1967. Licenciado en Derecho (= JD; Universidad Autónoma de Madrid), 1991; Doctor en Derecho (= PhD; UAM), 1997. Alexander-von-Humboldt Research Fellow (Universität Bonn, Universität München, Universität Freiburg), 2002/2009. Dr. *honoris causa* (Universidad Peruana los Andes, Huancayo, Perú), 2008. Professor of Criminal Law at the Universidad Autónoma de Madrid (2000-2008: *profesor titular* [associate professor]; since

2008: *catedrático* [full professor]). His publications (books, chapters, articles, case discussions), regarding criminal law principles, criminal law legal theory, comparative criminal law studies, European criminal law and several single offences (sexual crimes, personal injuries, crimes against the environment, organised crime, terrorism), have been published in Spain, most countries of Latin America, Germany, the United States, Italy, Portugal, Great Britain, Turkey, Taiwan and the People's Republic of China. He is a member of the advisory boards of several Spanish, Latin American and German Journals on criminal law.

Luis E. Chiesa is an Associate Professor at Pace Law School, New York. He obtained his law degree from the University of Puerto Rico and his Master's in Law (LLM) and Doctorate in Law (JSD) from Columbia University. Professor Chiesa served as the Rembe Distinguished Visiting Professor at the University of Washington. He is currently a member of the visiting faculty at the Torcuato Di Tella University in Buenos Aires, Argentina, and at the Sergio Arboleda University in Bogota, Colombia. He has published over 20 scholarly articles on various topics, including substantive and procedural criminal law and comparative criminal law.

Claire de Than, BA (Hons) LLB, LLM is a Senior Lecturer in Law at City University, London, having previously held appointments at two London University colleges. A graduate of Queen Mary, University of London, she is the author or co-author of more than 15 books, including Heaton and de Than, *Criminal Law* (Oxford University Press, 2010), de Than and Shorts, *International Criminal Law and Human Rights* (Sweet and Maxwell, 2004). She has also published articles in a variety of national and international journals, including the *Modern Law Review*. Her research fields include human rights law, media law and criminal law. She has advised several governments and many organisations on human rights and law reform issues, with specialisation in the law of British Overseas Territories and Crown Dependencies.

Susan Edwards is Professor of Law and former Dean of Law of Buckingham Law School. She is currently University Dean of Research and is a practising barrister and a Door Tenant at Clarendon Chambers London. She has acted as an expert witness in both civil and criminal cases of domestic violence and also acted in a consultancy capacity with regard to domestic violence in Europe and elsewhere. Her work on domestic violence and homicide spans several decades during which time she has advised the police, the CPS and also trained police forces in Denmark, Spain and Germany. Her work explores the interface of gender and culture, ethnicity and identity as these concepts impose themselves on the construction and interpretation of criminal and human rights law.

Catherine Elliott, LLB, barr., DEA, is a Senior Lecturer at City University, London. She has written extensively on both English and French criminal law. Her publications include a successful text book entitled *Criminal Law* (Pearson, and now in its eighth edition); a monograph entitled *French Criminal Law* (Willan, 2001) and a chapter on French criminal law in *The Handbook of Comparative Criminal Law* (Stanford University Press, 2011).

Jesse Elvin graduated with a PhD in Law from the London School of Economics in 2005. He is a Senior Lecturer in Law at City University London, where criminal law is one of his specialist fields. He has published in a number of leading journals, including the *Modern Law Review*, the *Cambridge Law Journal*, the *Law Quarterly Review*, the *King's Law Journal* (formerly known as the *King's College Law Journal*) and *Feminist Legal Studies*.

Rudi Fortson QC, LLB (Lond.), barrister, has been a criminal law practitioner for over 30 years at 25 Bedford Row, London, and a Visiting Professor of Law at Queen Mary, University of London. He has written and lectured extensively on criminal law issues. He was a member of the Police Foundation Independent Inquiry into the Misuse of Drugs Act 1971 and a member of the Criminal Justice Forum for the Institute of Public Policy Research (IPPR). He is a member of the Criminal Bar Association of England and Wales, the Proceeds of Crime Lawyers Association, the Forensic Science Society and the British Academy of Forensic Science.

Alisdair Gillespie is Professor of Criminal Law and Justice at Lancaster University. He is qualified as a member of the Bar (Middle Temple) and he has previously taught at the universities of Durham and Teesside and De Montfort University in Leicester. His primary research interest is the law relating to the sexual exploitation of children, particularly when facilitated by information and communication technologies. He has written several books and articles on this topic and regularly advises national and international governments, NGOs and law enforcement. Professor Gillespie sits on the Advisory Board of INHOPE, the International Association of Internet Hotlines, and is the case note editor for the *Journal of Criminal Law*.

Ana M. Garrocho Salcedo concluded her LLM in 2007 and is in her final year as a PhD student at Carlos III University (Madrid), where she is currently working as a teaching assistant in the Department of Criminal Law, Procedural Law and History Law. She was Visiting Researcher at Georg-August Universität Göttingen and at Universität zu Köln (2006, 2008) and has been a qualified lawyer at the Madrid Bar Association since October 2011. Her research interests are connected to criminal law and international criminal law, which are also the areas in which she teaches. Her doctoral dissertation focuses on superior responsibility in international criminal law.

Mohammad Hedayati-Kakhki graduated from Durham University in 2008 with a PhD in Middle Eastern Politics and Law. He qualified from Shahid Beheshti University in Tehran in 1990 with a Law degree and subsequently completed a Master's in International Law at the University of Shiraz (Iran) in 1999. He practised both civil and criminal law as a First Class Attorney within the Islamic legal system of Iran. Alongside teaching LLM modules including Islamic Law at Durham Law School, he continues his involvement in legal practice by acting as an expert in human rights and asylum cases. He is frequently appointed to conduct research and provide commentary into various aspects of Islamic law. He is also a special advisor to the Centre for Criminal Law and Criminal Justice at Durham University.

Jonathan Herring is a Fellow in Law at Exeter College, Oxford University and university Lecturer in Law at the Law Faculty, Oxford University. He has written on family law, medical law, criminal law and legal issues surrounding old age. His books include: *Older People in Law and Society* (Oxford University Press, 2009); *European Human Rights and Family Law* (Hart, 2010) (with Shazia Choudhry); *Medical Law and Ethics* (Oxford University Press, 2010); *Criminal Law* (4th edn, Oxford University Press, 2010); *Family Law* (4th edn, Pearson, 2009); and *The Woman Who Tickled too Much* (Pearson, 2009).

Michael Hirst is Professor of Criminal Justice at Leicester De Montfort Law School. He writes on a wide range of issues in criminal law, evidence and road traffic law and has been a major contributor to each edition of *Blackstone's Criminal Practice*. Other recent work includes: *Jurisdiction and the Ambit of the Criminal Law* (Oxford University Press, 2003); *Halsbury's*

Laws of England, vol. 11 (2006, with R. Card); *Sexual Offences* (with A. Gillespie and R. Card) (Jordan Publishing, 2008) 'Interpreting the New Concept of Hearsay', *Cambridge Law Journal*, with D.J. Birch, 2010); and articles in the *Criminal Law Review* and *Journal of Criminal Law* on the sentencing of road traffic homicide offenders, Sir Edward Coke's famous definition of murder, hearsay evidence, and jurisdiction over complicity in suicide abroad.

Gerhard Kemp, BA LLB LLM LLD (Stellenbosch) ILSC (Antwerp) is Professor of Criminal Law and International Criminal Law in the Faculty of Law, University of Stellenbosch, South Africa and advocate of the High Court of South Africa. He is Visiting Lecturer in International Criminal Law at the Nelson Mandela Metropolitan University, Port Elizabeth and at the University of Cape Town. Gerhard is the author of various books, chapters in books and journal articles in the fields of criminal justice and international criminal law. He serves on the editorial boards of the *African Yearbook of International Humanitarian Law* and the *Law and Justice Review* (Turkey). Gerhard serves on the board of directors and the executive committee of the Institute for Justice and Reconciliation (Cape Town) and serves as expert consultant to the Institute for Security Studies' Southern Africa curriculum development project for training courses in international criminal justice

Fiona Leverick is a Senior Lecturer in Criminal Law and Criminal Justice at the University of Glasgow, Scotland. She has published extensively in the field of criminal law and procedure, including two books on criminal defences, *Killing in Self-Defence* (Oxford University Press, 2006) and *Criminal Defences and Pleas in Bar of Trial* (W. Green/Scottish Universities Law Institute, 2006). Her work has been published in law journals including the *Modern Law Review* and the *Criminal Law Review*. She has been commissioned (along with James Chalmers) to write the fourth edition of the leading Scottish text on criminal law, Gordon's *Criminal Law*, for publication in 2014.

Ben Livings is Senior Lecturer in the Department of Law at the University of Sunderland. His research centres on socio-cultural conceptions of crime and examinations of the relationship between notions of culpability and the role of policy in the criminal justice system.

Barry Mitchell is Professor of Criminal Law and Criminal Justice at Coventry University. One of his principal research interests is in the arena of homicide law on which he has published widely. Barry's research has been both theoretical and empirical, and he has worked with various government departments including the Law Commission, the Ministry of Justice, the Home Office and the Crown Prosecution Service. He has conducted public opinion surveys on homicide and the law and recently, in collaboration with Julian Roberts (Professor of Criminology at Oxford University) carried out the first survey of attitudes towards the mandatory life sentence for murder.

R. Murat Önok, BA (Izmir Dokuz Eylul University, 2000), LLM (Izmir Dokuz Eylul University, Social Sciences Institute, 2002), PhD (Izmir Dokuz Eylul University, Social Sciences Institute, 2005), is currently an Assistant Professor in the Law School at Koç University, Istanbul. Dr Önok's fields of research are criminal law, human rights law and international criminal law. He has also been teaching international law since 2007. Dr. Önok is the author of two books (*The International Criminal Court and Its Historical Perspective* (Turhan, 2003), *The Crime of Torture within Its International Dimension* (Seckin, 2006)), and co-author of three textbooks (*Theory and Practice of the Special Part of Penal Law* (7th edn, Seckin, 2010), *International Criminal Law* (Seckin, 2009),

Handbook on Human Rights (4th edn, Seckin, 2011)). He has also written three book chapters, including 'Penal Law', in *Introduction to Turkish Law* (6th edn, Kluwer International, 2011).

Alan Reed graduated from Trinity College, Cambridge University with a first class honours degree in Law, and was awarded the Herbert Smith Prize for Conflict of Laws and the Dr Lancey Prize. Cambridge University awarded him a full Holland Scholarship to facilitate study in the United States and he obtained an LLM Master's of Law (Comparative Law) at the University of Virginia. After completion of the Law Society Finals Examinations he spent three years in practice in London at Addleshaw Goddard, and also acted as a tutor in Criminal Law at Trinity College, Cambridge. He spent seven years as a lecturer in Law at Leeds University, and from 2001 to 2012 was engaged as Professor of Criminal and Private International Law and Director of Research at Sunderland University. In April 2012 he commenced new roles as Associate Dean (Research and Innovation) and Professor of Law at Northumbria Law School. Alan has published over 200 monographs, textbooks and articles in the substantive arena in leading journals in England, Australia, New York, Florida and Los Angeles. For the last 10 years he has been editor of the *Journal of Criminal Law*.

Kent Roach is a Professor of Law and Prichard-Wilson Chair of Law and Public Policy at the University of Toronto Faculty of Law, with cross-appointments in criminology and political science. He is a graduate of the University of Toronto and of Yale, and a former law clerk to Justice Bertha Wilson of the Supreme Court of Canada. Professor Roach has been editor-in-chief of the *Criminal Law Quarterly* since 1998. In 2002 he was elected a Fellow of the Royal Society of Canada. Professor Roach's books include: *Constitutional Remedies in Canada* (winner of the 1997 Owen Prize for best law book), *Due Process and Victims' Rights: The New Law and Politics of Criminal Justice* (short-listed for the 1999 Donner Prize for best public policy book), *The Supreme Court on Trial: Judicial Activism or Democratic Dialogue* (short-listed for the 2001 Donner Prize), *September 11: Consequences for Canada* (named one of the five most significant books of 2003 by the *Literary Review of Canada*) and (with Robert J. Sharpe) *Brian Dickson: A Judge's Journey* (winner of the 2004 J.W. Dafoe Prize for best contribution to the understanding of Canada). He is also the author of *The Unique Challenges of Terrorism Prosecutions: Towards a Workable Relation Between Intelligence and Evidence* (2010) and *Criminal Law* (4th edn, 2009) and co-author (with Robert J. Sharpe) of *The Charter of Rights and Freedoms* (4th edn, 2009), (with Ken Jull and Todd Archibald) of *Regulatory and Corporate Liability: From Due Diligence to Risk Management* (2005) and (with Bibi Sanga, and Robert Moles) of *Forensic Investigations and Miscarriages of Justice* (2010). His most recent book is *The 9/11 Effect: Comparative Counter-Terrorism* (Cambridge University Press, 2011). Professor Roach is also the co-editor of several collections of essays including *Global Anti-Terrorism Law and Policy* (2nd edn, 2011) (1st edn, 2005), *Taking Remedies Seriously* (2010), *Access to Care: Access to Justice* (2005) and *The Security of Freedom* (2001) and several published casebooks. He has also written over 160 articles and chapters published in Australia, China, Hong Kong, India, Israel, Italy, Singapore, South Africa, the United Kingdom and the United States, as well as in Canada.

Emma Smith is Lecturer in Law at Northumbria University. Emma obtained a first class honours degree at Sunderland University, was awarded the Morton's Solicitors Award for Outstanding Achievement in Law and also obtained the faculty Criminal Law Prize. She commenced a new role as Postgraduate Academic Assistant in Law at the University of Sunderland in 2011 subsequent to an LLM distinction in Criminal Law and Procedure and the award for Best Student Performance of that year. Emma is now an academic at Northumbria University and is studying for her PhD at the same institution. Research interests centre predominantly around the law of criminal evidence, focusing specifically on evidence of bad character and expert evidence and on complicity principles. Emma has a number of forthcoming articles to be published in this area. Emma is also a member of the Socio-Legal Studies Association, the Society of Legal Scholars and the European Association of Psychology and Law.

John Stannard is a graduate of Oxford University, and has been on the staff of the Queen's University of Belfast since 1977. He has written widely on criminal law topics in a variety of journals including the *Irish Jurist*, *Legal Studies* and the *Law Quarterly Review*, and is the author of a textbook on Northern Ireland criminal procedure. He is a member of the Society of Legal Scholars, of the Irish Legal History Society and a Fellow of the Institute of Teaching and Learning. He is also a Past President of the Irish Association of Law Teachers.

Bob Sullivan is Professor of Criminal Law at University College, London. His research interests are in the fields of substantive criminal law and criminal law theory. He is co-author of Simester and Sullivan's *Criminal Law: Theory and Doctrine* (4th edn, Hart, 2010, with Simester, Spencer and Virgo). He has published widely in the leading general and specialist journals.

Julia Tolmie (LLB (Hons) (Auckland), LLM (Harvard)) is an Associate Professor at the Faculty of Law, University of Auckland. Prior to taking up her position with the University of Auckland in 1999 she was an academic on the Faculty of Law, University of Sydney for 10 years. She has researched and published extensively on issues arising within criminal law, family law and feminist legal theory across a number of jurisdictions and has spent brief periods of time as a visiting scholar at the University of Ottawa, Golden Gate University and Berkeley University.

Magnus Ulväng is Professor of Criminal Law at Uppsala University.

William Wilson is Professor of Criminal Law at Queen Mary, University of London. He is the author of *Criminal Law: Doctrine and Theory* (4th edn, Longmans, 2011) and *Central Issues in Criminal Theory* (Hart, 2002).

Hein Wolswijk is a Senior Lecturer in Criminal Law at the University of Groningen. He studied law at the University of Utrecht and graduated in 1991, with special focus on criminal law and legal theory. He obtained his doctorate in 1998 *cum laude* with a thesis on 'Locus Delicti and Criminal Jurisdiction'. From 1996 until 2000 he was a Lecturer in Environmental Law and Criminal Law at the University of Amsterdam. Since 2001 he has worked at the Department of Criminal Law and Criminology at the University of Groningen.

Preface

We are pleased to be able to present the second volume of our joint cooperation in areas of substantive criminal law, following on from the previous collection on *Loss of Control and Diminished Responsibility*, also with Ashgate. At the same time, this volume is the start of a new major series called 'Substantive Issues in Criminal Law', which will over the next few years systematically address areas of the criminal law in the UK that are in need of reform or which belong to the core areas of law where doctrinal abstraction or greater analysis is required. One part of each book will be dedicated to an in-depth look at the situation in the UK, with individual chapters analysing points of current interest. A second feature of each volume will be a major comparative section of, we hope, mostly the same foreign (and occasionally international) jurisdictions. These foreign contributions will all be written to a uniform research grid provided by the editors in order to ensure a maximum degree of ease of comparison. In this manner we intend to produce a major library of reference works to which all actors in the wider criminal justice and policy community in the UK and elsewhere will have recourse for academic, judicial and policy purposes.

As with the previous volume, we thank our contributing authors for their willingness to commit to such a time-consuming and demanding project, and for putting up with the manifold requests from the editors in the process of putting their manuscripts together into a coherent volume. We owe a great debt of gratitude to Nicola Wake and Emma Smith, who provided cheerful, unflappable and above all meticulous and sterling support in the collation, proof-reading and formatting of the final manuscript. We could not have done it without them.

We have endeavoured to state the law as in force in each jurisdiction on 31 August 2012.

Alan Reed
Michael Bohlander
Northumbria; Durham/Groningen, September 2012

Introduction

For a long time, issues of inculpatory engagement concomitant with disparate thresholds of complicitous behaviour have plagued the legal system of England and Wales. The criminal justice system has struggled in vain to extrapolate overarching principles that can apply effectively to various types of participatory involvement and any general basis of attributing criminal liability for the acts of others. The plethora of recent cases before the Supreme Court and the Court of Appeal have raised more questions than they provided answers in terms of comprehensive guidance. Our aim in editing this volume, as with the earlier edition on *Loss of Control and Diminished Responsibility*, is to produce a point of reference in the substantive arena relating to participation in crime. The Law Commission Paper *Participating in Crime*[1] revealed significant problems in the adoption of consistent approaches to doctrinal and theoretical underpinnings of complicity liability, and their proposals, although emboldening the debate, have yet to be adopted for secondary party liability. In a similar vein, the Law Commission Report,[2] outlining proposed reforms to the extant law on conspiracy and attempts, continues to gather dust on the Government's library shelves. Such piecemeal reform as has occurred has been in the limited context within Part 2 of the Serious Crime Act 2007, replacing common law incitement with new offences embracing acts of assisting or encouraging crime. Even here it is arguable that legislative development has simply created a range of offences delineated more by mud than by crystal, their interpretation hampered by imprecise and tautological drafting. This book's chapters by individual contributors, domestic and comparative, explore the fundamental precepts of participatory engagement, including a range of key issues within the spectrum of complicity liability. This includes chapters on England and Wales, Scotland and Ireland, as well as alternative approaches from several foreign jurisdictions. In Chapter 1, entitled 'Participating in Homicide', Barry Mitchell commences with an analysis of English law which has been littered with controversial issues regarding secondary liability, especially those relating to accessorial behaviour and foresight of the principal's conduct. Most of the issues are concerned with the substantive law but they also raise matters of evidence. The problems relating to participation in crime are particularly acute in homicide where the law recognises more than one offence. As the Law Commission and various commentators have demonstrated, there is the added complication of fixing the exact locus in the hierarchy of offences of an accessory's liability. The chapter critically examines the arguments and incorporates relevant comparative material from both common law and civil jurisdictions.

Bob Sullivan, in Chapter 2 entitled 'Accessories and Principals after *Gnango*', considers in depth the case of *R v Gnango*, in which D and P, each armed with a revolver, confronted each other in a public place and exchanged several rounds of fire. A shot aimed by P at D hit and killed V, a passer-by. For reasons unknown, P was not brought to trial. D was tried and convicted for the murder of V. He appealed successfully to the Court of Appeal. By a majority the Supreme Court restored the murder conviction. Lords Phillips, Judge and Wilson found that D was P's accomplice in the murder of V. Lords Brown and Clarke found that D had murdered V as a principal offender. It is argued that all members of the majority construed the facts of the case in a manner that went beyond the evidence. Further, it is argued that doctrinal conceptions of accomplices and principal offenders were taken beyond their proper limits.

---

1 Law Com. No. 305, 2007.
2 Law Com. No. 318.

Chapter 3, 'Locating Complicity: Choice, Character, Participation, Dangerousness and the Liberal Subjectivist', co-authored by Ben Livings and Emma Smith, suggests that the imposition of criminal liability for complicity runs counter to the prevailing liberal political ethos of the criminal law, whereby responsibility is incurred by the autonomous individual, with the capacity and freedom to exercise choice and control. The individual who is to be subjected to the harsh regime of criminal law is normatively presumed to be able to bring about or avoid the consequences of her actions; to engage or disengage from the behaviour that might form the causative element of an offence. Criminal liability is thus rooted in the idea of the autonomous individual; its foundation in the subsequent behaviour of another is problematic. Tied to these moral and philosophical issues, there are also doctrinal problems, insofar as it is difficult to fix both the type and extent of liability to be incurred by the complicit individual. As a result of this, complicity and the concept of the 'joint enterprise' are subjects that have greatly exercised the minds of the legal community in recent years. They have been addressed repeatedly by the Law Commission and resulted in a recent consultation paper on behalf of the Justice Committee. The chapter examines the place of complicity within the criminal law, and examines the moral and political foundations underpinning its existence.

Chapter 4, '"The Straw Woman" at Law's Precipice: An Unwilling Party', by Susan Edwards highlights that women's role in participation is historically ambiguous. Statute has presumed since 1925[3] a defence of marital coercion. Regarded as a quaint relic of past times, it was once considered that, since women had no personhood or agency, when a woman committed a crime then she must be acting under her husband's influence. The notion of women as passive within crime commission, or else mad or in some way mentally deficient, has been challenged by feminism as detrimental to women's agency. In contemporary times it is far less the case that the marital bond exerts a coercive influence and far more the case that the duress under which women sometimes find themselves flows from a partner's violence and the persistence of structural inequality which leads women to economic dependency. Indeed, these structural inequalities and differences are raised by feminist jurisprudence as relevant and necessary considerations to constructing participation and women's engagement in some spheres of criminal activity.

To recognise that women are coerced by men where there is domestic violence is merely to recognise the physical difference between the sexes in all but a minuscule portion of the cases. This 'coercion' leads to women's complicity not only through active participation but through omission especially in the spheres of criminal activity which involve women as parties with regard to a partner's or husband's domestic violence and sexual abuse against children. Indeed, the law recognised this and instituted the offence of failure to act where children become the victims of murder by one of the parties (Domestic Violence, Crime and Victims Act 2004).

As victims of domestic violence themselves, women are also parties to a wide range of criminal offences. However, defence lawyers in the US have developed this to a finer degree than in the UK and in this regard the expert witness has played a major role. In some spheres, however, to rob them of agency as secondary parties or accomplices is to deny women the quality as free agents and so the question must be asked with regard to the role women play in a joint enterprise, as, for example, in so-called honour killings: is it the case that here they also act under a kind of duress of so-called 'customary patriarchy'? In considering women's role in participation one must also consider how defences to crime as both principal and secondary parties have evolved particularly with regard to the battered woman syndrome 'defence', which has functioned in the UK to mitigate the harshness of the law in the context of murder, whilst in the US has a much wider influence across a range of offences. Duress is in the author's view also inherently gendered as the factors which have been

---

3   s 47 Criminal Justice Act 1925; see *R v Shortland*, *R v Darwin*.

included in its ambit have traditionally considered primarily the use or threat of force to act in mitigation. To rob women of agency as secondary parties to crime is to eclipse some of the very questions about the way in which gender functions in this area of the law.

Jonathan Herring, in Chapter 5, 'Victims as Defendants: When Victims Participate in Crimes against Themselves', addresses the well-known *Tyrrell* principle, but looks more broadly at cases where the victim has played a role in the injuries caused to them. This also includes the *Kennedy* case law (prosecution of drug dealers in cases where the drug user has died); gross negligence manslaughter cases involving 'contributory negligence' (for example *Wacker*); the case law on transmission of HIV; and cases on drunken victims of sexual assault. It is argued that the courts have struggled to secure the divide between who is the victim and who is the defendant. A bipartite approach has developed and the law is currently structured so that either the victim becomes responsible for their own injuries, or their blameworthiness is irrelevant. As a result, criminal law is in stark contrast with the law of tort where through the notion of contributory negligence blameworthiness can be divided between the claimant and defendant. The approach of the criminal law, however, is supported; indeed the fact that the victim has contributed to their injuries in many cases can be seen as an aggravating, rather than mitigating, feature.

Alan Reed, in Chapter 6, entitled 'Repentance and Forgiveness: Withdrawal from Participation Liability and the Proportionality Test', explores the ways in which English law has always recognised that a person who has embarked on a criminal enterprise may withdraw from it and save him or herself from a criminal liability in respect of it. This applies, of course, unless they have already reached the stage of an inchoate offence such as conspiracy or attempt for which English law does not recognise the possibility of withdrawal. The ambits of such a defence are unfortunately extremely unclear, providing another illustration of the uncertainty pervading the whole substantive area of the law on complicity. The limits of the defence remain controversial, and it is also opaque as to whether it operates within the sphere of presenting an inducement for a defendant to withdraw or alternatively as an iteration of their reduced level of blameworthy engagement. However, as stated by the Law Commission,[4] considerations of social policy support the argument that if an accessory counters their assistance with equally obstructive measures, an acquittal ought to follow given their efforts to right the wrong. The chapter examines the underlying bases upon which this extant defence ought to be constructed, evaluates the precedential edifice currently in place, and suggests a reformulated template for the future. It considers the most recent Law Commission proposals set out in *Participating in Crime*[5] wherein the contours of the defence were mechanistically set as, 'negating the effect of the assistance, encouragement or agreement', and the jury as fact finders were promoted to determine this prescribed threshold. It is necessary to re-examine the putative search currently engaged in a proportionality test for the constituents of an effective withdrawal as a defence to liability, and this focus may be aided by extirpation of comparative US and Australian doctrinal analysis.

William Wilson, in Chapter 7, 'Participating in Crime: Some Thoughts on the Retribution/ Prevention Dichotomy in Preparation for Crime and How to Deal with It', identifies and considers questions arising from the current law on attempts. Most jurisdictions have a law of attempt. They tend to grapple with the same problems; when does an attempt begin; can there be an attempt when the substantive offence is impossible; what *mens rea* is appropriate and so on. The conclusions which these different jurisdictions come to are often quite similar. The question posed in this chapter is: what does the law of attempts do that could not be equally well done by some other device? This is becoming increasingly pertinent due to a significant change in the way law enforcement

---

4 Law Com. No. 131.
5 Law Com. No. 305.

is conceived. Recent developments in criminal justice indicate that control and prevention are replacing retribution as the primary basis for state intervention. The chapter considers whether, given the conceptual difficulties of reconciling issues of law enforcement and desert, it is time to refashion the law's approach to preparatory crime to reflect this emphasis?

In Chapters 8 and 9, 'Conspiracy' and 'Attempt', by Jesse Elvin and Claire de Than, the authors argue that within the field of secondary participation in crime, it is important not to ignore the key and close relationship that such liability has with inchoate offences. Where D participates in a joint illegal enterprise or is otherwise complicit in a crime, a single course of conduct could lead to liability under the rules relating to both complicity and inchoate offences, depending on the stage at which D was arrested, and whether the full offence can be proved. For example, as the Law Commission has stated, 'If D1 and D2 agree to commit a crime (say, murder), and the murder is consequently carried out either by D1 alone, by D2 alone, or by D1 and D2 acting together, D1 and D2 are guilty of murder, and of conspiracy to murder'.[6] Conversely, D may think that he or she is participating in a joint enterprise that will amount to a crime, but not be caught by either set of rules: as the Law Commission has pointed out, 'secondary liability is a derivative form of liability in that D's liability derives from and is [generally] dependent on an offence committed by P ... If P does not commit or attempt to commit the offence that D has encouraged or assisted, D may still be liable but only if his or her conduct amounts to an "inchoate" offence'.[7] There has been commentary about the relationship between complicity and inchoate liability; for example, in relation to the Law Commission's 1993 proposal that, with the possible exception of the retention of the joint enterprise liability, the doctrine of secondary liability should be abolished. However, further work needs to be done on the interplay between inchoate offences and participation in crime. The authors seek to explore this interplay with reference to 'hard cases' and the use of hypothetical scenarios. Developments in other relevant jurisdictions will also be examined.

The Serious Crime Act 2007 introduced new offences relating to encouraging or assisting an offence. However, it did not reform the law relating to secondary liability or to two major inchoate offences: attempt or conspiracy. The Law Commission recommended reform to these two offences in 2009, proposing a series of amendments to the statutory law on conspiracy (it was not asked to consider common law conspiracy) and attempt but abandoning its 2007 provisional suggestion that there should be 'a newly defined offence of "attempt", complemented by a new offence of "criminal preparation"'.[8] One significant issue to be considered is the extent to which these 2009 recommendations would improve the law. Another important issue is whether the Law Commission was correct to abandon its 1993 proposals and decide that 'there are compelling reasons for retaining secondary liability in many cases where P goes on to commit or attempt to commit an offence that D has encouraged or assisted'.[9] Chapter 8, 'Conspiracy', analyses the law relating to conspiracy and its relationship to the participation offences. The authors argue that there are strong reasons in favour of streamlining the law between inchoate offences and participation in crime. Again, the statutory version of the offence under the Criminal Law Act 1977 removed various problems in the law, but it is argued that there is still work to be done. Unlike attempt, conspiracy continues to be governed partially by the common law with the result that parallel structures of common law and statutory conspiracies exist, yet with different definitional elements. The rules relating to common law conspiracy raise human rights concerns with their lack of clarity and predictability. Chapter 9, 'Attempt', examines

---

6   *Conspiracy and Attempts* (Law Com No 318, 2009) 1.58.
7   *Inchoate Liability for Assisting or Encouraging Crime* (Law Com No 300, 2006) 1.8.
8   Law Com No 318 (n 1) 1.90.
9   Law Com No 300 (n 2) 1.18.

the law relating to attempt, with reference to assisting and encouraging crime where relevant. The Criminal Attempts Act 1981 significantly reformed the law, but there are still some unresolved issues. What amounts to going beyond 'mere preparation' varies a great deal in cases; this variation may mean that the law is not compliant with Articles 5 and 7 of the European Convention on Human Rights. Furthermore, there is duplication of offences on the facts of many cases: for example where D committed inchoate offences and participated in a joint enterprise. This issue is not unique to the boundary between inchoate offences and secondary participation, but it is important to consider whether this duplication is desirable. Moreover, there is a lack of clarity as to precisely what it is that is being criminalised with attempt. One view is that 'the essence of the offence of attempt is intention … [and that] the acts which may amount to the *actus reus* derive their significance from the accused's intention'.[10] However, this does not sit easily with decisions such as *Taafe*,[11] where the House of Lords held that D cannot be liable for attempting to commit an act believing it to be a criminal offence when it is not. It is easy to understand the argument of the prosecution that D was morally blameworthy and deserving of criminal punishment 'because: (a) he knew that he was involving himself as the crucial instrument in a sophisticated operation to deceive customs; and (b) he knew that deception was operated to bring in prohibited goods and/or (c) he did not care to find out, though he could have done, the precise nature of the prohibited goods'.[12] Should D have been convicted under the rules relating to inchoate offences for his part in the operation to deceive customs?

Chapter 10, 'Inchoate Liability and the Part 2 Offences under the Serious Crime Act 2007', by Rudi Fortson QC, posits that three offences enacted under Part 2 of the Serious Crime Act 2007, were introduced as part of a scheme to modernise the law of incitement and law relating to secondary liability. In particular, the Act was intended to fill a gap in the law where a person (D) *assisted* another (P) to commit an offence, which P did not then go on to commit. However, the reach of these offences is considerably widened by embracing acts of *encouraging* crime, and widened even further by s 49(1) of the Act, which makes it immaterial whether the anticipated offence was committed or not. Technically complex, to the point of creating an almost impenetrable structure, the offences have rarely been used by prosecutors. But attitudes are changing and prosecutors are gaining confidence – especially in drug cases – to charge a Part 2 offence. Seen through the eyes of a criminal law practitioner, and noting the emerging case law, this chapter discusses the considerable potential of Part 2, its weaknesses and its incoherence.

In Chapter 11, 'Participation on the Internet', Alisdair Gillespie notes that the internet and related communication technologies allow individuals to communicate with one another easily. Whilst the benefits of the internet are well recognised, it is increasingly recognised that it is also possible to commit crimes on, or facilitated by, the internet. The fact that the internet is a global network of users means that this criminality can just as easily be by more than one party and so issues of participation arise. The chapter examines the application of participation on the internet by examining two key issues: the first is known as 'cybersuicide', that is the behaviour whereby a person provides assistance or encouragement to another person who wishes to commit suicide. The second issue is the liability of internet service providers (ISPs) for the hosting and distribution of child pornography material which requires the use of an ISP to gain access to the internet itself. Should these bodies be liable through participation for the actions of their customers who access or distribute child pornography? It is argued that rather than relying on traditional conceptions of participation the law has sometimes reacted by the introduction of specific rules governing this behaviour.

---

10   Michael Allen, *Textbook on Criminal Law* (Eleventh Edition, Oxford University Press, 2011).
11   [1984] AC 539.
12   Ibid. 541.

Chapter 12, by Michael Hirst, on 'Territorial and Extraterritorial Dimensions', performs an examination of the issue of territorial and extraterritorial jurisdiction. It examines jurisdiction over complicity in substantive offences and also jurisdiction over inchoate crimes involving solicitation, encouragement or the provision of assistance in respect of proposed offences. The author is currently involved in a project on conflicts of criminal jurisdiction within the European Union and use is made of some comparative material gleaned from the jurisdiction project. Although almost always referred to as 'jurisdiction', the real issue as far as English law is concerned is the ambit of the criminal law itself, or in other words the breadth of the relevant *actus reus*. If English law applies (either on a territorial or extraterritorial basis) there will be a court with jurisdiction to convict and punish the offender. Cases of complicity or solicitation etc. frequently give rise to cross-frontier jurisdiction/ambit issues because with modern technology and communications a person in one country can very easily assist or encourage the actions of a person in another country. The crime may indeed take effect in a third country and the local laws of each such country may differ significantly.

Chapter 13, by Fiona Leverick, 'Participation in Crime under Scots Law: The Doctrine of Art and Part', considers the ways in which Scots criminal law recognises three forms of general participatory liability: complicity, conspiracy and incitement. The chapter focuses primarily on the first of these: liability incurred through participation or, as it is termed in Scotland, art and part liability. Art and part liability was recognised in Scotland as early as the twelfth century and traces of this early law can be seen in its modern conception. The Scots law of art and part is, on the face of it, deceptively simple as it recognises no formal distinction between the parties involved in an enterprise (there is, for example, no formal distinction between principals and accessories). All that is required is some form of assistance and a 'common purpose'. Upon closer examination, however, the law is anything but straightforward. The case law has developed in a piecemeal manner with inconsistencies between recent judgments and a general lack of clarity. A distinction has developed in the case law between antecedent concert and spontaneous concert, but the law lacks a clear definition of each category alongside its accompanying requirements for liability and some recent judgments do not refer to the distinction at all. In addition, on a more general level, in failing to recognise distinctions between levels of liability, the law can also be criticised on fair labelling terms.

Chapter 14, 'Bishops in the Dock: Child Abuse and the Irish Law of Complicity', by John Stannard, puts forth the argument that one of the most striking scandals of recent years in Irish public life has been the failure of the Roman Catholic Church and of other responsible authorities to deal adequately with the problems of child abuse. There have been calls for the arrest and prosecution of bishops and cardinals, and even of the pope himself. Indeed, a Bill has recently been introduced in the Irish Parliament with the aim of imposing a legal duty to report such conduct to the police, even where the information has been obtained under the seal of the confessional. The purpose of the chapter is to examine how the criminal law of Ireland, both North and South, imposes liability in this situation to parties other than the actual wrongdoer. In particular, three issues are addressed, the first being liability as an accomplice to the crime, the second being liability for assisting offenders, and the third liability for failing to disclose criminal conduct to the authorities. The chapter seeks to explore whether and to what extent the present law strikes an appropriate balance between the legitimate interests of the various parties concerned.

These chapters on individual *foci* in the UK debate are followed by comparative expositions across a broad range of foreign legal systems. These are all written to a uniform research grid to allow a maximum degree of comparability, and span jurisdictions as diverse as Australia, Canada, France, Germany, the Netherlands, New Zealand, Shari'ah law, South Africa, Spain, Sweden, Turkey and the United States.

Chapter 1
Participating in Homicide

Barry Mitchell

Introduction

This chapter is ultimately concerned with the possible liability of people who do not actually perpetrate the fatal assault in a homicide, but they have done something that in some way 'links' them with the victim's death, albeit indirectly. Unfortunately, determining the precise nature of their liability is potentially complicated by the fact that English law currently recognises three distinct but related forms of criminal liability that might be appropriate. In some instances, the prosecution may even have a choice as to which charges to pursue.

Résumé of Secondary (or Accessorial) Liability for Homicide

Under section 8 of the Accessories and Abettors Act 1861 D may be liable as a secondary party (or accessory) to a homicide by aiding, abetting, counselling or procuring the homicide. If D gives help or support he may aid it. If he encourages P (the principal) to commit a homicide, perhaps by inciting or instigating it, he may abet homicide. Counselling homicide also involves encouraging it, though whereas abetting traditionally implies encouragement whilst the homicide is being committed, counselling is more likely for encouragement before the homicide. In all three cases, D need not cause P to commit homicide.[1] P should be aware of D's encouragement but there need be no consensus between them.[2] D procures a homicide if he causes its commission, though again there is no need for any consensus between D and P.[3] Hiring a 'hit-man' to kill someone might be thought to come close to procuring, but it is more likely to be treated as a form of counselling.[4]

D will not be a secondary party to homicide simply by being present at the scene and, unless he is under a legal duty to act, doing nothing to prevent it. But he may be liable if he assists or encourages its commission.[5] If D is present at the scene in pursuance of a prior agreement he has made with P that a homicide be committed, that would suffice. If there is no such prior agreement and no positive act by him, D may only be liable if he is present at the scene with the intention of giving assistance or encouragement.[6] Some act of assistance or encouragement must also be established.[7] If D voluntarily commits a positive act of assistance or encouragement, knowing of

---

1   For example, *Luffman* [2008] EWCA Crim 1752.
2   *Calhaem* [1985] QB 808.
3   *Luffman* (n 1).
4   *Richards* [1974] QB 776; *Calhaem* (n 2).
5   *Coney* (1882) 8 QBD 534.
6   *Clarkson* [1971] 1 WLR 1402.
7   *Allan* [1965] 1 QB 130.

the circumstances that constitute the homicide, he is still a party to it even if he acted without the desire or aim that the homicide be committed.[8]

This can lead to some rather surprising results. Suppose, for example, two groups of young men meet. There is a verbal exchange between them and two men, A and B (one from each group) start fighting. A punches B knocking him to the ground. C, a member of A's group, stands by and makes no attempt to get physically involved but he shouts encouragement to A – 'Go on, let him have it'. As B lies on the ground A kicks him several times in the head, and B dies. If the prosecution can show that A intended to cause B at least serious injury, he may be convicted of murder. But so too might C, as A's accessory.

The Accomplice's State of Mind

The rules regarding the required state of mind of accessories are complicated, partly at least because they relate not only to the accessory's awareness of what he is doing and the implications of that but also to the principal's conduct and intentions. There are two basic strands to the accomplice's state of mind that are crucial to his criminal liability. First, he must intend to carry out the acts of assistance or encouragement, and some authors have interpreted this as meaning that he must intend to carry out the acts in the belief that they *will* or *may* encourage or assist in the principal offence.[9] Second, he must be aware of the 'essential matters' that constitute the principal offence.[10] However, it is unclear just how much of the detail must be known to him. These rules requiring intention and awareness[11] apply even though the principal offence (such as involuntary manslaughter) may only call for recklessness on the part of the principal offender.

It is worth acknowledging that where D assists or encourages P *before* the offence is committed, he invariably has no control over P's actions and is really having to predict what will or is likely to happen, so that it is probably more appropriate to talk about his awareness of the risk of what is likely to happen. Thus, in *Webster*,[12] the defendant had been driving a vehicle and then allowed his co-accused to drive, knowing that he (the co-accused) had been drinking. The co-accused drove erratically and at excessive speed resulting in a passenger being thrown from the vehicle and subsequently dying. The co-accused was convicted of causing death by dangerous driving and the defendant of aiding and abetting that crime. The Court of Appeal held that the defendant merely had to believe that it was *likely* that his co-accused would drive dangerously.

The fact that the law permits secondary liability to arise where D merely realises that his acts *may* assist or encourage the principal offence can lead to seemingly harsh outcomes. For example, a shopkeeper (D) who sells a kitchen knife to P may overhear P saying to another person that he intends to use it to kill V. If D completes the sale of the knife to P – sales are down and the shopkeeper is in danger of going bankrupt – and P subsequently uses the knife to kill V, D may be convicted as an accessory to murder.[13]

---

8   *NCB v Gamble* [1959] 1 QB 11.

9   Ibid.

10   *Johnson v Youden* [1950] 1 KB 544.

11   It is almost certainly true that liability will arise in cases where D was 'wilfully blind' – that is, he deliberately shut his eyes to the obvious. On the other hand, mere negligence through failing to make reasonable enquiries will not suffice; see *J.F. Alford Transport Ltd* [1997] 2 Cr App R 332.

12   [2006] EWCA Crim 415.

13   A very similar scenario as considered by Devlin J in *NCB v Gamble* (n 8).

The Accomplice's Awareness of and Thoughts about the Crime

Since by definition an accessory is more remote from the actual commission of the crime than the principal, he need not be aware of all the details of it. Put simply, the accomplice need only be aware of the 'type of offence' that the principal commits; he need not know the precise details of the offence that the principal commits.[14] This principle was then developed in *DPP for Northern Ireland v Maxwell*[15] where the House of Lords held that D could be liable as an accessory to P's crime if it was one of a range or list of offences that D had foreseen (even though he was not sure exactly which offence would be committed). It is also important to point out that the essential matters of which D must be aware include P's state of mind, or *mens rea*. D must foresee that P will commit the conduct element of the offence and have the necessary *mens rea*. So D will only be liable for a murder committed by P if D believes that P will or might fatally assault V intending to kill or to cause serious harm: if D thinks P will or might kill through being merely negligent that is not enough.

However, the decision in *Maxwell* left the law in an uncertain state. As the Law Commission explained, there were apparently conflicting authorities that, where there is no agreement between the parties to commit a crime (which is considered in 'Withdrawal', below), D should believe either that P *would* commit the crime or that he *might* commit it.[16] Where the courts have indicated that D need only foresee that the crime might be committed, they have expressed the law's requirement using language that is not necessarily consistent – for example:

(1) he believes the principal might commit the conduct element;
(2) he foresees the risk of a strong possibility that the principal might commit it;
(3) he contemplates the risk of a real possibility that the principal will commit it; and
(4) he foresees that it is likely that the principal will commit it.[17]

Thus, there is a lack of clarity in the law and of parity of culpability between the accessory and principal – in many cases D may be liable as an accessory because he foresaw that the crime *might* be committed, even though P, the actual perpetrator of the crime, was only liable because he believed that the harm *would* result.

Joint Enterprises, Homicide and the Fundamental Difference Rule

The Joint Enterprise Principle

An accomplice may enter into some form of agreement with the principal that a crime should be committed – there may be a common purpose or joint enterprise between them. As a general principle all parties to such agreement will be criminally liable for offences committed within the scope of the agreement. If one party does something outside the scope of the agreement, the other parties will not be liable unless they foresaw it.[18] Liability arises on a collective rather than individual basis. The courts are not concerned with individual contributions to the venture: the acts

---

14 *Bainbridge* [1960] 1 QB 129.
15 [1978] 1 WLR 1350.
16 Law Commission, *Participating in Crime* (Law Com No 305) [3.70-3.169] [B101-B123].
17 Ibid. 2.65.
18 *Anderson and Morris* [1966] 2 QB 110, 118-19.

of any individual are attributed to all parties to the agreement. This principle is interpreted strictly so that:

D will be liable for all acts actually committed by P in the course of the venture even if D has expressly indicated his opposition to them in advance, provided:

a. he foresaw them (and did not discount the risk that they would occur as negligible);
b. as will be subsequently explained, P's acts are not 'fundamentally different' from what D had envisaged; and
c. as will also be subsequently explained, D has not effectively withdrawn from the joint enterprise.

The rationale for this is that by entering into the agreement with P, D has voluntarily associated himself with the criminal venture. He has thereby supported other participants in the venture and so may be liable for offences even though he may not have actively encouraged or assisted them.

It is interesting to note some points of contrast between joint enterprise and accessorial liability. First, accessorial liability relates to the crime actually committed by P, but there is only the one crime – both P and accessories are liable for the same offence. In joint enterprise, the parties may be liable not only for the 'agreed' crime but also for any further crime committed by the principal that the secondary party foresees. Second, in reality, it may be that D and P have a shared or common purpose – which is obviously an essential ingredient of a joint enterprise – but no agreement is required by law and in some cases there is none. Third, the aider and abettor must have intended to encourage or assist the commission of the crime, but in joint enterprise mere foresight that the further crime might be committed is sufficient. The implication is that the decision to enter into the common purpose 'compensates' for the difference between the two.

Joint Enterprise and Homicide

Unfortunately, the joint enterprise principle is especially problematic in cases of homicide, and commentators have argued that it sometimes leads to harsh outcomes. Although it is relatively uncontroversial in cases where D is convicted of murder on the basis that he foresaw that P might kill with the intent to kill, it is much more debateable that a conviction for murder is justified where D merely foresaw that P would intentionally cause serious injury. Admittedly, in one of the earlier leading authorities, *Powell and Daniels; English*,[19] the House of Lords said that D must foresee not only that P *might attack* V, but also that he might *cause V's death*. But this does not sit comfortably with the later view expressed in other appellate cases such as *Chan Wing-Siu*[20] and *Hyde*,[21] which indicate that foresight of the possibility of *attacking* V is enough. This latter interpretation has more recently been supported in *Neary*,[22] *Rahman*[23] and *A, B, C & D*[24] and almost certainly reflects current judicial thinking. There is, unfortunately, yet further complication in the case law. For Lord Hutton, in the House of Lords in *Powell and Daniels; English*, said that the *Chan Wing-Siu*

---

19   [1999] 1 AC 1.
20   [1985] 1 AC 168.
21   [1991] 1 QB 134.
22   [2002] EWCA Crim 1736.
23   [2007] EWCA Crim 342.
24   [2010] EWCA Crim 1622. Hughes LJ expressly approved comments made in *Chan Wing-Siu* by Sir Robin Cooke to this effect.

principle required not that D foresee the actual act P commits, but 'an act of the *type*' (emphasis added) which P commits.[25] This extends D's potential liability that bit further.

Unfortunately, as indicated earlier, the courts have articulated the principle in different ways and this has created uncertainty as to both its precise meaning and its function. Commentators such as Krebs have pointed out that whereas formerly the courts referred to the significance of what D 'authorised' (*Anderson and Morris*) or the extent of the 'understanding' between D and P (*Slack*[26]), more recent judicial statements emphasise the importance of 'contemplation' (*Chan Wing-Siu*) or 'foresight' (*Powell and Daniels*). The effect of this has been to move from an exculpatory principle that seeks to limit D's liability to an inculpatory principle which is more likely to extend it.

The Fundamental Difference Rule

The situation should be fairly straightforward where the principal does what the accomplice expected, but what if the principal does something different? Suppose P and D agree to rob a bank and D knows that P has a gun. But in the course of robbing the bank the cashier presses the alarm button and P fatally shoots her. D would probably be convicted of robbery, but is he also a party to the murder committed by P? Case law indicates that he may be if he realised there was a real risk that P might act as he did with the *mens rea* for murder and the murder was not *fundamentally different* from what D had envisaged. So the 'fundamental difference' rule effectively acts as a potential defence (or limitation to D's liability). In *English*, D and P, in pursuing their common purpose, attacked a police officer with wooden posts. But in the course of the attack P pulled out a knife and stabbed the officer with it; D stated that he had been unaware that P was carrying a knife. Death resulted from the stab wound, not from the assault with the wooden posts. The House of Lords ruled that P's act of stabbing the officer was beyond the common purpose as envisaged by D; even though wooden posts could be lethal, the use of the knife was fundamentally different from what D had expected and he was not guilty of the officer's murder (or manslaughter).

Whether P's act was fundamentally different from what D had foreseen is a question of fact in each case and will be determined objectively. However, it is not always easy to know what 'fundamentally different' means. Cases such as *Rahman*, *Mendez and Thompson*[27] and *A, B, C & D* stress that the phrase is not a term of legal art and the words should be construed according to their ordinary natural meaning. In *Rahman*, Lord Brown remarked:

> If D realises (without agreeing to such conduct being used) that P may kill or intentionally inflict serious injury, but nevertheless continues to participate with P in the venture, that will amount to a sufficient mental element for D to be guilty of murder if P, with the requisite intent, kills in the course of the venture unless (i) P suddenly produces and uses a weapon of which D knows nothing and which is more lethal than any weapon which D contemplates that P or any other participant may be carrying and (ii) for that reason P's act is to be regarded as fundamentally different from anything foreseen by D.[28]

Obviously, using a different weapon is not the only possible way in which the principal's fatal act might be fundamentally different from what the accomplice foresaw. An alternative illustration of

25 *Powell and Daniels; English* (n 19) 28.
26 [1989] QB 775; and see Beatrice Krebs, 'Joint Criminal Enterprise' (2010) 73 Modern Law Review 578.
27 [2010] EWCA Crim 516.
28 [2009] 1 AC 129, 129.

fundamental difference was offered in *A.G'.s Reference (No.3 of 2004)*;[29] firing a gun *at* the victim when it was envisaged that the gun would be fired *near* the victim. In *Mendez and Thompson*, the Court of Appeal thought that 'what matters is not simply the difference in the weapon but the way in which it is likely to be used and the degree of injury which it is likely to cause'.[30]

In applying the fundamental difference principle the court's attention is likely to be on P's acts rather than on his intent or state of mind. In *Rahman*, the House of Lords expressly rejected the argument that D should escape liability for murder if he foresaw that P would intend no more than serious injury but P in fact intended to kill. Lord Bingham thought it would be too much to expect a jury to distinguish whether D foresaw that P would act with the lesser of these intents or the greater: focusing on what P might *do* is much more feasible. As Simester et al. suggest, in homicide cases at least, the key criterion seems to be the degree of *dangerousness* that D envisaged and that was inherent in P's acts.[31] This sits comfortably with the Court of Appeals' comment in *Mendez and Thompson* about the importance of the way in which a weapon is likely to be used rather than the weapon itself. In *English*, Lord Hutton explained that if the weapon used by P 'is different to, but as *dangerous* as' that which D contemplated P might use, then D should not escape liability (emphasis added).[32]

Criticism of the Joint Enterprise Law

The Law Commission quite recently urged the Government to reform the law[33] and the Justice Committee of the House of Commons offered a series of recommendations including statutory intervention.[34] The Law Commission suggested that secondary liability became unduly extended because of the limitations on inchoate liability (that is, for incitement, conspiracy and attempts).

Practitioners argued in evidence to the Justice Committee that it is relatively easy for the prosecution to show that D foresaw what P *might* do – easier than showing foresight of what P *would* do! Little more than evidence of association, such as through membership of the same gang, and presence at the scene are all that is needed. This suggests there is a real danger that defendants are convicted on 'weak and tenuous evidence'.[35] The Committee was also told that the joint enterprise principle is being used increasingly, especially in cases involving children and young adults, and that there has recently been a high number of appeals in such cases. Murder trials are a particular concern because of the mandatory life sentence. The lack of what the Law Commission called 'parity of culpability' between the secondary party and the principal is problematic because the court has a limited sentencing discretion.[36] The Director of Public Prosecutions admitted that the mandatory life sentence can at least 'appear disproportionate' in cases where the defendant

---

29   [2005] EWCA Crim 1882.

30   *Mendez and Thompson* (n 27) 888.

31   Andrew Simester, John Spencer, Bob Sullivan and Graham Virgo, *Simester and Sullivan's Criminal Law: Theory and Doctrine* (4th edn, Hart 2010) 238.

32   *Powell and Daniels; English* (n 19) 30.

33   Law Commission (n 16).

34   House of Commons Justice Committee, *Joint Enterprise: Eleventh Report of Session 2010-12* (HC 1597, 17 January 2012).

35   Ibid. 11. These concerns echo the words of Professor Wilson, that '[a] person may be liable as an accessory to murder by dint of an act as innocuous as driving the getaway car, providing the murder weapon in the ordinary course of business supply, or, it appears, saying "oh goody" upon hearing the principal's lethal plan; William Wilson, '(1) A Rational Scheme of Liability for Participating in Crime' [2008] Criminal Law Review 3.

36   House of Commons Justice Committee (n 34) 26.

played only a very minor role.[37] Recent survey research also reveals public dissatisfaction with the current law.[38]

Is There Any Possible Justification for the Joint Enterprise Law?

Krebs re-examined potential justifications for the status quo but rightly rejected them.[39] They are essentially concerned with the idea that by entering into the agreement with P, D has changed his normative position and has accepted collective moral responsibility for the risk that some further crime(s) might be committed in pursuance of the venture. Simester et al. explain that D 'becomes, through her own deliberate choice, a participant in a group action to commit a crime', the 'moral significance' of which is that 'she associates herself with the conduct of the other members of the group …'.[40] Furthermore, the law is rightly concerned that groups of offenders constitute a particular threat to society's wellbeing. As Lord Steyn remarked in *Powell and Daniels; English*, 'experience has shown that joint criminal enterprises only too readily escalate into the commission of greater offences'.[41] The Law Commission also felt that in addition to foresight there is research evidence to show that joint offending is likely to lead to increased criminality.[42]

The alleged rationale for the joint enterprise principle, which is based on a combination of (1) D's foresight that P may commit the offence and (2) society's concern that group offending tends to lead to greater criminality, is tested most severely in cases where D has expressed his opposition to the very conduct/crime that P then commits. This has been recognised by senior members of the judiciary. In *Powell and English* Lord Mustill referred to the situation 'where S foresees that P may go too far; sincerely wishes that he will not, and makes this plain to P; and yet goes ahead, either because he hopes for the best, or because P is an overbearing character, or for some other reason'. His Lordship asked, 'How can a jury be directed at the same time that S is guilty only if he was party to an express or tacit agreement to do the act in question, and that he is guilty if he not only disagreed with it, but made his disagreement perfectly clear to P? Are not the two assertions incompatible?'[43] Kirby J, delivering his dissenting judgment in the High Court of Australia in *Clayton*, put it more bluntly: '[t]o hold an accused liable for murder merely on the foresight of a possibility is fundamentally unjust'.[44]

Supporters of the alleged rationale would presumably argue that if D and P agree that a burglary be committed and, having expressed his opposition to any violence, D continues with the venture, he cannot then exclude his liability for violence because he still chose to take the risk (that the level of criminality might increase). The problem with this argument is that it is too open-ended. The nature and extent of the risks associated with any joint enterprise will vary, according to the nature of the agreement, and D's foresight of what might happen will vary according to his knowledge and beliefs about P. Krebs argued that by agreeing to be party to the enterprise D has (only) accepted 'those choices and actions on the part of P which are intrinsically linked to the furtherance of the

---

37   Ibid. 28.

38   Ibid. Eva w2, w16.

39   Krebs (n 26).

40   Simester et al. (n 31) 244.

41   *Powell and Daniels; English* (n 19) 14.

42   This was recently underlined by Horder; see Jeremy Horder, *Homicide and the Politics of Law Reform* (Oxford University Press, 2012).

43   *Powell and Daniels; English* (n 19) 11.

44   [2006] HCA 58, 108.

purpose crime'.[45] This led her to suggest that D should only be liable for those further crimes (committed by P) to which he has *acquiesced*.[46]

This argument sounds promising – D should only be liable for those things that he has chosen to risk creating, rather than simply for whatever he foresaw. But much is likely to depend on the particular facts and circumstances of the case. If D continues with, say, a burglary venture after expressing opposition to violence, he may have difficulty in denying acquiescence (in the use of violence), at least unless he can show that he had dismissed the risk of it as negligible. Suppose D knows that P has a short temper and tends to react violently when under stress. D's plea that he had not agreed to violence is likely to fall on deaf ears. In such circumstances the court may well conclude that whilst D would much prefer that there should be no violence, he nonetheless must have accepted that P might be violent. In Krebs's terms, P's violence *in this instance* was 'intrinsically linked' to the burglary. If the circumstances – the nature of the personalities involved and what they believed about each other – were different, D might stand a better chance of showing that he genuinely believed there was no risk of violence.

Can D Be Guilty of Manslaughter if P is Guilty of Murder?

A further potential complication with the application of the joint enterprise principle in homicide arises where D foresees P's possible conduct (which results in V's death) but lacks the *mens rea* – that is, D did not foresee that P would act with the *mens rea* of murder – to make him guilty of murder. Regrettably, it is unclear from the case law whether, assuming P is guilty of murder, D may nonetheless be convicted of manslaughter. Some authorities suggest that an 'all or nothing' approach should be taken, whereas others indicate that D's liability depends on the nature of his *mens rea*. In *Powell and Daniels; English* the House of Lords took the former approach. Similarly, in *AG's Reference (No.3 of 2004)*[47] the victim was fatally shot. The defendant envisaged that the principal would deliberately discharge a gun near the victim but had not expected any physical injury to be caused at all – he thought the gun would be used solely to cause fear or alarm. The Court of Appeal held he was guilty of neither murder nor manslaughter.

But the Court of Appeal in *Yemoh and others*[48] took a different view. There D joined in an assault on V in the course of which V was fatally stabbed. D knew that P might use a knife with the intention of causing injury – *not necessarily serious injury* – and so did not foresee that P would act with the intent for murder. The fact that P did act with the *mens rea* for murder did not enable D to rely on the fundamental difference rule, and D had foreseen the elements of unlawful and dangerous act manslaughter. Whereas in *Rahman* D had foreseen that P would act with intent to cause *serious* injury, in *Yemoh and others* D had foreseen a slightly lesser intent. Basing his liability on that lesser intent, D was guilty of manslaughter.

A similar approach was adopted by the Northern Ireland Court of Appeal in *Gilmour*[49] where D drove P to a house knowing that P intended to plant a petrol-bomb. The bomb that was used was unusually large and it resulted in three deaths as well as much damage to property. The Court quashed D's conviction for murder and substituted one of manslaughter, on the ground that P had done what D foresaw and so the latter's liability depended on his *mens rea*. However, this is arguably a very dubious approach; P did not do what D foresaw; D had not realised that it was an

---

45   Krebs (n 26) 595.

46   Ibid. 604.

47   The House of Lords took the same view in *English*.

48   [2009] EWCA Crim 1775.

49   [2000] 2 Cr App R 407.

unusually large bomb that was likely to cause so much harm and damage. Indeed, petrol-bombs only rarely lead to personal injury.

Nevertheless, whatever reservations there may be about the decision in *Gilmour*, the approach taken in Y*emoh and others* cannot be dismissed simply as an isolated example or as confined to exceptional circumstances. The Court of Appeal had previously reached the same conclusion in *Stewart and Schofield*[50] in which the joint venture was the robbery of a shop. The defendants were armed with a scaffolding bar with the intent to cause non-serious injury. But a co-accused beat the victim to death, and was convicted of murder. This was found to be within the joint venture, but the Court held that the accessory was guilty of manslaughter because he had not anticipated the intentional use of serious (let alone fatal) injury. He, in effect, had the *mens rea* for unlawful and dangerous act manslaughter – he had expected his co-accused to inflict a battery on the victim.

Withdrawal

Accessorial liability, including joint enterprise liability, may be nullified if D withdraws from it. K.J.M. Smith suggested two possible rationales for this: (1) It provides an incentive to individuals to reconsider what they have done and the likely consequences thereof, and that in turn may reduce the likelihood of the offence being committed. (2) Withdrawal may constitute evidence of reduced culpability and perhaps that the individual represents no danger to society.[51] A potential deficiency with the first of these putative rationales is that, unlike most defences, it is reliant on D's awareness of the law. Ironically, if D is familiar with the law (and thus open to the incentive), he may also be aware that alternative forms of liability exist – for example, for encouragement and/or assistance under the Serious Crime Act 2007, or for statutory conspiracy (see 'Further Potential Forms of Criminal Liability for Participants in Homicide', below) – that may attach to him regardless of whether he withdraws!

As to the alternative rationale, implied reduction in culpability, much depends on D's motives for withdrawing. The courts will generally be uninfluenced by D's perceived motives for withdrawing – he may have had a genuine change of heart and sincerely regret his assistance or encouragement, or he may decide the intended offence is too 'risky' and is likely to be detected. Or he may have fallen out with his accomplices and chosen to 'spill the beans' out of spite. K.J.M. Smith, however, argued there are good reasons to exclude the defence where the motives for so doing are 'unmeritorious'. Limiting the availability of the defence in this way would be undesirable in that it discourages individuals from withdrawing in circumstances where withdrawal might reduce the likelihood of the offence ultimately being committed. Yet unmeritorious withdrawals do not imply any significant reduction in culpability. Those who seek to withdraw solely because of the fear of apprehension can hardly claim thereby to present any less danger to society.

The withdrawal must be both *unequivocal* and *timely*.[52] In *Otway*,[53] the Court of Appeal affirmed this, adding that effective withdrawal must be 'real' and 'communicated to the other party in good time'. A simple change of heart or mere repentance by D is insufficient.[54] To benefit from a plea of withdrawal D must show that he has communicated his unequivocal withdrawal, either to the

50 [1995] 1 Cr App R 441.
51 Keith Smith, 'Withdrawal in Complicity: A Restatement of Principles' [2001] Criminal Law Review 769, 772-74.
52 *O'Flaherty and others* [2004] EWCA Crim 526.
53 [2011] EWCA Crim 3, 32.
54 See, for example *Croft* [1944] 1 KB 295; and *Becerra and Cooper* (1976) 62 Cr App R 212.

principal offender or, where there are several principal offenders, to all of them, or possibly to the law enforcement agency.[55]

The timing of the withdrawal is important; it must take place *before* the offence is committed and preferably before the first steps in the commission of the offence have been executed.[56] In *Becerra and Cooper*,[57] D and P were in the process of burgling V's house. D had previously given a knife to P so that it might be used if they were disturbed. When they were confronted by V, D said to P 'Come on, let's go', and left the premises. But P ignored this and stabbed V. Not surprisingly, the Court held there had been no effective withdrawal. Having left it so late it was probably necessary for D to have physically intervened to prevent P from using the knife if the withdrawal plea was to succeed. If, though, unequivocal withdrawal is communicated in a timely fashion, the general view is that there is no need for D then to take reasonable steps to prevent the offence being committed.[58] Where D is unable to communicate his withdrawal to the other parties, taking preventative steps – perhaps giving a timely warning to the police – would be strong evidence of withdrawal.

The Court of Appeal in *O'Flaherty* stressed the need for D to have made an *effective* withdrawal, though it can often be very difficult to attach any truly useful meaning to this. 'Effective withdrawal' might be thought to require D somehow to nullify or undo the assistance or encouragement he has given. But if, for example, D has already communicated valuable information and advice about how the offence might be committed, it is difficult (if not impossible) to see how this could be achieved. In practice, the courts are likely to look closely not only at what D has done in his attempt to withdraw but also at what D did to assist or encourage the crime, and the time gap between the assistance/encouragement and the commission of the offence. If D had simply advised P about how to commit the crime, he may be able to effectively withdraw by telling P not to commit it or by trying to dissuade P from doing so.[59]

In *Grundy*,[60] D gave P1 and P2 information that would be helpful in the commission of a burglary. About two weeks before the burglary was due to be committed, however, D changed his mind and spent some time trying to stop them from carrying it out. The Court of Appeal took the view that the trial judge had been wrong not to leave a possible defence of withdrawal to the jury. Even though the burglary was subsequently committed, D may have effectively withdrawn by his efforts to prevent it. D's attempts to countermand his advice and encouragement failed but the Court did not then insist that he should have tried to prevent the burglary from being committed – such as by warning the police. The implication is that the courts will not look for real 'undoing' or 'neutralisation' of the assistance or encouragement given by D. It is probably sufficient for D to show that he has taken reasonable timely steps to withdraw. Similarly, in *Whitefield*,[61] another case in which D had assisted others in the planning of a burglary, D told Ps that he was withdrawing from the venture before it was carried out. The Court of Appeal said that the trial judge had been wrong to reject a plea of no case to answer on the basis that D's communication of withdrawal was insufficient.

The discussion thus far has focused on cases where the offence is planned or premeditated. Should the law be less strict where the offence is spontaneous? In *Mitchell and King*,[62] a murder case, the Divisional Court thought that where Ds aid or abet one another in a spontaneous attack

55   *O'Flaherty* (n 52).
56   *Perman* [1996] 1 Cr App R 24.
57   (1976) 62 Cr App R 212.
58   David Ormerod, *Smith and Hogan's Criminal Law* (13th edn, Oxford University Press, 2011) 238.
59   See *Saunders and Archer* (1573) 2 Plowd 473.
60   [1977] Criminal Law Review 534.
61   (1984) 79 Cr App R 36.
62   [1999] Criminal Law Review 496.

on V, any of them can simply physically withdraw by ceasing to continue the assault, and incur no liability for injuries caused thereafter. This suggests that in cases of spontaneous violence there is no requirement to express any form of communication to the other party.

As Sir John Smith remarked, the problem is that whilst D may change his mind and walk away, ceasing to give any further *assistance* to P, D may not necessarily thereby cease to give *encouragement* to P.[63] In principle, it appears that in such cases D does not deserve to be relieved of the responsibility for what P then does. The significance of the decision in *Mitchell and King* seems to have been severely restricted by the later decision in *Robinson*.[64] Although that case involved a planned attack, so that what was said about spontaneous attacks were strictly obiter, the Court of Appeal approved Professor Smith's criticism of *Mitchell and King* and made it clear that that case should be regarded as exceptional. Even in cases of spontaneous violence the general rule is that withdrawal must be communicated, unless it is not practicable or reasonable to do so. Unfortunately, however, in *O'Flaherty and others* the Court of Appeal was not referred to *Robinson* and (although strictly obiter) expressed its general approval of *Mitchell and King*! Thus, there is a frustrating lack of clarity from the case law. Nevertheless, it is respectfully suggested that the concerns about *Mitchell and King* remain valid and that it will only be in very rare, truly exceptional cases that a failure to communicate withdrawal will be accepted – that is, where it is neither reasonable nor practicable to expect D to have done so.

When considering whether D has done enough to have effectively withdrawn, the courts have never made it entirely clear how far the withdrawal requirements should be related or proportional to the original encouragement or assistance. It may well be said that the benefit of some acts of assistance, such as the provision of a weapon that is then used in a homicide, can be relatively easily erased – thus enabling D to extricate himself from the venture. If P nonetheless persists and finds some other means of committing the crime, then it cannot be said that P was being assisted by D. Yet where D has given words of encouragement or advice to P, the benefit thereof simply cannot be erased as easily, or perhaps by any means. In those circumstances, it may be that the only course of action open to D who is bent on withdrawing would be to alert the police and/or the intended victim

Proposals for Law Reform

The Government initially accepted that the law on complicity is complicated and uncertain, and that reform is particularly needed in relation to homicide because of the seriousness of the cases and the fact that a high proportion of homicides involve more than one offender.[65] In their consultation paper the Government accepted the need to amend the fundamental difference rule, so that if D foresaw that P might intentionally cause serious injury he could be convicted of murder if P's act was within the joint enterprise, the latter being satisfied if P's act did not 'go far beyond' what was agreed and so on. But the Government subsequently decided not to proceed with these proposals because they decided to focus on the law of complicity generally and not just that relating to homicide.[66]

---

63   John Smith, 'Commentary on *R v Mitchell and another*' [1999] Criminal Law Review 496, 497.

64   3 February 2000.

65   Law Commission, *Murder, Manslaughter and Infanticide: Proposals for Reform of the Law* (Consultation paper Law Com CP 19/08, 2008).

66   Law Commission, *Murder, Manslaughter and Infanticide: Proposals for Reform of the Law: Summary of Responses and Government Position* (Law Com CP(R) 19/08, 2009).

The Law Commission have undertaken two distinct but related projects concerning the criminal liability of those who encourage or assist in the commission of crime. The first was concerned with inchoate (incomplete) liability – what has traditionally been liability for incitement, conspiracy and attempts – and this culminated in recommendations being made in 2006.[67] The second was published in the following year and focused on amending the law relating to secondary liability.[68] The Commission was acutely aware that, assuming he had the relevant *mens rea*, as soon as D gives encouragement or assistance to P he may be liable for an offence (of what was formerly incitement), even though the crime he encouraged or assisted was not ultimately committed. Conversely, secondary (or accessorial) liability for P's crime could only arise if that crime was carried out.

The Commission's 2006 report was followed shortly afterwards by the Serious Crime Act 2007 which is discussed below in the section on Further Potential Forms of Criminal Liability for Participants in Homicide . Although it did not strictly replicate the Commission's recommendations, the Act abolished the old common law offence of incitement and effectively replaced it with three principal new offences of encouraging or assisting in the commission of an offence. But the Commission's 2007 report contained some additional proposals that have not thus far prompted any legislation by the Government. Nevertheless, it is worth briefly looking at some of the principal recommendations in the 2007 report.

At the end of the report there is a draft Bill containing two new crimes that are intended to replace the existing law on secondary or accessorial liability. They state as follows:

1. Assisting or encouraging an offence

> (1) Where a person (P) has committed an offence, another person (D) is also guilty of the offence if –
> > (a) D did an act with the intention that one or more of a number of other acts would be done by another person,
> > (b) P's criminal act was one of those acts,
> > (c) D's behaviour assisted or encouraged P to do his criminal act, and
> > (d) Subsection (2) or (3) is satisfied.
>
> (2) This subsection is satisfied if D believed that a person doing the act would commit the offence.
>
> (3) This subsection is satisfied if D's state of mind was such that had he done the act he would have committed the offence.

2. Participating in a joint criminal venture

> (1) This section applies where two or more persons participate in a joint criminal venture.
>
> (2) If one of them (P) commits an offence, another participant (D) is also guilty of the offence if P's criminal act falls within the scope of the venture.

---

67   Law Commission, *Inchoate Liability for Assisting and Encouraging Crime* (Law Com No 300, 2006).
68   Law Com No 305 (n 16).

(3) The existence or scope of a joint criminal venture may be inferred from the conduct of the participants (whether or not there is an express agreement).

(4) D does not escape liability under this section for an offence committed by P at a time when D is a participant in the venture merely because D is at that time –
    (a) absent,
    (b) against the venture's being carried out, or
    (c) indifferent as to whether it is carried out.

It is difficult to avoid the criticism that these proposals are complex and lacking in clarity, especially when looking at the culpability requirements. Under clause 1, D must intend the act or conduct element of the offence committed by P. 'Intend' here is to be construed either in its purposive or oblique sense.[69] Wilson criticised this, arguing that whilst there is a good case for a broad definition of principal liability for crimes such as murder, secondary liability should be confined to cases of purposive intent.[70] With regard to any consequences or circumstances required in the definition of the principal offence, D must either believe that P will satisfy the definitional requirements, or had he been committing the conduct element himself D would have satisfied the *mens rea* requirements of that principal offence.[71] As Simester et al. remark, this addresses the Commission's concern for 'parity of culpability' even though D's conduct may well have been much less harmful than P's.[72]

The culpability elements in joint criminal ventures would also appear complex and uncertain. D must either intend that P (or another party to the venture) should commit the conduct element, or believe that P (or another party) would or might commit the conduct element.[73] In place of the much-criticised fundamental difference rule the Commission proposed that D would not be liable if P's act fell outside the scope of the venture. But, as Professor Sullivan has remarked, one of the striking features of clause 2 is that it actually tells us very little about the things that we really want and need to know.[74] There is no definition, or indication of the meaning, of what constitutes a joint criminal venture, or how one may be inferred from the parties' conduct. And there is no definition of the scope of a joint venture, and no indication of the *mens rea* requirements. Sullivan also argued that clause would fall foul of Article 7 of the European Convention on Human Rights, that there can be no crime without a legal rule creating it.[75] The clause has, though, been defended against this and the allegation that it lacks sufficient clarity and explanation by Horder.[76]

The general tenor of their report indicates that the Commission were in favour of largely preserving the current situation. The joint enterprise principle would certainly continue to have broad impact. Though clause 2 offers no guidance on the nature or scope of 'joint venture', it seems that the Commission regard it as encompassing cases where there is no agreement provided there is a 'common intention … to commit an offence'.[77] Sullivan complains that this goes too far;

---

69   Ibid. 3.88.

70   Wilson (n 35) 15-16.

71   Law Com No 305 (n 16) 3.122.

72   Simester et al. (n 31) 259.

73   Law Com No 305 (n 16) 3.151.

74   Bob Sullivan, '(2) Participating in Crime: Law Com No. 305 – Joint Criminal Ventures' [2008] Criminal Law Review 19, 20.

75   Ibid. 21.

76   Horder (n 42) 165-68.

77   Law Com No 305 (n 16) 3.59.

it does not make the parties 'criminal partners'.[78] Yet if the Commission's proposal is adopted, it would have significant implications for homicide cases. As the report states, it could apply to 'spontaneous ventures' where there was no implied agreement but there was a shared intent, such as spontaneous violence involving groups of youths.[79]

The Commission also favoured retention of the current rule whereby D may be guilty of any 'collateral' offence committed by P even though D has previously expressed unequivocal opposition to it.[80] Thus, suppose D and P agree to burgle V's house and (aware of P's quick temper and propensity to strike out in the heat of the moment) D tells P that on no account should any violence be used. Nevertheless, when confronted by V, P pulls out a knife and fatally stabs V. The Commission thought D should be guilty of V's murder because (a) D chose to enter into the venture and (b) groups or associations of offenders tend to lead to an increase in criminality,[81] though the minimalist approach adopted in the drafting of clause 2 means there is no clear indication of how far the collateral offence rule would stretch. But as indicated earlier in this chapter, there is a real likelihood that this can lead to over-criminalisation of D. This is not to imply that D should never bear liability for a collateral crime; rather, the point is that there should be a stronger link between what D has agreed to and the collateral offence.

Further Potential Forms of Criminal Liability for Participants in Homicide

As indicated in the Introduction, apart from secondary liability for the principal offence there are two further bases of potential liability for those who participate in homicide. These are encouraging or assisting homicide under the Serious Crime Act 2007, and conspiracy to murder, to which the discussion now turns.

Encouraging or Assisting Homicide under the Serious Crime Act 2007

The three principal crimes under the 2007 Act[82]   It used to be an offence at common law to incite another person to commit a crime. That common law offence has been replaced by Part 2 of the Serious Crime Act 2007 which created new offences of encouraging or assisting in the commission of crimes. The new law has been heavily criticised for its excessive complexity[83] and its overlap with secondary liability.[84] There are differences between the provisions in the Act and the Law

---

78   Sullivan (n 74) 23.
79   Law Com No 305 (n 16) A18.
80   Ibid. 3.49.
81   Ibid. 3.58.
82   The law relating to these new offences came into force on 1 October 2008.
83   The Court of Appeal in *S and H* [2011] EWCA Crim 2872 [33] took this view in relation to section 46 of the Act.
84   See for example John Spencer and Graham Virgo, 'Encouraging and Assisting Crime' (2008) 9 Archbold News 7; and David Ormerod and Rudi Fortson, 'Serious Crime Act 2007: The Part 2 Offences' [2009] Criminal Law Review 389.

Commission's recommendations published in 2006[85] which preceded it.[86]

There are three main offences under the 2007 Act each of which involves the commission of an act which is *capable* of encouraging or assisting in the commission of a crime. Immediately this clearly indicates that no actual assistance or encouragement is necessary and, as Ormerod and Fortson remark, '[t]he most marginal acts suffice'.[87] Section 44 deals with cases where D intends to encourage or assist in the commission of a crime. Section 45 applies where D believes that the crime will be committed and that the act will encourage or assist its commission. Finally, section 46 arises where D's act is capable of encouraging or assisting the commission of one or more of a number of crimes and D believes that one or more of those crimes will be committed and that his act will encourage or assist one or more of them. Liability can arise under each of these sections even though the substantive crime (which is encouraged or assisted) is not actually committed,[88] and even though the person (P) who was encouraged or assisted was unaware that he was being encouraged or assisted. Thus, D may be liable for encouraging or assisting P in the commission of murder even though P may be acquitted of that murder. The fact that P is acquitted does not negate the point that D has nonetheless committed an act of encouragement or assistance.

Although the primary concern is with inchoate crimes, liability is stretched so that it may attach to those who actually carry out the principal offence. Section 56(1) states that a person can be convicted of a Part 2 offence if he can be shown to have committed either the inchoate crime or the 'anticipated offence' where the prosecution cannot prove which one he committed but the court is sure he committed one of them. How, therefore, ought we to regard D if he supplies a weapon to P which P then uses to murder V? Is D an assister/encourager, or an accessory (to murder), or a murderer? This muddying of the waters is further exacerbated in that the Part 2 offences have been created alongside the pre-existing common law on secondary liability and section 8 of the Accessories and Abettors Act 1861. One effect of this is to give the prosecution a broad discretion as to the charges they should bring, a matter that is of particular interest in homicide cases. There may well be a choice between charging an inchoate offence (assisting or encouraging), or a secondary offence.

If a person encourages or assists in murder, by section 58 the maximum penalty is life imprisonment – there is no mandatory life sentence.

Conduct elements   The Serious Crime Act 2007 does not define 'encouragement', but as under the old common law concept of incitement, it requires some form of persuasion or influencing of another person to do something. Neither is there any definition of 'assistance' in the 2007 Act, and it is likely that the courts will look to the case law on aiding and abetting for guidance. Assistance can be provided indirectly, so if D gives information of the whereabouts of V to A who then repeats that to P, and P then kills V, D may have assisted in the murder or manslaughter of V. The Act also makes it clear that assistance may be provided by omitting to act,[89] so if D deliberately omitted to

---

85   Law Com No 300 (n 67).

86   The Commission had been working on three related projects that culminated in reports published in 2006 and 2007 containing proposals for law reform – the two concerned with secondary liability and inchoate liability were obviously very closely linked – and between them the Commission offered a coherent set of proposals. Since the 2007 Act does not follow the Commission's 2006 recommendations, it would not be appropriate to implement the 2007 recommendations if Parliament decides to amend the law on secondary liability – some further adjustments would be necessary.

87   Ormerod and Fortson (n 84) 391.

88   Section 49(1) Serious Crime Act 2007.

89   Section 65(2)(b).

switch on a house alarm so that P was able to enter and kill V, D may have assisted in V's murder or manslaughter.

Mens rea   There are *prima facie* two elements of *mens rea* liability under the 2007 Act. Firstly, it is implicit that D intends to commit the act of encouragement or assistance. Secondly, D must have *mens rea* with regard to the crime that he is encouraging or assisting, and the details of that will vary according to the particular section under which he is charged. Ultimately, the fault requirements can be highly complex.

Section 44 of the Act requires D to have intended to encourage or assist the commission of a crime, and such intent will not be assumed simply because it was foreseeable that D's act would provide encouragement or assistance.[90] It is unclear whether the defendant must be aware of the possibility that his act might encourage or assist a crime, or whether it suffices that any reasonable person in his position would have been so aware.

Section 45 requires D to believe the crime *will* be committed, and that his act *will* encourage or assist that crime that he thinks *will* be committed, even if he believes certain conditions must be fulfilled before the crime is completed.[91] D may be liable under section 45 if he supplies P with a weapon in the belief that P will use it to kill V.

The offence in section 46 is the most complex of the three,[92] and is designed to apply where D believes that P might commit any one of a range of offences but is unsure precisely which. D must believe that one or more of a range of crimes *will* be committed and that his act *will* encourage or assist one or more crimes in the range – again, even though certain conditions may have to be met before the crime is committed.

The 2007 Act provides alternative forms of *mens rea* for liability under sections 44 to 46. Where the section refers to D intending to encourage or assist the commission of an offence, or believing an offence would be committed and so on, the word 'offence' can be substituted by 'act'.[93] The concept of an 'act' is used here to denote the *actus reus* or conduct elements of a crime. If, as in murder and manslaughter, the *actus reus* includes the causation of a consequence, some further element of *mens rea* must be proved. Even if he did not intend to encourage a specific murder, D may still be guilty of encouraging murder if he intended to encourage the commission of an act believing that it would or might result in a person's death.[94]

Additionally, where (as in murder), the crime that D encourages or assists itself requires proof of moral blame, the prosecution must also prove one of three further forms of *mens rea*.[95] Again, assuming D did not intend to encourage a particular murder, he may be convicted of encouraging murder if he deliberately encouraged P to commit an act that he thought or suspected might result in the death of another, and either (i) he thought P *would* kill with some form of malice aforethought; or (ii) he thought P *might* kill with malice aforethought; or (iii) if D had committed the act himself he would have acted with malice aforethought.

From time to time courts are faced with cases where one young male (D) has encouraged another (P) to 'beat up' (or something similar) a third (V). Even if P did not kill V, D could be liable

---

90   Section 44(2).
91   Section 49(7).
92   In *S and H* (n 83) the Court of Appeal rejected a claim that section 46 is so badly drafted that it breaches Article 7 of the European Convention on Human Rights on the ground of uncertainty.
93   Section 47(2), (3) and (4).
94   Sections 44 and 47(5)(b).
95   Section 47(5)(a).

for encouraging murder if he thinks that V will or might die as well as thinking that P will or might intend to kill or cause serious injury.

The relationship between inchoate and accessorial liability   Liability for encouraging or assisting a crime may arise regardless of whether the principal crime is ultimately committed, whereas accessorial liability depends on the principal offence being committed. As Spencer forcefully pointed out, it seems 'very strange' that I should be liable as an accessory if 'you commit the crime I knew you intended with my help to commit ... but if you do not, I may well commit no offence at all'.[96] The law appears to place extraordinary reliance on the element of luck, that the principal offence may or may not be committed. The 2007 Act offences thus seem to address this by providing the prosecution with alternative charges to pursue.

Where the principal offence is committed there is clearly a potential overlap between the encouraging or assisting offences and accessorial liability for the principal crime. If, for example, D provides P with a knife which P subsequently uses to murder V, whilst there may be a choice of charges to bring against D, conviction as an accessory to murder is, as Simester et al. suggest, preferable to one of intentionally encouraging or assisting an offence because it is a more precise reflection of D's criminality.[97]

Conspiracy to Murder

Where there is a common purpose (joint enterprise) between two or more individuals that a crime be committed, those involved may be liable for the statutory offence of conspiracy to commit an offence.[98] Conspiracy requires an agreement between the parties to pursue a course of conduct; the parties must have a criminal purpose. Indeed, the significance of this need for an agreed criminal purpose should not be underestimated. Suppose D1 agrees with D2 that V should be killed, and D1 provides the weapon that D2 uses to kill V, there is no difficulty in convicting D1 of conspiracy to murder V. But if, for example, D1 simply sells a weapon to D2 in the knowledge or belief that D2 will use that weapon to kill V, and D2 does so, D1 is not guilty of conspiracy to murder because there is no agreement with D2 that V should be killed.

What if the parties are in agreement as to the offence to be committed but disagree as to the identity of the victim? Suppose D1 and D2 agree to commit murder, but D1 thinks that V1 is the victim whereas D2 thinks their target is V2. In commenting on a case involving conspiracy to produce controlled drugs, Sir John Smith argued that the victim's identity is a significant issue and the disagreement negates liability for conspiracy.[99] Indeed, this view is consistent with the House of Lords' decision in *Powell and English* where the fact that P killed V with a knife when D expected wooden staves to be used was regarded as sufficiently fundamentally different to take the murder of V outside the scope of the joint enterprise so that D was not guilty of V's murder. It is arguable that a disagreement about the expected victim's identity is at least as if not more fundamental to the enterprise than the method used to inflict the violence. However, others argue that such disagreement is irrelevant because the legal definition of murder does not refer to the victim's identity; it merely refers to the causing of death of another human being with one of two

---

96   John Spencer, 'Trying to Help Another Person Commit a Crime' in P Smith (ed.) *Criminal Law: Essays in Honour of J.C. Smith* (Butterworths 1987) 148.

97   Simester et al. (n 31) 258.

98   Section 1 Criminal Law Act 1977.

99   John Smith, 'Commentary on *R v Broad*' [1997] Criminal Law Review 666, 668.

intentions.[100] In the example above therefore, D1 and D2 still agreed to commit murder, albeit different murders.

As to the *mens rea* requirements, section 191 of the Criminal Law Act 1977 clearly indicates that D must intend that the agreement be carried out, that is, that the crime they agree to commit should be committed. That said, there is (strictly speaking) a House of Lords' authority – *Anderson*[101] – to the effect that D need only intend to fulfil his/her role in the conspiracy. However, as commentators have suggested,[102] the debates that preceded the enactment of the 1997 Act together with various recent appellate decisions strongly suggest that nothing short of an intent that the offence be committed will suffice. There should therefore be no difficulty in convicting D of conspiracy to murder V if D agreed with E and intended that V be killed. What if V's death was a known side-effect of the agreement between D and E – as where D and E agree to destroy a house by fire and V is killed in the process? Provided D foresaw V's death as a virtual certainty, it matters not that he was only motivated to act by the desire to destroy the house and collect the insurance money.[103]

Summary and Conclusions

The law relating to the encouragement and assistance of crime is crying out for clarification, especially regarding D's culpability, and it is hoped that the House of Commons Justice Committee's report will ultimately prompt further review by the Government.

There is a real fear that secondary liability for murder can arise too readily. A young lad (D) stands and watches his mate (P) fighting with another lad (V). D may or may not shout general words of encouragement, but P then draws a knife and fatally stabs V. Having heard that D had agreed with P to use violence against V, it is easy to imagine that the jury would infer that D had foreseen what P did (even if D had not uttered any encouragement during the fight). D's conviction for murder, despite his protestations that he only foresaw some (not serious) injury being caused to V, would not be unduly surprising.

Furthermore, the current rationale for the joint enterprise principle, based on foresight that the crime might occur together with the risk of an escalation in criminality through group offending, is too far-reaching. The Law Commission's suggested reforms in 2007 appear not to have addressed this satisfactorily. Something more is needed, especially in homicide where the consequences for all those concerned are so serious. Krebs' suggestion that that something should be acquiescence merits serious consideration. The link between D's encouragement or assistance and P's crime needs to be strengthened in order to justify D's liability for a crime that was not the object of the venture. Potential injustices are particularly acute in homicide, especially as long as the mandatory life sentence for murder remains in force. In addition, there is a need for a resolution of the current uncertainty in the case law, whether D should be liable for manslaughter if he lacks the *mens rea* for murder.

Finally, it will naturally be interesting to see how the Serious Crime Act 2007 offences are used in practice, especially in relation to secondary (and principal) liability, and how far the culpability requirements cause difficulties. When applied to homicide, the likely complications are even greater.

---

100   For example Simester et al. (n 31) 306-307.
101   [1986] AC 27.
102   For example Simester et al. (n 31) 313-15.
103   This is implied from the Privy Council's decision in *Yip Chiu-Cheung* [1995] 1 AC 111.

Chapter 2
Accessories and Principals after *Gnango*

Bob Sullivan

Introduction

Magda Pniewska (V) was walking home from work across a South London car park talking to her sister by phone. Suddenly and shockingly she was dead, killed by a bullet fired by someone known only as 'Bandana Man' (P) in the reports of *R v Gnango*.[1] The bullet had been directed at Armel Gnango (D) who had responded to a shot from P by firing back at him, prompting several exchanges of gun fire, an event described as a 'shoot-out' in judgments shortly to be scrutinised. Four days later P was arrested but then released and never brought to trial for reasons unknown. Had P been brought to trial for murder, from the facts to hand, it should have been a simple case. That the victim was in some thin sense an unintended victim would not have made for any complication. P was shooting to kill and did kill by shooting. One could reference the doctrine known as transferred malice to emphasise the irrelevance of the fact that it was D rather than V who was the intended victim of P. But that seems unnecessary. The death of V was in no sense an unpredictable outcome. It was exactly the kind of thing that might happen when persons fire guns at each other in places where members of the public are present. It should suffice simply to say that P killed V, acting with an intent to kill.[2] The only conceivable plea was anticipatory self defence but as the exchange of fire was found at the trial of D to be a case of mutual aggression, there would have been no basis for such a plea.

Had there been a joint trial of P and D, resolving D's liability would seem an equally straightforward matter. Most obviously he was guilty of attempting to murder P and equally clearly possession of a firearm with intent to endanger life. It is a mere speculation but it might well have been the case that the prosecution at a joint trial would have been content with a verdict for those offences against D. Given the seriousness of his crimes, D may well have received a life sentence although probably he would have received a lesser minimum term than P in the light of the usual discount given for attempt by contrast with the completed crime. But at a trial where D was the sole defendant, the prosecution sought a verdict of murder in addition to attempted murder and the possession offence. What might have been a simple case became in the words of Lord Dyson, 'a very difficult case'.[3]

---

1   [2011] UKSC 59. For a trenchant critique of the decision see Richard Buxton, 'Being an Accessory to One's Own Murder' [2012] Criminal Law Review 275 and for a more favourable view see Graham Virgo, 'Joint Enterprise Liability is Dead, Long Live Accessorial Liability' [2012] Criminal Law Review 850.

2   As will be examined below, D was convicted for murder on the basis that he was a secondary party or a joint principal in P's murder of V. The Supreme Court applied the doctrine of transferred malice in order to, in the terms of the doctrine, transfer the *mens rea* of P with respect to D to the victim V. But it seems more straightforward to say that there was a coincidence of *mens rea* and *actus reus*, the identity of the victim being irrelevant to proof of the offence of murder.

3   [2011] UKSC 59 [106].

At trial D was convicted of murder on the basis that he was a secondary offender to the offence perpetrated by P. D's conviction was based on his being a party to a joint enterprise with P, a form of liability that the Supreme Court designated, 'parasitic accessory liability'.[4] The jury were directed that if they found that D and P had agreed in advance or spontaneously on the spot to exchange fire in a public place they were parties to a joint enterprise to commit the offence of affray. It followed that D was party to P's murder of V if he foresaw the risk that P in participating in the violent affray might kill or seriously hurt someone other than D.

The Court of Appeal quashed D's conviction for murder because (briefly), it considered that the agreement to commit an affray was simply another way of describing the agreement to shoot and be shot at. The affray and the shooting were not in substance two different things.[5] The Supreme Court agreed that D could not be found guilty of murder as parasitic accessory. However, by a majority of six to one the conviction for murder was restored. For Lord Phillips and Lord Judge (with whom Lord Wilson agreed) D's liability was based on direct, or, if you will, true complicity on the basis that he had encouraged the conduct of P which caused the death of V. Because of the way the case was argued below, Lords Brown and Clarke thought that liability on that basis was not an available option for the Supreme Court.[6] But they did consider it possible to restore the conviction of D on the basis that he was a joint principal in murder alongside P. Lord Dyson was happy to adopt either theory believing that there was no difference of substance in the circumstances of this case between convicting D as a principal or as an accomplice.[7] Lord Kerr, in his compelling dissent, considered that D could not be convicted of murder on any ground.

Below, arguments will be made against convicting D for murder either as a secondary party or as a principal. But first, a preliminary word about the nature of these arguments is in order. It will not be argued that any injustice of substance was suffered by D. To label D a murderer, particularly a principal in murder, was somewhat forced and unnatural. But only chance factors made P rather than D the true principal to the crime. D behaved in a very culpable and very dangerous way. That he was implausibly labelled a murderer does not entail that the punishment he received was in any way excessive.[8] The critique to be offered is predominantly doctrinal rather than normative.

---

4   Ibid. [15].

5   [2010] EWCA Crim 1691 [48]-[70].

6   Their position has considerable force. The prosecution at trial and before the Court of Appeal had confined itself to arguing that D murdered V on the basis of joint enterprise. Only before the Supreme Court was an argument based on direct complicity developed. Factual matters of relevance to that form of liability such as the intentional encouragement by D of P's conduct were taken by Lords Phillips and Judge to be established by inference from the jury's verdict following a direction limited to parasitic complicity, a direction that, unsurprisingly, did not include any reference to the elements of direct complicity.

7   '... in my view Lord Phillips and Lord Judge are right to say that in this case the difference between holding the respondent liable as a principal to an agreed joint activity rather than as an accessory is not a difference of substance. Either way the Crown had to prove that the respondent and Bandana Man agreed to shoot and be shot at with the necessary intent' [105]. But in convicting D as a principal the focus is on D's conduct and his *mens rea* in relation to that conduct. In convicting him as a secondary offender one must ask questions about D's state of mind in relation to P's conduct, particularly the matter of whether D intended to encourage that conduct. As Lord Dyson observed, 'The judge was right to distinguish between encouragement [to shoot] and provocation' [100].

8   If D had been convicted for attempted murder rather than murder itself it is highly likely that he would have escaped a life sentence or received a lesser minimum term in the event of a life sentence. That need not be an embarrassment for persons who hold that culpability is exclusively a function of the state of mind in which acts or omissions are done rather than changes in the world brought about as a consequence of the acts or omissions. For a sophisticated defence of the view that results do matter for assessments of culpability see

The Supreme Court's decision in *Gnango* places a useful limit on the scope of the joint enterprise doctrine. However, the decision expands core complicity and enlarges the concept of the principal offender in doctrinally flawed ways. And there is a normative sting in the tail of this doctrinal argument. This expansion of the categories of principals and accomplices may implicate persons in crimes for which, in moral terms, they should not be convicted.

The impact of *Gnango* on parasitic accessory liability, direct or 'true' accessory liability and the conception of principal offenders will be examined in that sequence. Before that there must be a consideration of a question of fact rather than law. It concerns what is perhaps the most important aspect of the case.

'To Shoot and Be Shot at'

Crucial to the majority opinions of the Supreme Court was the characterisation of the exchange of fire between P and D as something more than a sudden gunfight. The exchange was not merely a coincidence of aggressive, individual intents. On the basis of the trial judge's direction, the majority were sure that the jury found an agreement between D and P 'to shoot and be shot at' by the opponent. Indeed the exchange of fire was likened to a duel. With that take on the facts of the case in place, the way was opened for a (problematic) finding by Lord Phillips and Lord Judge, in which Lord Wilson concurred, that D was encouraging P to shoot at him and vice versa. That paved the way for the startling conclusion that each man was complicit in the violence that his opponent aimed at him. Similarly, the finding that D and P were quasi duellists made them for Lords Brown and Clarke, joint participants in a dangerous event making each man a principal to any harm associated with the event caused by the opponent (as well, of course, a principal to any harm he caused directly).

This majority construction of the facts was a great puzzle for the dissentient Lord Kerr. The straw the majority used to make the brick amounted to this: D had entered a large, residential car park with a revolver concealed on his person and had told the occupants of a parked car that he was looking for P because he was owed money by P. Suddenly P appeared at the head of steps leading down to the car park, and immediately drew his revolver and fired at D who in turn fired back at P. Further exchanges of fire ensued. In directing the jury on a joint enterprise to commit an affray Cooke J required the jury to find, '… that Bandana Man and the defendant joined together to commit such unlawful violence by having a gunfight, whether pre-planned or whether on the spur of the moment on the top of the steps and the side of the car and that this joint enterprise came into being before Magda was killed …'. Even though Cooke J thought that a finding to that effect would establish merely coincident but antagonistic intents to kill the opponent, the majority were content that the jury must have found an agreement 'to shoot and be shot at'.

Lord Kerr's analysis of the nature of the interchange between D and P is confined to the proven facts:

> Can it be said that solely because there was an exchange of fire it must be on foot of a plan? Agreement to shoot it out with an opponent would be such a plan but there is no evidence that this is what happened here. But where there has been what has been described as a 'spontaneous agreement' to engage in a shoot-out, the question arises whether this can truly be said to be the

---

Antony Duff, *Criminal Attempts* (Oxford University Press, 1996) chapter 12. If persuaded by Duff, then one would consider that D has suffered an injustice of substance as well as form.

product of an agreement in any real sense. Is it not at least as likely to be the result of a sudden simultaneously reached coincident intention by the two protagonists to fire at each other.[9]

The fact that P and D were armed with revolvers might be suggestive of mutually planning a shoot-out. But those involved in the drug commerce of South London are habitually armed, mostly with knives but not infrequently guns. On the evidence all that can be plausibly assumed is that if D met P on that day he was likely to shoot him and that P, aware of that risk, got the first shot in. There will be many occasions when D knows that if he meets P at a particular time and place there might be violent trouble from P and he resolves to meet force with force. That does not amount to proof of an agreement between D and P to 'shoot or be shot at' or 'hit and be hit' as the case may be.

Further consideration of *Gnango* will assume for the sake of the legal analysis the existence of a genuine agreement between D and P to shoot and be shot at. The case is a challenge to received doctrine even on that assumption. It will be even more disruptive if trial judges apply the new learning to be found in *Gnango* to cases where there is no genuine agreement, spontaneous or otherwise, to exchange acts of violence.

Parasitic Accessory Liability, aka, Secondary Liability Based on Joint Enterprise

D's conviction for murder was based on this well established yet controversial form of liability.[10] The prosecution case was as follows: by planning or agreeing spontaneously to exchange fire, D and P agreed to commit the offence of affray. As commission of the affray would involve shooting guns in a public place, D must have foreseen a risk that a passing member of the public would be killed or seriously hurt. So commission of the predicate offence carried the risk of a further more serious offence. On well established principle, on proof of an agreement to commit the predicate offence, D would be implicated as a secondary offender in P's further offence, if he foresaw a risk that P would commit the offence with the *mens rea* for the offence, in circumstances related to the commission of the predicate offence.

The artificial construction of a joint enterprise at trial was well exposed by the Court of Appeal. In substance there was no separate predicate offence with a further, subsequent offence disclosed by the facts. There was just one event, namely shooting at each other in public. At trial, it was common ground that if there was proof of an agreement to have a shoot-out, actual participation in the shoot-out involved coincident but individual intents; the possibilities of an agreement to 'shoot and be shot at' theory went unexplored. The particulars of offence on the count of affray consisted of a description of the agreed shoot-out. Essentially, the Court of Appeal decided that the predicate crime (violent affray) was indivisible as an event from the murder of V.

---

9   [2011] UKSC 59 [121].

10   The controversy is both doctrinal and normative. In terms of doctrine there is a division of opinion as to whether parasitic accessory liability is an organic extension of direct accessory liability or whether it is a free-standing form of liability. In normative terms there is a division of opinion whether it is ever justifiable to impose liability for a crime B on the basis of awareness that participation in crime A may result in one or more of one's fellow participants in that crime going on to commit crime B. The standard texts diverge on these questions: contrast David Ormerod, *Smith and Hogan's Criminal Law* (13th edn, Oxford University Press 2011) 213-30 with Andrew Simester, John Spencer, Bob Sullivan and Graham Virgo, *Simester and Sullivan's Criminal Law: Theory and Doctrine* (4th edn, Hart 2010) 233-44.

The Court of Appeal judgment was unanimously endorsed in the Supreme Court.[11] This further example of a heavy handed use of the joint enterprise doctrine might have led to a radical review of the doctrine by the Supreme Court. After all the House of Lords in *R v Rahman*[12] could find no theory to fold parasitic accessory liability into the body of rules comprising direct or true complicity. In *Rahman*, Lord Bingham accepted that the joint enterprise doctrine 'lacks logical purity' and rests not on firm legal principle but on 'earthy realism'.[13]

However, there was little prospect of a radical review: for decades defendants have been imprisoned because of convictions obtained under joint enterprise, including it would have to be said some very bad people who might otherwise have received far less than their full quantum of justified punishment.[14] The Supreme Court fully endorsed parasitic accessory liability as an acceptable form of criminal liability in the most plain of terms. If D forms a joint enterprise with P to commit crime A and foresees a risk that as an incident of crime A, P will go on to commit crime B with the requisite *mens rea* for crime B, then should P commit crime B, D will be complicit in crime B. D need not do or say anything that encourages or assists P in his commission of crime B.[15] Following a joint select committee report which in substance endorsed the joint enterprise doctrine,[16] the coalition Government announced that it had no plans to reform joint enterprise.[17] It is here to stay. All that *Gnango* offers by way of limitation is an insistence that crime B is a separate event from crime A as would be the case for instance where D and P agree to burgle V's home and P murders V when disturbed during the burglary .

Direct or True Accessorial Liability

Direct[18] or true complicity, historically based on intentional acts of direct assistance or encouragement of the principal offence, is far less controversial than the parasitic variant of

---

11   There was unanimity that D's murder conviction could not be restored on the basis of the joint enterprise doctrine.

12   [2008] UKHL 45, [2009] 1 AC 129.

13   [2008] UKHL 45 [25].

14   Perhaps the most telling example is the conviction for murder of two defendants present (along with others not brought to trial) at the racially motivated killing of the schoolboy Stephen Lawrence. Recall that it could not be proved as against either defendant that he directly participated in the attack on Stephen. The most that could be proved – and it was enough under the joint enterprise doctrine – was that they were present at the scene of the crime in support of the attackers, foreseeing that one or more of the attackers would seriously hurt Stephen with intent to do so: *Dobson* [2011] EWCA Crim 1255. Many persons will be content that no injustice was done to the defendants on the basis of video footage, ruled admissible at trial, that showed the defendants to be virulent racists. By contrast other persons convicted of murder on the basis of joint enterprise seem to be little more than persons in the wrong place at the wrong time. See note 54 and associated text below.

15   [2011] UKSC 59 [42]. Lord Phillips and Lord Brown do not offer any doctrinal or normative justification of parasitic accessory liability. Their brief black letter rendition of the elements of this form of liability underscores the fact that in doctrinal terms this form of liability is firmly entrenched.

16   House of Commons Justice Committee, *Joint Enterprise*, HC 1597 (2012).

17   Justice Committee, *First Special Report: Joint Enterprise: Government Response to the Committee's Eleventh Report of Session 2010-12* (HC 2010-12) Appendix A: Government Response. This is available at http://www.publications.parliament.uk/pa/cm201012/cmselect/cmjust/1901/190102.htm (date last accessed 22/3/2013 at 11:53am).

18   While all forms of complicity are derivative in that they are dependent on the commission of the principal offence, the term 'direct' is used in the text to identify those cases where the assistance or

complicity. To be sure, some very peripheral acts of encouragement or assistance can suffice to establish complicity.[19] But typically if D assists or encourages P to commit crime A, intending[20] his conduct to assist or encourage the commission of crime A, he will be P's true partner in crime. But the boundaries of direct complicity are threatened. There is now a body of dicta allowing recklessness on the part of D as to the circumstances and consequences of P's conduct, in addition to intent and knowledge, as a sufficient form of culpability. So take D, a retailer, who may now be P's accomplice to an act of violence if he suspects that P wants the kitchen knife he bought from him for violent purposes even if he is unsure that P will use the knife in any violence he inflicts on others. The bounds of complicity may encompass persons who do not act in order to assist or encourage crime provided they are aware that their acts of assistance or encouragement may assist P if and when he commits an offence of the type that D has contemplated that P might commit.[21] And now comes a further threat to the integrity of direct complicity in the shape of Lords Phillips's and Lord Judge's judgment (Lord Wilson agreeing) in *Gnango*. They ruled that D had been an accomplice to P's murder of V by encouraging him to shoot, notwithstanding that the target of the shot was D himself.[22]

Recall the trial judge had directed the jury that before they could find a joint enterprise to commit affray they had to find that either in advance, or spontaneously, D and P agreed to have a shoot-out. For Lord Phillips and Lord Judge this direction implied a jury finding that D and P agreed to shoot and be shot at. An agreement to that effect proved to their satisfaction that D was encouraging P to shoot at him thereby making him an accomplice to P's shot at himself and, applying the doctrine of transferred malice, an accomplice to the killing of V.[23]

This glossing of the trial direction has been criticised above on the ground explained by Lord Kerr that the sudden eruption of shooting was equally compatible with coincident, individual intents rather than an agreement to shoot and be shot at. The majority analysis that an agreement to fight entails that each man is an accomplice of his opponent is better tested against facts which incontestably establish a prior agreement to fight prior to the fight. In *Attorney General's Reference (No 6 of 1980)*,[24] D and P quarrelled in a pub and agreed to settle their difference by going outside to fight. Unquestionably, an agreement to hit, and risk being hit in return. Recall that each man was guilty of assaulting the other, their respective consents to the fight affording no defence. It must now be considered *post Gnango* whether each man was complicit in the violence of the other and thereby a party to the assault upon himself.[25]

---

encouragement flows directly to the principal offence, which is not the case for parasitic complicity.

19   See further, Joshua Dressler, 'Reforming Complicity Law: Trivial Assistance as a Lesser Offence' (2011) 5 Ohio State Journal of Criminal Law 427.

20   As complicity in its direct form should be confined to persons who act in true concert, encouragement or assistance should be provided in order that it should assist or encourage P's crime but it will suffice even on classic, restrained accounts of the limits of complicity that D assists P in the certain knowledge that he will assist P's crime even though it was not his purpose to do so: *National Coal Board v Gamble* [1959] 1 QB 11.

21   See the authorities gathered and analysed by Ormerod (n 10) 206-13.

22   [2011] UKSC 59 [42]-[65].

23   D's argument that he was protected by the victim immunity established by *R v Tyrrell* [1894] 1 QB 710 was rightly rejected: [47]-[54].

24   [1981] 1 QB 715.

25   In *Gnango*, the strangeness of this idea is muted by its deployment as a transmission mechanism to find D guilty of an offence against V rather than himself. But in theory at least this new take on the bounds of complicity could be used creatively by prosecutors. Say D and P agree to fight and D comes out second best. He is only able to give his opponent a bloody nose while he suffers a broken jaw. D's woes may be

To find complicity on these facts we must find encouragement in fact and intent to encourage. Make the assumption that the fight was P's idea and that D was a reluctant participant but anxious not to lose face. Until the fighting starts it would be very hard to say that D had encouraged P to fight. Of course when they start fighting D knows that P will try to hit him, something that P would not have done had D declined to fight. But no-one outside a court of law would say that to stand up to a bully is to encourage the bully. That the fight is agreed rather than spontaneous does not of itself bring P and D into concert regarding the blows aimed by the opponent. This was well recognised in another context by the Supreme Court of Canada when ruling that D a purchaser of drugs did not become a party to the seller's drug trafficking when agreeing the time and place for the sale. The activities of buyers and sellers have to be co-ordinated by agreement but they are counterparties on different sides of the same fence.[26] And the same is surely true of fighters, even when they fight by agreement.

For sure, by participating in the fight D knows his blows will induce reciprocal blows inflicted by P. But as recognised by Lord Clarke who declined to restore D's conviction for murder on the basis that he was P's accomplice[27] there is a difference between encouraging a blow and provoking a blow.[28] But assume if merely for the sake of argument that any participant in a fight who cannot claim self defence is in terms of his conduct encouraging his opponent to fight back. But of course, this is not enough. A conviction based on complicity in the opponent's violence requires proof of an intent to encourage.

Returning to the reluctant fighter D, he lacks an intent to encourage P's violence in the core sense of the meaning of intent. He is not fighting in order to allow P to hit him. As far as D is concerned the less blows from P the better. Of course, he knows that when he starts fighting P it is virtually certain that P will fight back. Does this open the way for a finding of intent on the basis of a *Woollin* direction?[29] No, for two reasons. First, finding intent merely on the basis of knowledge that some outcome (here blows from P) is virtually certain does not sit well with a finding of intent to *encourage*. Secondly, the *Woollin* direction was devised for a context where the issue was D's knowledge of the impact of his conduct on a passive victim – did he know that it was virtually certain that he would seriously hurt the baby when he threw the baby against a hard surface? It is ill-adapted to the issue of whether D intended to bring about a certain form of conduct on the part of a voluntary human agent. For instance, the fact that D knows that if he enters a certain room that it is virtually certain that he will be hit by P (it is D's own room currently occupied by burglar P) does not warrant a finding that D intended to be hit by P.[30]

The judgment of Lord Phillips and Lord Judge does not descend to any detailed consideration of whether on the facts of the case there was encouragement in fact together with an intent to encourage. They acknowledged a difference between provoking a shooting and encouraging a shooting. But that was without substance or impact. Their finding of complicity is premised on but one thing, namely the trial direction requiring a finding from the jury that the exchange of shots was a planned or spontaneously agreed event. This allegedly agreed exchange of fire is then

---

compounded by being made a party to the serious offence committed against him by P. Should D receive the same sentence as P?

26   *Sokoloski* [1977] 2 SCR 523.
27   As will be examined below he restored D's conviction on the ground that D was a principal to V's murder.
28   [2011] UKSC 59 [76].
29   [1999] 1 AC 82.
30   See *R v Redmond-Bate* [1999] Crim LR 998 where the Court of Appeal held that D could not be arrested to prevent a breach of the peace if his conduct was lawful however likely it was to induce a violent response on the part of others. And see *Beatty v Gillbanks* (1882) 9 QBD 308.

transmuted into an agreement, 'to shoot and be shot at'. Then everything is in place. It is taken to be self evident that parties to such an agreement encourage their counter party to shoot and intend to do so. They were undaunted that the jury, directed on joint enterprise liability alone, were not required to find that D encouraged P to shoot with the intention of encouraging P to shoot.[31]

It is, it is hoped, fair comment that Lords Phillips, Judge and Wilson were determined that the tragic death of V should be marked by a verdict of murder. Before this judgment it would not have occurred to criminal lawyers that D and P were accomplices in the direct, true sense. The reason for that is that that their relation was one of fierce antagonism. Even if, questionably, it is allowed that the shooting was a concerted shoot-out, it was still an occasion set up to give vent to a murderous intent toward an opponent. But now the bounds of direct complicity bring together murderous opponents with potentially novel and startling findings of liability.[32]

Principal Offenders

In English and Welsh criminal law the concept of a principal in a criminal offence is closely tied to persons who directly perpetrate the offence. For that reason, pre *Gnango*, one would have ruled out categorically any possibility that D could be found liable for V's murder on the basis that he was a principal offender. Yet Lords Brown and Clarke, found that he was a principal in V's murder. Lord Dyson thought that D's involvement in V's murder could take both forms, either as a principal or as an accomplice.

Lord Brown's judgment is extremely brief. For him this was a simple case. It sufficed to say that D and P had jointly agreed to do something very reprehensible and dangerous to the public. Because of their agreement to act in this fashion they were jointly responsible for any bad outcome that arose irrespective of who was directly responsible for what. They were equally responsible in moral terms for V's death, a responsibility best expressed by finding both men were principals in the matter of her death. No further refinements were necessary.[33]

Essentially, Lord Clarke is at one with Lord Brown. But he showed a little more concern for the structure and form of the criminal law than his colleague. He was not convinced that D was an accessory to the shots fired by P. Although concurring with the majority's finding that D and P had agreed to shoot and be shot at he was not sure that D could be said to be encouraging rather than provoking P to shoot. So, how to express D's liability?

> the victim was shot and killed in the course of the respondent carrying out the agreement between the two men as principals to shoot and be shot at just as in a duel. I am not disposed to analyse the respondent's liability for murder in accessory terms but as a principal to a joint enterprise.[34]

As a statement of where moral responsibility lies for V's death there is much to commend in this straightforward approach, an approach that avoids the counter-intuitive step of concluding that D

---

31   Lord Kerr in his dissenting judgment was particularly critical on this point: 'I do not consider that the verdict of the jury can be upheld on the basis that it was founded on their conclusion that [D] had either had the requisite intention or that the virtually certain result of his firing at [P] was that he would return fire and that [D] knew that this was virtually certain to occur' [125]. It should be noted that Lord Kerr does consider that a finding of an intent to encourage can be based on oblique intent, contrary to the view taken in the text above.

32   See (n 25).

33   [2011] UKSC 59 [69]-[71].

34   Ibid. [76].

was an accessory to a crime directed against him.[35] Even if it is thought that finding an agreement to shoot and be shot at is contrived and that D and P were shooting at each other independently, they must have been aware of the dangers they were creating for persons far removed from the violent drug culture they inhabited. Particularly in the matter of a gunfight in a public place, there is much to be said for the proposition that voluntary participation in such an event engages responsibility for any harm caused to third parties either by oneself or by a fellow participant, including harms caused by opponents.

But the conversion of moral responsibility into legal liability must be routed through the existing rules of the criminal law. Under those rules there are three pathways for liability for murder: as a principal offender; as a direct or true accessory; as a parasitic accessory. It is bedrock doctrine that the principal offender is the perpetrator, the person directly responsible for bringing about the *actus reus* of the offence.[36] That person was P not D. On the face of it, Lords Brown and Clarke have created a significant enlargement of the class of principal offenders. For them, all parties to an agreement to commit a dangerous crime may be principal offenders in respect of harms caused by any party to the agreement on committing any crime of the type agreed. So the crooked accountant who in advance of the violent robbery agrees to launder the proceeds may be a principal in the murder of the security guard. As alluded to already, there may be arguments in favour of re-shaping the criminal law to enable such a verdict. But such radical change would seem a decision for a legislature rather than a court. A major omission in the judgments of Lord Brown and Lord Clarke is the absence of any discussion of the requirement for a causal relationship between the principal and his crime. The matter is not even addressed let alone finessed.[37]

By way of a postscript to his judgment Lord Clarke addressed another way of finding D liable as a principal for V's murder. In his opinion D by shooting at P caused P to shoot back at him. By that token D was a joint principal in any shot made by way of response to his shots (and, presumably shots made by way of response to D's threatening presence given that P fired the first

---

35   This is not to advocate extension of the *Tyrrell* principle but to maintain that outside special circumstances such as sado-masochistic encounters, persons do not encourage or assist the infliction of harms upon themselves.

36   'Principals cause, accomplices encourage (or otherwise influence) or help. If the instigator were regarded as causing the result he would be a principal and the conceptual division between principals (or, as I prefer to call them, perpetrators) and accessories would vanish. Indeed, it was because the instigator was not regarded as causing the crime that the notion of accessories had to be developed' (Lord Bingham in *Rahman* [2008] UKHL 45 [17]).

37   There have been departures from the position so clearly set down by Lord Bingham in the note above. In *Mendez and Thompson* [2010] EWCA Crim 516, Hughes LJ concluded a major survey of secondary liability with these words: 'At its most basic level secondary liability is founded on a principle of causation, that a defendant (D) is liable for an offence committed by a principal actor (P) if by his conduct he has caused or materially contributed to the commission of the offence (with the requisite mental element); and a person who knowingly assists or encourages another person to commit an offence is taken to have contributed to its commission'. In the leading English academic work on complicity, common law secondary liability which results in an unqualified conviction of the secondary party for the offence committed by the principal is taken to be normatively and doctrinally incoherent unless a causal connection is established between the accessory's conduct and the principal's crime (Keith Smith, *A Modern Treatise on Criminal Complicity* (Oxford University Press, 1991). If these views are soundly based then the common law accepts that voluntary conduct can at least sometimes be caused by encouragement or assistance and the line between perpetrators and accessories is not sharp. Lord Bingham's view is favoured here but the point to be made is not who has the better view but the failure of the judgments of Lord Brown and Lord Clarke to engage with these doctrinal issues.

shot). He came to a firm conclusion that his analysis was correct but declined to base his judgment on it because of a lack of argument by counsel on the point.[38]

Should Lord Clarke's take on causation prove influential there would be a radical expansion of the class of principal offenders. To date a major restraint on causal findings has been a fundamental assumption that absent special circumstances, such as deception or coercion, our choices arise from the exercise of our free will and that we alone are responsible for our voluntary and informed choices and the natural and probable outcomes resulting from those choices. If P decides to shoot at D, any attempt on his part to deflect responsibility for his act by saying, 'D made me do it – he disrespected me' would be curtly dismissed. More attention would be paid if P said, 'I had to do it – it was kill or be killed', but full responsibility would be attributed to P if following examination of his claim it is concluded that he was not acting in self defence. In *Gnango*, P was not shooting in self defence and neither was D when he returned fire.

What has just been described is a theory of responsibility rather than a theory of causation as such. And it must be allowed that it is simply not true to say that conduct considered voluntary in law cannot be caused by the interventions of other human agents. It is not at all unreasonable to hold, for instance, that drug suppliers are morally responsible for drug induced deaths arising from supplying dangerous drugs. There is nothing in conceptual terms to prevent a legal system from cashing out that moral responsibility by making the supply of the drug a legal cause of the death physically caused by the drug. And a legal system can do this even if at one and the same time it holds that the drug taker is also morally responsible for taking the fatal drug and thereby an agent in the causing of her own death. There is no reason of causal logic which entails that the subsequent, voluntary taking of the drug takes the supplier out of the causal story. Indeed, there were a series of Court of Appeal decisions ruling that suppliers of illegal drugs had caused drug induced deaths, albeit consumption of the drug was taken to be a voluntary, informed act on the part of the deceased.

Be that as it may, the House of Lords in *R v Kennedy (no 2)*[39] reasserted the legal dogma that voluntary choices are uncaused choices, holding that the supplier had not caused the death of the addict as the decision to take the drug was a voluntary decision and therefore supervened in causal terms over the supply of the drug. Lord Clarke has posed a new challenge to the dogma but, remarkably, when doing so he did not reference the decision in *Kennedy*. The one criminal law case he cited was *R v Pagett*[40] where the Court of Appeal confirmed D's conviction for the manslaughter of his hostage V even though the shots that killed her were fired by police officers. But they were firing in self defence as he acknowledged but without taking the point that if D creates a situation where P must act in self defence, P's actions are no longer voluntary and in law may be said to be caused by D. It is hard to see how *Pagett* assists Lord Clarke and the same applies to authorities he cites from the law of tort,[41] a branch of law which does not use the concepts of principals and accessories.

Vindicating the Victim

In accounts of the virtues of the English criminal justice system, the neutrality of prosecutors and judges concerning the outcome of criminal cases is taken to be a prime value.[42] An acquittal is not

38　[2011] UKSC 59 [83]-[92].

39　[2007] UKHL 38.

40　(1983) 76 Cr App R 279.

41　*Gray v Thames Trains Ltd* [2009] EWHL 33, [2009] 1 AC 1339; *Corr v IBC Vehicles Ltd* [2008] UKHL 13, [2008] AC 884.

42　Patrick Devlin, *The Criminal Prosecution in England* (Oxford University Press, 1960).

a system failure. If a defendant is acquitted by raising a reasonable doubt on the basis of unperjured evidence, it shows that the presumption of innocence is working well. If conduct thought likely to be criminal by a prosecutor is shown to fall outside the bounds of the offences charged, this demonstrates that criminal law is a system of stable rules and not ad hoc judgments on the day. At least in public, officials of the criminal justice system would not challenge these claims. And yet prosecutors and judges also conceive of themselves as guardians of public safety and security. As public safety and security are utterly legitimate concerns for public officials and judges there is an inevitable tension between adhering strictly to legal principles and legal values and the realities of securing safety and security.[43]

The majority were committed to marking the tragic death of V with a murder conviction. The most forceful expression of this sentiment comes from Lord Brown:

> The public would in my opinion be appalled if in those circumstances the law attached liability for the death only to the gunman who fired the fatal shot (which, indeed, it will not always be possible to determine). Is he alone to be regarded as guilty of the victim's murder? Is the other gunman really to be regarded as blameless and exonerated from all criminal liability for that killing? Does the decision of the Court of Appeal here, allowing [D's] appeal against his conviction for murder really represent the law of the land?[44]

Even if one had read only that part of his Lordship's judgment one would assume, without more, that he would conclude that D was a murderer. But, until enlightened by Lord Brown, it was far from obvious that D was a murderer. It was obvious that P was a murderer but given the vagaries of the criminal justice system he was a ship that passed in the night. For a prosecutor determined to press for a murder conviction against D it was worth taking a punt on joint enterprise. But once that usually trusty sword had buckled many criminal lawyers would have agreed with the Court of Appeal that it was game over as far as a murder verdict against D was concerned. Speaking just for this criminal lawyer, it was startling to learn from Lords Phillips, Judge and Wilson that D was complicit in shots fired at him by P and by that token complicit in P's murder of V. And even more startling to learn from Lords Brown and Clarke that he was a principal in V's murder just as if he had shot V himself.

To be sure, it was a mere fortuity that it was P rather than D who killed a member of the public. But such fortuities are endemic to result crimes such as murder. And it is not true to say, as Lord Brown does, that not to find D guilty of V's murder would leave him, 'blameless and exonerated' in respect of V's death. The fact that V died demonstrates how dangerous to the public gun fights are, and how blessed we are that such events are rarities in England and Wales.[45] All the more reason to do what is necessary to suppress gunfights, particularly through tough gun control legislation. If D had been punished for attempting to murder P it would have been entirely in point to impose a life sentence with a minimum term reflecting the fact that he participated in an event culminating in the death of V. It is far from ideal that P was arrested but released without being charged. The absence at the trial for the murder of Magda Pniewska of 'Bandana Man' (as he was irritatingly called) discredits the criminal justice system. Such system failures are not best addressed by freehand reconstruction of the facts and wrenching the rules of substantive criminal law from their moorings.

---

43 See further, Bob Sullivan and Ian Dennis (eds), *Seeking Security: Pre-empting the Commission of Criminal Harms* (Hart Publishing 2012).

44 [2011] UKSC 59 [68].

45 *Firearm Crime Statistics*, www.parliament.uk/briefing papers/SNO 1940.pdf.

How Influential Will *Gnango* Be?

From time to time, a decision by our highest appellate court on matters of substantive criminal law causes surprise, consternation even, to practising and academic criminal lawyers. But such decisions can be in the nature of a storm in a teacup in the sense that the disruption to doctrine presaged by the decision fails to materialise or, if it does, for, in legal historical terms, a relatively brief period of time. Perhaps the best example of a case of this type is the decision of the House of Lords in *DPP v Smith*,[46] where the House of Lords ruled that proof of an intent to kill or cause grievous bodily harm for the purposes of murder could be found against D if a reasonable person placed in the same circumstances as D would have foreseen the probability that his conduct would cause death or serious bodily harm to V. For many criminal lawyers this decision lacked legitimacy in the broadest sense of that term. There was a professional and moral commitment to the idea of murder as a crime of subjective intent and a strong sentiment among criminal lawyers that this conception of murder was sundered by the House of Lords to ensure a murder conviction on the particular facts of the case.[47] In the immediate aftermath of the decision all manner of casuistic interpretations were offered to demonstrate that the House of Lords did not mean what it might, ostensibly, have said,[48] a reaction which emboldened trial judges to give directions to juries in terms that they must find that D himself must have intended to kill or cause serious harm.[49] The decision was finally put out of its misery by the Privy Council declaring that the decision in *Smith* had never been part of the common law.[50] A similar rise and fall attended the decision of the House of Lords in *MPC v Caldwell*[51] where recklessness was, controversially, in large part assimilated to negligence only for the sharp differentiation between the two concepts to be re-established by the House of Lords in *R v G*.[52]

There are grounds for thinking that *Gnango* will be without significance beyond the instant decision. The potentially expansive features of the majority judgments will be briefly revisited, together with reasons for thinking that their practical effect may well be negligible.

(a) Where P and D spontaneously and contemporaneously shoot at each other (or aim armed or unarmed blows at each other) a jury can legitimately infer an agreement between P and D to fight.

At trial the jury were directed on evidence going no further than a contemporaneous exchange of fire between P and D that they might find a prior agreement or a spontaneous agreement to fight with guns. The presence of an agreement to fight was essential at trial to a finding of a joint enterprise to commit the offence of affray and subsequently, before the Supreme Court, that D was an accomplice of P and/or that D was a joint principal with P by agreeing a dangerous act with P. But, as Lord Kerr complained, there was no evidence of a prior agreement and the sudden

46   [1961] AC 290.

47   V was a police officer who wished to question D about goods he suspected were in the boot of D's car. D reacted to V's order to pull over by driving off at speed with V standing on the running board of the car, V falling to his death some 30 seconds later. D claimed to be in a state of panic, unaware of the danger to V.

48   Readings dissected by Glanville Williams in *The Mental Element in Crime* (Oxford University Press, 1965).

49   Richard Buxton, 'The Retreat from Smith' [1966] Criminal Law Review 195.

50   *Frankland and Moore v R* [1987] AC 576.

51   [1982] AC 341.

52   [2003] UKHL 50, [2004] AC 1034.

exchange of fire was equally compatible with coincident, individual intents. There is no legal constraint preventing trial judges from directing juries on the lines of Lord Kerr in cases involving similar facts to *Gnango*.

(b) When P and D agree to fight (with guns, other weapons, other means) there is an agreement to shoot and be shot at, to hit and be hit and so on.

There are, of course, situations where P and D truly agree to fight as when P challenges D to step outside and sort things out. But does such an agreement entail an agreement by both opponents to be hit by the other opponent? If D accepts P's challenge he has not agreed to a choreographed event such as a professional wrestling match. Both opponents accept the risk, the near certainty, of being hit. But they will try their best to avoid being hit. Positing an agreement to shoot and be shot at was an essential predicate for a finding that that D was complicit or a principal in the shots that P aimed at him. But juries should be left free to decide for themselves whether an agreement to fight constituted an agreement to be shot at or to be hit, by contrast with the acceptance of the risk of injury by such means.

(c) An agreement to shoot and be shot at or hit and be hit and so on constitutes encouragement to one's opponent to shoot or to hit with the intention to encourage the opponent to shoot or hit.

There was one final step to take in concluding that D was P's accomplice or a joint principal in the shots that P fired at him. The majority assert that by agreeing to shoot and be shot at, D and P respectively are encouraging the opponent to shoot with an intention to encourage the opponent to shoot. But this is an unexamined assumption which may not stand up to scrutiny even in the plainest cases of agreeing to fight. Take a professional boxing match between P and D. P may be delighted if D is daunted by the occasion and shows little aggression. Most people like an easy pay day. There is nothing to compel a finding that P by agreeing to the match was encouraging and intending to encourage D to hit him. On facts similar to *Gnango* trial judges should in their jury directions fully address the question of encouragement with intent to encourage.

(d) If P and D agree to shoot and be shot at or hit or be hit in circumstances which threaten the safety of V, if in the course of the violent acts exchanged between P and D, V is killed or harmed, P and D will both be principal offenders in any offence committed against V, irrespective of whether it was P or D who directly caused the death or the harm to V.

This was the explanation of D's murder conviction favoured by Lords Brown and Clarke. Particularly in the case of shoot-outs in public places, it has great intuitive appeal. Furthermore, it does not rest on any unnatural assumptions making P a principal offender in any offence that D commits against him and vice versa. With a free hand one might go further and drop the requirement for any agreement for a shoot-out. If P shoots at D without any justification or excuse for doing so it is not unreasonable to say that P should be held responsible for the consequences to any third party of any return shot he provokes from D.

But there is a major doctrinal problem that cannot be dismissed by judicial fiat. For better or worse English/Welsh criminal law tightly ties the concept of the principal offender to the direct perpetrator of the *actus reus* of the offence. So entrenched is the identity between principal offenders and perpetrators, legislation looking at matters in the round is surely required to displace it. As Lords Brown and Clarke are a minority within the majority, trial judges may well decline to make use of this putative expansion of the class of principal offenders.

(e) Where P fires at D without justification or excuse and D returns fire thereby prompting P to fire again each man causes the other man to shoot at him. This causal connection entails that each man is a principal to the other man's shots. So if V is killed or harmed by a shot that P or D fired at his opponent, each man will be a principal offender in the offence committed against V.

Only Lord Clarke thought that this route to a finding that D murdered V was open. If Lord Clarke is correct and is found to be correct in future cases a radical shift in what can make for a crime will occur. If say P and D start fighting with knives even before any harm is done each is in serious trouble with the law in terms of carrying offensive weapons, attempting to murder/cause serious bodily harm and so on. Prior to *Gnango* if D was stabbed and disabled by P before he could do any harm to P at least D would not add to his list of offences beyond that point. But now prosecutors must seriously address the possibility that D as well as P is a principal offender in any offence based on the harm that P has done to him. Because Lord Clarke's analysis of causation is highly disputable it is unlikely that these possibilities will be explored by prosecutors and trial judges.

(f) Conclusion.

> It is not uncommon for groups of youths, supporters of rival football clubs for example, to plan to meet to do battle. It may be that most involved in such a skirmish have no wish to cause any serious injury. There will however be an obvious possibility that one or more of those involved may go beyond the common intention of the majority of the combatants and deliberately cause serious injury … We would consider undesirable however if a practice developed of relying on the doctrine of parasitic accessory liability to charge with murder parties to an affray who had not themselves intended that it would result in serious injury.[53]

In this passage Lord Phillips and Lord Judge are referencing the temptations for prosecutors to resort to joint enterprise in cases of multi-party violence. Take a case where V a City supporter was killed by a United supporter in circumstances highly indicative of an intention to cause V serious injury. But which United supporter? There were many parties involved, the murder weapon is never found and no-one is saying anything. No matter: there is evidence that all United supporters present at the crime scene participated in the affray. A prosecutor can seek murder convictions against all the United supporters on the basis of proof of a joint enterprise to participate in an affray, foreseeing the risk that one or more of their co-fighters might use serious violence against an opponent. Given the large number of young men serving life sentences for murder without proof of an intention to kill or cause serious harm, it is unsurprising that Lord Phillips and his concurring colleagues advise restraint on the part of prosecutors.[54]

But they have given further temptations to prosecutors. They postulate a planned fight, in other words an agreement to hit and be hit. By their reckoning, all the participants are encouraging the blows aimed at them by their opponents. By dint of the agreement to fight and by participating in

---

53   [2011] UKSC 59 [41].

54   The campaigning group Justice for Families have an informative database detailing the circumstances of many young men serving life sentences as a consequence of murder convictions based on joint enterprise. Available at http://www.justice-for-families.org.uk. (Date last accessed 22/3/2012 at 12:10pm)

the fight they intend to encourage the violence of their opponents. The way is open in the terms of their judgment to charge not only the United supporters but also the City supporters as direct accomplices in V's murder. It may be objected that this is to draw too bleak a picture as in the case of true or direct accessory liability in murder it must be proved that D intended to encourage serious violence on the part of P whoever P was. On a historically correct interpretation of the *mens rea* for complicity, in order to convict D as a direct accomplice in murder in the scenario under discussion there must be proof that D's participation in the affray constituted an intentional encouragement of serious violence. But the correct view is losing its grip. There are a significant number of modern cases that merely require that D intentionally does an act aware of the risk that it may encourage P to commit the crime in question should the crime be committed. It seems that the risk that the crime of the crime being committed need only be slight.[55] So D can be implicated in any murder of a City or United supporter if in 'encouraging' the violence of all the fighters by participating in the fighting he foresaw a risk that one of the participants might be seriously violent. The effect of their take on complicity is an extension of the prosecutor's armoury in just the very kind of case that caused him concern. Because their concern is a matter of public record it may discourage prosecutors from exploring these further possibilities.

The prosecutor's problem in *Gnango* was that the perpetrator of the killing was not before the court and the attempt to obtain a murder conviction against a non perpetrator by the usually dependable route of joint enterprise failed in the Court of Appeal. The Supreme Court restored the conviction by a creative application of the law of complicity which brought into concert people trying to kill each other or, alternatively, by extending the class of principal offenders. There are reasons for hoping that neither of these innovations will bed down and become part of received doctrine.

---

55   (n 21).

Chapter 3

Locating Complicity: Choice, Character, Participation, Dangerousness and the Liberal Subjectivist

Ben Livings and Emma Smith

Introduction

The dominant liberal subjectivist account of the criminal law presupposes a nexus between the conduct and culpability of the defendant, the type and extent of any liability imposed, and the concomitant punishment. As such, liability should attach only where this accords with the requirements of individual justice.[1] This priority manifests itself in the doctrinal structuring of criminal offences, which comprise a sufficiently causative *actus reus* in coincidence with the appropriate level of mental culpability, as signified by the requisite *mens rea*, and the absence of a justificatory or excusatory defence. As has often been noted, however, this central ideal is in competition with a parallel need; that of regulating society and preventing harm.[2] The tension inherent to addressing these twin aims is evident in a consideration of accomplice liability, which has long posed problems for the operation of the criminal law, and has been revisited on numerous occasions by the appellate courts, the Law Commission and scholars.

Whilst the manifestation of this disjunction within the law of complicity has been widely acknowledged,[3] most examinations of the subject have sought either to explain the doctrinal basis for the extant principles, or to reconcile accomplice liability with the normative foundations of criminal responsibility.[4] General theories that seek to locate and explain criminal responsibility tend to derive from those based in choice, capacity or character,[5] with the first two of these often elided

---

1   There are numerous statements of this. For Kutz, this means: 'Paradigmatically, individual moral agents are reproached, or reproach themselves, for harms ascribable to them and them alone, on the basis of their intentional actions and causal contributions' Christopher Kutz, *Complicity: Ethics and Law for a Collective Age* (Cambridge University Press, 2000) 4.

2   At one level, this 'regulatory function' may manifest as elements of preventive justice, such as the imposition of civil orders (the most widely known of which is the ASBO); at another it simply inheres within the criminal law. See, generally: Alan Norrie, *Crime, Reason and History* (Cambridge University Press, 2001).

3   Simester notes: 'The pull of judgments about culpability must be reconciled with the demands of criminalisation; Andrew Simester, 'The Mental Element in Complicity' [2006] Law Quarterly Review 578. Sayre points to the conflict between the 'social interest in the general well-being and security' and 'the individual interest of the particular defendant' in the context of complicity. Francis Sayre, 'Criminal Responsibility for the Acts of Another' (1930) 43 Harvard Law Review 689.

4   Although, for substantial expositions of the subject, see, Keith Smith, *A Modern Treatise on the Law of Criminal Complicity* (Oxford University Press, 1991); Kutz (n 1).

5   For an explanation of these, see, Victor Tadros, *Criminal Responsibility* (Oxford University Press, 2004) 44-70.

and counterposed to theories based in character. These choice-capacity theories dominate within the liberal tradition, as they purport to distance the law from the moral and the political, whilst theories based in character are sometimes difficult to align with the ostensible value-neutrality of the criminal sanction.[6] In this chapter, we contend that the inadequacies and incoherence that are evident in a misshapen conception of accomplice liability derive in large part from attempts to locate its tenets in the normative bases of culpability and liberal subjectivism, and we assert that an understanding of the current operation of accomplice liability is more readily found in the regulatory aspects and function of the criminal law, and in conceptions that look to the character and dangerousness of the complicit individual.[7] Here, we suggest that choice and character theories coincide over the matter of criminal liability for complicity,[8] in grounding justification in a conception of criminality that derives from the dangerousness of an individual as manifested in their voluntary participation in crime. Thus, it is an appraisal of that individual based in choice and character that propels policy and provides the impetus for the imposition of accomplice liability.[9] This conception, whilst less concerned with ascribing criminal liability on the basis of culpability, nevertheless vests in the individual; in this case, on the basis of an idea of dangerousness.[10]

In order to navigate the law of complicity, we look first to the way in which the doctrines have come to operate, and their normative foundations. We assert that the rules of criminal complicity are not easily accommodated by the doctrinal function of the criminal law, and nor are they accounted for by its generally accepted normative foundations. From here, we move on to examine recent developments within the law relating to complicity, and argue that what has emerged is a heuristic measure of liability, where the regulatory function of the criminal law predominates over its concern for individual justice, and is in turn shaped by socio-political influences.

Before turning to a doctrinal examination of complicity, there is a need to discern the type of offences that are our concern here. There is significant overlap between inchoate offences (that is, involvement in criminal conduct derived from an incomplete offence) and complicity in relation to offences that have been committed.[11] The forms of complicity considered in this chapter are limited to those which accompany a completed crime; in essence, those which amount to assisting or encouraging an offence,[12] and the unlawful joint enterprise, whether that be considered as separate

---

6   A leading proponent of the choice-capacity approach, Herbert Hart held that punishment should only be imposed where the defendant 'broke the law by an action which was the outcome of his free choice' (HLA Hart, 'Prolegomenon to the Principles of Punishment' [1959] Proceedings of the Aristotelian Society 22). Wilson describes character theories as 'less plausible ... in the context of criminal responsibility generally' William Wilson, *Criminal Law: Doctrine and Theory* (Pearson, 2011) 124.

7   For an account of the limitations of the 'individualistic conception' in relation to complicity, see, Kutz (n 1) 1-16.

8   For Hume, moral judgement founds in character, which is in turn signalled by action: 'If any action be either virtuous or vicious, it is only as a sign of some quality or character; David Hume, *A Treatise of Human Nature* III.iii.1.

9   A model of responsibility ostensibly based in character, but drawing substantially from choice, is proposed by Tadros (n 5). Duff regards the differentiation between the two conceptions as resting on a false dichotomy; 'a spurious distinction between what a person "is" and what she "does"'; Antony Duff, 'Choice, Character, and Criminal Liability' (1993) 12(4) Law and Philosophy 345. It should be clarified that, when we refer to character, we are not stating manifestation of character as an empirical, social or scientific fact, but rather as a justification for the marker of criminality that a conviction represents.

10   Michael Bayles, 'Character, Purpose and Criminal Responsibility' (1982) 1 Law and Philosophy 5.

11   This is even more so the case since the coming into force of the Serious Crime Act 2007, which made sweeping changes to the law of inchoate offences.

12   As covered by the Accessories and Abettors Act 1861, s 8.

or as a component part of the former. In common with much of the work that has been undertaken relating to complicity, we choose here to concentrate on the offence of murder.[13]

Complicity: A Doctrinal Perspective[14]

Statutory authority for accomplice liability is found in s 8 of the Accessories and Abettors Act 1861,[15] which provides four separate conduct elements: aiding, abetting, counselling or procuring the commission of an offence.[16] Although attempts have frequently been made to distinguish between them, it is unsurprising that the four elements have come to be seen as broadly synonymous and interchangeable.[17] It has been described as 'artificial to analyse the terms as independent, alternative, *actus reus* elements',[18] and the consensus is that they signify 'assisting or encouraging'.[19] Alongside the development of these forms of complicity, or subsumed within them, exists the concept of joint enterprise liability.[20] The fictional scenario presented below allows for an examination of joint enterprise liability, and of its accommodation within the wider conception of complicity, upon which we will draw in the ensuing argument:

A person dies as a result of a beating carried out by two men wielding baseball bats, who had planned in advance what they meant to do. Their involvement could take a number of forms:

---

13 Murder brings unique problems to accomplice liability, explored in: Richard Buxton, 'Joint Enterprise' [2009] Criminal Law Review 233. These include the mandatory life sentence, and the potentially constructive nature of the *mens rea* for murder. Largely as a result of these factors, many of the leading cases (and especially in relation to joint enterprise) are concerned with convictions for murder. Jeremy Horder (Law Commissioner at the time the Law Commission most recently examined complicity) said of the relationship: 'It would have been a bit like "Hamlet" without the prince, if you did complicity without murder; House of Commons Justice Committee, *Joint Enterprise* (Eleventh Report of Session 2010-12, HC 1597) ev 16.

14 In what follows in this section, we do not have the space to address exhaustively the range of issues relating to the doctrines of accomplice liability. For a fuller exploration, see Sullivan's chapter in this volume (Chapter 2).

15 As amended by the Criminal Law Act 1977. This applies to indictable offences; summary offences are provided for by the Magistrates' Courts Act 1980, s 44.

16 As Jefferson states, 'Aiding (etc.) is not itself a crime but a way in which a crime is committed'; Michael Jefferson, *Criminal Law* (10th edn, Pearson, 2011) 180. As such, they amount to quasi-*actus reus* requirements.

17 Lord Widgery held that these terms are also interchangeable to an extent in *A-G's Reference (No 1 of 1975)* [1975] QB 773, 779, stating that only procurement seemed to be substantially different due to the necessity for a causal link. For discussion, see: David Ormerod, *Smith and Hogan's Criminal Law* (13th edn, Oxford University Press, 2011) 192-96.

18 Andrew Simester, Bob Sullivan, JR Spencer and G Virgo, *Simester and Sullivan's Criminal Law: Theory and Doctrine* (4th edn, Hart 2010) 210.

19 As Smith states, 'what they mean in practice is "assists or encourages"', although he does add the rider that it may sometimes be necessary to add 'or causes' to these terms (John Smith, 'Criminal Liability of Accessories: Law and Law Reform' [1997] Law Quarterly Review 453). In *Bryce* [2004] 2 Cr App R 35, it was said that 'the shades of difference between [these terms] is far from clear'.

20 A considerable amount has been written about whether liability for engaging in a joint enterprise is a discrete doctrine, separable from that which derives from s 8, or whether it is a subsidiary category of the latter, operating within the limits of s 8. Whilst accepting that there are valid arguments for both sides of this debate (Smith makes a convincing argument for the latter (n 19)), we contend that joint enterprise is in fact distinct from assisting or encouraging. Although some engagement in this debate is inevitable, it is our contention that it is largely moot, and need not interfere overly with the argument we propose.

a. both take part fully in the attack, each intentionally causing serious injury to the victim, and the victim dies as a result of the joint attack; or

b. only one of the men uses the baseball bat, intentionally causing serious injury which results in the victim's death. As agreed, the other restrains the victim in order that he cannot fight back; or

c. the plan may have involved merely causing minor injuries to the victim, and one of the defendants goes beyond this by intentionally causing the death of the victim (here we are concerned with the liability of the defendant who did not exceed the original plan).

To each of these alternative scenarios, we can add another two characters. The first is a shopkeeper, who sells the baseball bats to the men, the second a woman who sees them entering the house of the victim, and shouts, 'Do it! He deserves it!'

In the three scenarios detailed above, the two men wielding baseball bats have set out together with a criminal purpose. In scenario A, ascription of liability for murder appears unproblematic; the conduct of both men is likely to fulfil the *actus reus* of murder, and they can also be said to have the *mens rea* required for this offence. There is therefore no need to invoke the doctrines of complicity, as both can be tried as principal offenders. In scenario B, only one of the men has (individually) fulfilled the *actus reus*. Here, there is a divergence of views as to the applicability of complicity principles. For some, this is an example of what has become known as 'plain vanilla' joint enterprise;[21] 'a plan to commit the actual offence charged'.[22] For others, however, the use of joint enterprise principles in this instance is unnecessary, and even damaging to the coherence of complicity more broadly.[23] In either event, a murder conviction for both men, whether viewed as joint enterprise or co-perpetration, is relatively unproblematic.[24]

Scenario C is, to some, the only one of these that truly warrants the label joint enterprise.[25] In cases such as these, where one of the parties has exceeded the agreed plan,[26] the demarcation of a joint enterprise acts as a mechanism by which to determine whether both should be held liable. In short, liability will be found where the offence is not 'fundamentally different' from that which

---

21   Horder is of the view that there are three types of complicity, although he acknowledges the dispute that exists in relation to this, and concedes that 'the whole law has got very complicated'; House of Commons Justice Committee (n 13) ev 16-17. The Law Commission also considered this to be part of joint enterprise; Law Commission, *Participating in Crime*; Law Com No 305, 2007 1.10, 1.21.

22   *Brown and Another v The State* [2003] UKPC 10, 13, per Lord Hoffmann.

23   Krebs refers to 'joint enterprise analysis' in such cases as 'redundant', holding that the rules around co-perpetration cater to it, and that resort to joint enterprise may 'undermine the well-established rules and requirements of aiding and abetting' Beatrice Krebs, 'Joint Criminal Enterprise' (2010) 73 Modern Law Review 578. We disagree with this, and suggest that this more straightforward example of joint enterprise provides a logical platform upon which to build the more complex form exemplified in scenario C.

24   In scenarios A and B, any disjunction between the formal requirements of murder and the conduct of the men is simply a matter of an agreed division of labour between them. The murder convictions likely to be imposed are unproblematic both legally and morally (according to the subjective view, both men are culpable).

25   For Krebs, this is 'the proper domain of the joint enterprise doctrine' (Krebs (n 23)). Virgo agrees: 'This situation, where D1 has departed from the common purpose and commits an additional offence, is the only one which should properly be designated "joint enterprise"'; Graham Virgo, 'The Doctrine of Joint Enterprise Liability' [2010] Archbold Review 6. It is referred to in *R v Gnango* [2012] 1 AC 827 as 'parasitic accessory liability', a term coined by Smith (n 19).

26   The 'agreed plan' need not be articulated. See: *DPP v Nedrick-Smith* [2006] EWHC 3015 (Admin).

comprised the common purpose,[27] and where the conduct of the principal perpetrator was foreseen as likely by the defendant.[28] We shall refer to this type of joint enterprise as 'joint enterprise+'.

The ancillary characters in the above scenarios (the shopkeeper and the woman who shouts to the main protagonists) may properly be caught by the essence of s 8, in that they have offered either assistance or encouragement. Horder refers to these as 'cases in which, with murder in mind, D assists or encourages P from the sidelines to commit the murder P intends to commit, without being part of P's murderous plan as such'.[29] Complicity of this type involves the defendant contributing to the offence by intentionally assisting or encouraging.[30] Wilson identifies potential grounds for concern:

> [Liability] derives from and is dependent upon the liability of the principal. It requires merely that the secondary party associate himself, by giving intentional help or encouragement, with a person who commits a criminal offence … A person may be liable as an accessory to murder by dint of an act as innocuous as driving the getaway car, providing the murder weapon in the ordinary course of business supply, or, it appears, saying 'oh goody' upon hearing the principal's lethal plan.[31]

In order that accomplice liability does not cast its net too wide, specific *mens rea* requirements serve a limiting function, so that, in the words of Krebs, '[t]he *actus* … only becomes *reus* if the *mens* is *rea*'. This is necessary to preclude the innocent seller of baseball bats, for example, from its purview.[32] Following *R v Bryce*,[33] it must be shown that the defendant's act in fact assisted the later commission of the crime, that it was done deliberately, that the defendant realised it was capable of assisting the commission of the offence, and foresaw its commission as a real possibility, and that when doing the act he intended to assist the principal in what he was doing.[34] The apparent simplicity of these stipulations belie their inherent controversies and complexities;[35] what can be stated with some certainty, however, is that the *mens rea* requirement in assisting or encouraging is higher than that for

---

27 The 'fundamental difference' rule is therefore of the utmost importance and significance, and yet it is itself clouded in uncertainty, to such an extent that Horder has recently written of it: 'most of the problems were left unresolved, and were arguably exacerbated, by the decision of the House of Lords in *Rahman* … I believe that little if anything was settled by the decision'; Jeremy Horder, *Homicide and the Politics of Law Reform* (Oxford University Press, 2012).

28 It is unclear how the idea of 'fundamental difference' and the requirements around foresight interact, as they will often fulfil largely the same function. The requisite degree and precision of foresight is arguable, and the case law is not consistent. For discussion, see: Ormerod (n 17).

29 Horder (n 27) 157. Horder regards the basis of such liability as 'analogous to, but not the same as, the basis of liability [in joint enterprise]'.

30 That is, the accomplice must intend to do the act of assistance or encouragement, with the intention that it assist or encourage the commission of the offence.

31 William Wilson, 'A Rational Scheme of Liability for Participating in Crime' [2008] Criminal Law Review 3. Although it may appear far-fetched, the latter example Wilson offers derives from the facts in *R v Giannetto* [1997] 1 Cr App R 1.

32 In *Johnson v Youden* [1950] 1 KB 544, 546, it was held: 'Before a person can be convicted of aiding and abetting the commission of an offence he must at least know the essential matters which constitute that offence'.

33 *Bryce* (n 19).

34 The Law Com No 305 (n 21) stated succinctly: 'The law relating to the fault element of secondary liability is complex and difficult' (B.67).

35 For a more detailed overview of the *mens rea* requirements of assisting or encouraging, see: Ormerod (n 17) 201-13; Wilson (n 6) 565-73. For Wilson, '[o]ne of the great infelicities of the current law is the lack

joint enterprise.[36] This is because there is no requirement for a common purpose; as Krebs puts it, the '*actus reus* deficit is usually counterbalanced by a *mens rea* "surplus"'.[37]

In joint enterprise+, and in cases of those who provide assistance or encouragement, the accomplice stands to be convicted of the same offence as the principal offender (in this case murder),[38] and yet the defendant's liability is effectively determined by the autonomous action of another. This is the nub of the problem for the orthodox subjectivist view of criminal responsibility, and the reason why complicity is so difficult to reconcile with the liberal, culpability-based criminal law; as Simester notes: 'The criminal law draws upon a limiting principle that D should not be convicted of an offence unless he is *responsible* for a *wrong*'.[39] Against this ideal is juxtaposed a doctrine that imposes liability in a 'parasitic' fashion, deriving from the offence of another, and imposed following any of a range of potential degrees of participation.

There is extensive debate over the existence, operation and interrelation of the principles described above, and the structure of complicity is far from settled or agreed. It is, for example, quite easy to characterise the two main protagonists in the above scenarios as involved in mutual assistance or encouragement, rather than acting in pursuit of a joint enterprise, and therefore to fit them more easily within the literal meaning of s 8. Smith proposes exactly this interpretation: 'If D and P set out together to rape (or to murder), how does D "participate" in P's act of sexual intercourse with V (or P's pulling of the trigger and shooting V) except by assisting him or encouraging him (*i.e.* aiding, abetting, counselling or procuring him) to do the act? It is submitted that there is no other way'.[40] The existence of a joint enterprise then assumes little more than evidential significance, in that its existence can be used to prove the assistance or encouragement, and the accompanying mental states.[41] Whilst Smith's logic is irrefutable, it is nevertheless the case that there is something very different about the relationship of the participant in scenario C (joint enterprise+) to the offence than that of those who shout encouragement or who sell a baseball bat, even where this is done with the *mens rea* for complicity.[42] Other commentators have agreed that there is a conceptual difference to be marked between joint enterprise and assisting or encouraging; for Herring, the

---

of doctrinal precision in relation to the degree of fit necessary between the offence committed and the state of knowledge/intention of the secondary party' (571).

36   Although see below for the doubt cast over this in the wake of *R v Gnango* [2012] 1 AC 827.

37   As Krebs (n 23) puts it, the '*actus reus* deficit is usually counterbalanced by a *mens rea* "surplus"'.

38   The rules of complicity allow for the accomplice to be charged and sentenced for the same crime, and to the same extent, as the principal offender. Although it has been held preferable that a case brought should specify what role the defendant played, this is not always the case; see *R v Giannetto* (n 31). This has obvious advantages for the prosecution, to which we will turn below.

As the Law Com No 305 (n 21) notes: 'the principle that section 8 embodies is a common law principle, namely that aiding, abetting, counselling or procuring another person to commit an offence is not, and never has been, a distinct offence. Rather, a person who, with the requisite state of mind, aids, abets, counsels or procures the commission of an offence is guilty of the principal offence that he or she has aided, abetted, counselled or procured (provided that the offence is subsequently committed)' (B.2).

39   Simester (n 3).

40   Smith (n 19). Smith's view is broadly shared by David Ormerod (n 17).

41   For Elliott and Quinn, the principal significance lies *tout court* in its evidential function, as making it 'easier to find the elements of helping or encouraging and the relevant *mens rea*'; Catherine Elliott and Frances Quinn, *Criminal Law* (8th edn, Pearson, 2010) 292. Jefferson appears to agree that the principle function of joint enterprise is evidential; Michael Jefferson, *Criminal Law* (10th edn, Pearson, 2011) 196.

42   That is not to say that there will not be grey areas; in cases of joint enterprise+, for example, it will frequently amount to little more than a legal fiction that there was a plan, especially when trying to distinguish it from a more simple case of assisting or encouraging.

'difference between a joint enterprise and aiding etc. is that in a case of joint enterprise at the time of the offence the accomplice was committing an offence with the principal, while in the case of aiding, abetting, counselling, and procuring the accomplice has left the commission of any offence up to the principal'.[43] Simester and Sullivan, writing both individually and together, have asserted the separate grounds of s 8 and joint enterprise for ascertaining liability;[44] for Simester, '[j]oint enterprise is a quite distinct source of complicity liability, one rooted in centuries of common law'.[45] The disparate views on this, and on other fundamental aspects of accomplice liability, are symptomatic of the confusion that pervades the doctrines.

Normative Foundations for Complicity

The conceptual contortions necessary in order to navigate and bring an approximation of order to the doctrines described above mean that complicity is hard to account for from a doctrinal perspective.[46] In light of this, it is pertinent to ask whether this is simply a doctrinal failing; an inability coherently to translate the normative work of the criminal law into mechanisms that can accommodate those who are to be found guilty of complicity, whether by reference to their involvement in a joint enterprise+, or through assisting or encouraging.[47] This does not appear to be the case, as doctrinal confusion in relation to complicity is mirrored in attempts to locate its normative roots.[48] In this section, we contend that the normative explanations called upon to explain the existence of accomplice liability are unsatisfying.[49] Although others have come to similar conclusions,[50] there remain pervasive and insistent attempts to justify accomplice liability according to the individual justice model. We argue that complicity is better explained as a manifestation of the regulatory function of the criminal law, influenced by policy aimed at curtailing 'dangerous' elements within society, and is responsive both to this demand and to the political expediencies that attach to so controversial an area.

At its base level, the criminal law tends towards retributivism,[51] and the orthodox tradition privileges theories of criminal responsibility based on a coincidence of conduct and mental

---

43   Jonathan Herring, *Criminal Law: Text, Cases and Materials* (4th edn, Oxford University Press, 2010) 855.

44   See, for example: Sullivan's chapter in this volume. See also, Simester (n 3); Simester et al. (n 18).

45   Simester (n 3).

46   The Law Com No 305 (n 21) described complicity as 'a doctrine characterised by uncertainty and incoherence', stating: '[t]he doctrine of secondary liability has developed haphazardly and is permeated with uncertainty. Crucially, these features affect not merely the margins of the doctrine but key concepts' [1.12].

47   For reasons that are suggested above, cases of 'plain vanilla' joint enterprise are relatively easily accounted for, both doctrinally and normatively.

48   Although for an emphasis on the importance of conceptual and linguistic clarity in this area, see: Daniel Yeager 'Helping, Doing, and the Grammar of Complicity' (1996) 15 Criminal Justice Ethics 25.

49   The extent to which this individualising process feeds directly into the shape of the law is not absolute. As Norrie explains: 'Legal categories should essentially reflect moral judgments of wrongdoing. However, legal categories only indirectly distil moral issues, which they mix with other considerations in a process of political, state-based judgment; Alan Norrie, 'Between Orthodox Subjectivism and Moral Contextualism: Intention and the Consultation Paper' [2006] Criminal Law Review 486.

50   Wilson (n 6) states: 'If desert alone formed the scope of accessorial liability we might expect then a distinction to be drawn between certain forms of participation in crime'. Also see Christopher Kutz (n 1).

51   According to Moore's theory of retribution: 'Retributive justice demands that those who deserve punishment get it. To deserve punishment, two things are necessary: one must have done a wrongful action,

culpability. There are some well-worn exceptions to this, such as the profusion of offences for which liability is strict;[52] the vast majority of these are minor offences, which may be said to amount to quasi-regulatory offences.[53] Although a justification of accomplice liability as an extension of strict liability is perhaps a little far-fetched, it remains the case that its existence is anomalous within the criminal law. As Simester notes, '[i]n a liberal society, the right to be treated as separate individuals is fundamental. If the law is to acknowledge this, it must judge its citizens according to their own actions and not according to what others do'.[54] It is immediately apparent that a criminal law committed to finding liability on the basis of correspondence between culpability and offence will struggle to accommodate accomplice liability; as Wilson notes, 'liability as an accomplice departs markedly from [the] standard model in that the basis of the accomplice's liability is not what he has done but what someone else has done'.[55] In scenario C, the defendant has embarked upon a plan to cause minor injury, and it is through the conduct of another that he is to be charged with murder. The shopkeeper and the woman who shouts encouragement find themselves in a similar position; in the event of a murder charge, they will be tried according to the conduct of somebody else.

A variety of accounts of the normative foundations of accomplice liability have been given, in an attempt to accommodate complicity within the broader framework of the criminal law. Krebs presents four potential avenues:[56] 'change of normative position',[57] 'assumption of risk', 'enhancement of risk' and 'liability for an omission'.[58] All of these amount to attempts to ground accomplice liability in culpability on the part of the accomplice; the first two also depend upon a causal element as underpinning liability.

The possibility of a causative explanation for the imposition of criminal liability is an attractive proposition, and may go some way towards ameliorating liberal subjectivist objections to complicity.[59] As with most aspects of accomplice liability, opinions are divided on the subject of causation;[60] as Smith states, '[c]ommon law authorities offer little beyond contradictory and, at best, half-articulated theoretical explanations of the nature of the connection between the accessory's conduct and the principal offence'.[61] The Law Commission, meanwhile, summed up

and one must have done so culpably'; Michael S Moore, *Placing Blame* (Oxford University Press, 1997) 33.

52   Other examples might include the more limited remit of vicarious and corporate liability.

53   Although see, for example, s 5 of the Sexual Offences Act 2003, which imposes strict liability for the rape of a child under the age of 13. This offence carries a penalty of life imprisonment. As noted above, we are looking at accomplice liability in the event of murder, which can by no means be deemed to be a regulatory offence.

54   Simester (n 3).

55   William Wilson, *Central Issues in Criminal Theory* (Hart 2002) 195.

56   These have been offered in relation to joint enterprise+ in particular, but have a broader application; given the bleed between doctrinal categories, they could arguably be applied across accomplice liability.

57   Prominent advocates of the concept of a 'change of normative position' are Gardner and Horder; see: John Gardner, 'Rationality and the Rule of Law in Offences against the Person' (1994) 53 Cambridge Law Journal 502; Jeremy Horder, 'A Critique of the Correspondence Principle' [1995] Criminal Law Review 759.

58   Freer suggests that the defendant in *R v Gnango* [2012] 1 AC 827 was 'punished for an omission' (Elaine Freer, 'R v Gnango: The Curious Case of Bandana Man – Part 2' (2012) 176 Criminal Law and Justice Weekly 218).

59   For Wilson, 'objections wither away if it is possible to conceive of both mechanical helpers and instigators as bearing causal responsibility' Wilson (n 55) 200.

60   For Smith, the issue of causality is central to the theory of complicity: 'non-causal explanations, either singularly or jointly, fail to produce an adequate theoretical account of complicity's derivative structure' Smith (n 4) 55; Yeager (n 48) describes the search for a causal explanation as 'pointless'.

61   Smith (n 4) 88.

the case law as revealing no causal requirement: 'it is clear that D can be convicted as a secondary party despite the fact that his or her assistance or encouragement has made no material difference to the "outcome"'.[62] Shorn of the possibility of a causative justification, the principles of complicity must look elsewhere.[63]

Neither the 'change of normative position' nor 'assumption of risk' theses are dependent upon establishing causation; both seek effectively to found justifications for complicity in a conception of the defendant's culpability.[64] According to the former, the defendant changes his normative position in relation to the victim by acting as an accomplice. Thus, in scenario C, by entering into a joint enterprise to cause minor injury to the victim, the defendant changes his normative position, and thus legitimates the possibility of the imposition of liability for the much greater harm (murder) caused by the other perpetrator. The idea of an assumption of risk is similar; by entering into the joint enterprise, the defendant assumes the risk of the greater offence occurring. As such, both justifications act as gateways to greater liability, facilitated by the voluntary commission of an ostensibly lesser offence.[65]

On close inspection, however, neither the assumption of risk nor the change of normative position explains very much in relation to the extent of the defendant's culpability, and both are descriptively and normatively wanting as justifications for the existence or shape of accomplice liability. In the case of joint enterprise+, Krebs puts this failing down to the legal fiction that links the defendant's behaviour with the offence on which liability founds: 'The problem that most of the different attempts at justification have in common is that they seem to presuppose a stronger link between purpose crime and collateral crime than the tenuous connection currently deemed sufficient by the doctrine of joint enterprise'.[66] As such, 'those justifications that have been put forward to defend this development are simply not persuasive and cannot bear the load of such a significant extension of criminal liability'.[67] Writing in the analogous context of strict liability offences, Simons asserts that 'it is empirically absurd and normatively unacceptable to interpret every decision to commit a serious crime as an intentional waiver of the right to proportional treatment'.[68] Explanations for accomplice liability that are founded in an assumption of risk or change of normative position may therefore amount to an effective principle of forfeiture that is anomalous when considered alongside the broader function of the criminal law; the drive to accommodate it within the culpability paradigm leads to a mechanism that allows for disproportionate judgments, based on minimally culpable conduct.

---

62   Law Com No 305 (n 21) B.50. For discussion of the issue of causation, see: Law Commission (n 21) B48-B66. The Law Commission noted the exceptional case of 'procuring', which may require causation, citing *A-G's Reference (No 1 of 1975)* (n 17). Smith explains the lack of a causal requirement on the basis of expediency: 'policy demands for a wide-ranging coverage by complicity combined with inevitable limitations of proof of causal influence or effect necessitates the criminal law's adoption of an implicit rule of presumed cause'; Smith (n 4) 89.

63   This is not to say that there may not be provable causative elements to particular instances of complicit conduct. In individual cases, it may provide impetus for prosecution, and may have evidential value.

64   For a more in-depth appraisal, and a similar dissatisfaction with these normative bases for complicity liability, see, Krebs (n 23).

65   A similar account underlies the decision in *R v Hasan* (2005) UKHL 22, where duress was not accepted as a defence, and in relation to self-induced intoxication; *R v Bailey* [1983] 1 WLR 760.

66   Krebs (n 23).

67   Ibid.

68   Kenneth Simons, 'Is Strict Criminal Liability in the Grading of Offences Consistent with Retributive Desert?' [2012] Oxford Journal of Legal Studies.

Gnango and a Further Retreat from Liberal Subjectivism

In the preceding sections, we have sought to locate accomplice liability, both in terms of its doctrinal function and its normative foundations. We looked at some of the confusion that subsists within the principles of complicity and suggested that they may stem from an impossibility properly to found them in the normative function of the criminal law. We now move to an examination of the way accomplice liability has fared recently, culminating in the Supreme Court's judgment in *R v Gnango*,[69] which is symptomatic of the direction in which complicity liability appears to be moving.

It is perhaps surprising to see near-consensus in refuting the idea of joint enterprise as a separate ground, but a slew of recent cases together seemingly confirm that the authority for joint enterprise lies in s 8, and that it is simply a means of finding the assistance or encouragement that this provision requires.[70] This is a view that has been adopted by the majority of commentators and was recently stated unequivocally in *R v Stringer*:[71] 'Joint enterprise is not an independent source of liability'.[72]

The observation that the authority for joint enterprise emanates from s 8 is of relatively little import if the doctrine is nevertheless accorded its own principles, which are then kept separate from assisting or encouraging. If, however, the finding of a joint enterprise is simply evidence of factual assistance or encouragement, there is scope for a more interesting development, whereby the respective conduct and mental elements of these forms of complicity merge or become interchangeable. In *R v A and Others*,[73] the court appeared to conflate the principles,[74] and it is with some prescience that Krebs outlines the invidious steps taken in Australia in the case of *Clayton*.[75] Here, she remarks the degradation of the *mens rea* requirement for complicity, as a result of the effective conflation of the Australian equivalent of joint enterprise with other forms of complicity, which usually demand a higher form of *mens rea*.[76] In *Gnango*, the Supreme Court appears to have brought the same approach to the law of England and Wales.

The *Gnango* judgment is likely to occupy scholars for some time, especially if it stands to point the direction of travel for accomplice liability. As the court conceded, the case raised particular problems because of an unusual confluence of factors.[77] The question for the court was whether or not the defendant should be held liable in the following circumstances:

---

69   [2012] 1 AC 827.

70   See: Ormerod, House of Commons Justice Committee, *Joint Enterprise* (Eleventh Report of Session 2010-12, HC 1597) ev 42.

71   [2012] QB 160.

72   Ibid. 173 (Toulson L.J.).

73   [2011] QB 841.

74   In the judgment, the terms 'common enterprise' and 'joint enterprise' were given an expansive remit; alongside the instances of joint enterprise familiar from the above scenarios, the court included the example where 'D2 aids and abets D1 to commit a single crime, as for example where D2 provides D1 with a weapon so that D1 can use it in a robbery' *A and Others* (n 73) 845. Here, rather than viewing joint enterprise as a subsidiary category of assisting and encouraging, the court appears to advocate its use as embracing elements of the latter; aiding and abetting has become a variety of joint enterprise.

75   [2006] HCA 58.

76   Krebs (n 23).

77   The facts of *Gnango* are reported in some detail elsewhere in this volume. In order to lay the ground for what follows, we will only give a short description of the facts that confronted the Supreme Court. Armel Gnango was convicted of murder after meeting with another man, referred to throughout the judgment as 'bandana man' (BM), in a car park. BM began shooting at the defendant, who returned fire. During the 'shoot

If (1) D1 and D2 voluntarily engage in fighting each other, each intending to kill or cause grievous bodily harm to the other and each foreseeing that the other has the reciprocal intention, and if (2) D1 mistakenly kills V in the course of the fight, in what circumstances, if any, is D2 guilty of the offence of murdering V?[78]

After the defendant's successful appeal to the Court of Appeal, the Supreme Court reinstated the murder conviction, with six of the seven justices of the view that a murder conviction was appropriate. They did not agree amongst themselves on the basis for this, with both joint enterprise and liability for assisting or encouraging finding judicial favour;[79] Lords Phillips and Judge approved fluidity and flexibility in the doctrines,[80] and the court held that 'B was liable for the murder of the passer-by whom he had accidentally shot and killed and the defendant would also be party to the murder if he had aided, abetted, counselled and procured B's actions ... [or alternatively via] an agreement to shoot and be shot at ... as a principal to a joint enterprise to engage in unlawful violence'.[81]

Rogers and Buxton express a degree of disquiet at the diverse routes to a conviction,[82] and others have doubted the conclusion arrived at by the Supreme Court.[83] Beyond this, however, *Gnango* hails a development that takes the interrelationships between the respective strands of complicity far past their largely case-specific complaints. Whilst a conviction on the basis of mixed findings of joint enterprise on the one hand, and assisting or encouraging on the other, may raise

---

out' a passerby was shot and killed. The shot came from the gun of BM, who was not subsequently charged. In *Gnango*, there were technical objections relating to the ability to be convicted of an offence of complicity where the defendant is the intended victim, which shall not detain us. Nor shall we be detained in the argument that, if the joint enterprise that was planned was the killing of Gnango, this was, on his part, suicide, and thus legal.

78 [2012] 2 WLR 17, 19-20.

79 Lords Clarke and Brown favoured joint enterprise as a route to a murder conviction, whilst Lord Clarke also suggested a direct route of causation. The remainder of the justices chose assisting or encouraging as the route to the reinstatement of the murder conviction. The characterisation and treatment of Armel Gnango and BM as accomplices is, in itself, problematic for more logical and intuitive reasons than there is here space to document. For discussion of these, see: Jonathan Rogers, 'Shooting (and Judging) in the Dark?' [2012] Archbold Review 8; Richard Buxton, 'Being an Accessory to One's Own Murder' [2012] Criminal Law Review 275.

80 They cited *Archbold, Criminal Pleading, Evidence and Practice* (2011), 18.6: 'the distinction between a joint principal and an abettor is sometimes difficult, and unnecessary, to draw'; [2012] 1 AC 827, 849). Lord Dyson agreed that this was 'not a difference of substance'; [2012] 1 AC 827, 859.

81 [2012] 2 WLR 17, 17-18, per Lords Phillips and Judge. Parts of the judgment in *Gnango* may therefore stand as authority for the proposition that joint enterprise stands as a discrete set of principles; for Rogers (n 79), '[o]ne gratifying point which runs throughout the litigation is that [joint enterprise] was recognized to be a distinct form of complicity'. This is contestable, and, in light of the conflation of principles evident in the judgment, largely a moot point.

82 Rogers (n 79); Buxton (n 79). Buxton states: 'Where the two routes to a conviction depend on different analyses of complex facts, the prosecution at the trial should be required to nail its colours to one or other of those different theories. The fair charging rules in art.6(3)(a) of the European Convention require no less'.

83 Freer states: 'It is very hard to see under what common law rule or legislation Gnango is guilty of murder. He is certainly guilty of other things – an affray for starters, as the Court of Appeal identified, not to mention a host of firearms offences'; Elaine Freer, 'R v Gnango: The Curious Case of Bandana Man – Part 1' (2012) 176 Criminal Law and Justice Weekly 181.

legitimate concerns,[84] it is an entirely different proposition to allow an effective mixing of the component parts of the respective doctrines, so that, for example, the lesser *mens rea* requirement of joint enterprise becomes sufficient for a finding based in assisting or encouraging. And yet, it appears that this is what has happened in *Gnango*, as is evident in the judgment of Lord Clarke:

> [O]nce the defendant became aware that Bandana Man had a gun and was willing to use it, even assuming that there was no joint enterprise, it was undoubtedly foreseeable that, if the defendant continued shooting at Bandana Man, he would shoot back with intent to kill him or cause serious harm. Indeed, the jury's verdict shows that the defendant foresaw precisely that. In these circumstances, it was open to the jury to conclude that the defendant's firing at Bandana Man was a cause of the latter shooting back. It was the very thing that might have been expected.[85]

Similarly, Lords Phillips and Judge held:

> [BM and Gnango had] chosen to indulge in a gunfight in a public place, each intending to kill or cause serious injury to the other, in circumstances where there was a foreseeable risk that this result would be suffered by an innocent bystander. It was a matter of fortuity which of the two fired what proved to be the fatal shot. In other circumstances it might have been impossible to deduce which of the two had done so. In these circumstances it seems to accord with the demands of justice rather than to conflict with them that the two gunmen should each be liable for Miss Pniewska's murder.[86]

In both of the above excerpts from *Gnango*, the justices intimate that a finding of complicity based on assisting or encouraging can use an objectively calibrated 'foreseeability' as its *mens rea* standard.[87] This goes beyond even the previously accepted *mens rea* for joint enterprise: the subjective measure of 'foresight'. In so doing, it considerably broadens the net by which may be caught those who assist or encourage,[88] and further distances accomplice liability from the individual justice model of criminal law. The conflation of doctrinal structures may also create technical problems of application for the jury,[89] in that it is hard to imagine how the jury could be

---

84   The Supreme Court held that 'it did not matter by which of those two routes the members of the jury had arrived at that finding'; [2012] 1 AC 827, 828, and '[w]hether the defendant is correctly described as a principal or an accessory is irrelevant to his guilt'; ([2012] 1 AC 827, 849 (Lords Phillips and Judge).

85   [2012] 1 AC 827, 855, per Lord Clarke.

86   [2012] 1 AC 827, 848, per Lord Phillips and Lord Judge. It should be emphasised that this passage is concerned with the extension of the doctrine of transferred malice and is not offered as a formula by which to establish accomplice liability. Nevertheless, we contend that it is a statement that demonstrates the thinking of the court in this latter regard.

87   Whether or not they were held to be applicable, it is interesting that, as the major qualifiers to the 'foresight' test that has pertained in relation to joint enterprise, the 'fundamentally different' and 'withdrawal' principles were not referred to at all by the Supreme Court.

88   Krebs (n 23) notes the implications in relation to joint enterprise: 'There is a real danger, then, that the foresight test, not very demanding in and of itself, is in practice further diluted to one of foreseeability. Taking all this into account, the doctrine of joint enterprise as understood today seems to have very little in common with its historical predecessor: it is inculpatory in nature rather than exculpatory'.

89   In *R v A and Others*, the trial judge was commended for having given the jury 'both (commendably brief) written directions and, even more helpfully, a "route to verdicts"' [2011] QB 841, 844 (Hughes LJ); it is hard to see how this could be easily achieved, following *Gnango*.

instructed, without simply referring to an intuitive sense of whether the defendant's conduct was worthy of criminal sanction.[90]

Why Punish Complicity? Dangerousness and the Politics of Accomplice Liability

Much of what has been written in relation to complicity seeks to rationalise the doctrines, attempting to impose order onto the disparate constructions that emerge from case law and commentary. In the foregoing, we have criticised the doctrinal and normative bases for accomplice liability, insofar as the doctrinal basis for the ascription of liability remains confused and problematic, and attempts to locate it within the normative framework of culpability have proven unsatisfactory. In light of the arguments presented above, and the trajectory suggested by recent developments, liability for complicity is increasingly difficult to reconcile with the liberal tenets of much of the rest of the criminal law. Given this apparent disjunction, the existence and operation of accomplice liability must be accounted for. Our contention is that the current drift to a wide and inclusive law of complicity can best be explained by reference to two, interrelated drivers: the role of the criminal law as a regulatory force that seeks to protect society from danger and harm; and the political expediency that attaches to the imposition of accomplice liability. In what follows, we consider these two factors behind the development of complicity liability. We look first to the regulatory function as a basis for the imposition of liability. Whereas the individual justice paradigm looks to an assessment of culpability as a justification for the imposition of criminal sanction, we contend that the regulatory model is more interested in the dangerousness of the individual, and that such concerns find a target in those who are complicit in crime. Alongside this, and in some ways inextricable from it, are the political imperatives, whereby purported public demand and the nebulous requirements of justice fuel policy in shaping doctrine.

Character, Choice, Complicity and 'Dangerousness'

'Dangerousness' is a concept that is difficult to define, but one which necessarily and inevitably suffuses the regulatory function of the criminal law.[91] Were a definition possible, it would still prove difficult to quantify, and an attempt to do either necessitates the use of intuitive and heuristic judgements.[92] Floud outlines the problems this presents for use of the idea in criminal justice: 'Dangerousness is a thoroughly ambiguous concept and we may well ask whether it has any place in the administration of criminal justice; and, if it be conceded that it has, how we are to define and identify "dangerous" offenders for legal purposes'.[93] In spite of this, the concept is one that has informed the criminal law's response to the problem of complicity.

---

90   In the context of complicity trials, Horder remarks: 'I would support [the view] that juries listen to all the rush of words, look at what would do justice and then try to do that, because they know that if they tried to follow the rules they would get into an awful muddle'. He continues: 'That, though, in the end is not really a very satisfactory outcome' (House of Commons Justice Committee (n 13) ev 18).

91   '[T]he concept of dangerousness in English criminal justice is prevalent but elusive. It is not used consistently or with any precision and the nature of the risk to which it refers is never clearly defined'; Jean Floud, 'Dangerousness and Criminal Justice' (1982) 22(3) The British Journal of Criminology 213.

92   For an examination of the rationale underlying a system of criminal justice predicated on the dangerousness of individuals (a 'prediction-prevention' model), see: Alan Dershowitz, 'The Law of Dangerousness: Some Fictions about Predictions' (1970-71) 23 Journal of Legal Education 24.

93   Floud (n 91).

Offenders acting in concert are thought to pose more of a threat than those who act alone. In *Powell*, Lord Steyn stated: 'Experience has shown that joint criminal enterprises only too readily escalate into the commission of greater offences', and that the rules of accomplice liability exist 'in order to deal with this important social problem'.[94] As a generalised account, this may help to justify the existence of the complicity regime within the criminal law. In order to give any insight into the topography of its doctrines, and their operation on the level of particular cases, this must translate into individual contributions.

Following *Gnango*, the *mens rea* criteria for complicity have collapsed into a broad requirement that may amount to foreseeability of the offence that subsequently occurs. In addressing the particular problems raised by complicity, the Supreme Court appears to have accepted bare volition allied to the eventuation of a foreseeable risk; Lords Phillips and Judge asserted that the defendant had 'chosen to indulge in a gunfight ... in circumstances where there was a foreseeable risk that this result would be suffered'.[95] The justifications for such a widening of the law are found in policy. Whilst under the traditional subjectivist conception, direct intention is privileged as the highest form of *mens rea*, Lord Steyn noted in *Powell* that 'practical and policy considerations' mean that there are limits on the *mens rea* requirements that can be employed in complicity.[96] In locating the mental element of complicity in a broad conception of choice, the courts may assess what Simester refers to as 'bad deliberative preferences' on the part of the defendant.[97] It is arguable that the decision to join a criminal enterprise or encourage or assist the commission of an offence exhibits just such a 'bad deliberative preference', which manifests itself in a choice to participate in criminality. Yeager characterises the accomplice as follows: 'The helper is an excessive risk-taker whose subjective, not manifest criminality, is what warrants punishment, regardless of whether his aid or encouragement glances off his principal'.[98] Thus, for Sullivan, it is possible to 'locate the essence of complicity not in the conduct of A but in A's attitude to the conduct of P'.[99] Under the somewhat amorphous concept alluded to above, choice and attitude manifest a character that may be held to be a marker of dangerousness.

In light of the undoubted dangerousness of group offending, it could be argued that deterrence is a powerful utilitarian justification for punishing complicity. The existence or otherwise of a deterrent effect is difficult to demonstrate, and Robinson and Darley have asserted that the deterrent effect of the substantive criminal law is minimal: 'Given the rarity of the situations in which the prerequisites of deterrence are present and of non-negligible effect, the standard use of deterrence analysis to formulate criminal law doctrine seems wildly misguided'.[100] Robinson and Darley are particularly sceptical about the deterrent effect as it may be thought to apply to groups: 'group processes shift its

---

94   [1999] 1 AC 1, 14. Ashworth points out that 'joint criminal ventures tend to have a momentum of their own that makes the commission of crimes more likely'; Andrew Ashworth, *Principles of Criminal Law* (6th edn, Oxford University Press, 2009) 421.

95   [2012] 1 AC 827, 848.

96   [1999] 1 AC 1, 14.

97   Simester has disputed the 'moral primacy' of intention, asserting that '[both] intended and foreseen wrongful actions are *chosen*, and merit blame because their doing reflects bad deliberative preferences' (Andrew Simester, 'Why Distinguish Intention from Foresight' in Andrew Simester and Bob Sullivan, *Harm and Culpability* (Oxford University Press, 1996) 71).

98   Yeager (n 48).

99   Bob Sullivan, 'Intent, Purpose and Complicity' [1988] Criminal Law Review 641.

100   Paul Robinson and John Darley, 'Does Criminal Law Deter? A Behavioural Science Investigation' (2004) 24(2) Oxford Journal of Legal Studies 173.

members toward taking more risky actions, and deindividuates them, facilitating the commission of destructive behaviours. It is difficult to fit this to the image of a person who is affected by complex rational deterrence considerations'.[101] Horder has also expressed scepticism about the extent to which the rules of joint enterprise possess a deterrent effect, casting doubt on whether those who commit such crimes are aware of the extant rules, or that they would turn their minds to them 'when a confrontation is going on'.[102] The empirical value of deterrence is thus uncertain, but it is likely to continue to play a role in the demarcation of accomplice liability. Kahan has suggested that the language of deterrence also serves a 'discourse management function', whereby its invocation can serve to distract from substantive discussion of contentious issues.[103] In the context of complicity, it is certainly easier to assert that the undoubtedly dangerous behaviour of Armel Gnango should be deterred, than it is to explain, in the context of a murder conviction, why exactly it is that he is guilty.[104]

Complicity and the Politics of Criminal Justice

The politics of criminal justice are close to the surface in *Gnango*, and their presence can cloud the justicial questions that arise in this and in other cases of complicity.[105] Lord Brown's contribution in *Gnango* is punctuated throughout with references to policy considerations, and the wider societal impact of the Supreme Court's judgment:

> [T]o my mind the all-important consideration here is that both A and B were intentionally engaged in a potentially lethal unlawful gunfight ... in the course of which an innocent passerby was killed. The general public would in my opinion be astonished and appalled if in those circumstances the law attached liability for the death only to the gunman ... The public interest in criminalising the violence engaged in is yet more obvious: here there were others about so that the risk of harm was by no means confined merely to the protagonists themselves ... whichever analysis is adopted, A's liability for C's murder seems clear to me and I would regard our criminal law as being seriously defective were it otherwise.[106]

---

101   Ibid.

102   House of Commons Justice Committee, *Joint Enterprise* (Eleventh Report of Session 2010-12, HC 1597) ev 18-19.

103   Daniel Kahan, 'The Secret Ambition of Deterrence' (1999-2000) 113 Harvard Law Review 413.

104   Freer (n 58) exhibits disquiet at the grounds for the reinstatement of the murder conviction: 'However reprehensible Gnango's conduct in going armed with a gun to meet someone with whom he had a disagreement, it would have been more appropriate to prosecute him for firearms offences than for a murder that he was practically involved in but for which he was not legally culpable'.

105   A similarly naked policy move, in the other direction, can be seen in cases such as *Gillick v West Norfolk and Wisbech Area Health Authority* [1985] 3 All ER 402, where apparent offences of complicity are ruled non-criminal by reference to the public interest. Public policy plays a large part in other areas of the substantive criminal law, such as that relating to consensual physical harm; see: *R v Brown* [1994] 1 AC 212. In December 2012, the Crown Prosecution Service published a document titled *CPS Guidance on: Joint Enterprise Charging Decisions*, in response to recommendations made by the House of Commons Justice Committee (*Joint Enterprise* (Eleventh Report of Session 2010-12, HC 1597)). A significant part of the guidance emphasises 'participation' as a concept central to the exercise of prosecution; whether it will bring any clarity to the operation of the law in this area remains to be seen. The guidance can be found at: http://www.cps.gov.uk/legal/assets/uploads/files/Joint_Enterprise.pdf (Date last accessed 22/3/2013 at 14:35pm).

106   [2012] 1 AC 827, 850.

Here, Lord Brown engages with some of the notions of dangerousness we have explored above, but his primary concern is the requirements of public policy, based largely in an intuitive belief that the public would demand that Armel Gnango be held accountable for the death of the victim.[107] In a robust criticism of the judgment of the Supreme Court, Buxton suggests that the populist tone expressed by Lord Brown betrays much of the motivation for the court's decision; whilst Lord Brown's judgment marks its most obvious example, considerations of policy permeate throughout the case.[108]

That the logic of complicity doctrine is corrupted by political concerns is broadly acknowledged; Smith notes that 'internal coherence and relational consistency with general principles of liability are, in one sense, compromised by the distorting pressures of satisfying more general policy needs'.[109] The normative explanations that have been offered in order to bridge the evident gap between the operation of complicity and the wider function of the criminal law fail to achieve this satisfactorily. This is because, *inter alia*, they cannot satisfy the normative demands of correspondence between culpability and offence, and seem to amount to little more than a qualified principle of forfeiture. Whilst this may not align well with the liberal philosophical demands of the criminal law, it is potentially more palatable from a political perspective; Simons explains:

> Having knowingly or intentionally crossed the line into criminality, how can the criminal complain if the results or circumstances are worse than he believed them to be, and if he is punished accordingly? There is a widespread contemporary public attitude of contempt and loathing towards perpetrators of serious crimes, fuelled by inflammatory media coverage of especially grisly or horrific acts of violence. Serious criminals are often viewed as outlaws ... Consistent with this 'outlaw' perspective is the position that proportionality principles within the criminal law itself should not be rigorously applied to those who choose to violate the law.[110]

Freer suggests that a strong driver behind the decision of the Supreme Court to reinstate the murder conviction in *Gnango* was 'because it felt someone should be liable for the death ... or because it did not want to pave the way for gang violence to go unpunished'.[111] If there is a political imperative to establish liability in the case of *Gnango*, this is likely to manifest a lack of public sympathy for those who put themselves in the position of Armel Gnango. In the face of this, Buxton points to the 'dangers of appellate courts thinking that a certain result is required by the public'.[112] Resort to public sentiment as a guide to shaping the criminal law is not without its obvious shortcomings; as Robinson observes, '[l]ay intuitions of justice hardly produce a distribution of criminal liability that maximizes the traditional crime control mechanisms of deterrence, incapacitation

---

107   Whilst criticising the lack of clarity in the judgment, Ormerod appears to agree with Lord Brown in respect of public expectations; David Ormerod, 'Worth the Wait?' [2012] Criminal Law Review 79. Buxton (n 79) considers the possibility of an additional public concern: 'We may perhaps wonder whether the general public was equally concerned that the law enforcement agencies had not succeeded in bringing to justice ... the gunman who actually fired the fatal shot'.

108   For example: 'We have considered whether to hold the defendant guilty of murder would be so far at odds with what the public would be likely to consider the requirements of justice as to call for a reappraisal of the application of the doctrine in this case' [2012] 1 AC, 827 848 (Lord Philips and Lord Judge).

109   Smith (n 4) 89.

110   Simons (n 68).

111   Freer (n 58).

112   Buxton (n 79).

or rehabilitation'.[113] Insofar as public demand is raised as an argument in favour of a murder conviction for the defendant, it is apposite to ask whether or not this would be the case had the law enforcement agencies involved been successful in apprehending the man whose gun had killed the victim, and bringing him to trial. It could cogently be argued that the Supreme Court was filling in the gaps left by an unsuccessful investigatory process.[114]

In 1994, Sullivan wrote: 'At present, we are governed by a very broad conception of complicity, considerably tempered by a lack of full enforcement'.[115] The concessions to policy, and the lack of doctrinal coherence and consistency witnessed in *Gnango*, and in other recent appellate decisions, emphasise the continuing relevance of such a statement.[116] The malleability of the substantive criminal law affords a great deal of latitude to the courts to address policy concerns when assessing the liability that may arise through complicity.

As is the case throughout the criminal law, the substantive doctrines are important, both to individual defendants and as a wider signalling mechanism to society, However, insofar as it can impact directly on society, it is easy to overstate the importance of the substantive law in areas and cases such as these; other parts of the system also feed into the outcome for a potential defendant.[117] Stuntz is forthright in his views on this:

> We need to think of criminal law as having less to do with codes and court opinions than with policing strategies and press coverage and prosecutors' charging patterns. That in turn requires careful attention, of a sort scholars have not yet paid, to why enforcers make the decisions they do, and why the public pays attention when it does.[118]

Stuntz's statement carries particular import when applied to an area where the substantive criminal law lacks determinacy. Whilst the existence of indeterminate doctrines promotes discretion in court judgments, it can also heighten the importance of decisions made across the various agencies that constitute the criminal justice system. When it comes to accomplice liability, there is an appetite to take advantage of this on the part of the prosecuting authorities; in his evidence to the House of Commons Justice Committee on Joint Enterprise, the Director of Public Prosecutions Keir Starmer gave evidence, in which he stated that prosecutors can and should charge an individual both as a principal and a secondary party in the same indictment. This was described as advantageous to the prosecution, as it enables them to avoid having to 'nail their colours to the mast until slightly later

---

113   Paul Robinson, 'Why Does the Criminal Law Care What the Layperson Thinks Is Just? Coercive versus Normative Crime Control' (2000) 86(8) Virginia Law Review 1839.

114   A point that Freer (n 58) makes: 'Arguably, the significant problem the courts were all trying to surmount in *Gnango* was that the police had not managed to apprehend Bandana Man'.

115   Bob Sullivan, 'The Law Commission Consultation Paper on Complicity: Part 2: Fault Elements and Joint Enterprise' [1994] Criminal Law Review 252. See *CPS Guidance on: Joint Enterprise Charging Decisions* (n 105) for an idea of the current and future direction of prosecutorial policy.

116   As Wilson notes, '[t]he common law's typically pragmatic response, rather than legislate for different levels of involvement, is to make this a matter of prosecutorial and judicial discretion'; Wilson (n 6) 551.

117   A fact that is in itself open to criticism, as the less than democratic forces of prosecutorial discretion and charging practices shape the contours of real-life liability.

118   William Stuntz, 'Self-Defeating Crimes' (2000) 86 Virginia Law Review 1871.

in the process'.[119] Although undoubtedly expeditious from a prosecution point of view, this exposes indeterminate criminal law doctrine to the whims and forces of prosecutorial discretion.

Conclusion

A little over two decades ago, Smith wrote of accomplice liability: 'Common law's almost infinite capacity eventually to adapt and (usually) muddle through, with occasional statutory intervention when judicial inventiveness falters, has implicitly established in complicity a theoretical *Modus Vivendi* that demonstrably works to a reasonable level of satisfaction but which leaves the theorist unsatisfied'.[120] More recently, Ashworth offered the following criticism of the law of accomplice liability: '[it is] replete with uncertainties and conflict. It betrays the worst features of the common law: what some would regard as flexibility appears here as a succession of opportunistic decisions by the courts, often extending the law and resulting in a body of jurisprudence that has little coherence'.[121] It is clear that Ashworth's criticism still pertains; that the law of complicity continues to find itself bereft of doctrinal coherence or solid normative foundations.

Whether Smith's statement might also amount to a fair characterisation of the law as it currently operates is contingent upon judgements as to the proper role and function of the criminal law and the wider criminal justice system. Locating accomplice liability is complicated by the effective division of labour that takes place in an offence carried out by multiple parties, and the difficulty in attributing culpability for the resultant criminal harm. The present law of complicity is in a state of some confusion, and navigation by reference solely to doctrine is a fraught, even impossible, task. The subjectivist model, relying upon correspondence between level of fault and the extent of liability, is inadequate to explain this, and the theorist who attempts to align complicity with its requirements is bound to be frustrated. Detached from normative justification, the substantive doctrines fade into the background, replaced by heuristic measures of culpability based in the perceived demands of justice and the manifest volition of the defendant.

In *Gnango*, the Supreme Court has crystallised further degradation and conflation of the doctrinal structure of accomplice liability. This has the inevitable corollary of shifting decision-making about the types of conduct that require criminal sanction away from the substantive law. Whilst factors such as deterrence and the potential dangerousness of accomplice offenders are hard to assert with any accuracy, the political drivers are evident. Whether the law functions to a reasonable level of satisfaction is currently far from certain, and dependent upon the perspective from which it is viewed. If the judgment in *Gnango* is a portent of the future of accomplice liability, it appears that the complicity principles, such as they remain identifiable, are moving towards a system in which high levels of prosecutorial and judicial discretion are able to facilitate a finding of guilt where it is felt to cohere with public policy objectives.

---

119   House of Commons Justice Committee, *Joint Enterprise* (Eleventh Report of Session 2010-12, HC 1597) ev 2.
120   Smith (n 4) 90.
121   Ashworth (n 94) 443.

Chapter 4

'The Straw Woman' at Law's Precipice: An Unwilling Party

Susan Edwards

Introduction

A consideration of the legal framing of women's participation in crime requires a simultaneous consideration of defences to crime, since participation turns on a particular construction of complicity which is determined, in law, by individual and external circumstances including duress. Women commit crimes as principals and as accomplices and in many circumstances are, like men, fully responsible. But as secondary parties the part they play as accessories should take into account contemporary understanding of domestic and family violence and family pressures which in some instances may be of significance. Case law and legal commentary, including the Law Commission's Report on Participation,[1] have not considered such experiences. Participatory liability has widened through the development of new principles including *mens rea* by association, and a concept of foresight which is broad, ill-defined and runs contrary to general criminal law principles. At the same time, following the House of Lords judgment in the case of *R v Hasan*,[2] participants wishing to rely on duress find that the opportunities for pleading this defence have been further restricted. One can only hope that Baroness Hale's prediction in this case – that the restrictions placed on the duress defence would not apply to victims of domestic violence – is more than an expression of her own wishful thinking. In addition, efforts to abolish the defence of marital coercion will further exclude women's experience of violence and coercion from law's consideration.

Women parties to crime are at the precipice of law which promises miscarriages of justice where participatory liability has been extended and defences to crime have been restricted. This juxtaposition arises in a context where public policy concerns for enhanced protection from street and gang violence have taken precedence over public policy concerns to protect victims from domestic violence. However, it is acceded that the law has provided a defence for women who kill violent men where the defendant is in fear, thereby acknowledging and accommodating women's fear of male violence especially in the domestic context (Coroners and Justice Act 2009 s 55(3)), but this development in itself is not enough and such consciousness requires comprehensive application throughout all branches of the criminal law.

This chapter makes a plea for the development of a coherent approach within the law with regard to gender-based violence and coercion in considering its impact on women's involvement and participation in crime. What is required is a harmonisation of the criminal law in its framing of participation especially in consideration of accessories and innocent agents, together with the provision of defences to accommodate those circumstances where women as defendants are actually the victims of abuse and coercion. In approaching these twin concerns I first provide an

---

1 Law Commission, *Participating in Crime* (Law Com No 305, 2007).
2 [2005] 4 All ER 685 (HL).

overview of the prevailing law on participation with reference to women victims of violence, and second, examine the defences of marital coercion and duress, the rules which apply in both defences and the effect the eligibility criteria have on women parties to crime. The third aspect considers the doctrinal incoherence in the conceptualisation of duress across the law, focusing particularly on the difference in the test and definition of duress as between criminal and family law. The law on participation collides with duress when, in the fourth aspect, I consider the role played by family and 'cultural' pressures as well as violence, which may compel women to commit crime as participants whilst the law on participation ignores such exculpatory aspects as it is bent on its own expansionist project. In this regard, I make a plea for the law's expansion in such circumstances.

Participation and Unwilling Women

Women are implicated in crimes as principals, joint principals and parties. Whilst the question of gender victimisation has been considered across several areas of law, most notably with reference to homicide defences, it must be assumed that its absence with regard to participation suggests that no gender question arises at all. This is curious, as elsewhere there is a recognition that women may act and fail to act because of violence and/or fear of violence. In this regard, the academic discourse on women's silence as victims and witnesses to crime and their compunction as criminal actors has been noted.[3] It is suggested then, that the rules regulating participation might adversely or unfairly affect women since this vulnerability to coercion and other related pressures is eschewed.

Case law has developed as public policy on crime prevention has driven legal principles demonstrating an expansion in the accessory *mens rea* and a contortion of present common law doctrines in an attempt to mollify public opinion. Following *R v Rahman and others*,[4] the test for accessory contemplation extended liability to those circumstances where the principal's intention, when moving from causing V serious injury to killing V, is also ascribed to the secondary party, provided the secondary party foresaw the outcome as a possibility. As the Court of Appeal in *R v Roberts, Day and Day*,[5] had earlier expressed it: 'The subject matter of a joint enterprise is not a state of mind or intention but an objective act which it is contemplated will or might be done'.[6] Extending liability further in *R v Gnango*,[7] the Supreme Court held that where two parties engage in a gunfight and one party inadvertently kills a passer-by, the other party who neither fired the shot nor had the requisite intention should be liable for murder. Samuels argues, '[t]he basic problem is how far association amounts to complicity'.[8]

The response of the Law Commission on participation[9] (pre-*Gnango*), whilst critical of the expansion of the case law missed an opportunity to consider for example, the gendered implication of threats and pressures on women, added to this the way in which the construct of reasonableness is predicated on circumstances which men consider reasonable and not on what women placed under violence or its threat might consider reasonable. In its recommendations is recognised that encouraging may include, 'doing so by emboldening, threatening or pressurising another person

---

3   Janet Loveless, 'Domestic Violence, Coercion and Duress' [2010] Criminal Law Review 93.
4   [2008] 4 All ER 661.
5   [2001] Crim LR 984.
6   Jonathan Rogers, 'Shooting (and Judging) in the Dark?' [2012] Archbold Review 1, 8-9.
7   [2011] 2 All ER 129.
8   Alec Samuels, 'Joint Enterprise' (2012) 176(7) Criminal Law and Justice Weekly 91.
9   Law Commission No 305 (n 1).

to do a criminal act'. Women are especially vulnerable to threats and pressure, however the gender aspect was not considered in their deliberations. At paragraph 7.3 is also recommended 'that encouraging or assisting … should include doing so by failing to take reasonable steps to discharge a duty'. It is here that the construct of reasonableness, where women are victims of domestic violence, needs to be considered from a subjective standpoint. Again, the issue of reasonableness arises at paragraph 7.16 where is considered defences to liability as a secondary party. The Law Commission states: 'We recommend that it should be a defence to liability for an offence as a secondary party if D proves that: (2) it was reasonable to act as D did in the circumstances'. Here, too, a gendered question arises since it is relevant that domestic violence and related pressures can undermine a person's ability to take reasonable steps. At the same time negation of participation requires withdrawal. In this regard women may find withdrawal even more difficult than men because of pressures both physical and psychological. As the law on participation widens its net, the law on defences to crime contracts and women who find themselves compelled to act because of what they perceive as duress fall outside a duress defence and are then caught by the rules regulating participation.

Unwilling Parties: Women under Coercion and Duress

If women may be more vulnerable to involvement in crime because of domestic violence and other pressures, the rules regulating defences to crime have clearly not accommodated the reality of their experience. Whilst duress is not an available defence for murder, both the defences of marital coercion and duress are available but in certain clearly defined circumstances for female (and some male) defendants . The defence of marital coercion is currently being challenged on the grounds of inequity in that it offers a defence only to married women, since the rules governing duress have now been severely restricted[10] it is even more imperative that the marital coercion defence is retained.

Marital Coercion: Unwilling Wives

With reference to marital coercion, whilst accepting that inequality flows from a special plea for women on the grounds of involuntariness merely because of the marriage contract, nonetheless, since there remains a need for the law to recognise women's systematic victimisation and vulnerability at the hands of violent men, including spouses, retaining a defence of marital coercion addresses this reality. The Criminal Justice Act 1925 s 47, created a complete defence of marital coercion, for wives who had committed a crime (other than treason or murder) and could prove that the crime was committed in the presence, or under the coercion, of the husband.[11] (The unmarried woman in a relationship with a man was, by exclusion from this provision, perhaps considered neither coerced nor under his control such that she was capable of independent *mens rea*). This notion of the non-agent wife evolved from the historic perception of wives as lacking independent legal status and under the rod of the husband, *sub virgo*, based on an antiquated model of wifehood as subservient, ever obedient and complicit.[12] The 1925 Act reversed this earlier common law

---

10   *Hasan* (n 2).

11   *R v Shortland* [1996] 1 Cr App R 116; *R v Cairns* [2003] 1 Cr App R 662; Crim LR [2003] 403; *R v Darwin* [2009] EWCA Crim 860.

12   See the case of *R v Peel* (1922) *The Times*, 8 March 1922.

presumption. Although in Bracton's[13] time, if the wife was voluntarily a party to the commission of a crime, marriage provided no defence: 'Quid erit si uxor cum viro conjuncta fuerit, vel confessa fuerit quod viro suo consilium præstiterit et auxilium? Numquid tenebuntur ambo? imo ut videtur,' and he goes on to add, 'sic ut sunt participes in crimine, ita debent esse participes in poenâ'.[14] [What will it be if a wife shall have joined her husband in a crime and admits a common intent with assistance offered? Will both be held guilty – so it seems. (And he goes on to add) Just as they are both partners in crime so should they both share the punishment.[15]] The wife defendant bears the burden of proving the defence, the standard is one on the balance of probability and the test is a subjective one. However, perhaps surprisingly at appellate level, very few cases have been brought pleading marital coercion as a defence. Edwards,[16] writes that by 1951 the Court of Appeal had offered no authoritative definition of marital coercion, reflecting further the fact that it had probably been only occasionally considered by the lower courts.[17] Although Xavier McCoy's breathtakingly thorough research on this question demonstrates that the defence was far more frequently employed than had been hitherto acknowledged.[18] Well known is the case of *R v Bourne*,[19] where a husband had forced his wife to allow a dog to vaginally penetrate her. The husband and not the wife was charged with the offence. The wife stated in her evidence that she had been terrorised into submission and her participation was entirely against her will. In *R v White (Heather)*,[20] the wife successfully pleaded marital coercion where her husband was a domestic violence abuser, and so there has been some limited recognition of innocent parties under such circumstances. The defence of marital coercion is also broader than duress in that it recognises both physical and psychological coercion. By 1982, in *R v Gary Richmond and Ann Richmond*,[21] the Court of Appeal approved the judge's direction to the jury that a distinction should be drawn between duress and coercion when he said:

> ... coercion did not necessarily mean physical force or the threat of physical force, it could be physical, or moral, she had to prove that her will was overborne by the wishes of her husband. ... coercion was different from persuading someone out of loyalty ... and that the jury should try and put themselves in the position of the wife and ask themselves whether from what they had heard she had proved that she was forced unwillingly to participate ... It seems to us that there must be,

---

13   Bracton, *Bracton's Note Book 3: A Collection of Cases Decided in the King's Courts during the Reign of Henry the Third* (Cambridge University Press 2010).

14   Cited in *Annie Brown Appellant; and Attorney-General for New Zealand Respondent New Zealand* (1898) AC 234, 237.

15   Translation, Michael Anthony L Bowyer, MA (Oxon).

16   JLJ Edwards, 'Compulsion, Coercion and Criminal Responsibility' (1951) 14 Modern Law Review 297, 309.

17   Edwards cites two cases: *R v McGrowther* (1746) 18 St Tr 391 and *R v Critchley* (1831) 5 C & P 133. See also *R v Torpey* (1871) 12 Cox CC 45, 47. See also Avory Committee, *Report on the Responsibility of the Wife for Crimes Committed under the Coercion of the Husband* (Avory Com No 1, Cmd 1677, 1922). See also, *R v Mabel Smith* (1916) 12 Cr App R 42, 43, *R v Green* (1913) 9 Cr App R 228, 231.

18   Gerard John Xavier McCoy, *Uxorial Privileges in Substantive Criminal Law: A Comparative Law Enquiry* [2007] a thesis submitted in partial fulfilment of the requirements of the degree of Doctor of Philosophy in the Faculty of Law in the University of Canterbury, New Zealand, 110-14. See also *R v Grondkowski and Malinowski* (1946) 1 All ER 559, 560H.

19   (1952) 36 Cr App R 125.

20   *The Times*, 16 February 1974, 3.

21   [1982] Crim LR 507; *R v Cope, The Times*, 11 April 1922; *R v Foster, The Times*, 27 April 1922, 11; *R v Jenkins, The Times*, 17 August 1922, 5.

as the learned judge in that case accepted, a distinction to be drawn between duress and the defence of coercion.

The requirement that the 'will be overborne' was the language used by the court in the later case of *R v Shortland*[22] where, '[t]he appellant signed, in her husband's presence, two application forms for passports in the name of a dead child'. The court approved a direction that coercion did not necessarily mean physical force or the threat of physical force, coercion could be physical or moral. It was for the wife to prove that her will was overborne and clearly distinguishable from willing participation or loyalty. Convictions have also been quashed where the jury have been misdirected or the defence improperly withheld from them. In *R v Cairns*,[23] where the defendants were charged with conspiracy to supply a class A drug, the Court of Appeal following *Shortland* held, that coercion must be given a broader meaning than duress:[24]

> We revert therefore to the argument about the misdirection on the meaning of 'coercion'. It was clearly unfortunate that in an otherwise excellent summing up the judge used the word 'just' instead of the word 'necessarily,' or some equivalent, that would have left the jury in no doubt that something less than physical force or the threat of such force would suffice. There was, moreover, no explicit reference by him to any kind of coercion less than physical force, such as moral force or emotional threats. We accept that there was some ambiguity here and an ambiguity of importance … capable of leading the jury astray.

Whether the defence was available to a wife of a polygamous marriage arose to be decided in *R v Ditta, Hussain and Kara*.[25] In this case, Khatiza Begum was stopped at Heathrow airport on a plane arriving from Pakistan. She was found to have heroin in her suitcase. Mahmoud Hussain was stopped shortly afterwards although no heroin was found on him, but he did admit that he had arranged for Khatiza Begum and another woman (Sarifa Kara) to carry the drugs for him. Alla Ditta was also arrested after he agreed to meet Mahmoud Hussain at Piccadilly station in Manchester to pick up a bag from the left luggage office. Khatiza Begum was acquitted on the basis that she was acting under the duress of Hussain. Kara appealed and said she was acting under the duress of Hussain who, she said, was her husband – the marriage, however, was polygamous. The prosecution contended that the marriage, even under Islamic law, was no longer in existence as it had been dissolved. The case for the appellant was that the defence in respect of coercion should be extended to a woman who mistakenly believed that she is married to the coercer even when she is not. The Court of Appeal rejected this argument and stated: 'before a woman can bring herself within the terms of this section it must be shown that she is a wife in the strict sense of the term and that the person who coerced her was her husband in the strict sense of the term'.[26] Whilst a mistaken belief it appears was accepted in law it was held that polygamous marriages should be

---

22   *Shortland* (n 11).

23   *Cairns* (n 11).

24   Ibid.

25   [1988] Crim LR 42.

26   Ibid. See also the case of *Anne and John Darwin*, *The Times*, 1 April 2009, [2009] EWCA Crim 860, where a married couple engaged in a fraudulent conspiracy (John Darwin staged his apparent drowning at sea in a canoeing accident) and where the wife's defence of marital coercion failed on the ground that she was not coerced (Loveless (n 3)). See also *R v Quissamba (Jacqueline)* 6 July 1998, Manchester Crown Court; letter from Circuit Judge Peter Lakin, 22 cited in Xavier McCoy (n 18) 174, where marital coercion was relied upon in a prosecution for fraud and the prosecution offered no evidence.

excluded, a decision which flies in the face of the acceptance of polygamy in other areas of the law (family)[27] and is contrary to *R v Caroubi*.[28]

There has been considerable opposition to the retention of this defence of marital coercion. Viscount Simon in *Holmes v DPP*[29] said, 'we have left behind us the age when the wife's subjection to her husband was regarded by the law as the basis of the marital relation'. By 1977, the Law Commission called for its abolition[30] and reflected its rejection of the defence by excluding it from the Draft Criminal Code.[31] However, as I argue later in this chapter, some wives, particularly wives from some non-Western cultures, continue to remain even more so under the patriarchal rule of the husband, for whom this defence may be especially important when charged with offences of participation.[32] and the retention of this defence may mitigate some of the harshness of the restrictions placed on the duress defence.

Duress: A Male Construct

The defence of duress, unlike marital coercion, potentially applies to all parties to crime, depending not on the relationship but on the circumstances. The defence is however hugely constrained by a series of qualifying features.

What kind of threats? The duressed must demonstrate that '… threats of immediate death or serious personal violence so great as to overbear the ordinary powers of human resistance should be accepted as a justification for acts which would otherwise be criminal'.[33] Where the threat(s) falls outside the threat of death or serious violence the defence does not operate, nor is duress a defence to murder or attempted murder.[34] The threshold and nature of the threat embodies a male view of the degree of force necessary to coerce or compel and thus sets a very high standard for women who may be put under duress by a lesser degree of physical force, and, in addition, psychological force and other family pressures.

Whose characteristics? The law on duress is founded on a construct of the individual's ability to resist, hence references to the moral will of the individual are prominent in the judgments. Specific characteristics may be taken into account when considering whether a reasonable person would have been capable of resisting such pressure. Whilst the law on provocation[35] (now loss of

---

27   The Criminal Law Commentator (n 25) in this case writes, 'Dicey and Morris Conflict of Laws (11th ed, 1987) states "Rule 77. A marriage which is polygamous under Rule 73 [which defines polygamous marriages] and not invalid under Rule 75 [marriage celebrated in England with polygamous forms] or Rule 76 [where either party is domiciled in England at the time of the ceremony] is a valid marriage unless there is some strong reason to the contrary"'.

28   [1912] 7 Cr App R 149.

29   [1946] AC 588, 600.

30   Law Commission, *Report on Defences of General Application* (Law Com No 83, 1977).

31   Law Commission, *Draft Criminal Code* (Law Com No 177, 1989). See also Lord Simon in *DPP v Lynch* [1975] 61 Cr App R 6, 29.

32   See Stanley Yeo, 'Coercing Wives into Crime' (1992) 6 Australian Journal of Family Law 214, 217.

33   *Attorney-General v Whelan* [1934] IR 518.

34   Law Commission, *Murder, Manslaughter and Infanticide* (Law Com No 304, 2006) [6.21].

35   Homicide Act 1957, s 3.

control manslaughter)[36] conceded the characteristic of battered woman syndrome as relevant to an assessment of the reasonable person, by contrast, the understanding of the human will in duress is somewhat locked in a time past.[37] Characteristics considered relevant to a defendants ability to resist include age; the courts have also said 'possibly sex'. In this regard sex is considered only of relevance with regard to pregnancy. The Court of Appeal in *Bowen*[38] said this, 'Obvious examples are age, where a young person may well not be so robust as a mature one; possibly sex, though many women would doubtless consider they had as much moral courage to resist pressure as men; pregnancy, where there is added fear for the unborn child'.[39] Also included, is serious physical disability, and a recognised mental illness or psychiatric condition.[40] Rather than interrogating the judicial opinion that resisting the duressor is simply a matter of moral courage or moral will, the concerns of the legal and academic community have almost exclusively focused on the impact of duress on the mentally and psychiatrically vulnerable.

Always on her mind   It is conceded, however, that it was gender considerations that provided the underlying impetus with regard to the expansion of the law when the question of whether for a defence of duress to be satisfied the threat is to be immediately carried out. *R v Hudson and R v Taylor*,[41] (Parker LCJ, Lord Widgery and Cooke J) is the leading case, where two female teenage defendants pleaded duress to a charge of obstructing the course of justice where they had been threatened by a person who was in the public gallery at the time of the trial in which they were material witnesses. The Court of Appeal stated that whilst the threat was not one that could be carried out immediately, that is executed in the courtroom, it could be carried out in the streets of Salford that same night, and accepted that the threat was operative on the mind of the witnesses. The Court of Appeal stated, 'It is wholly artificial and unrealistic to say that duress could operate if a gun is pointed at the witness in the box, but not if she thinks that she may be seriously injured shortly after leaving the box', and 'The simple test which should have been left to the jury is: at the time when each appellant committed the offence was her mind so overborne that she was not an independent actor?' Clearly *Hudson* was by no means the first, or the only case where witnesses had been threatened prior to, and during, the trial.[42] Undoubtedly, the fact that the two witnesses' 'circumstances' were their teenage years of 17 and 19 influenced the court in its assessment of the

36   Coroners and Justice Act 2009 s 55(4) now expressly excludes sexual infidelity. Section 54(3) includes fear. On this matter, the explanatory note states, 'Subsection (3) deals with cases where the defendant lost self-control because of his or her fear of serious violence from the victim. As in the complete defence of self-defence, this will be a subjective test and the defendant will need to show that he or she lost self-control because of a genuine fear of serious violence, whether or not the fear was in fact reasonable. The fear of serious violence needs to be in respect of violence against the defendant or against another identified person. For example, the fear of serious violence could be in respect of a child or other relative of the defendant, but it could not be a fear that the victim would in the future use serious violence against people generally'.
37   Interestingly the Law Commission said, 'we believe it would be anomalous if there were to be a significant distinction between the characteristics that are relevant to provocation and duress ...' (Law Commission (n 34) [6.84]).
38   *R v Bowen* [1996] 4 All ER 837.
39   Ibid. 844.
40   Ibid.
41   [1971] 2 All ER 244 (Parker LCJ, Lord Widgery and Cooke J)
42   Criminal Justice and Public Order Act 1994, s 51. See also Roger Tarling, Lizanne Dowds and Tracey Budd, *Victim and Witness Intimidation: Findings from the British Crime Survey* (Crown Copyright Home Office 2000). This study found 'female respondents reported significantly more incidents of intimidation than male respondents' (6).

ability of young women to resist such threats. Glanville Williams, however, considered *Hudson* 'an indulgent decision'[43] and Lord Bingham in the House of Lords in *Hasan* said this, '… it [Hudson] has in my opinion had the unfortunate effect of weakening the requirement that execution of a threat must be reasonably believed to be imminent and immediate if it is to support a plea of duress …'.[44] This understanding and application of the concept of 'operative on the mind', however, is by no means unique to the law of duress. It is to be noted that in self-defence and provocation cases where abused women have responded to the fear of the aggressor and killed him in circumstances where there was no immediate threat, in that for example, she killed a sleeping man, the courts have accepted expert testimony on her psychological perception of imminence and foreseeability of imminent violence.[45] In such circumstances the courts have conceded that fear and her perception of future violence operates on the mind and impacts on behaviour thus bringing her within the immediacy requirement for self-defence and provocation.

Since *Hudson*, the notion of 'operative on the mind' rather than 'in fact' has been accepted as relevant to a defence of duress in two in extremis situations involving certain torture and death. In *R v Abdul-Hussain and others*,[46] the contention that the threats of death were 'operative on the mind' and therefore brought the defendants within the requirement of imminence was accepted by the Court of Appeal. The appellants were Shia Muslims from southern Iraq, who were convicted of hijacking a plane. They had fled Iraq to live in Sudan, their passports were confiscated, and they feared deportation to Iraq where they were certain to be executed. The issue for the court was whether the defence of duress by threat of circumstances was correctly withdrawn from the jury because the threat could not be carried out immediately. The Court of Appeal, in quashing the convictions, stated:

> The peril must operate on the mind of the defendant at the time when he commits the otherwise criminal act so as to overbear his will and this is essentially a question for the jury. But the execution of the threat need not be immediately in prospect. [Rose LJ V-P said]: 'If Anne Frank had stolen a car to escape from Amsterdam and been charged with theft, the tenets of English law would not, in our judgment, have denied her a defence of duress of circumstances, on the ground that she should have waited for the Gestapo's knock on the door'.

In *R v Safi and others*,[47] the concept of 'operative on the mind' was revisited in a case which turned on similar facts. The Court of Appeal ruled the convictions 'unsafe' because the law relating to whether the men had acted under duress had been wrongly applied at their trial. However, the Court of Appeal, in *Abdul-Hussain* also observed that 'legislation relating to the defence of duress was urgently required as the law had evolved on a case by case basis and the scope of the defence was uncertain', whilst in *Safi* the Court of Appeal observed that, 'In 1999 this Court, for the fourth time in five years emphasised the urgent need for legislation to define duress with precision'. Academic comment reflected similar concerns.[48]

---

43   Glanville Williams, *Textbook of Criminal Law* (Stevens and Sons 1983) 636.

44   *Hasan* (n 2) [27].

45   See David Faigman, 'Battered Woman Syndrome and Self-Defense: A Legal and Empirical Dissent' (1986) 72 Virginia Law Review 619. See also Lenore Elizabeth Walker, *The Battered Woman Syndrome* (Springer 1984).

46   [1999] Crim LR 570 (Mustafa Shakir Abdul-Hussain, Saheb Sherif Aboud, Hasah Saheb Abdul Hasan, Maged Mehdy Naji, Mohammed Chamekh Muhssin, Adnan Hoshan, Sabah Nouri Nagi).

47   *R v Safi* (Ali Ahmed) [2004] 1 Cr App R 157.

48   Ian Dennis, 'Duress, Murder and Criminal Responsibility' (1980) 96 Law Quarterly Review 208.

Excluding not excusing women However, it was not legislation but a decision of the House of Lords that brought to an end the acceptance of 'operative on the mind' as falling within the requirement of imminence. In *R v Hasan*[49] *(R v Z*[50]*)*, the defendant was convicted of aggravated burglary, and had worked as a driver and minder for a woman who ran an escort agency and was involved in prostitution. He said that threats of violence were made to him and his family by a drug dealer if he did not commit the offence. His appeal against conviction was allowed on the basis that the trial judge had misdirected the jury on the question of whether (1) the accused voluntarily put himself in a position in which he knew he was likely to be subject to threats to commit a crime, and (2) that such a direction should refer to threats to commit a crime of the type charged. The prosecution appealed to the House of Lords, who restored the original conviction. The decision of the House of Lords in *Hasan* limited the defence in two significant ways and effectively overturned the ruling in *Hudson*.[51] First, the threat must be reasonable and not subjectively assessed and second, the threat of death or serious injury must be capable of being carried out immediately (in fact). Lord Bingham in his judgment said '… I must acknowledge that the features of duress to which I have referred in paras 18 to 20 above incline me, where policy choices are to be made, towards tightening rather than relaxing the conditions to be met before duress may be successfully relied on'. Baroness Hale raised her concern that women victims made vulnerable to duress because of gender-based violence and coercion might be adversely affected. Notwithstanding her intervention, neither gender nor the circumstances of domestic violence have had any role in the development of the law on duress nor were discussed by their Lordships.

Duress: not a question of moral will but of the prospect of violence The House of Lords effectively undertook the revision of the law that was properly a matter for Parliament. As *Hasan* was the only occasion when the question of the law on duress was considered by the House of Lords one might have expected that this case was joined by third party interveners to argue for women who act involuntarily under duress. That such an opportunity was missed might be explained by the fact that *Hasan* appeared at the appellate stages as centring on confessional evidence and whether duress should be excluded where the defendant voluntarily involves himself with criminal others and thereby should have foreseen that pressure would be brought to bear upon him to engage in criminal acts. In *Hasan*, it was left to Baroness Hale to make any special pleadings. If the Court of Appeal in *Bowen* had said that the ability to resist was a question of 'moral courage', Baroness Hale in *Hasan* pointed out that ability to resist was a matter far beyond the gymnastics of the moral will. Baroness Hale expressed reservations with regard to the tightening of the law on duress particularly with regard to the objective test and voluntary participation, expressing the concern that the limitations placed on the defence would mean that women parties to crime who experienced domestic violence and were essentially victims would be unable to use it. Her remarks impliedly suggested the need to expand the present characteristics of the reasonable person of duress beyond its present remit. In this regard she said:

> This solution, coupled with the Commission's 'sell-out to subjectivism', has been strongly criticised: see Jeremy Horder, 'Occupying the moral high ground? The Law Commission on duress' [1994] Crim LR 334. The moral basis of the defence remains a hot topic of debate: see, for

---

49   *Hasan* (n 2) (Lord Bingham of Cornhill, Lord Steyn, Lord Rodger of Earlsferry, Baroness Hale of Richmond, Lord Brown of Eaton-under-Heywood).

50   *R v Z* [2003] 1 WLR 1489.

51   *Hudson* (n 41).

example, Professor William Wilson, 'The Structure of Criminal Defences' [2005] Crim LR 108. ... I accept that even the person with a knife at her back has a choice whether or not to do as the knifeman says. The question is whether she should have resisted the threat. But, perhaps because I am a reasonable but comparatively weak and fearful grandmother, I do not understand why the defendant's beliefs and personal characteristics are not morally relevant to whether she could reasonably have been expected to resist.

In offering a glimmer of hope to women victims of domestic violence subject to duress who are parties to crime, she further said, 'I do not believe that this limitation on the defence is aimed at battered wives at all, or at others in close personal or family relationships with their duressors and their associates, such as their mothers, brothers or children'.[52] Certainly, it is to be hoped that women who experience domestic violence and commit criminal offences under the influence of their aggressors will not be subject to the limitations imposed in *Hasan* and that legal argument will seek to distinguish future cases from the strictures of this rule.

Of course I am not arguing here that women per se are especially vulnerable, this would be to deny all criminal women agency, and as Carol Smart[53] so rightly identified in 1975 the erstwhile contention that all women criminals lacked agency led to their infantilisation and medicalisation. Women have struggled against such pathologisation and essentialism within the law itself.[54] Women have also challenged the claimed existence of so called judicial chivalry in sentencing pointing out that such leniency operated only when women committed crimes considered to be congruous with the ideal image of femininity and conversely that women were punished more harshly when their crimes deviated from this stereotype.[55] Zoora Shah's original prison term provides an example of how presumptions about, and expectations of, gender and culture intersect, where the judge handed down a harsher sentence to a (South Asian) woman who was convicted of murdering an abusive partner.[56] On the one hand the courts essentialised Zoora Shah as a South Asian woman and sentenced her in accordance with their expectation of such women, but at the same time selectively disregarded the role her culture played in putting her in fear and silence.

Three points need to be made, first, women per se should be recognised as being placed in a vulnerable position because of their lack of physical strength compared with men,[57] making women ideal candidates for male duressors and participation in crime.[58] Second, some women in intimate relationships, both as partners and as wives, may come under very the specific influence and pressure of domestic violence. Third, given the multicultural composition of modern society women (and occasionally men) may be subject to family pressure. In this sense, some women live within a more pervasive patriarchal structure than others. Some have called this aspect 'cultural', although one should be cognisant of the point made by Anne Phillips who writes '... many of the world's traditions are quite distinctly patriarchal'.[59] It is by no means clear cut at what point, and

---

52   *Hasan* (n 2) [73] and [78].

53   Carol Smart, *Women, Crime and Criminology: A Feminist Critique* (Routledge 1976).

54   Susan Edwards, *Women on Trial* (Manchester University Press 1984); Hilary Allen, 'At the Mercy of Her Hormones: Premenstrual Tension and the Law' (1984) 9 m/f 19.

55   Edwards (n 54).

56   See Samio Bano and Pragna Patel, 'R v Zoora (Ghulam) Shah' in Rosemary Hunter, Clare McGlynn and Erika Rackley (eds), *Feminist Judgments from Theory to Practice* (Hart 2010).

57   See, *State of Washington v Wanrow* (1977) 88 Wash, 2D 221, 559 P.2d where the court accepted that self defence instructions are prejudicial to women.

58   Loveless (n 3).

59   Anne Phillips, *Gender and Culture* (Polity 2010) 14.

when, cultural factors should be accommodated in law. Certainly, the 'cultural defence' so called has figured in jurisprudence and law where invalid excuses/justifications have been advanced by the defence and entertained by the courts when men have killed wives or where male family members have killed other family members.[60] Yet valid cultural considerations, including women's silence, and the fact that they may be less able to resist pressures from within their relationships, families and communities, have been less readily articulated and accommodated in considerations of participation and duress. Certainly the proposition that a wife's unquestioning compliance is outmoded does not pertain uniformly across all cultures and communities. To ignore this is to ignore a significant reality of many women's lives.

Participation: Threatening and Emboldening and Other Pressures

Gender and culture are both important aspects where women as victims remain silent, and acquiesce and thereby appear complicit. Here, I want to focus on the duress experienced by the woman party to crime, that category of persons Baroness Hale hoped will be excluded from the harshness of the limitations following the ruling in *Hasan*. In the ordinary sense of the word women experience duress from violent men and from coercive families in multifarious ways including, pressures to conform, to submit, to marry and so on, and also to commit crime. Indeed, any consideration of cultural diversity and family structure and pressures might have led to a more inclusive definition of domestic violence. With regard to the role of family members in domestic violence Siddiqui notes with reference to the government strategy on domestic violence *Safety and Justice*[61] that it '... fail[ed] to address a number of issues affecting black and minority women, including by its narrow definition of domestic violence as concerning only intimate partners'.[62] Such misunderstanding and cultural stereotyping may lead to adverse conclusions. In South Asian families, for example, power and authority is vested in male members including brothers and also in-laws. In the case of *Begum*,[63] where a schoolgirl wished to wear a jilbab (long dress) to school, the brother of the applicant, because of his prominent presence, was considered as the orchestrator of her struggle to wear Islamic dress. An understanding of family structure and authority may have led to a different conclusion since both her parents were dead and a brother's role in South Asian culture, under such circumstances, is to act in *loco parentis*.

---

60   See the following commentaries: Jeroen Van Broec, 'Cultural Defence and Culturally Motivated Crimes (Cultural Offences)' (2001) 9 European Journal of Crime, Criminal Law and Criminal Justice 1; Simon Bronitt and Kumaralingam Amirthalingam, 'Cultural Blindness: Criminal Law in Multicultural Australia' (1996) 21(2) Alternative Law Journal 58; Anne Phillips, 'When Culture Means Gender: Issues of Cultural Defence in English Courts' (2003) 66 Modern Law Review 510; Charmaine Wong, 'Good Intentions, Troublesome Applications: The Cultural Defence and Other Uses of Cultural Evidence in Canada' (1999) 42(2-3) Criminal Law Quarterly 367; Deborah Woo, 'Cultural "Anomalies" and Cultural Defenses: Towards an Integrated Theory of Homicide and Suicide' (2004) 32 International Journal of Soc L 279; Pieter Carstens, 'The Cultural Defense in Criminal Law: South African Perspectives' (2004) 2 De Jure 312.

61   Home Office, *Safety and Justice*, The Government's Proposals on Domestic Violence (2003, Cm 5847).

62   Hannana Siddiqui, 'There Is No "Honour" in Domestic Violence, Only Shame! Women's Struggles against "Honour" Crimes in the UK' in Lynn Welchman and Sara Hossain (eds), *Honour Crimes, Paradigms, and Violence against Women* (Zed 2005) 275.

63   *Begum R (on the application of Begum (by her litigation friend, Rahman)) (Respondent) v Headteacher and Governors of Denbigh High School (Appellants)* [2006] 2 All ER 487.

Cultural Pressure, Duress and Forced Marriage

With regard to forced marriage however, recent family law judgments have indeed recognised the culpability of family members in perpetrating a far wider panoply of duress, where judges have been sensitive to the intersectionality of culture, tradition, family pressures and the overarching patriarchy in creating a climate of 'duress'. Family law has recognised, for example, for the purpose of annulment of marriage, psychological duress exercised by future spouses and by parents and relatives. The common law in *Wharton*'s case,[64] held that a rebuttable presumption of coercion could be maintained without any demonstration of actual or threatened physical violence with regard to the consent of the parties to their marriage.[65] In *Scott v Sebright*,[66] Butt J established a subjective test for duress; the test was whether pressure is such as to destroy the reality of consent and overbear the will of the individual. He said:

> It has sometimes been said that in order to avoid a contract entered into through fear, the fear must be such as would impel a person of ordinary resolution and courage to yield to it. I do not think that is an accurate statement of the law. Whenever from natural weakness of intellect or from fear, – whether reasonably entertained or not, – either party is actually in a state of mental incompetence to resist pressure improperly brought to bear, there is no more consent than in the case of a person of stronger intellect and more robust courage yielding to a more serious danger.

Of course, it was anticipated that it was women who would be subject to fear and threats and forced into a marriage. In some cases men too have been forced into marriage, particularly when following sexual liaisons or where promises of marriage had been made. *Buckland*[67] was such a case and established an objective test for annulment. This objective test was applied in a series of cases including *Szechter*.[68] The Matrimonial Causes Act 1973 s 12(c) followed, but merely to assert that a spouse who enters a marriage because of threats, force or duress had not freely consented thereby vitiating the marriage, and that the threat need not emanate from the respondent spouse but may come from another source. In *Singh v Singh*,[69] under the new objective test, family pressure was not enough, and in *Singh v Kaur*,[70] it was held that only where physical violence prevailed could a petition for nullity succeed. But in 1983 in *Hirani*,[71] the objective test with its strict requirement of physical violence for duress in marriage was overruled. The court was enabled to revert to the subjective test in *Scott v Sebright* by drawing on a case before the Privy Council which dealt with duress and its effect on a contract. Lord Scarman said, 'Duress, whatever form it takes, is a coercion of the will so as to vitiate consent'.[72] In recent years, the courts have increasingly encountered

---

64   (1690) 10 Commons Journals 14, Lords Journals 538, 585, 591.

65   In *Cooper v Crane* (1891) P 369, 378, the woman consented to marriage because the future husband said he would blow his brains out if she refused. See also Joseph Jackson, 'Consent of the Parties to Their Marriage' (1951) 14(1) Modern Law Review 1.

66   (1887) LR 12, PD 21, 24.

67   [1968] P 296, [1967] 2 WLR 1506. See also Sundari Anitha and Aisha Gill, 'Coercion, Consent and the Forced Marriage Debate in the UK' (2009) 17(2) Feminist Legal Studies 165.

68   *Szechter (otherwise Karsov) v Szechter* [1971] P 286, [1970] 3 All ER 905.

69   [1971] 2 All ER 828.

70   (1981) 11 Fam Law 216.

71   [1983] 4 FLR 232.

72   Ibid. 234, citing *Pao On v Lau Yiu Long* [1980] AC 614.

forced marriages where duress has manifested in various forms.[73] Duress by extended family members (parents and the bride's brother) was evident in *P v R (Forced Marriage: Annulment: Procedure)*[74] which included threats and psychological blackmail in that she was told she would bring shame to her family. In *NS v MI*,[75] her family had morally blackmailed her and threatened to commit suicide if she disobeyed them. Munby J said that there can be no consent to marriage where the person marrying is able to say '… my tongue has sworn but my mind [that is, the mind as the seat of the mental faculties, perception, thought] is unsworn'.[76] Munby J acknowledged that parental influences may be very subtle and reiterated his words in *Re SA (Vulnerable Adult with Capacity: Marriage)*:[77]

> … where the influence is that of a parent or other close and dominating relative, and where the arguments and persuasion are based upon personal affection or duty, religious beliefs, powerful social or cultural conventions, or asserted social, familial or domestic obligations, the influence may be, as Butler-Sloss LJ put it in *In re T (Adult: Refusal of Treatment)*,[78] '… subtle, insidious, pervasive and powerful'. In such cases, moreover, very little pressure may suffice to bring about the desired result.

Forced marriage is now also provided for under the Forced Marriage (Civil Protection) Act 2007, amending Part IV of the Family Law Act 1996 empowering courts to make Forced Marriage Protection Orders to prevent forced marriages and to offer protection to victims.[79] From 2012, a criminal provision is to be included.[80] Shafilea Ahmed contacted social services with regard to her parents forcing her into an arranged marriage, and she swallowed bleach in her efforts to escape this marriage. She had plenty of moral will but could not resist the physical violence to which she was subjected. Her parents were convicted of killing her.[81] And so with regard to a contract of marriage, a reluctant spouse may be considered to lack free will and capacity in the face of family pressures, but should she commit a criminal offence she is expected to have the 'moral' capacity to resist and no special consideration is made for her or for the victim of domestic violence. Are we really to believe that coercion stops with marriage and plays no part in criminal participation!?

---

73   Javaid Rehman, 'The Sharia, Islamic Family Laws and International Human Rights Law: Examining the Theory and Practice of Polygamy and Talaq' (2007) 21(1) International Journal of Law, Policy and the Family 108.

74   [2003] 1 FLR 661.

75   [2006] EWHC 1646 (Fam).

76   *Scott (falsely called Sebright) v Sebright* (1886) 12 PD 31 [24].

77   [2006] 1 FLR 867 [78]. See also *Allcard v Skinner* (1887) 36 ChD 145, 183.

78   [1993] Fam 95, 120.

79   A total of 340 applications for an FMPO have been made since their introduction up to the end of 2011, with 414 orders made in the same period. See *Judicial and Court Statistics* July 2011 (Ministry of Justice, 28 June 2012) 30 <http://www.justice.gov.uk/downloads/statistics/courts-and-sentencing/jcs-2011/judicial-court-stats-2011.pdf>.

80   *Forced Marriage*, SN/HA/1003 (Home Affairs Section, 8 June 2012). <www.parliament.uk/briefing-papers/SN01003.pdf> accessed on 10/01/2013.

81   Helen Carter, 'Shafilea Ahmed's Tragic History of Violence' (*The Guardian*, 3 August 2012) <http://www.guardian.co.uk/uk/2012/aug/03/shafilea-ahmed-history-of-violence> accessed 10/01/2013.

72 Participation in Crime

Criminal Participation: Culture and Coercion

Since the present law on participatory liability has widened to include those only tangentially involved and also those unable to escape the influence of the principal, inevitably injustice will follow. Gender is indeed a relevant characteristic in assessing accessory liability where a history of domestic violence may affect the gravity of the threat necessary to crush the will. The gravity of the threat is perceived by her to be greater where the duressor is a partner or family member. 'Cultural pressures', as well as violence, may affect her ability to resist, and effectively to withdraw. Women from certain communities may live outside their country of origin but 'cultural' practices with regard to patriarchy and gender relations are reproduced within these communities.[82]

The case of *Hussein and others*,[83] provides one such example where culture and gender were both relevant to the circumstances of both participation and duress in which a woman (Nyla Hussein) found herself, when jointly charged with principal(s) in a murder, in which her involvement, the prosecution conceded, was only peripheral. In December 1999 seven members of the same family were charged with the abduction and murder of Amjad Farooq. Farooq was the uncle of three of the accused. Nyla Hussein – one of the co-defendants – was the niece of the deceased and had been having an affair with him. The other defendants were her father, Khadim Hussein, her brothers Shazad and Shabaz, her husband Imran Farid (by an arranged marriage) and Ashiq and Pervaz – Khadim Hussein's brothers. At the time of the killing, Nyla was 200 miles away from where the killing took place but was charged as one of the parties and according to the Crown aided and abetted the murder by 'supplying' the address of Farooq to the others, thereby 'recruiting' them. The defence case was that she revealed Farooq's whereabouts only under duress and coercion and was an innocent victim.

Cultural stereotyping was played out by both defence and prosecution. Nyla, by her affair with the deceased, the Crown argued, had brought dishonour to the family. The prosecution 'recruitment' theory was an impossibility as her position and status within a traditional South Asian family demanded her subordination. She would have had no authority or responsibility for avenging perceived transgressions of 'honour' and would have had no role as orchestrator or 'recruiter' or indeed any influence in providing encouragement. The prosecution alleged: 'She knew the anger and hostility the family felt towards him and she knew how carefully he had kept his address secret. She set out to recruit members of her family to remove the obstacle of Amjad Farooq from their lives'.

A scenario of family honour was painted dictating precisely which family members could redeem lost honour and whose place it was to avenge it. Shazad (Nyla's brother) said in his evidence, 'Once she gets married seniority comes to the husband. I have no right! It is the husband and his wife. It's the culture, that's how it is'. Although clearly he thought he had at least some right to avenge shame and thereby redeem honour, as he said, 'I was going to give him a beating'. In the same vein, counsel for Shabaz relied on these cultural typifications in his closing speech: 'It was the primary responsibility of the husband to meet the shame, it was not his place to wipe away dishonour. He (Shabaz) is not the head of the family it is not his problem. He would be pressurized into going along'. Nyla Hussein chose to remain silent throughout the trial and so no evidence was brought in her defence. She appeared in the court at the commencement of trial when charges were

82   See Ravi K Thiara and Gill Hague, *Bride-Price, Poverty and Domestic Violence in Uganda* 6 <http://www2.warwick.ac.uk/fac/soc/shss/swell/bride_price_report_-_executive_summary_-_final_fin.pdf> accessed 31 August 2012.

83   From author's own court transcribed notes. See also <http://news.bbc.co.uk/1/hi/uk/510255.stm> accessed 31 August 2012. See also *Farid* [2007] EWHC 2413.

read and then only when ordered to do so during the judge's summing up. Such was the duress and coercion to which she was subjected, it robbed her of all agency, including the will even to defend herself. The jury could not reach a verdict and she was acquitted, no retrial was ordered.

Duress of family members through coercion of the will is also relevant in analysing the murder of Shafilea Ahmed. Farzana and Iftikar Ahmed were convicted on 3 August 2012 of killing their daughter, Shafilea. With the exception of Alesha (Shafilea's younger sister), who said in her evidence that she had witnessed the killing (but also changed her evidence during the trial indicating her dissonance in giving evidence against her parents), the other siblings, Mevish and Junyad, kept the knowledge of what their parents had done secret and supported their parents' defence. Mr Justice Evans said, 'As to Junyad, he remains supportive, especially of you Iftikhar Ahmed ... Whether that is simply out of filial affection or the result of the warped values you instilled in him is impossible to tell'.[84] Clearly offences of perverting the course of justice by giving false evidence, and obstructing justice and assistance after the commission of the crime (Criminal Law Act 1967 s 4), may have been committed by other family members; including the Domestic Violence and Crime Victims Act 2004 s 5; understanding the silencing of family members requires an understanding of cultural pressures which fall outside threats of physical violence.

Extending participatory liability led to the Domestic Violence Crime and Victims Act 2004, s 5(1)(DVCVA), which created a new offence of 'causing or allowing the death of a child or vulnerable person'. Section 5(1) provides:

> A person ('D') is guilty of an offence if – (a) a child or vulnerable adult ('V') dies as a result of the unlawful act of a person who – (i) was a member of the same household as V, and (ii) had frequent contact with him, (b) D was such a person at the time of that act, (c) at that time there was a significant risk of serious physical harm being caused to V by the unlawful act of such a person, and (d) either D was the person whose act caused V's death or – (i) D was, or ought to have been, aware of the risk mentioned in paragraph (c), (ii) D failed to take such steps as he could reasonably have been expected to take to protect V from the risk, and (iii) the act occurred in circumstances of the kind that D foresaw or ought to have foreseen. (2) The prosecution does not have to prove whether it is the first alternative in subsection (1)(d) or the second (sub-paragraphs (i) to (iii)) that applies.[85]

This provision was designed to address the difficulty which presented the prosecution in *R v Lane and Another*,[86] where the Court of Appeal in quashing convictions for manslaughter held that it could not be established which of two defendants (in this case a mother and stepfather) were responsible for the death of a 22-month-old baby.[87] In 2003, the Law Commission issued a consultation document followed by a report outlining their concern that co-accuseds could, and did, evade conviction in such circumstances.[88] The new provision in the DVCVA, addresses this

---

84 Mr Justice Evans cited in the *Guardian*, 4 August 2012. See also Rupa Reddy, 'Gender, Culture and the Law: Approaches to "Honour Crimes" in the UK' (2008) 16 Feminist Legal 305.

85 Sections 5 to 8 in force 21 March 2005, SI 2005/579.

86 [1985] 82 Cr App Rep 5.

87 See also *R v Aston and another* [1991] Crim LR 701; *R v Akinrele* [2010] EWCA Crim 2972; *R v Ikram and Parveen* [2008] EWCA Crim 586; *R v Jason Reid, The Times*, 19 July 2010; *R v Laura-Jane Vestuto* (2010) 2 Cr App R (S) 108; *R v James Watt, Natasha Jane Oldfield, Nichola Roberts, Richard Watt* (2012) 1 Cr App R(S) 31; *R v Khan and Others* [2009] EWCA Crim 2.

88 Law Commission, *Children: Their Non-Accidental Death or Serious Injury (Criminal Trials) A Consultative Report* (Law Com No 279, 2003).

problem, although there was a concern that the provision may be too broad. The 'ought to have foreseen the risk' element embodies an objective test and is driven by the difficulties presenting the prosecution in cases where two parties either blame each other for the death of a child or vulnerable person or where both simply deny any involvement. The (DVCVA), places a duty on the household member to protect the child or vulnerable person and implemented the direction of the trial judge in *Lane* (which the Court of Appeal had held was a misdirection). The burden of proof is on the prosecution (section 5(1)(d)(ii)(a)), to prove that D failed to take steps, he could reasonably have been expected to take, to protect the victim. The Home Office Circular, however, did acknowledge that a participant may act or fail to act under coercion fear and duress. It noted, '… Depending on the facts of the particular case the court may find that the defendant may have been too frightened to take some of the steps which in other circumstances might have been available to them' but it also goes on to state, 'The fact that the defendant may be young …, feel intimidated or have suffered violence, will not in itself be conclusive evidence that it was reasonable for the defendant not to take any steps to protect the victim'.[89]

There have been circumstances where parties are 'unable to take reasonable steps' to protect a child and a lesser sentence has been imposed.[90] The provision has also been used to protect vulnerable adults. In *R v Khan and others*,[91] K was convicted of the murder of his 19-year-old wife, S. K's mother (who was also S's aunt), two of his sisters (S's cousins) and the husband of one of the sisters were convicted of allowing the death of S, a vulnerable adult. In such cases, a defence of coercion will fall short of the requirements of duress as currently constructed. This provision has now been extended under the Domestic Violence, Crime and Victims (Amendment) Act 2012 where the offence will also apply where there is 'serious physical harm' to a child or vulnerable adult.

Participation: Duress and Sentencing

Whilst all these circumstances then are excluded from a duress defence falling outside its new strictures Lord Bingham addresses the moral dilemma created by the House of Lords judgment in *Hasan* which makes such victims criminally liable. He asserts that the harshness of a failed duress defence can always be 'remedied' in mitigation at the sentencing stage, 'If it appears at trial that a defendant acted in response to a degree of coercion but in circumstances where the strict requirements of duress were not satisfied, it is always open to the judge to adjust his sentence to reflect his assessment of the defendant's true culpability'.[92] Even if victims, or vulnerable parties, subject to duress fall short of the legal requirements, it will mean that women victims in fear will still incur a criminal conviction.[93] In this regard, Baroness Hale noted:

> The Commission also saw practical difficulties in the way of treating duress as mitigation. The Law Commission said this: If duress is rejected as a defence, that must be either because the defendant who acts under duress is at some way at fault, albeit it only by not behaving heroically;

89   Home Office Circular, *The Domestic Violence and Victims Act 2004: The New Offence of Causing the Death of a Child or Vulnerable Adult* (HO/Circ 2005) 9 [18]-[24].

90   'Father Jailed for "Possessed Baby" Murder' (*The Guardian*, 23 December 2005) <http://www.guardian.co.uk/uk/2005/dec/22/ukcrime1> accessed 2 January 2013.

91   [2009] EWCA Crim 2.

92   *Hasan* (n 2) [22].

93   See Loveless (n 3).

or because there is some public policy reason for convicting him even though he is not at fault. If he is at fault, the law should mark his fault by a penalty, or at least should not assume that in no case will an effective penalty be imposed. If the reasons for rejecting duress as a defence are ones of public policy, it is hard to see that that policy is forwarded by a regime that assumes that convictions are to be purely nominal in nature; or, even more, that assumes that in some cases the law will not be enforced at all.[94]

And so how have legal arguments attempted to remedy injustice at this stage? The leading case is *R v Emery*.[95] Sally Emery was charged with neglect for failing to protect her daughter who died at 11 months of age from the violence of her partner. Her defence to the charge was that her fear of the [child's] father meant that she had totally lost her capacity to act independently of him. She was recognised as suffering from 'post traumatic stress disorder' including an inability to stand up to the abuser, coupled with a dependence on him which made her unable to seek help. Her defence of duress was rejected by the jury. The duress arguments were repeated in an appeal against sentence. Lord Taylor (LCJ), in the Court of Appeal, in deciding whether the sentence of four years was excessive, said, 'the question for the doctors was whether a woman of reasonable firmness with the characteristics of Miss Emery, if abused in the manner which she said, would have had her will crushed so that she could not have protected her child'. The Court of Appeal reduced her sentence to 30 months accepting that her fear of the abuser might well have 'sapped her will'.[96] But should such women as Emery have been convicted at all?

Laws' Fractured Consciousness: Participation, Duress and Gender-Based Violence

Women as wives, partners and family members may well face particular circumstances of coercion implicating them as criminal participants. Marital coercion remains an intransigent aspect of some ethnic/cultural backgrounds as does the coercion of intimates and family members, which compels wives to participate in crime. With regard to marital coercion, whilst it is true that since its enactment in 1925 many married women have achieved independence through economic and political emancipation, there is also a very strong argument for its retention since the situation in which some married women continue to find themselves is indeed characterised by physical and mental coercion and duress. Partner homicide, which includes spousal homicide, continues unabated.[97] The retention becomes especially important following the restriction of the defence of duress following *Hasan*, because at least a marital coercion defence recognises psychological duress albeit it is limited to wives. In addition, the increasing multicultural nature of modern society reflects a diversity of family and cultural arrangements which are resistant to challenges to patriarchy, and mitigate against the more general trend of development in women's personal and social status, with the consequence that family members can exert a variety of oppressive pressures which do control women (and some men) who are neither weak minded nor feeble nor lacking in moral will. An understanding of the way in which gender and ethnicity intersect is required and it is here that a case is to be made for taking into account valid cultural pressures.

---

94   Cited in *Hasan* (n 2) [69].

95   *R v Emery* (1993) 14 Cr App R (S) 394.

96   See also *R v Bibi* [1980] 1 WLR 1193; *R v Bainton* [2005] EWCA Crim 3572; *R v Gutierrez-Ruiz* [2005] EWCA Crim 2917.

97   Kevin Smith, Sarah Osborne, Ivy Lau and Andrew Britton, *Homicides, Firearm Offences and Intimate Violence 2010/11* (Supplementary Volume 2 to Crime in England and Wales) (2012) Table 1.05.

Whilst there have been significant developments in other areas of criminal and family law with regard to the understanding of women's fear and violence perpetrated against them compelling them to commit crime, the law governing participation and the law governing duress has been hermetically sealed. Elsewhere, including the criminal law on homicide, and recent developments in the Policing and Crime Act 2009, with regard to sexual offences and coercion, family law on marriage, and international and human rights law, such considerations have occupied a central position.[98] It is pleaded that the law on participation considers the predicament of some women and that the law on duress expands the characteristics of the reasonable person so as to be consistent with jurisprudential understanding elsewhere in the criminal law to include gender-based violence and coercion. It is simply not logical to argue as Lord Bingham has done, in efforts to justify distinguishing the approaches to provocation from duress, that:

> Duress affords a defence which, if raised and not disproved, exonerates the defendant altogether. It does not, like the defence of provocation to a charge of murder, serve merely to reduce the seriousness of the crime which the defendant has committed. And the victim of a crime committed under duress is not, like a person against whom a defendant uses force to defend himself, a person who has threatened the defendant or been perceived by the defendant as doing so. The victim of a crime committed under duress may be assumed to be morally innocent, having shown no hostility or aggression towards the defendant.[99]

As to participation, Lord Kerr of Tonaghmore, in his dissent in *R v Gnango*,[100] sums up the current problems with the recent expansion in participatory liability:

> In any event for parasitic accessory liability to arise, Gnango and B *would have to have a common intention* to commit an affray, if affray is the crime on which Gnango and B are to be said to have jointly embarked. Whether or not a common intention is required for a joint offence of affray, it is most certainly required for parasitic accessory liability. Even if it were possible, therefore, for them to be convicted of joint affray without a common intention to commit that offence, for the offence to provide the basis of parasitic accessory liability, it would have to be proved that they had a shared intention [and] … To speak of joint principal offenders being involved in a joint enterprise is, at least potentially, misleading. The essential ingredient for joint principal offending is a contribution to the cause of the *actus reus*. If this is absent, the fact that there is a common purpose or a joint enterprise cannot transform the offending into joint principal liability.

Vulnerable women are now caught in the crossfire of participatory liability and duress principles. Law's consciousness in the development of criminal law principles and their intersectionality with gender and other factors of relevance cannot be held simply in the heads of the one or two judges who understood in the past and those few judges who understand in the present. Lord Taylor in *Emery* understood duress when he spoke of a will being crushed.[101] But then Lord Taylor (CJ) understood the predicament of abused women and was able to bring this understanding and compassion to

---

98   Hilary Charlesworth and Christine Chinkin (eds), *The Boundaries of International Law: A Feminist Analysis* (Juris 2000).

99   *Hasan* (n 2) [19].

100   *Gnango* (n 7).

101   *Emery* (n 95) 398.

his judgments.[102] Lord Scarman in *Hirani*[103] similarly understood when he expanded the law on nullity and duress to achieve a greater justice. There is a need to raise in the wider political arena this issue of women's unwilling participation in crime and their inability to avail themselves of the masculinist duress defence. Part of this intransigence in the law on participation and duress and the exclusion of gender and cultural considerations can in part be attributed to a judiciary where women and women of diversity are under-represented and invisible. Only five women have ever sat in the Court of Appeal, the House of Lords or Supreme Court such that Baroness Hale is a lone voice.[104] Thus, whilst legal reasoning and conversations about participation and duress are fuelled, quite rightly, about social policy concerns, policy about women's experiences is still left knocking at the door of these debates. The law needs to take into account cultural differences with regard to the way in which cultural conventions impose themselves on women's ability to withstand duress resulting in their participation in crimes through omission and silence or through commission. The current rejection of anything other than immediate physical threats and the requirement of an objective test is inherently masculinist. As Loveless has argued, 'The defence is based on the way in which men may more typically experience identifiable specific threats of serious harm rather than the incremental destruction of self-esteem characteristics of prolonged domestic violence'.[105] The law, at the same time, must also recognise valid cultural differences in women's responses to resisting duress and coercion if justice is also to be delivered to some of the most vulnerable women unwilling parties in crime.

---

102   See *R v Ahluwalia* [1992] 4 All ER 889; *R v Thornton* [1992] 1 All ER 306.
103   *Hirani* (n 71).
104   See Hunter, McGlynn and Rackley (n 56) 8.
105   Loveless (n 3) 95.

Chapter 5
Victims as Defendants: When Victims Participate in Crimes against Themselves

Jonathan Herring

Introduction

The criminal law typically focuses on an individual defendant and asks whether that defendant caused the victim an identified kind of harm. This has led to a powerful critique from a critical studies perspective that this "snapshot" approach disguises the complex causes of crime. It excludes, for example, consideration of the extent to which socio-economic forces or genetic factors may be responsible for the injury.[1] I do not intend to enter those debates.[2] I will focus on another aspect of such a complaint, that by casting the parties as defendant and victim this renders invisible and irrelevant questions about the extent to which the victim might be responsible for the harm they suffer.

There is a notable distinction between civil law and criminal law in this regard. Under civil law an attempt is made to apportion blame for the loss between the claimant and the defendant. Under the doctrine of contributory negligence the court will assess the extent to which the victim and defendant share responsibility for the loss.[3] The criminal law undertakes no such assessment.

The defendant will have no defence based on the fact the victim contributed to their own injuries and victims are rarely, if ever, prosecuted for causing themselves injury. This presentation of the law, as we shall shortly see, is somewhat over-simplified because, in fact, the blameworthiness of the victim can be relevant in relation to certain defences. Nevertheless as a general observation it is correct that questions of the fault of the victim are not seen as relevant.

Some commentators, most notably Vera Bergelson,[4] have argued that the law needs to be far more open to the idea of sharing blame for injuries between defendants and victims. One way of doing this, which she advocates, is allowing a partial or complete defence or mitigation based on the contributory blame of the defendant. I will explain later why I do not find this convincing. More plausible is a suggestion that the victim should be regarded as an accessory to the crime against themselves.

This chapter, then, will focus particularly on the circumstances in which a victim might be said to have been an accomplice to injuries against themselves.[5] It is extremely rare for prosecutions to be brought based on such an argument. It will be argued in this chapter that the law is right to be very reluctant to prosecute victims who contribute to injuries against themselves. The chapter

---

1   Arthur Ripstein, 'Justice and Responsibility' (2004) 17 Canadian Journal of Law and Jurisprudence 361.

2   See for example, Victor Tadros, 'Poverty and Criminal Responsibility' (2009) 43 Journal of Value Inquiry 391.

3   Law Reform (Contributory Negligence) Act 1945.

4   Vera Bergelson, *Victims' Rights and Victims' Wrongs: Comparative Liability in Criminal Law* (Stanford University Press 2009).

5   Alon Harel, 'Efficiency and Fairness in Criminal Law: The Case for a Criminal Law Principle of Comparative Fault' (1994) 82 California Law Review 1181.

will start by putting the issue of the criminal responsibility of victims in its broader context, before considering the current law. It will look at the more theoretical issue surrounding victim responsibility as an accomplice in the law, before concluding that only very rarely should victims be found to be liable as accomplices.

The Broader Picture

The fact that the victim's blameworthiness is not generally relevant in the criminal law is not surprising. First, and obviously, the fact the victim is an unpleasant character is utterly irrelevant. If Anne picks Tom's pocket, then the fact Tom abuses his son, will provide Anne with no defence. It is as irrelevant to the charge as the fact that Anne abuses her son would be to a charge of pickpocketing. A good application of the principle can be found in *R v Wacker*,[6] where the fact the victims were engaged on an unlawful enterprise with the defendant when they were killed offered no defence for the defendant to a charge of manslaughter. The criminal law protects the right to life of those embarked on criminal enterprises as much as anyone else.

Second, the fact that the victim may have made a causal contribution to their own injuries is irrelevant to the charge facing the defendant. This is entirely in line with the general approach to the criminal law on causation. Once it is shown that the defendant's act was an operating and substantial cause of the harm to the victim it is no defence for the defendant to show that others (including the victim) were also an operating and substantial cause.[7] The only argument that such a defendant can successfully make in terms of the causation was that the victim's act broke the chain of causation.[8] The defence in such a case is based on the fact that the defendant's act was not a substantial and operating cause of the injury. The fact it was the victim, as opposed to anyone else, who broke the chain of causation is of no relevance so far as the defendant's trial is concerned. Hence, the fact the victim had left their car unlocked with the keys in the ignition and so enabled a theft, or walked down a dark alley facilitating the mugging, would be utterly irrelevant to the conviction of the defendant.

However, it would be false to suggest that the victim's contribution is irrelevant for the purposes of the substantive criminal law. Indeed Douglas Husak argues: 'anyone who contends that victim fault is and ought to be irrelevant in all cases simply does not know what he is talking about'.[9] Vera Bergelson[10] has argued that the criminal law takes account of the behaviour of the victim through the defences of consent, self-defence and provocation.[11] She uses this to make a broader argument which we will explore later. For now I simply note that her examples show that there can be cases where the conduct of the victim is relevant in assessing the criminal liability of the defendant.

The focus of this chapter will not be on the issue of when the victim's conduct affords a defence to the defendant, but rather to ask when, if at all, might a victim be found to have been an accessory to the crime committed against him. To give a practical example, if the victim leaves the windows of their house open, enabling a defendant to enter the house and commit burglary, there is no

---

6   [2003] QB 1207.
7   *R v Mellor* [1996] 2 Cr App R 245.
8   *R v Kennedy* [2007] UKHL 38.
9   Douglas Husak, 'Comparative Fault in Criminal Law: Conceptual and Normative Perplexities' [2005] Buffalo Criminal Law Review 523.
10   Bergelson (n 4) 4.
11   In England the defence of provocation has been replaced with the defence of loss of control; Coroners and Justice Act 2009, ss54-56.

doubt that the acts of the victim will provide no defence to the defendant. But what about the victim's criminal responsibility as an accomplice? A person who opens a neighbour's windows foreseeing that doing so might assist a burglar could face inculpation as an accessory; should it be any different if they open their own? Before explaining why there should be a difference, I will set out the current law.

The Victim as an Accomplice in English Law

The law on the extent to which a victim can be an accomplice to crimes committed against them is somewhat vague. One point that stands out is that there have been very few prosecutions. In one leading textbook[12] it is stated that a victim can be an accomplice to an offence against themselves, but the only authority cited is *Wright*'s Case,[13] in which a defendant agreed to cut off the victim's hand so that the victim could beg more effectively. Both the defendant and 'the victim' were convicted of mayhem. It is submitted this is not a strong enough authority to establish the general principle that a victim can be an accomplice for offences against themselves. If authority is to be found in support for such a claim it might be identified in the '*Tyrrell* principle'.

The *Tyrrell* principle[14] is commonly expressed as an exception: it sets out when a victim will not be determined to have been an accomplice to their own injury. This suggests that generally the rule is that the victim can be found to be an accomplice to their own injury. However, it will be argued that the issue is not that straightforward.

The Law Commission state the *Tyrrell* principle in this way: 'Under the current law, if an offence is enacted to protect a category of persons and D falls within that category, D cannot be convicted of committing the offence as a secondary party (or of inciting P to commit the offence)'.[15]

In *Tyrrell*[16] itself the charge was that Jane Tyrrell, aged 15, unlawfully aided and abetted, counselled and procured the commission by Thomas Ford of a misdemeanour of having unlawful carnal knowledge of her when she was between the ages of 13 and 16. There was evidence that she had encouraged him to have sex with her. Lord Coleridge concluded that Jane Tyrrell could not be convicted of the charge under the Criminal Law Amendment Act 1885. He explained:

> The ... Act was passed for the purpose of protecting women and girls against themselves. At the time it was passed there was a discussion as to what point should be fixed as the age of consent. That discussion ended in a compromise, and the age of consent was fixed at 16. With the object of protecting women and girls against themselves the Act of Parliament has made illicit connection with a girl under that age unlawful; if a man wishes to have such illicit connection he must wait until the girl is 16, otherwise he breaks the law; but it is impossible to say that the Act, which is absolutely silent about aiding or abetting, or soliciting or inciting, can have intended that the girls for whose protection it was passed should be punishable under it for the offences committed upon themselves.[17]

---

12   Andrew Simester, JR Spencer, Bob Sullivan and Graham Virgo, *Simester and Sullivan's Criminal Law* (4th edn, Hart 2011) 251.

13   (1603) 1 Co Lit 127a.

14   This is helpfully discussed in Michael Bohlander, 'The Sexual Offences Act 2003 and the Tyrrell Principle: Criminalising the Victims?' [2005] Criminal Law Review 701.

15   Law Commission, *Participation in Crime* (Law Com No 305, 2007) 1.52.

16   [1894] 1 QB 710.

17   Ibid. [712].

While the judgment is brief, it was clear Lord Coleridge saw the matter as one of statutory interpretation and did not appear to be creating a general common law principle.

In *R v Whitehouse*,[18] *Tyrrell* was interpreted as a case about statutory interpretation. The defendant was charged with inciting his 15-year-old daughter to commit incest with him. This was a flawed charge. As the court concluded, his daughter could not be convicted of committing incest as was made clear under section 11 of the Sexual Offence Act 1956 (since abolished), nor could she be said to aid and abet his commission of incest. That was an appropriate interpretation of the 1956 Act, bearing in mind the way the statute in *Tyrrell* had been interpreted.[19]

Most recently, the doctrine was considered in the decision of *Gnango*.[20] The case, in short, involved a shoot out between Gnango and 'bandana man', in the course of which 'bandana man' shot a bystander. The case centred on Gnango's liability for the murder. The prosecution alleged that Gnango was liable as an accomplice to the murder, by aiding, abetting, counselling or procuring the firing of shots at himself which led to the victim's death. The defence raised the *Tyrrell* principle, or 'victim rule' as the Supreme Court preferred to call it. Their Lordships denied the application of the principle to this case. The *Tyrrell* principle only applied where the offence was created for the protection of a particular class of vulnerable people. Murder was not such an offence and so a person could be charged with aiding, abetting, counselling or procuring their own murder. In any event the victim in this case was the bystander, not Gnango, and so the *Tyrrell* principle was not engaged.

This latter point is not entirely convincing. The prosecution in this case was clearly relying on the principle of transferred malice. Bandana man was aiming at Gnango and missed and killed the bystander. His conviction of murder, to which it was said that Gnango was an accomplice, depended on a finding of intention to kill Gnango, which could be transferred to the victim. However, it is questionable that if a person intends to kill person A in circumstances in which it would not be a crime, and in fact, by chance, kills person B that the doctrine of transferred malice could be used to ensure a conviction.[21] It was, therefore, a legitimate question whether the *Tyrrell* principle could be used to prevent a murder conviction had P in fact killed Gnango.

That is slightly by the by if the *Tyrrell* principle has no application because the offence of murder has no identified class of protected vulnerable people. That point is central to this article and needs further analysis. Their Lordships in their discussion of *Tyrrell* relied upon an article by Professor Glanville Williams, and his definition of the principle:

> where the courts perceive that the legislation is designed for the protection of a class of persons. Such people should not be convicted as accessories to an offence committed in respect of them when they co-operate in it. Nor should they be convicted as conspirators.[22]

It is respectfully suggested that this is the correct way of formulating the *Tyrrell* principle. It is a principle of statutory definition, not a matter of common law or foundational justice. Significantly, as formulated by Professor Williams, it leaves open the question of whether generally the law recognises that a victim cannot be an accomplice to an injury against themselves.

The Supreme Court held there was no such general principle. In *Gnango*, Lords Phillips and Judge, with the agreement of Lord Wilson, confirmed that generally there is no common law rule

---

18   [1977] QB 868.
19   See also *Pickford* [1995] 1 Cr App R 420.
20   [2011] UKSC 59.
21   *Attorney General's Reference (No 3 of 1994)* [1998] AC 245.
22   Glanville Williams, 'Victims and Other Exempt Parties in Crime' (1990) 10 Legal Studies 245.

preventing conviction of a defendant as a party to a crime of which he or she was the intended victim. As their reasoning is key to this chapter it is worth citing it at length:

> The fact that Parliament found it necessary to enact section 2(1) of the 1977 Act and section 51 of the 2007 Act is cogent indication that there is no common law rule that precludes conviction of a defendant of being party to a crime of which he was the actual or intended victim. We are satisfied that there is no such rule. This is evident from the fact that, under common law, attempted suicide was a crime, as was aiding and abetting suicide. The victim of a successful suicide attempt could not, of course, be prosecuted, but if in an attempt to commit suicide, the defendant killed a third person, he committed the crime of murder under the doctrine of transferred malice: see *R v Hopwood* (1913) 8 Cr App R 143 and *R v Spence* (1957) 41 Cr App R 80 .

> We can see no reason why this court should consider extending the common law so as to protect from conviction any defendant who is, or is intended to be, harmed by the crime that he commits, or attempts to commit. Such an extension would defeat the intention of Parliament in circumscribing the victim rule in section 51 of the 2007 Act. In *R v Brown (Anthony)* [1994] 1 AC 212 sado-masochists were held to have been rightly convicted of causing injury to others who willingly consented to the injuries that they received. There would have been no bar to conviction of the latter of having aided and abetted the infliction of those injuries upon themselves. It is no doubt appropriate for prosecuting authorities to consider carefully whether there is justification for prosecuting anyone as party to a crime where he is the victim, or intended victim of that crime, but that is not to say that the actual or intended victim of a crime should on that ground alone be absolved from criminal responsibility in relation to it. As Lord Lane CJ observed in *Attorney-General's Reference (No 6 of 1980)* [1981] QB 715, 719: 'it is not in the public interest that people should try to cause, or should cause, each other actual bodily harm for no good reason'.[23]

Their Lordships' approach could be supported by reference to section 8 of the Accessories and Abettors Act 1861:

> Whosoever shall aid, abet, counsel, or procure the commission of any indictable offence, whether the same be an offence at common law or by virtue of any Act passed or to be passed, shall be liable to be tried, indicted, and punished as a principal offender.

This appears to indicate that the liability for accomplices is general. The wording would seem to apply to victims as much as any other accessories. However, the stark fact is that apart from the *Wright* case mentioned previously, we have no recorded case of a victim being prosecuted as an accomplice. In *Brown*,[24] mentioned by their Lordships, it was notable that the 'victims' were not prosecuted, only those who actually inflicted harms. There is something a bit odd about a positive statement that victims can be accomplices when there has not been a recorded prosecution for nearly 400 years.

Let us consider further one of the arguments developed here by their Lordships, before going on to look at the theoretical issues. First, their Lordships refer to Section 51 of the Serious Crime Act 2007 which states that a person does not commit an offence if:

---

23   *Gnango* (n 20) [52] [53].
24   [1994] 1 AC 212.

(a) he falls within the protected category; and

(b) he is the person in respect of whom the protective offence was committed or would have been if it had been committed.

(2) 'Protective offence' means an offence that exists (wholly or in part) for the protection of a particular category of persons ('the protected category').

In short their Lordships' argument is that this provision would not be necessary if there was a general rule that victims could not be liable as accomplices. However, it is always dangerous to assume a common law principle from a statute. The mere fact that a statute creates a particular offence or defence does not necessarily amend the common law as it applies in similar situations. The criminal law is replete with examples of where the statute and common law overlap.[25]

The discussion of this issue in *Gnango* was *obiter* and as suggested there was no precedent support for it. A deeper consideration of the issues might have explained why no prosecutions have been brought. We need to explore further the theoretical issues, before I conclude that it is not appropriate to charge a victim as an accessory to an offence against themselves, save in very unusual cases.

Theoretical Issues

The starting point in analysing this issue should be to consider why generally people should not be subject to harming themselves under the criminal law.[26] It is crucial to distinguish a case of self-harm and harm to others. There are six reasons I would highlight why self-harm should not be criminalised *per se*. I say '*per se*' because I am leaving aside cases where self-harm in a public place might cause distress to others of the kind that would justify a public order offence. In such a case the justification for criminalisation would rest on the harm caused to the public, not the self-harm caused to the victim.

Why We Should Not Punish Self-Harm

The first reason against criminalising self-harm is that doing so interferes with the 'harm principle'. In *On Liberty*, Mill[27] asserts:

> The only purpose for which power can be rightfully exercised over any member of a civilized community, against his will, is to prevent harm to others. His own good, either physical or moral, is not a sufficient warrant.

While that formulation has been subject to much debate over its exact interpretation it is widely respected as providing a useful starting point in debates over criminalisation. It is notable in this

---

25   The law governing self-defence is a good example where both the common law and Criminal Law Act 1967, section 3(1) apply. Both are also governed by Criminal Justice and Immigration Act 2008, s 76.

26   Dennis Baker, 'Moral Limits of Consent as a Defence in the Criminal Law' (2009) 12 New Criminal Law Review 93; Joel Feinberg, *The Moral Limits of the Criminal Law: Harm to Self* (Oxford University Press, 1986).

27   John Mill, *On Liberty* (Roberts and Green 1869).

formulation that it is harm to others which justifies the harm principle. Causing harm to oneself, whatever the morality of doing that, is not sufficiently harmful to justify criminalisation.

Second, a central aspect of the wrongfulness of harming another is that it involves, typically, a breach of the Kantian imperative of not treating others as a means to an end. In harming another you are typically using their body to pursue your own goals. In harming oneself one is not using another as an object for oneself. A person is using their own body in order to pursue their goals, but that is how bodies are typically used. There may be arguments over whether a particular individual's use of their body might infringe conceptions of dignity.[28] However, that will require an exceptional kind of case.

The third reason against criminalising self-harm is the social meaning that is attached to a particular act. The significance of an act can take on a particular meaning in a social context.[29] A gesture or words can in a particular society carry with it serious negative meaning and can play a significant part in assessing the harmfulness of the act. Part of the reason why being squashed by others in a tube train is not a crime is in our society such behaviour is understood as part of everyday life. If there is a justification for not criminalising boxing it may lie in the same point. This is why self-harm is different. Where a person is harming themselves we do not see this as being an act requiring the intervention of the criminal law. Self-harm may engender pity or horror but not the call for punishment that crimes normally would. Censure is not required.

The fourth arises by analogy with the Suicide Act 1961. When attempted suicide was made no longer a crime, Parliament determined that those who attempt to commit suicide require the ministrations of the medical professional not a criminal prosecution. It was a therapeutic response. The same is generally true of self-harm. There too the therapeutic concerns about the self-harmer should outweigh any claims for punishment. This is why self-harm and suicide are seen to create civil intervention to prevent such behaviour, rather than criminal sanctions punishing it.[30] This is particularly so when much self-harm is a symptom of psychological ill health, rather than being blameworthy conduct.[31] Victor Tadros captures this well in his explanation of why it might be appropriate to punish those who kill with consent of the victim, but not to punish suicide:

> The duty that I have not to kill myself, while important, is unenforceable. Your duty not to kill me, in contrast, is both important and enforceable. But why should this be so? Perhaps because an enforceable duty against suicide would typically be intrusive in a way that enforceable duties on others not to assist would not be, or perhaps because enforcing the self-regarding duties of suicidal people would harm a person who is already in distress. It would typically make a person who is very badly off even worse off.[32]

Fifth, there are arguments based on autonomy. To many commentators, we should be free to do with our bodies what we will. We should be free to adorn, tattoo and redesign our bodies because they are ours. If a person, with capacity, wishes to cut their bodies that is their choice and the

---

28   See for a detailed discussion, Charles Foster, *Human Dignity in Bioethics and Law* (Hart 2011).

29   See further Jonathan Herring and Michelle Madden Dempsey, 'Why Sexual Penetration Requires Justification' (2007) 27 Oxford Journal of Legal Studies 467.

30   Andrew von Hirsch, 'Direct Paternalism: Punishing the Perpetrators of Self-Harm' (2008) 5 Intellectum 7.

31   For a discussion of the causes of self-harm see Kerry Gutridge, 'Safer Self-Injury or Assisted Self-Harm?' (2010) 31 Theoretical Medical Bioethics 79.

32   Victor Tadros, 'Consent to Harm' (2011) 64 Current Legal Problems 23, 49.

criminal law should not intervene. Joel Feinberg, for example, argues in favour of the ultimate principle of respect for autonomy:[33]

> If, on the other hand, our ultimate principle expresses respect for a person's voluntary choice as such, even when it is the choice of a loss of freedom, we can remain adamantly opposed to paternalism even in the most extreme cases of self-harm, for we shall be committed to the view that there is something more important (even) than the avoidance of harm. The principle that shuts and locks the door leading to strong paternalism is that every man has a human right to 'voluntarily dis-pose of his own lot in life' whatever the effect on his own net balance of benefits (including 'freedom') and harms.

The issue is not quite straight-forward. There are limits to autonomy. This is a complex issue, but even the best case for limiting autonomy is likely to be where a defendant has shown an utter lack of respect for the value of personhood that we think society should value. As Baroness Hale put it in one context:

> It is not for society to tell people what to value about their own lives. But it may be justifiable for society to insist that we value their lives even if they do not.[34]

But, and this is a key point, if cases where an individual is showing no regard for the value of their life are the cases where there may be a case for overriding autonomy, those are the very cases where the therapeutic argument made above is the strongest.

The sixth argument is that there are often strong policy arguments against opening up the question of the blameworthiness of the victim in a criminal trial. An analysis of *Tyrrell* demonstrates this issue. Parliament has determined in relation to sexual offences that those under 16 cannot give effective consent to sexual intercourse. There are a number of reasons why this might be so. It cannot be that all those under 16 lack the actual capacity to consent.[35] It must rather be that there is a public policy protection that sexual behaviour with those under 16 should be prohibited. The way this is expressed is that those under 16 cannot consent because this is a particularly powerful way of expressing society's condemnation. It sends a strong clear message to those who might abuse children, claiming children consent to the experience. Of course, there will be those who disagree with the way the law has dealt with this issue and space prevents a detailed discussion.

If the explanation for the law lies along those lines, it seems the public policy is even stronger in cases where the defendant claims the victim incited sex. If we do not want people to think that those under 16 consent to sex, we certainly do not want them thinking that those under 16 are inciting or encouraging others to have sex with them.

A similar kind of argument can be made in relation to rape trials. Rape trials are replete with examples of where the victims end up being blamed for their rapes.[36] Again there are good reasons why the law might want to shut out even a discussion of the extent to which the victim might

---

33   Joel Feinberg, 'Legal Paternalism' (1971) 1 Canadian Journal of Philosophy 120.

34   *R (Purdy) v DPP* [2009] UKHL 45, 68.

35   *Gillick v West Norfolk and Wisbech Area Health Authority* [1986] 1 **AC** 112.

36   Jennifer Temkin and Barbara Krahé, *Sexual Assault and the Justice Gap: A Question of Attitude* (Hart 2008).

be to blame for the rape.[37] The six arguments just made provide, I suggest, a strong case against criminalising self-harm.

Why We Should Not Share Responsibility for Crime between Victims and Defendants

Professor Bergelson has made a radical argument in favour of 'comparative liability', taking into account the blameworthiness of the victim in assessing the blame of the defendant. She summarises her argument in these words:

> Criminal liability of the perpetrator should be reduced to the extent that the victim, by his own acts, has diminished his right not to be harmed. The victim may reduce his right not to be harmed either voluntarily, by consent, waiver, or assumption of risk, or involuntarily, by an attack on some legally recognized rights of the perpetrator. The reduction of the victim's right not to be harmed correlates with the reduction of the perpetrator's liability.[38]

She provides five reasons in favour of her approach:

> (a) The just desert argument. Under the principle of just desert, individuals should be responsible only for the amount of harm they caused. Accordingly, to the extent the victim is responsible for a portion of the harm, the offender's liability should be reduced;

> (b) The efficiency argument. The law should be efficient. I do not view that principle as the ultimate organizing consideration of criminal law and utilize it only to the extent that it does not contradict the just desert principle. Accordingly, I do not rely on the economic efficiency line of reasoning. On the other hand, I agree with arguments that, in order to be efficient, the law should (i) not overuse criminal sanctions, and (ii) develop in a dialogue with community perceptions of right and wrong. In that sense, it is important to recognize that the community (acting through jurors) has already incorporated comparative fault into criminal law. To maintain a fair and lawful system of criminal justice, a theory of comparative fault must be worked out to guide people in their decision making;

> (c) The consistency argument. The law is a system in which various rules are interdependent. To be consistent, the law must treat similar states of affairs in a similar fashion. At this point, the law recognizes the victim's fault as a mitigating circumstance in a number of specific situations, and, at the same time, refuses to recognize it as a general principle. That leads to illogical, incoherent, and unfair decisions;

> (d) The penalty argument. The victim's fault is a valid penalty mitigator in a number of circumstances. Since the victim's fault is a 'fault mitigator', it should be allowed at the guilt adjudication stage, and not only at the penalty stage; and

---

37   Michelle Madden Dempsey, 'Sex Trafficking and Criminalization: In Defense of Feminist Abolitionism' (2010) 158 University of Pennsylvania Law Review 1729.

38   Vera Bergelson, 'Victims and Perpetrators: An Argument for Comparative Liability in Criminal Law' (2005) 8 Buffalo Criminal Law Review 385, 387.

(e) The torts argument. Tort and criminal law doctrines have significant similarities. Tort theory has recognized the principle of comparative responsibility and continues to broaden the scope of its application. The comparative responsibility reform in torts supplies arguments and criteria for conducting a similar reform in criminal law.[39]

I will not consider this proposal in depth as it is rather different from the one focused on in my chapter and has been discussed at length elsewhere.[40] There are a range of difficulties with it. It is notable, for example, that Bergelson's proposals are somewhat unclear as to how the liability of the perpetrator should be reduced. While murder might be reduced to manslaughter it is unclear what an assault occasioning actual bodily harm should be reduced to, for example. It may be that she imagines a rewriting of the criminal law to have two versions of each offence so that the reduction she seeks can be made. It may be she also has in mind mitigation, but that would not be a radical claim.

It has also received criticism from Hedi Hurd for being over-inclusive in its use of the notion of assumption of risk. A victim who walks in a dangerous part of town late at night, realising the dangers of mugging should not be seen as responsible for the attack on her.[41] This is part of a larger concern. Many examples of cases where a victim might be said to have casual responsibility for the attack would constitute an improper interference in the rights of the victim. Simply because the victim puts themselves in a position where a crime is likely, be that by not locking their house at night, or not keeping their bank account details secret, does not mean that the victim has consented to the risk and certainly not be seen in criminal law as partly to blame for the crime.

Bergelson deals with these points by making it clear that 'the offender's liability may be mitigated by the conduct of the victim only if the offender has the right that the victim does not behave that way'.[42] This is an important limitation, but is opaque. She suggests it is left to the jury in those terms. That is dangerous as the surveys of rape trials indicate. In any event, it severely restricts the application of her suggested principle. The circumstances in which the offender has a right that the victim does not behave in a particular way are likely to be limited to where self-defence or, perhaps, provocation apply.

At the heart of Vera Bergelson's argument is the claim that there should be a defence for a defendant when the victim 'by his own acts, has waived or reduced his right not to be harmed'.[43] The difficulty is that, as Husak notes, the idea that rights are forfeited or reduced is a controversial one. A more convincing approach is that rights are conditional. He argues:

> Conditional rights, like categorical rights, are either implicated or they are not; construing rights as conditionals does not help to explain how one's right can be reduced by the behavior of others. When White provokes Green, he does not reduce his right not to be assaulted, for such a right did not exist in the first place. As we have seen, an accurate description of White's right must include more detail; it is the right not to be assaulted if he refrains from provocative behavior.[44]

39   Ibid. 427.
40   Hedi Hurd, 'Blaming the Victim: A Response to the Proposal that Criminal Law Recognize a General Defence of Contributory Responsibility' (2005) 8 Buffalo Criminal Law Review 503.
41   Ibid.
42   Bergelson (n 38) 421.
43   Bergelson (n 4).
44   Husak (n 9).

Seeing self-defence as the victim forfeiting their rights gives too much power to the victim. The victim is prohibited from attacking another person. It is not a choice they can exercise if they are willing to forfeit their rights.[45]

Vera Bergelson makes much of the distinction between civil and criminal claims.[46] She calls for consistency of approach between these. However, there is a substantial difference between the two. One major difference is, of course, that the criminal proceedings are brought by the Crown on behalf of society generally against the defendant, whereas civil cases are brought by an individual. The wrong doing of the claimant may legitimately be taken into account as affecting what remedy she receives. However, in a criminal trial the wrong is one for society and this is not necessarily reduced by the blameworthiness of the victim.[47] In *Wacker*,[48] the Court of Appeal held that even though the victims would not have been able to sue the defendant in the law of tort because of the principle of *ex turpi causa* that was no bar to the conviction of the defendant of gross negligence manslaughter in criminal law. Their explanation is instructive:

> Why is there, therefore, this distinction between the approach of the civil law and the criminal law? The answer is that the very same public policy that causes the civil courts to refuse the claim points in a quite different direction in considering a criminal offence. The criminal law has as its function the protection of citizens and gives effect to the state's duty to try those who have deprived citizens of their rights of life, limb or property. It may very well step in at the precise moment when civil courts withdraw because of this very different function. The withdrawal of a civil remedy has nothing to do with whether as a matter of public policy the criminal law applies. The criminal law should not be disapplied just because the civil law is disapplied. It has its own public policy aim which may require a different approach to the involvement of the law.[49]

The question in a criminal trial is whether the defendant has behaved in a blameworthy enough way to justify punishment. This involves consideration of multiple factors, only one of which is causal responsibility. It never has been required that the defendant is the sole or even main cause of the injury. In a civil case the primary focus is on the extent to which the defendant's negligence caused the injury. This is revealed by the fact that a criminal charge can be brought even where there is no injury to the victim, that would never be true in the case of a civil claim.

But at the heart of my objections to Bergelson's approach is that it fails to place sufficient weight on the reasons why self-harm are seen as very different from harming others, outlined in the six points above. For those reasons the law legitimately treats differently a case where the person has caused themselves harm and where they have caused another harm. For those reasons, it seems to me a far more convincing case for those sympathetic to the kind of arguments Bergelson makes to seek to peruse accomplice liability. Then we can keep the wrong doing to others as the focus of criminal harm, and attach liability, if at all, of victims to the assistance or encouragement of that harm.

---

45 Iñigo Ortiz de Urbina Gimeno, 'Old Wine in New Wineskins? Appraising Professor Bergelson's Plea for Comparative Criminal Liability' (2008) 28 Pace Law Review 815.

46 Kenneth Simons, 'The Relevance of Victim Conduct in Tort and Criminal Law' (2005) 8 Buffalo Criminal Law Review 541.

47 Anthony Duff, 'Responsible Victims and (Partly) Justified Offenders' (2010) 8 Ohio State Journal of Criminal Law 209.

48 [2003] QB 1207.

49 Ibid. [33] [34].

Victims as Accomplices to Their Own Harm

So far I have provided reasons for why if X cuts herself there should be no criminal liability. For those same reasons we should not entertain an argument that X should be seen as partly responsible for her injuries. But what if X has asked or helped Y to cut her? It might be argued that in such a case the arguments above play out rather differently. Now we do have a case where a person has harmed another, being a harm of sufficient seriousness to justify criminalisation. X has used Y as a means to an end, and X has encouraged Y to do that. The act of cutting of Y by X will have a negative social meaning and X will have encouraged that. So, arguably the first three of the arguments listed above against punishing self-harm do not necessarily argue against accessorial liability. However, the last two do, as we shall see shortly.

Dennis Baker has considered this issue and argues that while these points show moral blame for the person encouraging another to harm them, they do not justify punishment as an accomplice:

> If X, a sadomasochist, consents to Y (who is also a sadomasochist) poking her eyes out, she has not only used herself as a mere means, but has also allowed Y to use (wrong and harm) her to a grave degree. Y has used X as a mere means and is criminally liable for wrongfully harming her without excuse or justification. In effect sadomasochists and gladiators wrong not only themselves, but each other.[50]

Nevertheless he does not support criminalisation for the 'victim' because to him criminalisation is only justified in the case of harm-doer. His central principle is:

> Masochism is not a mere case of self-harm and we do not criminalise the consenter. Instead it is the actions of the harm-doer that are criminalized .... The degree of moral wrongdoing involved in serious self-harm and harm to others is equal, but self-wrongs are not criminalizable because they do not wrong or harm others.[51]

I do not agree with Baker that the harms are equal. That is because of the social meanings attached to the acts. Nevertheless, more importantly I think he moves too quickly in his argument. If we punish the masochist for harming the 'victim' and that is a recognised legal wrong, why should the 'victim' not be liable as an accomplice to the wrong the principal has done. The fact we do not punish self-harm is somewhat beside the point in the accessorial argument. We are punishing X not for harming himself, but encouraging someone to harm another.

The best arguments against accessorial liability require us to return to the arguments generally against criminalising self-harm. The first concerns autonomy. If there is respect for the principles mentioned above, that people should be entitled to shape their lives and treat their property as they wish, the criminal law should be reluctant to criminalise what is done. Where the actors only harm themselves it is not clear that the harm is sufficient to justify criminal liability, save, maybe, in cases of serious harm. That argument is as powerful in cases where the defendant has harmed him or herself as it is in cases where the defendant has persuaded another to harm him.

As suggested above, there will be cases which arguably are not protected by the principle of autonomy. These are cases where serious harm is done or the behaviour is seen as showing a particular lack of respect for the dignity of the individual. But in those cases the therapeutic

---

50   Dennis J Baker, *The Right Not to Be Criminalized* (Ashgate 2012) 184.
51   Ibid. 185.

principle will nearly always come into play. These are likely to be cases where the individual is in a sorry state and needs support and help, rather than punishment of the criminal law.

There may be a small band of cases where the individual has encouraged or helped in causing themselves a serious injury, but there is no therapeutic case for not intervening. Perhaps the *Wright* case,[52] in which the person had their arm removed to assist in begging, is an example. But those will be very rare indeed.

Conclusion

This chapter has considered the circumstances in which it appropriate to punish a victim as an accessory to a harm they have suffered. It has looked at the current law and noted that although the Supreme Court has recently suggested *obiter* that in theory a victim can be liable as accomplice to behaviour which has harmed them, there is only one very old reported case where that has happened. This chapter has sought to explain and justify that. It has started by setting out the reasons behind the principle that the law should not punish those who harm themselves. It has argued that these reasons also explain why the victim should not share blame with the defendant even when they have contributed to their own injuries. It has also argued that some of the arguments against self-harm are sufficient to mean that except in a few cases where very serious harm is inflicted and there are no therapeutic reasons against a proscution a victim should not be liable as an accomplice to acts which harm them.

---

52   (1603) 1 Co Lit 127a.

Chapter 6

Repentance and Forgiveness: Withdrawal from Participation Liability and the Proportionality Test

Alan Reed

I came not to call the righteous, but sinners to repentance.[1]

Introduction

It is important that we can justify our reasons for temporally defining the offence elements and harm prevention nexus that pervades criminal liability.[2] This criminalisation process takes on heightened significance when we factorise redemptive conduct on the part of an individual that may or may not act as a withdrawal defence to neutralise earlier complicitous behaviour, and consequential derivative inculpation.[3] In considering these principles we are not entering into *terra incognita*; fellow academicians have found some tillable soil for deconstruction,[4] but it is very surprising how limited treatment this fertile landscape has received in recent times. This stands in contradistinction to extensive distillation of other hardy perennials within the criminal justice garden. The recent Law Commission Report on *Participating in Crime*,[5] by way of illustration, devoted little coverage to withdrawal in any real sense.[6] The qualitative redemptive conduct of a criminal actor is addressed in three particularised sections: the conceptual nature of withdrawal as a quasi-excusatory affirmative defence with foundational tenets of reduced culpability; extirpation of relevant substantive principles and comparative evaluation of other common law juridical precepts; and the propagation of a new standardised template for withdrawal predicated on aligning together a reasonableness–imputed proportionality normative assessment for exculpation.

---

1   Luke 5:32, King James Version of the Holy Bible, The New Testament.

2   See generally, Paul Hoeber, 'The Abandonment Defense to Criminal Attempt and Other Problems of Temporal Individuation' (1986) 74 California Law Review 377; Stanford Kadish, 'Complicity, Cause and Blame: A Study in the Interpretation of Doctrine' (1985) 73 California Law Review 324; Daniel Rotenberg, 'Withdrawal as a Defense to Relational Crimes' [1962] Wisconsin Law Review 596; and SJ Schulhofer, 'Harm and Punishment: A Critique of Emphasis on the Results of Conduct in the Criminal Law' (1974) 122 University of Pennsylvania Law Review 1497.

3   See generally, Richard Taylor, 'Complicity and Excuses' [1983] Criminal Law Review 656; Bob Sullivan, 'Intent, Purpose and Complicity' [1988] Criminal Law Review 641; Glanville Williams, 'Complicity, Purpose and the Draft Code' [1990] Criminal Law Review 98; and Paul Robinson, 'Element Analysis in Defining Criminal Liability: The Model Penal Code and Beyond' (1983) 35 Stanford Law Review 681.

4   See generally, David Lanham, 'Accomplices and Withdrawal' (1981) 97 Law Quarterly Review 575; KJM Smith, 'Withdrawal from Criminal Liability for Complicity and Inchoate Offences' (1983) 12 Anglo-American Law Review 200; KJM Smith, 'General Defences and Withdrawal' in KJM Smith (ed.), *A Modern Treatise on the Law of Criminal Complicity* (Clarendon Press 1991); and KJM Smith, 'Withdrawal in Complicity: A Restatement of Principles' [2001] Criminal Law Review 769.

5   See Law Commission, *Participating in Crime* (Law Com No 305, 2007).

6   Ibid. 3.60-3.65.

Withdrawal: The Conceptual Edifice of a Quasi-Excusatory Defence and Reduced Culpability

English law has recognised that an individual who has embarked on a criminal enterprise may withdraw from it and save him or herself from liability.[7] A pre-inculpatory interlude prevails, wherein a redemptive change of heart aligned with appropriate reductive criminal depredation may exculpate via reverse conduct prophylaxis. This applies, of course, unless the defendant has already reached the stage of an inchoate offence such as conspiracy or attempt, and liability exists separately for this misfeasance.[8] The limits of the withdrawal defence remain controversial, and a sustainable rationale that underpins neutralisation of accessory liability is still ill-defined and subject to conjecture.[9] Mere repentance subsequent to the commission of the offence is irrelevant, but for centuries our law has to some degree recognised an escape from liability by countermand before the crime is committed. Plowden's commentary on *Saunders and Archer* way back in 1576 stated:

> If I command one to kill JS and before the fact is done I go to him and tell him that I have repented and expressly charge him not to kill JS and he afterwards kills him, there I shall not be accessory to this murder, because I have countermanded my first command, which in all reason shall discharge me ... but if he had killed JS before the time of my discharge or countermand given, I should have been accessory to the death, notwithstanding my private repentance.[10]

The acceptance that *unequivocal* withdrawal may absolve a repentant sinner who negates complicitous support by direct and active steps is juxtaposed with the opaqueness that surrounds the conceptual edifice for actual exculpation.[11] In determining prohibited and reductionist behaviour there are dilemmatic choices to be made in terms of temporal individuation of liability across an extended time-frame, and layered within a continuum of conjoined events.[12] This broader kaleidoscopic appraisal of inchoate and derivative liability has been advanced by Kelman as an explanation underpinning adoption in US jurisdictions of multi-faceted abandonment principles:

> [T]he basic decision to allow [an] abandonment defense follows a wide time-framed interpretive construction. The defendant has already committed some act which, if interrupted by external

---

7   A number of international commentators have also endorsed this concept; see Rollin Perkins and Ronald Boyce, *Criminal Law* (3rd edn, Foundation Press 1982) 656 who assert, 'it would be sound to recognize the possibility of a *locus penitentiae* so long as no substantial harm has been done and no act of actual danger committed'; and Hyman Gross, *A Theory of Criminal Justice* (Oxford University Press, 1979) 165 who states, 'there is much in principle as well as in authority to support the defence of renunciation if the actor has voluntarily and effectively abandoned his criminal activity before doing any harm'.

8   Note also that the Serious Crime Act 2007 in ss 44-46 imposes inchoate liability for acts capable of assisting or encouraging the principal (D1), and are not derivative from offence completion.

9   See generally, David Ormerod, *Smith and Hogan's Criminal Law* (13th edn, Oxford University Press 2011) 436; Andrew Ashworth, *Principles of Criminal Law* (6th edn, Oxford University Press 2009) 430; and Dennis Baker, *Glanville Williams: Textbook of Criminal Law* (3rd edn, Sweet & Maxwell 2012) 506.

10   (1576) 2 Plowd 473 at 476.

11   See generally, Smith, 'Withdrawal in Complicity' (n 4) 772-74; and Lanham (n 4) 576-81.

12   See generally, Mark Kelman, 'Interpretive Construction in the Substantive Criminal Law' (1981) 33 Stanford Law Review 591, 593 who articulates the expression 'time-framing' with reference to 'the way we view disruptive incidents'.

forces, would constitute ... an attempt ... Yet we judge the act innocent [that is, not attempt] because of the defendant's *subsequent* failure to consummate the harm.[13]

The precise legal topography, however, of the basis for withdrawal exculpation has polarised debate centred around diverse frameworks: (i) incentivisation for an individual to withdraw from his criminal pathway and facilitate crime prevention; or (ii) a reflection of reduced culpability and/ or societal dangerousness of the actor.[14]

The incentive premise is buttressed by the argument that an inducement opportunity can be presented to individual non-coerced participants to prevent consummation of complicitous liability, and expunge their guilt.[15] A voluntary pathway is left open to desist from earlier criminal engagement, and embrace a righteous re-birth of character.[16] The provision of this 'escape' mechanism will arguably enhance the likelihood of a criminal actor renunciating their earlier conduct, thereby extricating themselves from inculpation, and consequently propagating substantive crime reduction to benefit the state.[17] The potentiality of a new direction that is kept ajar, absolution via incentivisation, has been expressed as, 'socially desirable in giving criminals an interest to prevent the consequences of their actions';[18] and, moreover, that renunciation rests in part, 'upon policy of the law that aims at providing an incentive for abandonment of criminal projects by those who pursue them before they do harm. It is thus the carrot of immunity whose complementary stick is punishment'.[19] The incentive rationale, as presented, is of a *quasi-justificatory* nature in that the prescribed harm (D2's complicitous behaviour to date) is outweighed by the need to avoid an even greater harm or to further a greater societal interest (the avoidance

---

13   Ibid. 611.

14   See generally, William Wilson, *Criminal Law: Doctrine and Theory* (4th edn, Longman 2011) 587; Bob Sullivan, Andrew Simester, John Spencer, and Graham Virgo, *Criminal Law: Theory and Doctrine* (4th edn, Hart 2011) 254; Richard Card, *Card, Cross and Jones Criminal Law* (18th edn, Oxford University Press 2008) 785.

15   See Model Penal Code and Commentaries s 5.01 comment at 359-60 (Official Draft 1962 and Revised Comments 1985). The comment in relation to attempt renunciation states: 'The basis for allowing the defence involves two related considerations. First, renunciation of criminal purpose tends to negative dangerousness. As previously indicated, much of the effort devoted to excluding early "preparatory" conduct from criminal attempt liability has been based on the desire not to impose liability when there is an insufficient showing that the actor has a firm purpose to commit the crime contemplated. In cases where the actor has gone beyond the line drawn for defining preparation, indicating *prima facie* sufficient firmness of purpose, he should be allowed to rebut such a conclusion by showing that he has plainly demonstrated his lack of firm purpose by completely renouncing his purpose to commit the crime .... The second reason for allowing renunciation of criminal purpose as a defence to an attempt charge is to provide actors with a motive for desisting from their criminal designs, thereby diminishing the risk that the substantive crime will be committed ... on balance it is concluded that renunciation of criminal purpose should be a defence because ... it significantly negatives dangerousness of character, and, as to later stages, the value of encouraging desistance outweighs the net dangerousness shown by the abandoned criminal effort'.

16   See Oliver Wendell Holmes, 'The Path of the Law' (1897) 10 Harvard Law Review 457, 459: 'If you want to know the law and nothing else, you must look at it as a bad man, who cares only for the material consequences which such knowledge enables him to predict, and not as a good one, who finds his reasons for conduct, whether inside the law or outside of it, in the vaguer sanctions of conscience'.

17   See generally, Daniel Moriarty, 'Extending the Defense of Renunciation' (1989) 62 Temple Law Review 1.

18   Gerald Gordon, *The Criminal Law of Scotland* (W. Green 1976) 183.

19   Gross (n 7) 166.

of a completed substantive offence).[20] The essence of this presupposition is made explicit in the Model Penal Code's general justification defence in the US which provides a defence if, 'the harm or evil sought to be avoided by such conduct is greater than that sought to be prevented by the law defining the offence charged'.[21] The English Law Commission has previously offered support for this justificatory basis for withdrawal, highlighting that considerations of social policy support the argument that if an accessory counters assistance with equally obstructive measures, an acquittal ought to follow given the reductionist efforts to right the wrong.[22]

Incentivisation, as an overarching template for a withdrawal defence, seems inherently counter-intuitive, and not reflective of real-world criminal practices. Presumptively, it is the apotheosis of absurdity to iterate that an accessory modifies their criminal behaviour in relation to criteria of which they are highly likely to be unaware.[23] Even more redolent for an informed actor, in any event, will be continuing liability attached to conduct and fault coalescence for inchoate crimes; it is unrealistic to contend that an individual '[w]ho decides not to commit [an offence] would change his mind again and then decide to carry on since he realizes that he is guilty of the attempt anyway as no defence of withdrawal is available'.[24] More realistically, it is the conceptual basis of reduced social dangerousness that presents a logically compelling redemption analysis of withdrawal as a rehabilitative adjunct.[25]

The reduced social dangerousness model of withdrawal exculpation takes as a starting proposition that individuals who have commenced upon a criminal enterprise are amongst a cadre to be feared by society in that they have failed to control internal regulatory intuitions of right and wrong as a bulwark to set against criminal propensity.[26] In essence, they have exposed themselves as requiring external societal control mechanisms imposed by criminal law. Their injudicious

---

20   See Paul Robinson, *Structure and Function in Criminal Law* (Clarendon Press 1997) 95: '[A] defense is given under the common theory of all justification defences: although the conduct ordinarily constitutes an offence, when the justifying circumstances exist we are content to have the conduct performed. The existence of the justifying circumstances means that, while the harm prohibited by the offence does occur, it is outweighed by the avoidance of a greater harm or by the advancement of a greater good. In other words there is net reduction of societal harm'.

21   Model Penal Code s 3.02(1).

22   See Law Commission Consultation Paper, *Assisting and Encouraging Crime* (Law Com No 131, 1993) 4.133; and Law Commission Working Party Paper, *Inchoate Offences* (Law Com No 50, 1973) 150: 'Since the object of the criminal law is to prevent crime it is equally important to give reasonable encouragement to a conspirator, attempter or inciter to withdraw ... The absence of such a defence may operate to dissuade an individual who might otherwise decide to cease participating in the planning of a crime from taking that decision since having become a party to the inchoate offence there is no inducement for him to cease his activities before commission of the substantive offence takes place'.

23   Smith, 'Withdrawal in Complicity' (n 4) 773.

24   Martin Wasik, 'Abandoning Criminal Intent [1980] Criminal Law Review 785, 793; and see, Smith, 'Withdrawal from Criminal Liability' (n 4) 204.

25   See Wilson (n 14) 589; Andrew Simester, Bob Sullivan, John Spencer and Graham Virgo (n 14) 255; and Smith, 'Withdrawal in Complicity' (n 4) 773.

26   See Richard Buxton, 'The Working Paper on Inchoate Offences: (1) Incitement and Attempt' [1973] Criminal Law Review 556, 660: '[P]ersons who threaten to commit acts forbidden by the substantive criminal law ... are, by reasons of their intentions, socially dangerous'; and Walter Ullmann, 'The Reasons for Punishing Attempted Crimes' (1939) 51 Judicial Review 353, 363: '[T]he external criminal act is considered as a mere symptom of the destructive tendencies; the offender appears ... already so dangerous that the law dare not wait for further proofs of his dangerous character'; and Herbert Wechsler, 'The Challenge of a Model Penal Code' (1952) 65 Harvard Law Review 1097, 1105: '[T]he object is control of harmful conduct in the

proclivities and skewed lack of control functionality, evidenced by initial engagements, has been recalibrated to a degree if they unequivocally and genuinely take steps of cessation.[27] Their penitent behaviour may counter-act complicitous activity, and consequently in terms of present or future depredations they do not present as great a societal danger, or at least present a reducibly minimum threat.[28] Their rebalanced internal controls have correspondingly been presented as meeting a more acceptable threshold gradation, and thus the necessity of external control via criminal sanction has been obfuscated: 'spontaneous abandonment show[s] that the offender is not dangerous, or is so in an insignificant degree'.[29]

The redemptive change of heart of the accessory means that derivative criminal liability for complicity may be inapposite as the 'flame of dangerousness', created by initial attitudinal behaviour, has been doused by voluntary choice to undo or prevent harm.[30] The reasoning here is that the individual, considered inwardly on a prognostic basis, has revealed him or herself as possessing more limited socially dangerous characterisations, and therefore should be inculcated a *quasi-excuse*.[31] In general terms an excuse is a defence that involves concession that the action is wrong, but nonetheless the individual's characteristics or prevailing state of affairs indicate that they should not be inculpated for their infractions.[32] It is not that the acts of withdrawal are

---

future. The legislative question therefore is: What past behaviour has such rational relationship to the control of future conduct that it ought to be declared a crime?'

27   See Henry Seney, 'A Pond as Deep as Hell: Harm, Danger and Dangerousness in Our Criminal Law' (1972) 18 Wayne Law Review 569, 571 criticising the derivations of the social dangerousness argument: 'This yields the preposterous inference that an unsuccessful effort at one crime proves some special disposition to general crime-doing …. The little gods of evidence who try wisely, if unsuccessfully, to keep evidence of past crimes out of trials for present crimes because of the dubious inferences which might be drawn from past guilt to present guilt, would surely "laugh themselves mortal" at the proposition that a man should be found guilty of a present crime on the basis of inferences about future crimes'.

28   See generally, Joshua Dressler, *Understanding Criminal Law* (M. Bender 1987) 357 (contending that punishment is not deserved if an individual renounces their criminal enterprise); and Gross (n 7) 105 (arguing that the full course of conduct that includes an effective renunciation is not a criminal act sufficiently dangerous to warrant liability). 'There is a very profound axiom in law … and it is this … human nature is repelled by crime. However civilisation has given us needs, vices and artificial appetites which sometimes cause us to repress our good instincts and lead us to wrongdoing' (Alexandre Dumas, 'The Count of Monte Cristo' (Robin Buss translation, Penguin 2003) XVII, 161). The actor's renunciation potentially indicates a restoration of human instinct and, therefore, indicates that D2 is less socially dangerous than D1 who goes on to complete the substantive offence.

29   See Royal Commission for the Reform of the Penal Statutes, *Report and Preliminary Project for an Italian Penal Code* (1921) 214; and Michael Bayles, 'Character, Purpose and Criminal Responsibility' (1982) 1 Law and Philosophy 5, 13-14 (stressing that abandonment of attempt may negate the inference of an undesirable disposition or character trait). See generally, Hoeber (n 2); and Moriarty (n 17).

30   Wilson (n 14) 591; and see generally, Joshua Dressler, 'Reassessing the Theoretical Underpinnings of Accomplice Liability: New Solutions to an Old Problem' (1985) 37 Hastings Law Journal 91; A Katz, 'Dangerousness: A Theoretical Reconstruction of the Criminal Law, Part I' (1970) 19 Buffalo Law Review 1; Paul Robinson, 'A Theory of Justification: Societal Harm as a Prerequisite for Criminal Liability' (1975) 23 University of California Los Angeles Law Review 266; and Schulhofer (n 2).

31   Smith, 'Withdrawal in Complicity' (n 4) 773; and see generally, Smith, 'General Defences and Withdrawal' (n 4).

32   See generally, Stanford Kadish, 'Excusing Crime' in S Kadish (ed.), *Blame and Punishment* (Macmillan 1987) 81; Michael Moore, 'Choice, Character and Excuse' in E Paul, F Miller and J Paul (eds), *Crime, Culpability and Remedy* (Blackwell 1990) 29; and George Vouso, 'Background, Responsibility and Excuse' (1987) 96 Yale Law Journal 1661.

justified in terms of net harm, but rather that the penitent and redemptive situation presented by the actor should potentially excuse, and this is for adjudicative interpretation by fact finders.[33] The recalibration is intrinsically demonstrative of a quasi-excuse in that, although the defendant 'cannot be said to be subject to some form of internal incapacity or external impairment preventing his actions from being broadly characterised as the free exercise of informed choice',[34] a positive premium should exist for a genuine change of heart that is driven by a voluntary motivation of contrition. This provides a more satisfactory conceptual basis for lack of criminal penalty in that as a defendant of lower culpability who is less socially dangerous, a different threshold categorisation should apply.[35]

The arguments presented thus far, that withdrawal needs to be viewed through a legal prism reflective of quasi-excuse, and predicated upon reduced culpability or societal dangerousness of the accessory, cuts across our overall appraisal of the overarching basis of the defence *per se*.[36] The operational underpinning of the withdrawal defence has been beset by conflicting jurisprudence, and equivocality has impacted Anglo-American and Commonwealth traditional perspectives with successful prediction of outcome as likely as tattooing soap bubbles. The arguments have been distilled around three alternative templates.[37] First, that the withdrawal defence is only applicable where D2 totally neutralises their egregious conduct (*actus reus*) as part of their complicitous penitence.[38] The recent Law Commission proposals, articulated in *Participating in Crime*, somewhat mechanistically set out the contours of the defence as, '*negating* the effect of the assistance, encouragement and agreement', and the jury as fact-finders are promoted to determine this prescribed threshold.[39] A difficulty, however, with this unduly narrow construction is a failure properly to accord redemptive effect to the change of heart of the initially culpable actor, unless it totally abrogates and negates the assistance or encouragement provided. If this neutralisation has occurred then withdrawal as a defence is an empty vessel in any event as the causal influence of D2's behaviour at the point of commission of the substantive offence has disappeared into the ether, and derivative liability is inapt.[40] Interpretational problems also underscore a secondary viewpoint that withdrawal may operate to negate *mens rea* to provide a defence.[41] A number of precedential authorities in this regard have tended to be circumscribed by variation from the

---

33   See generally, Robinson (n 20) 81-87; HL Schreiber, 'Problems of Justification and Excuse in the Setting of Accessorial Conduct' [1986] Brigham Young University Law Review 611; and John Smith, *Justification and Excuse in the Criminal Law* (Sweet & Maxwell 1989).

34   Smith, 'Withdrawal in Complicity' (n 4) 773.

35   Smith, 'General Defences and Withdrawal' (n 4) 253-54.

36   See generally, Paul Robinson, 'Criminal Law Defenses: A Systematic Analysis' [1982] Columbia Law Review 199; Donald Horowitz, 'Justification and Excuse in the Program of the Criminal Law' (1986) 49 Law and Contemporary Problems 109; and WH Dray, 'Causal Judgment in Attributive and Explanatory Contexts' (1986) 49 Law and Contemporary Problems 13.

37   See Ormerod (n 9) 237.

38   See Wilson (n 14) 588; and see generally, Lanham (n 4).

39   Law Commission (n 5) 3.60.

40   See generally, Baker (n 9); and in terms of derivative liability at the point of commission of the substantive offence consider *Calhaem* [1985] QB 808; *Gianetto* [1997] 1 Cr App R 1; and *Luffman* [2008] EWCA Crim 1739.

41   See generally, Luis Westerfield, 'The Mens Rea Requirement of Accomplice Liability in American Criminal Law: Knowledge or Intent' (1980) 51 Mississippi Law Journal 155; and Graham Strong, 'Fault, Threat and the Predicates of Criminal Liability' [1980] Wisconsin Law Review 441.

original common plan by principal offenders, as in *Rafferty*[42] considered below, and are better viewed as part of the fundamentally different rule in joint enterprise theory, and wholly outwith withdrawal constituents.[43]

A supererogatory perspective on the basis for withdrawal, rejecting the strictures of neutralisation of *actus reus* or *mens rea* offence elements, is to view it as an affirmative defence that is *sui generis*.[44] It is this latter perspective within our triumvirate of rationale-section, ascription as a 'true' defence, that accords with previous explanations and key embodiments of withdrawal as a quasi-defence.[45] It is a defence, as Robinson has partially indicated, that is independent in nature as constitutively it does not necessarily operate to diminish the normal rules for proof of offence elements (negating *actus reus* or *mens rea*), but rather it operates within the spectrum of offence-modification as an element of the criminalisation reflection underpinning the offence.[46] The defence is *sui generis* in that it cannot be pigeon-holed into the traditional justification/excuse dichotomy revealed by dissection of other general defences, including self-defence, involuntary intoxication, diminished responsibility or duress: 'It is not a defence of reasonable reaction. Neither is it a defence of impaired voluntariness'.[47] In terms of the balancing of legitimate social interests, appropriate thresholds of culpability, and overarching public policy concerns withdrawal most closely mirrors consent as an individuated defence.[48] It is distinctive as a defence in that complicity liability as an accessory is derivative in nature from completion of the full substantive offence.[49] Accessory liability may attach to D2 from pre-offence defalcations where constitutive external and fault elements are adduced, but a defence of withdrawal may be superimposed *ex-post facto* to conduct during the brief pre-inculpatory interlude to exculpate.[50] The defence should, in such a context, be available to reflect redemptive behaviour and reduced levels of culpable dangerousness.[51]

The consequence of accepting withdrawal as an offence-modification defence, rather than simply as a mitigation of sentence as some have suggested,[52] is that a coherent set of crystallised principles need to be drawn *vis-à-vis* exculpatory conduct. A shifting continuum ought to apply, dependent

---

42 [2007] EWCA Crim 1846; [2008] Crim LR 218; and see generally, Chris Clarkson, 'Complicity, *Powell* and Manslaughter' [1998] Criminal Law Review 556; and Richard Taylor, 'Complicity Legal Scholarship and the Law of Unintended Consequences [2009] Legal Studies 1.

43 See *Powell, English* [1999] 1 AC 1; *Rahman* [2009] 1 AC 129; and *Gnango* [2011] UKSC 59; and see generally, Alan Reed and Ben Fitzpatrick, *Criminal Law* (Sweet & Maxwell 2009) 127-44; Richard Buxton, 'Joint Enterprise' [2009] Criminal Law Review 389; and Beatrice Krebs, 'Joint Criminal Enterprise' (2010) 73 Modern Law Review 578.

44 See Law Commission, *Conspiracy and Criminal Law Reform* (Law Com No 76, 1976) 1.79: 'We think that withdrawal as a defence to a charge of complicity in crime would be a defence of general application and should be considered in that context'.

45 See generally, Ormerod (n 9); and Smith, 'Withdrawal from Criminal Liability' (n 4).

46 Robinson (n 20) 68-69.

47 Wilson (n 14) 589.

48 See Reed and Fitzpatrick (n 43).

49 See generally, D Unterhalter, 'The Doctrine of Common Purpose: What Makes One Person Liable for the Acts of Another?' (1988) 105 South African Law Journal 671.

50 See generally, Andrew Simester, Bob Sullivan, John Spencer and Graham Virgo (n 14) 254-56.

51 See generally, Katz (n 30).

52 See generally, Richard Buxton, 'The Extent of Criminal Complicity' (1979) 42 Modern Law Review 315; Edward Griew, 'Consistency, Communication and Codification: Reflections on Two Mens Rea Words' in PR Glazebrook (ed.), *Reshaping the Criminal Law: Essays in Honour of Glanville Williams* (Stevens 1978); Meir Dan-Cohen, 'Decision Rules and Conduct Rules: An Acoustic Separation in Criminal Law' (1984)

upon the nature of the assistance or encouragement to others provided by D2, the complicitous offence to be avoided, and the stage reached in the criminal enterprise. The greater the level of support that the accessory has lent in the complicity and furtherance of unlawful activity, the higher the threshold needed for an effective countermand. A natural correlation is flexibly drawn in the context of irreducible requirements of 'reasonable' or 'proper efforts' to withdraw, set against the parameters of responsibilities engendered by creation of a dangerous situation, and motivational indicia for 'genuine' withdrawal. A reformulated template is subsequently provided in this chapter, addressing the requirements of a proportionality test for fact-finders in terms of gradations of excusing action, and identifying a manifestly normative question of whether the individual actor's repentant behaviour was reasonable in the circumstances. The 'price of exculpation' should be standardised and contextualised against an individuated normative assessment predicated upon an imputed proportionality test of withdrawal.[53] Our extant law is considered in the next section, and developed further by examination of US and Commonwealth comparative extirpations. These articulated principles provide succour to identification of withdrawal as an affirmative defence with proportionality and reasonableness at the epicentre.

Withdrawal: Substantive Principles and Comparative Evaluations

The withdrawal defence has developed in a haphazard fashion in English law, the by-product of a limited range of precedential authorities that are delineated more by mud than by crystal in terms of providing an overarching standardised template.[54] Initiatives have occurred in a solipsistic and *ad hoc* manner by judicial sleight of hand, rather than through any comprehensive legislative engagement. The extant position is comparatively evaluated herein with Australian and US juridical precepts to formulate a sustainable recalibration of guiding principles, and efficacious and universal treatment of accessorial criminal actors.[55]

The modern law on withdrawal was addressed in *Becerra and Cooper*.[56] The common design was one of burglary from an elderly householder. While in the house, the tenant of a flat on the first floor surprised the defendants during the course of their intrusion. Becerra, calling 'let's go', climbed out of a window and ran away. Cooper, meanwhile, who had been handed a knife by his co-adventurer, stabbed and killed the tenant. They were both charged with murder. Becerra (D2), as an accessory, contended by his words and actions he had withdrawn from the joint enterprise before the attack on the tenant, thereby negating complicitous behaviour, and therefore was not liable to be convicted of murder. The defence of withdrawal was rejected by the appellate court, relying on

---

97 Harvard Law Review 625; and P Doherty, 'A New Crime: Criminal Facilitation' (1971) 18 Loyola Law Review 103.

53   See generally, Smith, 'Withdrawal in Complicity' (n 4); and Antony Duff, 'Can I Help You?' (1990) 10 Legal Studies 165.

54   See *Mitchell and King* (1998) 163 JP 75; [1999] Crim LR 496; *O'Flaherty* [2004] EWCA Crim 526; [2004] Crim LR 751; *Mitchell* [2008] EWCA Crim 2552; *Campbell (Andre)* [2009] EWCA Crim 50; and *Otway* [2011] EWCA Crim 3.

55   See generally, Robin Stanley O'Regan, 'Complicity and the Defence of Timely Countermand or Withdrawal under the Griffith Code' (1986) 10 Criminal Law Journal 236; Brent Fisse, *Howard's Criminal Law* (5th edn, Law Book Company 1990); and Mirko Bagaric, Ken Arenson and Peter Gillies, *Australian Criminal Law in the Common Law Jurisdictions: Cases and Materials* (Oxford University Press 2011).

56   (1976) 62 Cr App R 212.

the earlier authority of *Whitehouse*[57] before the Court of Appeal of British Columbia. Roskill LJ stated an effective withdrawal must: 'serve *unequivocal* notice on the other party to the common unlawful cause that if he proceeds upon it he does so without the further aid and assistance of those who withdraw'.[58] It is essential that, in order to allow the principal offender (D1) the opportunity to desist rather than complete the offence, the co-adventurer must make a timely and unequivocal communication to D1 of his change of heart and of the fact that, if continuance of liability occurs, it is on the principal offender's own account, without the aid and assistance of the person who is purporting to withdraw.

The fundamental principle of 'unequivocal notice' to facilitate the potentiality of a withdrawal defence was affirmed in *O'Flaherty*:[59] 'a person who unequivocally withdraws from the joint enterprise before the moment of the actual commission of the crime of murder should not be liable for that crime'.[60] It remains a consideration easier to state than to apply. The determinant was not satisfied in *Baker*,[61] in a scenario where the accessory, a co-adventurer in a joint unlawful enterprise to kill the victim, had said, after starting the attack, 'I'm not doing it', and then moved a few feet away, whereupon the other parties effected the unlawful killing. The words uttered were far from serving unequivocal notice that he was dissociating himself from the entire enterprise, and could simply have meant, I will stay but not do anything after having struck my blows. No doubt the lack of timeliness of the countermand was also an implicit factor. The relevant evidence was also too vague to anthropomorphise an unqualified withdrawal in *Fletcher, Fletcher and Zimnowodski*;[62] a complicitous actor sought to withdraw from a planned arson by telling the principal offender, 'Don't do it' or 'Don't be a fool', before the latter set off for the premises with the petrol. In similar vein, the bland statement by the defendant in *Nawaz*,[63] to the effect that he 'withdrew' from the joint enterprise, was also insufficient. To be effective, as recently interpreted in *Otway*,[64] the withdrawal must be voluntary, real, communicated in some form in good time, and incorporate an effort to dissuade others from continuing.

The very question of what may constitute an effective withdrawal was indirectly raised in *Rook*.[65] The defendant contended that his absence on the day of the murder amounted to an effective withdrawal. This was rejected by the court which held that where an individual had merely changed his mind about participating in the commission of the actual offence, and had failed to communicate his intention to the other persons engaged in the homicide, he did not thereby effectively withdraw, and was liable as a secondary party. In order to escape liability for derivative complicity the accessory had at least unequivocally to communicate his withdrawal to the other party. His simple absence on the day of the murder did not amount to unequivocal communication of his withdrawal to constitute redemptive disengagement.

The basis and requirements of an effective withdrawal will depend very much on the assistance or encouragement that the accessory has provided. This imputed proportionality standardisation has developed in an unstructured and individuated manner to disparate modes of participatory

---

57 [1941] 1 WWR 112 (Sloan JA).
58 *Becerra and Cooper* (n 56) 218.
59 [2004] EWCA Crim 526.
60 Ibid. at [58] (Mantell LJ).
61 [1994] Crim LR 444.
62 [1962] Crim LR 551.
63 Unrep. May 13, 1999.
64 [2011] EWCA Crim 3.
65 [1993] 2 All ER 955.

engagement.[66] More redemptive disavowal is required where an individual has supplied the very means of the crime as in *Becerra and Cooper*: 'retracting assent is a fish from a very different kettle from neutralising assistance'.[67] The defendant had provided the weapon and lent support as a co-adventurer. The appellate court determined that conduct 'vastly different' and 'vastly more effective' was required than merely stating, 'come on, let's go', and decamping through the window.[68] As a co-adventurer an express countermand was needed that may have only been effected by direct and active physical intervention. A far greater threshold applied to withdrawal in terms of positive conduct to prevent the criminal effectuation: 'once the mortar is set it may indeed take a sledgehammer rather than a gentle tap to bring down the wall of co-operative criminal enterprise'.[69]

It will be easier to withdraw, as in *Grundy*,[70] where the defendant had simply aided the principal through the supply of information concerning a burglary. Here efforts to prevent the principal offender actually committing the offence, and attempts to dissuade in the two weeks prior to commission of the substantive crime, were sufficient evidence of a valid withdrawal to have been left to the jury. Verbal communication of withdrawal sufficed without the necessity to warn either the police or the owners of the premises. An indirect countermand constituted an adequate withdrawal without the need for additional steps facilitative of crime prevention. The variable requirements of effective neutralisation of complicitous behaviour was also raised in *Croft*.[71] The defendant, as part of a suicide pact, had procured the killing of another, but a simple verbal communication of disengagement sufficed as a countermand. This forms part of a 'reasonableness' standardisation in terms of behaviour that may or may not be tantamount to effective withdrawal.

The reasonableness–proportionality nexus that underpins withdrawal as a defence has been subjected to a degree of consideration in Australian jurisprudence.[72] A diversity of views prevail more broadly in Australian law as to whether withdrawal is only applicable where the actor's behaviour negates the conduct requirement of complicity or whether it should be viewed as an affirmative defence by itself.[73] The matter was considered by the High Court in *White v Ridley*,[74] albeit that the defendant therein was a constructive principal offender in reliance upon the doctrine of innocent agency and so not complicitously engaged. Nonetheless the perspectives adduced were analogous to secondary participation liability in abstraction. The defendant was convicted of an offence of importing prohibited goods into Australia. These goods had been despatched to an airline in Singapore for putative consignment to Australia, and this delivery occurred despite a last minute attempt by the importer (a telegram was sent to the airline's office in Singapore) to circumvent forward carriage. Gibbs J (drawing an analogy with earlier precedential authorities related to the cessation of accessorial involvement) determined that positive and timely actions to counteract earlier conduct was required:

---

66   See generally, Lanham (n 4).

67   Wilson (n 14) 590.

68   *Becerra and Cooper* (n 56) 218 (Roskill LJ).

69   Wilson (n 14) 590.

70   [1997] Crim LR 543.

71   [1944] KB 295.

72   See generally, O'Regan (n 55); and Bagaric, Arenson and Gillies (n 55).

73   Lanham (n 4) 578-79; and see generally, Peter Gillies, *The Law of Criminal Complicity* (Law Book Company 1980).

74   (1978) 140 CLR 342.

> It seems entirely reasonable to insist that a person who has counselled another to commit a crime, or who has conspired with others to commit a crime, should accompany his countermand or withdrawal with such action as he can reasonably take to undo the effect.[75]

The perspective in *White*, acknowledging withdrawal as an affirmative and independent defence in its own right in reliance on 'reasonable' efforts of redemptive conduct and change of heart to undo complicitous behaviour, was subsequently accepted as extant law by the New South Wales Court of Criminal Appeal in *Tietie v The Queen*.[76] A recalibrated defence of withdrawal ought to adopt similar balanced principles, rather than the more stringent threshold advocated in the recent Law Commission Report,[77] and by Murphy J in *White* that D2 must effectively neutralise all aspects of their act of complicity.[78] An accessory should be exculpated if reasonable steps are proportionately taken to undo the overarching effect of their complicitous behaviour. The implications from *White*, that withdrawal must be voluntarily motivated and not causally related to simple detection-avoidance after arousing the suspicions of Australian customs officers, resonates with articulated English principles on genuineness of independent action.[79]

A clear division applies in terms of general US principles relating to abrogation of liability for inchoate offences or complicity; inchoate offence liability, in more constrained terms, requires that the individual has 'directly' prevented the harm from occurring.[80] A more relaxed and generous standardisation applies to complicitous derivative liability where D2 can effectively withdraw by making 'proper effort' to prevent D1 from committing the substantive offence, and failure to prevent that commission does not constitute a total bar to defence applicability provided 'reasonable efforts' to desist can be promulgated before fact finders.[81]

A modified proportionality test is supported by the Model Penal Code s 2.06(6)(c)(ii) which provides a defence where the defendant terminates his complicity prior to the commission of the offence, and gives timely warning to the law enforcement authorities or otherwise makes 'proper effort' to prevent the commission of the offence.[82] By way of illustration, in *Commonwealth v Huber*,[83] where D2 had provided assistance through supply of the tools of the trade (a rifle for use in a robbery) the court determined that an escape route from liability was provided to D2 via reporting the actions of D1 to the police in time to thwart the robbery. This 'escape' mechanism appears more generous than our extant law, but less generous than the Australian position adopted in *White*, in the requirement that redemptive efforts *must* be aimed at crime commission prevention rather

---

75   Ibid. 350-51. Note that this perspective was followed by Thomas J in *Mennitti* [1985] 1 Qd R 520, 527; and *Heaney* (1992) 61 A Crim R 241, 274.

76   (1988) 34 A Crim R 438. Note that contrary views were expressed in *White* (n 74) 357-63 by Stephen J and Aickin J determining that withdrawal did not exculpate unless it directly broke the chain of causation.

77   See Law Commission No 305 (n 5) 3.60.

78   *White* (n 74) 363 per Murphy J asserting that for exculpation the issue was whether D2 had 'done all he reasonably could to prevent the importation'.

79   See *Otway* (n 54); *Becerra and Cooper* (n 56); *O'Flaherty* (n 54); *Campbell (Andre)* (n 54); and *Mitchell* (n 54).

80   See Gross (n 7) 165; and see generally, *State v Smith*, 409 NE 2d 1199, 1202 (Ind Ct App 1980); accord *Sheckles v State*, 501 NE 2d 1053, 1055 (Ind 1986); *Barnes v State*, 378 NE 2d 839, 843 (Ind 1978), *State v Eagle*, 611 P 2d 1211, 1213 (Utah 1980); and see generally Moriarty (n 17).

81   See generally, Paul Robinson, *Criminal Law Defences* (West 1984).

82   Ibid.

83   (1958) 15 D and C 2d 726, noted in George E Dix and Michael Sharlot, *Criminal Law: Cases and Materials* (West 1973) 638-41.

than simply undoing the efforts of the original behaviour.[84] In general terms a reasonableness-proportionality of remedial action standard is imposed, requiring a duty of reasonable negation that charts a pathway for an English reformulated template:

> Most formulations of this defence permit it only if the defendant terminates his complicity and does one of a variety of other things ... All of these formulations permit the defense for conduct short of prevention of the offense. They essentially require, in the words of the catch-all clause, a 'proper effort' to prevent the offense ... [This standard] is clearly more lenient than the 'actual prevention' standard that must be satisfied in many jurisdictions to gain a renunciation defense to attempt, conspiracy, solicitation and facilitation.[85]

Imputed proportionality is significant in English law in that where the defendant decides to withdraw long before the commission of the offence, it may suffice that the accessory makes it very clear to the others than any further activity will go ahead without their assistance.[86] Where the offence is about to be committed it may well be that the accused must try, by force if necessary, to prevent the commission of the offence.[87] If the assistance has been in the form of supplying a gun for a murder, then the court would certainly require something more than mere communication by the accessory to the would-be killer that D2 wants nothing more to do with the offence. In such a case, or where communication with the other parties is impossible, it may be that the only effective action the individual can take to withdraw is to inform the police so that the crime can be stopped.[88] The position is unclear as in *Perman*[89] the Court of Appeal stated, *en passant*, that it was questionable whether once the criminal activity contemplated in a joint enterprise had commenced, it was possible for a party to the joint enterprise to withdraw.[90] A similar statement, albeit *obiter* again, was made by the Northern Ireland Court of Appeal in *Graham*.[91] The defendant, part of a group of terrorists, had transferred a kidnap victim from a house he had used following an earlier escape, to another house where he realised the terrorists were staying, appreciating the risk that they may kill the terrified hostage. Despite the protestations of Graham, and his refusal to assist the terrorists further, the hostage was subsequently killed. Carswell LJ, who delivered the leading judgment, asserted *obiter* that in such circumstances even informing the police would most likely fail to constitute an effective withdrawal in the scenario were terrorist murderers were close to committing the homicide:

> We consider that at the late stage which the murder plan had reached and after the appellant had played such a significant part in assisting the killers to accomplish their aim, it could not be a sufficient withdrawal to indicate to them that he no longer supported their enterprise. Something more was required, and the judge was amply justified in holding that what the appellant did was not enough. His pleas were useless and the withholding of co-operation ... was of minimal effect. We

---

84   Note that, as stated, the limited Australian jurisprudence on this issue suggests that the putative accessory may redemptively escape liability if reasonable steps to 'undo' the effectiveness of their complicitous behaviour are carried out, but such actions must be timely and proportionate.
85   Robinson (n 81) s 81(e) at 363-64.
86   See generally, Lanham (n 4) 579-85.
87   Ibid.
88   Ormerod (n 9) 237-39.
89   [1996] 1 Cr App R 24.
90   Ibid. 34 (Roch LJ).
91   [1996] NI 157.

do not find it necessary to attempt to specify what acts would have been required of the appellant in the circumstances. It is sufficient for present purposes for us to say that the steps which he did take cannot be regarded as sufficient for withdrawal.[92]

Our extant principles, contrary to comparative doctrinal extirpations, have drawn a perplexing dichotomy between pre-planned and spontaneous violence, and the requirements of exculpatory conduct. In *Mitchell and King*,[93] the Court of Appeal determined that communication of withdrawal (the *Whitehouse*[94] *direction),* while necessary when violence was planned, was not a requirement when the violence was spontaneous; the unlawful homicide had been effected by two separate violent attacks and D2 had desisted from engagement in the latter. A direction as to the test of communication of withdrawal was not appropriate, since such communication was only a necessary condition for dissociation from pre-planned violence. Subsequently, in *O'Flaherty*,[95] Mantell LJ stated that a jury must be satisfied that the fatal injuries were sustained when the joint enterprise was continuing and, 'that the defendant was still acting within that joint enterprise';[96] moreover, in a case of spontaneous violence where there has been no prior agreement the jury will have to make inferences as to the scope of the joint enterprise from the knowledge and actions of individual participants.[97]

A series of appellate decisions,[98] quite legitimately, have limited the breadth of the pre-planned/spontaneous violence diversification. It has been extrapolated that where an individual has given encouragement to others to commit an offence it cannot be withdrawn once the offence has commenced; in this sense *Mitchell and King* can be viewed as an exceptional case since generally communication of withdrawal must be given in order to provide the principal offenders the opportunity to desist rather than complete the crime. This principle is pre-eminent, even in situations of spontaneous violence, unless it is not practicable or reasonable so to communicate as in the exceptional circumstances pertaining in *Mitchell and King* where the accessory threw down his weapon and moved away before the final and fatal blows were inflicted. It seems that if the very attack of personal violence which D2 has initiated has come to fruition then it is too late for him effectively to withdraw: the exculpatory interlude available for quasi-excusatory extrication from complicity liability has passed.[99] This applied to the defendant in *O'Flaherty* who was present during the infliction of violence, and at the very least providing encouragement or prepared to lend support to the attack. The corollary is that the exculpatory withdrawal limits enunciated in *Mitchell and King* remain overly generous to the co-adventurer. Apart from the unfortunate need to make nebulous distinctions between 'spontaneous' and 'pre-planned' violence,

---

92   Ibid. 169.

93   (1998) 163 JP 75; [1999] Crim LR 496. See John Smith, 'Case Commentary on *Mitchell and King*' [1999] Criminal Law Review 496-98.

94   [1941] 1 WWR 112 (Sloan JA).

95   [2004] EWCA Crim 526.

96   Ibid. at [65].

97   See Andrew Ashworth, 'Case Commentary on *O'Flaherty*' [2004] Criminal Law Review 753, 754-55 who asserts: 'If the foundations of complicity and of withdrawal lie chiefly in B's culpability, a definite withdrawal from spontaneous violence (even if not accompanied by communication) should suffice. But if the foundations lie chiefly in B's contribution to A's offence, B's withdrawal in those circumstances may be no more effective than an uncommunicated withdrawal from a non-spontaneous offence'.

98   See *Mitchell* (n 54); *Gallant* [2008] EWCA Crim 1111; *Campbell (Andre)* [2009] EWCA Crim 50; and *Otway* [2011] EWCA Crim 3.

99   See generally, Reed and Fitzpatrick (n 43).

irrelevant to joint enterprise principles, there is a failure to address concerns over effectiveness and universality of withdrawal.[100] There is also a failure to accord tacit recognition to the element of the principal offender's encouragement in the commission of the crime through the accessory's overall involvement which is not directly countermanded:

> Secondary participation consists in assisting or encouraging the principal offender in the commission of the crime. A party who withdraws from an enterprise, spontaneous or not, usually ceases to assist but he does not necessarily cease to encourage. Suppose that A is encouraged in the fight because he knows that B is there with him. If B decides that he has had enough and quietly slopes off without attracting A's attention, the external element of secondary participation still continues. B's encouragement of A is still operative. Does mere withdrawal then relieve B of responsibility? In principle, it seems that it should not do so. A person who has done an act which makes him potentially liable for a crime cannot relieve himself of responsibility by a mere change of mind. Once the arrow is in the air, it is no use wishing to have never let it go – 'Please God, let it miss!' The archer is guilty of homicide when the arrow gets the victim through the heart. The withdrawer, it is true, does not merely change his mind – he withdraws – but is that relevant if the withdrawal has no more effect on subsequent events than the archer's repentance?[101]

It is disconcerting to note that our courts have been confused, on occasion, as to the very applicability of withdrawal as a determinant. In *Rafferty*,[102] the defendant and other co-adventurers, carried out an attack on the victim at a beach. Rafferty elbowed the victim in the back and stole his debit card (elements of robbery). Before decamping from the scene for over 40 minutes to find a cash dispenser he called out, 'come on boys, leave it'. In his absence the violence escalated, the victim was stripped down then drowned. The trial judge left for jury consideration whether D2 had withdrawn from the unlawful joint enterprise. In reality, this was a non-issue. The appellate court, quite appropriately, concluded that D2 was not a principal offender as he was not a substantial cause of the unlawful homicide. The application of joint enterprise principles meant that Rafferty could also not be categorised as a secondary party – the act of drowning effected by the principals was of a fundamentally different nature from the unlawful robbery enterprise contemplated by D2 and within which he was engaged. Concomitantly, this meant that any consideration of withdrawal principles were rendered otiose.[103] It reveals again in sharp focus the requirement for a comprehensive review and reformulation of our withdrawal determinants.

---

100   Ibid.
101   Smith (n 93) 497.
102   [2007] EWCA Crim 1846; [2008] Crim LR 218.
103   See David Ormerod, 'Case Commentary on *Rafferty*' [2008] Criminal Law Review 218, 220 who states: 'The defence of withdrawal would only seem to be relevant if the acts of P1 and P2 were not fundamentally different from those which D had foreseen. If the jury reached that conclusion, it would be highly questionable whether merely walking away from the scene to fulfil part of the robbery can properly be described as a withdrawal'.

Withdrawal: A Normative Affirmative Defence Standardised on Proportionality and Reasonableness Principles

The preceding section has revealed a beguiling fog of obscurity, and a lack of clarity or consistency of approach to withdrawal as a defence across judicial systems; successful prediction of outcome throughout the limited pantheon of arcane cases remains as likely as determining how many angels can dance on the head of a pin. A new reappraisal is needed which ought to view withdrawal as a bespoke and individuated defence, engaging a normative assessment utilising an imputed proportionality test. The central tenet for the fact finders should engage a flexible examination of 'reasonableness', and whether the individual actor's redemptive behaviour matches a qualitative gradation (reasonable in all of the circumstances) properly to undo accessorial liability, and furnish a 'sufficiency' of diminished culpability to avoid criminal sanction.[104] The reasonableness standard and proportionality test are intertwined, and a correlation prevails between D2's mode of participation in criminal activity (inculpatory conduct) and requirements for a successful withdrawal (exculpatory disengagement).[105]

A continuum scale may beneficially be promulgated in terms of threshold levels of engagement and comparative redemptive abatement. Juridical precepts revealing a higher threshold level will apply to those who provide material assistance or instigation to D1, but reduced threshold levels of 'proper efforts' to undo previous harm will qualitatively apply to those who have simply provided encouragement.[106] Flexibility may apply to individual circumstances in terms of required direct or indirect countermands. Consider, by way of illustration in this regard, a hypothetical postulation involving a multi-party common enterprise to effect a bank robbery. The level and mode of participatory engagement may vacillate across a wide continuum, and the reasonableness–proportionality nexus requirement for qualitative acts of accessory withdrawal will shift according to normative fact-finder deliberations: (i) A, with knowledge of purpose, makes the clothes for the gang; (ii) B, again with direct contemplation, sells the balaclava disguise; (iii) C instigates and counsels the plan of criminal action; (iv) D supplies the gun and bullets; (v) E cleans the weapon in preparation; (vi) F supplies the petrol for the get-away vehicle; (vii) G drives the car to the bank; and (viii) H and I enter the bank, but are apprehended by a security guard; H shouts to I to leave, but I shoots the guard and steals property. The scenario reveals that different levels of participatory engagement (A to I) will be coterminous and coalesce together with determinative redemptive behaviour to facilitate withdrawal. The required countermands for different modes of participation may be direct or indirect, and incorporate direct physical intervention or weapon retrieval at one end of the scale, to warnings to law enforcement authorities or to potential victim(s) at the reduced level.[107] It is suggested herein that the following gradations and demarcations form part of our proportionality–reasonableness nexus:

1. A dichotomy exists between co-adventurers and 'mechanical assisters'[108] in that a higher threshold level of renunciatory conduct applies to the former category of participants

---

104 See generally, Smith, 'General Defences and Withdrawal' (n 4); and in terms of effective manifestation of withdrawal requirements see *O'Flaherty* [2004] 2 Cr App R 20 [60]: 'To disengage from an incident a person must do enough to demonstrate that he or she is withdrawing from the joint enterprise. This is ultimately a question of fact and degree for the jury'.

105 See Wilson (n 4) 589-90.

106 Ibid.

107 See Smith, 'Withdrawal in Complicity' (n 4) 780-82.

108 See Wilson (n 4) 591.

in crime. If D2 is acting as a co-adventurer and provided material assistance then direct countermand should be required in terms of retrieval of the weapon or physical intervention proactively to protect the victim, including restraint of D1.[109] If the 'tools of the crime' are supplied by D2 then more is needed proportionally for an effective withdrawal. The reasonableness standardisation dictates that an enhanced level of redemptive counter-action is needed effectively to absolve D2.[110]

2. A more onerous standard will apply to the instigator of criminal activity. The apposite guiding principles in such a scenario were established in *Gallant*,[111] where D2 had instigated the violence and it was legitimately determined that, 'In those circumstances, assuming that the attack started as a joint enterprise, he clearly would have had to do more than merely walk away in order to demonstrate that he was withdrawing from any further participation'.[112] A higher threshold is presumptively engaged herein as the instigator needs to withdraw from a duality of inculcated and coterminous participatory engagements; this duality embraces both the common purpose itself and effectively countermands the initial encouragement (emboldenment) to others that was furnished at the outset.

3. A different perspective ought to apply where D2 has simply provided encouragement, or basic agreement to the commission of a crime, and in such limited circumstances the price of exculpation should be lowered.[113] The 'cost' may not be as high as taking additional steps to prevent the commission of the crime, but penitent behaviour may involve strictures of indirect countermand. The countermand, dependent on prevailing factual variants in different circumstances, may incorporate either notification to law enforcement authorities or to the victim, or attempted comportment with both sets of reductionist disengagement.[114] The preferred analysis of withdrawal as a quasi-excuse, extrapolated from derivations of reduced social dangerousness, should allow fact-finders to consider an individuated proportionality standardisation within a normatively compartmentalised set of indicators to indirect countermands.

4. The proportionality test will clearly not apply when the pre-inculpatory interlude has expired, and the possibility of withdrawal is no longer timely as in *White v Ridley*: 'a countermand which comes so late as to be incapable of influencing the actions of the perpetrator cannot be regarded as breaking the chain of causation'.[115] The constitutive timeliness (or otherwise) of an attempt to withdraw from complicitous joint enterprise activity arose recently in *Campbell (Andre)*,[116] in a case of spontaneous violence inflicted by a group of participants. D2 had engaged in the first attack, not the second, but only a short time span accrued

---

109   See Lanham (n 4) 572; and Andrew Simester, Bob Sullivan, John Spencer and Graham Virgo (n 14) 256.

110   See Law Commission Report, No 177, [4.135-4.137] which appears to draw a dichotomy between different culpability gradation thresholds between assisting and encouragement, indicating that encouragement at a lower threshold may be negated by 'discouragement' which is less of a stricture than measures impacted for assistance withdrawal. Interestingly, the report appears rather schizophrenic in this regard: at one point the withdrawal defence seems predicated upon D2 seeking to 'undo' the effect of an earlier act of participation, but the actual proposals iterate redemptive action aimed at preventing the principal offence; see Vol. 2 [9.41].

111   *Gallant* (n 98).

112   Ibid.

113   See Lanham (n 4) 584-85.

114   Ibid.

115   Ibid. 589.

116   *Campbell (Andre)* (n 98).

between the two assaults, and the Court of Appeal determined that the conduct during the course of the earlier attack still represented a significant and operating cause of death. Similarly, in *Eldredge v United States*,[117] in a memorable statement, the court determined that an expressed intent to withdraw from a conspiracy to use dynamite to destroy a building is insufficient if the fuse is set, and at that juncture verbal communication is inadequate, so the individual to withdraw must step on the fuse.

5. Finally, in terms of the correlation between mode of participation and proportionality of withdrawal behaviour, conduct of an irreducibly minimal nature is inadequate to meet the threshold test: perfunctory verbal disclaimers of liability;[118] failure to attend on the day of commission of criminal purpose (omission);[119] or fleeing the scene of the crime[120] are all ineffectual manifestations of imputed countermand. Normatively, these types of limited remedial disengagement are not sustainable or adequate as a vignette of redemptive behaviour: the cost of exculpation has not been satisfied.

The attitudinal motivation that lies behind an individual actor's withdrawal, part of the price of exculpation calculus, should also form an essential pre-requisite element of fact-finder assessment of the reasonableness–proportionality nexus, and normative enquiry. Our criminal law, more broadly, should present an opportunity to complicitous actors to disengage for genuine reasons to diminish liability, and seek voluntarily to undo the effects of earlier criminality. This rationale does not adhere to a defendant who is compelled to refrain from commission of the substantive crime for nefarious inducements or improper situational pressures. The central importance of motivation as part of a newly formulated withdrawal defence is greatly enhanced by earlier presuppositions that base this quasi-excuse defence on grounds of reduced culpability.[121] The individual's ratiocination to withdraw, for good or ill reasons, constitutes an important diagnostic tool for fact-finders in terms of a reduced risk of societal dangerousness, both currently and prospectively.[122]

Attitudinal motivation should play a crucial role in the calibrations of withdrawal as an affirmative defence on a preponderance of the evidence (see below), and exculpation must be based on a 'genuine' decision taken by the participant to independently and voluntarily desist their criminal pathway, derived from legitimate and verifiable phenomenological calculations.[123]

---

117   (1932) 62 F 2d 449.

118   See *Fletcher, Fletcher and Zimnowodski* (n 62); *Nawaz* (n 63); and *Baker* (n 61).

119   *Rook* (n 65); see also *Goodspeed* (1911) 6 Cr App R 133.

120   *Becerra and Cooper* (n 56); and *O'Flaherty* (n 59).

121   See Smith, 'Withdrawal in Complicity' (n 4) 783-84 asserting: '[T]he alternative view (to the incentive rationale) that withdrawal is a strong indicator of the lack of (or diminished) culpability, or future social dangerousness, would more clearly favour distinguishing true repenters from opportunist or inveterate sinners. Withdrawal motivated solely by the belief that the police have become aware of the planned offence hardly indicates a level of reduced culpability or dangerousness appropriate to the award of a complete defence. Much the same comments would be justified where, for example, an accessory withdraws with the firm intention of transferring his assistance to a similar but financially more rewarding criminal enterprise'.

122   See Moriarty (n 17) 22 who states, 'Yet as beauty lies in the eye of the beholder, so too the possibly intensively subjective question of the moral quality of the renouncing defendant's motive may lie in the personal psyche of the judge, to be determined quite differently by different officials'.

123   Ibid. Note that Moriarty also stresses: 'The Model Penal Code Commentary argues that a man who has begun a criminal enterprise may be judged dangerous because he is likely to cause criminal harm in the future. It is a sensible use of the criminal law to neutralize his threat before it materializes. A man who has renounced his crime, on the other hand, has revealed the error of our prediction of future harm at his hands. We have no reliable basis to judge him a danger and it would be wrong to subject him to criminal sanctions'.

An improper motive can be of constitutive significance to abrogate the redemptive quality of D2's conduct. Illustratively, this has been supererogatory in a number of US precedential authorities. In *People v Kimball*,[124] the defendant was engaged in the attempted robbery of a convenience store, but when accosted by a female operator he decided to abandon the venture declaring, 'I won't do it to you; you're good looking and I won't do it to you this time but if you're here next time it won't matter'.[125] Clearly, where the defendant's motivation for withdrawal relates simply to the physical appearance of the victim, or the defendant awaits a more opportune moment for criminal engagement, then this needs to frame part of the normative assessment of culpability. It would, for example, be disingenuous to allow a withdrawal defence if the rationale for disavowing further criminal behaviour centred on a relationship with the partner of a co-adventurer. An improper motive can be identified, as in *Commonwealth v Doris*,[126] where D2 only seeks to withdraw to avoid imminent arrest or to attempt to expunge liability during the actual furtherance of a robbery. The flame of culpability is not duly doused in such circumstances, and effectual motive is causally linked diagnostically to enduring social dangerousness.

Withdrawal because of fear of apprehension is cognitively different from the redemptive quality of behaviour that springs from the genuine pricking of conscience,[127] highlighted by the court in *Weaver v State*,[128] and delineated by 'whether [the defendant] was frightened by the approach of the officers or deterred by the voice of conscience and repented of his wicked intentions'.[129] Inculcated motivations for disaggregation of criminal behaviour are addressed in the draft commentaries to the Model Penal Code[130] and adopted in a plethora of US state legislatures:

> A renunciation is not 'voluntary and complete' [in respect of complicity and inchoate liability] if it is motivated in whole or in part by: (a) a belief that circumstances exist which increase the probability of detention, or which render more difficult the accomplishment of the criminal purpose, or (b) a decision to postpone the criminal conduct until another time or to transfer the criminal effort to another victim or another but similar objective.[131]

Further grist to the mill can be added by directly comparing the reasonableness–proportionality standardisation attached to the withdrawal defence, and individual liability created by supervening fault, appurtenant to the principles laid out in *Miller*[132] and *Evans*.[133] An actor who has set in motion a dangerous situation, in *Miller* it was arson and in *Evans* the risk effected by drug administration (gross negligence manslaughter), then comes under an incumbent duty to prevent the harm accruing

---

124 109 Mich App 273, 311 NW 2d 343, *modified on other grounds*, 412 Mich 890, 313 NW 2d 285 (1981).

125 Ibid. 276, 311 NW 2d 344.

126 (1926) 135 A 313.

127 See Smith, 'Withdrawal in Complicity' (n 4) 783.

128 42 SE 745 (1902).

129 Ibid. 747.

130 See Model Penal Code s 5.01(4) (Proposed Official Draft 1962) (complete and voluntary renunciation is an affirmative defence).

131 New York Penal Code 1965, as amended, s 40.10 para 5; and see further Connecticut Penal Code s 53a-106.

132 [1983] 2 AC 161; and see Reed and Fitzpatrick (n 43) 32-34.

133 [2009] 1 WLR 1999: [2010] 1 All ER 13; and see Glenys Williams, 'Gross Negligence and Duty of Care in Drugs Cases: *R v Evans*' [2009] Criminal Law Review 631.

by taking effective and 'reasonable' remedial steps to prevent inculpatory liabilities.[134] The harm–offence–reasonableness nexus correlates with the 'proper efforts' of negation required for a withdrawal defence. A defendant who has created a dangerous situation was held to be under a 'responsibility' to mitigate the harm via proportionate reciprocal acts of disengagement: in *Miller* when D1 accidentally set alight a mattress he became under a responsibility to counteract the damage to the property at risk by telephoning the fire brigade or householder; and in *Evans* the drug supply to a younger half-sister engendered prospective duties focused upon contacting hospital authorities or other effective care obligation.[135] The responsibilities to take 'reasonable' efforts of abatement in a pre-inculpatory interlude, and set normatively against the danger created, mirror the withdrawal defence rationale.

Interestingly, the Court of Appeal in *Evans* have determined that an offence–harm–reasonableness standardisation for determination by fact-finders does satisfy the legal certainty requirements of Article 7 of the European Convention of Human Rights.[136] A template that the court applies in addressing the issue of certainty within Article 7 is the test of notional legal advice – could the defendant find out, using a lawyer if needs be, whether his or her conduct would render him or her liable?[137] As was stated in the European Court of Human Rights, in the context of a statutory provision in *Kokkinakis v Greece*,[138] the criminal law must not be construed excessively to the disadvantage of an accused, but the requirement of certainty is met, 'where the individual can know from the wording of a relevant provision and, if need be, with the assistance of the courts' interpretation of it, what acts and omissions will make him liable'.[139] It is contended that, on a similar perspective, the reasonableness–proportionality standard adduced herein for withdrawal would, contemporaneously, satisfy legality and certainty constituents as a true defence.

The final reformulation that is proposed to extant withdrawal principles must also be sufficiently robust to withstand Convention challenges. This relates to the burden of proof attached to the defence. It is contended that withdrawal needs to be viewed as an affirmative defence, operating *sui generis* as an independent offence-modification defence, and cathartically as a quasi-excuse on a reduced culpability framework.[140] Controversially, however, optimisation principles indicate that a reverse burden of proof should apply on a preponderance of evidence standard, and that it is for the recalcitrant defendant to satisfy the court of their redemptive actions. This is reflective of practice in a majority of US jurisdictions, and in this regard Robinson has concluded: '[t]he burden of production for defences of renunciation, abandonment, and withdrawal is always on the defendant. The burden of persuasion is generally on the defendant by a preponderance of the evidence'.[141] A number of defendants have challenged the constitutionality of this reversal, but to no avail.[142]

In essence, the withdrawal defence ought not to be viewed as a negation of either the external or fault element of an offence that has presumptively already been completed, but rather as a separate circumstance that may or may not modify existing liability. This facilitative determinant is outwith offence completion, and consequently the burden of proof as to the 'new' derivation is to be

---

134   See Alan Reed, 'Criminal Law' [2010] All England Annual Review 131.

135   Ibid. 136-37.

136   *Evans* (n 133) [45] (Lord Judge CJ).

137   See Reed (n 134) 140-41.

138   (1993) 17 EHRR 397.

139   Ibid. at [52].

140   See generally, Robinson (n 20).

141   See Robinson (n 81) 349-50.

142   See *Vera* 153 Mich App at 418, 395 NW 2d at 341 (burden of proving affirmative defence shifted to a defendant was held constitutional); and *Cowart* 136 Ga App at 531, 221 SE 2d at 651 (burden of proof *vis-à-vis* the abandonment defence placed upon the defendant).

allocated as most appropriate.[143] The court is addressing the question of whether D2 has effectively demonstrated a reduced culpability and abrogated complicitous behaviour via redemptive conduct (a reasonableness–proportionality nexus). In this regard three separate arguments highlighted in the commentary to the Model Penal Code support a reverse defence burden: (1) most importantly the constitutive facts and attitudinal behaviour that support the defence are within the ambit of the individual actor fruitfully to produce for the court, including motivational pathways to disengagement; (2) instances of withdrawal will occur very infrequently, and when they do arise the defence is often unlikely, subject to correction by the defendant; and (3) viewing withdrawal as an affirmative defence of reduced culpability and social dangerousness improves the likelihood of wider acceptance for a contested principle, and lends credence to viewing it as a true defence not merely relevant to mitigation of sentence.[144] A further ingredient, as part of the refrain that underscores this chapter, is the conceptualisation of a new lodestar model of qualitative proportionality standardisations across diverse complicitous behaviour that may normatively be established for determination by relevant fact-finders. This template may efficaciously advance a reverse burden presumption to reflect appropriate changes of heart by a recalcitrant criminal actor.

Conclusion

The precise legal topography of the withdrawal defence ought to be distilled within a newly formulated standardisation. The guiding principles that are promulgated in this chapter may be crystallised in the following terms:

1. It is the conceptual basis of reduced societal dangerousness not incentivisation that presents a logically compelling redemptive behaviour analysis of withdrawal. The reasoning herein is that the accessory, considered inwardly on a prognostic rationale, is less culpable, and a lower danger to the state both currently and prospectively.
2. It is the quasi-excuse framework that underpins the defence in that D2's actions are not justified in terms of net harm or utilitarian calculus, but the actor is not inculpated to the same degree. The correlation is that it presents an independent type of defence that is *sui generis* in nature, and akin to consent in some constituent elements, as it is not predicated on internal incapacity or external impairment but reflects a positive premium for redemptive and genuine change of heart. This is determinable by the adjudication of fact-finders.
3. Withdrawal is not a defence predicated upon neutralisation of either *actus reus* or *mens rea* components of complicitous behaviour, to which separate principles are determinative. It represents, however, an affirmative defence which operates within the spectra of offence-modification as an element of the criminalisation reflection underpinning the charged offence. It is distinctive in ambit as a defence in that complicity liability in general operates as a derivation from completion of the full substantive offence.
4. A normative assessment should apply of individuated withdrawal behaviour, predicated upon an imputed proportionality test. To be effective the withdrawal needs to be unequivocal, timely, voluntary, and incorporate a genuine effort to undo earlier complicitous action. The normative assessment adduced is developed by examination and evaluation of comparative

143   See generally, George Fletcher, *Rethinking Criminal Law* (Little, Brown 1978).
144   See Model Penal Code and Commentaries s 5.01 comment 361 (Official Draft 1962 and Revised Comments 1985).

juridical precepts. These perspectives acknowledge withdrawal as an affirmative and independent defence in reliance upon reasonable efforts of disengagement, as in Australia, as part of the 'price' of exculpation. In US jurisdictions that mirror the Model Penal Code a more relaxed attitude to withdrawal from accessory liability has been promulgated, in contrast to renunciation from inchoate liabilities. D2 can effectively withdraw by making 'proper efforts' to prevent D1 from effecting the substantive offence, and failure to prevent that commission does not constitute a total bar to defence applicability provided 'reasonable efforts' to desist can be purveyed before fact-finders. Redemptive efforts to withdraw, including the provision of timely warning to law enforcement officers, must be aimed at crime prevention rather than simply undoing the effects of the complicitous behaviour. In general terms, the US indicia points to a reasonableness–proportionality standard, importing a duty of reasonable care, that charts a pathway for an English reformulated standard.

5. A correlation should exist between D2's mode of participation in criminal activity (exculpatory conduct) and requirements for a successful withdrawal (inculpatory disengagement). In this regard demarcations ought to apply in terms of a qualitative proportionality standardisation across different gradations of complicitous behaviour. A higher threshold categorisation will apply to those who provide material assistance or crime instigation but lower levels of reductionism will coalesce together to individuals who have simply provided encouragement. A reasonableness test will allow sufficient flexibility to examine individuated circumstances in terms of required direct or indirect countermands. Required modes of countermands for different modes of participation can be identified and equated across a continuum; direct physical intervention or weapon retrieval to prevent the substantive offence may be inculcated at one end of the scale, but reduced levels of indirect warnings to police authorities or potential victims may apply at a lower equipoise.

6. The proportionality test will clearly not apply when the pre-inculpatory interlude has expired, and the possibility of withdrawal is no longer timely.

7. The attitudinal motivation that lies behind an actor's withdrawal should form an essential element behind our normative assessment of imputed proportionality. The individual's ratiocination towards withdrawal, for good or ill reasons, constitutes an important diagnostic tool for fact-finders in terms of reduced societal dangerousness. Motivation should be based on a genuine decision taken by the participant to desist independently and voluntarily their criminal pathway.

8. A direct comparator for complicity withdrawal principles is provided by individual liability attached to supervening fault and creation of a dangerous situation. In the latter scenario standardisations of consequential 'reasonable' steps of remedial disengagement have been evaluated in *Evans*, adopting *Miller* precepts. The discursive considerations therein of the legality and certainty constituents of our harm–offence–reasonableness nexus is applicable to the overarching withdrawal template.

9. Finally, it is contended, perhaps controversially, that optimisation principles suggest that a reverse burden of proof should apply on a preponderance of evidence standard, and that it is for the recalcitrant defendant to satisfy the court of their redemptive actions, reflective of practice in a majority of US jurisdictions. This reflection, as the chapter began, is imbued with biblical intonations of an individual's redemptive change of heart to facilitate a withdrawal defence: 'He that covereth his sins shall not prosper: but whoso confesseth and forsaketh them shall have mercy'.[145]

---

145 Proverbs 28:13, King James Version of the Holy Bible, The New Testament.

Chapter 7

Participating in Crime: Some Thoughts on the Retribution/Prevention Dichotomy in Preparation for Crime and How to Deal with It

William Wilson

Introduction

It is usual these days to talk of a crisis of criminalisation. The State is portrayed as thrashing around in a vain attempt to reconcile opposing interests and interest groups, enacting and proposing all kinds of ineffectual, unnecessary and inappropriate measures to give the impression that something is being done to combat or neutralise whatever moral panic has currently seized the imagination of the media and public. A common point of attack for much recent criminal legislation is that it is weak and ineffective, unprincipled, even divisive, offending liberal ideals such as the rule of law, fair labelling and the harm principle.[1] Growing up alongside the overuse of the substantive criminal law the criminal law's model of success has shifted from process to outcome. Efficient, cost effective management of crime and disorder is the order of the day, rather than the just disposal of offences. Ashworth and Zedner have described the ways in which the criminal justice system has remodelled itself so as to achieve this end, namely increasing the use of diversion, fixed penalties, summary trials, hybrid orders, prevention orders, and strict liability and increasing incentives to plead guilty. Such developments are underpinned by the state prosecuting an unstable and largely incoherent mixture of prevention, managerialism and authoritarianism.[2]

In this chapter the view is presented that although many contemporary aspects of criminal law and procedure are indeed best understood as opportunistic and politically expedient we would do well to understand these developments as recognition of changes in social relations which demand novel responses to the problems and conflicts these changes engender. Instead we should identify areas where control and prevention may properly complement retribution as an agreed basis for state intervention. In this chapter I shall concentrate upon the law of criminal attempts. Given the conceptual difficulties of reconciling issues of law enforcement and desert is it time to refashion the law's approach to preparatory crime to reflect this emphasis?

---

1 Thanks are due to the helpful comments of James Chalmers, Lindsay Farmer and the participants in the Gerald Gordon Seminar Series at Edinburgh, and Nils Jareborg and Magnus Ulvang and the participants in a seminar at Uppsala University. See generally, Andrew Ashworth, 'Is the Criminal Law a Lost Cause?' [2000] Law Quarterly Review 116; Andrew Ashworth and Lucia Zedner, 'Defending the Criminal Law: Reflections on the Changing Character of Crime, Procedure, and Sanctions' (2007) 2(1) Criminal Law and Philosophy 21-51; Rowan Cruft, 'Liberalism and the Changing Character of the Criminal Law: Response to Ashworth and Zedner' (2008) 2(1) Criminal Law and Philosophy 59; Adam Crawford, 'Governing through Anti-Social Behaviour: Regulatory Challenges to Criminal Justice' (2009) 49(6) British Journal of Criminology, 810-31.
2 Ashworth and Zedner (n 1).

The chapter is organised as follows: in the following section I shall outline the established view of the structure of the criminal justice system as comprising two separate but complementary paradigms of liability, prevention and retribution. I shall follow this up with an examination of the doctrinal problems posed by the failure of the criminal justice system to determine the true nature of criminal attempts, the reasons for this and the various solutions which have been proposed to improve the situation. I shall argue that a possible way of reconciling the preventive and retributive aspects is to exploit the potential of the civil prevention order so as to ensure that the retributive response is limited to those who deserve to be punished for what they have done while leaving room for non-retributive, coercive interventions for those whose conduct poses a threat to the community's dominion. Central to such an initiative is developing principles of application and due process appropriate for the task.

Paradigms of Criminal Justice

Criminal law as filtered through the lens provided by traditional crimes such as murder, theft, assault and other stigmatic crimes protective of personal interests lends an imperfect view of the nature of criminal law and its social function. We cannot say, for example, that coercive norms necessarily embody collectively agreed moral standards. Clearly the core of criminal law does embody such standards – intentional killing, stealing, hurting, defrauding are obvious examples. This core seeks to express and enforce society's core values, most notably the liberal values of individual freedom and autonomy. It prohibits wrongful interference with property and person and censures us when we do so, typically expressed in stigmatic punishment such as imprisonment. However, one cannot expect morality to do all the work society would wish of it, namely to set and enforce standards of obligatory behaviour. For this to be possible there must, at the very least, be an overwhelming consensus guaranteeing the authority of the norm, which in turn demands a high degree of social homogeneity, a social structure which offers offenders no hiding place from officialdom and whose mechanisms of social control are sufficiently responsive to incentivise compliance. It goes without saying that modern liberal society tends to lack such conditions. Even core wrongs such as murder elicit contradictory moral responses depending upon the individual's moral stance on the permissibility of autonomy overriding the sanctity of life. The criminal law cannot sit on the fence. It embodies political choices which are not reducible to any consensually agreed norm.

The position is, of course, further complicated by the existence of a separate and more modern paradigm of liability, reflecting the criminal justice system's two complementary objectives – preventing harm and censuring wrongdoing. Over a significant area of social life the state, on our behalf, restricts freedom of action to promote those collective goods of welfare and security whose realisation is central to a meaningful sense of individual mastery of their environment.[3] Thus the contemporary scope of criminal offences includes a vast and ever increasing raft of offences whose function is to regulate our social and economic activities. The activities prohibited by such offences we acknowledge to be wrong but they are wrong by virtue of being declared wrong rather than any immorality intrinsic to them. It is easy to overlook, however, that even such wrongs have some moral reference point in the sense of being declarations of socially appropriate ways of behaving which hold good whatever social or economic function the individual has, whatever community

---

3   See generally on this point Alan Brudner, 'Agency and Welfare in the Penal Law' in Stephen Shute, John Gardner and Jeremy Horder (eds), *Action and Value in the Criminal Law* (Clarendon Press 1993) 22-27; Grant Lamond, 'What Is a Crime' (2007) 27 Oxford Journal of Legal Studies 609.

the individual inhabits, whatever values that community espouses. Speeding offences, health and safety regulations, environmental offences embody the moral obligation not to subject our fellow citizens to any risk of harm from our activities which a properly conscientious attitude would remove.

Although once widely criticised for subverting the ethical foundation upon which the state obtains its warrant to punish – the requirement that the defendant knowingly and inexcusably committed an act of serious wrongdoing – regulatory offences are now generally accepted as comprising a separate and complementary paradigm of liability.[4] The function of sanction is forward looking, not to communicate disapproval for past wrongdoing – proof of fault is not required – but to prevent future harm by exacting compliance whether through deterrence, education or incapacitation. Both liability paradigms have in common, however, normative claims about power relations existing primarily between individual and the state. Obligations of compliance derive in the former case from the force of collectively accepted and internalised moral norms and in the latter case from a morality of cooperation fostered by the reciprocal benefits and burdens of living in a well regulated secure and predictable society in which the primary value of individual autonomy is respected and protected.

There is little argument, however, that the existence of this complementary paradigm has had deleterious effects on the quality of justice delivered by the criminal justice system as whole. Even today, there is little legislative appetite for ensuring that criminal offences are assigned to the right paradigm.[5] But a more important complaint in this context is how, by judicious selection of the regulatory paradigm, defendants may be stripped of the protection of the fault requirement for stigmatic crimes and some of its procedural safeguards. Obvious examples include sex offences, some of which, although highly stigmatic and capable of seriously affecting a person's quality of life, contain strict liability elements.

Although there is now greater understanding of the internal connection between these elements in relation to regulatory crime, the confused interrelationship between the criminal justice system's retributive and other purposes continues to surface in other areas. In *McCann*, where the central question was whether it was permissible to augment the penalty for breach of an ASBO on the basis of the same conduct which had first invoked the ASBO, is a good contemporary illustration.[6] In this case Lord Steyn represented as the aim of the criminal law 'not punishment for its own sake but to permit everyone to go about their daily lives without fear of harm'.[7] No doubt the statement is true for the purpose of understanding the ASBO amongst the panoply of coercive rules and techniques but it is hardly a statement which is true of the system as a whole.[8]

A similar confusion bedevils the law of criminal attempts. Here, as elsewhere, commentators and judges have tried in vain to secure an accommodation made between the preventive and the retributive aspects of the criminal law by dint of a careful balancing of its internal doctrinal

---

4   For a general exploration of this issue see Brudner (n 3) and Lamond (n 3).

5   For example, activities causing or generating the risk of causing substantial social harms are typically enacted as part of a regulatory framework, with prosecutions typically initiated by the public authorities rather than the police. The rules governing environmental pollution are an obvious example of a crime at once regulatory and yet comparable in terms of potential to harm to traditional crimes of violence or endangerment suggesting that its place within a solely regulatory framework is debatable.

6   Created by Section 1 Crime and Disorder Act 1998.

7   *R v Manchester Crown Court* ex parte *McCann* [2002] UKHL 39, [2003] 1 AC 787.

8   Brudner (n 3).

elements.[9] The view presented here is that such an accommodation is neither possible nor desirable. The law of criminal attempts can only achieve part of this project, the retributive part. We must look elsewhere to achieve prevention.

Two Theories of Criminal Attempts

The prevention/retribution dichotomy maps directly onto the two ruling approaches to criminal attempts, subjectivism and objectivism. Subjectivists generally espouse doctrine which optimises its preventive potential. They may do this either with the explicit purpose of creating preventive doctrine fit for purpose or, in more nuanced versions, by insisting that the wrongdoing against which retributive punishment is concretised in the performance of some act indicating the defendant's commitment to the criminal project. The act is not important in its own right but simply serves to provide the evidence of the dangerous and blameworthy inclinations which subjectivists hold to be the cornerstone of attempt liability. In this respect subjectivism in criminal attempts exhibits the theoretical template of all the general inchoate offences. It is of passing interest that Glanville Williams, a principled subjectivist on matters relating to the fault element in criminal law exploits that subjectivism for the less principled purpose of adding bite to the preventive aspect of criminal attempts. Discussing the case of *Jones*, in which a man who, following a preconceived plan, entered a car and pointed a firearm at the driver with murderous intent, he asserts 'I do not think it an abuse of language to say that (the defendant) started his attempt as soon as he set out with his firearm, his disguise and his Spanish money, or even when he acquired the firearm and his disguise with the firm object of using it in the offence'.[10]

Pure objectivists repudiate this approach as contrary to the ethical premises which underpin and justify state coercion. Our membership of a free society behoves the state not to subject us to coercion unless we have done something wrong. The state's warrant to punish demands at the very least, then, an act of 'manifest criminality', that is an act which 'shows criminal intent on the face of it'.[11] This is objectively wrongful behaviour because it has harmful effects on the material world, specifically the alarm and apprehension experienced by the community. In Fletcher's classic analysis, it is the fact that criminal conduct is unnerving which justifies affected individuals taking defensive or pre-emptive measures and agencies of the state law enforcement measures. The

---

9   The following statement of Andrew Ashworth is representative: 'the law should not only provide for the punishment of those who have culpably caused … harms but also penalize those who are trying to cause the harms. A person who tries to cause a prohibited harm and fails is, in terms of moral culpability, not materially different from the person who tries and succeeds: the difference in outcome is determined by chance rather than by choice, and a censuring institution such as the criminal law should not subordinate itself to the vagaries of fortune by focusing on results rather than on culpability. There is also a consequentialist justification for the law of attempts, inasmuch as it reduces harm by authorizing law enforcement officers and the courts to step in before any harm has been done, so long as the danger of the harm being caused is clear' (Andrew Ashworth, *Principles of Criminal Law* (Oxford 2009) 438).

10   *R v Jones* [1990] 3 All ER 886; Glanville L Williams, *Textbook of Criminal Law* (2nd edn, Stevens & Sons 1983) 19 TCL, 422. The Tasmanian Criminal Code affords one of the more extreme versions of the subjectivism which, emphasising its preventive function, requires neither proximity of the act to the intended crime nor any manifest wrongdoing. The conduct element simply requires an act or omission which is 'part of a series of events which if it were not interrupted would constitute the actual commission of the crime'.

11   Per Salmond J in *The King v. Barker* [1924] NZLR 865. See generally, Antony Duff, 'Criminal Attempts' in George Fletcher, *Rethinking the Criminal Law* (Little Brown 1978) 139-57.

corollary is that if an act is so equivocal that it does not generate apprehension, then any basis for either private or public intervention disappears.[12]

Neither approach conduces to a state of affairs in which the law's retributive and preventive functions are effectively balanced. The former allows intervention at a stage well before any sign of danger or wrongdoing is made manifest by an act which is objectively innocent of wrongdoing.[13] Getting into a car, walking down a street, donning a pair of gloves could all form 'part of a series of acts which if it were not interrupted would constitute the commission of a crime'.[14] On the other hand there is little pre-emptive potential in a conduct element which requires the defendant to have committed the last act necessary to effect the offence or, if not the last act, an act so unequivocal as 'to declare and proclaim the guilty purpose with which they are done'.[15]

In England and Wales the Criminal Attempts Act 1971 is representative of the general approach which is to seek a midway point between acts of preparation and acts of perpetration to constitute the attempt.[16] Proximity to the completed offence is required but, in order to ensure a practical marriage of prevention and retribution, the test for proximity is couched in terms which avoid specifying the degree of proximity required.[17] The 'fudge' is effected by requiring an act which is 'more than merely preparatory to the commission of the offence'. Ireland, Canada, Victoria, Singapore, and Australian Capital Territory all use a similar formula. The emphasis in each case is upon what remains to be done. Is he/she 'on the job' or simply preparing for it?

The indeterminacy of this test has been described as both its strength and its weakness. It is a strength in that it embodies sufficient flexibility to deal with the infinite variety of act situations which attempts to commit different crimes may involve – perpetrating fraud tends to involve a longer time period and more complicated and equivocal processes than murder for example – but a weakness in that it leaves what counts as an attempt very much up for grabs. Has a person who follows another on a crowded street intending to garrotte her when he gets the chance gone beyond mere preparation? Is the answer any different if the intended offence was rape or theft or if he lay in wait? Applying the natural meaning of the words is not the answer since this is only uncovered through the conceptual filter of an objectivist or subjectivist attitude. Using the former, the words 'more than merely preparatory' require an act bearing the hallmark of the consummated offence. Using the latter, the words require simply an act of a nature to support the prosecution claim that the offence is due to take place unless it is thwarted.

An examination of case law, moreover, indicates that the conceptual filter may also vary according to the context of the actor's deeds. Those who have 'burned their boats; or 'crossed the Rubicon' are more likely to be deemed to be 'on the job' than some who are nearer to executing their criminal

---

12   Fletcher (n 11) 144; Antony Duff has 'the attack' as the threshold for intervention, arguably a more analytically secure notion than 'manifest wrongdoing' (Antony Duff (n 11) 221-28).

13   Daniel Ohana, 'Desert and Punishment for Acts Preparatory to the Commission of a Crime' (2007) 20(1) Canadian Journal of Law and Jurisprudence 113.

14   Stephen's classic formulation of the subjectivist approach, *Stephen's Digest of Criminal Law* (5th Edition, 1894) Act 50.

15   This latter test, although it thoroughly reflects the common law's concern to punish wrongdoing specifically rather than criminal disposition generally, is not even cogent in its own terms as apart from the last act necessary to effect the offence very few actions directed towards the commission of an offence are that unequivocal.

16   KJM Smith, 'Proximity in Attempt: Lord Lane's Midway Course' [1991] Criminal Law Review 576.

17   For general discussion of the problems of definition see Law Commission, *Criminal Law: Attempt, Conspiracy and Incitement* (Law Com No 102, 1980) 2.40; Ian Dennis, 'The Criminal Attempts Act 1981' [1982] Criminal Law Review 5.

adventure.[18] This is particularly apparent in attempted rape cases. So, in *Dagnall* it was attempted rape where the defendant had dragged a woman by the hair and pushed her against a fence and told her he wanted to 'fuck her' and then 'rape her'.[19] Lord Justice Latham referred to perhaps:

> the most important aspect ... that by the end of the incident she was so convinced that she was about to be raped that she indicated to him that she would be prepared to do anything he wanted provided that he did not hurt her ... He had overcome her resistance and it was only, it would appear, the arrival of the police car that prevented the ultimate offence from taking place.[20]

This conviction, that she was about to be raped, seems here to be acting as the psychological proxy for the Rubicon test. On the other hand, in *Geddes*, a man who had trespassed in a school lavatory equipped with knife, rope and masking tape intended to be used in the abduction of a boy pupil was held not to have committed attempted false imprisonment since, although putting himself in the position to commit the offence, he had not 'actually tried' to commit it. Again using the 'crossing the Rubicon' metaphor what the defendant had done was just as easily undone and this seemed to be the filter through which the court decided whether what had been done was a criminal attempt.

The problem is not so much the words themselves, therefore, but the conceptual resources of the judges who interpret those words. If these conceptual resources are not to thwart the avowed policy of criminalising attempts, it is necessary for that policy, whatever it is, to be articulated clearly within the definition of an attempt. Whether we use a subjectivist form of words for example 'substantial steps'[21] or an objectivist form, for example 'on the job', the furtherance of that policy probably then requires a precise blueprint of what it is which converts thought into deed in as many potential attempt scenarios as possible. Probably the best example of such a blueprint is to be found in the Model Penal Code. The Model Penal Code encapsulates its own fudge, although here proceeding from a subjectivist premise in which the act undertaken by D is not merely one of a 'series of acts ' but rather is a *substantial step toward the commission* of that offense. Proximity to that offence is not of the essence so long as the steps taken 'strongly corroborate' the actor's criminal purpose to effect the substantive crime. It continues:

> (2) The following, if strongly corroborative of the actor's criminal purpose, shall not be held insufficient as a matter of law:

> (a) lying in wait, searching for or following the contemplated victim of the crime;

> (b) enticing or seeking to entice the contemplated victim of the crime to go to the place contemplated for its commission;

---

18   These metaphors have been commonly used to describe, from both objectivist and subjectivist points of view, but usually the line between preparatory action and an actual attempt. See, for example, *Director of Public Prosecutions v. Stonehouse* [1978] AC 55.

19   Cf. *Attorney-General's Reference (No 1 of 1992)* (1993) 96 Cr App R 298 (CA).

20   Clarkson prefers the filter of 'confrontation'. There is something to be said for this. However, the court's notion of an attempt has always involved metaphors and the Rubicon test does much of the line-drawing work that the 'on the job test' signally fails to do and arguably does so with an analytical focus absent from the confrontation requirement. CMV Clarkson, 'Attempt: The Conduct Requirement' (2009) 29(1) Oxford Journal Legal Studies 25-41.

21   This is Glanville Williams' preferred option. Glanville Williams, *Criminal Law: The General Part* (Stevens 1961) 632.

(c) reconnoitering the place contemplated for the commission of the crime;

(d) unlawful entry of a structure, vehicle or enclosure in which it is contemplated that the crime will be committed;

(e) possession, collection or fabrication of materials to be employed in the commission of the crime, which are specifically designed for unlawful use or which can serve no lawful purpose of the actor under the circumstances;

(f) soliciting an innocent agent to engage in conduct constituting an element of the crime.[22]

The Law Commission originally embraced this approach before proposing the proximity test which was incorporated into the Criminal Attempts Act.[23] Deploring this change of heart Williams complained that the list of examples of actions corroborating a criminal purpose 'beautifully clarifies nearly all the matters that have been litigated in England, most of which we have either failed to settle or settled in an impolitic way'.[24] True to be sure, but such an approach is hardly a recipe for sustaining the moral authority of a criminal paradigm centred upon state retribution for culpable wrongdoing.

A Fudge too Far?

The Law Commission has recently reported on inchoate offences. Most of the useful theoretical work underpinning the analysis of a criminal attempt occurs in the Consultation Paper and it is this paper which will feature most heavily in the succeeding pages. In the Consultation Paper[25] the Commission acknowledged that the 'more than merely preparatory' formula was too vague and uncertain, such that the Court of Appeal has had the task of drawing the line between acts of mere preparation and criminal attempts. With 'too little regard being paid to the underlying rationale for the offence' the result has been a narrowing of the intended meaning of a criminal attempt in many cases, with too much emphasis on the offence's label ('attempt') – and therefore on the notion of 'trying' to commit an offence.

The Law Commission's solution was a reformulated definition of the conduct element in a criminal attempt together with a new offence of criminal preparation. It concluded that it would be rational to particularise two different forms of wrongdoing in order to achieve both retributive credibility and preventive efficacy. The offence of criminal attempt would be limited to the last acts needed to commit the intended offence. The offence of criminal preparation would cover acts of preparation but only those which are 'properly to be regarded as part of the execution of the plan to commit the intended offence'. The overall ambition is to render more clear what counts as proximity in attempt, while leaving the back-up offence for those remaining cases where doubt

---

22   Section 5.01(2). The above list contains merely examples of what the judge as a matter of law is not entitled to remove from the jury. It is, therefore, still open to it to decide that a person reconnoitring a bank with the avowed purpose of robbing it, is not guilty of attempted robbery because, say, the quality of the acts concerned and the mentality of the defendant left them unsure as to his commitment.

23   Law Commission (n 17).

24   Glanville Williams, 'Wrong Turnings on the Law of Criminal Attempts' [1971] Criminal Law Review 416, 421.

25   Law Commission, *Conspiracy and Attempts* (Law Com CP No 183, 2008).

may remain. It leaves room for pre-emptive action for those less but still proximate acts which are nevertheless part of the execution of the plan rather than preparation for it. So the overall scheme of liability will have a person committing attempted murder if he pulls a gun and releases the safety catch prior to aiming and firing it. She commits criminal preparation for murder if she lies in wait with the intention of so doing when the opportunity arises.

In order to add focus and definition to the offences the Law Commission adopted a list of statutory illustrations of criminal preparation in like fashion to the Model Penal Code. However, since the avowed purpose of the exercise was to keep faith with the proximity approach to the *actus reus* the illustrations are necessarily different. So, such activities as reconnoitring or possessing/manufacturing articles to be used for a criminal purpose count neither as attempts nor as criminal preparation. More generally none of the actions listed count as criminal preparation unless performed with a view to 'there and then' committing the offence or 'as soon as an opportunity presents itself'.[26]

Back to the Drawing Board

The Law Commission proposals came under immediate challenge from commentators. These challenges fall into two main categories. The first, espoused by Jonathan Rogers, bemoaned the fact that having identified the problem – the prevention/retribution dichotomy – and having identified the method for reaching a solution – two offences rather than one – the solution identified – make the present law criminalise who it was intended to criminalise – was the wrong solution.[27] This confounds the very purpose of particularising the two inchoate offences. The new offence is surely not needed for the purpose of condemning what the accused has done, which quite properly requires an immediate and close connection with the substantive offence. Rather it is geared towards the need to incapacitate the accused before he executes his plan. The solution then must be geared towards ridding the law of its narrow retributive focus by including an offence designed with prevention in mind. By exploiting the subjectivist and objectivist approach as proxies, one offence should address the wrongdoing inherent in trying to commit a criminal offence. The other offence, by contrast, should address the quite separate wrongdoing of endangerment, inherent in taking steps sufficient to manifest a commitment to the offence. So activities such as disabling an alarm for the purpose of committing burglary later that day or arriving early at a health spa for a swim prior to executing the plan to commit robbery therein, which fall foul of the 'then and there' requirement, should fall within the catchment of the offence.

The second challenge, mounted by Clarkson, agrees that the two-offence approach is the wrong solution but this time because the second offence is superfluous and is proposed simply to ensure a properly operational test of proximity. Even on the Commission's own analysis, there is only one wrong addressed, namely that an actor with the moral culpability of trying to commit an offence has embarked on a course of action that has brought him or her sufficiently near to the commission of the offence as to present a 'vivid danger of intentional harm'.[28] If only one wrong is being addressed, only one crime label is necessary. What is driving the proposal is the pragmatic concern that the law is being construed too narrowly with the result that defendants like those in *Geddes*

---

26   Ibid. 12.39.

27   Jonathan Rogers, 'The Codification of Attempts and the Case for "Preparation"' [2008] 12 Criminal Law Review 937-54.

28   CMV Clarkson, 'Attempt: The Conduct Requirement' (2009) 29(1) Oxford Journal of Legal Studies 25, 36.

are escaping liability. This could easily be achieved by a reformulation of the definition of attempt, with a list of statutory illustrations as guidance, to ensure that such defendants are caught by the offence which would better advance the communicative moral clarity of the scheme of liability and prevent unwanted judicial sabotage.[29]

In this criticism, of course, Clarkson is at one with Rogers. Both deplore the legislative sledgehammer used to crack a pretty small penological nut. The difference between them is that Rogers has more radical ambitions for a scheme of liability for preparatory offences which *would* justify the creation of this separate offence. However, neither of these critics adequately resolve the retribution/prevention dichotomy which the Law Commission identified, yet failed, to solve. Clarkson outlines how to solve the problem of pinning down the *actus reus* of attempt, which solution involves an improved definition and a list of statutory illustrations as guidance. Disappointingly, however, his solution to the wider preventive question is to strike a careful balance between the preventive and retributive rationales, that is, 'between the competing interests of individual freedom and the countervailing interests of society'. Unfortunately, balancing exercises of this character have proved either ineffective or ethically controversial in addressing conduct which has not yet crystallised in executory criminal action but is sufficiently advanced to present a substantial threat to the personal dominion of individuals and their community. Rogers, by contrast, advocates a redefinition of criminal attempts which might be effective in this regard but which fails to address the central problem in the subjectivist approach to criminalisation, namely that a general offence of preparing to commit a crime is liable to over criminalise. While we may approve an offence which criminalises a stalker committed to raping his victim if the opportunity arises would we be similarly disposed if the intended offence was handbag robbery, a minor assault, sexual or otherwise?

A third challenge predates the Law Commission Consultation paper and report but is addressed here because it was considered seriously by the Law Commission and will inform later discussion of the way forward. The challenge is that the law of criminal attempts is not fit for purpose and should be abandoned. Peter Glazebrook, for example, has long complained that an impromptu preventive device to address the problem of duelling by criminalising acts of preparation has transmuted into a general offence of attempt, with none of its specific applications subjected to the appropriate legislative scrutiny. Given this opportunistic, coercive, pedigree liability for attempts is undesirable, lacking sufficient conceptual precision to sustain moral authority[30] since no one formula is capable of distinguishing between preparation and perpetration for the full range of attemptable crimes. Moreover, even if it could, it would leave untouched the problem of sucking into the criminal justice system those whose actions are worthy of condemnation and discouragement, perhaps, but not state punishment.

On this view the prevention/retribution dichotomy is better resolved using existing features of the criminal process. Individuals and the police can already intervene to prevent an offence being committed irrespective of whether the attempt has been launched, and indeed at a much earlier stage than addressing an attempt would allow.[31] The retributive aspect of the present law

---

29   In the Report the Law Commission (n 25) 8.60 concedes that the present law of attempts does everything the proposed two offences do and for the reason that Clarkson gives but, strangely, proposes no substantive changes to the present test for proximity.

30   See generally Peter Glazebrook, 'Should We Have a Law of Attempted Crime?' (1969) 85 Law Quarterly Review 28.

31   Citizens may be arrested on reasonable suspicion that a criminal offence is imminent as a means of preventing its occurrence. s 24(1)(c) PACE 1984; individuals and police officers may use reasonable force in defence of self or property or to prevent the commission of an offence. s 3(1) CLA 1967, s 76 CJIA 2008; penalty notices for disorder.

of criminal attempts, on the other hand, should involve individuated penal laws, filtered via the usual legislative scrutiny, taking into account the gravity of the harm threatened, the culpability of the actor, the availability of other mechanisms of control and all the other limiting principles governing criminalisation. In short, if what A has been arrested for is worthy of criminalisation in its own terms then this should be a legislative outcome. If it is not the state has no business with what A has done. Indeed, a number of legislative initiatives of recent vintage suggest that the law of criminal attempts may become of marginal future relevance in addressing the problems posed by preparing for crime.[32]

The broad question as to whether these arguments suffice to support the wholesale abolition of criminal attempts is still to be answered. The merits of Glazebrook's proposal are that it seeks to limit the reach of inchoate crime, rescue from the law of criminal attempts that which is properly criminalised but not as an attempt, and remove the inherent instability of a scheme of liability that is not informed by a universally agreed rationale. Beyond this, however, there remains an important function which only the label of a criminal attempt can discharge, namely to communicate precisely the moral disapproval which certain forms of unconsummated crime engenders. Attempting to commit a crime is a form of moral wrongdoing. If it is a wrong to rape someone it must also be a wrong to attempt to rape someone, and for the same reason. If it is a wrong to kill someone it must also be a wrong to attempt to kill someone, and for the same reason. This judgement needs to be communicated with exactly the same vigour as that of the substantive offence both in terms of the offence label and the punishment it involves. However inexact present doctrine is; however over inclusive the present scope of liability for attempted crime is, it is unavoidable, if criminal justice is about communicating moral disapproval of wrongdoing, that there is room for criminalising attempts in contradistinction to mere criminal preparation.[33]

Reconciling the Criminal Law's Retributive and Preventive Functions

Despite the numerous attempts made to square the circle we seem to be no nearer a solution to the problem of how to ensure a scheme of liability for preparatory crime which is both effective and yet true to the ethical principles underlying the criminal law. The major questions which must be addressed in this regard are, first, how to ensure the scope of liability is limited to those substantive offences the attempt of which is worthy of criminalisation on grounds of the social condemnation attracted, utility and so on. The second question is the inevitably thorny one of definition. How do we ensure that the criminal label fits the basis upon which we wish to express disapproval through punishment? These questions will be covered below. At this stage it is necessary to herald what will be the overriding theme for resolving the prevention/retribution dichotomy. This is that the law of criminal attempts should not attempt to strike a balance between the communication of wrongdoing and the prevention of harm. If communication is to be effective and just it must

---

32   The Fraud Act 2007 largely dispenses with the need to rely on the notion of an attempt to commit fraud by encompassing what once were attempts in the substantive offence. The Bribery Act 2009 follows a similar template with a conduct element of offering, promising or giving a financial or other advantage with intent to induce or reward improper conduct. More broadly a number of preparatory offences are created under the Sexual Offences Act 2003 (including luring, grooming and lying in wait) and the Terrorism Act 2006 which afford law enforcement agencies both the opportunity and incentive to intervene before harm occurs or is threatened.

33   See generally Antony Duff, 'Whose Luck Is It Anyway?' in CMV Clarkson and S Cunningham (eds), *Criminal Liability for Non-Aggressive Death* (Ashgate 2008) 61.

identify what it is about the attempter's conduct which we find so deplorable. Concentrating on the preventive side of the attempt function compromises that purpose. On the other hand, the law's preventive ambitions should not be compromised by retributive ethics. This requires consideration to be given to the overall scheme of liability and enforcement.

Attempts: Questions of Definition and Scope

One of the problems with which the Law Commission wrestled was the judicial tendency to use an 'ordinary language' approach to the constitution of a criminal attempt. This tendency looks for an event, a 'trying' to commit the offence, rather than seeking a practical template which satisfies the 'common sense intuition' that the actor is in the process of executing his criminal plan.[34] Attempting to do something, as A.R. White has described, is performed by doing something else. So we attempt to catch a fish by baiting a hook and throwing it in the water. We do not make an attempt simply by baiting the hook. Similarly, one attempts murder by aiming and pulling the trigger of a loaded gun, not by loading it. One attempts rape or burglary, both, by seeking to effect penetration, not by pushing one's victim to the ground or examining a lock, as the case may be. This ordinary language approach, to the constitution of criminal attempts is, in the view of this writer, inevitable if the criminal label is to be effective as a form of moral communication. Only in respect of completed attempts are there, uncontroversial grounds for making a direct moral connection between what the accused has done and the consummated offence.[35] That ground is that if condemnation is warranted for commission of the substantive offence then it is also equally warranted for trying to commit that offence. The wrong which demands addressing is that the actor has tried to do what he is forbidden to do. It is worth remembering, in this context, that if we are to have a general law of criminal attempts, *applicable to all indictable crimes*, it is of central importance to maintain this kind of conceptual link between the substantive offence and the attempt. Only if the 'attempt' is as reprehensible as the substantive offence in terms of both its conduct and culpability is there any ground for treating the two as equally deserving of censure and punishment.

Where the defendant has not done all the acts necessary on his part to bring about that offence the moral connection between the two is obviously less clear since, not only has he time to repent, but until that point is reached, he has, in effect tried nothing.[36] In the United States the problem of repentance is addressed by having a defence of voluntary withdrawal. A cognate defence of voluntary withdrawal is an important antidote to a test for attempts drawn so widely.[37] Indeed, it confirms the incoherence of a test for attempts in which the time frame within which liability can be founded is so stretched that a person can have attempted to commit a crime and yet have the excuse of not having gone too far as to change his mind. In domestic law, which demands proximity, this is not needed. An actor's change of mind, say in desisting from killing or robbing a bank, is used to indicate that the attempt had not yet been launched and that the necessary commitment to

---

34   *Moore v DPP* [2010] EWHC 1822 (Admin); [2010] All ER (D) 195 and see (n 41).

35   So, some argue that liability for attempts should be limited to completed attempts. See Larry Alexander, 'Duff on Attempts' (San Diego Legal Studies Research Paper Series, Research Paper No. 11-069 September 2011).

36   'When successful the attempt to do so and so becomes the doing of so and so; the turning of the handle and pushing is opening the door ... So the orders "Try to do this" and "Do this" are obeyed in the same way' (Alan White, *Misleading Cases* (Oxford Clarendon Press 1991) 15). Cf. Larry Alexander (n 35) generally.

37   And so it is recognised by the MPC s 5.01(4).

go through with the offence was never formed, reflected by the ease with which the project was ultimately abandoned.[38]

The question, then, is whether to attempt to commit an offence means to perform the last act necessary to effect it. Must the actor have 'tried' to commit the offence or is it enough that he was 'trying' to do so? The difference is crucial. If the former constitutes the *actus reus* then only completed attempts will pass the threshold for liability. If the latter is enough then the time frame is extended to include cases, the majority one would hazard, where the method adopted to achieve one's aim involves further acts, perhaps a number of directly and immediately connected acts as in *Tosti*,[39] or *Jones*, or the steps to be taken are cumulative, as in *White*,[40] rather than simply a necessary precursor to that 'doing' as in *Campbell*.[41]

The definition arrived at in the Consultation Paper centres the *actus reus* in the last 'acts' rather than 'act' to capture this idea of 'trying'. A tidied up approximation of the test, which was not fully defined, might look like this: A must have performed 'an act which was immediately and not merely remotely connected with its commission and which was one of the last acts needed to commit the intended offence'. Although a lot more focused than the more than merely preparatory formula, this itself falls short of encompassing with precision what the 'on the job' or 'trying to commit the offence' tests do with imprecision. For example, it lacks a form of words capable of criminalising Mr White who had many more acts of the same nature to perform and the safe breaker who is on the job but may need to commit any number of different acts before he is in a position to execute the offence. Compare the following more analytically sound, though inevitably imprecise, formulation of this 'on the job' test to be found in *Moore v DPP* where the *actus reus* is described as follows:

> For conduct by an individual to constitute an attempt to commit an offence under the Criminal Attempts Act 1981, and not an act that was merely preparatory to the commission of an offence, the conduct by the individual had to be sufficiently close to the final act that it could, on the application of common sense, be properly regarded as part of the execution of the individual's plan to commit the intended offence.[42]

---

38   George Fletcher (n 11) at 188; Donald Stuart, 'The *Actus Reus* in Attempts' [1970] Criminal Law Review 519-41; cf. Antony Duff, *Criminal Attempts* (Oxford 1996) 65-75.

39   *R v Tosti and another* [1997] Crim LR 746.

40   [1910] 2 KB 124, 127, W's method of killing his mother was to place small amounts of poison into her daily drinks. Bray J for the Court of Criminal Appeal stated: 'Here seems no doubt that the learned judge in effect did tell the jury that this was a case of slow poisoning the appellant would be guilty of the attempt to murder. We are of opinion that this direction was right, and that the completion or attempted completion of one of a series of acts intended by a man to result in killing is an attempt to murder even although this completed act would not, unless followed by the other acts, result in killing. It might be the beginning of the attempt, but would none the less be an attempt'.

41   The appellant who planned to rob a post office was apprehended by police within a yard of the post office carrying an imitation gun and a written demand for cash intended for the cashier. In a classic example of the retribution/prevention dichotomy Watkins LJ, allowing C's appeal against conviction, insisted that 'a number of acts remained undone' and that, at least until the post office was entered, his acts were merely preparatory.

42   *Moore v DPP* [2010] EWHC 1822 (Admin); [2010] All ER (D) 195.

A possible working definition which addresses the problems of scope of the Consultation Paper's proposal and the imprecision of the latter might be as follows: To constitute an attempt A must have done an act:

> which was directly connected with its commission and which was the last act the actor contemplated as necessary to commit the intended offence, , or was a more remote act which, without being an act of mere preparation, formed part of a sequence of connected acts designed for the execution of the offence.

To ensure some clarity and consistency of application this would be supported by a list of statutory illustrations.

Substantive Offences

This definition places the conduct element in criminal attempts firmly in the camp of the objectivists. I have explained why this is necessary and desirable, namely to uphold the communicative nature of criminal convictions, and to rid the law of the kind of functional instability which indeterminate definitions produce. This leaves unaddressed cases where criminalisation may still be thought appropriate either because, although falling short of an attempt, the action deserves punishing on the basis of the gravity of the substantive offence and/or because the steps taken present a real danger that the offence may be committed.

Is the solution a general offence of criminal preparation similar, reaching beyond the Law Commission's proposed offence to embrace the subjectivist premises espoused by Rogers? The answer must be a qualified no. As Duff insists, punishing on the basis of merely preparatory action does not respect the autonomous person's freedom to comply with the law. The criminal law is not there 'to make us better people' but to punish us for our bad choices as reflected in individuated chosen action.[43] Attempts are different. They are criminalised as a reflection of the state's obligation to the individual and the community he inhabits to safeguard autonomy and security and to take the side of the victim against the person who has wronged him/her. For this to be possible the wrong must have crystallised. In Duff's analysis, this occurs when an attack is launched on the victim. This attack marks the basic threshold for state intervention. As will be seen, this does not leave the state without preventive options.

Further, a general preparatory offence will fall foul of the basic ethical principles governing the power relationship between individual and the state. A recent statement of limiting principles, reflecting the increased attention given to the propriety of state sponsored coercion, is provided by Husak:[44]

> (1) Since punishment expresses condemnation, only conduct worthy of condemnation should be criminalised.

---

43   Antony Duff, 'Dangerousness and Citizenship' in Andrew Ashworth and Martin Wasik (eds), *Fundamentals of Sentencing Theory* (Clarendon 1998) 141.

44   Douglas Husak, *Overcriminalisation: The Limits of the Criminal Law* (Oxford University Press 2008); Douglas Husak, 'Limitations on Criminalisation and the General Part of the Criminal Law' in Stephen Shute and Andrew Simester, *Criminal Law Theory: Doctrine of the General Part* (Oxford University Press 2002) 13.

(2) Criminal laws should not punish innocent conduct.

(3) Each criminal law must do more good than harm.

(4) Conduct should not be criminalised unless the state has a compelling interest in punishing those who engage in it. Non-criminal means must be used if this would be effective.

(5) The criminal law should be narrowly tailored to serve the state's compelling interest; criminal laws should be neither over inclusive or under inclusive.

(6) Each criminal law must be designed to prevent a non-trivial harm or evil.

On any balanced assessment, a *general* offence of criminal preparation would fall foul of every one of these restrictions.[45] Such an offence should not be adopted as a means of avoiding a rigorous analysis of what kinds of preparatory conduct needs to be criminalised and why. For this, it is necessary to redraw the map of inchoate offences so as to map more clearly the different moral connections which can be made between substantive offences and acts performed in furtherance of such offences.

Preparing for Crime: Justifying Criminalisation in Its Own Terms

In recent years a number of specific offences have been created, for example, in the case of terrorism, sexual offences[46] and fraud, which criminalise as wrongful in themselves certain templates of preparation by which the committed wrongdoer can be confidently distinguished from the fantasist. Since *Geddes* was decided the problem of whether he was attempting to falsely imprison the intended victim has been sidestepped, as it surely should have been, by making his conduct a criminal wrong in itself. The Sexual Offences Act 2003 describes that wrong as committing an offence or trespass with intent to commit a relevant offence. Similar action sequences are incorporated in forms of wrongdoing captured, albeit in some cases too broadly, by the Fraud Act 2006, for example, phishing, and the Terrorism Act 2000, for example, possession of articles for terrorist purposes.

The merits of much of this legislation have been questioned as themselves criminalising activities too remote or too innocuous to justify state sanction. However, the concept of enacting properly scrutinised and evaluated individual offences rather than a general inchoate offence is a good one and should be the agreed model for the next level down in the pyramid of preparatory actions worthy of punishment or prevention, of which attempts form the apex. The ambition should be to create out of the present disorder a functional hierarchy. That hierarchy should have, at the apex, a narrowly focused law of criminal attempts including completed attempts and all but completed attempts. Beyond criminal attempts the task is to decant the more serious activities into crimes of endangerment and crimes of ulterior intent, and through the more systematic deployment of possession offences. The prototypes for this response are the crime of assault with intent to rob, offences under the Computer Misuse Act, Terrorism Act 2000, and sections 61-63 of the

---

45   The Law Commission's proposal for an offence of preparing for crime is less objectionable because of its restricted scope.

46   ss 61-63 Sexual Offences Act 2003.

Sexual Offences Act 2003. In the attempted rape cases discussed earlier, for example, the kind of moral connection which can be made between what the actor means to achieve and what he has done is misrepresented by the use of the word attempt given the enormous gap existing between the two. The better characterisation of the wrongdoing is assault with intent to rape, as exists in other common law jurisdictions, such as in the United States and Australia.[47] This offence label communicates with precision what we find so deplorable in the actor's conduct.

Assuming agreement that the overall model for criminalisation will conform to the ethical limits on criminalisation outlined above there are two key threshold questions which must be posed and answered in any potential crime of criminal preparation falling short of an attempt. The first question is whether the wrong intended is sufficiently serious to justify criminalising acts of preparation? This must take account of course the specific substantive wrong to be addressed. In the *Geddes* type of case, this might be abduction, sexual assault, rape, the sexual assault of a child under 13. One assumes that each of these potential wrongs would pass this threshold test, although section 57 does not cover abduction, and there are no other statutory offences to cover this (or other offences against the person). But each substantive crime would need to pass this first threshold test. If criminalisation is a measure of last resort the crime intended must be so serious that the state, in opposition to the usual presumption that it should not, is permitted, if not obligated, to criminalise acts of preparation. There are no doubt grounds for criminalising appropriate conduct preparatory to sexual assault on a child, or rape, abduction or murder, but this is not to say the same threshold should be adopted for other wrongs, say assault, criminal damage or theft.[48]

If the first test is satisfied the second threshold question, mirroring the position for criminal attempts, is whether a coherent and meaningful basis for intervention has been established. The Sexual Offences Act section 63 provides two, namely committing an offence or committing trespass. The point of this intervention threshold is that it forms part of a typical action sequence, along with grooming, for those intending to commit sexual offences against children[49]. Significantly, other possible action templates in the *Geddes* type scenario are eschewed. It does not criminalise a person who chooses a public park, a deserted alleyway, or his own back garden for the commission of the offence, or if the defendant was a caretaker in the school where he lay in wait for his victim. The purpose of this observation is to clarify why this should be. On the face of it it is because such action templates would too easily criminalise the fantasist and the uncommitted. Using less morally ambiguous action templates, however, this problem could be avoided by characterising such templates as follows:

1. Has D done something wrongful in itself? The Sexual Offences Act 2003 largely adopts this threshold test to cope with the Geddes problem. I say largely because the forms of wrongdoing specified are arguably unnecessarily restrictive, leaving out of account other action sequences by which a person could prepare for sexual assault. Other forms of non-criminal wrongdoing such as causing alarm or anxiety, or breach of contract could, with some degree of ingenuity, all past muster. For example, 1. A frightens B, a house guest,

---

47 Glazebrook (n 30); Jeremy Horder, 'Crimes of Ulterior Intent' in Andrew Simester and ATH Smith (eds), *Harm and Culpability* (Oxford University Press, 1996) 153.

48 A major criticism of the fraud act is that this threshold was not crossed, leading to the conclusion that this is a crime which requires no proof of harm but simply criminalises lying. David Ormerod, 'Criminalising Lying' [2007] Criminal Law Review 19.

49 For discussion of the concept and value of action sequences as a basis for intrvention see Daniel Ohana, 'Desert and Punishment for Acts Preparatory to the Commission of a Crime' (2007) 20(1) Canadian Journal of Law and Jurisprudence 113

by dressing up as a ghost in order to encourage B to seek shelter in A's bedroom where he intends to rape her. 2. A, a hotelier, locks the door of guest B's *en suite* bathroom, in breach of contract, in order to give himself the opportunity of raping B in the public bathroom. In principle, each of these action sequences could satisfy the second threshold requirement although not constituting an offence or a trespass. The argument against extending the threshold to include other forms of wrongdoing is that the action sequence in each case is possibly too farfetched to justify criminalisation, so although the wrong aimed at is serious there would be too few instances to warrant the state's intervention.[50]

This objection does not exclude action templates which have been adopted in other offences to enable swift police intervention in advance of an intended offence. In particular:

2. Has D equipped him/herself for the purpose? For example, has D been not at his place of abode equipped with handcuffs, rope, chloroform, disguise and so on. This threshold is adopted for section 25 Theft Act 1968 and could have been used profitably to convict Mr Geddes, whether or not he had first committed trespass.[51]
3. Is D in possession of articles for the purpose? Such a threshold is adopted in the Terrorism Act 2000. Under s 57, it is an offence[52] for a person to possess an article in circumstances which give rise to a reasonable suspicion that his possession is for a purpose connected with the commission, preparation or instigation of terrorist acts.[53]

Arguably, the action template governing potential criminalisation in the *Geddes* type of case could include either of the above thresholds. The determining factor will be whether criminalisation should require the defendant to be in possession of the relevant articles otherwise than in 'his place of abode'. This in turn should depend upon the type of crime, its seriousness and form. So 'the equipped' threshold may be considered appropriate where the offence intended is less serious in terms of the harm threatened and where the items themselves are relatively innocuous as in theft, whereas the possession threshold may be appropriate where the harm threatened is severe and/ or the items less amenable to innocent explanations as in the possession of items to be used for terrorist purposes. Again, it may be considered justified to criminalise the possession of chloroform to assist sexual assault, but not the possession of a skeleton key to commit criminal damage or theft due to the relative seriousness of the respective offences.[54]

4. Has D done something which, given the crime charged, manifests a settled intention to commit the offence and is not amenable to an objectively innocent explanation? An offence which instantiates this kind of threshold is child grooming under the Sexual Offences Act 2003, whose action template is easily extendable to other wrongs.[55] Other action sequences meet for adoption in relation to substantive offences which pass the first threshold of gravity,

---

50   Cf. above item 6 on Husak's list (n 44) of limits on criminalisation.
51   Which does require the actor to be away from his place of abode for a relevant purpose.
52   It is a defence to prove that the possession was not for such a purpose.
53   Which does not require the actor to be away from his place of abode for a relevant purpose.
54   I deliberately include theft here due to the relative weakness of the justificatory arguments in favour of section 25.
55   Section 15.

such as rape or murder, and might include damaging one's own property[56], having a false computer identity, or arranging to meet an intended victim at an isolated place, or at a time when a building is empty of people, and/or exacting a promise to keep the arrangement secret. Many of the activities characterising failed prosecutions for criminal attempts, such as Robinson,[57] Comer and Bloomfield,[58] Gullefer,[59] Campbell,[60] or misguided convictions such as Dagnall[61] either have been or could be effectively addressed by such mechanisms.

If criminalisation cannot be justified on the basis of gravity of offence and/or having breached a threshold of intervention, A's criminal preparation may be dealt with by means of regulatory offences, such as crimes of possession , where the function of the offence changes from retribution to prevention. Penalties may accrue for non compliance so long as the actor could have avoided offending by exercising due diligence.[62] In theory, belonging to the harm prevention paradigm, they should not involve stigmatic penalties unless an ulterior intent is present or they are inherently dangerous and admit of no innocent explanation, such as being in possession of an explosive or radioactive substance[63] in which case they belong in the upper part of the pyramidic scheme of liability.

This leaves, however, a large range of preparatory actions which bespeak conduct which, without constituting a present and vivid threat to security and dominion nevertheless is of a nature to justify state intervention for the purpose of preventing the materialisation of the threat. The range is neatly encapsulated in the list of illustrations provided in the Model Penal Code[64] which, it will be remembered, presented these instances, which include lying in wait, possession of articles and reconnoitring, as potentially a criminal attempt, if strongly corroborative of the actor's criminal purpose. By contrast with Glanville Williams who advocated a similar position in English Law,[65] Glazebrook's solution, assuming the absence of manifest and serious wrongdoing sufficient to justify retributive condemnation, is that it should be addressed by the usual preventive mechanisms of the criminal process,[66] Citizens may be arrested on reasonable suspicion that a criminal offence is imminent as a means of preventing its occurrence,[67] and individuals and police officers may use reasonable force in defence of self or property or to prevent the commission of an offence.[68] Although the actor will often have begun to embark upon the substantive offence when such intervention

---

56 As where a hotelier, breaks the lock on the door of guest B's *en suite* bathroom, in order to give himself the opportunity of raping B in the public bathroom

57 *Robinson* [1915] 2 KB 423 CCA. R staged a break in at his jeweller's shop intending to commit fraud against his insurance company. Held not sufficiently proximate to be an attempted fraud.

58 *Comer v Bloomfield* (1970) 55 Cr App R 305. D contacted his insurance company to ascertain whether he could claim for the theft of his van although his van had not in fact been stolen. Held not sufficiently proximate to be an attempted fraud.

59 *R v Gullefer* [1990] 3 All ER 882. G jumped on a race track in an attempt to have the race called off so that he would not lose on the bet he had wagered. Held not sufficiently proximate to be an attempted theft of the wager.

60 *R v Campbell* (1991) 93 Cr App R 350.

61 [2003] All ER (D) 86.

62 This is a key feature supporting the legitimacy of regulatory crime.

63 Such offences would, however, require a defence of lawful excuse.

64 MPC s 5.01(2). See above (n 37).

65 See generally Glanville Williams, 'Wrong Turnings on the Law of Criminal Attempts' [1971] Criminal Law Review 416.

66 Glazebrook (n 30).

67 s 24(1)(c) PACE 1984.

68 s 3(1) CLA 1967, s 76 CJIA 2008.

takes place the legality of the intervention does not depend upon that point having been reached. However, the key point about the powers of arrest afforded by these enactments is that they afford the opportunity not merely of preventing the harm threatened there and then but also of protecting at risk communities from similar activities in the future if combined with the criminal justice system's other coercive techniques. This prospect provides a potentially promising means of addressing preparatory conduct of insufficient gravity or proximity to justify criminalisation.

Other Coercive Techniques

A central element in the analysis which has taken place over the ethical boundaries governing criminalisation ever since J.S. Mill is the recognition that the mechanisms of social control we have at our disposal are not limited to criminal law.[69] A widespread view is that moral censure and education act as a line of first resort; the civil law a midway point when harm has occurred or threatened but not so grave a harm or threat for the State to take ownership, and the criminal law the technique of last resort, reflecting the state's role of taking the side of the injured party in expressing disapprobation for the disrespect show to him.[70]

In this regard, the recent proliferation of Civil Prevention Orders seems to mark a shift towards a form of social control which is irreducible to the two-paradigm approach discussed earlier, as it has control and compliance as its justification rather than punishment or penalty. Of increasing interest in this respect is the idea that coercive responses to different forms of misconduct should form a 'regulatory pyramid' in which civil and criminal law combine to effect a functional hierarchy in which, at the base of the pyramid, interventions take the form of communication and persuasion and rely on the cooperation and active involvement of the parties. Only if this intervention fails will the need for movement up the pyramid arise to more coercive forms of intervention.[71] Such a model signals a different attitude towards wrongful behaviour in its various forms, namely to manage it, and the situations out of which it arises, rather than concentrating on responding to individual acts of wrongdoing. The significant feature characterising these orders is that there is no need to show the actor was on the point of committing an offence to entitle coercive intervention. They aim rather to address acts which signal an indifference to the autonomy and dominion of the victims. Non-molestation orders show this at their most uncontroversial, constituting the base of a clear ladder of coercive response with individuated sets of rules designed to protect the victim while communicating how an individual must behave in order to show respect to, and help rebuild a loss of autonomy/security/dominion in, another.

There are particular reasons why, in the context of preparing for crime, at least, the traditional divisions between informal (morality/education) and formal (law), criminal and civil mechanisms of social control, should not apply. First, the inherent difficulty of rendering determinate, in a form appropriate for retributive punishment, what can and cannot be done by way of preparing to commit crime is a reason in itself to place outside the direct range of the criminal sanction conduct which

---

69   JS Mill, 'On Liberty' in John Gray (ed.), *On Liberty and Other Essays* (Oxford University Press, 1991).

70   '... punishment is a conventional device for the expression of attitudes of resentment and indignation, and of judgments of disapproval and reprobation, on the part either of the punishing authority himself or of those "in whose name" the punishment is inflicted. Punishment, in short, has a symbolic significance largely missing from other kinds of penalties' (Joel Feinberg, 'The Expressive Function of Punishment' reprinted in *Doing and Deserving* (Princeton University Press 1970) 98).

71   John Braithwaite, *Restorative Justice and Responsive Regulation* (Oxford University Press 2002). For critique see Adam Crawford (n 1).

is at the margins of criminality. The avowed philosophy of civil and hybrid orders is to pre-empt the possibility of criminal sanction for conduct which lies in the grey area between innocuous and wrongful activity. As A.T.H. Smith explains in another context: 'The criminal law is the system of rules by which he must live under pain of opprobrium and penalty should he fail to conform to its dictates. It follows as a matter of principle that he should be able to know in advance precisely what it enjoins him to do or abstain from doing. As an American court pithily put it, "the right to test a statute by submitting to arrest is not a remedy." Where a citizen wishes to know the limits of the permissible, some mechanism ought to be available to enable him to ascertain them'.[72] The Judicial Studies Board guidance on ASBOs, the most controversial of these orders since it is a hybrid order permitting criminal punishment for breach, make this communicative requirement central to its functioning and legitimacy.[73] Like a declaratory judgment the ASBO will not only communicate what A must not do but also the underlying system of values which underpins this – it should embody moral guidance rather than simply an order not to cause harm. Significantly, although he would doubtless deprecate the idea, this bears comparison with the view advanced by Duff that in the ideal criminal code, rather than representing a prohibition imposed by the state, the law becomes a declaration regarding the wrongfulness of a particular action, which wrongfulness 'properly concern[s] the whole community and … must be recognised and condemned as such by the community'.[74]

The second reason why some pre-criminal response is justified for criminal preparation is that this also addresses Duff's argument, considered earlier, that punishing on the basis of action which lacks the required degree of proximity to the substantive offence does not respect the autonomous person's freedom to choose to comply with the law. Until the defendant gets to the point of committing the offence proper the state has no business coercing him/her.[75] This may be so, but this essentially moral objection lacks practical usefulness given the enormous potential for harm posed by preparatory crime and the availability of non-stigmatic forms of authoritative communication. Daniel Ohana has made the interesting suggestion that civil prevention or hybrid orders such as the ASBO are, in principle, actually consistent with the constructive dialogue which Duff recommends as the alternative to a punitive response to acts preparatory to crime. He argues that statutorily defined acts of preparation such as luring, stalking, acquiring tools or information with the intent to commit a designated crime could be the trigger for such an order.[76] Analysed in this way, ASBOs and similar orders are the pre-criminalisation counterpart of probation and supervision orders. With the latter the message is, 'You've done something wrong, we're going to help you keep out of trouble' with the CPO it is, 'You've nearly done something wrong, we're going to help you keep out of trouble'. Whatever one's view as to the CPOs worth and legitimacy in targeting anti-social behaviour generally there is a strong argument that some such order is the best solution to the problem posed by imperfect attempts. If a person has not done anything objectively wrongful it is wrong to punish him as though he or she had. CPOs enable us to avoid this injustice. They offer a mechanism for protecting communities by preventing crime without imposing undeserved

72   ATH Smith, 'Clarifying the Criminal Law: Declarations in Criminal Proceedings' in P Smith (ed.), *Criminal Law: Essays in Honour of J.C. Smith* (Butterworths 1987) 132, 138.

73   'Each separate prohibition must be targeted at the individual and the specific form of anti-social behaviour it is intended to prevent. The order must be tailored to the defendant and not designed on a word processor for generic use' (Judicial Studies Board Guidance).

74   Antony Duff, *Punishment, Communication and Community* (Oxford University Press 2003) chapters 2-3. See also Antony Duff, 'Rule Violations and Wrongdoings' in Shute and Simester (n 44) 56.

75   Duff (n 38) 387.

76   Daniel Ohana, 'Responding to Acts Preparatory to the Commission of a Crime: Criminalization or Prevention?' (2006) 25(2) Criminal Justice Ethics 23.

punishment, while respecting the principle of minimal criminalisation which extensions to the range of preparatory offences would offend.[77]

The Legality Challenge

The challenge, of course, is that the state does this, not for such reasons of principle, but for the unprincipled convenience of it. As Crawford argues, in the context of the ASBO:

> Government interpretation of the 'regulatory pyramid' departs appreciably from that advanced by regulation scholars. Its idea of an incremental tiered approach conforms more closely to a ladder (or escalator!), where each subsequent intervention is more serious than the first. Each step may be missed out whilst going up, but movement is always upwards.[78]

In this respect the ASBO's major structural weakness is that, although nominally a civil order, its breach results in criminal penalty, not, as in the case of contempt of court, for defiance of the authority of the court but for the wrongfulness of the action which the order prohibits. This enables criminal penalties to attach to conduct which is not inherently criminal and although the rules of evidence and procedure characterising criminal trials are not complied with. Given that they are used most profitably in areas of urban deprivation to tackle various levels of disorder and bad behaviour in the youth,[79] the charge is that this process facilitates the targeting for coercion of the disempowered in order to secure the security and autonomy of the majority, but at the price of compromising the human rights of the former. In essence they appear to be the modern equivalent of the vagrancy laws, made only slightly more palatable by the two-stage process.

Although a cogent criticism, it does not, however, stack up as a compelling argument against prevention orders *per se*. Rather, it presents an important admonition against their potential misuse as a means of bypassing the usual procedural safeguards against unjust conviction. The development of regulatory crime underwent similar problems of legitimacy with stigmatic criminal liability sometimes not attended by a requirement of fault, as has already been described. As has also been noted, its recent development has brought with it a general, if regrettably still too often ignored, recognition of the need to marry form and substance to secure the individual's right to fair treatment.[80] Already proposals are finding favour that this structural weakness in ASBOs is best addressed by making them a purely civil order.[81] Max Weber characterised this transitional dynamic as one involving formal justice inevitably having to play catch up in the context of rapid

---

77   See generally Peter Ramsay, 'Why Is It Wrong to Breach an ASBO?' LSE Law, Society and Economy Working Paper Series (WPS 20-2009); Peter Ramsay, *The Insecurity State: Vulnerable Autonomy and the Right to Security in the Criminal Law* (Oxford University Press 2012); under this third criminal justice paradigm criminal responsibility and methods of coercion derive not specifically from the wrongful decision to attack the interests of another but more generally from a breach of the principles which sustain the relevant host community for which the state acts as ultimate guarantor.

78   Crawford (n 1).

79   Andrew Ashworth, John Gardner, R. Morgan, ATH Smith, A von Hirsch and M Wasik, 'Neighbouring on the Oppressive: The Government's "Anti-Social Behaviour Order" Proposals' (1998) 16(1) Criminal Justice 7.

80   A presumption of *mens rea* applies in cases of stigmatic crime. See for example *B (a minor) v DPP* [2000] 1 All ER 833; *M and B* [2009] EWCA Crim 2615.

81   Simon Hoffman and Stuart Macdonald, 'Should ASBOs Be Civilised?' (2010) 6 Criminal Law Review 457.

substantive reform. Philip Selznick, more recently, has used Weber's insights to describe the dynamics behind changes in the legal form in a way which offers a more positive vision of the context underpinning the development of such orders:

> The concept of legality does not settle the rules of pleading evidence, or judicial discretion. Legality is a master ideal, not a specific set of injunctions. This ideal is to be realised in history not outside of it and history makes its demands, offers its own opportunities … In this perspective the achievement of legality is seen as the refinement of basic principles, their application in depth, and their extension to new social settings. As this evolution takes place however, *the line between the legal and the political is blurred.*[82]

In an analysis which anticipates the kind of legal challenges which arise when legality lags behind following substantive change, Selznick describes how changes in social and economic organisation make the switch from coercive to restitutive and other methods of social control first desirable and then inevitable. One of the key features in that change is that of the community replacing the state as the locus of power and the different control responses this necessitates.[83] What is this 'community', however? It clearly cannot be simply be synonymous with the ahistorical and decontextualised notion of society often used by criminal theorists to skate over the problem of who 'owns' moral or criminal wrongs.[84] The more analytically focused notion of 'community' is rather more complex. It refers to individuated social networks, based on such variables as geography, ethnicity, occupation, and shared interests as in social networking sites, which interact and interpenetrate and whose organising ethic of social solidarity is one of interpersonal cooperation and trust rather than shared values underpinned by a common world view. For Selznick, all communities of this nature,[85] – he limits his discussion to families, universities, businesses and corporations but clearly extends far wider,- have governance at their heart and have accordingly developed methods of governance which head off and manage potential sources of conflict as a means of maintaining the integrity of the institution or community.[86]

Managerialism as a response to conflict and disorder is often disparaged as a process. It is typically treated as a purely technical phenomenon in which institutional goals are prosecuted through forward planning and setting targets rather than in a reactive pragmatic fashion. At worst, the achievement of the target takes priority over the substance of the goal. However, underpinning such strategies is typically a moral ideal. In the present context, reflected in ideologies of human rights, autonomy, dominion and welfare, this ideal represents a retreat from punitiveness. In the

---

82   P Selznick, *Law Society and Industrial Justice* (Holt Saunders 1980) 28.

83   As Duff acknowledges: 'The "community" figures as the victim of crime: we must build safer communities and protect them against criminal depredations. It figures as an agent of crime prevention: it should be involved in "situational crime prevention" and help to police itself. It figures as a locus of punishment: more punishments should be administered "in the community". It figures as the beneficiary of punishment; and "punishments in the community", such as Community Service Orders, enable offenders to make reparation to the community. It figures, less frequently, as the offender's proper place: even if rehabilitation is no longer a central penal purpose, one supposed benefit of "punishment in the community" is that it allows offenders to retain their place in the community – a place that imprisonment threatens to destroy' (Antony Duff, *Punishment, Communication and Community* (Oxford University Press 2003) 39, 40).

84   See for example Grant Lamond, 'What Is a Crime' (2007) 27 Oxford Journal of Legal Studies 609, who uses the terms 'the public', 'society', 'the state' and 'the community' interchangeably.

85   Selznick (n 80) calls these 'associations' to delineate their separate powers and sources of governance.

86   Selznick (n 80) 28-29.

workplace techniques such as the giving of informal and formal warnings which once developed in an ad hoc and informal fashion to manage conflict arising out of disciplinary matters and which might once have resulted in summary dismissal, are now mandatory. Schools have likewise become typically less punitive, despite increasingly disorderly behaviour. It is acknowledged that one cannot simply pile punishment upon punishment as a mechanism for responding to challenges of authority. Not only is this ineffective but, unless the standards upon which it is based is internalised, it compromises the very legitimacy of the authority it is designed to uphold. Schools have therefore sought to manage disorder, disruption and lack of attentiveness, rather than punish it. A common technique, well known to parents, is putting pupils on report by which they are given certain targets and a mechanism is set up to monitor the achievement of those targets. Other mechanisms of managing potential sources of disorder and conflict include parent–school–student contracts. Many families attempt to achieve similar results by house rules and restricting access to sources of conflict and disorder. And crucially for our purposes, those methods of governance which begin informally, may be later adopted and formalised in positive law, when its principles become integrated into political culture through the interpenetration of community and state. The hybrid order, as instantiated in the ASBO, on this view, may be far from a simply historically contingent and unprincipled item of state coercion, rather a reflection of underlying moral ideals in the pursuit of maintaining social order in the context of rapid social change.

Developing Due Process

Let us assume then that the present historical contingency is one in which legal evolution is taking place to address a new power relation, namely that existing between the individual and the various interpenetrating communities by which social life in the modern world is constituted. On this assumption the state acts as guarantor for such communities when faced with activities, such as preparation for crime, which threaten community dominion, and that for this reason the civil law takes on, in the first instance, the task of managing social relations[87]. Let us assume also that the line between the political and the legal is blurred because of the absence of clarification as to how to ensure that the message immanent in the civil order is communicated, heeded and enforced, with justice. The task is, then, to effect this clarification to ensure that the individual is protected from the arbitrary exercise both of state power and community power; to ensure that at the base of the framework by which communities and individuals are protected against the self interested actions of other individuals is a system for communicating the principles surrounding membership of a community.[88]

At the root of the dissatisfaction with the hybrid order is its capacity to draw a person into the criminal justice system without the protection of the rules of criminal procedure and evidence.[89] This dissatisfaction presupposes, rightly or wrongly, a clear distinction between civil and criminal wrongs such that distinctive legal processes and distinctive legal responses characterise and, moreover, should characterise the two kinds of wrongs.[90] In fact, it is passing strange that in the early years of the twenty-first century, after a period of unprecedented social and economic change, the old ideas about

---

87   See generally Peter Ramsay, *The Insecurity State: Vulnerable Autonomy and the Right to Security in the Criminal Law* (Oxford University Press 2012)

88   Cruft (n 1).

89   See discussion (n 80).

90   See for example, Carol Steiker, 'Punishment and Procedure: Punishment Theory and the Criminal-Civil Procedural Divide (1997) 85 Georgetown Law Journal 775, 780; John M Coffee, 'Paradigms Lost: The Blurring of the Criminal and Civil Law Models – And What Can Be Done About It' (1992) 101 Yale Law

the criminal law/civil law divide still constitute the lens through which methods of social control are typically evaluated.[91] The critics of these orders have tended to ignore or underestimate the degree of fluidity and overlap between the civil and the criminal law. As is well known, civil courts, operating within the civil standards of proof and process, have long had the power to award punitive damages, aiming at deterring the defendant rather than compensating the victim. Civil injunctions and court orders are underpinned by the authority of the criminal sanction for contempt of court. Bankruptcy is a civil order with a penal effect. The power of magistrates to bind over a defendant to be of good behaviour or to keep the peace does not require proof of criminal wrongdoing. It is a civil order geared at preventing a potential threat of harm. It is not a conviction or a punishment. But it is supported by the criminal sanction. Such phenomena have led other commentators to conclude that the civil and the criminal aspects of social control are better analysed not as separate with their distinctive rules and procedures but as being on a continuum in which ever more stigmatic, condemnatory sanctions attach[92] and rules of procedure and evidence may vary accordingly. On this view these rules and procedures are, and should be, tailored towards the function of the norm – to punish – to compensate – to prevent – to protect – to declare – to instruct, as the case may be. Due process is everywhere essential but what satisfies the ethical demands of due process is contingent. The demands of due process are generally more rigorous in the criminal trial than the civil trial for obvious reasons. The criminal law is a communicative endeavour, communicating society's disapproval of culpable wrongdoing through conviction and punishment. Due process is integral to that communication. It only carries moral authority where the process which delivers it is transparent and fair. In other settings, particularly if the potential effect of the trial outcome on the defendant is more tolerable, and the purpose has a protective, educative or preventive aspect, a greater risk of acting unfairly may be taken . Likewise if the relative power of one of the parties is disproportional there are grounds for redressing that balance by changes in the rules of evidence and procedure if such rules may sustain that inequality. This is so even in the criminal trial, particularly if one of the parties is a corporation or agency of the State. The rule of law is not about due process as a purely abstract concept, it is also about ensuring through the rules and procedures of law, that power is not abused and that litigants are treated equally.[93]

A Model of Due Process

An example from employment law reflects this type of concern where form is wedded to function and power differentials apply. Here, the fairness or otherwise of dismissal for disciplinary

---

Journal 1875, 1876; Paul H Robinson and John M Darley, 'The Utility of Desert' (1997) 91 Northwestern University Law Review 453, 471.

91   Selznick (n 80) 32.

92   See for example Issachar Rosen-Zvi and Talia Fisher, 'Overcoming Procedural Boundaries' (2008) 94(3) Virginia Law Review 79. It is of passing interest that Glanville Williams in chapter 2 of the second edition of his Textbook of Criminal Law makes no bones about the existence of such a continuum and nowhere deplores the system for being unprincipled

93   '[T]he fulfilment of the promise of the rule of law requires not only the universal protection of law rights of all citizens to participate as members of the polity as a whole but also the specific protection of degrees of autonomy of groupings of citizens in partially regulating communities of many kinds. The possibility of citizens to take more control of their lives can be enhanced though conditions of self regulation, but only in so far as law ensures possibilities for all members to participate as full members of the communities to which they belong' (Roger Cotterrell, 'The Rule of Law in Transition: Revisiting Franz Neumann's Sociology of Legality' (1996) 5 Social and Legal Studies 451, 464).

reasons depends upon the employer following an agreed process which each organisation is expected to consult upon, draw up and publicise.[94] There is no sense in which these procedures act as an escalator to dismissal and indeed are intended to serve the contrary purpose. They are designed to maximise the possibility of the employer and employee settling their differences. Article 20 of the ACAS code advises that a first or final written warning should set out the nature of the misconduct or poor performance and the change in behaviour or improvement in performance required (with timescale). The employee should be told how long the warning will remain current. The employee should be informed of the consequences of further misconduct, or failure to improve performance, within the set period following a final warning. For instance that it may result in dismissal or some other contractual penalty such as demotion or loss of seniority. All of these procedures are consistent with the maintenance of a communicative endeavour in which the ultimate goal is that of managing and restoring relationships rather than restitution or punishment.

The pursuit of this goal could profitably form the basis of the development of non criminal interventions, including the foregoing orders and the managed use of cautions, within an overall civil hierarchy of response to address the problems posed by preparation for crime. Using a similar template non compliance could be dealt with by a further or final caution, in which the consequences of non compliance are spelt out. These could be punitive, if the misconduct involves a criminal offence, or preventive, in the form of a civil prevention order.

Putting Some Flesh on the Bones

The following constitutes a rough prototype of a scheme of liability for preparatory crime together with some suggestions on the matter of due process. As has been suggested, the retributive purpose of the criminal law demands an *actus reus* which reflects and communicates the moral basis upon which the defendant is arraigned. I have suggested the following explicitly objectivist definition, which would be backed up by a list of examples. To constitute an attempt A must have done an act:

> which was directly connected with its commission and which was the last act the actor contemplated as necessary to commit the intended offence, or was a more remote act which, without being an act of mere preparation, formed part of a sequence of connected acts designed for the execution of the offence.

Included in this list of examples would be, crucially, examples of acts more remote than the last act which illustrate sequences of connected acts. Some sample illustrations, reflecting existing case law, might include:

- Breaking into a compound with a view to stealing from a building within the compound
- Putting a non-lethal amount of poison in the victim's drink in furtherance of a plan to poison by cumulative effect.
- Making a request at school gates to take a child to the dentist in furtherance of an intention to abduct.
- Pouring petrol on a door in furtherance of an intention to commit arson.

---

94   Guidelines appear in the ACAS Code of Practice No 1 Disciplinary and Grievance Procedures (2009).

Acts worthy of criminalisation in their own right include, or would include, such acts as

- Staging a false robbery or drowning with a view to perpetrating an insurance fraud, chargeable as fraud.
- 'Phishing' and similar activities, chargeable as fraud.
- Standing, prior to entry, outside PO with imitation firearm and threatening note for cashier, chargeable as possession with intent.
- Forcing V against a fence intending rape, chargeable as assault with intent to commit rape
- Pointing a gun at V (safety catch on/finger off trigger), chargeable as possession with intent to kill.
- Luring a person to a venue for the purpose of abduction or sexual assault – (s 14,15 Sexual Offences Act 2003).
- Possession of radioactive (and similar substances) with intent, chargeable as per section 9 Terrorism Act 2006.
- Harassment as per sections 1 and 4 Protection from Harassment Act 1997.
- Stalking as per The Protection of Freedoms Act 2012.

Acts worthy of criminalisation as a regulatory offence would include crimes of possession such as, most obviously, possessing a dangerous weapon, possessing dangerous substances, and possessing articles designed for the commission of specified offences.

Illustrations of acts not worthy of criminal response for which a civil order would be appropriate, based, as explained above, upon failing to satisfy one or both of the threshold questions might include, therefore

- Following a vehicle with intent to steal therefrom.
- Following a person with intent to commit sexual assault/rape/steal.
- Possessing information and equipment to be used for production of LSD.
- Reconnoitring a bank for later robbery.
- Examining a bolt of a door with a view to committing burglary.
- Lying in wait for theft/rape/assault.

These should, as at present, be dealt with by offence specific orders designed, like a declaratory judgement or an idealised criminal code, to communicate not only what A must not do but specific guidance restricting the kind of behaviours and context which might precipitate the commission of a future offence such as prohibiting certain specified locations and activities. In effect, such an order would communicate also the underlying system of values embodied in the order, Due process requires the consequences of breaching the civil order to be incorporated into the order and to be tailored to the type and gravity of the misconduct alleged against the defendant. For example, an order prohibiting the following of a security/goods vehicle without reasonable excuse, might involve loss of driving license as the primary sanction. A breach of an order prohibiting the possession of information and/or equipment capable of being used for the production of classified drugs might involve confiscation, Orders addressing stakeouts might be deal with by curfews, and so on. In each case such sanctions should be supported, if necessary, by community service, supervision, citizenship, or restorative programmes either in addition to the primary sanction or as a secondary sanction implemented for a subsequent breach. The coercive apex of this system should, unlike the present hybrid order, be punishment for contempt to ensure a proper insulation of the civil from the criminal mechanisms of social control.

Conclusion

In *Law Society and Industrial Justice*, Philip Selznick made the following observation:

> The anti-formalist posture of legal sociology encourages interest in the problem solving practices and spontaneous orderings of business or family life. *While this approach has tended to deprecate formal law, and has been indifferent to legal ideals, it just as easily supports an emphasis on the emergence of formal law out of the realities of group life.* Incipient law may be created by a stabilised public sentiment or pattern of organisation; it refers to a compelling claim of right or a practice so viable and so important to a functioning institution as to make legal recognition in due course highly probable. Thus some of the private arrangements worked out in collective bargaining especially seniority rights and protection against arbitrary dismissal, may be seen as incipient law.[95]

One of the realities of group life is the loss of dominion experienced by communities when faced with threats to their security as crystallised in preparatory crime. Another reality is the increasing emphasis on non-punitive methods of social control as a means of resolving problems and sources of disorder. Such methods have become realised to a certain extent in such phenomena as hybrid orders. So far such orders have failed to operate in a manner which safeguards the rights of individuals to fair treatment. Liberal theory has taken the view that since they are essentially coercive and are underpinned by the criminal sanction for breach they fall foul of principles of criminal justice such as generality, legality and fair labelling. Moreover they have rules of evidence and procedure to match. I have suggested that this criticism fails to acknowledge the positive dynamic nature of the orders, ignoring the perhaps inevitable fact that formal justice has always had to play catch up in the context of rapid substantive reform. This particular game of 'catch up' will cease when such orders lose their criminal character and become the coercive apex of a civil system designed for communicating and enforcing the moral basis of citizenship. In the specific field of preparatory crime such a development can achieve what any amount of tinkering around with the definition of a criminal attempt cannot. It, along with a systematic mapping of the range of criminal wrongdoing involved in attempts, crimes of ulterior intent, crimes of endangerment and regulatory crime, may finally deliver something approaching a rational mechanism for reconciling coercive law's retributive and protective functions.

---

95   Philip Selznick, *Law, Society and Industrial Justice* (Transaction 1980) 32.

Chapter 8

Towards a Rational Reconstruction of the Law on Secondary Participation and Inchoate Offences: Conspiracy

Claire de Than and Jesse Elvin

Introduction

In this chapter and the following one, we will focus on the complex relationship between the so-called 'inchoate offences' of attempt and conspiracy on the one hand and the law of complicity on the other.[1] Within the field of secondary participation in crime, it is important not to ignore the key and close relationship that such liability has with inchoate offences. Where D participates in a joint illegal enterprise or is otherwise complicit in a crime, a single course of conduct could lead to liability under the rules relating to both complicity and inchoate offences, depending on the stage at which D was arrested, and whether the full offence can be proved. For example, as the Law Commission have stated, 'If D1 and D2 agree to commit a crime (say, murder), and the murder is consequently carried out either by D1 alone, by D2 alone, or by D1 and D2 acting together, D1 and D2 are guilty of murder, and of conspiracy to murder'.[2] Conversely, D may think that he or she is participating in a joint enterprise that will amount to a crime, but not be caught by either set of rules: as the Law Commission have pointed out:

> secondary liability is a derivative form of liability in that D's liability derives from and is [generally] dependent on an offence committed by P … If P does not commit or attempt to commit the offence that D has encouraged or assisted, D may still be liable but only if his or her conduct amounts to an 'inchoate' offence.[3]

There has been some commentary about the relationship between complicity and inchoate liability; for example, in relation to the Law Commission's 1993 proposal that, with the possible exception of the retention of joint enterprise liability, the doctrine of secondary liability should be abolished.[4] However, further work needs to be done on the interplay between inchoate offences and participation in crime. We will explore this interplay with reference to 'hard cases' and the use of hypothetical scenarios. Developments in other relevant jurisdictions will also be examined.

This area of criminal law has been subject to repeated, partial reforms. The Serious Crime Act 2007 introduced new offences relating to encouraging or assisting an offence. However, it did

---

1   It must be noted that D cannot be liable for one of these 'inchoate offences' in the abstract: for example, D must be charged with 'attempted murder' rather than just with 'criminal attempt', since there is no such offence as 'criminal attempt' in the abstract.

2   Law Commission, *Conspiracy and Attempts* (Law Com No 318, 2009) 1.58.

3   Law Commission, *Inchoate Liability for Assisting or Encouraging Crime* (Law Com 300, 2006) 1.8.

4   For a summary of reaction to this proposal, see ibid. 2.7-2.19.

not reform the law relating to secondary liability or to two major inchoate offences: attempt and conspiracy. The Law Commission recommended reform to these two offences in 2009, proposing a series of amendments to the statutory law on conspiracy (it was not asked to consider common law conspiracy) and attempt but abandoning its 2007 provisional suggestion that there should be 'a newly defined offence of "attempt", complemented by a new offence of "criminal preparation"'.[5] One significant issue we will consider is the extent to which these 2009 recommendations would improve the law. Another important issue is whether the Law Commission were correct to abandon their 1993 proposals and decide that 'there are compelling reasons for retaining secondary liability in many cases where P goes on to commit or attempt to commit an offence that D has encouraged or assisted':[6] We will consider this in the context of the interplay between inchoate offences and joint enterprise, but we will have to continue that argument in a future publication for space reasons, since it is only one of many strong arguments for a different and more comprehensive approach to reform in this field of law.

Our first chapter will examine the law relating to conspiracy and its relationship to the participation offences. Most conspiracies, if carried out, would result in liability for joint enterprise or as an accomplice; we will argue that there are hence strong reasons in favour of streamlining the law between inchoate offences and participation in crime. Again, the statutory version of the conspiracy offence under the Criminal Law Act 1977 removed various problems in the law, but we will argue that there is still work to be done. The Law Commission's 2009 Conspiracy and Attempts Draft Bill recommended a suite of reforms to the statutory offence,[7] but these will not be brought into force, with the result that gaps and grey areas will remain in the law. Unlike the law of attempt, the law of conspiracy continues to be governed partially by the common law. Common law conspiracy has been deliberately excluded from some key reform attempts, with the result that we have parallel common law and statutory conspiracies, with different definitional elements. The rules relating to common law conspiracy raise human rights concerns with their lack of clarity and predictability; for example in the context of conspiracy to defraud. The latter offence continues to criminalise participation in behaviour which, if carried out by D alone, would be lawful. In addition, the availability of common law conspiracy in the realm of morality remains questionable after repeated statutory intervention, and the Law Commission have recently recommended abolishing the offence of outraging public decency in its present common law form.[8] Given that at least one of the common law offences – conspiracy to defraud – has proved to be very commonly charged, this chapter will argue that it was illogical to exclude it from existing and proposed statutory reforms if their aim was to produce a coherent, effective codified and human rights-compliant law.

Our second chapter (Chapter 9) will examine the law relating to attempt, with reference to assisting and encouraging crime where relevant. The Criminal Attempts Act 1981 reformed the law, but there are still some unresolved issues. What amounts to going beyond 'mere preparation' varies a great deal in cases; this variation may mean that the law is not compliant with Articles 5 and 7 of the European Convention on Human Rights. Furthermore, there is duplication of offences on the facts of many cases: for example where D committed inchoate offences and participated in a joint enterprise. This issue of duplication is not unique to the boundary between inchoate offences and secondary participation, but it is important to consider whether this duplication is desirable

---

5   Law Com No 318 (n 2) 1.90.

6   Law Com No 300 (n 3) 1.18.

7   Law Com No 318 (n 2) appendix A.

8   Law Commission, *Simplification of Criminal Law: Public Nuisance and Outraging Public Decency* (Law Com CP 193, 2010) 6.15. However, it should be noted that the Law Commission have provisionally proposed restating the offence 'in statutory form, while altering the fault element' (ibid.).

here. Moreover, there is a lack of clarity as to precisely what it is that is being criminalised with attempt. One view is that 'the intent is the essence of the crime',[9] or, to put it slightly differently, that 'the essence of a criminal attempt lies in the defendant's firm intention to commit the substantive offence'.[10] However, this focus upon D's intention to commit a crime does not sit easily with decisions such as *Taaffe*,[11] where the House of Lords held that D cannot be liable for attempting to commit an act believing it to be a criminal offence when it is not. It is easy to understand the argument of the prosecution that D was morally blameworthy and deserving of criminal punishment 'because: (a) he knew that he was involving himself as the crucial instrument in a sophisticated operation to deceive customs; and (b) he knew that deception was operated to bring in prohibited goods and/or (c) he did not care to find out, though he could have done, the precise nature of the prohibited goods'.[12] One issue we will consider in Chapter 9 is whether D should have been convicted under the rules relating to inchoate offences for his part in the operation to deceive customs.

Conspiracy, Attempt, Part 2 of the Serious Crime Act 2007 and the Law of Complicity

It is logical to begin by considering the relationship between the main inchoate offences and the law of complicity, which will require some examination of the definition of each inchoate offence. The main inchoate offences are conspiracy, attempt, and the three offences relating to encouraging or assisting crime under the Serious Crime Act 2007. A conspiracy is an agreement by two or more people on a course of conduct. The statutory version of the offence defines conspiracy as an agreement between two or more persons to pursue a course of conduct that will amount to a crime if carried out in accordance with their intentions or which 'would do so but for the existence of facts which render the commission of the offence or any of the offences impossible'.[13] The common law versions of conspiracy are vague, but it is clear that they concern agreements to defraud, to corrupt public morals or to outrage public decency. A conspiracy to defraud has been described as an agreement to 'deprive a person dishonestly of something which is his or of something to which he is or would or might but for the perpetration of the fraud be entitled'.[14] There is no consensus about the precise definition of a conspiracy to corrupt public morals, but Lord Simon characterised it as an agreement to engage in conduct that is 'destructive of the very fabric of society'.[15] In contrast, a conspiracy to outrage public decency is an agreement to do something that could be seen by at least two other people that is likely to disgust and annoy ordinary members of the public if they witness it. As Lord Simon put it in the leading case of *Knuller v DPP*: '"Outraging public decency" goes considerably beyond offending the susceptibilities of, or even shocking, reasonable people. Moreover, the offence is … concerned with recognised minimum standards of decency, which are likely to vary from time to time'.[16] Even at this stage in the chapter, it can be observed that the common law conspiracy offences raise concerns about clarity, certainty and over-inclusive

---

9   *Whybrow* (1951) 35 Cr App R 141, 147, per Lord Goddard.

10   Andrew Ashworth, 'Criminal Attempts and the Role of Resulting Harm Under the Code, and in the Common Law' (1987-88) 19 Rutgers Law Journal 725, 733.

11   [1984] AC 539.

12   Ibid. 541.

13   Criminal Law Act 1977, s 1(1), as amended by s 5 of the Criminal Attempts Act 1981.

14   *Scott v Metropolitan Commissioner* [1975] AC 819, 839, per Viscount Dilhorne.

15   *Knuller v DPP* [1973] AC 435, 491, per Lord Simon.

16   Ibid. 495.

scope. These concerns are not unique to our jurisdiction. For example, some of the common law conspiracy offences currently found in English law also exist in similar, if not identical form, in Ireland. In recommending the abolition of the common law conspiracies to corrupt public morals and outrage public decency, the Law Reform Commission of Ireland have stated: 'Not only do they have the extraordinary function of rendering criminal quite lawful activity merely because two or more agree to pursue it, there is also great uncertainty as to what constitutes, for example, the corruption of public morals'.[17]

The contemporary rationale behind the doctrine of conspiracy is a matter of debate. This doctrine was developed to punish agreements directed against the administration of justice; it was originally not a general inchoate offence, but rather a specific offence confined to 'combinations only to procure false indictments or to bring false appeals or to maintain vexatious suits'.[18] Some would still argue that conspiracy is a social wrong in its own right, rather than a step along the way towards a complete offence;[19] this view is understandable in historical context, since at common law conspiracies were often perceived as threats to the social order, whether they took the form of plots to blow up Parliament, to harm the financial interests of others or to do things regarded as unspeakably shocking. According to the Law Commission, the modern justification for the existence of the doctrine of conspiracy is the need to prevent unlawful harm ('the harm principle'):

> The forming of a conspiracy does not itself cause harm. Nonetheless, the achievement of the criminal law's principal aim would be substantially undermined if there could be no criminalisation of acts directed at causing harm, however determined the would-be criminals, however many people were drawn in to preparing to perpetrate the harm or however close they came to perpetrating it.[20]

This is not uncontroversial. In relation to terrorist conspiracies or organising riots via Facebook and Twitter, for example, the social wrong analysis still bears weight, especially given the reality that many conspiracies are charged when the plotted offence has actually been completed and hence charging conspiracy cannot possibly prevent the plotted harm, although it might have a deterrent effect for other plots.[21] However, the Law Commission believe that the harm principle also justifies the existence of other inchoate offences such as attempt and encouraging or assisting crime.[22] Liability for attempted crimes is governed by s 1(1) of the Criminal Attempts Act 1981, which states: 'If, with intent to commit an offence to which this section applies, a person does an act which is more than merely preparatory to the commission of the offence, he is guilty of attempting to commit the offence'.[23] Liability for encouraging or assisting crime is governed by the Serious Crime Act 2007, which abolished the common law offence of incitement to commit crime and created three offences relating to encouraging and assisting crime. The first of these offences

---

17   Law Reform Commission of Ireland, *Inchoate Offences* (LRC 99, 2010) 3.91. For discussion of relevant Irish law, see ibid. 3-91-3.92.

18   Francis Sayre, 'Criminal Conspiracy' (1921-22) 35 Harvard Law Review 393, 396, referring to English law in the late thirteenth and early fourteenth centuries.

19   See D Hodgson, 'Law Com. No 76: A Case Study in Criminal Law Reform' in P Glazebrook (ed.), *Reshaping the Criminal Law* (Stevens & Sons 1978).

20   Law Commission, *Conspiracy and Attempts: A Consultation Paper* (Law Com CP 183, 2007) 1.5.

21   Of course it remains possible (if dubious) to charge both conspiracy and a complete offence in such situations.

22   Law Com No 318 (n 2) 1.3.

23   The law on attempt is considered in detail in our next chapter (Chapter 9), and is thus not the subject of extensive discussion here.

is intentionally encouraging or assisting the commission of an offence,[24] the second is encouraging or assisting an offence believing that this offence will be committed,[25] and the third is encouraging or assisting offences believing that one or more will be committed.[26]

Since we are about to examine the relationship between inchoate offences and complicity, some explanation of the current law on the latter is helpful at this point, although it is of course dealt with in much greater detail in other chapters of this book. Like the law on inchoate offences, the law of complicity is a mixture of common law and statute. Section 8 of the Accessories and Abettors Act 1861, as amended by the Criminal Law Act 1977, states: 'Whosoever shall aid, abet, counsel or procure the commission of any indictable offence … shall be liable to be tried, indicted or punished as a principal offender'. There is a similar provision relating to summary offences in a section of the Magistrates' Courts Act 1980. Liability under these provisions will only arise where the prosecution prove that the accessory (the person who allegedly aided and so on) performed the *actus reus* of aiding and so on with the relevant *mens rea*. Moreover, the prosecution must also generally prove that someone committed the crime that the accessory allegedly aided and so on. One argument for this form of liability is that it fulfils 'the condemnatory and labelling function of the law' by adequately connecting D with the consequences of his or her conduct.[27] Nonetheless, there is an additional, common law, form of complicity with much older origins. The doctrine of joint enterprise applies where D and others have a shared common purpose to commit a crime; in this sense, it deals with conspiracies that have been brought to fruition. Each party to the plan is liable for the crime if the plan is carried out; it does not matter who actually committed the *actus reus* of the offence, since it was part of the common plan to which each had 'signed up'. If one party departs from the scope of the plan and commits a second offence without the agreement of D, liability will not necessarily be imposed upon D for this second offence. There has been much debate about the precise rules relating to joint enterprise; as Beatrice Krebs put it in 2010, 'the doctrine's proper scope, appropriate doctrinal basis and function in relation to other modes of complicity remain uncertain and continue to generate diverging opinions in the courts and literature'.[28] No records are even kept of the number of joint enterprise prosecutions, nor of the type of offence to which they related. Since the highest-profile cases reaching the highest courts have tended to be where the common purpose was murder or manslaughter, these areas have a stronger body of case law, with the result that there is less certainty about whether the same *mens rea* applies to all other joint enterprise offences. However, it currently appears that the general rule is:

> that where two parties embark on a joint enterprise to commit a crime, and one party foresees that in the course of the enterprise the other party may carry out, with the requisite *mens rea*, an act constituting another crime, the former is liable for that crime if committed by the latter in the course of the enterprise.[29]

Thus, 'it is sufficient to found a conviction for murder for a secondary party to have realised that in the course of the joint enterprise the primary party might kill with intent to do so or with intent to

---

24 Serious Crime Act 2007, s 44.
25 Ibid. s 45.
26 Ibid. s 46.
27 Law Com No 300 (n 3) 2.14.
28 Beatrice Krebs, 'Joint Criminal Enterprise' (2010) 73 Modern Law Review 578.
29 *R v Powell and English* [1999] 1 AC 1, 18, per Lord Hutton.

cause grievous bodily harm'.[30] Nonetheless, D will not be liable for an act that is 'fundamentally different' from anything s/he foresaw;[31] that is, 'if ... [the principal's] act was of a different kind from, and much more dangerous than, the sort of acts which D intended or foresaw as part of the joint enterprise'.[32] The courts currently favour the view that joint enterprise liability is an aspect of the ordinary principles of secondary liability; that is, that it builds upon the law relating to aiding and so on.[33] As the Court of Appeal put it in *R v Stringer*, 'Joint enterprise is not a legal term of art ... joint enterprise as a basis of secondary liability involves the application of ordinary principles; it is not an independent source of liability. Participation in a joint criminal adventure involves mutual encouragement and assistance'.[34] A recurrent theme in this pair of chapters (Chapters 8 and 9), uncertainty in the common law modes of liability, has drawn comment recently regarding joint enterprise; in June 2012 the House of Commons Justice Committee noted that there was evidence of inconsistency in the application of the doctrine, and concluded that statutory codification of the principles for all joint enterprises, not just those involving death, was required in order to ensure clarity.[35] Our submission is that while that is indeed the case, it does not go far enough; considered and internally-consistent codification of the whole body of principles applying to inchoate and secondary liability is required. Backed by reports from senior academics, the Committee stated:

> The lack of clarity over the common law doctrine on joint enterprise is unacceptable for such an important aspect of the criminal law. We therefore recommend that it be enshrined in legislation. We do not make this recommendation lightly. We fully appreciate the pressures on the parliamentary timetable but the evidence we have heard on joint enterprise has convinced us that legislative reform is required.[36]

We argue that the same could be said of common law conspiracies and much of the case law on both conspiracy and attempt.

As we explained above, where D is complicit in a crime, a single course of conduct could lead to liability under the rules relating to both complicity and inchoate offences. Let us suppose that D1 decides to bomb a public building, recruits other parties to help him, and successfully implements his plan, or that D2 plans a riot, using Twitter to recruit other participants, who join D2 in carrying out the riot. In both cases, the defendants could be liable for various offences under the rules relating to secondary liability, as well as for numerous inchoate offences, such as conspiracy, and full offences relating to terrorism and public order. Where this is the case, the prosecution will often prefer to argue for secondary rather than 'just' inchoate liability, since, in the words of the Law Commission, '[s]econdary liability is a more serious form of liability than inchoate liability. If D is secondarily liable, D, as well as P [the principal], is convicted of the principal offence. D is labelled in the same way as P and may be subject to the same penalty as P'.[37] However, a conviction for inchoate liability is sometimes much more straightforward to secure than one for secondary

---

30   Ibid. 27, subsequently approved by the House of Lords in *Rahman* [2009] UKHL 45, as explained by the Court of Appeal in *R v A* [2010] EWCA Crim 1622, [24]-[26].

31   *Rahman* (n 30) [68], per Lord Brown (with whom Lords Scott and Neuberger agreed).

32   *R v Mendez and Thompson* [2010] EWCA Crim 516, [47].

33   Ibid. [17].

34   [2011] EWCA Crim 1396, [57].

35   House of Commons Justice Committee, *Joint Enterprise* (11 January 2012, Eleventh Report of Session 2010-12).

36   Ibid. [36].

37   Law Commission, *Participating in Crime* (Law Com No 305, 2007) 1.2.

liability, and the reasons behind this may not stand up to close scrutiny. The most common situation in which this occurs is that conspiracy to defraud is charged more often than is fraud, for the reasons examined below, but there are similar patterns elsewhere in criminal law. *Gnango* is an excellent illustration of this point.[38] D armed himself with a gun and approached B to settle a dispute about debt. B began firing at D, who returned fire. A passer-by, V, was unintentionally killed by a bullet from B's gun. Convicting D for attempted murder would have been relatively uncomplicated on the facts; indeed, attempted murder was one of the offences for which D was convicted at his trial. However, the Supreme Court controversially held that D was also liable for V's murder. Some of their Lordships imposed liability by a combination of the principles relating to aiding and abetting and the doctrine of transferred malice. As Lord Phillips put it, B was liable for V's murder under the doctrine of transferred malice because he had attempted to murder D and killed V, and D was liable for V's murder because he had aided, abetted, counselled or procured the attempted murder of himself by B.[39] However, other members of the Supreme Court imposed liability upon D as a principal party to a joint enterprise; for instance, Lord Brown's view was that 'A is liable for ... [V's] murder as a principal – a direct participant engaged by agreement in unlawful violence (like a duel, a prize-fight or sado-masochism) specifically designed to cause and in fact causing death or serious injury'.[40]

Gnango raises various concerns which are outside the scope of these chapters, but we will return to it in order to examine its interpretation of the 'victim exception' in criminal law at a later point in the discussion. Two further concerns are relevant to the present inquiry. Firstly, this case has not aided the certainty or clarity of the criminal law of homicide, which the Law Commission already regarded as a 'mess'[41] and a 'rickety structure set upon shaky foundations',[42] and it will be some time before its significance can be evaluated since it does have facts unusual enough for it to become a footnote in legal principles. Secondly, it could be argued that what the Supreme Court does in *Gnango* is to introduce a new felony murder offence by the back door, unjustifiably[43] expanding joint enterprise doctrine to plug the gap left by the statutory abolition of that offence in the Homicide Act 1957. The latter point will be examined elsewhere, but adds weight to another theme of this pair of chapters, the advantages of statutory codification of the entire field of inchoate offences and complicity. Expansions and contractions of common law principles are adding to the mess.

What's Wrong with the Law of Conspiracy?

As we stated above, the rules relating to common law conspiracy raise human rights concerns with their lack of clarity and predictability. It has long been recognised that ambiguous laws are not good laws. For H.L.A. Hart, '[T]he characteristic technique of the criminal law is to designate by rules certain types of behaviour as standards for the guidance ... of members of society. [T]hey are

---

38   [2011] UKSC 59; [2012] 1 AC 827.

39   Ibid. [55].

40   Ibid. [71]. For critical analysis of this decision, see Richard Buxton, 'Being an Accessory to One's Own Murder' [2012] Criminal Law Review 275; and David Ormerod, 'Worth the Wait?' [2012] Criminal Law Review 79.

41   Law Commission, *Partial Defences to Murder* (Law Com No 290, 2004) 2.74.

42   Law Commission, *Murder, Manslaughter and Infanticide* (Law Com No 304, 2006) 1.8.

43   See *Zemmel* (1985) 81 Cr App R 279 as one potential basis on which the expansion may be unjustifiable.

expected without the aid or intervention of officials to understand the rules and to see that the rules apply to them and to conform to them'.[44] Human rights law has taken this further. Articles 5 and 7 of the European Convention on Human Rights are particularly pertinent here. Article 5 stipulates that 'Everyone has the right to liberty and security of person' and that any interference with this right must be in accordance with a procedure prescribed by law and on certain specified permissible grounds. This Article requires that any detention be in accordance with domestic law, and that this domestic law is itself sufficiently clear to satisfy the principle of rule of law.[45] The Convention is a 'living instrument', and from time to time the European Court of Human Rights has 'interpreted in' to Article 5 a principle that the scope of every criminal offence should be certain. While it is true that few offences have been found to be too uncertain in the Court, that is often due to finding a violation on other grounds, not to rejection of such arguments.[46] With far more case law to support it, Article 7 requires that there should be no punishment without law, which amongst other things means that the criminal law should be sufficiently clear so that 'the individual can know from the wording of the relevant provision and, if need be, with the assistance of the courts' interpretation of it, what acts and omissions will make him criminally liable'.[47] As Lord Bingham summarised the relevant Article 7 principles in *R v Rimmington and Goldstein*, 'It is accepted that absolute certainty is unattainable'.[48] All law must be reasonably clear, accessible and foreseeable. Accordingly, Article 7 allows the 'gradual clarification of the rules of criminal liability … provided that the resultant development is consistent with the essence of the offence and could reasonably be foreseen'.[49] Beyond Articles 5 and 7, there has long been a general requirement of legal certainty in ECHR law. This is implied into the concepts of 'prescribed by law' and 'according to law'. A relevant example is that of *Sunday Times* v *UK*,[50] where the European Court of Human Rights found the common law of contempt of court lacking in this respect, requiring '… sufficient precision to enable the citizen to regulate his conduct: he must be able – if need be with appropriate advice – to foresee to a degree that is reasonable in the circumstances, the consequences which any given action may entail'.[51] The existence of conflicting case authority on the same issue, particularly when it increases over time, may violate Article 6 of the Convention,[52] again on grounds of uncertainty, ambiguity and inconsistent application of legal principles. Statutory inchoate offences have recently withstood such a challenge; in *S* the Court of Appeal rejected the claim that s 46 of the Serious Crime Act 2007 failed the tests for certainty and clarity,[53] but that says nothing about a challenge to the offences which the 2007 Act was originally intended to replace. English courts have so far been reluctant to find that common law offences are too uncertain to meet human rights standards but the Strasbourg court could still do so, given the lack of consensus as to the elements of these offences.[54] It is true that in *G v UK* the Strasbourg court stated:

44   *The Concept of Law* (Clarendon Press 1961) 38-39.
45   D Harris, M O'Boyle, E Bates and C Buckley, *Harris, O'Boyle and Warbrick: Law of the European Convention on Human Rights* (2nd edn, Oxford University Press 2008) 133, citing *Ilaşcu v Moldova* (2004) 40 EHRR 1030, [461].
46   For example *HL v UK* [2005] 40 EHRR 42.
47   *CR v UK* (App No 20190/92) [1995] ECHR 51, [33].
48   [2005] UKHL 63, [35].
49   *SW v UK* (App No 20166/92) (1996) 21 EHRR 363, [36].
50   [1979] 2 EHRR 245.
51   Ibid. [49].
52   *Tudor v Romania* (App No 21911/03); *Stefanica v Romania* (App No 38155/02).
53   [2011] EWCA Crim 2872.
54   *Misra* [2005] 1 Cr App R 21; *Goldstein* [2003] EWCA Crim 3450.

in principle the Contracting States remain free to apply the criminal law to any act which is not carried out in the normal exercise of one of the rights protected under the Convention and, accordingly, to define the constituent elements of the resulting offence. It is not the Court's role … to dictate the content of domestic criminal law, including whether or not a blameworthy state of mind should be one of the elements of the offence or whether there should be any particular defence available to the accused.[55]

However in that case the Court was able to define the relevant statutory offence and its defences readily, which cannot be said to be possible with the common law conspiracies, as we shall see.

It is a difficult point whether the common law conspiracy offences are sufficiently precise to satisfy the requirements of Articles 5 and 7, but they are by no means becoming clearer and more consistent over time. The Law Commission have noted that the courts have settled upon a broad, vague definition of conspiracy to defraud 'so that any dishonest agreement to make a gain at another's expense could form the basis of conspiracy to defraud'.[56] As they point out, 'It is only the element of "dishonesty" which renders it a criminal fraud. In other words, that element "does all the work" in assessing whether particular facts fall within the definition of the crime'.[57] This is a problem, since it is arguable that 'the current formulation [of dishonesty] fails the "certainty" test prescribed by the European Court of Human Rights'.[58] The definitions of conspiracy to corrupt public morals and to outrage public decency are similarly unsatisfactory. The former offence relies upon the jury to 'apply the current standards of ordinary decent people – a vague and unpredictable test'.[59] Furthermore, the latter offence also relies upon 'recognised standards of propriety'.[60] In *Hamilton*, the Court of Appeal explained that the offence of outraging public decency is designed to protect the public 'from lewd, obscene or disgusting acts which are of a nature that outrages public decency and which are capable of being seen in public'.[61] According to the Court, the notion of 'outraging public decency' sets 'a standard which the jury must judge by reference to contemporary standards'.[62] Since there may be no social consensus about many matters, such as whether it is acceptable to exhibit earrings made from freeze-dried human foetuses at an art gallery,[63] it can be argued that the scope of conspiracy to outrage public decency is 'vague and unpredictable in the extreme'.[64] Even if the common law conspiracy offences satisfy the requirements of Articles 5 and 7 as they are currently interpreted in the case law, this does not mean that they are acceptable. As Arnold Enker puts it, the function of criminal law is to secure 'a high measure of protection from harmful acts. But since society achieves such protection by inflicting harm on those who would

---

55   Application no. 37334/08, Admissibility Decision, 30 August 201 [27].

56   Law Commission, *Fraud* (Law Com No 276, 2002), 3.6.

57   Ibid.

58   Russell Heaton and Claire de Than, *Criminal Law* (3rd edn, Oxford University Press 2011) 361, referring to the 'dishonesty' test established in *Ghosh* [1982] QB 1053.

59   Ibid. 569.

60   [2007] EWCA Crim 2062, [30].

61   Ibid. [39].

62   Ibid.

63   In *Gibson* [1990] 2 QB 619, two defendants were convicted for outraging public decency in relation to such facts.

64   Heaton and de Than (n 58) 570.

commit such acts, it must take care not to offset this gain in security by unduly increasing the risks that persons will be subjected to official harm unpredictably'.[65]

Substantive Issues in the Law of Conspiracy

This part of the chapter will examine some of the difficulties which span inchoate offences and the various forms of complicity. There are strong arguments in favour of consistency in criminal law,[66] again backed by human rights arguments and the rule of law. As will be seen, in some of the themes there is at least partial consistency of approach, but in others there is incoherence or illogicality. We will return to each of the issues examined here in the next chapter, in the context of attempt and complicity, and conclude on them there.

Proof of the Agreement

As David Ormerod observes, '[t]he question of what conduct amounts to a sufficient agreement to found a charge of conspiracy is one of several questions in the criminal law aggravated by a confusion between the substantive law and the law of evidence'.[67] The dominant view is that a conspiracy is an agreement to pursue certain conduct and does not need to be carried out – the agreement is enough in itself to found liability. However, Lord Diplock stated that 'it is legal fiction that the offence lies not in the overt acts themselves which are injurious to the common weal but in an inferred anterior agreement to commit them'.[68] In practice, it may be impossible to prove conspiracy without evidence that the defendants have taken actions to implement it, and some recent cases have blurred the distinction between conspiracy and attempt by failing to find the necessary intention without steps being taken to carry out the plan. In *Goddard and Fallick*, the defendants were charged with conspiracy to rape a child under the age of 13.[69] The prosecution argued that a series of text messages between the defendants discussing a plan to rape a 6 year old, whose description matched a boy known to one of the defendants, proved an intent to carry out the plan. When questioned by the police, neither defendant stated that the discussion had just been a fantasy. However, the Court of Appeal concluded that 'no reasonable jury, taking the prosecution evidence at its highest, could surely infer that the defendants intended to carry out the agreement. The evidence is all equivocal; it is as consistent with fantasy as with an intent to carry out the plan'.[70] The danger is that this approach effectively requires evidence of steps taken to implement the plan, which would convert conspiracy into a preparatory offence. Given that (as we shall see in Chapter 9) there is no clear point at which sufficient steps have been taken to found attempt, gaps and overlaps between the inchoate offences are almost certain to occur by that analysis. It is also arguable that the Court of Appeal failed to appreciate the rapid and accelerating developments in

---

65   Arnold Enker, 'Impossibility in Legal Attempts: Legality and Legal Process' (1989) 53 Minneapolis Law Review 665, 688, discussing the *mens rea* requirement in criminal law but making a point of general relevance.

66   Examined in detail in Catherine Elliott and Claire de Than, 'The Case for a Rational Reconstruction of Consent in the Criminal Law' [2007] Modern Law Review 225.

67   David Ormerod, *Smith and Hogan's Criminal Law* (13th edn, Oxford University Press 2011) 431.

68   *DPP v Bhagwan* [1970] AC 60, 79.

69   [2012] EWCA Crim 1756.

70   Ibid. [40].

the technology of communication; if letters and oral words can found conspiracy in thousands of cases, so can text messages, and the latter is no more likely to be a fantasy than the former.

The Continued Existence of Common Law Liability for Conspiracy to Defraud

The abolition of common law conspiracy offences has been proposed on several occasions, as will be discussed in the next chapter, yet they remain in existence and their elastic nature has been stretched repeatedly to encompass new forms of behaviour. This has the advantage of allowing the law to keep pace with developments in society and technology, but also the dangers of over-criminalisation, inconsistency in approach and the creation of conflicts in policy between Parliament and the common law. We will focus in this section on conspiracy to defraud, which has proved to be a particularly popular offence with those involved in the prosecution of offences since it is supremely useful in practice, but the broadness and flexibility which make it so popular with prosecutors are related closely to the reasons for the calls for its repeal. Its definition lacks precision and has varied over time, which has led to some surprising cases such as *Vickerman*, discussed below. In June 2012 the Ministry of Justice published a post-legislative assessment of the Fraud Act 2006,[71] which found that the new statutory fraud offences had simplified the law and were very useful, yet also recommended the retention of conspiracy to defraud since it continues to criminalise behaviour which does not fall within the statutory fraud offences and is broad enough to allow a single charge when the statutory offences would require several. With respect, these arguments raise serious concerns and possibilities for abuse. Although the Attorney General issued guidance for the CPS in 2007 which '… has resulted in additional care being exercised by prosecutors and increased scrutiny of charging decisions by experienced lawyers'[72] and which requires a prosecutor to justify the use of the common law charge, this guidance is not being applied in the recent rash of private prosecutions for conspiracy to defraud. Given that the guidance notes that it was drafted to regulate prosecutions in the light of the concerns that the offence is 'unfairly uncertain, … wide enough to have the potential to catch behaviour that should not be criminal [and] it can seem anomalous that what is legal if performed by one person should be criminal if performed by many',[73] it is surely a matter of urgency to ensure that the guidance's balancing exercise is applied in all prosecutions, including those brought by private organisations or companies. The dangers of the continued existence of the common law conspiracy offences can be seen in *Vickerman*.[74] Anton Vickerman was convicted of conspiracy to defraud after a private prosecution was mounted by the Federation Against Copyright Theft in relation to his website, Surfthechannel, which listed links to copyrighted and out-of-copyright material held elsewhere on internet sources. He was not charged with copyright offences under the Copyright Designs and Patents Act 1988 for the simple reason that there was insufficient evidence that he had committed any, and the CPS declined to prosecute for conspiracy to defraud, presumably after applying the AG's guidance. The conviction sits particularly uneasily with earlier cases such as *Rock and Overton*,[75] where the trial judge threw out charges of conspiracy to defraud as well as statutory copyright offences, and possibly *Ellis*,[76] where the jury acquitted. In *Rock and Overton*, Mr Justice Ticehurst found that under regulation

---

71   Cm 8372, Memorandum to the Justice Select Committee.

72   Ibid. [40].

73   Guidance available at: <www.gov.uk/use-of-the-common-law-offence-of-conspiracy-to-defraud--6> accessed 10 January 2013.

74   Sentenced to four years' imprisonment at Newcastle Crown Court on 14 August 2012.

75   6 February 2010, the TV-Links case, Gloucester Crown Court, unreported.

76   January 2010, unreported, the OiNK case.

17 of the Electronic Commerce (EC Directive) Regulations 2002 there was a complete defence for any website which did not itself upload copyrighted material but merely acted as a 'conduit of information' by linking to other sites containing copyrighted material. On that basis and others[77] the conviction in Vickerman is questionable and demonstrates both that greater scrutiny is required over private prosecutions in general, and that the concerns over common law conspiracies could reach new heights. One man's flexibility and ease may be another man's human rights violation. The trend is particularly worrying since the Court of Appeal has stated, in fact twice,[78] that complex matters of copyright law should be decided by specialist Chancery judges and not in jury trials since 'They can be so tried much more efficiently in terms of cost and time than before a jury, and questions of law can if necessary be determined on appeal on the basis of clear findings of fact'.[79]

Although common law conspiracies criminalise an agreement to behave in a way which would be lawful if done alone, they do have one limitation: if a statute criminalised a type of behaviour but the statute was repealed, then an agreement to do that thing will no longer be a conspiracy to defraud, as seen in *Zemmel*.[80] In the latter case, the Court of Appeal was unwilling to accept arguments that 'by a side wind the common law has suddenly re-emerged to reinstate or create as a crime that which Parliament thought it right to take off the statute book as a crime'.[81] By analogy, surely changes in European law as incorporated in the UK via the 2002 Regulations, in combination with the introduction of the Fraud Act 2006, should mean that conspiracy to defraud should not recriminalise lawful behaviour in the field of copyright law.

Even if the arguments advanced for the retention of conspiracy to defraud were unassailable, they would not hold water as arguments for its continuation as a common law offence. Codification would enable greater control over consistency in use and interpretation of the offence and could render the current guidance mandatory. If there is truly a gap in the offences under the Fraud Act 2006, the fairest answer would be to amend the statute. We submit that this should be done as part of the bigger picture – a comprehensive codification of inchoate offences and complicity.

Status-Based Exemptions from Liability for Conspiracy

The victim   As explained above, a conspiracy is an agreement by two or more people on a course of conduct. However, there are certain restrictions about who can be liable for conspiracy. According to s 2(1) of the Criminal Law Act 1977, D cannot be guilty of statutory conspiracy 'if he is an intended victim of that offence'. Similarly, where the only other party to an agreement to commit an offence is an intended victim of that offence, D will not be guilty of statutory conspiracy.[82] There are no relevant common law conspiracy authorities on this issue. In practice, this may not be a problem. 'It is difficult to envisage how there could be a common law conspiracy to defraud where the "intended victim" agrees to commit the fraud!'[83] Furthermore, conspiracy to corrupt public morals and outrage public decency are by their nature directed against the public, rather than specific individuals, who might be a party to the conspiracy. Nonetheless, there is a major potential discrepancy here between the law on complicity and the law on statutory conspiracy. It has long been clear that D cannot be guilty as

---

77   The basis on which dishonesty and intention were found, as well as the method by which losses to the film industry were calculated, to name a few.

78   In *Higgs* [2008] EWCA Crim 1324 and *Gilham* [2009] EWCA Crim 2293.

79   In *Gilham* (n 78), per Stanley Burton LJ [30].

80   *Zemmel* (n 43).

81   Ibid. per Watkins LJ [284].

82   Criminal Law Act 1977, s 2(2).

83   Heaton and de Than (n 58) 554.

an accessory where the offence was created to protect him or her.[84] What is not so clear is whether s 2(1) of the Criminal Law Act 1977 applies this so-called 'victim rule' to statutory conspiracy. Lord Phillips PSC and Lord Judge made obiter remarks, with which Lord Wilson agreed, about this matter in the leading judgment in *Gnango*. In their words, section 2(1) can be read literally, as applying 'a wider principle than [the traditional interpretation of the "victim" rule] if "victim" is given the wide meaning of any person who will be harmed by the offence'.[85] The problem with this interpretation was explained by Lord Phillips PSC and Judge CJ:

> if 'victim' in s 2(2) is given the wide meaning of any person who will be harmed by the offence it would seem to produce the surprising result that a conspiracy by two persons that one will commit a terrorist atrocity as a suicide bomber, or to set fire to a house owned by one of them in furtherance of some ulterior motive, would not subject either to criminal liability.[86]

Their Lordships thought that there is a case for confining the meaning of victim to persons of a class that the relevant Act is intended to protect, thus bringing s 2(1) into accord with the 'victim rule' which applies in respect of statutory offences under the law relating to accomplices to crime under the *Tyrrell* principle. In their opinion, 'The case for giving a narrow construction to "victim" in section 2(1) of the Criminal Law Act 1977 is perhaps strengthened by the limited exemption from criminal liability conferred by section 51 of the Serious Crime Act 2007'. Section 51 specifically applies the *Tyrrell* rule to the encouraging and assisting offences created by Part 2 of the 2007 Act, referring to offences that exist '(wholly or in part) for the protection of a particular category of persons ("the protected category")'. However, since section 2(1) of the Criminal Law Act 1977 does not use this terminology, it can be plausibly argued that Parliament intended this section to apply more widely than the common law *Tyrrell* principle.

Spouses   Section 2(1) of the Criminal Law Act 1977, as amended by the Civil Partnership Act 2004, states that an agreement confined to spouses or civil partners will not constitute a statutory conspiracy. There is authority for the view that this rule about spouses also applies to common law conspiracy. In *Mawji*,[87] the Court of Appeal accepted that it is a general rule in English criminal law that a husband and wife cannot conspire alone, stating that 'the rule is an example of the fiction that husband and wife are regarded for certain purposes, of which this is one, as in law one person'.[88] It can be argued that 'the common law would presumably now take the same approach [as the 1977 Act], although there has not been a leading case on this point'.[89] However, the law would benefit from certainty here. The continuing relevance of the exemption regarding spouses is evident in *Singh*,[90] a 2011 case where the trial judge directed the jury on the point. It cannot be assumed that the common law would take the same approach as the amended 1977 Act. In 1982, when invited to extend the scope of the spousal exemption to cover conspiracy in tort, the Court of Appeal declined on the basis that it was based on an outdated fiction: as Lord Denning put it, 'the doctrine of unity and its ramifications should be discarded altogether, except in so far as it is retained by judicial

---

84   *Tyrrell* [1984] 1 QB 710; *Whitehouse* [1977] All ER 737.
85   *Gnango* (n 38) [49].
86   Ibid. [50].
87   [1957] AC 126.
88   Ibid. 135.
89   Heaton and de Than (n 58) 554.
90   [2011] EWCA Crim 2992.

decision or by Act of Parliament'.[91]

The Effect of Conditional Intention

It is clear that it is no defence to a statutory conspiracy charge that the agreement to commit a crime was subject to a condition: for example that A and B would rob a bank if it seemed safe to do so.[92] The Law Commission believe that a conditional intent to commit a crime is also regarded as an intention to commit the crime at common law.[93] However, conspiracy to defraud does not necessarily involve an agreement on a course of conduct that is itself criminal – the planned conduct might well be entirely lawful.[94] Thus, it is arguable that conditional intention is of limited relevance in relation to conspiracy to defraud. As the Law Commission put it, 'The approach should be different if the nature of the condition is such as, to use Lord Nicholls words, to "cast doubt on the genuineness of a conspirator's expressed intention to do an unlawful act"'.[95]

Do All Parties Have To Intend That the Plan Will Be Carried Out and
To Participate in the Conduct That Constitutes the Substantive Offence?

The rules in this respect seem to be the same for all conspiracies, but they are the subject of debate. In *Anderson*,[96] Lord Bridge, giving the leading judgment in the House of Lords, stated obiter: 'It is … necessary that any party to the agreement shall have assented to play his part in the agreed course of conduct … knowing that the part to be played by one or more of the others will amount to or involve the commission of an offence'.[97] However, his Lordship added that it was unnecessary for D to intend to participate in the conduct that constitutes the substantive offence or that this offence should occur; for example where D intended to provide a car to be used for a bank robbery, but was indifferent as to whether the robbery occurred. In *Siracusa*, the Court of Appeal expanded the notion of participation to include 'passive participation', whereby D's intention to participate is 'established by his failure to stop the unlawful activity'.[98] *Anderson* and *Siracusa* were considered in *King*, where the Court of Appeal observed that that there is still uncertainty: 'It is a controversial question whether the defendant must harbour an intention to participate in the conduct which constitutes the substantive offence … For reasons which will appear, this is not a debate into which it is necessary for this court to enter on the present occasion'.[99] Contrary to Lord Bridge's obiter in *Anderson* is the view that 'there is nothing in the … [1977 statute], nor in the common law, to require participation in the carrying out of the agreement by each conspirator',[100] and 'all that need be contemplated is the commission of the offence "by one or more of the parties to the agreement"'.[101] Thus, the law would benefit from statute-imposed clarity here. Furthermore, as the Law Commission point out, the law as stated in *Anderson* draws an unjustified distinction 'between

---

91   *Midland Bank Trust Co. Ltd. and Another v Green and Another (No.3)* [1982] Ch. 529, 539.
92   *R v Reed* [1982] Crim LR 819; *R v Jackson* [1985] Crim LR 442; *O'Hadhmaill* [1996] Crim LR 509.
93   Law Commission (n 2) 2.104.
94   See *Scott v Metropolitan Police Commissioner* [1974] 3 All ER 1032.
95   Law Commission (n 20) 5.13, citing *Saik* [2006] UKHL18; [2007] 1 AC 18, [5].
96   [1987] 2 AC 27.
97   Ibid. 38.
98   [1990] 90 Cr App R 340, 349.
99   [2012] EWCA Crim 805.
100 Ormerod (n 67) 441.
101 Ibid.

an undercover officer (say) who intends to play some part in the fulfilment of the conspiracy, and one who simply agrees to take part but intends to do nothing further'.[102] As the Commission state, 'The former can be convicted of conspiracy, whereas the latter cannot be convicted, even though both may share the same ulterior intention to expose the conspiracy'.[103]

The Effect of Impossibility

Even within the field of conspiracy, there are two sets of rules in operation in relation to impossibility. For common law conspiracies,[104] if the agreement would be impossible to carry out, then there will be no liability under the rule in *DPP v Nock*,[105] unless the reason for the impossibility is that D has insufficient means to carry out the plan; legal or factual impossibility are complete defences at common law. However for statutory conspiracies, s 1(1)(b) of the Criminal Law Act 1977 (as amended) states that if the agreed course of conduct *would* necessarily amount to or involve the commission of an offence 'but for the existence of facts which render the commission of the offence … impossible' then there is a statutory conspiracy. There is no logical basis for this distinction to be maintained, and it would be helpful to have statutory confirmation of the position in respect of impossibility and the other common law conspiracy offences.

Withdrawal?

A conspiracy is complete once the agreement is reached; it is impossible to withdraw from it.[106] However, seeking to prevent it being carried out appears to prevent a conspiracy from existing at all.[107] As we shall see, the impossibility of withdrawal conflicts with the approach taken in complicity, which is a conspiracy carried out; surely the same principles should apply to both forms of liability in this respect. On public policy grounds, it is better to encourage conspirators to thwart plots and to alert the authorities than to encourage them to keep quiet and do nothing.

A Duress Defence?

On public policy grounds, duress is no defence to murder,[108] attempted murder[109] and probably treason,[110] at least encompassing the death of the sovereign. There is a dearth of reported cases directly on the point of duress as a defence to conspiracy to murder,[111] but there has been a very recent development: *Ness*.[112] The defendants (accomplices of Raoul Moat) were charged with

---

102   Law Commission (n 2) 6.21.

103   Ibid.

104   Clearly for conspiracy to defraud, and probably for the other two categories, although there is a dearth of case law.

105   [1978] AC 979.

106   *Saik* [2006] UKHL18 [?], per Lord Hope; [2007] 1 AC 18.

107   *Yip Chiu-Cheung* [1994] 2 All ER 924 per Lord Griffiths [928], see below.

108   *Howe* [1987] 1 AC 417.

109   *Gotts* [1992] 1 All ER 832.

110   Although the cases do conflict, see *Steane* [1947] KB 997; *Purdy* (1945) 10 JCL 18; and *Pommell* [1995] 2 Cr App R 607.

111   Charges of conspiracy to murder were made in many of the leading cases, including *Howe*, but since the defence of duress was left to the jury in relation to that charge, it has not featured in appeals.

112   [2011] Crim LR 645.

murder, attempted murder, robbery, a firearms offence and conspiracy to murder, and argued duress to those charges where it was clearly available at law – robbery and the firearms offence. The court then had to consider whether duress was available to the conspiracy to murder charges, and found that it was. Relying on Lord Lane LCJ in *Gotts*,[113] the trial judge found that there was logic in drawing a line between mere preparation for murder (conspiracy) and attempting it, allowing duress as a defence to the former but not the latter. However, *Gotts* was far from a unanimous decision: there was powerful dissent as to whether duress should apply to homicide offences, and four of the judges urged that Parliament should consider whether, as a matter of policy, duress should continue to be a complete defence to crimes generally or simply be regarded as a mitigating factor, seemingly preferring the latter. What united Lord Justices Lane (in the majority) and Lowry (dissenting) was that allowing duress as a defence in some crimes but not others would create anomalies wherever the boundary was drawn. In addition, we have already seen that there is blurring of boundaries between conspiracy and attempt, in which case the distinction regarding duress seems arbitrary and difficult to justify.

The Effect of Mistaken Beliefs

As seen above, in *Taaffe*,[114] the House of Lords held that D cannot be liable for attempting to commit an act believing it to be a criminal offence when it is not. Logically, the same should be true of other inchoate offences; where Ds mistakenly believe that the planned conduct is criminal but it is not, they should no more be guilty when caught at the plot stage than when going beyond mere preparation. The statutory definition of conspiracy has the same effect as *Taaffe* since it criminalises agreement on a course of conduct which would involve a criminal offence if carried out. However common law conspiracies do not seem to have the same approach, since it is in their nature that they would not be crimes if carried out, and so D's beliefs as to that issue are not relevant except in the opposing sense argued in Vickerman's trial for conspiracy to defraud, that is that a D who believes he is breaking the criminal law is dishonest even when his actions are in fact lawful. Since it has already been demonstrated in this chapter that in practice there are significant overlaps between conspiracy to defraud and statutory conspiracies, surely the same rules should apply to them all. Yet again, codification could bring resolution.

Interim Conclusions

In this chapter, we have focused upon the law of conspiracy, and argued that it needs comprehensive statutory reform in order to produce a clear, coherent, and human rights-compliant system that fits logically with the law on secondary participation. As we shall show in our next chapter (Chapter 9), many of the problems we have examined in relation to conspiracy and its fit with complicity also plague the law of attempts. We will also demonstrate that there has been a recurrent tendency throughout this field to go only part of the way towards a sensible reform, with partial codification and simplification or improvement of the law, which does little for the clear, effective and fair law we seek.

---

113   *Gotts* (n 109).
114   *Taaffe* (n 11).

Chapter 9

Towards a Rational Reconstruction of the Law on Secondary Participation and Inchoate Offences: Attempt

Claire de Than and Jesse Elvin

Introduction

In Chapter 8, we examined the law on conspiracy, and suggested that a comprehensive review of its principles is an urgent concern. As we will show in this chapter, the law of attempt is equally complex and driven by incoherent policy. Therefore, we submit that it is only by an inclusive reform of all forms of secondary and inchoate liability that a workable set of legal principles may be achieved.

Historical Issues in the Law of Attempt

In order to appreciate the current state of the law and the potential impact of reform proposals, it is helpful to examine its development. The English law on attempt has undergone a number of significant changes over the centuries. 'In the days of Edward III and for a time thereafter, the law punished one who lay in wait ... to commit murder or robbery as though he or she had committed the full offence, on the basis that the will was taken for the deed'.[1] It was not until later that attempt became a distinct area of criminal law. The modern common law on attempt can be traced back to two cases from 1855. In the former, *Eagleton*, Parke B stated: 'Acts remotely leading towards the commission of the offence are not to be considered as attempts to commit it; but acts immediately connected with it are'.[2] As the Law Commission note, this decision 'established what came to be known as the "proximity" test for attempt' whereby an act is an attempt if it is immediately connected with the intended offence.[3] In the second case from 1855, Parke B similarly defined an attempt as 'an act directly approximating to the commission of an offence'.[4] *Eagleton* has also been interpreted as authority for the view that D must have attempted the last act dependent upon him or her.[5] However, as the Law Commission has noted, the best interpretation of *Eagleton* is that it stipulates that D will have committed the *actus reus* of attempt where s/he has performed

---

1   David Lanham, Bronwyn Bartal, Robert Evans and David Wood, *Criminal Laws in Australia* (Federation Press 2006) 428, citing Yearbook 13 Hen 4 Mich pl 20; (1412) Coke 3 Inst 5, and W. Holdsworth, *History of English Law Volume 3* (3rd edn, revised, Methuen 1923) 373.

2   *Eagleton* (1855) 6 Cox 559, 571.

3   Law Commission, *Conspiracy and Attempts: A Consultation Paper* (Law Com CP 183, 2007) 13.2.

4   *Roberts* (1855) Dears 539.

5   KJM Smith, 'Proximity in Attempt: Lord Lane's "Midway Course"' [1991] Criminal Law Review 576, 578.

the last act, but that this is not required for attempt.[6] Some subsequent common law cases used other definitions of attempt: for example, in *Hope v Brown*, the High Court adopted the definition in *Stephen's Digest of the Criminal Law*: 'An attempt to commit a crime is an act done with intent to commit that crime, and forming part of a series of acts, which would constitute its actual commission if it were not interrupted'.[7] Lord Reid subsequently doubted that the courts could devise a definitive test, stating in the 1973 case of *Haughton v Smith*: 'no words, unless so general as to be virtually useless, can be devised which will fit the immense variety of possible cases. Any attempted definition would, I am sure, do more harm than good. It must be left to common sense to determine in each case whether the accused has gone beyond mere preparation'.[8] The House of Lords returned to this matter in *DPP v Stonehouse*, where Lord Diplock stated: 'The constituent elements of the inchoate crime of an attempt are a physical act by the offender sufficiently proximate to the complete offence and an intention on the part of the offender to commit the complete offence ... the offender must have crossed the Rubicon and burnt his boats'.[9] However, the common law never settled on a clear definition of the *actus reus* of attempt, which made the law unpredictable.[10]

There were two other main problems with the common law on attempt. First, notwithstanding Lord Diplock's statement about the requisite *mens rea* in *Stonehouse*, there was still doubt about this matter. It was clear that D must intend whatever act and consequences are required by the crime. However, *Khan* held that intention or knowledge is not required in relation to any prescribed circumstances.[11] This case concerned attempted rape. At the time, D could not be liable for rape unless he knew that V was not consenting or was reckless as to whether she consented. Russell LJ rejected the appellant's argument that the prosecution must prove that D intended the act to be non-consensual and stated instead that 'the intent of the defendant is precisely the same in rape and in attempted rape and the *mens rea* is identical, namely, an intention to have intercourse plus a knowledge of or recklessness as to the woman's absence of consent'.[12] There is no post-Sexual Offences Act 2003 authority directly on point, but, following the logic in *Khan*, the *mens rea* for attempted rape under the current law is an intention to have intercourse in the absence of a reasonable belief in consent.[13] Further clarity could be helpful, particularly since this divergence from the general principle applies to a category of serious offences.

Another major problem with the common law on attempt concerned impossibility. As one textbook puts it, 'The situation contemplated here is where, unknown to D, the prevailing circumstances make it impossible for him to complete the offence he is trying to commit. Prior to the 1981 Act, the courts made unconvincing distinctions and excluded from the law of attempt cases which most people thought ought to be included'.[14] In *Haughton v Smith*, the House of Lords held that D 'could not be convicted of attempting to do that which it had not been possible for him to do'.[15] Lord Morris stated that to take the alternative approach would be to 'punish

---

6   Law Com CP 183 (n 3) 13.3.
7   [1954] 1 WLR 250, citing *Stephen's Digest of the Criminal Law* (9th edn, Sweet and Maxwell 1950) 24.
8   [1975] AC 476, 499.
9   *DPP v Stonehouse* [1978] AC 55, 68.
10   Law Com CP 183 (n 3) 1.73.
11   [1990] 1 WLR 813.
12   Ibid. 819.
13   After considering this decision, the New Zealand Supreme Court adopted a similar approach in *L v The Queen* [2006] NYSC 18 in relation to a charge of attempted sexual violation, sexual violation being a New Zealand offence involving lack of a reasonable belief in V's consent.
14   Russell Heaton and Claire de Than, *Criminal Law* (3rd edn, Oxford University Press 2011) 549.
15   *Haughton* (n 8) 502, per Lord Morris.

people for their guilty intention'.[16] According to him, 'The man who stabs the corpse may be as deserving of punishment as a man who attempts to murder a living person … But such a radical change in the principles of our law should not be introduced in this way [at common law] even if it were desirable'.[17] As many commentators have pointed out, this approach was indefensible: '"Impossible" attempts are no more thought crimes than are other attempts. D must do something which is more than merely preparatory on the facts that he assumed'.[18] Parliament intervened in this matter in the Criminal Attempts Act 1981; sections 1(2) and 1(3) of this Act make it clear that D can now be guilty of an attempt to achieve the impossible.[19] Thus, this aspect of the law has now been resolved in a manner that many people would think is sensible.

Current Issues in the Law of Attempt

In this section, we will return to many of the issues which we debated in the conspiracy chapter (Chapter 8), and also highlight some further remaining problems in the law of attempt. We argue that these issues should be re-examined with an eye to consistency and coherent principle throughout the field of inchoate offences and complicity.

The Issue of Evidence: Proving an Attempt

In a 1980 Report, the Law Commission recommended the definition of attempt adopted in the Criminal Attempts Act 1981.[20] Section 1(1) of the 1981 Act provides: 'If, with intent to commit an offence to which this section applies, a person does an act which is more than merely preparatory to the commission of the offence, he is guilty of attempting to commit the offence'. As we stated in our previous chapter, this Act significantly reformed the law, but this does not mean that the current law is perfect, nor that judges have stopped applying the previous law. It is clear from cases such as *Jones*[21] that judges continue to seek guidance from cases decided under the old common law test (whatever that was exactly!). In the latter case, the Court of Appeal construed as capable of being 'more than merely preparatory' only behaviour very close to D's last possible act.[22] Some of the problems with the law on attempt are specific to certain offences: for example, in the context of offences such as rape and sexual assault, it is anomalous that statutory presumptions about consent and reasonable belief in consent may apply where D is charged with the full offence but not where s/

---

16 Ibid. 500.

17 Ibid.

18 Andrew Simester, Bob Sullivan, John Spencer and Graham Virgo, *Criminal Law: Theory and Doctrine* (3rd edn, Hart 2007) 326.

19 See *Shivpuri* [1987] AC 1, overruling *Anderton v Ryan* [1985] AC 560 on the correct interpretation of s 1 of the Criminal Attempts Act 1981.

20 Law Commission, *Attempt and Impossibility in Relation to Attempt, Conspiracy and Incitement* (Law Com No 102, 1980).

21 [1990] 1 WLR 1057.

22 Ibid. at 890-91, 'Clearly his actions in obtaining the gun, in shortening it, in loading it, in putting on his disguise, and in going to the school could only be regarded as preparatory acts. But, in our judgment, once he had got into the car, taken out the loaded gun and pointed it at the victim with the intention of killing him, there was sufficient evidence for the consideration of the jury … it was a matter for them to decide whether they were sure those acts were more than merely preparatory'.

he is charged with attempting to commit such an offence.[23] However, other issues are more general. Perhaps the most important general problem with the law on attempt is that what amounts to going beyond 'mere preparation' still varies a great deal from case to case. For example, in *Griffin*, D was convicted for attempting to take her two children, who were in local authority care, out of the jurisdiction without the local authority's permission: the attempt occurred when D went to the children's school and told a teacher that she had come to take the children to the dentist; it was not required that the children were in D's control embarking upon a journey to another country.[24] In contrast, in *Geddes*,[25] the Court of Appeal held that D, aged 29, had not committed an act that was more than merely preparatory to false imprisonment after he was found waiting to abduct a child in a school toilet with a knife, rope and masking tape: the Court of Appeal held that D had merely placed himself in a position where he could attempt an offence if a child approached and hence had not 'moved from the realm of intention, preparation and planning into the area of execution or implementation'.[26] The rights of the children in that school would now surely be engaged by the presence of a threat on the premises, in which case some human rights rebalancing of similar cases might well be necessary in future. The lack of clarity on what constitutes an attempt may additionally mean that the law is not compliant with Articles 5 and 7 of the European Convention on Human Rights. We have already outlined the rules relating to these Articles in Chapter 8, and do not intend to repeat them in detail here. However, it is important to note that the law of attempt may be inconsistent with the principle of rule of law enshrined in both of these Articles. We accept that absolute certainty is unattainable, and that Article 7 accordingly allows the 'gradual clarification of the rules of criminal liability … provided that the resultant development is consistent with the essence of the offence and could reasonably be foreseen'.[27] However, a significant problem with the English law on attempt is that the case law is inconsistent on the meaning of 'more than merely preparatory', and that the law of attempt has not been gradually clarified in this respect. Thus, there is significant confusion as to the practical application of the law, which makes it difficult to foresee the results of many cases.

Another issue with the law on attempt is that there is duplication of offences on the facts of many cases; for example, where D was part of a conspiracy that came to fruition. As we stated in our previous chapter, this issue of duplication is not unique to the boundary between inchoate offences and secondary participation, but this does not mean that it is desirable.

Status-Based Exemptions from Liability

Victims   In *Gnango*,[28] Lord Phillips PSC and Judge CJ observed, obiter, that it is clear that the so-called victim rule applies to statutory conspiracy, the inchoate offences created by the Serious Crime Act 2007, and complicity in connection with statutory offences designed to protect members of a class to which D belongs. However, as they also noted, its precise parameters remain unclear.

---

23   Daniel Rodwell, 'Problems with the Sexual Offences Act 2003' [2005] Criminal Law Review 290.

24   *R. v Griffin* (Unreported) (CA). 'Abduction: Criminal Attempts Act 1981, s 1(1), Child Abduction Act 1984, s 1 – Attempt to Take Child out of Jurisdiction without Appropriate Consent' [1993] Criminal Law Review 515 (case comment).

25   *Geddes* [1996] Crim LR 894. 'Attempt: Attempted False Imprisonment' [1996] Criminal Law Review 894 (case comment).

26   Ibid.

27   *SW v UK* (App No 20166/92) (1996) 21 EHRR 363, [36].

28   [2011] UKSC 59; [2012] 1 AC 827.

There is no reference to it in the Criminal Attempts Act 1981.[29] Lord Phillips PSC and Judge CJ stated that the victim rule is based upon the intention of Parliament, rather than of common law origin, and concluded that D was liable for V's murder because he had aided, abetted, counselled or procured the attempted murder of himself by B.[30] If they are correct, then the victim rule potentially applies to complicity in relation to attempted statutory offences, but not to complicity in relation to attempted common law crimes. This is contentious. If there is a valid reason for the victim rule to apply to statutory conspiracy, then it is arguable that this rule should also apply to complicity in relation to an attempt to commit a common law offence; after all, an attempt is often just a conspiracy to commit a crime taken to the next stage. It is true that the Criminal Attempts Act 1981 does not expressly state that the victim rule should apply to complicity in relation to all criminal attempts, but Parliamentary intention can be implied. It must be remembered that the victim rule ultimately originates from *Tyrrell*,[31] a decision that 'can best be interpreted as being based on a term to be implied into the Criminal Law Amendment Act 1885, based as the reasoning was on the implied intention of Parliament'.[32]

Spouses   An agreement confined to spouses or civil partners will not constitute a statutory conspiracy. It could be argued that there ought to be a similar exemption for spouses and civil partners in relation to complicity and the encouraging or assisting inchoate offences under the Serious Crime Act 2007. If this exemption to liability for statutory conspiracy is based upon the notion that spouses and civil partners 'are regarded for certain purposes as in law one person',[33] then one can argue that it should also extend to complicity and the 2007 Act inchoate offences.[34] Let us return to one of our hypothetical examples from Chapter 8. D1 decides to bomb a public building, and successfully implements his plan with D2's help: as the law currently stands, neither will be liable for statutory conspiracy to commit, say, criminal damage if they are spouses or civil partners and the only parties to the plan. However, both will be liable if the plan is implemented; for instance, D2 could be liable for aiding criminal damage committed by D1. Similarly, D2 could be liable for an inchoate offence under the Serious Crime Act 2007. Our point here is not that the law on complicity needs reform in this respect, but simply that it is inconsistent with the law on statutory conspiracy and the inchoate offences under the 2007 Act.

Conditional Intention

We discussed the rules relating to conditional intention as they apply to conspiracy in Chapter 9. It is clear that conditional intention is sufficient for liability for attempt: for example where D enters a house with the intention of stealing if he finds money in it.[35] In contrast, the law of complicity is less settled as it relates to conditional intention. With joint enterprise, liability is based upon D1's foresight that D2 might commit a crime. Thus, if D1 is aware that D2 has a conditional intention

---

29   Ibid. [47]-[53].
30   Ibid. at [52].
31   [1894] 1 QB 710.
32   Ibid. [48].
33   *Mawji* [1957] AC 126, 132.
34   Although there is no space to discuss this matter here, we would argue that the same argument could be made in relation to most, if not all, of the potential public policy reasons put forward in favour of this exemption discussed in *Midland Bank Trust Co Ltd v Green (No 3)* [1982] Ch 529, 535.
35   *Attorney-General's References (Nos 1 and 2 of 1979)* [1979] 3 WLR 577.

to commit a crime, D1 will be liable if this crime or an attempt to commit it occurs.[36] However, with non-joint enterprise secondary liability, the law is not so clear-cut. The weight of authority suggests that liability for aiding and so on, may be imposed where D realises that the crime *may* be committed, but that D does not need to know that it *would* be committed.[37] However, there is also authority against this view.[38] This lack of clarity is undesirable. Moreover, if joint enterprise liability builds upon the law relating to aiding and so on, it is not obvious why there might be a distinction between these two forms of secondary liability in relation to D's foresight that the crime may be committed; for example where D foresees that the principal may kill or attempt to kill 'if necessary'. It also does not seem particularly logical that the law on joint enterprise has a 'fundamental difference' rule, whereas the law on aiding and so on does not seem to grapple with the issues raised by such a rule. Let us suppose that D1 foresees that D2 might use a knife to kill or intentionally inflict serious injury upon V 'if necessary', but D2 actually uses a gun – a much more dangerous weapon – to kill V. D1 is less likely to be liable for V's murder under the doctrine of joint enterprise than s/he is under the rules relating to aiding and so on. Another problem with the law on joint enterprise is that there has been a disproportionate focus upon the rules relating to joint enterprise murder and manslaughter, with the result that there is little clarity of the rules in relation to other types of joint enterprise liability.[39]

The Effect of Impossibility

The law of statutory conspiracy is similar to the law of attempt in relation to impossibility. As David Ormerod summarises the rules, 'once ... intention [to commit the offence contemplated] is proved, it is immaterial that it is in *fact* impossible to commit the substantive offence if, in the case of conspiracy, there has been an agreement to commit it and in the case of attempt, a more than merely preparatory step towards its commission'.[40] In contrast, common law conspiracies are governed by the common law rule in *Nock* that there can be no conspiracy where there is 'an agreement upon a course of conduct which could not in any circumstances result in the statutory offence alleged'.[41] This inconsistency between these different areas of inchoate liability is illogical and undesirable. There is a further problem when one considers the Serious Crime Act 2007. As Ormerod says, this Act 'makes no reference to the position regarding impossibility'.[42] Thus, it is unclear how it would apply 'in a case where D provides P with an article which he thinks is capable of assisting in the commission of a crime, but is never going to be of assistance in committing any crime'.[43] D might be liable for *attempting* to assist or encourage in such a situation,[44] but it is not obvious whether D has committed an offence under the 2007 Act. It is also important to consider

---

36   *Rahman* [2009] UKHL 45.

37   *Bryce; Gilmour* [2000] 2 Cr App R 407; *Carter v Richardson; J.F. Alford Transport Ltd; Reardon* [1999] Crim LR 392.

38   *Bainbridge* [1959] 3 All ER 200.

39   See House of Commons Justice Committee, 'Joint Enterprise' (Eleventh Report of Session 2010-12, 11 January 2012) [34]-[35], for academic and other criticism of the law on joint enterprise as a whole.

40   David Ormerod, *Smith and Hogan's Criminal Law* (13th edn, Oxford University Press 2011) 481-82, referring in particular to s 1(1)(b) of the Criminal Law Act 1977 and s 1(2) of the Criminal Attempts Act 1981 respectively.

41   [1978] AC 979, 998.

42   Ormerod (n 39) 485.

43   Ibid.

44   Ibid.

the law on complicity here. Let us suppose that D1 leaves a bomb where D2 can find it with the intention of aiding D2 in killing V. D2 finds the bomb, unaware that D1 has left it to help him, and attempts to use it to kill V. It is possible to aid an attempt,[45] although the Criminal Attempts Act 1981 rules out liability for attempted 'aiding, abetting, counselling, procuring or suborning the commission of an offence'.[46] Thus, if D2 plants the bomb and it explodes, D1 might be liable for aiding attempted murder even if V was already dead before the explosion. In contrast, D1 will not be liable for aiding attempted murder if it is impossible for D2 to kill V with the bomb because it simply does not work, since D1 has not in fact assisted D2. In the latter situation, D might be liable for attempting to intentionally assist or encourage a crime contrary to section 44 of the Serious Crime Act 2007. There is a fierce debate here about whether there is at least a conceptual clash between section 44 of the 2007 Act and the section in the 1981 Act that rules out secondary liability for what might be 'attempted complicity'.[47]

Withdrawal and Complicity

As examined in Chapter 8, it is impossible to withdraw from a conspiracy[48] but seeking to prevent it being carried out appears to prevent a conspiracy from existing at all.[49] The latter approach seems to be broadly parallel to the rules on withdrawal from a joint enterprise, but the former conflicts with those rules. The lack of a similar rule applying to attempt is in the nature of that form of liability, since going beyond preparation is not reversible and a solo would-be criminal who changes his mind does not need to communicate his withdrawal to anyone else. The harm threatened to society is removed simply by his decision not to continue with his plan, whereas the harm in a conspiracy might still be carried out by others. However matters are not always so simple because many crimes are attempted by two or more people acting together. The complexity is compounded if we consider two people who plot to commit a crime, attempt to do so, then begin to carry it out together. If one of them changes his mind and tries to withdraw from the planned crime, different legal principles may apply depending on how far they manage to proceed before being arrested or charged.[50] An accomplice can avoid liability for an offence which he has assisted or encouraged by making an effective withdrawal from participation before the offence is committed. The rationale for this is not clear but it may be because A is deemed to be less culpable (he will remain liable for an offence, if any, committed before the point of repentance) and/or because the law wants to encourage accessories to withdraw. Where the crime is planned in advance, withdrawal is easier if the planned crime is not yet in the process of being committed, with unequivocal communication of withdrawal being sufficient and no requirement of seeking to prevent the crime being carried out.[51] There is a lack of clarity as to whether and when a joint enterprise party may withdraw once the

---

45   *Hapgood and Wyatt* (1870) LR 1 CCR 221, CCR.

46   s 1(4)(b).

47   See, Michael Bohlander, 'The Conflict Between the Serious Crime Act 2007 and Section 1(4)(b) Criminal Attempts Act 1981: A Missed Repeal?' [2010] Criminal Law Review 483; and John Child, 'The Differences Between Attempted Complicity and Inchoate Assisting and Encouraging: A Reply to Professor Bohlander' [2010] Criminal Law Review 924.

48   *Saik* [2006] UKHL18.

49   *Yip Chiu-Cheung* [1994] 2 All ER 924 per Lord Griffiths at 928.

50   Although they could of course be charged with inchoate offences even after completing the full offence successfully.

51   *Grundy* [1977] Crim LR 543; *Whitefield* (1983) 79 Cr App R 36; cf. *Becerra* (1975) 62 Cr App R 212.

crime has begun[52] and it appears that different rules apply when a joint enterprise is spontaneous.[53] In the latter situation, the test seems to be fluid depending on the extent and importance of A's contribution to the crime as well as the timing and manner of his withdrawal; according to Mantell LJ in *O'Flaherty*,[54] 'To disengage from an incident a person must do enough to demonstrate that he or she is withdrawing from the joint enterprise. This is ultimately a question of fact and degree for the jury'. Account will be taken of, *inter alia*, the nature of the assistance and encouragement already given and how imminent the infliction or the fatal injury or injuries is, as well as the nature of the action said to constitute withdrawal.

One arguably illogical aspect of the current rules is that it is easier for him to withdraw from the plan the closer he moves towards its commission, since he may withdraw from a joint enterprise in limited circumstances but cannot withdraw from conspiracy. Of course this means that a joint principal who withdraws could still face liability for the earlier conspiracy, but not every joint enterprise involves a conspiracy.[55] If it were possible to withdraw from a conspiracy, that would often have the surely desirable effect of the plot falling apart or becoming known to the police.

A Duress Defence?

We saw in Chapter 8 that duress may be argued as a defence to conspiracy to murder, but not to any murder charge.[56] We noted in that chapter that there have been powerful dissenting judgments in the leading cases, that judges have spoken out repeatedly about the undesirability of anomalies in this area of the law, and that the blurred boundary between conspiracy and attempt makes the distinction even more difficult to justify; it sometimes seems as if there is less than one 'step' between the two inchoate offences. Duress is not the only defence where such anomalies might arise, and so defences should form part of a re-evaluation of this entire field of law. It is also worth noting that the statutory defence of acting reasonably under the SCA 2007 should arguably also apply to all inchoate offences and forms of complicity or none at all.

The Effect of Mistaken Beliefs

As we stated in our previous chapter, an important matter is that it is unclear precisely what is being criminalised with attempt. Many commentators believe that 'the intent is the essence of the crime',[57] or, to put it slightly differently, that 'the essence of a criminal attempt lies in the defendant's firm intention to commit the substantive offence'.[58] However, this does not sit easily with the rule that D cannot be liable for attempting to commit an act believing it to be a criminal offence when it is not.[59] If the essence of the offence is indeed an intention to commit criminal conduct, then it is arguable that, contrary to the current law, D should be punished even when the act in question is not an offence; for example, of 'a new offence of "contempt of law", consisting

---

52   *Perman* [1996] 1 Cr App R 24.

53   *Mitchell and King* [1999] Crim LR 496; *O'Flaherty* [2004] EWCA Crim 526 (approved and applied in *D* [2005] EWCA Crim 1981).

54   *O'Flaherty* (n 52).

55   Since a joint enterprise may, rarely, be spontaneous.

56   *Howe* [1987] 1 AC 417; *Gotts* [1992] 1 All ER 832.

57   *Whybrow* (1951) 35 Cr App R 141, 147, per Lord Goddard.

58   Andrew Ashworth, 'Criminal Attempts and the Role of Resulting Harm Under the Code, and in the Common Law' (1987-88) 19 Rutgers Law Journal 725, 733.

59   *Taaffe* [1984] AC 539.

in acting in a way that one believes to be criminal'.[60] After all, in such circumstances, D has demonstrated a commitment to perpetrate a crime, and is thus arguably a future threat 'to interests that the law seeks to protects'.[61] Nonetheless, the problem with imposing liability on this basis is that 'if guilt becomes a function of future dangerousness, actors will be blamed for something that has nothing to do with blame – namely for what actors are predicted to do in the future'.[62] Thomas Weigend argues that the function of the law of attempt is to protect 'an intangible good – the public peace',[63] and that the potential harm to the public peace 'is the apprehension and fear of the victim as well as the alarm of the community about the fact that someone has set out to do serious damage to a fellow citizen and to break the accepted rules of social life'.[64] Weigend's analysis suggests that a case like *Taaffe* should not result in liability.[65] D claimed that he had attempted to import foreign currency into the UK, mistakenly believing it to be a crime, but unknowingly imported prohibited drugs instead. The House of Lords held that he could not be liable, since he was to be judged on the facts as he believed them to be, and clandestinely importing foreign currency into the UK is not an offence. Adopting Weigend's analysis, it could be said that the House of Lords reached the correct result because D had not engaged in conduct likely to create alarm, since his conduct 'seen in the light of his statements accompanying the acts he deemed necessary for achieving his purpose, would [not] cause alarm, or apprehension to an average observer'.[66] However, the better view seems to be that the primary purpose of the English law of attempt is to prevent the harm that would or could be caused by a successful attempt.[67] As Antony Duff puts it, the criminal law should seek to prevent such harm and it 'would be a less effective deterrent [if it did not punish attempt]: people would be more likely to embark on criminal enterprises and to carry them through'.[68] Furthermore, as Duff adds, 'in so far as punishment also aims at reform or incapacitation, such a system would fail to capture many who merited such coercive attention'.[69] This approach to the rationale underpinning the law of attempt also suggests that the House of Lords reached the correct decision in *Taaffe*. In this case, D displayed a willingness to break what he believed to be the law, at least on one occasion, but he did not deserve punishment because he did not 'display a willingness to injure any … substantive interest which the law actually protects, or to do anything which the law otherwise actually prohibits'.[70] However, it needs to be noted here that the common law offence of conspiracy to defraud is so wide that it criminalises agreements that do not necessarily involve the commission of a substantive crime or even a tort; that is, anything that the law actually prohibits. Thus, we have an anomalous situation where an agreement to perform a plan might be unlawful, but attempting to

---

60   Antony Duff, *Criminal Attempts* (Oxford University Press, 1997) 157 (ultimately concluding that the law should contain no such offence).

61   Peter Westen, 'Impossibility Attempts: A Speculative Thesis' (2007-2008) 5 Ohio State Journal of Criminal Law 523, 542.

62   Ibid. 543.

63   Thomas Weigend, 'Why Lady Eldon Should Be Acquitted: The Social Harm in Attempting the Impossible' (1977) 27 DePaul Law Review 231, 264.

64   Ibid.

65   *Taaffe* (n 58).

66   Weigand (n 62) 269, explaining the relevant test. See too ibid. 272, discussing an analogous hypothetical smuggling case.

67   See for example Law Com CP 183 (n 3) 14.8, framing the debate about attempt in terms of the desirability of preventing this type of harm.

68   Duff (n 59) 133.

69   Ibid. 134.

70   Ibid. 159.

carry out the goal of the plan or even successfully implementing it might not be an offence even if the defendants think that carrying out their plan is a crime

Other significant current issues   There are other significant issues in the current law of attempt. The Law Commission have pointed out that there is an important debate about the appropriate fault element for attempt 'in relation to the circumstance element of the substantive offence';[71] for example, whether 'the test for fault in relation to a circumstance element in the law of attempts [should be] … whether D possessed the fault element (if any) required for the completed offence'.[72] Finally, as the Law Commission state, the statutory definition of attempt would seem to preclude an attempt via omission. However, it is arguable that this is wrong as a matter of principle where, as a matter of law, 'the offence intended is capable of being committed by an omission'.[73] Moreover, while it would also appear to be impossible to commit a conspiracy by omission, there is an inconsistency here between the law on attempt, on the one hand, and the rules on complicity and encouraging or assisting crime contrary to the Serious Crime Act 2007 on the other. This situation does not appear to be logical. It is clear that an omission can be a sufficient *actus reus* of secondary liability[74] and of encouraging or assisting crime under the 2007 Act.[75] However, there is no obvious reason why secondary liability and encouraging or assisting crime under Part 2 of the 2007 Act can occur through an omission, but an attempt cannot.

Alternative Approaches on Attempt

The sheer volume of reform proposals which have been made in recent decades concerning attempt and conspiracy would indicate that the existing law is far from ideal, and hence it is helpful to examine such proposals. There have been so many law reform proposals on attempt that it is impossible to consider them all in detail here; instead, we shall concentrate on the main elements of the most important ones, and on relevant alternative approaches in other jurisdictions. A Working Party assisting the Law Commission on the General Principles of the Criminal Law examined the English law of attempt in 1973.[76] One of their most radical proposals concerned the *actus reus* of attempt. Believing that attempts should be criminalised on the basis of the harm principle and that the law at that time was too generous to certain defendants, the Working Party recommended a 'substantial step' as the *actus reus* in attempts. Furthermore, they proposed to clarify the phrase 'substantial step' by reference to 'a number of illustrations such as appear in the Australian Draft Code and the Model Penal Code'.[77] Their recommendation was that legislation should adopt these illustrations as a non-exhaustive list of 'examples of what are substantial steps if the requisite intent is proved'.[78] This would have reformed the law in a manner similar to the United States Model Penal Code, which has long contained 'the most commonly used "attempt" definition'

---

71   Law Com CP 183 (n 3) 1.81.

72   Ibid. 1.82.

73   Ibid. 1.86.

74   See for example *Tuck v Robson* [1970] 1 WLR 741, DC.

75   See s 47(8).

76   Law Commission Working Party on the General Principles of Criminal Law, *Inchoate Offences: Conspiracy, Attempt and Incitement* (Working Paper No 50, 1973).

77   Ibid. 78.

78   Ibid.

in United States jurisdictions.[79] This Code defines attempt as a 'substantial step in a course of conduct planned to culminate in [the defendant']s commission of the crime'.[80] However, the Law Commission subsequently rejected the Working Party's 'substantial step' recommendation in the 1980 Law Commission paper that led to the 1981 Act. The Law Commission thought that the phrase 'substantial step' was inherently vague, and that 'If, as we believe, provision of … [illustrative] examples is necessary because it is inherently impossible to define further what is meant by a "substantial step", the test in our view stands self-condemned'.[81] The Law Commission also considered four other alternative approaches to the definition of the *actus reus* of attempts. First, they considered what they called 'the "first stage" theory'.[82] As they summarised it, 'The "first stage" test in its pure form seizes on the first overt act done towards the commission of the offence as the criterion. It appears to be adopted by some Continental Codes, which refer to "acts exhibiting the commencement of the execution" of crimes … It also met with a measure of approval in the English draft code of 1879, Stephen's *Digest of the Criminal Law* Article 29, and the Indian Penal Code'.[83] The Law Commission rejected the 'first stage' theory because they thought that it put too much emphasis on D's intention 'in that, given proof of intention to commit an offence, many quite innocent acts can be regarded as overt acts done towards the commission of the offence'.[84] The Law Commission also rejected the 'final stage' or 'last act' theory, which 'admits of no attempt unless and until the intending offender has done all that is necessary for him to do in order to bring his crime to completion'.[85] Some English common law cases can be interpreted as authority for this 'final stage' approach; for example, Lord Diplock's speech in *Stonehouse* where he stated that 'the offender must have crossed the Rubicon and burnt his boats'.[86] However, the Law Commission rejected this 'last act' approach for a variety of reasons, including because they believed it would allow D to advance too far towards his or her objective before effective intervention could take place. Similarly, the Law Commission rejected the 'unequivocal act' theory. As they put it, 'This theory in its pure form requires that the act itself, without regard to any statement of intention, either contemporaneous or subsequent, must unequivocally demonstrate the intention to commit the relevant offence. It was propounded by Salmond and was enacted in the New Zealand Crimes Act 1908, but was found not to work satisfactorily in practice'.[87] Pointing out that this test was discarded by the New Zealand Crimes Act 1961, they claimed that one significant problem with it was that in some cases 'the conduct was clearly carried out in execution of the offence but could not be regarded as unequivocally pointing to the intention'.[88] The Law Commission also considered the 'proximity test', noting that 'no precise test has been evolved for determining whether an act is sufficiently proximate to the offence to constitute the *actus reus* of an attempt'.[89] Observing that 'there is no magic formula which can now be produced to define precisely what constitutes an attempt', they proposed to modify the proximity test and recommend 'as the most appropriate

---

79   *Sui v Immigration & Naturalization Serv.*, 250 F.3d 105, 116 (2d Cir. 2001). See too *US v Jose Guadalupe Hernandez Galvan* No 09-40872, January 31, 2011 – US 5th Circuit, making the same point.

80   Model Penal Code, s 5.01(1)(c).

81   Law Com No 102 (n 20) 2.33.

82   Ibid. 2.22.

83   Ibid.

84   Ibid.

85   Ibid. 2.24.

86   *Stonehouse* (n 9).

87   Law Com No 102 (n 20) 2.26.

88   Ibid. 2.26.

89   Ibid. 2.31.

form of words to define the *actus reus* of attempt *any act which goes so far towards the commission of the offence attempted as to be more than an act of mere preparation*'.[90] This formulation was adopted in the 1981 Act.

The Law Commission returned to the issue of attempt again in their Draft Criminal Code of 1989. Their Criminal Code would have changed the law on attempt in two respects. First, they would have clarified the fault element of attempt to make it clear that 'recklessness with respect to a circumstance suffices where it suffices for the offence itself' (the law on this point was subsequently addressed in *Khan*, discussed above).[91] Secondly, they would have amended the law on attempt to include attempts via omission where the substantive offence could be committed via omission,[92] since they believed that this was the correct approach as a matter of principle. This would have moved the English law of attempt closer to the Australian common law and to the statutory regimes in Tasmania, Canada and New Zealand, all of which define attempts as including omissions.[93]

Concerned by inconsistency in the interpretation of the 'more than merely preparatory' provision in the Criminal Attempts Act 1981, as well as the narrow reading of this provision in cases such as *Geddes*,[94] the Law Commission returned to the issue of attempts again in their 2007 consultation paper on conspiracy and attempts.[95] This time, they provisionally proposed 'the creation of two offences to replace the single offence in the 1981 Act'.[96] The first of these offences would still be called 'attempt' but 'confined to those who, with intent to commit a substantive offence, were engaged in the last acts needed to commit it'.[97] The second offence would be '"criminal preparation" applying to those who, with intent to commit the offence, were still only preparing to commit it but had proceeded beyond the stage of mere preparation'.[98] The two offences would carry the maximum penalty now available for an attempt to commit the substantive offence. The Commission thought that the creation of an offence of criminal preparation would not extend the scope of criminal liability imposed by the 1981 Act, correctly interpreted, but that it might be helpful to deal with 'the reluctance of some courts to extend the scope of the crime of attempt beyond a "trying" that involves D having done all he or she needs to do or believes he or she needs to do to bring about the completion of the offence: a "completed attempt"'.[99] They provisionally proposed that 'Illustrations would be provided of the kinds of conduct which ought to be regarded as going beyond mere preparation and as amounting to criminal preparation'.[100] The Law Commission also proposed other changes to the law on attempt; for instance, that 'attempt and criminal preparation should cover omissions where, as a matter of law, the offence intended is capable of being committed by an omission'.[101]

---

90   Ibid. 2.49.

91   Draft Criminal Code, s 49(2).

92   Ibid. s 49(3).

93   See *Britten v Alpogut* [1987] VR 929 (Vic CA), the Tasmanian Criminal Code Act 1924, s 2(1), s 25 of the Canadian criminal code, and s 72(1) of the New Zealand Crimes Act 1961 respectively.

94   *Geddes* (n 25).

95   Law Com CP 183 (n 3).

96   Ibid. 1.76.

97   Ibid. 1.77.

98   Ibid. 1.78.

99   Ibid. 12.21.

100   Ibid. 17.27.

101   Ibid. 1.86.

The Law Commission's provisional proposal to create two offences to replace the single offence in the 1981 Act encountered much opposition. In their 2009 Report on conspiracy and attempt, the Law Commission identified 11 objections in this respect.[102] Persuaded by the argument that the present offence of attempt is not fundamentally flawed and that it has not 'been rendered unworkable by the courts having adopted a consistently narrow approach when interpreting the 1981 Act',[103] they decided not to propose fundamental reform to the law of attempt in their Report and abandoned the idea of creating two offences. We would argue that abandoning significant reform was a mistake. The law on attempt is inherently unclear and contextual, but the duty is to make it as a clear as possible, and the use of illustrative examples to explain what is meant by going beyond mere preparation would be a major improvement. As should be clear from this pair of chapters, we would argue for more significant reform than any so far proposed by the Law Commission. However, the Law Commission did recommend certain reforms. For instance, they proposed:

> [F]or substantive offences which have a circumstance requirement but no corresponding fault requirement, or which have a corresponding fault requirement which is objective (such as negligence), it should be possible to convict D of attempting to commit the substantive offence only if D was subjectively reckless as to the circumstance at the relevant time.[104]

This recommendation would require amendment to the 1981 Act and clarify the law in relation to, say, attempted rape, where D would not be liable for attempted rape unless he was subjectively reckless as to lack of consent. This would mean that the English law of attempt would extend its reach beyond the equivalent law in certain other common law jurisdictions: for example, the law of attempt in Victoria requires that D 'intend or believe that any fact or circumstance the existence of which is an element of the offence will exist at the time the offence is to take place'.[105] Limited justifications have been advanced to support such a development. To introduce one of the most extensive laws of attempt in the Commonwealth in this respect without ensuring a good fit with other obviously related modes of liability would surely be myopic. We would argue that this is yet another proposal for piecemeal reform without a view to the bigger picture.

In their 2009 Report, the Law Commission also proposed to amend the law to specifically include attempted murder by omission, but abandoned the notion that 'it is necessary or desirable to extend the law of attempt in *general* terms to encompass omissions'.[106] They made this decision about omissions in general for a variety of reasons, including 'the paucity of plausible factual scenarios [of potential injustice] beyond the example of attempted murder ... [and] the additional complexity a general omissions provision would bring to the law of attempt'.[107]

---

102   Law Commission, *Conspiracy and Attempts* (Law Com No 318, 2009), 8.33-8.66.
103   Ibid. 8.60.
104   Ibid. 8.133.
105   Crimes Act 1958, s 31N(2). For similar approaches in Canada and Ireland, see *Ancio* (1984) 1 SCR 225 (SC), where the Supreme Court of Canada interpreted s 24 of the Canadian criminal code, and *People (Attorney General) v Thornton* [1952] IR 91, 93 where the Irish Court of Criminal Appeal held that a criminal attempt is an act done with 'specific intent to commit a particular crime'.
106   Law Com No 318 (n 101) 8.150.
107   Ibid. 8.148.

The Law Commission's Proposals on Conspiracy

To conclude our pair of chapters and tie together our arguments for principled reconsideration of this entire field of law, we will now take a look at past reform proposals for conspiracy.

The Law Commission has considered the issue of criminal conspiracy on many occasions. Its 1976 report on conspiracy and criminal law reform led to the enactment of statutory rules relating to conspiracy introduced in the Criminal Law Act 1977.[108] This 1977 legislation specifically preserved the common law offences of conspiracy to defraud, conspiracy to corrupt public morals, and conspiracy to outrage public decency.[109] The Law Commission returned to the issue of conspiracy in their Draft Criminal Code of 1989, clause 48 of which would have retained much of the existing law but made certain changes to it: for example, 'Clause 48 did not provide for the continuation of the exemptions from liability for a conspiracy formed by D with a spouse or a child under the age of criminal responsibility'.[110] Clause 48 was of course never implemented, since the Draft Criminal Code was itself never implemented. The Law Commission produced another report relating to conspiracy in 2002, when they considered law on conspiracy to defraud in the course of reviewing the criminal law on fraud in general.[111] This time, they recommended the abolition of conspiracy to defraud, concluding: 'The advantages of abolishing it … greatly outweigh any possible advantage that might accrue from retaining it alongside the new offences we recommend. We believe that those offences cover enough of the ground presently covered by conspiracy to defraud to make it unnecessary to retain that offence any longer'.[112] Parliament enacted the majority of the Law Commission's 2002 recommendations in the Fraud Act 2006. However, although the then Government ultimately wanted to repeal the common law offence of conspiracy to defraud, it chose to retain it temporarily 'at least until we have experience of how the new offences operate in practice, [since] it would be rash to repeal conspiracy to defraud as it provides flexibility in dealing with a wide variety of frauds'.[113] The Law Commission returned once again to the issue of conspiracy in 2006 and 2007, when they considered the issues of inchoate liability for encouraging and assisting offences and secondary liability for participating in crime.[114] Their focus in considering these areas of law was understandably not on the general law of conspiracy. However, in response to a Government request in 2006, they finally returned to the general rules relating to conspiracy in a 2007 consultation paper on reform to the law of conspiracy and attempt.[115] This time, they did not review the common law on conspiracy, since the Government had not asked them to do so. The Law Commission made 16 recommendations on the law of conspiracy in their 2009 report on the inchoate offences of conspiracy and attempt.[116] Some of these recommendations would retain elements of the existing statutory law of conspiracy. For example, their first 2009 recommendation is that the law on conspiracy must remain focused upon the element of agreement and that this leaves no room for a defence of withdrawal: as they put it, conspiracy 'must involve an agreement by two or more persons to engage in the conduct element of an offence and (where relevant) to

---

108   Law Commission, *Report on Criminal Conspiracy and Law Reform* (Law Com No 75, 1976).
109   Criminal Law Act 1977, ss 5(2)-5(3).
110   Law Com CP 183 (n 3) 3.33.
111   Law Commission, *Fraud* (Law Com No 276, 2002).
112   Ibid. 9.4.
113   Home Office, *Fraud Law Reform: Government Response to Consultations* (2005) 40.
114   Law Commission, *Inchoate Liability for Assisting and Encouraging Crime* (Law Com No 300, 2006) and Law Commission, *Participating in Crime* (Law Com No 305, 2007) respectively.
115   Law Com CP 183 (n 3).
116   For a summary, see Law Com No 318 (n 101) Part 9.

bring about any consequence element of the substantive offence'.[117] As the Law Commission states, this recommendation 'is already generally understood to be the law'.[118] Other recommendations in this 2009 Law Commission report would make significant substantive changes to the law of statutory conspiracy. For instance, although the Commission proposed retaining the 'need to prove intention with regard to a conduct or consequence element',[119] they concluded that 'the law is now operating in a way too generous to those who agree on conduct that they know may end in the commission of criminal offences',[120] and accordingly proposed changes in this respect so that 'The prosecution should no longer be required to show knowledge on the part of an alleged conspirator that a circumstance element would be present at the relevant time, unless proof of such knowledge is required by the substantive offence'.[121] The Government 'has accepted the recommendations contained in this report',[122] but it has chosen to prioritise other matters, announcing in 2012 that, although the recommendations are 'worthwhile projects for the future',[123] they will not 'be implemented during the lifetime of this Parliament'.[124] Given that the Law Commission's 2009 proposals do not address common law conspiracy, they would not solve the problems with this offence, even if they were implemented.

The most recent Law Commission proposals relating to conspiracy concern the common law. In 2010, the Commission chose to examine public nuisance and outraging public decency in the light of 'a new programme of "simplification" of the criminal law'.[125] They provisionally concluded that the offence of outraging public decency should be retained, and that its conduct element should remain unchanged. However, they recommended reform to the fault element of the offence so that 'D must be shown to have intended to generate, or realised that he or she might generate, outrage, shock or disgust in ordinary people'.[126] Their provisional recommendation regarding the offence of conspiracy to outrage public decency is that the existing common law offence should be abolished and replaced with a restated offence in statutory form with a new fault element of intention or recklessness as to the two elements of the *actus reus* of the substantive offence:

performing any activity or creating any display or object:

(a) which is of such a nature as to be likely to cause a reasonable person witnessing it shock, outrage or humiliation (the indecency requirement),

(b) in such a place or in such circumstances that it may be witnessed by two or more members of the public (the publicity requirement).[127]

---

117   Ibid. 2.45.
118   Ibid. 2.31.
119   Ibid. 2.47.
120   Ibid. 1.46.
121   Ibid. 1.47.
122   Ministry of Justice, *Report on the Implementation of Law Commission Proposals* (HC 1900, 2012) 29.
123   Ibid.
124   Ibid.
125   Law Commission, *Simplification of Criminal Law: Public Nuisance and Outraging Public Decency* (Law Com CP 193, 2010) 1.1.
126   Ibid. 5.52.
127   Ibid. 6.13.

The Law Commission concluded in their 2010 report that outraging public decency and conspiracy to outrage public decency cover the same conduct (which surely needs to change). They provisionally recommended abolishing the conspiracy form of the offence.

Conclusion: Time for a Coherent, Unified Approach

In our pair of chapters we have examined many of the arguments for streamlining the law between inchoate offences and complicity. We have traced issues across this field of criminal law and found many instances where further consideration would be welcome. The need for clarity and consistency is too strong for this to be left to judges or piecemeal reform. While the Law Commission's many existing proposals have many admirable aspects, the one thing that they have always missed is the opportunity to consider the bigger picture for which we have argued. This is, of course, understandable given their narrower remit and the fact that the Government has never asked them to do so. We have demonstrated that there are significant disagreements and grey areas in the case law, which, in some areas, have persisted for hundreds of years. Partial reform in the law of conspiracy has created substantial grey areas and worrying new trends. If statutory schemes allow the prior common law to continue to develop, then there are dangers of further such problems. Surely it is undesirable to repeatedly leave a common law form of liability while codifying an area of law, for the same reasons that common law attempt was abolished by the Criminal Attempts Act 1981. As we have demonstrated, the present fit between common law and statute is far from ideal in various parts of this field of law. Although prosecutors are very fond of common law conspiracy, they have made no case for it remaining uncodified. Many a judge would welcome similar codification of joint enterprise liability, which is essentially the same crime as conspiracy but at a later stage in events. It is now time to codify the whole of the law of conspiracy and complicity.

Chapter 10

Inchoate Liability and the Part 2 Offences under the Serious Crime Act 2007

Rudi Fortson QC

Background and General Matters

Introduction

In search of a comprehensible code for Participation in Crime: a pipedream? Part 2 of the Serious Crime Act 2007, which creates three inchoate offences of encouraging or assisting the 'commission of an offence', came into force on 1 October 2008.[1] The offences do not extend to Scotland. Each offence is successively more widely drawn and, unhappily, increasingly complex in its structure.

Common to each offence is the element that D 'does an act capable of encouraging or assisting the commission of an offence' by P.[2] As we shall see, Parliament's use of the word 'offence' is often misplaced. At the heart of each Part 2 offence is D's subjective attitude[3] with regards to conduct that D contemplates P will carry out. At the risk of over simplification, whereas s 44 criminalises D who *intentionally* encourages or assists P to act criminally, ss 45 and 46 are founded on D's *belief* that his act will encourage or assist P to commit a crime. Importantly, each Part 2 offence remains subject to further *mens rea* elements set out in s 47 of the Act.

The Part 2 offences are primarily intended to deal with cases where D does an act (for example, providing a ladder, knife, or firearm, to P) that was 'capable of encouraging or assisting' P to commit an offence which the latter was unable to commit (for example, P was arrested before he could do so).[4] There can be cases where it is not open to the prosecutor to charge an offence of conspiracy, attempt, or common-law incitement.[5] In the event that the anticipated offence was not completed, D cannot be convicted on a secondary liability basis. Part 2 of the 2007 Act therefore

---

1 SI 2008/2504.

2 s 44(1)(a), s 44(a) and s 46(1)(a). Note that the s 46 of the Serious Crime Act 2007 offence is triable only on indictment: s 55(2), Serious Crime Act 2007.

3 The expression 'subjective attitude', employed (and perhaps coined) by Sir Richard Buxton, in his article, 'Joint Enterprise' [2009] Criminal Law Review 233, neatly and usefully summarises the various descriptors that could be applied in respect of a defendant's *mens rea*.

4 Note that the expression 'anticipated offence', is used in this chapter as a convenient way of referring to P's future offence (that is, the offence which D contemplates that P will go on to commit), but it is also an expression that is defined by s 47(9) of the Serious Crime Act 2007 for the purposes of the 'remaining provisions of [Part 2] (unless otherwise provided) …'.

5 Common law incitement has been repealed: s 59, Serious Crime Act 2007.

fills a gap in the pre-existing law, but it is a gap that (arguably) could have been filled by a carefully crafted offence of 'facilitating' the commission of an offence.[6]

The three Part 2 offences take subject to a statutory defence, namely, that D knew or believed that 'certain circumstances existed'[7] *and* that it was reasonable for him to have acted as he did.[8] No liability arises under Part 2 if D falls within the 'protected category', that is to say, 'he is a person in respect of whom the "protective offence"[9] was committed or would have been if it had been committed'.[10] Furthermore, a person cannot be guilty of a Part 2 offence in respect of corporate manslaughter.[11]

Despite the breadth of the Part 2 offences, prosecutors have tended to resist the temptation to use them[12] due, in large part, to the conceptual and practical complexities of Part 2, which many commentators have remarked is 'over detailed, convoluted and unreadable'.[13] What may appear to be a straightforward structure in the creation of each offence, will be demonstrated to be nothing of the sort. This is particularly evident in respect of the s 46 offence, which was examined by the Court of Appeal in *S and H*,[14] but which has attracted strong criticism[15] as well as supportive comments.[16] Accordingly, confidence in the s 46 offence has not been bolstered by the problems identified by the Court in that case notwithstanding the Court's best efforts to resolve them. There is little doubt that another Division of the Court of Appeal will be required to look again at the

---

6   See, for example, David Ormerod and Rudi Fortson, 'Serious Crime Act 2007: The Part 2 Offences' [2009] Criminal Law Review 389; Glanville Williams, 'Complicity, Purpose and the Draft Code' [1990] Criminal Law Review 4; Dennis Baker, 'Complicity, Proportionality and the Serious Crime Act 2007' (2011) 14(3) New Criminal Law Review 403.

7   Serious Crime Act 2007, s 50(1)(a). The Act provides no assistance as to the range or kind of circumstances that can be taken into account for the purposes of this statutory defence.

8   Ibid. s 50. Assuming that s 50 is ECHR compliant, the burden of proof is on the defendant: see Rudi Fortson, *The Serious Crime Act 2007*, para.6.131 to 133 (n.13).

9   '… an offence that exists (wholly or in part) for the protection of a particular category of persons ("the protected category")' (ibid. s 51(2)).

10   Ibid. s 51.

11   Ibid. s 62.

12   The same point has been made by Professor Virgo: see Graham Virgo 'Encouraging or Assisting More Than One Offence' [2012] Archbold Review 6, who cites *R v Blackshaw* [2011] EWCA Crim 2312 as an example of use being made of the Part 2 offences (riot). However, there is clear evidence that since 2009, the number of offences charged under Part 2 of the 2007 Act has increased (13 (2009), 47 (2010), and 121 (2011)): para.52, Memorandum prepared by the Home Office and the Ministry of Justice (November, 2012), to the Home Affairs Select Committee and Justice Committee (Post Legislative Scrutiny of the Serious Crime Act 2007). Part 2 of the 2007 has been deployed creatively, see, for example: *Khan v The Secretary of State for Foreign and Commonwealth Affairs* [2012] EWHC 3728 (Admin).

13   See Ormerod and Fortson (n 6); David Ormerod, *Smith and Hogans Criminal Law* (13th edn, Oxford University Press 2011) 460-79; John Spencer and Graham Virgo, 'Encouraging and Assisting Crime' (2008) 9 Archbold News 7; David Ibbotson, 'Encouraging or Assisting an Attempt' [2009] Archbold News 8; Michael Bohlander, 'The Conflict between the Serious Crime Act 2007 and Section 1(4)(b) of the Criminal Attempts Act 1981: A Missed Repeal?' [2010] Criminal Law Review 483; John Child, 'The Differences Between Attempted Complicity and Inchoate Assisting and Encouraging: A Reply to Professor Bohlander' [2010] Criminal Law Review 925; Rudi Fortson, *The Serious Crime Act 2007* (Blackstone's Guide, Oxford University Press 2008); and Rudi Fortson (Note) *R v S and H* [2012] Criminal Law Review 449, 450.

14   [2011] EWCA Crim 2872.

15   Virgo (n 12); and John Child, 'Exploring the *Mens Rea* Requirements of the Serious Crime Act 2007: Assisting and Encouraging Offences' [2012] Journal of Criminal Law 220.

16   Albeit from this author: see Fortson, *R v S and H* (n 13) 450.

scope of the s 46 offence and, as seems likely, to review its own decision in *S and H*. Although a number of *sentencing* appeals have been heard by that Court, there have been no significant judicial pronouncements in respect of appeals against conviction that have critically examined offences under s 44 or s 45. Prosecutors will doubtless be mindful of the 'CPS Guidance on: Joint Enterprise Charging Decisions' (December 2012). However, that guidance may need to be revised in the light of judicial decisions made in respect of Part 2 of the 2007 Act. The guidance ought not to be regarded as the 'last word' (or even definitive) so far as this difficult area of the law is concerned.

This chapter has been written from the perspective of a criminal law practitioner (for which no apology is made) and it aims not only to guide the reader through the maze of legal complexities in Part 2, but also to attempt to bridge what may be seen as a growing divide between legal theorists and practitioners with regard to rules that give rise to criminal liability for participation in the commission of an offence.

It is in the nature of case law that rules develop in a piecemeal fashion as the experience of the judiciary widens to address novel situations.[17] For at least 200 years, cases of murder and manslaughter in respect of which the victim was killed during a fight involving several persons, in circumstances where the evidence may disclose two or more contributing causes of death,[18] have proved to be very problematic for the courts.[19] Yet, attempts by some of the finest legal minds to devise a coherent, comprehensible, and workable set of rules relating to participation in crime have not produced the reforms hoped for.[20] Unfortunately, Part 2 overlaps with rules relating to other inchoate offences and secondary liability, which thereby introduces further incoherence into the legal structure, as well as making the task of trial judges more difficult when directing juries.[21] Given that it will be rare to find instances where the facts of a particular case cannot be appropriately dealt with by one or more offences drawn from among the array of offences that exist,[22] it is arguable that the enactment of Part 2 was unnecessary or, at least, untimely. The better course (it is submitted) would have been for Parliament to have deferred enacting that Part until such time as it was able to incorporate its provisions as part of a comprehensive code relating to secondary liability and, only then, in conjunction with modified rules pertaining to homicide. But

---

17 As recently as 2011 the Supreme Court of England and Wales gave consideration to liability in cases of a shoot-out between two or more persons in a public place that killed an innocent bystander – a thankfully rare occurrence in the UK but familiar in some jurisdictions: see *R v Gnango* [2011] UKSC 59.

18 Giving rise to more than just a theoretical possibility that there could be two 'chains' of liability, that is, D1 who aided or abetted P1 to stab V, and D2 who aided and abetted P2 to stamp on V's head: both acts of violence contributing to the cause of V's death.

19 In *R v Mendez* [2010] EWCA Crim 516, Toulson LJ cited legal materials dating as far back as 1762: Foster, *Crown Law* (3rd edn, republished, 1809); and more recently, *Anderson* [1966] 2QB 110; *Chan Wing-Siu* [1985] AC 168; *Powell and English* [1999] 1 AC 1; *Rahman* [2009] AC 129; *Yemoh* [2009] EWCA Crim 930; and *Carpenter* [2011] EWCA Crim 2568.

20 See, Law Commission, *Inchoate Liability for Assisting and Encouraging Crime* (Law Com No 300); Law Commission, *Murder, Manslaughter and Infanticide* (Law Com No 304); Law Commission, *Participating in Crime* (Law Com No 305).

21 The reasons are only touched upon in this chapter but they are discussed in detail in writings elsewhere; see, for example, Ormerod and Fortson (n 6); Fortson (n 13); Ormerod (n 13); Spencer and Virgo (n 13); Ibbotson (n 13); Bohlander (n 13) (and reply by John Child (n 13)); Buxton (n 3); Baker (n 6); House of Commons Justice Committee, 'Joint Enterprise', 11th Report, 2012, HC1597.

22 Other than under Part 2 of the 2007 Act.

such a code, even if based on the proposals of the Law Commission in three reports,[23] is unlikely to bring us to a state akin to *nirvana*.[24]

Part 2 Offences: An Overview

Common law offence of 'incitement' abolished   Although the common law offence of incitement has been abolished,[25] a number of statutory offences that are expressed in terms of 'incitement',[26] 'assisting', 'encouraging', 'inducing', 'soliciting', have been retained. Many such offences are specified in schedule 3 to the 2007 Act ('listed offences'). The effect of s 49(4)-(6) is to exclude the operation of ss 45 and 46 in respect of any 'listed offence', so that only the s 44 offence[27] may be used on an inchoate-upon-inchoate basis (for example, where D *intentionally* encourages P1 to incite P2[28] to commit an offence contrary to the Misuse of Drugs Act 1971).[29]

Rules relating to secondary liability   Nothing in Part 2 of the 2007 Act modifies rules relating to secondary liability,[30] or modifies (still less, repeals) s 8 of the Accessories and Abettors Act 1861.

Immaterial whether the anticipated offence was committed by P or not   In order to avoid a defendant successfully defending a charge under ss 44-46 by showing that P had actually committed the anticipated offence, Parliament enacted s 49(1), which provides that D may commit a Part 2 offence 'whether or not any offence capable of being encouraged or assisted by [D] is committed'. Thus, even in cases where the evidence is inconclusive of whether P committed the anticipated offence or not, the effect of s 49(1) is that a judicial resolution of this issue is rendered unnecessary. Accordingly, it appears to be open to prosecutors, subject to the exercise of sensible prosecutorial discretion, to prefer one or more offences under Part 2 notwithstanding that there is plain evidence that P committed the anticipated offence. This has attracted the criticism that a conviction for an offence under Part 2 in such circumstances pays scant regard to the 'principle of fair labelling'.[31]

Immaterial that it cannot be resolved whether D was a perpetrator, encourager, or assister   By s 56(1) of the 2007 Act, a defendant may be convicted under Part 2 if it is proved that D must have committed a Part 2 offence *or* the anticipated offence,[32] *but* 'it is not proved which of those

---

23   Namely Law Com Nos 300, 304 and 305 (n 20).

24   Even Law Commissions (past and present) have not been *ad idem* as to the best model for reform: see, for example, Buxton (n 3); and see William Wilson, 'A Rational Scheme of Liability for Participating in Crime' [2008] Criminal Law Review 3.

25   Serious Crime Act 2007, s 59.

26   For example, s 19 of the Misuse of Drugs Act 1971; s 1 of the Incitement to Disaffection Act 1934.

27   But not the ss 45/46 offences.

28   The statutory offence under s 19, Misuse of Drugs Act 1971, of inciting the commission of a Misuse of Drugs Act offence, is listed in schedule 3 to the 2007 Act.

29   Note that since 1 February 2010, s 44 does not apply to an offence under s 2(1) of the Suicide Act 1961, or s 13(1) of the Criminal Justice Act (Northern Ireland) 1966 (offence of encouraging or assisting suicide). And see s 177(1), sch 21, Part 2, para 61(1), (2), of the Coroners and Justice Act 2009.

30   Including rules relating to 'joint enterprise'.

31   See Ormerod and Fortson (n 6).

32   See Serious Crime Act 2007, s 56(1)(a).

offences he committed'.[33] However, s 56(2) provides, somewhat ambiguously, that:

> [f]or the purposes of this section, a person is not to be treated as having committed the anticipated offence merely because he aided, abetted, counselled or procured its commission.[34]

It is submitted that the effect of s 56 is that in cases where D is *proved* to have committed the anticipated offence as a joint principal *in the first degree*, D ought to be convicted on that basis rather than under Part 2. For example, if (without lawful excuse) D and P each repeatedly kick and damage the bodywork of a car belonging to another, intending to do so, they act as joint principals because each contributed to the *actus reus* of the offence of criminal damage. However, if it cannot be proved whether D was a principal offender in the first degree, or had acted as a secondary party then he falls to be convicted under that Part. The purpose of s 56(2) appears to be a deeming provision so that, *for the purposes of Part 2 of the 2007 Act*, even if it is proved that D had committed the anticipated offence *as a secondary party*,[35] s 56(2) treats him as *not* having done so and, therefore, D may be convicted under that Part as a person who had encouraged or assisted its commission.

Traps and Pitfalls

Before discussing the elements of each of the Part 2 offences, practitioners need to be alert to a number of potential pitfalls.

The use of the word 'offence'; a misnomer in places in Part 2   First, the word 'offence' as it appears in ss 44-46, being the 'offence' which D contemplates P will commit, is a misnomer. The potential for error is compounded by the use of the word '*commission*', which appears in conjunction with the word 'offence'. In everyday speech, the expression 'commission of an offence' suggests criminal wrongdoing, but it is less natural to refer to a person who does an *innocent* act as having 'committed' it (for example, applying paint stripper to a painted surface). However, a close reading of ss 44-46[36] reveals that references to 'the *commission of*' and '*committed*', are actually references to the performance by P of the *conduct element* of the anticipated offence. For example, the conduct element of criminal damage is the act that causes the damage. This construction becomes apparent when ss 44-46 are read together with other provisions, notably, s 47 of the 2007 Act.[37] Section 47, is concerned with D's *mens rea*. Subsections 47(2), (3) and (4) of the Act[38] make it clear that D's *mens rea* relates to the 'doing of an *act*' by P. Further (and frequent) references in s 47 to 'the act' and 'his act' put beyond doubt that the proper construction of the word 'offence', as it appears in ss 44-46, is confined to P's *conduct* – regardless of P's *mens rea*. This is not an accident of Parliamentary drafting. The Law Commission's proposed offences, on which Part 2 is modelled, were drafted in terms of something done by D which was capable of encouraging or assisting P's '*criminal act*'. Presumably, the

---

33   Ibid. s 56(1)(b).
34   It is submitted that by 'a person' in s 56(2) of the 2007 Act, is meant the 'defendant'.
35   That is to say, applying s 8 of the Accessories and Abettors Act 1861.
36   And certain other provisions in Part 2, but not all of them!
37   Section 47(1) requires ss 44-46 to be read 'in accordance with that section', and s 65 of the Act provides that 'a reference in [Part 2] to encouraging or assisting the commission of an offence is to be read in accordance with section 47'.
38   Which relates to the Serious Crime Act 2007, s 44(1)(b), s 45(b) and s 46(1)(b), respectively.

reason why Parliament opted for the word 'offence', rather than the phrase 'criminal act', was to emphasise the headline policy/political message, namely, that Part 2 outlaws encouraging or assisting the commission of *crime*.

Unfortunately, Parliament has not been consistent in its use of the word 'offence' in Part 2. For example, in both s 47(a) and (b) the word 'offence' is used in its everyday sense.[39]

Who is it who 'does an act': D or P?   The second trap is the use in Part 2 of the expressions, 'does an act',[40] 'doing of an act',[41] 'act to be done'.[42] The Parliamentary draftsman has left it to the reader to work out for himself or herself whether the provision in question refers to the acts of D or P. It is submitted that the parties should be identified as follows. The person in ss 44-46 who 'does an act' is D. The 'doing of an act', in s 47(2), relates to the acts of P. The act which 'if done, would amount to the commission of an offence',[43] relates to acts done by P. Similarly, references in s 47(5) to, 'were the act to be done' are references to the acts of P – and not D.

A further trap[44] is s 47(8),[45] which might well be thought to refer to the doing of an act by D, but which relates to acts done by P.

Significance of 'which would amount to the commission of an offence': s 47   It is important to note that references in s 47(2), (3) and (4), to acts done 'which would amount to the commission of [that/an] offence' (or, in relation to s 46, 'one or more of them') cross-refer to s 47(5) because it is that provision which particularises the matters that the prosecution must prove in relation to D's awareness of P's conduct with regard to fault, circumstances or consequences. These provisions are discussed in greater detail in relation to the *mens rea* elements of the Part 2 offences.

Interpretation and Sources

As a general rule, the primary task of the Court is 'not to analyse the Commission's report, but to construe the statute'.[46] However, there are exceptions.[47] In *S and H*, the court derived some support for its analysis of Part 2 (with particular reference to s 46) from the Law Commission papers.[48] Although there has been some criticism of the Court for doing so,[49] it is submitted that there are at least two reasons why the approach was appropriate:

---

39   Thus, by s 47(5)(a), if the 'offence' – now used in its everyday sense – is one requiring proof of *fault*, then consideration must be given to subparagraph (i)-(iii). Section 47(5)(b) relates to any *circumstances* or *consequences* (or both) that must be proved for a given offence.

40   For example, Serious Crime Act 2007, ss 44-46.

41   Ibid. s 47(2).

42   Ibid. s 47(5). See, Ormerod and Fortson (n 6); and Fortson, *The Serious Crime Act 2007* (n 13) ch. 6.47.

43   Serious Crime Act 2007, s 47(5).

44   And a trap that almost ensnared one of the counsel in *S and H*, [60].

45   Section 47(8) reads: 'Reference in this section to the doing of an act includes reference to – (a) a failure to act; (b) the continuation of an act that has already begun; (c) an attempt to do an act (except an act amounting to the commission of the offence of attempting to commit another offence)'.

46   *R v Y* [2008] EWCA Crim 10 (Hughes LJ).

47   Consider *R v Chinn* [2012] EWCA Crim 501.

48   See, for example, judgment, [2011] EWCA Crim 2872, paragraphs [7] and [8, 55]. Law Com No 300 (n 20).

49   Child (n 15).

1. First, there is the issue of why Part 2 exists at all. Quite apart from Part 2, there is a wide array of inchoate and substantive offences. A trial judge is entitled to explore with the prosecution why an indictment includes a Part 2 offence rather than another offence. A defendant is entitled to know the basis on which a conviction is sought and, if convicted, the basis on which he may be sentenced. If guilty, the defendant is entitled to have his offending conduct appropriately described on the face of the indictment ('fair labelling').

2. Secondly, Part 2 will not be properly construed and applied without appreciating that its structure involves a departure from the taught-tradition of criminal lawyers that a criminal offence usually consists of two broad elements, namely, the *actus reus* and the *mens rea*. By contrast, Part 2 follows the approach taken by the Law Commission that analyses the *actus reus* of an offence by reference to one or more of its three external elements, namely, (a) conduct, (b) circumstances and (c) consequences. It is therefore essential not to disregard this form of element-analysis when considering the offence which it is alleged D contemplated P would commit. It is this analysis that helps us to understand why the word 'offence' in ss 44-46 is a misnomer in respect of the performance by P of the *conduct element* of the *actus reus* of the anticipated/future offence. Furthermore, it is the above-mentioned analysis that explains the structure and purpose of s 47(5), namely, to determine D's state of mind (rather than P's) with regards to any *fault*, *circumstances*, or *consequences* which it is necessary for the prosecution to prove were an act to be done by P which would amount to the commission of an offence by him.

Offence Element Analysis: Which Model?

Conduct, circumstances, consequences and fault Most criminal law practitioners will not routinely analyse a criminal offence beyond distinguishing between its *actus reus* and *mens rea* elements, but there will be occasions when greater refinement is required. Although Part 2 of the 2007 Act is not alone in requiring *mens rea* with regards to circumstances[50] or consequences, Part 2 is unique in placing at the heart of its offence-structure the three possible external elements of the *actus reus* of an offence (that is *conduct*, *circumstances* and *consequences*) and *fault*. Practitioners

---

50   For example, s 1(2) of the Criminal Law Act 1977, which provides: 'Where liability for any offence may be incurred without knowledge on the part of the person committing it of any particular fact or circumstance necessary for the commission of the offence, a person shall nevertheless not be guilty of conspiracy to commit that offence by virtue of subsection (1) above unless he and at least one other party to the agreement intend or know that the fact or circumstance shall or will exist at the time when the conduct constituting the offence is to take place'. It is submitted that commentators should be slow to say that *R v Mir and Beg* (22 April 1994, CA, unreported) had been decided *per incuriam* (see the commentary to that case by Edward Griew, Archbold News 1994). That case (in which the author of this chapter appeared for B) was heavily dependent on its facts and it was decided at a time when *Caldwell* recklessness prevailed (see *Caldwell* [1982] AC 341). Although proof of the existence of actual endangerment to life is not an essential element of being reckless as to whether the life of another would be thereby endangered, it was necessary to prove (for the full offence) that 'an ordinary prudent bystander would have perceived an obvious risk that property would be damaged and that life would thereby be endangered' (see *Sangha* [1988] 2 All ER 385). That perceived risk was and remains (it is submitted) an 'objective circumstance' element of the offence which, by reason of the Criminal Law Act, s 1(2), it was necessary for the prosecution to prove. It is conceded that this analysis is contentious (see, for example, Smith and Hogan's 'Criminal Law' (n 13) 444). There had been an exchange of correspondence between this author and Professor Griew shortly after the latter's commentary appeared, concerning the decision in *R v Mir* but, unfortunately, only one letter (from Professor Griew) remains in the author's possession.

and, importantly, fact finders, will need to keep the distinction between each element well in mind.

Analysing offences in this way is not without its critics,[51] and there is force in the complaint that not all offences can be easily subdivided into three elements of the *actus reus*: indeed, not every offence has all three elements.[52] Thus, although the offence of theft involves the appropriation of property (conduct), belonging to another (circumstance), it is unnecessary to prove permanent deprivation which would otherwise be a consequence element. But, it will not always be easy to determine whether the ingredient under consideration is a circumstance, or a consequence, or merely an incidental feature of D's conduct. However, the distinction between *acts, circumstances* and *consequences* is essential in relation to D's *mens rea* requirements under Part 2. For example, under s 44, D must *intend*[53] to encourage or to assist the performance of an *act* by P, or (under s 45) that D *believes*[54] that his act will encourage or assist P to perform the conduct element of an offence. By contrast, it may be sufficient to prove that D was reckless whether P would act in the *circumstances* and/or with the *fault* and/or *consequences* necessary for the commission of the offence.[55] The question of whether or not recklessness dominates D's *mens rea* requirements is considered later in this chapter.[56]

Although the aforementioned offence-element-analysis[57] may seem daunting, it is unlikely to pose significant difficulties in practice. In *Att-Gen's Reference (No. 3 of 1992)*,[58] the distinction between *consequences* and *circumstances* was, arguably, material for the purposes of applying s 1(1) of the Criminal Attempts Act 1981,[59] but such difficulties are less evident for the purposes of Part 2 of the 2007.

Over-criminalisation   Child and Hunt advance powerful arguments for improving the model by which criminal offences are analysed,[60] but notwithstanding that model's imperfections, of greater practical importance is how D's *mens rea* is defined in respect of a particular element. On that issue, Child shares the concern held by this author that there is a danger of over-criminalisation by imposing inchoate liability on a basis that '[criminalises] the defendant for believing or intending to create the risk that a future offence will be committed'.[61] This is particularly pertinent in respect of s 47(5) of the 2007 Act, which specifies alternative *mens rea* requirements as low as being 'reckless' with regard to any element of fault, circumstance or consequence that is an essential ingredient of the anticipated/future offence. Given the concern expressed, it is perhaps surprising to find criticism being made of the means by which the Court of Appeal, in *S and H*, has reached conclusions that render at least s 46 (and, arguably, ss 44

---

51 Child (n 15).
52 See, Ormerod and Fortson (n 6).
53 Serious Crime Act 2007, s 44.
54 Ibid. s 45/46.
55 Ibid. s 47(5).
56 For the argument that recklessness *does* dominate D's *mens rea* requirement, see Child (n 15).
57 That is to say, conduct, circumstances, consequences and fault.
58 [1994] 1 WLR 409.
59 Noting *R v Khan* [1990] 1 WLR 813. In *AG-Ref (No. 3 of 1992)* (1994) 98 Cr App R 383, it was held that 'the crime here consisted of doing certain acts in a certain state of mind in circumstances where … in short … the danger to life arose from the damage to the property which the defendant intended to damage' ((Schiemann J) 388).
60 John Child and Adrian Hunt, 'Mens Rea and the General Inchoate Offences: Another New Culpability Framework' (2012) 63(2) Northern Ireland Law Quarterly 247.
61 Child (n 15).

and 45) less risk-based than a strict, literal, interpretation of Part 2 (and particularly s 47) might require.[62]

The Part 2 Offences: Elements

The traditional approach to this topic would be to describe each offence in terms of only two elements, namely, the *actus reus* and *mens rea*. However, given the extended offence-element analysis that Part 2 requires (described above), such an approach would not be helpful and, therefore, it is not adopted in the presentation of this chapter.

Common to each Part 2 offence is the requirement that the defendant 'does an act that is capable of encouraging or assisting' the commission of an 'offence' by P. Each Part 2 offence focuses primarily on D's state of mind with regard to *acts* that D intends or believes P will do, in the *circumstances*, *consequences* and, *fault* necessary for the completed offence. In short, each of the Part 2 offences is in the nature of a 'thought crime'. Accordingly, a description of each Part 2 offence has been given (below) on that basis.

Intentionally Encouraging or Assisting an Offence: Section 44

It is submitted that the essential elements of section 44 are:[63]

(1) D must intend to encourage or to assist P to commit the anticipated offence (that is, that it is D's purpose to encourage or to assist P to carry out the conduct element of the *actus reus* of the anticipated offence);

(2) D must have one of the states of mind set out in s 47(5):
    (a) if the offence is one requiring proof of *fault*, it must be proved that:
        (i) D *believed* that, were the act to be done, it would be done with that fault;
        (ii) D was *reckless* as to whether or not it would be done with that fault; or
        (iii) D's state of mind was such that, were he to do it, it would be done with that fault; and
    (b) if the offence is one requiring proof of particular *circumstances* or *consequences* (or both), it must be proved that:
        (i) D *intended or believed*[64] that, were the act to be done, it would be done in those circumstances or with those consequences; or
        (ii) D was *reckless* as to whether or not it would be done in those circumstances or with those consequences.

---

62   Ibid. The decision of *S and H* is discussed in detail later in this chapter.

63   Section 44, Serious Crime Act 2007, reads: '(1) A person commits an offence if – (a) he does an act capable of encouraging or assisting the commission of an offence; and (b) he intends to encourage or assist its commission. (2) But he is not to be taken to have intended to encourage or assist the commission of an offence merely because such encouragement or assistance was a foreseeable consequence of his act'. Despite its apparent simplicity, this section must be read together with s 47(2), (5), (7), (8), s 49(1), (2) and s 67. See Fortson, *The Serious Crime Act 2007* (n 13) ch. 6.59.

64   Note s 47(7)(a) of the Serious Crime Act 2007, which modifies the wording of s 47(5)(b)(i) for the purposes of s 44 of the Act.

Acts that Are capable of encouraging or assisting P   D's act must be *capable* of encouraging or assisting the 'commission of an offence' (more accurately, the performance by P of the *conduct element* of the *actus reus* of the anticipated offence). For example, giving a prisoner a game card marked 'Get out of Jail' would not be capable of assisting P to effect an escape, and D's act is unlikely to constitute more than token 'encouragement'.

It is submitted that there is an important distinction between, (a) cases where D's defence is that his acts were *incapable* of encouraging or assisting P, and (b) cases where D pleads that the principal offence was impossible of commission (for example to kill V who was already dead). The latter is *not* a defence whereas the former would be.[65] The test (it is submitted) is to consider the inherent quality of D's purported act of encouragement or assistance. The Law Commission gave the following example:[66]

> [D] having heard that P intends to commit a burglary, sends P a package believing that it contains D's notes on how to break into buildings. In fact, the package contains his mother's cookery recipes. P has no intention of committing burglary and reports the matter to the police.

In the opinion of the Commission, the recipe notes 'were clearly not capable of encouraging or assisting the criminal act of entering a building as a trespasser'.

It is important to note that if it would have been impossible, *as a matter of law*, for P to have committed the offence anticipated (e.g. the offence which D has in contemplation does not exist) then D cannot be liable under Part 2 of the SCA 2007.[67]

It is submitted that the question of whether an act is capable of encouraging or assisting [the commission of an offence] will usually be one of fact.[68]

Note that s 65 of the Act describes various kinds of acts that are 'capable of encouraging or assisting' P, including cases where D threatens another person to commit an offence, or reduces the possibility of criminal proceedings being brought in respect of the anticipated offence, or fails to take steps to discharge a duty. But, *excluded* are instances where D 'fails to respond to a constable's request for assistance in preventing a breach of the peace'.[69]

D's act of encouragement need not be communicated to P, for example, where D shouts 'hit him!', but P fails to hear the remark, which is lost in the midst of other chants. D's act was nonetheless capable of encouraging P. The fact that D's efforts were ineffective is irrelevant. Accordingly, it is immaterial that P disregarded D's act of encouragement or assistance.

Example:

> D, at P's request, drafted a document detailing a chemical formula as well as the process for producing (illegally) amphetamine sulphate (a Class B controlled drug). However, the document, although posted, never reached P. On those facts, D did an act that was capable of assisting P to produce a controlled drug contrary to s 4 of the Misuse of Drugs Act 1971.

---

65   For the reasons given by the Law Commission: see Law Com No 300 (n 20) [6.61]-[6.62].

66   Ibid. [5.28] example 5J.

67   Ibid. [5.28] example 5J, and, for the distinction, see Ormerod (n 13) 13.5.1; and consider *R v Taaffe* [1984] AC 539.

68   And see Law Com No 300 (n 20) [5.28], which is to this effect.

69   Serious Crime Act 2007, s 65(3). See *R v Brown* Car & M 314; see Law Com 300 (n 20) [5.66]; and see Fortson, *The Serious Crime Act 2007* (n 13) ch. 6.57.

The above example illustrates two further points. First, given that D can be held liable for ineffective 'attempts' to encourage or assist P to commit an offence, there is no need to charge D with the statutory offence[70] of attempting to commit a Part 2 offence, *provided*, of course, that the remaining elements of the Part 2 offence are capable of being proved. Secondly, it is important to note that s 47(8)(c) of the 2007 Act has no relevance here. That provision states that references to 'the doing of an act include a reference to … (c) an attempt to do an act …' However, those words refer to the acts *of P* – and not D.

It is no defence for D to say that P completed the anticipated offence and, therefore, D's acts should not give rise to 'inchoate liability'. This is because s 49(1) of the 2007 Act provides that a person may commit an offence under Part 2 'whether or not any offence capable of being encouraged or assisted by his act is committed'.

'Intentionally Encouraging': s 44, Serious Crimes Act 2007   What is meant by the expressions '*intentionally* encouraging'[71] and, '*intend* to encourage or assist',[72] as those expressions appear in s 44 of the 2007 Act? It is submitted that neither expression implies a requirement that it must be D's purpose that P will act with the *fault*, or *consequence*, or in the *circumstances*, necessary for the commission of the anticipated offence. Were that the case, there would be no need for s 47(5), and it would make a nonsense of s 47(2) which provides:

> … it is sufficient to prove that [D] intended to encourage or assist the doing of *an act* [that is by P] which would amount to the commission of that offence.[73]

It is submitted that the words 'commission of that offence' in s 47(2), refer to P's *act* which, if carried out, *would* (not might) constitute the *conduct element* of the anticipated offence. Section 47(2) must therefore be read together with s 47(5)-(7),[74] noting that the operation of s 47(5)(a) and (b) is *conditional*,[75] that is to say that the provisions apply '*if*' the anticipated offence requires proof of fault and/or circumstances, and/or consequences, as the case may be.[76]

What does the element of 'intending' to encourage or assist add to the s 44 offence? Suppose D sold a gun to P, aware that P wished to use it to shoot a person (V). One interpretation of the

---

70   Pursuant to the Criminal Attempts Act 1981, s 1.

71   See the heading to s 44 of the Serious Crime Act 2007.

72   Serious Crime Act 2007, s 44(1)(b).

73   Author's emphasis added.

74   Section 47(5)-(7) of the Serious Crime Act 2007 provides, '(5) In proving for the purposes of this section whether an act is one which, if done, would amount to the commission of an offence – (a) if the offence is one requiring proof of fault, it must be proved that – (i) D believed that, were the act to be done, it would be done with that fault; (ii) D was reckless as to whether or not it would be done with that fault; or (iii) D's state of mind was such that, were he to do it, it would be done with that fault; and (b) if the offence is one requiring proof of particular circumstances or consequences (or both), it must be proved that – (i) D believed that, were the act to be done, it would be done in those circumstances or with those consequences; or (ii) D was reckless as to whether or not it would be done in those circumstances or with those consequences. (6) For the purposes of subsection (5)(a)(iii), D is to be assumed to be able to do the act in question. (7) In the case of an offence under section 44 – (a) subsection (5)(b)(i) is to be read as if the reference to "D believed" were a reference to "D intended or believed"; but (b) D is not to be taken to have intended that an act would be done in particular circumstances or with particular consequences merely because its being done in those circumstances or with those consequences was a foreseeable consequence of his act of encouragement or assistance'.

75   Noting that paras (a) and (b) to subs. 47(5), of the Serious Crime Act 2007, opens with the word 'if'.

76   Section 47(5)-(7) is discussed in detail later in this chapter.

word 'intends' in s 44(1)(b) is that it is sufficient that D merely acted *deliberately* by assisting P in providing him with the gun even if D had advised P not to use it to injure someone but anticipated that P would do so. But, if that is all that the word 'intends' means, then the distinction between the ss 44 and 45 offences would be so slight as to be insignificant. However, there is no reason to suppose that in relation to the s 44 offence, Parliament's foundation reasoning diverged from that of the Law Commission, which had recommended that (in relation to its cl.1 offence) the Crown must prove that D acted 'with a particular purpose',[77] adding that '[in] this context intention does not include foresight of the consequences of one's conduct'.[78] It is submitted that D must not only *deliberately* encourage or assist P, but D must also *intend* that P will perform the *conduct element* of the *actus reus* of the anticipated offence. It is for that reason that s 44(2) makes it plain that by 'intend' is meant 'purpose'. Oblique intention is not sufficient.[79] If D lends P a car so that the latter can take and transport goods from a warehouse, D has intentionally assisted P with the purpose (direct intention) that P *will* (not might) appropriate property (the conduct element of the offence of theft).

Is It Sufficient for s 44, That D Was Reckless as to P's Future Act Element?   In a thoughtful article, Child suggests that the preferred interpretation of the s 44 offence is that it is sufficient that D is merely reckless as to P's 'future act element'. Child takes issue with the proposition attributed to Ormerod that an intention to assist or encourage P's act element implies that D must also intend that that act element be *completed*.[80] Ormerod certainly implies that D intended that the *act* element of the anticipated offence should be 'done' by P,[81] but with respect, this seems to be the natural construction of s 44(1)(b). It is relevant to note that 'in the case of an offence under section 44', s 47(7)(b) excludes oblique intention, in relation to D's *mens rea*, so that D is not to be taken to have intended that P would act in the *circumstances* and/or with the *consequences* necessary to prove the commission of the anticipated offence by P "merely because its being done in those circumstances or with those consequences was a foreseeable consequence of his act of encouragement or assistance".[82] There seems little purpose enacting s 47(7)(b), and s 44(2), if it is sufficient that D can be merely reckless as to whether or not P performs the conduct element of the anticipated/future offence. Furthermore, the Law Commission was anxious to limit the extent to which D would be liable for unforeseen or 'unlooked-for' outcomes. There is scant information that suggests that Parliament took a different view from that of the Commission. Insofar as this author may be understood to have stated in other

---

77   Law Com No 300 (n 20) [A.26].

78   Ibid. [A.26] [fn 20].

79   Unfortunately, the 2007 Act fails to make this point sufficiently clear: see, Ormerod and Fortson (n 6) 404. For further discussion regarding 'oblique intention', see Glanville Williams, 'Oblique Intention' [1987] Criminal Law Journal 417; Richard Buxton QC, 'Some Simple Thoughts on Intention' [1988] Criminal Law Review 484; Alan Norrie, 'Oblique Intention and Legal Politics' [1989] Criminal Law Review 793, 806-807 (and see the response, Duff [1990] Criminal Law Review 637); Andrew Simester, 'Intention Thus Far' [1997] Criminal Law Review 704; Andrew Simester and Bob Sullivan, *Criminal Law: Theory and Doctrine* (Hart 2010) 421.

80   Child (n 15), citing Ormerod (n 13) where it is said that 'unlike s 44 [for s 45 and 46] D need not intend that the criminal act should be done'.

81   'Doing' of an act being the expression that tends to be used in the Serious Crime Act 2007, rather than 'completing' an act (if there is a distinction with a difference).

82   Section 47(7)(b), Serious Crime Act 2007, reads: 'D is not to be taken to have intended that an act would be done in particular circumstances or with particular consequences merely because its being done in those circumstances or with those consequences was a foreseeable consequence of his act of encouragement or assistance'.

writings[83] that it is sufficient that D *believed* that P would perform the conduct element of the *actus reus* of the anticipated offence, that statement should be taken to be confined to ss 45/46.[84]

It is true, as Child points out, that s 44 does not explicitly set out in the statute 'in a manner reflecting the equivalent drafting of the section 45 and 46 offences'[85] that D must intend that P will carry out[86] the act element. However, it is submitted that we cannot treat intention and belief in the same way. It is in the nature of 'belief' that the person, who holds it, forms a view about things that may or may not happen. Whether the belief proves to be well founded, or not, may not be of particular interest to him. This is very different from 'intention' of a kind where a person purposefully seeks a particular state of affairs to come about. Parliament presumably saw no need to make explicit that which it had assumed would be implicit in the use of the word 'intention'.

For reasons given later in this chapter, there is a strong case to be made against interpreting the further *mens rea* requirements set out in s 47(5) of the 2007 Act[87] as giving rise to a general presumption that it is sufficient to prove *mens rea* founded on subjective recklessness. If subjective recklessness does dominate D's *mens rea* requirements, to the extent suggested by Child,[88] then this would constitute a substantial and radical departure from any scheme envisaged by the Law Commission in relation to inchoate liability.

Encouraging or Assisting an Offence Believing It Will Be Committed: s 45

The elements of the s 45 offence[89] are (it is submitted) as follows:

(1) D does an act which is 'capable of encouraging or assisting' P to perform the *conduct* element of the *actus reus* of the anticipated offence: s 45(a); and

(2) D *believes* that the conduct element of the anticipated offence *will* be performed: s 45(b)(i);[90] and

---

83   In *The Serious Crime Act 2007* (n 13) this author stated at ch. 6.100: 'Note in each case, it must be proved that D believed that an act would be done "*which would amount to the commission of that offence*" [author's emphasis added]. That expression is explained/defined by s 47(5) which (subject to subs (6) and (7) provides ... [statutory provisions set out])'. This passage is best read as the continuation of the preceding paragraph, '(2)' at 6.99, in that work, rather than referring to all three Part 2 offences. Other passages make it clear that for the purposes of the s 44 offence, D must intend to encourage or assist P to commit the anticipated offence (and note the example, at 6.58).

84   The author is indebted to Mr Child for identifying the inconsistency in the commentary (Fortson (n 13)).

85   Child (n 15) fn 32.

86   Child uses the word 'complete', which may be apposite in respect of offences that do not involve a continuing course of conduct (for example theft). However, offences such as 'cheating', or 'evading the prohibition ...', or 'evading the payment of ...' are continuing offences.

87   For the Serious Crime Act 2007, s 47(5)-(7), see (n 74), above.

88   Child (n 15) 229, fn 32.

89   Section 45, of the Serious Crime Act 2007, provides: 'A person commits an offence if – (a) he does an act capable of encouraging or assisting the commission of an offence; and (b) he believes – (i) that the offence will be committed; and (ii) that his act will encourage or assist its commission'.

90   Note that by the Serious Crime Act 2007, s 49(7), it is sufficient for the purposes of s 45(b)(i) that D believed that the offence will be committed 'if certain conditions are met'.

(3) D *believes* that *his* act *will* encourage or assist P to perform the conduct element of the anticipated offence; s 45(b)(ii); and

(4) D *believes* that an act *will* be done by P which 'would amount to the commission' of the anticipated offence [actually, the conduct element of the offence]: s 47(3)(a).

(5) It is sufficient to prove that D *believed* that 'his act' (that is D's act) would encourage or assist P to do his act: s 47(3)(b); and

(6) At the time that D believed that P would carry out the conduct element of the anticipated offence, D had one of the states of mind described in s 47(5), that is to say:

> (a) if the offence is one requiring proof of *fault*:
>> (i)   D *believed* that, were the act to be done, it would be done with that fault;
>> (ii) D was *reckless* as to whether or not it would be done with that fault; or
>> (iii) D's state of mind was such that, were he to do it, it would be done with that fault; and
>
> (b) if the offence is one requiring proof of particular *circumstances* or *consequences* (or both), it must be proved that:
>> (i)   D *believed* that, were the act to be done, it would be done in those circumstances or with those consequences; or
>> (ii) D was *reckless* as to whether or not it would be done in those circumstances or with those consequences.

Example:

D sold to P a high-speed seagoing boat, aware that P imports cannabis into the United Kingdom and believing that P will use the boat for that purpose. D does not intend to assist P to import cannabis. D's purpose is to make a profit on the sale of the boat.

In the above example, D did an act that was capable of assisting a person to import cannabis. It is immaterial that P had no intention of using a boat to import cannabis, or that P used another boat to do so. D's purpose was to profit from the sale of the boat. It is immaterial that it was not D's purpose that P should import cannabis into the UK. It would also be immaterial that D had hoped that P would not use the boat for that purpose: it was D's *belief* that P *would* do so. D's liability will ultimately turn on the application of s 47, Serious Crime Act 2007.[91]

Section 45 follows the reasoning of the Law Commission in relation to its proposed cl.2 of the draft Bill:[92]

A.22 For example, if D hands a jemmy over to P, in the belief that P will commit burglary by using the jemmy to effect his entry into a building,[17][93] D will be liable under clause 2(1) for encouraging or assisting burglary, regardless of P's own intentions. However, D would not be liable under clause 2(1) if he delivered the jemmy to P for an entirely innocent reason, anticipating no crime,

---

91   For the Serious Crime Act 2007, s 47(5)-(7), see (n 74), above.
92   Law Com No 300 (n 20) [A.22].
93   Theft Act 1968, s 9(1)(a).

even though the jemmy had the capacity to assist burglary and was in fact subsequently used by P to commit that offence.

It is crucial to follow the steps set out in the 2007 Act. Section 45 must be read together with s 47(3) which provides:[94]

> (3) If it is alleged under section 45(b) that a person (D) believed that an offence would be committed and that his act would encourage or assist its commission, it is sufficient to prove that he believed –
>> (a) that an act would be done which would amount to the commission of that offence; and
>> (b) that his act would encourage or assist the doing of that act.

To elaborate, by s 47(3)(a), it is sufficient to prove: (a) that D believed that an act *would* (not might) be done by P (not by D) which *would* amount to the conduct element (e.g. importation) of the anticipated offence[95] *and*, (b) by virtue of s 47(3)(b), that D believed that 'his act' (this time, D's act; e.g., the supply of a boat) *would* (not might) encourage or assist P to (e.g.) import cannabis into the United Kingdom.

Thus far, D's state of mind extends only to *conduct* that D contemplates P will perform. Viewed in isolation, the conduct may be legal (for example appropriating property belonging to another). However, the words in s 47(3)(a), namely, 'that an act would be done which *would amount to the commission of that offence*', take us to s 47(5) and to further matters that must be proved in relation to D's *mens rea* with regard to fault, circumstances or consequences necessary for the commission of the anticipated offence.[96] Those complex provisions are considered below. Of crucial importance is the extent to which recklessness is sufficient to found a conviction for any of the Part 2 offences.

Encouraging or Assisting Offences; Believing One or More Will Be Committed: s 46   Section 46 provides:

> 46 Encouraging or assisting offences believing one or more will be committed
>
> (1) A person commits an offence if–
>> (a) he does an act capable of encouraging or assisting the commission of one or more of a number of offences; and
>> (b) he believes–
>>> (i) that one or more of those offences will be committed (but has no belief as to which);[97] and
>>> (ii) that his act will encourage or assist the commission of one or more of them.
>
> (2) It is immaterial for the purposes of subsection (1)(b)(ii) whether the person has any belief as to which offence will be encouraged or assisted.

---

94   It is advisable to read the Serious Crime Act 2007, s 45, together with s 47(3), (5), (6), (8), (9)(b), s 49(1), (2)(b), (3), (4)(a), (5)-(7), s 50 and s 51. Other provisions may also be relevant.

95   For example, the Customs and Excise Management Act 1979, s 170 (unlawful evasion of the prohibition on importation of goods, for example, controlled drugs; Misuse of Drugs Act 1971, s 3).

96   For the Serious Crime Act 2007, s 47(5), see (n 74), above.

97   Note that by s 49(7) of the Serious Crime Act 2007, it is sufficient for the purposes of s 46(1)(b)(i) that D believed that the offence (or one or more of the offences) will be committed 'if certain conditions are met'.

(3) If a person is charged with an offence under subsection (1)–

    (a) the indictment must specify the offences alleged to be the 'number of offences' mentioned in paragraph (a) of that subsection; but

    (b) nothing in paragraph (a) requires all the offences potentially comprised in that number to be specified.

(4) In relation to an offence under this section, reference in this Part to the offences specified in the indictment is to the offences specified by virtue of subsection (3)(a).

This is the most complex of the three Part 2 offences. Section 46 should be read together with s 47(4), (5), (6), (8), s 48, s 49(1), (4)(b), (5)-(6), s 50, s 51 and s 58.[98]

The background to this offence begins with *DPP of Northern Ireland v. Maxwell*,[99] where it was held that D can be held liable as a secondary party if he assists P believing that the latter will commit one or more offences (for example, robbery, criminal damage, murder) but has no settled belief as to which. The Law Commission proposed that on such facts, a defendant should not escape liability if, for whatever reason, P did not go on to commit any of the offences that had been in D's contemplation. The Government agreed but, when framing s 46 of the 2007 Act, it departed from the Law Commission's approach, notably in relation to D's *mens rea*.[100]

Core elements of the s 46 offence   The defendant must do an act that is capable of encouraging or assisting P in the 'commission of one or more of a number of offences'.[101]

For the reasons given earlier, it is essential not to be misled by the words 'commission' and 'offence' as they appear in s 46. Section 46(1) is concerned with the performance *by P* of the *conduct element* of the *actus reus* of the offence or offences in question. Thus, D must believe that P *will* perform one or more *acts*, but has no settled belief as to which,[102] and that D *believes* that his [D's] act *will* (not might) encourage or assist P to perform the conduct element of one or more offences,[103] albeit that D has no settled belief as to which.[104] For example, D might be told that P *will* get money from V by way of the conduct and in the circumstances necessary to amount to (a) robbery, (b) blackmail or (c) theft, but he has no belief as to which offence P will commit.[105]

---

98   Other provisions may also have relevance to the application of the s 46 offence.

99   [1978] 1 WLR 1350.

100   'A person commits an offence if (a) he does an act capable of encouraging or assisting the doing of one or more of a number of criminal acts, and (b) he believes (i) that at least one of a number of criminal acts will be done (but has no belief as to which), and (ii) that his act will encourage or assist the doing of one of those criminal acts ("the act in question"). (3) If the principal offence requires proof of fault, a person is not guilty of an offence under this section unless (a) he believes that, were another person to do the act in question, that person would do it with the fault required for conviction of the principal offence, or (b) his state of mind is such that, were he to do it, he would do it with that fault. (4) If particular circumstances or consequences (or both) must be proved for conviction of the principal offence, a person is not guilty of an offence under this section unless he believes that, were another person to do the act in question, that person would do it (a) in those circumstances, (b) with those consequences' (Law Com No 300) (n 20) Draft Bill: Clause 2(2)).

101   Serious Crime Act 2007, s 46(1).

102   Ibid. s 49(1)(b)(i).

103   Ibid. s 49(1)(b)(ii).

104   Ibid. s 46(2).

105   Thanks are due to Professor David Ormerod for providing this example to the author.

Significantly, for reasons which will be explained in the context of the decision of the Court of Appeal in *S and H*, the indictment must specify the 'offences' that D is alleged to have contemplated P would commit.[106] For the purpose of penalties,[107] these are the 'reference offences', referred to in that section. Confusingly, the use of the word 'offence' in s 46(3)(a) and (b) is now being used in its everyday sense.

Although the point remains open, it seems likely that the offences should be of *different types* and description (for example, criminal damage, theft, murder) rather than multiple offences of the same kind (for example, multiple acts of supplying a controlled drug, or a series of robberies or murders).[108] There are at least two reasons that support that interpretation of s 46. First, the *Maxwell case* (on which decision s 46 appears to have been modelled) was not one that involved multiple offences of the same kind. Secondly, it is arguable that rule 14.2 of the Criminal Procedure Rules goes further than merely giving effect to *DPP v Merriman*,[109] and permits repeated offending acts to be charged by way of a single count (for example, theft, 'supplying a controlled drug'). Section 49(2)[110] does not apply in relation to the s 46 offence.

The issue of greatest complexity, in relation to the s 46 offence, concerns D's *mens rea* requirements.

Proving the Defendant's Mens Rea: and the Problems of s 47[111]

Summary of the mens rea elements specified in ss 44-46   For the purpose of s 44, D must *intend* to encourage or assist P to perform the conduct element of the *actus reus* of the anticipated offence, that is, that it was D's purpose to encourage or assist: oblique intention has no part to play here.[112]

For the purposes of s 45, D must at least *believe* that P *will* perform the conduct element of the *actus reus* of the anticipated offence, *and* D must believe that his [D's] act *will* encourage or assist P. Similar considerations apply with regard to the s 46 offence.

Example 1

D sells P a revolver and bulleted ammunition, believing that P will use the items (i) to cause grievous bodily harm and/or (ii) to kill, and/or (iii) to appropriate property belonging to another (by force).

D, who does not intend to act with P, cannot know precisely what P *will* carry out, but D does *believe* that P *will* do at least one or more of the aforementioned acts.

---

106   Serious Crime Act 2007, s 46(3).

107   Ibid. see s 58.

108   If so, it may be that this author went too far in leaving open the question of whether s 46 might be available in cases of multiple acts of supplying a controlled drug; Rudi Fortson, *Misuse of Drugs and Drug Trafficking Offences* (Sweet and Maxwell 2012) ch. 5.057.

109   [1973] AC 584.

110   'If a person's act is capable of encouraging or assisting the commission of a number of offences – (a) section 44 applies separately in relation to each offence that he intends to encourage or assist to be committed; and (b) section 45 applies separately in relation to each offence that he believes will be encouraged or assisted to be committed' (Serious Crime Act 2007, s 49(2)).

111   For the Serious Crime Act 2007, s 47(5)-(7), see (n 74), above.

112   Ibid. Serious Crime Act 2007, s 44(2).

Example 2

P told D that he was going to steal V's money 'even if I have to shoot him', not caring whether P
would use the gun or not: D's purpose was merely to profit from the sale of the gun to P.

It is submitted that on those facts, D's indifference is immaterial: he did an act which he *believed
would* assist P.[113] Furthermore, D *believed* that P *would* carry out the conduct element necessary to
prove one or more offences.

In *S and H*,[114] the question arose whether the wording of s 46 means that D must believe that
each reference offence *will* be committed, or whether it is sufficient that each offence *might* be
committed. The Court of Appeal held that, in the event of a contested trial, each reference offence
that the prosecution wish to include on the indictment[115] should be the subject of a discrete count
charged under s 46,[116] and that D can only be convicted of a given count if he believed that the
offence *will* be committed. The decision (which is discussed in greater detail below) has been
criticised on various grounds that include the Court taking a 'wrong turn' by relating the requirement
in s 46 that the offence *will* be committed, to each of the identified reference offences.[117] In defence
of the decision of the Court, it is submitted that ss 45 and 46 are not to be watered down in terms of
what D believed P *might* do or, worse, that D was subjectively reckless as to whether P would carry
out the conduct element of the *actus reus* of the anticipated offence. This would be contrary to the
language of s 45 and, similarly (it is submitted), s 46. Suppose, D believes that P *will* use a gun to
rob V, and that P *will* shoot V if the latter resists. P is arrested before either crime is committed. The
nature of the s 46 offence, being inchoate and rooted in D's belief, is that none of the matters that
had been in D's contemplation may actually come to pass. In that context, it may be said that the
word '*might*' is apposite. But to use the word 'might' as a basis of D's liability for the purposes of s
46 of the 2007 Act (or s 45), is to risk setting a threshold so low that it would be sufficient to prove
merely that D foresaw the possibility (no matter how speculative) that P might carry out the act that
is the essential ingredient of the reference offence. In the above example, D's belief is resolute, at
least in relation to robbery. By contrast, s 46 ought not to be satisfied if D believed that P would
use a gun *only* for the purpose of frightening V, although he feared that P *might* shoot V, *and* that
he 'wouldn't put it past P to rob someone' (that is, 'might' rob). Given that the Part 2 offences are
essentially 'thought crimes', it is submitted that there is no justification for criminalising D for his
speculative thoughts and fears.[118]

Mens rea and s 47 of the 2007 Act   In addition to the *mens rea* elements in ss 44-46, each offence

---

113   Ibid. Serious Crime Act 2007, s 46(1)(b)(ii).

114   [2011] EWCA Crim 2872; [2012] 1 WLR1700.

115   The prosecution is not obliged to charge by way of a separate count every reference offence that
could be identified on the facts of a given case, but only those reference offences on which the prosecution
wish to rely; ibid. [83].

116   Ibid. [84].

117   Virgo (n 12).

118   The Court also sought a practical solution to a serious problem, namely, where the s 46 offence
includes two or more reference offences each of which attract different maximum penalties (Serious Crime Act
2007, s 58) and that, in respect of trials on indictment, the factual basis for sentencing should be determined
by a jury. An offender is entitled to know the factual basis on which he or she falls to be sentenced. This
consideration alone amply justifies the Court's decision that each reference offence should be the subject of a
separate count on the indictment.

takes subject to the matters to be proved in accordance with s 47 of the 2007 Act. Note that s 47(2),[119] (3)[120] and (4)[121] concern ss 44, 45 and 46, respectively. At first sight, those subsections appear merely to reiterate the matters specified in ss 44(1)(b), 45(b) and s 46(1)(b):[122]

- section 44: D *intended* his act to encourage or assist P, or
- section 45/46: D *believed* that his act *would* encourage or assist P to perform the conduct element of the anticipated offence.

However, of central importance are the words 'would amount to the commission of that offence'.[123] Those words take us to s 47(5),[124] which specifies further matters which *may* need to be proved with regards to D's *mens rea* requirements.

'Would amount to the commission of an offence'   As stated above, each of subsections 47(2), (3) and (4) of the Serious Crime Act 2007, refer to an act which, if done by P, 'would amount to the commission of an offence'. Unfortunately, subs (2), (3) and (4) are further instances where the word 'offence' is a misnomer and refers only to P performing the conduct element of the *actus reus* of the anticipated offence.[125] Thus far, the approach in Part 2 is consistent with that of the Commission:

> D ought not to incur liability merely because D intends or believes that P should or will commit an 'act' that is criminal. The 'act' that is criminal in theft is the appropriation of property. It would be absurd if D could be criminally liable for doing nothing more than encouraging P to do that act ....[126]

Accordingly, the Commission proposed that D should be liable if:

> (a) In addition to a criminal act (that is, the *conduct* element of the offence), *if* a *circumstance* element or a *consequence* element (or both) must be proved for the commission of an offence, then

---

119   'If it is alleged under section 44(1)(b) that a person (D) intended to encourage or assist the commission of an offence, it is sufficient to prove that he intended to encourage or assist the doing of an act which would amount to the commission of that offence' (Serious Crime Act 2007, s 47(2)).

120   'If it is alleged under section 45(b) that a person (D) believed that an offence would be committed and that his act would encourage or assist its commission, it is sufficient to prove that he believed – (a) that an act would be done which would amount to the commission of that offence; and (b) that his act would encourage or assist the doing of that act' (Serious Crime Act 2007, s 47(3)).

121   'If it is alleged under section 46(1)(b) that a person (D) believed that one or more of a number of offences would be committed and that his act would encourage or assist the commission of one or more of them, it is sufficient to prove that he believed – (a) that one or more of a number of acts would be done which would amount to the commission of one or more of those offences; and (b) that his act would encourage or assist the doing of one or more of those acts' (Serious Crime Act 2007, s 47(4)).

122   Those provisions seem not to require D to *intend* (Serious Crime Act 2007, s 44), or to *believe* (ss 45/46) that P would actually *complete* that conduct. Indeed, by s 47(8), the 'doing of an act' includes 'the continuation of an act that has already begun'. It is submitted that s 47(8) relates to the doing of acts by P. The point is raised because in some academic writings, the word 'complete' tends to appear.

123   See Serious Crime Act 2007, s 47(2), (3)(a), (4)(a).

124   For the Serious Crime Act 2007, s 47(5)-(7), see (n 74), above.

125   The Law Commission had used the expression 'criminal *act*'. Author's emphasis added.

126   Law Com No 300 (n 20) [5.100].

D must have *intended* or *believed* that the criminal act would be done in those circumstances or with those consequences;[127] and,

(b) *If* the anticipated offence requires proof of *fault*, then D must have *believed* that, were P to do the criminal act, that P would do it with the fault required for conviction of the principal offence; or D's state of mind must be such that were D to do the criminal act, he would do it with that fault. In the latter situation, D is to be assumed to be able to do the criminal act in question [which explains the combined effect of s 47(5)(a)(iii) and s 47(6)].[128]

Each of subsections 47(2), (3) and (4) must therefore be read together with s 47(5),[129] which concern D's state of mind with regards to any element of fault, circumstances or consequences, that it is necessary for the prosecution to prove in relation to acts done by P in carrying out the anticipated offence(s).

Recklessness with regards to fault, circumstances, or consequences: s 47(5)[130]   Section 47(5) of the 2007 Act is both complex and controversial. *Complex*, because its scope is unclear and undefined. *Controversial*, because on a strict reading of s 47, it is sufficient to prove that D was reckless whether P would act in the circumstances, or with the fault or consequences, necessary for the commission of the anticipated offence. It is therefore unsurprising that commentators have been quick to suggest that 'recklessness dominates D's *mens rea* requirements',[131] or at least, it appears to do so. For example, Child suggests that the defendant will be guilty of the s 44 offence only if:

a. D intends that his act will encourage or assist the commission (of the act element) of X; and

b. D is *reckless* as to whether the act element of X will be completed; and

c. D is *reckless* as to whether, if the act element is completed, it will be completed with the necessary circumstance elements of X; and

d. D is *reckless* as to whether, if the act element is completed, it will be completed with the necessary consequence elements of X; and

e. D is *reckless* as to whether, if the act element is completed, it will be completed with the necessary fault for X. Or, where D holds the required fault for X.[132]

---

127   Law Com No 300 (n 20) [5.118].
128   Law Com No 300 (n 20) [5.105]. The wording in square brackets is an observation made by this author.
129   And subject to the Serious Crime Act 2007, s 47(6) and (7) – depending on the Part 2 offence in question.
130   For the Serious Crime Act 2007, s 47(5)-(7), see (n 74), above.
131   Child (n 15); and see Spencer and Virgo (n 13).
132   Child (n 15) 229 (fn 39): 'This final possibility in relation to the fault required for the principal offence is important to our sketching of minimum requirements because it allows for liability even where D does not intend that (and is not even reckless as to whether) P will act with the required fault (s 47(5)(iii))'. For discussion, see Ormerod and Fortson (n 6) 407.

But, if D need only be reckless, what purpose is served by Parliament enacting higher *mens rea* requirements where the words '[D] intended',[133] or 'believed',[134] appear? Although it is not unusual for Parliament to enact alternative *mens rea* requirements (for example, knowing or believing), it is submitted that there were four reasons (other than to extend the reach of the Part 2 offences) for including, what Parliament has styled, 'recklessness' in s 47(5).

1st reason: strict liability: The Law Commission believed that the law would be too severe if D could be convicted of encouraging or assisting a strict liability offence. The Commission acknowledged that this 'might be thought [to treat] D more favourably than the prospective principal offender, P'. However, 'as a general rule, P is in a better position to appreciate the nature of the risk that he is taking in committing the conduct element'.[135] Accordingly, the Commission concluded that 'for all offences that include a circumstance or consequence element, or both, D must be at fault in relation to the consequence or circumstance even if the offence is a constructive or strict liability offence'.[136]

2nd reason: constructive liability: There can be cases where an offence involves proof of a *consequence* (for example, death in respect of a murder), but it is *not* necessary to prove that P acted with *fault* with regard to that result. The question then becomes whether, as a matter of policy/ fairness, D should be inchoately liable without proof of *mens rea* with regard to consequences. The answer given by the Law Commission,[137] and by Parliament, was in the negative. The Explanatory Notes to the Serious Crime Act 2007 provide the following example:[138]

> 157. Requiring some degree of belief in relation to consequences ensures that a person would not be guilty of an offence that requires certain consequences to arise for it to be committed, unless he believes or is reckless as to whether those consequences should arise. For example, D gives P a baseball bat and intends P to use it to inflict minor bodily harm on V. P however uses the bat to attack V and intentionally kills V. It would not be fair to hold D liable for encouraging and assisting murder, unless he also believes that, or is reckless as to whether, V will be killed

Accordingly, by requiring that D should have *mens rea* with respect to consequences (or circumstances),[139] D's conduct is not otherwise criminalised on an inchoate basis in cases where P's liability would either have been 'constructive' (or 'strict'). The potential difficulty is that, construed strictly, s 47(5) appears to apply generally, regardless of whether the anticipated offence is one of strict liability or constructive liability, or not. However, for reasons given later in this

---

133   Serious Crime Act 2007, s 47(7)(a), (b).
134   Ibid. s 47(5)(a)(i); (5)(b)(i).
135   Law Com No 300 (n 20) [5.111].
136   Law Com No 300 (n 20) [5.112].
137   Law Com No 300 (n 20) [5.112].
138   The Law Commission had given a slightly different example, namely, where D provides P with the bat, unclear as to P's exact intention but *hoping that P will use it to cause V serious harm*. P does nothing with the bat. The Commission answered the example in the following way (the answer has been modified to reflect the effect of s 47 (5)): 'D is not liable under [s 44] for intentionally encouraging or assisting murder, even though he would have acted with the fault for murder if he himself had committed the conduct element of that offence. [D is, however, liable for intentionally encouraging or assisting the offence of causing grievous bodily harm with intent (Offences Against the Person Act 1861, s 18)]. Although [s 47(5)(a)(i)] is satisfied, [s 47(5)(b)] is not because D does not believe that V will be killed (and it was not D's purpose that V should be killed)'; see Law Com No 300 (n 20) [A 29] and [30].
139   Serious Crime Act 2007, s 47(5)(b).

chapter, it may be possible to construe s 47(5) in a manner that prevents recklessness dominating D's *mens rea* requirements. It is submitted that avoiding such an outcome may have formed part of the reasoning of the Court of Appeal's decision in *S and H*.

3rd reason: D's indifference: The Law Commission acknowledged that there could be situations where D should be liable on an inchoate basis if he acted not caring whether P committed the anticipated offence or not.[140] However, the Commission's draft Bill made no express provision to cater for such situations, seemingly on the grounds that the wording of clause 1(2)(a) and clause 2(3)(a) was sufficient to encompass such cases.[141] Cases of this kind typically arise in respect of a trader or service-provider who may, or may not, have the 'direct intention'[142] of encouraging or assisting P to commit an offence, but who *believes* that P will use the goods or services in order to commit a particular offence. In what circumstances should D be held inchoately liable? In respect of *intentional* encouragement, the Commission contrasted two examples which it introduced in the following terms:[143]

> … D must intend to encourage or assist a person to commit the conduct element of the principal offence. This definition [cl.1(1)] is broad enough to cover two types of intention. It covers the typical case where D's purpose is to see the conduct element of the principal offence committed; but it is also wide enough to encompass a case such as the following: …

Example 1

> D, a wholesaler for career criminals, encourages a customer (P) to commit burglary in order to persuade him to purchase expensive cutting equipment. D's purpose is to encourage P to commit burglary, but he is *indifferent as to the commission of that principal offence*.[144]

Given that cl.18(1) – now s 44(2) – states that a 'person is not to be taken to have intended to encourage or assist a criminal act to be done merely because such encouragement or assistance was a foreseeable consequence of his act', it may seem puzzling that the Commission was of the view that D had *intentionally* encouraged P to commit burglary, notwithstanding that D was *indifferent* 'as to the commission of that principal offence'. The answer is that 'indifference' is context specific. In Example 1, D's purpose was that P should perform the *conduct element* of burglary (for example cutting the warehouse door to the premises) but could not care less whether anything was appropriated by P or not. D's recklessness as to whether property would be taken or not, is irrelevant to the question of whether D intended that P would perform the *conduct element* of burglary (entering property).

---

140   Law Com No 300 (n 20) [5.124]. In his response to the Law Commission's Consultation Paper, Sir Edwin Jowitt, expressed his concern by way of the following example: 'The armourer who hires out a weapon may not be told by the criminal what crime is afoot. The armourer may prefer not to know. He may be indifferent as to whether this, that or any crime is committed providing he receives his hire. The criminal may take the view that the less the armourer knows the better' (Law Com No 300 (n 20) [4.16]).

141   See Fortson, *The Serious Crime Act 2007* (n 13) ch. 6.115-18.

142   That is to say that it is not D's *purpose* to encourage or to assist P to commit a criminal offence.

143   Law Com No 300 (n 20) [A 27]-[28]. Paragraphs [A 27]-[28] have been slightly modified for ease of explanation in this chapter.

144   Author's emphasis added.

However, the Commission drew a distinction between the above and, '… where D's only purpose is to do an act which, incidentally, he knows or believes will encourage or assist another person to commit an offence …'.[145]

Example 2

> D, an ironmonger, intentionally sells a piece of lead piping to a customer (P), believing that P will use it to commit murder.[146]

In Example 2, D would not have been liable under cl.1 (intentionally encouraging and so on) because:

> … it is not D's purpose to provide encouragement or assistance in relation to any conduct which could cause death. In other words, *clause 1(1) does not encompass individuals such as the 'indifferent' shopkeeper or householder* who sells or lends an item *in the* belief *that it will be used to achieve a particular criminal end.*[147]

However, there would seem to be no reason why D would not have been liable under the Commissions cl.2 offence or s 45 of the 2007 Act. D's *belief* relates to P's *conduct* – using the lead piping to hit V – but his *indifference* relates to any fault, circumstance or consequence, in the event that P used the piping to hit V. It is submitted that this is the context in which Parliament included, in s 47(5), liability based on 'recklessness'. It was not Parliament's intention (it is submitted) that recklessness should dominate D's *mens rea* requirements.

4th reason: the position in relation to secondary liability: It is conceivable that Parliament used the word 'reckless' in s 47(5) as a convenient, if not entirely apposite term that was intended to go no further than to give effect to the proposals, and the supporting reasoning, of the Law Commission in Report No. 300.[148] It is therefore arguable that the decision of the Court of Appeal, in *S and H*,[149] merely reflects that viewpoint. It will be recalled that the Law Commission's proposals, and the Part 2 offences under the 2007 Act, are intended to fill a gap in the law where an alleged accomplice would escape liability in respect of the principal offence if P failed to commit that offence. One also notes that s 49(1) of the 2007 Act provides that 'a person may commit an offence [under Part 2] whether or not any offence capable of being encouraged or assisted by [D's] act is committed'. It is easy to lose sight of the fact that a secondary party (D) may be liable if he aids, abets (and so on) P in the commission of an offence *and* that his [D's] *mens rea* requirements are satisfied in terms of what he *foresaw* P *might* do (*with mens rea*). Putting aside policy considerations of whether D ought to be convicted on the basis of mere foresight of what P *might* do (with *mens rea*), there is logic in giving a degree of symmetry to the elements of the Part 2 offences based on rules pertaining to accessorial liability. It is a point that ought not to be taken too far because there are sound policy reasons (it is submitted) why inchoate offences should not merely track the *mens rea* requirements for substantive offences[150] and, in any event, it must always be remembered that 'subjective recklessness' and 'foresight' are different concepts. That said, it is submitted that accessorial liability, in terms of

---

145   Law Com No 300 (n 20) [A 28].
146   Law Com No 300 (n 20) [A 28].
147   Law Com No 300 (n 20) [A 29] [author's emphasis added].
148   Law Com No 300 (n 20).
149   [2011] EWCA Crim 2872.
150   See, for example, the interesting discussion by Child and Hunt (n 60) 67.

D's foresight of the *possible* commission of the principal offence is itself too strict. Considerations of this kind appear to have influenced the reasoning of the Law Commission:[151]

> A.46 If the principal offence *is* committed by P, under our proposals for secondary liability *an 'indifferent' encourager or assister (D)* would be liable for P's principal offence only if he was a participant in a joint venture to commit an offence, and *he foresaw the possible commission of the principal offence in furtherance of the venture*. In other circumstances, indifferent encouragers or assisters acting with the required belief would be convicted of the clause 2(1) offence in relation to the anticipated offence. They would not be secondarily liable for the offence actually committed by P.

> A.47 The fault element for liability under clause 2(1) can be broken down as follows, for offences defined with a requirement of fault:

>> (1) D believes that another person will commit the conduct element of the principal offence in question;

>> (2) D believes that his own conduct will encourage or assist a person to commit the conduct element of the principal offence; and

>> (3) D believes that the conduct element of the principal offence, if committed, will be committed by a person acting *with the fault required for the principal offence (or D himself acts with such fault) in the circumstances and with the consequences, if any, required for the principal offence to be committed.*

> A.48 Given that clause 2 defines the parameters for inchoate liability, we expect the words 'will' and 'would' to be interpreted narrowly. In particular, D would not be liable under this clause if he merely believed that the principal offence might be committed.[152]

The decision of R v S and H   In *S and H*,[153] the two appellants were charged with assisting in the supply of Class A or Class B controlled drugs contrary to s 46 of the 2007 Act. The act of assistance was alleged to be the provision of 'cutting agents', sulphuric acid and other chemicals, 'believing that one or more of those offences would be committed, and that their act would assist in the commission of one or more of the said offences'. The Court held that the s 46 offence 'should only be used if it may be that it was D's belief at the time of his doing the acts that one or more offences will be committed but has no belief as to which';[154] that there should be a separate s 46 count for each reference offence (X, Y and Z) 'at least if there is to be a trial';[155] and (in para 87) that:

> D can only be convicted of (for example) offence X if:

> a. Either:

---

151   Law Com No 300 (n 20).
152   Author's emphasis added.
153   [2011] EWCA Crim 2872.
154   Ibid. [82].
155   Ibid. [84].

(i) D believes that X will be committed; or
(ii) D believes that one or more of the offences specified in the indictment (X, Y and Z) will be committed but has no belief as to which; and

b. D believes that his act will encourage or assist the commission of X; and

c. D believes that X will be committed with the necessary fault for X.[156]

Paragraph 89, of the 'CPS Guidance on: Joint Enterprise Charging Decisions', repeats the above ingredients of the s 46 offence. However, the decision of the Court has been criticised, chiefly on the grounds that para 87 of the judgment fails to state the 'true breadth' of the Part 2 offences that require mere recklessness 'if the act element is completed'[157] with regard to circumstances, consequences and fault, necessary for the commission of offence X (Y and Z). Child suggests that, correctly stated, the minimum requirements of the ss 45 and 46 offences are:

a) D believes that his act will encourage or assist the commission of (the act element of) X; and

b) Either:
i) D believes that the *act element* of X will be committed [section 45]; or
ii) D believes that one or more *acts* of the offences specified in the indictment (X, Y and Z) will be committed but has no belief as to which [section 46]; and

c) D is reckless as to whether, if the act element is completed, it will be completed with the necessary circumstance elements of X; and

d) D is reckless as to whether, if the act element is completed, it will be completed with the necessary consequence elements of X; and

e) D is reckless as to whether, if the act element is completed, it will be completed with the necessary fault for X. Or, where D holds the required fault for X.[fn 25] [158]

Sections 45 and 46 are capable of the above construction, but given what one understands to be the principal argument advanced by Child and Hunt with regard to the structure of inchoate liability, namely, that a higher level of fault is justified for inchoate liability than for the standard choate offences,[159] it is perhaps surprising to find that the same argument is not advanced in support of the pragmatic solutions offered by the Court of Appeal in *S and H*.[160]

In another critique of this decision, Professor Graham Virgo has argued that although the Court sought to make sense of the s 46 offence it has, in doing so, 'made the offence vague, uncertain and

---

156 Ibid. [87].
157 Child (n 15).
158 Footnote 25 reads, 'This final possibility in relation to the fault required for the principal offence is important to our sketching of minimum requirements because it allows for liability even where D does not believe that (and is not even reckless as to whether) P will act with the required fault (s 47(5)(iii)). For discussion, see Ormerod and Fortson (n 6) 407'.
159 Child and Hunt (n 60) 67; and noting the work done by several distinguished academics regarding this topic, for example, Professors Andrew Ashworth and Anthony Duff.
160 See, Child (n 15).

effectively redundant'.[161] The author of this chapter has responded in detail to these criticisms.[162] In *S and H*, the Court recognised that subjective recklessness is a component of the Part 2 offences, but it did not elaborate as to the circumstances in which subjective recklessness operates. It is submitted that whether subjective recklessness is left for the jury's consideration (or not) is a matter of judicial discretion.[163] In a typical case it will be sufficient (and just) to confine the *mens rea* requirements of s 47(5) to what D 'believed' the position to be. This approach is no different from that taken by trial judges in other contexts. For example, it is not every case of murder, involving a group attack, which requires a judge to cover every permutation of joint principalship and/or joint enterprise liability, from intention and oblique intention, to the foresight of P's acts as well as P's *mens rea*.

It is important to stress that the Court, in *S and H*, was required not only to make sense of the s 46 offence, but also to find practical solutions in respect of a count which, as originally framed, would have compelled the sentencer to decide whether a convicted defendant had committed the most, or least, serious reference offence (noting that trafficking in Class A and B drugs attracts different maximum statutory penalties).

Although not cited or discussed in the S *and H* judgment (or in the commentary to that case[164]), there is Strasbourg jurisprudence to support the proposition that a defendant is entitled to know the factual basis on which he has been convicted and falls to be sentenced.[165] As the court, in *S and H*, remarked, it is 'only by knowing what the specified offence is do we know what the maximum punishment is'.[166] This was not the situation that arose in the *Maxwell case*.[167] In that case, M was convicted of two specific substantive offences as a principal in the second degree (that is, placing a bomb, and being in possession of a bomb with intent). Unlike *S and H*, the indictment in *Maxwell*, specified a single offence in each count. Significantly, four of their Lordships (in *Maxwell*) opined that where the role of an accused person is that of a secondary party, then the Particulars of Offence in the indictment should make clear the nature of the case that the accused has the answer. As Lord Scarman pointed out, a secondary party may have in contemplation any one offence, or several: and the several he may see as alternatives.[168] Lord Scarman saw great merit in the principle that the relevant crime must be within the contemplation of the accomplice because it 'directs attention to the state of mind of the accused – *not what he ought to have in contemplation*, but what he did …'.[169]

---

161 Virgo (n 12).

162 Fortson, *R v S and H* (n 13).

163 Similarly, Serious Crime Act 2007, s 47(5)(a)(iii).

164 Fortson, *R v S and H* (n 13).

165 *Taxquet v Belgium* Nov 16, 2010 [97]; and consider *Canavan and Kidd* [1988] 1 Cr App R (S) 243; but consider *R v Mercer* [2001] EWCA Crim 638.

166 [2011] EWCA Crim 2872 [50] (Hooper LJ); and see [2011] EWCA Crim 2872 [77]-[80]. Also note, the Serious Crime Act 2007, s 58 (penalties).

167 (1979) 68 Cr App R 128.

168 (1979) 68 Cr App R 153. 'An accessory who leaves it to his principal to choose is liable, provided always the choice is made from the range of offences from which the accessory contemplates the choice will be made' ((1979) 68 Cr App R 152 (Lord Scarman)).

169 Author's emphasis added.

Inchoate-upon-Inchoate Liability

The effect of s 49(3)–(6) is that s 44, but not ss 45-46, may be applied on an inchoate-upon-inchoate basis.[170] Although common-law incitement has been abolished,[171] statutory inchoate offences have been retained. Many (if not all) of those offences appear as 'listed offences' in schedule 3 to the 2007 Act.[172] The Secretary of State may by order amend that schedule.[173] The 'listed offences' are to be disregarded for the purposes of ss 45 and 46.[174]

Accordingly, D may commit the s 44 offence by doing an act that intentionally encourages or assists P to:

(a) *incite* the commission of an offence under the Misuse of Drugs Act 1971,[175] or

(b) *attempt* the commission of an offence,[176] or

(c) enter into an agreement to commit a criminal offence.[177]

Section 5(7) of the Criminal Law Act 1977 provided that it was no offence to incite a conspiracy, but this provision was repealed by the 2007 Act[178] in line with the recommendations of the Law Commission.[179]

A person may commit a s 44 offence in respect of another Part 2 offence. Thus, D can be liable under s 44 for intentionally doing an act that is capable of encouraging P1 to do an act that is capable of encouraging P2 to commit an offence, and this is so even if P1 had no intention of heeding D's encouragement.

Example

D wrote to P1 asking him to persuade P2 to shoot and kill V: P1 received the letter but tore it up and thought no more about it.

In the above example it would be immaterial that D's words of encouragement not been communicated to P1.

---

170   Section 49(3)-(6) of the Serious Crime Act 2007, provides: '(3) A person may, in relation to the same act, commit an offence under more than one provision of this Part. (4) In reckoning whether – (a) for the purposes of section 45, an act is capable of encouraging or assisting the commission of an offence; or (b) for the purposes of section 46, an act is capable of encouraging or assisting the commission of one or more of a number of offences; offences under this Part and listed offences are to be disregarded. (5) "Listed offence" means – (a) in England and Wales, an offence listed in Part 1, 2 or 3 of Schedule 3; and (b) in Northern Ireland, an offence listed in Part 1, 4 or 5 of that Schedule. (6) The Secretary of State may by order amend Schedule 3'.
171   Serious Crime Act 2007, s 59.
172   Ibid. s 49(5).
173   Ibid. s 49(6).
174   Ibid. s 49(4).
175   Misuse of Drugs Act 1971, s 19.
176   Criminal Attempts Act 1981.
177   Criminal Law Act 1977, s 1.
178   Serious Crime Act 2007, schedule 6, Part 2 [54].
179   Law Com No 300 (n 20) [7.19].

The Trap in s 47(8)(c)   Where the allegation is that D committed the s 44 offence by intentionally doing an act of encouraging or assisting P to commit a *criminal attempt*,[180] it is important not to be misled by the wording of s 47(8)(c).[181] Two points should be noted. First, subsection (8) concerns the 'doing of an act' by P, and not by D. Secondly, it is submitted that the words 'attempt to do an act', as they appear in s 47(8), have their ordinary, everyday meaning. Accordingly, the word 'attempt' in that provision is not to be given its legal, technical meaning. P's preparatory acts might loosely be styled 'an attempt' and these fall within s 47(8)(c). The words within round brackets in (8)(c) ensure that the restriction imposed by s 49(4)-(6) in respect of inchoate-upon-inchoate liability (save for the s 44 offence) is maintained.

Section 1(4)(b) of the Criminal Attempts Act and Serious Crimes Act 2007   As Professor Michael Bohlander has pointed out,[182] the 2007 Act has not repealed s 1(4)(b) of the Criminal Attempts Act 1981, which (in effect) excludes from s 1 of that Act 'aiding, abetting, counselling, procuring or suborning the commission of an offence ...' (that is, attempts to aid, abet and so on). As interpreted in *Dunnington*,[183] the effect of s 1(4)(b) of the 1981 Act is that it prevents D 'being convicted of attempting to commit an offence that has been committed by P if, despite trying to encourage or assist P, D's conduct does not in fact do so'.[184] And yet, as Bohlander observes, this is precisely the sort of conduct that may be caught by Part 2 of the 2007 Act. For example, if D, in an effort to assist P, obtained a gun for the latter to use in a robbery, but failed to deliver it to P, who *nonetheless went on to commit that crime*, s 1(4)(b) of the Criminal Attempts Act 1981 prevents D being convicted on the basis that he attempted to aid and abet P's robbery. However, for the purposes of s 44 of the Serious Crime Act 2007, D did intentionally do an act that was capable of assisting P to commit robbery. D's liability need not be confined to the s 44 offence because none of the Part 2 offences requires D to have actually succeeded in encouraging or assisting P to perform the conduct element of the anticipated offence.

Bohlander's argument goes further, alluding to s 3 of the 1981 Act, which provides that 'any inconsistent provision in any other enactment' is to be applied in a manner consistent with the scheme of that Act.[185] By s 3(2)(b) of the Criminal Attempts Act, the inconsistent provision includes any offence that is 'expressed as an offence of *attempting* to commit another offence...'. But, none of the Part 2 offences is expressed as an offence of 'attempting' or is a 'special statutory provision' within the meaning of s 3 of the 1981 Act. Bohlander therefore suggests that s 1(4)(b) of the 1981 Act should be repealed in order to bring it into line with the Serious Crime Act 2007.[186]

Bohlander's analysis is compelling but one answer, as a matter of criminal practice, is that there will rarely be cases where the issue at trial is between whether D aided or abetted an offence, or merely *attempted* to do so (still less, whether in the latter case, D had acted contrary to Part 2 of the Serious Crime Act 2007). For what the point may be worth, it is doubtful that the existence of s 49(1) of the 2007 Act, which provides that D can be liable for the commission of a Part 2 offence

---

180   Notably, Criminal Attempts Act 1981, s 1.

181   See (n 45)

182   Bohlander (n 13).

183   [1984] QB 472.

184   Law Com No 300 (n 20) [3.3], [fn 2]; and see, Ormerod (n 13) 421.

185   Bohlander (n 13) 487.

186   See also Michael Bohlander's Letter to the Editor, 'Inchoate Offences', [2010] Criminal Law Review 934, in reply to John Child, 'The Differences Between Attempted Complicity and Inchoate Assisting and Encouraging: A Reply to Professor Bohlander' [2010] Criminal Law Review 925.

regardless of whether or not the anticipated offence was committed by P, bears on the question of whether s 1(4)(b) of the Criminal Attempts Act 1981 should be retained or not.

The fact remains that ss 1 and 3 of the 1981 Act are expressly included in schedule 3 to the Serious Crime Act 2007 (that is, the 'listed offences'), and a court may yet decide that s 1(4)(b) and s 3 of the 1981 Act have relevance in the context of the Part 2 offences. Even though those considerations may be a weak argument for retaining s 1(4)(b) of the Criminal Attempts Act 1981, the question of whether that provision ought to be repealed, or not, is one that ought (arguably) to be considered first by the Law Commission, perhaps as part of a further but wider review of secondary and inchoate liability.[187] Regard should be given to the reason for enacting the provision in the first place. If the answer is that it exists in order to limit criminalisation of inchoate acts then it is arguable that, rather than repealing protections, legislators and policy makers should seek to limit the reach of the Part 2 offences.

As a footnote, under this heading, nothing in Part 2 prevents D from being indicted under s 1, Criminal Attempts Act 1981 for attempting to commit a Part 2 offence. The provisions of s 47(4)-(6) have no relevance here because those provisions concern cases where D is alleged to have encouraged or assisted P to commit a 'listed offence',[188] rather than the other way round (that is, where D attempts, conspires and so on to commit a Part 2 offence). However, it is debatable whether it would be in the public interest to prosecute D on such a basis (given the remoteness of D's acts).

Issues of Policy, Practice and Procedure

The mens rea 'soup': joint enterprise, intention and recklessness   Nothing in this chapter seeks to (nor could) improve on the works of eminent commentators who have critically examined the circumstances in which it is appropriate to fix a person with criminal liability for conduct or consequences that he or she did not purposefully intend. What is offered here continues to be a practitioner's perspective, particularly in relation to cases that are presented before juries constituted almost entirely of persons with no knowledge of the criminal law. Although each legal rule must obviously be principled, and that a body of rules must have coherence, there is a point at which the refinement of rules, however principled, begin to have diminishing practical value and may work an injustice. To that end, judges will tailor jury directions and 'routes to verdict', in order that the directions are comprehensive, comprehensible, and fair to the accused, even if that means that the directions are more favourable to the accused than they need to be.

Rules relating to participation in crime, and the elements of an offence, are increasingly complex, particularly in cases of murder arising out of a gang attack, or where offences are committed by members of a group whose objectives may be disparate or antagonistic. In many cases, where an offence has been committed by more than one party, there is the potential for 'routes to verdict' to encompass too many issues, involving too many alternative bases of liability, with the result that a given case becomes bogged down and leaves the jury confused and perplexed.

At the risk of over-simplification, the array of rules pertaining to D's *mens rea*, include:

---

187   Section 1(4)(b) of the Criminal Attempts Act 1981 is barely mentioned in Law Com No 300 (n 20) [3.3], [fn 2]; and [B.5].

188   Note that para 6.85 of the Blackstone's Guide 'addresses only cases where D encourages or assists P to attempt to commit a crime, and not attempts to encourage or assist P to do so' (Fortson, *The Serious Crime Act 2007* (n 13)).

1. Proof that D *intended* (e.g.) acts, consequences.
2. D's intention may be direct – that is to say that it was his *purpose* to act as he did or as he contemplated that he would act; *purpose* is to be distinguished from desire and motive.
3. D's intention may be '*oblique*', that is to say, a 'kind of knowledge or realisation'.[189] Such intention may include awareness that a certain consequence was '*virtually certain*'.[190]
4. D (as a secondary party) may purposively intend to encourage/assist P to perform the conduct element of an offence, *and* that D had knowledge of the essential elements of P's offence.
5. 'Knowledge' may mean (a) actual knowledge, (b) belief,[191] (c) realisation or (d) foresight.[192]
6. For secondary liability, it is sufficient that D *foresaw* that P's offence *might* be committed.
7. Knowledge or foresight will usually extend to (a) the conduct element of P's offence, (b) P's *mens rea*, (c) the possibility of any consequence element flowing from Ps conduct.
8. Notwithstanding (7) above, although death is a consequence element necessary for the offence of murder, neither D nor P need have foresight that V would be killed.[193]
9. Where the allegation is murder, D (as a secondary party) will not be liable if it was not his purpose to kill V and he did not foresee P's lethal act, which was 'fundamentally different' from the act that D had foreseen P might carry out.[194]
10. Rules relating to manslaughter have 'chopped and changed' in cases where D did not foresee the manner by which P killed V, and where D did not have the *mens rea* for murder, and did not foresee that P would act with the *mens rea* for murder: *R v Carpenter*.[195]

'Joint enterprise': what is it?   To many legal scholars the expression 'joint enterprise' is confined to the circumstances in which D can be held jointly liable with P if the latter has committed crime X and caused crime Y, notwithstanding that D neither participated in crime Y, nor purposefully intended its commission. But, the expression is often used by practitioners to refer to any situation where two or more defendants are jointly charged.[196] Indeed, it is doubtful that there is consensus among criminal law practitioners as to what 'joint enterprise' means. This is hardly surprising. Not only have rules relating to participation in crime developed in a piecemeal way but, as Toulson LJ

---

189   G. Williams (n 79).

190   Precisely what is represented by the expression 'virtually certain' is unclear: see *R v Woollin* [1999] 1 AC 82; M. C. Kaveny, 'Inferring Intention from Foresight' [2004] Law Quarterly Review 81; the Andrew Ashworth (note) '*R. v Matthews and Alleyne*' [2003] Criminal Law Review 553; and the David Ormerod (note) '*R v Gnango*' [2011] Criminal Law Review 150.

191   What constitutes 'belief' has been expressed in various ways. In *R v Hall* (1985) 81 Cr App R 260, 264, Boreham J, giving the judgment of the Court over which Lord Lane CJ presided, distinguished between knowledge and belief as follows: 'Belief, of course, is something short of knowledge. It may be said to be the state of mind of a person who says to himself: "I cannot say I know for certain that these goods are stolen, but there can be no other reasonable conclusion in the light of all the circumstances, in the light of all that I have heard and seen"'. In *R v Forsyth* [1997] 2 Cr App R 299, Beldam LJ said (320) that the 'ordinary meaning of belief is the mental acceptance of a fact as true or existing'.

192   Query whether there is a material difference between 'realisation' and 'foresight'.

193   See, Ormerod (n 13) 227, and noting fn 313. See also, Buxton (n 3) 234.

194   In cases of murder, jury directions that must have regard to *English* [1999] 1 AC 1; *Rahman* [2008] UK HL 45; and *Yemoh* [2009] EWCA Crim 930, pose considerable difficulties.

195   [2011] EWCA Crim 2568.

196   See Ormerod (n 13) 213.

remarked in *Mendez*,[197] and in *Stringer*,[198] the expression 'joint enterprise is not a legal term of art' notwithstanding that there is a tendency among some scholars to treat it as such.[199] Distinguishing between situations, and labelling categories of conduct, will often assist legal analysis but it is often unwise to be dogmatic about what is meant by a particular label or about the circumstances that are encompassed within a category.[200]

Directing juries   Juries will readily comprehend that a defendant *intended* a result (for example, causing grievous bodily harm) if it had been his *purpose* to do so (that is, that he 'meant' to do so: direct intention). It will often not be necessary or desirable (in the interests of clarity) to modify jury directions in order to accommodate 'oblique intention' (that is, that the defendant must have foreseen/realised/been aware that a consequence was 'virtually certain'). Such directions require elaboration by trial judges lest juries equate intention with recklessness. Even in cases where two or more defendants are jointly charged, juries are often directed to decide whether the defendant whose case they are considering, shared the same intention (same 'purpose') drawing no distinction between joint principalship and secondary liability (whether on a 'parasitic liability' basis, or not). In cases where the offence alleged is less serious than that of murder, judges tend not to direct juries on the basis of what the defendant did, or did not, foresee.

It is doubtful that this pragmatic approach has worked to the detriment of the criminal trial process. If every criminal case had to be analysed and presented before a jury paying strict regard to rules relating to participation in crime, it is conceivable that the criminal trial process would be less efficient, with outcomes no more satisfactory.

Given the complexity of the Part 2 offences, particularly s 46, there will be an understandable reluctance on the part of prosecutors and judges to compound difficulties by including, on an indictment, Part 2 offences, especially if the jury must be directed to consider all of the *mens rea* alternatives that appear in s 47(5).

Inchoate liability, secondary liability and the risk of over-criminalisation   The arguments for and against setting D's *mens rea* requirement as low as foresight of what P *might* do (with *mens rea*) have been discussed in the literature, but it is submitted that persons ought not to be stigmatised as 'murderers', and sentenced as such, on mere foresight of what another might do.[201] Although it is 'judge made' law that has largely taken us to this position, it is also the judiciary that has qualified *mens rea* requirements in various ways, notably where P's act was 'fundamentally different' from that foreseen by D. However, there is a strong body of opinion that the existing state of the law is

---

197   [2010] EWCA Crim 511.

198   [2011] EWCA Crim 1396.

199   In *R v ABCD* [2010] EWCA Crim 1622, the Court of Appeal (Criminal Division) specified three instances of 'joint enterprise' (see para 9; the Court did not seek to limit the situations of 'joint enterprise' to three).

200   In this regard, consider, G.R. Sullivan, 'Doing without complicity', J.C.C. Law 2012, 2(Nov), 199-231; Graham Virgo, 'Joint Enterprise Liability is Dead: Long Live Accessorial Liability' [2012] Criminal Law Review 850, and see the 'Letter to the Editor' [2013] Crim. L.R.222 (Steven J. Odgers), and the reply by Professor Graham Virgo ([2013] Crim. L.R.224); see also, S. Parsons, 'Joint Enterprise and Murder' (2012) JCL 76 (463).

201   In essence, this is the 'parity of culpability' problem: and see Law Com no 304 (n 20) [1.7]-[1.11]; and see the House of Commons Justice Committee 11th Report, *Joint Enterprise* (HCJC, 1597).

unsatisfactory and unfair:[202]

> 11. In its 2007 report on aspects of secondary liability the Law Commission recognised that the principle was 'severe', although the Commission recommended its retention with certain safeguards. Tim Moloney QC and Simon Natas, both specialists in criminal law, argue that the principle should be abandoned because in some cases it can lower the bar for conviction:
>
> The prosecution will usually find it easier to adduce evidence that the defendant foresaw what the principal might do than to adduce evidence that he actually intended the principal to cause serious injury or to kill – indeed, such evidence may not go far beyond evidence of association (or alleged 'gang membership') added to alleged presence at the scene. For this reason, the *Chan Wing-siu* principle increases the likelihood that cases will be prosecuted on the basis of weak and tenuous evidence …
>
> 12. In addition, Professor Graham Virgo told us that the courts' approach to determining the mental state required for a finding of joint enterprise was 'inconsistent'. In some cases the secondary participant in the criminal venture was only required to foresee the commission of the offence. In others, the secondary participant was apparently required to foresee the state of mind of the principal offender, as well as foreseeing the criminal act itself.
>
> 13. One of the reasons the Law Commission recommended the retention of the *Chan Wing-siu* principle was the existence of two defences. A defendant can refute a charge under the joint enterprise doctrine either by showing that there is a 'fundamental difference' between the joint criminal venture agreed on and the crime committed during the course of that venture, or by showing clear and unambiguous withdrawal from the venture before the crime took place.[203]

The House of Commons Joint Committee heard evidence that 'the complexity of the law presented serious difficulties for juries' and that the complexity can be 'overwhelming' and (anecdotally) applied inconsistently.[204]

The Part 2 offences, with particular reference to s 47(5)-(7) are open to similar criticisms especially if juries are to be directed, in every case where a Part 2 offence is charged, that D's *mens rea* with regard to any fault, circumstances or consequences is satisfied if D was subjectively reckless.

There is much work to be done to improve the law regarding participation in crime. It is work that needs to be done sooner rather than later.

---

202   House of Commons Justice Committee (HCJC No 11, 2012).

203   See the House of Commons Justice Committee (HCJC No 11, 2012) [11].

204   House of Commons Justice Committee (HCJC No 11, 2012) [16]-[19]. The Committee also remarked that 'it is not the purpose of the law of joint enterprise to foster gang mentality or to draw people into the criminal justice system inappropriately' (ibid. [16]-[19] and [32]).

Chapter 11
Participation on the Internet

Alisdair A. Gillespie

This chapter considers how the law applies to participation that occurs on, or facilitated by, the internet. The internet is a global network of computers which makes instantaneous communication possible throughout the world. The internet allows for people to communicate and act in concert even though they are physically located thousands of miles apart, which clearly raises issues in terms of criminal liability for participation as a result of the actions of others.

It should be noted at the outset that the internet raises important jurisdictional issues. This chapter will not address these issues of jurisdiction but rather consider substantive law. This is not to downplay jurisdiction because it is arguably one of the most important aspects of cybercrime but issues of jurisdiction are considered elsewhere in this book[1] and the issue of internet jurisdiction has been the subject of discussion elsewhere.[2] This chapter will operate on the assumption that jurisdiction can be secured in these instances.

Most countries, but particularly common-law countries such as England and Wales, tend to operate on the principle that 'whatever is illegal offline is illegal online', in other words shy away from specific legislation to tackle online behaviour.[3] For this reason rather than examine general rules of participation as applied to the internet this chapter presents two examples of behaviour on the internet that raises issues of participation.

The first behaviour is that known as cybersuicide. It has been noted in recent years that there have been a number of cases of people committing suicide after accessing the internet and finding either information on how to do so or being encouraged by others on the internet to do so. The second issue to examine is the liability of internet service and content providers for the hosting or distribution of child pornography. Most laws have focused on liability of individuals but given that access to internet content is through providers what, if any, is their liability?

Cybersuicide

The first behaviour to examine is that of cybersuicide. It should be noted at the outset that this is a non-technical term that covers a broad range of behaviour. There are three forms of behaviour that would appear particularly relevant to our examination:

---

1   See Chapter 12, by Michael Hirst.

2   See, for example, Alisdair Gillespie, 'Jurisdictional Issues Concerning Online Child Pornography' (2012) 20(3) International Journal of Law and Information Technology 151; and Bernhard Maier 'How Has the Law Attempted to Tackle the Borderless Nature of the Internet?' (2010) 18 International Journal of Law and Information Technology 142.

3   Although there are, of course, exceptions to this general rule where specific issues are raised. The most obvious would be those that relate to computer-access crime under the Computer Misuses Act 1990 – for a general discussion on this see David Ormerod, *Smith and Hogan's Criminal Law* (13th edn, Oxford University Press 2011) 1047.

1. the creation of websites that offer general advice on how to commit suicide;
2. sites that include message boards or interactive chat facilities, allowing specific advice on how to commit suicide or encourage those who are contemplating it;
3. suicide pacts – where two or more people agree to kill themselves at the same time.

What will not be examined in this part of the chapter is the liability of those who cause people to commit suicide through bullying and harassment. Whilst it is clear that there are instances of suicide through bullying, including cyber-bullying,[4] it has been postulated that the ruling in *R v Kennedy (No 2)*[5] is such that the voluntary actions of a person to commit suicide would act as a break in the chain of liability for homicide.[6] This is, however, premised on the basis that a person voluntarily commits suicide. Where the actions are involuntary, compelled or performed under pressure then the chain of causation may not be broken.

The Court of Appeal, albeit *in dicta*, has accepted that there can be liability in homicide for those who cause a person to commit suicide,[7] although in that instance the court suggested it would be through physical assaults but it is submitted there is no reason why a death following the infliction of psychiatric harm through persistent bullying could not fall within the rule.[8] Clearly those who undertake such bullying could be criminalised either as a principal or through being tried as a principal where they were an accessory to such bullying.[9]

The abuse that compels someone to commit suicide should not be minimised but due to limitations of space this chapter will be limited to the more conventional forms of cybersuicide presented above. In respect of the behaviour discussed here the victim has sought out information or advice in respect of suicide. Whilst it is conceded that this could include those who have been the victims of (cyber-)bullying, the liability to be discussed here is not those who caused the victim to have suicidal thoughts but rather the liability of those who provide assistance or encouragement to attempt suicide.

Suicide Act 1961

The starting point of any inquiry into cybersuicide, at least under English law, is the resolution of a partial paradox. Whilst suicide was (and in some religions still is) considered a spiritual wrong, the (temporal) law no longer criminalises attempted suicide.[10] Therefore if suicide, and the attempt thereof, is lawful it could be legitimately questioned why there may be liability through participation. The general rule of participation is that where there is no principal offence there can

---

4   See, for example, Jocelyn Ho, 'Bullied to Death: Cyberbullying and Student Online Speech Rights' (2012) 64 Florida Law Review 789-816; and Keith Hawton, Kate Saunders and Rory O'Connor, 'Self-Harm and Suicide in Adolescents' (2012) 379 The Lancet 2373.

5   [2008] 1 AC 269.

6   Andrew Simester, Bob Sullivan, John Spencer and Graham Virgo, *Simester and Sullivan's Criminal Law* (4th edn, Hart 2010) 420.

7   *R v Dhaliwal* [2006] 2 Cr App R 24 [8] 351.

8   Especially since, of course, psychiatric injury is now recognised: *R v Ireland; R v Burstow* [1998] AC 147. The *ratio* of *Dhaliwal* was that a conviction could not be sustained for suicide through psychological harm but this was because psychological rather than psychiatric harm has not been recognised as bodily harm by the courts.

9   Accessories and Abettors Act 1861, s 8.

10   See Suicide Act 1961, s 1.

be no secondary liability.[11] Thus if it is legally permissible for A to commit suicide why should B, who assists or encourages A to do so, be held liable? Like all good rules it is perhaps defined by its exceptions. In the context of suicide the exception is contained in statute where, at least under English law, it is a criminal offence to do an act that is capable of encouraging or assisting suicide.[12]

The offence of encouraging and assisting suicide is an offence that was heavily amended by the recent Coroners and Justice Act 2009, in part because of concerns about cybersuicide.[13] The original offence was a straight-forward complicity offence where liability was based on aiding, abetting, counselling or procuring but the 2009 amendments altered it to one of causing or encouraging, using language similar to the offences contained in the Serious Crime Act 2007,[14] although as will be seen there are some differences. The *actus reus* of the offence is that D does an act[15] that is capable of either encouraging or assisting the suicide or attempted suicide of another person.[16] There is no requirement that the person actually does commit or attempt to commit suicide, simply encouraging a person to do so will suffice. The other person need not be a specific person, class of person or even known to or identified by the defendant.[17] This will be important in the context of cybersuicide where it could mean that generic information is caught by the provisions.

The *mens rea* of the offence is that D intended his act to encourage or assist suicide or attempted suicide.[18] There is some doubt whether the offences under the Serious Crime Act 2007 will permit or include oblique intent, that is the foresight that an act is virtually certain to lead to suicide or a suicide attempt,[19] but no such doubts exist in respect of the offence under s 2 and this may be relevant in respect of cybersuicide.

The offence was brought into the public spotlight as a result of the litigation of Debbie Purdy,[20] an MS sufferer who sought a declaration that if her husband were to help her commit suicide by, for example, helping her to board an aeroplane to Switzerland, that he would not be culpable.[21] The House of Lords ruled that Article 8 of the European Convention on Human Rights was engaged and that a person contemplating assisting a person to commit suicide should be aware of the

---

11   Simester et al. (n 6) 204.

12   Suicide Act 1961, s 2(1).

13   See the explanatory notes accompanying the Act, para 357 (available online at <www.legislation. gov.uk/ukpga/2009/25/notes> accessed 1 August 2012).

14   Serious Crime Act 2007, ss 44-49.

15   And, according to s 2B this includes a 'course of conduct'. Whilst that term is not defined it is inevitable that it will bear the same meaning as the Protection from Harassment Act 1997.

16   Note it is another person so it is not possible to do an act that is capable of assisting one's own suicide, for example by emailing instructions to oneself on how to tie a noose. Cf. the position in Australia where there is some doubt as to whether their law applies to self-assistance (Jennifer Prinz, 'The Phenomenon of Cybersuicide' (2008) 18 Indiana International and Comparative Law Review 477).

17   Suicide Act 1961, s 2(1A).

18   Suicide Act 1961, s 2(1)(b).

19   Discussed by Simester et al. (n 6) 421. The classic definition of oblique intent was provided by the House of Lords in *R v Woollin* [1999] 1 AC 82.

20   Culminating in the hearing before the House of Lords: *R (on the application of Purdy) v DPP* [2010] 1 AC 345.

21   Debbie Purdy was concerned that if she was unable to walk or move independently at that stage that the act of her husband (or another) to assist her in boarding an aeroplane to Switzerland (where assisted suicide is lawful) would be considered a causative act and thus liable under s 2(1). The House of Lords agreed that there was this risk (see the speech of Lord Hope, 382-87).

circumstances which the DPP would take into account when deciding to prosecute.[22] Whilst the decision of the House of Lords has been attacked as unconstitutional[23] the DPP complied with the decision and produced interim and then final guidance on the circumstances under which a prosecution is likely to be brought.[24] Again for reasons of space these will not be discussed here but rather the focus will be on the substantive law.

Suicide Websites

The first type of cybersuicide behaviour to consider is that of suicide websites. To an extent this was one of the earlier concerns about cybersuicide, that the internet provides people with the opportunity to create websites that either promote suicide or provide assistance on how to commit suicide.[25] This can potentially raise interesting issues of jurisdiction where the host country does not criminalise assisted suicide or the promotion of suicide but, for reasons explained previously this will not be discussed.

A variety of different types of suicide websites can be seen to exist[26] but they can be classified into key groups, such as:

- sites that are pro-suicide and provide detailed information about how to commit suicide,
- sites that provide information on how to commit suicide but do not actively encourage suicide,
- sites that are jokey in nature but which contain real information on how to commit suicide,
- sites that are anti-suicide.

In addition to these static sites there are more active sites that facilitate communication through chat, that is, the ability to talk to others about suicide.[27] These type of sites will not be discussed in this section but will instead be considered below.

Outside of the web there are other places to obtain advice using an internet connection, including the use of newsgroups/usenet discussion boards, which can also provide advice and assistance. One commentator has noted that a particular site produces a 'practical user's guide to suicide' which includes details on multiple methods to commit suicide, and offers advice on the drafting and editing of suicide notes.[28]

---

22   The Suicide Act 1961, s 2(4) provides that a prosecution can only be instigated with the permission of the DPP (often delegated to Crown Prosecutors) and thus the purpose of the litigation was to discover what the DPP would take into account when deciding whether to give permission.

23   See, for example, John Keown, 'Dangerous Guidance' (2009) 159 New Law Journal 1718; and Jonathan Rogers, 'Prosecution Policies, Prosecutorial System, and the Purdy Legislation' [2010] Criminal Law Review 543.

24   *Policy for Prosecutors in Respect of Cases of Encouraging or Assisting Suicide* (available online at <www.cps.gov.uk/publications/prosecution/assisted_suicide_policy.html> accessed 1 August 2012).

25   See, for example, L Biddle, J Donovan, K Hawton, N Kapur and D Gunnell, 'Suicide and the Internet' (2008) 336 British Medical Journal 800.

26   For an empirical analysis see ibid. 801.

27   Ibid.; and also Laura Pontzer, 'If Words Could Kill: Can the Government Regulate Any Online Speech?' (2011) 5 Pittsburgh Journal of Environmental Public Health 153, at 159 et seq.

28   Ellen Luu, 'Web-Assisted Suicide and the First Amendment' (2009) 36 Hastings Constitutional Law Quarterly 307.

Biddle et al. found that pro-suicide sites were the most common type of site, followed by those who provide advice on how to commit suicide.[29] What is the liability of those who create such a website? It will be remembered that the offence under s 2 requires that the defendant does an act that is capable of encouraging or assisting suicide or attempted suicide. Where a website simply glorifies suicide by, for example, making comments that suicide is a valid life-choice or praises those who have committed suicide, then it may be difficult to see how it could be said that this encourages or assists another to commit suicide, even accepting that, as noted above, it need not be directed towards a particular victim.[30] What if it can be shown that the website provides comfort to a person who was contemplating committing suicide? Could it be argued that this amounts to assistance or encouragement? Whilst neither term is defined in the Act it is submitted that it must require more than simply comfort. Whilst comfort may be relevant where there is a particular defendant it may perhaps be a step too far to say that writing a post that someone may find comforting amounts to an act of encouragement or assistance. In any event in such circumstances it would perhaps be difficult to show *mens rea*. It is unlikely that the person who writes the post that provides comfort intended for this to encourage or assist a person to commit suicide.

However what of those websites that, for example, provide assistance to a person who wishes to commit suicide? For example, if a website explains how to tie a noose and the best locations to hang oneself from (to ensure a quick and painless death) then these could presumably be considered to be an act that is capable of assisting suicide – it helps the person who wishes to commit suicide by providing detailed information on how to do it. Whilst there may be a question over the *mens rea* in that D may seek to claim that he did not intend to assist V in committing suicide, it is clear that oblique intent suffices. Therefore if the prosecution can prove that D foresaw that it was virtually certain that someone (anywhere in the world) may find their website useful in attempting to commit suicide then liability could arise.

Human Rights

The fact that the simple creation of a website could potentially lead to culpability does raise potential human rights issues which should be at least summarised. Whilst it is clear that most human rights instruments will prioritise the protection of life,[31] the creation and publishing of material will ordinarily raise issues of freedom of speech/expression,[32] which are often considered to be one of the most important rights.[33]

Notwithstanding the importance of the freedom of speech, it has generally been considered appropriate to criminalise speech where it can be shown that the content is harmful,[34] and clearly this will be of relevance to some suicide websites, but what of sites that simply provide general advice? Can this be considered sufficiently harmful to take it outside the scope of free speech/

---

29   Biddle et al. (n 25) 800.

30   Suicide Act 1961, s 2(1A).

31   See, for example, the jurisprudence of the US Supreme Court (the most relevant case being *Washington v Gluckenberg* 117 S Ct 2258 (1997)) and the European Court of Human Rights has been clear that Article 2 (Right to Life) does not include a right to end one's life (*Pretty v United Kingdom* (2002) 35 EHRR 1). The decision of the House of Lords in *Purdy* (n 20) did not alter this as it did not recognise a right to die but rather focused on prosecutorial discretion.

32   Perhaps the most notable of which are the First Amendment to the Constitution of the United States of America and Article 10 of the European Convention on Human Rights.

33   In the context of the ECHR see *Handyside v UK* (1979-80) 1 EHRR 737, 754.

34   See, for example, *Surek v Turkey* (1994) 8 BHRC 339.

expression? At least one commentator believes that the nexus can be shown: 'ordinarily benign words ... and counselling on the science of taking one's own life certainly inflict injury'[35] and should therefore be considered to exist outside of free speech protection. However, others disagree and suggest that it is necessary to divorce the generic cyber-comments from true assisted suicide and recognise that it may amount to a 'legitimate speech-related purpose'.[36] Expanding on this theme Luu notes that there should be a temporal link and that it is not appropriate to criminalise speech on the basis that the content 'increases the chance an unlawful act will be committed at some indefinite future time'.[37] Within the European context this can perhaps be supported by Article 10 which has been construed to include offensive, shocking and disturbing material,[38] albeit one that is qualified where, *inter alia*, it is shown that the material incites harm.[39]

There has been little jurisprudence on this point[40] and indeed the majority of academic analysis has been centred on the US constitutional position which is perhaps understandable given the importance of the First Amendment. In the context of English law, where the jurisprudence of Article 10 is more relevant, the position may be clearer since although Article 10 protects freedom of expression, including protecting material that is offensive, shocking and disturbing,[41] interference is permissible not only on the basis of potential harm but also of morality.[42] The key in deciding whether criminalisation can be justified is the necessity and proportionality of any action by the state, which the European Court of Human Rights has always considered key,[43] and the threshold for justifying interference in respect of Article 10 has always been set high.[44]

An important point is that suicide is not in itself criminal. It will be remembered that Luu believes that freedom of speech should not be compromised where there is some speculative belief that the material may, at some indeterminate point in the future, incite unlawful activity.[45] Presumably the position may be even clearer where the incited activity is not even criminal.[46] Certainly where there is no proof that a site actually incites persons (or a section of the public) to harm themselves, which may be the case with some generic suicide websites that simply glorify suicide, then it is quite possible that it would be considered disproportionate to criminalise those who created the site, thus leading to a breach of Article 10.[47]

---

35 Pontzer (n 27) 166.
36 Luu (n 28) 309.
37 Ibid. 312 citing *Brandenburg v Ohio* 395 US 444 (1969).
38 See DJ Harris, M O'Boyle, EP Bates and CM Buckley, *Harris, O'Boyle and Warbrick Law of the European Convention on Human Rights* (2nd edn, Oxford University Press 2009) 444.
39 Ibid. 452-55.
40 One of the few cases to refer specifically to this is *State of Minnesota v Melchert-Dinkel* A11-0987 (Court of Appeals, 17 July 2012) but this is not particularly helpful as that case involved the direct encouragement through interactive chat rather than generic websites.
41 Harris et al. (n 38) 444.
42 European Convention on Human Rights, Article 10(2).
43 Harris et al. (n 38) 349.
44 Ibid. 444.
45 See (n 37), above, and associated text.
46 An interesting case in this context is *Open Door Counselling and Dublin Well Woman v Ireland* (1993) 15 EHRR 244 where the European Court of Human Rights found a breach of Article 10 where the applicants' publishing of material that presented information, *inter alia*, on how to travel to England and Wales to procure an abortion, was prevented even though this was not illegal in Ireland (whereas abortion in Ireland is).
47 There is no evidence that Parliament, when considering the amendments to the Suicide Act 1961, actively considered Article 10 of the ECHR. This by itself is not problematic and it will be for the police and

Suicide Chat

The proliferation of general websites that discuss the issue of cybersuicide is a concern but perhaps the most notable difficulty is those that allow for chat, either asynchrously[48] or in real-time.[49] There are a wide number of suicide chat-rooms that are easily obtainable from the internet[50] and they are diverse in topic. Some simply provide information about suicide but others will allow users to talk to each other, either live or through message-boards.[51] There is considerable discrepancy over who actively participates in these sites. Whilst some will feature empathetic persons who are there to assist troubled persons[52] or indeed include professionals who are there to talk about why the viewer feels the need to visit such sites[53] others will include more sinister people and postings, including situations where there is the encouragement or even goading of a person to commit suicide or the facilitation of suicide pacts.[54]

Whilst examples can sometimes distort an analysis, since it is easy to concentrate on the extremes, they can help us understand the behaviour and how the law may apply.

Direct Encouragement

Perhaps the easiest example is that where there is direct encouragement to kill. A good example of this is the actions of William Melchert-Dinkel[55] who contacted a number of people on the internet he met on suicide websites and encouraged them to commit suicide,[56] including pretending to be willing to commit suicide himself.[57] To an extent this is the easiest form of liability to establish. Where someone provides specific advice to a person that assists them in committing suicide or provides specific encouragement to them to make a suicide attempt, then liability under the Suicide Act 1961 arises.

Believing V's Suicide Attempt

Some forms of encouraging suicide arguably cause difficulties. What is the position where a person sits at a computer and says that they are going to kill themselves by taking a series of pills?[58] Let us consider the liability of D who seeks to encourage V to consume these pills. Where D believes that the pills are real then liability is simple and is no different to that explained above: D has performed an act (encouragement) that was intended to encourage or assist an attempt at suicide. What should

---

CPS to decide, in each individual case, whether a prosecution may breach Article 10.

48 Usually considered to be 'message boards', that is, people leave messages in a 'thread' which others can contribute to and which remain for all to see.

49 Which can include so-called 'chatrooms'.

50 Pontzer (n 27) 159.

51 D Baker and S Fortune, 'Understanding Self-Harm and Suicide Websites' (2008) 29 Crisis 118, 118.

52 Ibid. 120.

53 Pontzer (n 27) 159.

54 Biddle et al. (n 25) 801.

55 See *State of Minnesota v Melchert-Dinkel* A11-0987 (Court of Appeals, 17 July 2012).

56 See, for example, ibid. [9]-[12].

57 Discussed further below.

58 For an illustration of this see the example of Abraham Biggs who killed himself by taking drugs whilst broadcasting his suicide attempt live on the internet (Pontzer (n 27) 159). A number of people viewed this attempt and encouraged him to take the tablets.

the position be where D does not know whether the pills are real (and thus that it is a real suicide attempt) but does not care whether they are?

The Suicide Act 1961 is quite clear that the *mens rea* is that of intention; that D's act was intended to encourage or assist suicide or attempted suicide. If D does not know that the pills were real then there can be no liability since D cannot possibly be intentionally encouraging suicide (as the pills, he believes, will not kill him). What about where D does not care whether the pills are real? Again it would seem difficult to argue that there is the intention to encourage suicide. There is no doubt that he is intending to encourage V to take the pills but that is not the same as saying he is encouraging suicide. Not caring about the result of one's actions is classic recklessness territory not intention.

If, as seems likely, culpability under s 2 could not be shown it would seem that the revised offence is more generous to a defendant than when it adopted the ordinary rules of participation. As is well-known, the *mens rea* for complicity is not only based on the intention to encourage but also knowledge of the circumstances of the offence.[59] Initially this was based on direct knowledge but the courts began to relax this, including situations where D thought the circumstances were probable[60] or where there was a 'real or serious risk' that the circumstances were true[61] or, perhaps more relevant for our determination, where there was a 'strong possibility'[62] that the circumstances were as he believed them to be. If this were to be applied to the example above a different result would occur. Where D closes his mind and simply does not care whether the tablets are real but accepts they may be, then intentionally encouraging V to take the tablets would be culpable.

Will the courts extend this ruling to s 2? Whilst the Suicide Act 1961 does refer to belief it does so only in the context of where the actions of D are *not* capable of assisting or encouraging suicide.[63] That is not the position here where D simply does not know. Nothing in the Act suggests that there is a need for belief although the courts may wish to consider implying it on the basis that it may be difficult to argue that there was the intention to encourage suicide or attempted suicide unless the defendant believed that the victim was capable of such an act.[64]

The difficulty, however, is whilst this may appear sensible in respect of encouragement it could cause a problem for assistance. It will be remembered that s 2 applies to both encouragement and assistance. Let us take an example: D is aware that V has had suicidal tendencies for some time. V asks D to borrow some weed-killer to kill some weeds in his garden. D believes that V wants it to kill weeds in his garden but contemplates that he may use it to kill himself. Under the existing definition there would be no liability – D clearly does not intend to assist V in committing suicide (nor foresee it as virtually certain). However if the extension discussed above was applied, then liability may arise. D contemplates that V may kill himself and so it must be said that it is a 'strong possibility'. Clearly in this example, however, it would be unjust to impose liability.

Perhaps the difficulty here is that we are concerned about the indifference of D in the first example. Reckless indifference is not currently recognised as a form of *mens rea* and instead is thought to be an aggravating factor where culpability can already be shown.[65] The Law Commission

59   See, perhaps most notably, *Johnson v Youden* [1950] 1 KB 544, 546 and see the explanation provided by Simester et al. (n 6) 226.

60   *Carter v Richardson* [1974] RTR 314.

61   *R v Rook* [1993] 2 All ER 955.

62   *R v Reardon* [1999] Crim LR 392.

63   See Suicide Act 1961, s 2A(2) discussed further below.

64   The phrasing of s 2A(2) may preclude this, however. Instead of simply referring to impossibility it relates to belief which may indicate that Parliament intended belief to exist only in respect of this issue.

65   Ormerod (n 3) 125.

proposed the adoption of reckless indifference in respect of second-degree murder but the proposal was dropped over concerns that it would over-complicate the definition of recklessness.[66] Thus, it is unlikely that indifference would assist us in identifying the appropriate culpability for the person who encourages a person to consume pills, not caring whether they are real or not. However, given that what is being discussed is whether there should be a requirement of knowledge of the circumstances perhaps a better question is to ask whether D is wilfully blind to the consequences of his actions?

The concept of 'wilful blindness' has existed for centuries[67] and is designed to tackle those who deliberately close their mind to an obvious risk. The precise definition is open to some question and it has been suggested that it applies 'where he suspected the truth but did not want to have his suspicion confirmed',[68] but others have suggested it is 'where the defendant intentionally chooses not to inquire whether something is true because he has no real doubt what the answer is going to be'.[69] The difference between the two definitions is not one of mere semantics, the latter definition requires 'no doubt' as to the answer whereas the former requires 'suspicion', a much lower threshold. Applying this to the drugs example it may be difficult to argue that there is 'no doubt' that the pills are real but it would be difficult to argue that D did not suspect that they are real because that is one of the reasons why he is encouraging their consumption.

Whilst there may be doubt over the definition of wilful blindness, there is more clarity over why the rule exists, '[b]roadly speaking, if there is an obvious way of finding something out and the defendant deliberately shuts his eyes to a risk by failing to find out, he will not be permitted to exculpate himself by claiming he did not know the truth'.[70] This is an important remark in the context of the consumption of pills. It would not be unreasonable to suggest that there is an obvious way of finding out whether the pills are real or not before encouraging their consumption, that is, by asking the victim what they are. By failing to do so then it could be argued that D should be culpable for deliberately not facing the consequences of his actions.[71]

There is obviously a similarity between 'wilful blindness' and recklessness but it has been argued that they are distinct, with the former being narrower.[72] Ormerod suggests the difference can be summarised thus:

> Wilful blindness is distinct from recklessness because, while recklessness involves knowledge of a danger or risk and persistence in a course of conduct which creates a risk that the prohibited result will occur, wilful blindness arises where a person who has become aware of the need for some inquiry declines to make the inquiry because he does not wish to know the truth. He would prefer to remain ignorant.[73]

This is a quote that can be easily applied to the scenario at issue. Whilst there may be some concern as to whether suspicion can be applied to all circumstances (for example, the weedkiller example presented above) the harshness is perhaps removed if the doctrine of 'wilful blindness' is applied.

---

66   Ibid. 126.
67   Ibid. 130.
68   Ibid. 130.
69   Simester et al. (n 6) 150.
70   Ibid.
71   Whilst the victim may lie and, for example, say they are fake when they are real this would not make D culpable because he now believes them to be harmless and thus he cannot intend V to commit suicide.
72   Ormerod (n 3) 132.
73   Ibid.

Those who deliberately close their mind to the risk because they are ambivalent as to the answer should be considered more culpable than those who did not contemplate this. Adopting the 'wilful blindness' test would assist in respect of the consumption of pills example presented above (which is arguably a paradigm of this approach) whereas it would not render D culpable in the weed-killer example, where there is no evidence of wilful blindness. This would seem the most prudent solution to the examples discussed above. If, as has been suggested, the 'doctrine'[74] of wilful blindness is narrower than recklessness then this should limit some of the harshness of implying foreseeability into the *mens rea* of s 2. It would also ensure that someone who encourages a person to commit suicide online, not considering the consequences of his actions, can be culpable where they intentionally do an act that could give encouragement to a suicide attempt.

Belief that the Tablets are Poisonous

As a final observation, what would the position be where the factual situation is reversed, that is, where D believes incorrectly that the tablets are poisonous? To expand: V has announced that he has some tablets in front of him and that he is going to take them to commit suicide. D, believing them to be toxic and capable of killing V, encourages him to take the tablets but, in fact, the tablets are placebos. What is the liability of D in this situation? Arguably it is simpler. Here, the act that is capable of encouraging suicide – telling him to take the pills – would not be factually possible to cause suicide. The legislation states in such circumstances the liability should be based on what D believed it to be,[75] that is, that the tablets were real. Accordingly D would be liable under s 2(1) irrespective of whether the pills could actually kill, presumably because it was D's intention to encourage V to kill himself. Permitting inchoate liability for impossible actions is, of course, not unusual in English law[76] and this is just another example of this rule.

The Best Interests of V?

What is the position where D, a medical practitioner, states that any advice or encouragement he gives is in the best interests of V? To put this into context, let us imagine a scenario. N is a medically-qualified nurse who visits suicide websites on the internet. There he meets V and they talk about suicide, including providing medical information about the best way to do so and condoning the choices that V is making. Should N be liable for this or is it subject to any qualification about whether he was doing so in the best interests of V? Does it matter why N wishes to commit suicide? For example, if V is suffering from a painful, terminal illness is that materially different from the position whereby V is depressed? The motivations for acting may also differ. So, for example, does the liability change if N believes that it is inevitable that V will commit suicide and he is providing his advice, for example, on how to tie and place a noose, because he is concerned that the manner in which V is going to do it will cause a slow, painful death through strangulation rather than a quick death through the breaking of the neck leading to paralysis (as occurs in capital punishment) or indeed the suggestion of using a combination of drugs because it is thought to be quicker, more effective and painless?

---

74   Simester et al. (n 6) place quotation marks around the word 'doctrine' (150) because it is far from certain that it can be considered a doctrine, not least due to its uncertain definition and imprecise application.

75   Ibid.

76   See most notably, s 1(2) Criminal Attempts Act 1981.

Certainly there is some evidence to suggest that some websites may have some benefit. Baker and Fortune reported that some users of websites found that they were able to talk to people in a way that they could not to health-care professionals.[77] They found that the sites helped form a type of community and that it provided emotional support and could reduce incidents of harmful behaviour.[78] This raises questions over the illegality of the sites. Assuming the sites contain information that allows a user to obtain information about committing suicide – including discussing suicide with others – then it would seem that liability under s 2 would be likely. Even if D did not create the website for the purpose of encouraging or assisting suicide, if it were a virtual certainty that the site could encourage or assist suicide, and the defendant appreciates that, then liability would arise through oblique intent. In the context of homicide the law has accepted the doctrine of double-effect in medical circumstances. The classic application of this rule is where a doctor gives a drug that will ease the pain of a patient even though he knows it will also hasten their death.[79] However, it is unlikely that this would apply. For a start the doctrine of double-effect is probably based on public policy grounds surrounding *bona fide* medical treatment,[80] something that may not be clear in these cases. For example, the Medical Defence Union has clearly stated that doctors should not discuss suicide[81] suggesting that the creation or operation of a website by a health-care professional is unlikely to be considered *bona fide* treatment. If so, this would almost certainly prevent the doctrine of double-effect from applying and liability could arise under s 2.

Whether this is appropriate is perhaps more open to question. The fact that medical practitioners are at risk of prosecution has led one commentator to question whether there will be 'an increase in botched suicides presided over by (hopefully) well-meaning, but ill-informed relatives'.[82] This statement does not immediately appear to be capable of being placed within the context of the internet since it envisions loved-ones (reluctantly) helping a terminally ill patient to die, but it does raise an important issue about the internet and medically qualified persons. If a person is determined to die and a medical practitioner is concerned that their choice of mode could cause prolonged pain and suffering (especially where, for example, it was unsuccessful) and provides neutral advice on the best way of committing suicide (without directly encouraging them to commit suicide) should that person be at risk of prosecution? The fact that suicide advice is considered unethical medically would seem to influence this decision and accordingly the answer is likely to be 'yes'.

Suicide Pacts

The final issue to consider briefly is that of suicide pacts. Until recently suicide pacts were generally considered to be in the context of mutual killing. D and V decide to kill themselves but decide D will kill V before killing himself. If, for whatever reason, D does not kill himself, or was unsuccessful in doing so, then instead of being liable for murder – since clearly D would have the intent to kill – he would be guilty of manslaughter as a result of a partial defence.[83] Suicide pacts on the internet are sometimes different. Whilst some will involve persons agreeing to meet up and do

---

77   Baker and Fortune (n 51) 120.
78   Ibid. 121.
79   For a discussion on this in the context of homicide see Ormerod (n 3) 495-97.
80   Discussed perhaps most extensively in *Airedale NHS Trust v Bland* [1993] AC 789.
81   A Mullock, 'Overlooking the Criminally Compassionate: What Are the Implications of Prosecutorial Policy on Encouraging Assisting Suicide?' (2010) 18 Medical Law Review 442, 466.
82   Ibid. 453.
83   Homicide Act 1957, s 4.

the above – in which case the ordinary rules would apply – it may also include the situation where D agrees with V to kill himself at the same time as V but in different locations: that is, D where he is based and V where she is based. If D fails to go through with the pact then, following the ruling in *Kennedy (No 2)*, discussed above, it is unlikely that liability for homicide could be found as it would seem a conscious decision to commit suicide. However, it would seem obvious that it can be considered, at the very least, to be encouragement and thus liability under s 2 may arise.

Liability for Child Pornography Content

The second matter that considers the issue of participation on the internet is that which relates to the liability of service and content providers for child pornography[84] content. The architecture of the internet, which is a global network of computers, means that it is necessary for a user to connect to the internet via an intermediary. The most common intermediary is that known as an Internet Service Provider (ISP) which, as its name suggests, is the person who allows the user to connect to the internet. Internet Content Providers (ICPs) are those companies that gather or produce material that is to be distributed or made available through the internet. Whilst some academics have suggested that academics and the courts confuse the distinction between ISPs and ICPs,[85] others have pointed out the distinction is not always easy, with some ISPs also being ICPs.[86] This is particularly true where, for example, an ISP provides space for a person to host their own website. Virtually all ISPs will provide some content (links to news stories, videos, information about their services) but this section is restricted to the examination of those who facilitate the distribution (by permitting access to the internet) or hosting (by making available space) of child pornography.

In England and Wales there is a variety of material that could be classed as child pornography,[87] but this section will consider only that material which can be classed as an indecent photograph or pseudo-photograph of a child.[88] It is a criminal offence, *inter alia*, to distribute or show an indecent photograph of a child[89] and 'distribute' includes exposing or offering material for acquisition by another.[90] It is also clear that there is no requirement for a user to actively send an image; allowing someone access to a (virtual) space where they can browse and download images is equally culpable.[91] This is relatively straightforward and the person who does actually distribute, or allows access to, the material will be liable as a principal.

The mechanics of the internet, however, raise an interesting question over what, if any, the liability should be for ISPs and ICPs. A person can only distribute an indecent photograph over the internet if they are connected to it by an ISP. Similarly, a person can only host indecent photographs

---

84   The term 'child pornography' is extremely controversial (see Alisdair Gillespie, *Child Pornography: Law and Policy* (Routledge 2011) 1-4) but is used here as it remains a term of ordinary usage.

85   Joseph Monaghan, 'Social Networking Websites' Liability for User Illegality' (2011) 21 Seton Hall Journal for Sports and Entertainment Law 499, 501.

86   Broder Kleinschmidt, 'An International Comparison of ISP's Liabilities for Unlawful Third Party Content' (2010) 18 International Journal of Law and Information Technology 332, 333.

87   Gillespie (n 84) 19-22.

88   Defined in Protection of Children Act 1978, s 7. Expanded upon ibid. 42-63.

89   Protection of Children Act 1978, s 1(1)(b).

90   Ibid. s 1(2).

91   *R v Fellows and Arnold* [1997] 1 Cr App R 244.

on the web[92] where an ICP provides space for him to host the material. In the language of complicity therefore it could be argued that the ISP and ICP aids[93] the distribution of an indecent photograph and/or the possession of such material with the intent to distribute,[94] in that it provides assistance in the commission of the offence.[95] Without the role of an ISP or ICP it would simply not be possible for the distribution or hosting to take place so should there be liability for complicity?

Innocent Agent?

Perhaps the first argument that should be considered is whether the ISP or ICP could be considered an innocent agent. The law recognises that sometimes an offender will seek to commit an offence by using a third party who is unaware that they are committing an offence. Its application has been summarised as applying 'where it is possible for P to fulfil the elements of the *actus reus* by the instrument of some other person'.[96] Could this apply here? If we look at the ISP situation first it could be argued that, whilst they perform the actual delivery, they are analogous to the ubiquitous postman who is often used as the paradigm of an innocent agent when he delivers a bomb that kills V,[97] they are simply a delivery mechanism.

An initial thought may be that there is a difference between the crime of homicide and a crime that actively criminalises delivery (distribution) but the above example can be easily altered. What of the postman who delivers a package that contains class A drugs? The package looks perfectly normal and there is no reason for S, the postman, to suspect anything. S would remain an innocent agent. It is the absence of *mens rea* that makes S the innocent agent in this example[98] and the same is likely to be true of the ISP or ICP. We must first decide whether they have any *mens rea* before deciding whether they are therefore an innocent agent.

Mens rea

For the reasons discussed above the *mens rea* of complicity is likely to be crucial. It would be extremely difficult to argue in the context of either an ISP or ICP that the *actus reus* has not occurred in that the very nature of these services is that they must be assisting the commission of a crime, the same cannot be said of the *mens rea*. The *mens rea* of complicity is twofold; the secondary party (S) must intend their own contribution (in this instance, the aiding) but they must also appreciate the nature of P's actions.[99] In many instances it may be difficult for this element to be satisfied. Whilst there is little doubt that the first element will be satisfied – that S must intend his own contribution – since an ISP or ICP certainly directly intends to allow users to distribute or

---

92 Note for the purposes of this article hosting will be limited to the web and not other internet services, for example Peer-to-Peer services.

93 Accessories and Abettors Act 1861, s 8. The classic definitions were given in *Attorney-General's Reference (No 1 of 1975)* [1975] 1 QB 773.

94 Protection of Children Act 1978, s 1(1)(c).

95 Simester et al. (n 6) 210.

96 Ibid. 208.

97 Ibid. See Ormerod (n 3) 189.

98 Ormerod (n 3) 188.

99 Ibid. 220.

host material, there must be a degree of doubt that exists over the second element, the appreciation of P's actions.

If we think of the major ISPs, for example the four main companies that supply domestic broadband to the public, they are large companies with millions of customers. The very nature of these companies is such that they cannot know what each of their customers is doing at any particular time. Accordingly, it is unlikely that unless they took steps to find out what each customer was doing – which would raise significant privacy issues – then they are unlikely to satisfy the *mens rea* for being an accessory to distribution meaning no liability should arise.

What of ICPs (including ISPs who are themselves ICPs)? The same position is likely to exist. Let us take, for example, Facebook. This is a classic ICP and is probably one of the largest ICPs on the internet. According to their latest statistics, there are approximately 955 million users,[100] each of which will have a profile webpage. Users can also create additional Facebook pages (so-called 'like pages') and Facebook has estimated that there are in excess of 42 million of these pages. It is unlikely therefore that they are able to monitor what is happening on nearly one billion pages. The same position will exist for other ICPs where the logistics of the content that they provide is that they are simply not able to identify what is happening all the time and accordingly it is unlikely that they will have the necessary knowledge required for the *mens rea* of complicity.

However the position may not always be as straightforward. One of the earlier concerns about child pornography on the internet related to newsgroups (sometimes referred to as usenet discussion groups). These still exist but were one of the earlier forms of internet content. They collated emails sent to the newsgroup and allowed users to either browse material or have it automatically emailed to them. Newsgroups were not as user-friendly as the web[101] and it meant that they were sometimes the more hidden element. There were (and are) thousands of newsgroups that cater for a wide variety of topics, including extremely specialist subjects. However a number are known to include child pornography and are actively used to facilitate the dissemination of child pornography.[102] Each newsgroup carries a name and the names of some, such as alt.binaries.pictures.erotica. children or alt.binaries.pictures.erotica.pre-teen[103] would seem likely to include child pornography. ISPs argued that it was not possible to know whether a group included illegal material unless it physically examines the contents of the group, and it would argue there were too many to do that.

Where there is the suspicion, or indeed belief, that content may include illegal material does that alter the position of complicity? It will be remembered from the first section of this chapter that the *mens rea* requirement of knowledge of the circumstances has been relaxed by the courts and liability can now exist where there is a 'strong possibility' or 'a real or substantial risk' would exist.[104] Where there is an obvious-sounding newsgroup that would appear to indicate this or, in the context of the web, a URL[105] that would seem to indicate illegal material,[106] then this may alter the liability for complicity. The first element – intentionally assisting – is obviously met by the provision of the internet access service, and if it can be shown that an ICP or ISP can foresee a risk

---

100   'Facebook Reports Second Quarter 2012 Results' (available online at <http://investor.fb.com> accessed 29 July 2012).

101   John Carr, *Child Abuse, Child Pornography and the Internet* (NCH 2003) 12.

102   P Jenkins, *Beyond Tolerance: Child Pornography on the Internet* (New York University Press 2001) 54-57.

103   Taken from Jenkins, ibid. 55.

104   Discussed more extensively in Simester et al. (n 6) 228.

105   Uniform Resource Locator, better known as the web-address, that is, www.[address].

106   For example, making reference to illegal images or pre-teen sex and so on. Such names do exist on the web.

that illegal content is present then the second element of the *mens rea* may be thought to be satisfied too, potentially leading to culpability.[107]

ISP and ICP Exemptions

However, the ISPs have one last card to play. As the internet began to expand it was clear to governments and international agencies that the role of the ISP was crucial and that there was a danger to expanding the market if ISPs were considered responsible for the content posted by others. Some countries had considered the criminalisation of ISPs in respect of illegal content, including child pornography[108] but arguments against criminalisation include the potential that this could raise free-speech concerns, with ISPs themselves having to 'police' what would be lawful or unlawful. Laws began to adapt to these concerns and restricted the liability of ISPs.

The USA arguably took the lead on this when passing the Communications Decency Act of 1996 which provided ISPs with immunity for third-party content,[109] although this was supposed to be restricted to civil matters and not provide immunity from criminal prosecutions.[110] The EU soon followed suit and introduced a series of measures that were designed to cater for the increased electronic marketplace. Arguably the most significant of these measures was the Directive on electronic commerce[111] which specifically addressed the issues of ISP liability because the EU believed that a failure to do so could harm the common market.[112] The Directive provides exemptions for ISPs where they act solely as a provider[113] or when transmitting or caching data[114] and the Directive also specifically addresses the issue of hosting which is relevant to ICPs and ISPs who also provide content.[115] The wording of the Directive has been carried forward into the UK's implementation of it.[116] Unlike the legislation in the USA the EU Directive specifically includes restrictions on criminal jurisdiction.

Looking at ISP liability first, that is, where the potential liability is for assisting in the distribution of material, the Directive makes clear that ISPs will ordinarily not be liable and will render them innocent agents. Article 12 of the Directive applies where the service 'consists of the transmission in a communication network of information provided by a recipient of the service, or the provision of access to a communication network', in other words where they are a mere conduit, facilitating the communications of another. The Directive requires Member States to exempt providers from liability so long as the provider does not initiate the transmission, select the receiver of the

---

107 The Protection of Children Act 1978, s 3 expressly provides for corporate liability.

108 For a discussion see Yaman Akdeniz, *Internet Child Pornography and the Law: National and International Responses* (Ashgate 2008) 228.

109 Section 230. For a discussion see Monaghan (n 85).

110 Section 230(e)(1). For a discussion on this see Ashley Ingber, 'Cyber-crime Control: Will Websites Ever Be Held Accountable for the Legal Activities They Profit From?' (2012) 18 Cardozo Journal of Law and Gender 423, 441.

111 Directive 2000/31/EC of the European Parliament and of the Council on certain legal aspects of information society services, in particular electronic commerce, in the Internal Market.

112 Discussed in Akdeniz (n 108) 234.

113 Article 12.

114 Article 13.

115 Article 14.

116 See *Electronic Commerce (EC Directive) Regulations 2002/2013* particularly regulations 17-19, regulation 19 being the domestic equivalent of Article 14.

transmission and does not select or modify the information contained in the transmission.[117] This is an unproblematic statement of the law. For the reasons discussed above it is unlikely that an ISP can know that they are distributing indecent photographs of children and this exemption merely recognises that this is the case.

Perhaps the more relevant for our purposes is Article 14 which applies where the service 'consists of the storage of information provided by a recipient of the service' and thus this will apply to the hosting of material and the newsgroup operators. The Directive requires service providers to be exempt from liability so long as they do not have 'actual knowledge of illegal activity or information'[118] and 'the provider, upon obtaining such knowledge or awareness, acts expeditiously to remove or disable access to the material'.[119]

The key effect of this Article is to ensure that ICPs and ISPs will not have criminal liability in respect of assisting in the hosting of material unless they have *actual* knowledge of the illegal material. As this rule is legislative it must trump the common law rules relating to complicity and accordingly it would seem that the *mens rea* requirement discussed above, potentially criminalising service providers where there is a risk that content is illegal, will not apply. The Directive and domestic regulations are clear that only actual knowledge will suffice and this must mean that the provider is aware that illegal material exists and not merely suspect it. In the context of websites and usenet groups this must mean that even where the description is such that it would seem inevitable that the material contained within is illegal, there will be no liability unless the provider looks at the material or receives a report stating that it contains illegal material.

Paragraph (b) is important in that it has created what has become known as the 'notice and takedown' system.[120] In the United Kingdom the Internet Watch Foundation operates a hotline that allows users to report illegal content.[121] If the material is hosted inside the UK then the IWF notifies the relevant service provider who will then take down the material.[122] This system is, in essence, backed by Article 14 of the Directive in that if a service provider is informed of the content they will then have actual knowledge of it and will lose their protection under Article 14 unless they disable the content expeditiously. If they do not and continue to allow the content to be accessed then it would seem liability for complicity could be established. The *actus reus* is satisfied, as noted above, and both elements of the *mens rea* would be satisfied because they are intentionally assisting (providing the service) and now have knowledge of the circumstance of the principal's actions. Save in this situation and in the absence of actual knowledge then both an ICP and ISP must be considered an innocent agent because they will not have *mens rea* and accordingly will ordinarily have no liability for complicity.

Conclusion

This chapter has concentrated on two examples of behaviour that demonstrate that the internet can raise issues of complicity. The internet is, at its most basic, a tool that allows for the exchange of

---

117 Article 12.1.
118 Article 14.1(a).
119 Article 14.1(b).
120 Akdeniz (n 108) 236 and 238-39.
121 See <www.iwf.org.uk> accessed 29 August 2012.
122 If it is hosted abroad but in a country that has a hotline then the IWF will notify that country that material is hosted there, the intention being that the relevant hotline will themselves notify the appropriate provider and get the material removed if it is illegal in the host country.

information and facilitates communication between individuals and so it is perhaps unsurprising that it can be a rich playground for those who wish to commit crime. Numerous crimes raise issues of participation on the internet, including denial of service attacks (a form of hacking), fraud and offences against persons (including bullying and harassment). This chapter could only examine two examples and both raise interesting questions as to our understanding of participation.

Cybersuicide demonstrates how new technology can put a different spin on existing behaviour. Encouraging a suicide attempt is a problem that has existed for many years but the internet allows for this behaviour to be more widespread. Not only is it possible to put detailed information into the public domain on how to commit suicide, the internet allows individuals to counsel suicide whilst feeling one-step removed from the consequences. Whilst some may try to persuade people to commit suicide on camera, many will simply resort to the anonymity of the keyboard and screen to provide advice or encouragement without having the emotional dependence that may exist in an off-line meet.

Internet Service and Content Providers are essential to the very architecture of the internet. The expanse of cyberspace requires the application of the innocent agent doctrine to many forms of online participation. Without the Internet Service and Content Providers there would be no cyber-crime. However, it is unrealistic to expect such providers to monitor the internet, even if it were technically feasible. Some have questioned, however, to what extent this is true innocent agency or the deliberate aversion or closing of eyes. It is likely that this is an issue that will be increasingly discussed, especially as technology advances and the real-time monitoring of behaviour becomes easier.

Where the crime involves the production or distribution of material or the facilitation of communication (which both examples raise) human rights issues quickly arise. It is widely accepted that the internet is one of the most valuable sources of information and arguably the tool most often used to search for information. Democracies tend to elevate the protection of freedom of speech/expression and these debates have progressed to the internet leading to debates about the extent to which content on the internet can be regulated. This is a debate that is unlikely to dissipate quickly, especially as laws recognise that freedom of speech/expression is not absolute. The extent to which online content and speech can be criminalised is a battle that will be fought for many years and participant liability is likely to feature heavily in these debates.

Chapter 12

Territorial and Extraterritorial Dimensions

Michael Hirst

Introduction

Criminal prosecutions relating to alleged acts of complicity in offences committed by other persons may be complicated by what are usually referred to as 'jurisdictional' issues, notably where some relevant acts or events take place abroad. As the Law Commission observed,[1] 'there are infinite ways in which encouragement or assistance may be sent to and from any place in the world'. A fraud or robbery committed by the principal offender (P) in England or Wales may have been masterminded by D in Scotland, or aided by the acts of E in Canada. It may be clear in such a case that P can be prosecuted under English law, but what of D or E, who may have remained at all times abroad? Are they nevertheless subject to English law? The converse type of scenario may also cause problems, as where D in England aids or procures P to rob a bank in Ireland. Robbery abroad is not ordinarily an offence under English law, but is it possible that D nevertheless commits an offence on the basis of what he does in England?

One can add an extra layer of complexity to such scenarios by postulating a substantive offence that is itself committed on an international or cross-frontier basis. The alleged principal offender may thus be in one country, the secondary party in another and the victim in a third. The proceeds or subject-matter of the crime (typically drugs, cash, bank balances or migrants) may be transferred or 'trafficked' from, through or into, a fourth. One of those countries may be England and Wales. If so, does it matter which?

Jurisdictional issues may even arise in cases of complicity that involve no territorial connection with England at all, as where the sexual abuse of a child prostitute in Bangkok by P, a British tourist, is committed with the encouragement or assistance of D, a US citizen living there. As a 'United Kingdom national',[2] P may in this case face prosecution in England, because the Sexual Offences Act 2003, s 72, expressly provides for extraterritorial jurisdiction over such nationals (and in some cases over foreigners who are UK residents), but what of D, who was a foreigner living abroad? One might suppose that English criminal law could not possibly apply to him, but foreigners abroad are not always beyond the reach of that law, as we shall see.[3]

Finally, jurisdictional issues may arise in prosecutions for inchoate offences of assisting or encouraging crime, contrary to one of the provisions of part 2 of the Serious Crime Act 2007, or for other inchoate offences such as soliciting murder, contrary to the Offences Against the Person Act 1861, s 4, or statutory conspiracy. Prosecutors may sometimes do well to consider such charges even where the alleged substantive offence appears to have been completed. Suppose, for example, that D, in England, solicits or encourages P, a foreign national, to murder V somewhere abroad. P does as D suggests. On such facts, P would not ordinarily be triable for murder under English

---

1   Law Commission, *Participating in Crime* (Law Com No 305, 2007) [6.1].
2   This term is explained at (n 16), below.
3   As to whether D would in this case commit any offence under English law, see pp 309-310, below.

law – we would need to know more about the circumstances of this murder in order to provide a firm answer[4] – but D may face a charge of soliciting that murder, encouraging the commission of a crime, or conspiracy to murder. Could such a charge succeed, even where a prosecution for the full offence would fail?

I will attempt here to identify the rules and principles that govern cases such as these, and suggest answers to the various problems that may arise. This will involve examination both of complicity in substantive offences and of liability for related inchoate offences. I will conclude by considering whether the relevant law is largely satisfactory as it stands, or whether there is a pressing case for its reform.

The Jurisdiction of the Courts and the Ambit of the Law

Questions such as those posed above are often said to relate to the 'jurisdiction of the English criminal courts'. If that were correct, they would be questions of criminal procedure; but the jurisdiction of the *courts* is no longer limited by any territorial or extraterritorial constraints. By the Senior Courts Act 1981, s 46(1):[5]

> The Crown Court of England and Wales has jurisdiction in proceedings on indictment for offences wherever committed, and in particular proceedings on indictment for offences within the jurisdiction of the Admiralty of England ....

By the Magistrates' Courts Act 1980, s 2(1), those courts are similarly free from any territorial limitations on their power to hear criminal cases. Jurisdiction over summary offences was previously limited (with some exceptions) to offences committed within a court's commission area, or within 500 yards of the boundary between its own and another commission area, but that limitation was removed when s 2(1) was amended by the Courts Act 2003, s 44.

Since such questions are not procedural, what then are they? The answer is that they relate to something more fundamental. They pertain to the ambit of the criminal law itself, or in other words to whether given acts or omissions can be governed by English law. To put it another way, they pertain to the *actus reus* of whatever offence is in question.[6]

If a farmer causes an accident when driving a tractor on his land, we at once recognise that the provisions of the Road Traffic Act 1988 have no application. An offence of careless or dangerous driving under that Act must necessarily be committed on a road or other public place. That is a basic *actus reus* element – and in much the same way an alleged offence must ordinarily be committed within England and Wales if it is to be punishable as an offence under English law. Lord Diplock emphasised this in *Treacy v DPP*,[7] when (in the context of a case involving the blackmail of a victim in Germany by the appellant in England) he said:

4   In particular, the answer might depend on P's nationality and/or on which other country the murder was committed in. See Michael Hirst, 'Murder as an Offence under English Law' (2004) 68 Journal of Criminal Law 315.

5   This was originally entitled the Supreme Court Act 1981, and s 46(1) derives from the Courts Act 1971, s 6.

6   Glanville Williams was probably the first writer to emphasise this distinction, notably in 'Venue and the Ambit of Criminal Law' (1965) 81 Law Quarterly Review 395.

7   [1971] AC 537, 559 [HL].

The question in this appeal is not whether the ... court had jurisdiction to try the appellant ... but whether the facts alleged and proved against him amounted to a criminal offence ....[8]

There can indeed be no question more fundamental to criminal liability, because it concerns what is arguably the first thing we should ask about any law, namely, 'To whom does it apply?' Unfortunately, it is a question that many works on English criminal law overlook or ignore.[9]

It is nevertheless difficult to avoid using the term, 'jurisdiction' in this context. Parliament often uses it, as do the courts themselves, and such use is acceptable as long as one understands that it refers to the ambit of the law itself. That is the sense in which international lawyers understand it, and in which I will use it here.

Ambit and Extent

The ambit of the criminal law must also be distinguished from its 'extent'. The extent of a given Act of Parliament is ordinarily specified in the final or penultimate section of that Act, and does not necessarily coincide with the ambit of any criminal offences it creates.[10] In the Accessories and Abettors Act 1861, for example, s 10 provides that, 'nothing in this Act contained shall extend to Scotland', yet in *R v Robert Millar (Contractors) Ltd*[11] a Scottish company and its managing director were each convicted, in accordance with s 8 of that Act, of counselling and procuring *in Scotland* an offence of causing death by dangerous driving in England. How so?

The explanation is simple. When an Act of Parliament (or any part of such an Act) 'extends' to a given part of the UK, it becomes law there, so if it extends only to England, Wales and Northern Ireland it does not become part of the law of Scotland and would not be applied by the courts in Scotland; but that does not tell us whether things done in Scotland can amount to offences under the Act as a matter of English law; nor indeed does it tell us whether things done in Northern Ireland can be the subject of a prosecution in England and Wales (or vice versa). Those are issues of ambit, and the ambit of the law may differ entirely from its extent. Thus, the Outer Space Act 1985, s 15(5) provides: 'This Act *extends* to England and Wales, Scotland and Northern Ireland', but s 1 provides:

This Act *applies* to the following activities whether carried on in the United Kingdom or elsewhere ... [including] ... (c) any activity in outer space.

---

8   It may sometimes be possible to say of an alleged offender that, 'he committed an offence, but we have no jurisdiction to try or punish him'. That, however, can be true only where the alleged offender possesses an immunity (such as diplomatic immunity) which has not been waived.

9   See generally on this topic Michael Hirst, *Jurisdiction and the Ambit of the Criminal Law* (Oxford University Press 2003); P Arnell, *Law across Borders* (Routledge 2012); Lord Justice Hooper and David Ormerod (eds), *Blackstone's Criminal Practice 2013* (Oxford University Press 2012) section A8.

10   The presumption is that Acts of the UK Parliament extend to the whole of the UK, but not to any other place for which Parliament has power to legislate. So, if the 'extent' of an Act is said to exclude Scotland, the presumption is that it applies to the rest of the UK. In practice, however, an Act extending to Northern Ireland is normally expressed to do so and in some cases express provision is also made for England, Wales and Scotland.

11   [1970] 2 QB 54, CA.

Where judges confuse ambit with extent, the results can be bizarre.[12]

Jurisdiction over Substantive Offences

Although the focus of this chapter is on jurisdictional issues concerning the ambit of complicity, conspiracy and statutory inchoate offences of encouragement, solicitation or assistance, we must briefly consider the law relating to substantive offences. This is because the liability of a secondary party ordinarily depends, in part at least, upon establishing that the alleged offence was indeed committed by the principal offender.[13] The position is now different (as we shall see) in respect of conspiracy, solicitation to murder and inchoate offences under part 2 of the Serious Crimes Act 2007, but that is because legislation has made specific and express provision for jurisdiction to exist on a wider basis in such cases.

In respect of substantive offences, the general rule remains as stated by Viscount Simonds in *Cox v Army Council*:[14]

> Apart from those exceptional cases in which specific provision is made in respect of acts committed abroad, the whole body of the criminal law of England deals only with acts committed in England.

In *Treacy v DPP*,[15] Lord Reid noted that this rule governs the drafting and interpretation of all penal legislation:

> There is a strong presumption that when Parliament, in an Act applying to England, creates an offence … it does not intend this to apply to any act done by anyone in any country other than England. Parliament, being sovereign, is fully entitled to make an enactment on a wider basis. But the presumption is well known to draftsmen, and where there is an intention to make an English Act or part of such an Act apply to acts done outside England, that intention is and must be made clear in the Act.

Extraterritorial and Cross-Frontier Offences

There are many offences in respect of which Parliament has indeed 'enacted on a wider basis', thereby creating offences of extraterritorial application or ambit. Most apply extraterritorially only to British citizens or persons holding some other form of British nationality,[16] but some apply

---

12   Lord Phillips, no less, made such an error in *R (Purdy) v DPP* [2009] UKHL 45, [2010] 1 AC 345 in concluding that since the Suicide Act 1961 did not 'extend' to Switzerland, the suicide of a British citizen in Switzerland must still be a crime of self-murder under English law. Thankfully, this was obiter. See below, p. 301.

13   There are cases in which a secondary party has been convicted even though the alleged perpetrator had a complete defence (*R v Bourne* (1952) 36 Cr App R 125, CCA), or lacked *mens rea* (*R v Cogan* [1976] QB 217, CA) but none in which the *actus reus* of the alleged offence was never committed.

14   [1963] AC 48, 67, HL.

15   [1971] AC 537, 551, HL.

16   The specified connection varies: older statutes typically refer to 'British subjects' or (after 1948) to 'citizens of the UK and colonies'. These now apply to British citizens, citizens of British overseas territories and British subjects or British protected persons under the British Nationality Act 1981, a group sometimes

universally to both British and foreign nationals.[17] The best known offence of universal ambit (albeit one that the British authorities seem reluctant to prosecute) is piracy on the high seas.[18]

Even if a given offence has no extraterritorial ambit, persons who remain at all times abroad may still be guilty of committing that offence 'in England and Wales' if they cause one or more of its constituent elements to take place there. The traditional approach in English law was that, in the absence of any specific statutory provision, a crime was deemed to be committed *only* where it was completed. This is known as the 'terminatory' approach to jurisdiction and is supported by numerous decisions of the Court of Appeal and House of Lords,[19] but it was arbitrary and often unsatisfactory in its operation.[20] The Criminal Justice Act 1993 introduced an alternative approach in connection with specified fraud and property offences, whereby jurisdiction is triggered by the occurrence of any 'relevant event' within England and Wales, regardless of whether the offender is British or was at any material time in England and Wales.[21] A relevant event is defined for most purposes as one that is an essential element of the offence in question, so in the case of a result crime it includes both the proscribed result and the unlawful conduct that produced that result.

Because this legislation is expressly limited to specified fraud and property offences,[22] the provisions of the Criminal Justice Act 1993 cannot be construed as laying down any general principle of English law, but in *R v Smith (Wallace Duncan) (No 4)*,[23] the Court of Appeal decided that the common law position is in fact much the same. Giving the judgment of the Court, Lord Woolf CJ held that a crime may be regarded as committed within the jurisdiction if 'any substantial part of the offence' was committed in England and Wales, even if the last constituent element took place abroad. This more flexible 'inclusionary' approach is (with respect) a judicial U-turn that cannot be reconciled with preceding authority, and if good law it renders the Criminal Justice Act provisions superfluous. But in other respects it makes good practical sense and was followed without hesitation by the Court of Appeal in *R v Sheppard*.[24] We cannot yet be sure which approach will prevail, but the impetus is with the new inclusionary approach and it thus seems likely that this will in time become the new orthodoxy.

---

referred to in later statutes as 'United Kingdom nationals'. In a few cases liability additionally extends to UK residents when abroad. See further Hirst (n 9) 204, 208.

17   As the House of Lords declared in *Air India v Wiggins* [1980] 1 WLR 815, the courts require the clearest possible wording from a statute before they interpret it as making criminal legislation applicable to things done by foreigners abroad.

18   Otherwise known as piracy *jure gentium*. See the Merchant Shipping and Maritime Security Act 1997, s 26 and sch 5). One factor which may discourage the UK from prosecuting Somali pirates seized by the Royal Navy is that they might be granted asylum here on their release.

19   See *R v Harden* [1963] 1 QB 8, CCA; *DPP v Stonehouse* [1978] AC 55, HL; *R v Nanayakkara* [1987] 1 WLR 265, CA; *R v Manning* [1999] QB 980, CA.

20   In *Manning* (n 19) Buxton LJ said, 'It is deplorable that … we find ourselves forced to conclude that plainly dishonest conduct with a strong connection with this country cannot be tried here'.

21   Criminal Justice Act 1993, s 3(1).

22   And only to those committed on or after 1 June 1999.

23   [2004] EWCA Crim 632, [2004] QB 1418.

24   [2010] EWCA Crim 65, [2010] 1 WLR 2779. See also per Lord Hope (obiter) in *R (Purdy) v DPP* [2009] UKHL 45, [2010] 1 AC 345 [23].

The Position of the Secondary Party

As previously explained, the liability of an alleged secondary party in English law is largely parasitic on the liability of the alleged perpetrator. In cross-frontier cases this means that if P commits an offence in England and Wales, or aboard a British ship or a British controlled aircraft in flight, with the encouragement or assistance of D, who remains abroad, D will be considered complicit in P's offence and punishable for it under English law, even if he is a foreigner who has never set foot here. As the Court of Appeal explained in *R v Robert Millar (Contractors) Ltd*,[25] those who participate abroad in the commission of such a crime:

> ... are guilty of participating in that crime and not of some self-subsisting crime on their own account and, therefore, they are in the same position as the principal offender and they are liable to be tried in this country.

In *Robert Millar (Contractors)* this meant that a Scottish road haulage company and its managing director were each properly convicted as secondary parties to an offence of causing death by dangerous driving in England on the basis that they had 'counselled and procured' the offence by instructing an employee (Hart) to drive into England in a heavy goods vehicle that Hart and Millar each knew was fitted with a seriously worn and defective front tyre. Six members of one family died when the tyre failed suddenly on the M6 motorway in Northern England, causing the HGV to crash through the central reservation and smash head-on into their car.

Giving the judgment of the court, Fenton-Atkinson LJ concluded:

> We are quite satisfied that it is not right on the facts of this case to say that the counselling and procuring was ... over and done with at the moment that Hart drove his lorry out of the garage at Bridge of Weir. The counselling and procuring was a continuing act which persisted so long as Hart in pursuance of his employers' orders was driving the vehicle on this particular trip in its known dangerous condition on the road. In our view, at the moment this accident happened in Lancashire the appellants were still counselling and procuring the dangerous driving by Hart which brought about this disaster.[26]

It would logically seem to follow that in a mirror image of the *Robert Millar* case, in which the assistance or procuring is provided by D in England, but the alleged 'offence' is committed by P abroad, in circumstances to which the relevant English criminal law has no extraterritorial application, then no offence under that law will be committed by either party. If D is indeed in the same position as P, and commits no 'self-subsisting crime' in England, then he cannot logically be convicted because P commits no offence within the ambit of English law.[27] In other words, there is no offence in which he can be complicit.

In practice, however, the position is somewhat uncertain. This is because in D's case the courts may perhaps invoke a variant of the inclusionary principle developed in *Smith (Wallace Duncan) (No 4)* and reason that if his own contribution was made in or from England that will suffice to

---

25   [1970] 2 QB 54, 73.

26   Ibid. The company was guilty on the basis that Millar's knowledge was imputed to it.

27   The company and its MD may each have been guilty of using (or of causing or permitting the use of) the HGV with its defective tyre in England, but not of any death by driving offence abroad.

make his conduct criminal under English law, even if the alleged perpetrator (P) commits no such offence.[28]

There is no reported case since *Smith* directly in point, but the inclusionary approach is a relatively new one and the right case to extend it may not yet have been heard. A similar issue has been considered in the House of Lords, in a closely analogous context, but as we shall see, no clear answer emerged.

Assisted Suicide and the *Purdy* Case

In *R (Purdy) v DPP*,[29] the House of Lords, in its last appellate case, was invited to consider a hypothetical question overlooked in the courts below, namely, whether a husband who might one day help his terminally ill wife travel from England to a clinic in Switzerland to commit assisted suicide there (lawfully under Swiss law) would thereby commit in English law an offence of 'aiding, abetting, counselling or procuring' that suicide, contrary to the Suicide Act 1961, s 2(1), as originally enacted.[30]

Committing or attempting to commit suicide is not itself a crime, so the s 2 offence differed in that respect from 'ordinary' cases of complicity. Because there is no offence in which the aider and abettor can be complicit, the conduct proscribed under s 2 must in some respects at least function as an offence in its own right (an offence of being complicit, rather than one of complicity in the offence of another). But as Lord Phillips explained:

> The words 'aids, abets, counsels or procures' are those used to define secondary participation in crime … [so] the interpretation of the words should be the same.[31]

Mrs Purdy suffered from primary progressive multiple sclerosis, and planned to end her life in Switzerland if and when it became unbearable to her. She sought clarification from the DPP as to whether her husband would face prosecution in England if he helped her, no such prosecution being possible without the DPP's consent. If, it was argued, the DPP could not go so far as to promise immunity in this case (and indeed he could not do that) he should at least be required to issue detailed guidance as to the circumstances in which a s 2 prosecution would be considered to be in the public interest, so as to avoid infringing her rights under the ECHR.

It had been assumed without question in the courts below that any assistance Mrs Purdy's husband might provide while in England (booking the journey, driving her to the airport, boarding the aircraft with her and so on) would give rise to liability under s 2 if and when she committed suicide in the Swiss clinic. In contrast, it was accepted that things done abroad, whether by him or by staff at the clinic, could not be caught by English law.

---

28   Law Com No 305 (n 1) [6.21] has recommended that if P commits an offence abroad, D may be guilty of it if he aided it and so on from within the jurisdiction and *either* P could be tried here; *or* could have been tried for it had he been a British citizen, and so on.

29   [2009] UKHL 45, [2010] 1 AC 345.

30   The s 2 offence was redefined by the Coroners and Justice Act 2009 and now takes a form akin to that of an inchoate offence under the Serious Crime Act 2007, s 44. See Coroners and Justice Act 2009, section 59 and schedule 12.

31   *Purdy* (n 29) [4].

I argued, in an article published shortly before the House of Lords hearing, that this assumption was misplaced,[32] because the weight of authority supported a terminatory approach to jurisdiction, on the basis of which the alleged 'offence' would be committed only if, when *and where* the suicide itself was committed, namely in Switzerland. I conceded that *Smith* might, if followed, support a different conclusion, but questioned whether it could stand against earlier authority and whether s 2 was ever intended to apply to complicity in foreign suicides. If such an ambit had been intended, it would (I argued) have been expressly stated, as in various other 'complicity' provisions where an extended ambit was required.[33]

This was not a 'loophole' argument based on accidental lacunae, but was based on principle. English law is not concerned with regulating suicides in Switzerland, whether committed with or without assistance. They are a matter for Swiss law and are none of our business. Parliament might have chosen to provide otherwise in respect of British citizens or United Kingdom nationals, but it has never expressly done so and the presumption must therefore be that it never intended to.

Had my argument been accepted, the other issues in the case would simply have fallen away. There would have been no potential offence to worry about and Mrs Purdy would no longer have needed guidance on prosecutorial policy. But although the Appellate Committee called for written submissions on the question and although Lord Phillips and Lord Hope each discussed it at some length, it was not discussed by the other law lords and was eventually left unresolved.[34] It was deemed too difficult to decide without a full hearing and for as long as it remained unresolved Mrs Purdy and her husband had a right to know what policy considerations the DPP would take into account before prosecuting.[35]

Lord Hope was minded to reject my argument, both on the basis that the inclusionary approach adopted in *Smith* should be adopted, and on the basis that one could, he said, be complicit for the purposes of s 2, even in an act that has not occurred:

> The language of [s 2(1)] suggests that it applies to any acts of the kind it describes that are performed within this jurisdiction irrespective of where the final act of suicide is to be committed … [or] even if the assisted person does not go on to commit suicide.[36]

With respect, this latter argument is impossible to square with the wording of the Act as then in force. As Sir Richard Buxton subsequently observed:

> By using language that was absolutely central to the law on accessory liability, the draftsman in 1961 showed that he thought that s 2(1) was creating an offence of complicity … suicide was to be judged according to the established and accessible principles that applied to accessory liability in crime.[37]

Lord Phillips, in contrast, was inclined to take my argument a whole stage further, but his arguments in so doing were also flawed. He argued that since the Suicide Act does not extend to Switzerland

---

32   'Suicide in Switzerland: Complicity in England?' [2009] Criminal Law Review 335.
33   See, the Misuse of Drugs Act 1971, s 20 (discussed at p. 303 below).
34   The jurisdiction issue was also ignored in all media reports of the case.
35   This was, as it later transpired, a good thing, because the law relating to assisted suicide was subsequently amended in a way that might otherwise have left Mrs Purdy and her husband (and others like them) back at square one.
36   *Purdy* (n 29) [23].
37   Michael Hirst, 'Complicity in Suicide Abroad' (2010) 126 Law Quarterly Review 1.

then suicide by a British citizen in Switzerland may still amount to self-murder, and a party complicit in that self-murder would be guilty of murder. But Lord Phillips was confusing the ambit of the law with its extent.[38] As previously explained, no statute of the United Kingdom Parliament ever *extends* to foreign countries by becoming part of their law, but such a statute may nevertheless apply English law (*in England and Wales*) to things done abroad, subject to the presumption that it will not criminalise such conduct without using express words to that effect. Thus, the Suicide Act 1961, s 1, decriminalised suicide (in English law) wherever it occurs, but in the absence of express words to the contrary, s 2 criminalises complicity in such a suicide only where the s 2 offence is committed in England and Wales.

So the proper question to ask was this: if assistance or encouragement is provided in England but the suicide is committed in Switzerland, can it still be said that the suicide is aided, abetted, counselled or procured *in England*? That question was not answered in *Purdy*, and in all probability will never be answered, because the law on assisting suicide has now changed. The s 2 offence, which previously mimicked one of secondary liability, now resembles an inchoate offence of encouragement or assistance under the Serious Crime Act 2007, s 44. The change was not intended to affect jurisdiction over the type of case discussed in *Purdy*, but if my arguments above (and those of Sir Richard Buxton) are correct, that is exactly what it has done.

I will briefly return to the revised s 2 offence in due course, once I have considered some other forms of complicity, inchoate assistance and incitement.

Complicity in Extraterritorial Offences

Where legislation provides an extraterritorial ambit, whether for a designated class of British citizens and so on, or on a universal basis, it usually refers only to those *committing* the offence. There are exceptions. Thus, the Suppression of Terrorism Act 1978, s 4, applies to any person, 'who does an act … which if he had done it in a part of the UK would have made him guilty … in that part'. That formula is clearly capable of extending to secondary parties, but at first sight the usual one is not. A secondary party does not commit the offence.

The Accessories and Abettors Act 1861, s 8, provides an answer. It may not have been enacted with jurisdiction issues in mind, but it ensures that a secondary party is liable to be 'tried, indicted and punished' on the same basis as a principal offender, and the Magistrates Courts Act 1980, s 44, makes similar provision in summary cases.

But if a secondary party to an extraterritorial offence is triable on the same basis as the principal offender, that implies that he must possess any qualifying status or nationality that would be required of a principal offender. If, in other words, D could not, as a foreigner, have been charged as a principal offender, then neither can he properly be indicted as a secondary party. The law creating the extraterritorial offence simply does not apply to him.

What then if D, a British citizen, is complicit in the commission abroad of a murder in circumstances where P, the actual murderer, commits no offence under English law? On such facts there would appear to be no substantive offence in which D can be complicit. According to the Accessories and Abettors Act 1861, s 8, the offence to which D is party must be an offence at common law or a statutory offence; it cannot therefore merely be an offence under foreign law, or

---

38   See Michael Hirst, 'Assisted Suicide after Purdy: The Unanswered Question' [2009] Criminal Law Review 870.

something that would have been an offence if committed in other circumstances (for example if committed in England).

Legislation has addressed this issue in the context of conspiracy and other inchoate offences,[39] but not in respect of actual participation. The Law Commission has, however, made proposals:[40]

> We recommend that if P commits an offence [*sic*] outside the jurisdiction, D may be tried within the jurisdiction if:
>
> (1) D's behaviour takes place wholly outside the jurisdiction;[41] and
>
> (2) irrespective of whether P can be tried within the jurisdiction, D could have been tried within the jurisdiction had he or she committed the offence in the place where P committed it.

The reference here to P committing an 'offence' for which he himself might not be triable in England must here mean an act that *would be* an offence if committed in England, or by a person subject to extraterritorial jurisdiction. Read in that way, the proposal makes good sense, although in such cases extradition will usually offer the best solution, both in respect of principal offenders and in respect of secondary parties. Few extraterritorial offences are ever actually prosecuted in England and Wales.

Complicity in Offences (or Proposed Offences) under Foreign Law

Some statutes make specific provision for cases of what might be termed 'complicity in a foreign offence'. Noteworthy examples can be found in the Misuse of Drugs Act 1971, s 20, the Criminal Justice Act 1993, s 71, and the Immigration Act 1971, s 25.[42] Each of these adopts a slightly different approach, but what they have in common is that each proscribes complicity in offences committed against foreign laws.

By the Misuse of Drugs Act 1971, s 20:

> A person commits an offence if in the United Kingdom he assists in or induces the commission in any place outside the United Kingdom of an offence punishable under the provisions of a corresponding law in force in that place.

A 'corresponding law' is defined in s 36 as:

> A law stated in a certificate purporting to be issued by or on behalf of the government of a country outside the United Kingdom to be a law providing for the control and regulation in that country of the production, supply, use, export and import of drugs and other substances in accordance with the provisions of the Single Convention on Narcotic Drugs signed at New York on 30 March 1961 or a law providing for the control and regulation in that country of the production, supply, use, export and import of dangerous or otherwise harmful drugs in pursuance of any treaty, convention

---

39 See *R v Abu Hamza* [2006] EWCA Crim 2918, [2007] QB 659 (discussed at p. 307 below).

40 Law Com No 305 (n 1) [6.26].

41 A separate recommendation (in para 6.22) addresses the position where D acts within the jurisdiction.

42 The current s 25 offence was substituted for the original by the Nationality, Immigration and Asylum Act 2002 and further amendments and substitutions were made by the UK Borders Act 2007, s 30.

or other agreement or arrangement to which the government of that country and Her Majesty's Government ... are for the time being parties.[43]

In *R v Panayi*,[44] the Court of Appeal held that (as in cases of aiding and abetting) this requires the relevant offence under foreign law to have been committed. O'Connor LJ said:

> If one asked in simple English, were these two men sailing the boat laden with cannabis resin ... on their way to Holland, assisting in the commission of what would be an offence when they got to Holland ... one might have perhaps answered 'yes'. But a little bit of thought will show that this cannot be right. A whole series of acts might be done preparatory to the commission of an offence, but if no offence is in fact committed, it is difficult to see how you can assist in its commission ....[45]

The Criminal Justice Act 1993, s 71, similarly makes it an offence for a person in the UK[46] to 'assist in or induce' conduct abroad that involves a serious offence (punishable with at least 12 months' imprisonment) under the law of another EU member state, in connection with 'community' (EU) taxation, subsidies, restrictions or prohibitions. The concept of 'assisting in or inducing' must here bear the same meaning as in the Misuse of Drugs Act 1971.

The Immigration Act 1971, s 25 (as amended) is different. It gives effect to the Schengen Convention, Art 27, by making it an offence for any person in the UK or elsewhere to 'do an act which facilitates' the commission by a person who is not an EU national of a breach of immigration law within any member state of the EU (or within Iceland or Norway, which are also 'Schengen Acquis' states[47]). The UK is itself a Schengen state, and s 25 thus applies equally to acts that facilitate breaches of the UK's own immigration laws, but its application to offences under foreign law is what makes it remarkable.

The s 25 offence differs from the other offences in two ways. The first is that it has full extraterritorial effect (nothing need be committed in England and Wales or relate to things happening there) but it also differs in that it involves 'doing an act which facilitates' the breach in question rather than 'assisting or inducing' that breach. Does this require any actual breach of a relevant immigration law? Or does it create an inchoate offence that may be committed even if the proposed offence never is?

The current wording is ambiguous, but as originally enacted,[48] s 25 made it an offence to be 'knowingly concerned in the making or carrying out arrangements' for securing or facilitating unlawful entry, and so on, into the UK. Clearly one can be 'concerned in arrangements' even if the event to which those arrangements relate never occurs, and the Court of Appeal so held in *R v*

---

43   Such a certificate is conclusive evidence of the law in question, but does not necessarily prove whether the conduct alleged by the prosecution amounts to an offence under that law.

44   (1988) 86 Cr App R 261. See also *R v Vickers* (1975) 61 Cr App R 48, CA; *R v Evans* (1977) 64 Cr App R 237, CA.

45   The corresponding foreign offence need not have any exact counterpart in English law. Sentencers must, however, look to the penalties applicable under the nearest equivalent English offence when sentencing under s 20. See *R v Faulkner* (1976) 63 Cr App R 295, CA.

46   Proscribed conduct in Scotland or Northern Ireland would, however, fall exclusively under the jurisdiction of Scots or Northern Irish law.

47   Immigration (Assisting Unlawful Immigration) (Section 25 List of Schengen Acquis States) Order 2004 (SI 2004 No 2877). The UK itself is such a state, so s 25 also applies to acts that facilitate breaches of the UK's own immigration laws.

48   See (n 42), above.

Adams[49] and *R v Eyck*.[50] It seems unlikely that the new version of s 25 was intended to change this, and *Adams* and *Eyck* are still widely cited as precedents, albeit without any reference to the change of wording.[51] Where, however, the breach of immigration law is frustrated or abandoned for any reason, charges of conspiracy to commit a s 25 offence will often be preferred, and the issue will not then need exploring.

Other Inchoate Forms of Complicity

At common law, acts of incitement, conspiracy or attempt were never punishable unless they related to a substantive offence which would itself, if committed, be triable in England and Wales, or in the case of conspiracy to defraud, to a fraud that would be practised there,[52] but most inchoate offences are now governed by modern legislation, which invariably includes provisions specifically addressing jurisdictional issues.[53] It follows that the doubts and uncertainties that bedevil complicity cases at common law can often be avoided if inchoate offences such as conspiracy are charged instead. But that does not mean this area is entirely free from difficulty. Far from it.

Conspiracy to Commit an Offence under English law

The offence of statutory conspiracy, contrary to the Criminal Law Act 1977, must ordinarily involve an agreement to commit an offence that would itself be triable under English law. That may be an offence which is to be committed within England and Wales, or one that is to be committed aboard a British ship or aircraft, but it may also be an extraterritorial offence, such as murder committed by a British citizen on land outside the UK, or the hijacking of an airliner by anyone, anywhere in the world.[54] What then if the conspiracy itself takes place exclusively abroad?

The position of those who conspire abroad to commit an offence within England was clarified by the Privy Council in *Liangsiriprasert v United States*,[55] where Lord Griffiths observed:

> In this century crime has ceased to be local in origin and effect. Crime is now established on an international scale and the common law must face this new reality. Their Lordships can find nothing in precedent, comity or good sense that should inhibit the common law from regarding as justiciable in England inchoate crimes committed abroad which are intended to result in the commission of criminal offences in England.

---

49   [1996] Crim LR 593, CA.

50   [2000] 1 WLR 1389, CA. Eyck drove a van containing asylum seekers onto a ferry at Calais. They were discovered on the ferry en route to Dover, before they could enter the UK. His s 25 conviction was upheld on appeal.

51   See *R v Javaherifard* [2005] EWCA Crim 3231. In *R v Kapoor* [2012] EWCA Crim 435, [2012] 2 All ER 1205 Hooper LJ also referred to s 25 as an inchoate offence.

52   *Board of Trade v Owen* [1957] AC 602, HL.

53   Even conspiracy to defraud (which remains a common law offence) benefits from jurisdiction provisions in the Criminal Justice Act 1993.

54   Much the same is true (*mutadis mutandis*) of criminal attempts to which the Criminal Attempts Act 1981 applies: see s 1(4) of that Act.

55   [1991] AC 225. See also *R v Manning* [1998] 2 Cr App R 461, CA; *R (Al-Fawwaz) v Governor of Brixton Prison* [2001] UKHL 69, [2002] 1 AC 556.

That doctrine was later extended by the House of Lords in *R v Bow Street Metropolitan Stipendiary Magistrate, ex p Pinochet Ugarte (No 3)*,[56] in which it was held that if an offence such as torture is triable in England even when committed abroad, a conspiracy to commit such an offence will be triable on the same extraterritorial basis. Lord Hope said:[57]

> I consider that the common law of England would, applying the rule laid down in *Liangsiriprasert* … regard as justiciable in England a conspiracy to commit an offence anywhere which was triable here as an extraterritorial offence in pursuance of an international Convention, even although no act was done here in furtherance of the conspiracy.

Lord Hope was specifically concerned with offences which implement international conventions and which typically impose liability on a universal basis, but his logic does not necessarily apply to conspiracies to commit substantive offences that apply extraterritorially only to UK nationals. The justification for asserting jurisdiction over foreigners in such cases is much weaker. Since they cannot in English law commit or be parties to such offences on a purely extraterritorial basis, it is difficult to see how one could properly charge or convict them of conspiracy to do so, even if other parties, being British, fall squarely within the ambit of that law.

Conspiracy to Commit an Offence under Foreign Law

Anyone who conspires in England to commit acts abroad which are punishable under the law of the country in question, and would also be punishable under English law if committed in England, may also be charged with a form of statutory conspiracy. This is possible because the basic offence under the Criminal Law Act 1977, s 1, is now supplemented by s 1A,[58] which ensures that the relevant law in part 1 of the Act applies to such agreements on the same basis as it applies to conspiracies that fall within s 1(1) itself.

Section 1A was considered in *Patel*,[59] where the object of the agreement was illegal entry to the USA, contrary to US federal law – an offence equivalent to one under the Immigration Act 1971, s 25. The Court observed that s 1A is not a stand-alone or offence-creating provision, but merely operates as an extension to, and in conjunction with, the s 1 offence. But s 1A does not apply to conspiracies to commit offences under English law abroad. If for example the offence in *Patel* had been one of conspiracy to facilitate illegal entry to a 'Schengen Acquis' country, it would then have been a conspiracy to commit an extraterritorial offence under English law. In such a case, s 1A of the 1977 Act would have no application. It would be a 'straightforward' case of conspiracy under s 1(1).

---

56   [2000] 1 AC 147. See also *R v Sansom* [1991] 2 QB 130, CA; *R v Manning* [1999] QB 980, CA.
57   [2000] 1 AC 147, 237.
58   Inserted by the Criminal Justice (Terrorism and Conspiracy) Act 1998, s 5.
59   [2009] EWCA Crim 67.

Solicitation in England of Murder Abroad

By the Offences Against the Person Act 1861, s 4:

> whosoever shall solicit, encourage, persuade, or endeavour to persuade, or shall propose to any
> person, to murder any other person, whether he[60] be a subject of Her Majesty or not, and whether
> he be in the Queen's dominions or not, shall be guilty of a misdemeanour and being convicted
> thereof shall be liable to … [imprisonment for life] ….

The survival of this offence is something of a mystery, because it does nothing that the new offences
of encouraging or assisting crime under part 2 of the Serious Crimes Act 2007 do not, and the
penalties it provides are significantly lower than those available under the 2007 Act.[61] But survive
it has, and it is of particular interest in this context because its jurisdictional ambit was considered
at some length by the Court of Appeal in *R v Abu Hamza*.[62]

The appellant in *Hamza* was a notorious imam whose sermons at the Finsbury Park Mosque
in London involved incitement to various acts of *Jihad* including murder. It could not, however,
be proved that he ever incited such murders to be committed in England and Wales or even that
the persons he incited were British. Since murder committed abroad by a person who is not a UK
national is not ordinarily punishable as murder under English law, an issue arose as to whether
Hamza had in fact committed any offence under the 1861 Act. Does the reference to 'murder' in s
4 mean 'the offence of murder under English law' or does it have the same meaning as it does in
the International Criminal Courts Act 2001, namely 'the killing of a person in such circumstances
as would, *if committed in England or Wales*, constitute murder'?[63]

It was argued on behalf of Hamza that it bore the usual, narrower, meaning, and in support of
that argument his counsel contrasted the wording of s 4 with that of the Criminal Law Act 1977, s
1(4), which (in its original form) stated:

> In this Part of this Act 'offence' means an offence triable in England and Wales, except that it
> includes murder notwithstanding that the murder in question would not be so triable if committed
> in accordance with the intention of the parties to the agreement.

Since s 4 of the 1861 Act says no such thing, such an extended meaning could not (he argued)
be inferred; but the Court of Appeal rejected that argument, relying instead on the fact that s 4
was derived, albeit indirectly, from Palmerston's Conspiracy to Murder Bill of 1858. This Bill,
which never became law, was inspired by French protests over the impunity enjoyed by Italian
émigrés in England, some of whom had recently been implicated in the 'Orsini bomb plot', in
which a number of bystanders had been killed in Paris when a bomb was thrown at Napoleon

---

60   This must be a reference to the proposed victim, as becomes apparent if one studies the original
wording of s 4, which also dealt with conspiracies and began, 'All persons who shall conspire, confederate,
and agree to murder any person, whether he be a subject of Her Majesty or not …'. But the nationality of the
victim would in any case be immaterial, so those words add nothing of substance.

61   Where the murder in question would be an act of terrorism, a more substantial penalty is also
provided under the Terrorism Act 2000, s 59.

62   [2006] EWCA Crim 2918, [2007] QB 659.

63   That definition is provided in s 53 (emphasis added). A broadly similar definition is provided in the
Terrorism Act 2000, s 59(1)(b) and (2): 'An act which would, if committed in England and Wales constitute
… murder…'.

III's carriage.[64] It would thus have made no sense, said Lord Phillips CJ, to have restricted the s 4 offence to situations where the murderers were to be British subjects or (in modern parlance) UK nationals. Hamza's appeal against his conviction under s 4 was accordingly dismissed.

Encouraging or Assisting Crime Abroad (or from Abroad)

The various inchoate offences created in part 2 of the Serious Crime Act 2007 have become notorious for their difficulty and complexity. At the time of writing, however, the jurisdiction provisions within part 2 had caused few problems, and despite their own complexity they do at least appear workable, which is more than can be said of some of the part 2 offences themselves.[65]

The key provision here is s 52, by which:

(1) If a person (D) knows or believes that what he anticipates might take place wholly or partly in England or Wales, he may be guilty of an offence under section 44, 45 or 46 no matter where he was at any relevant time.

(2) If it is not proved that D knows or believes that what he anticipates might take place wholly or partly in England or Wales, he is not guilty of an offence under section 44, 45 or 46 unless paragraph 1, 2 or 3 of schedule 4 applies.

(3) A reference in this section (and in any of those paragraphs) to what D anticipates is to be read as follows –
> (a) in relation to an offence under section 44 or 45, it refers to the act which would amount to the commission of the anticipated offence;
> (b) in relation to an offence under section 46, it refers to an act which would amount to the commission of any of the offences specified in the indictment.

Where s 52(1) applies, the position is relatively simple. D, whoever and wherever he may be, will commit one of the part 2 offences if he encourages or assists someone to commit a proposed offence (within the meaning of ss 44 to 46) and 'knows or believes' that the offence in question *might* be committed wholly or partly in England and Wales. The vast majority of part 2 offences will fall within its scope, including all purely domestic cases and many cross-frontier ones. If for example the crime D proposes or anticipates is the murder of V, who divides his time between England and Ireland, it suffices that D believes the proposed 'hit' *may* take place in England. But if D assumes that it will be done in Ireland (or if proof to the contrary is lacking), one must look instead to s 52(2) and sch 4. One of three sets of conditions postulated by sch 4 must then be satisfied before it can be said that a part 2 offence has been committed.

Schedule 4, para 1, applies where D acts wholly or partly within England and Wales, and the crime he anticipates would be punishable as an offence under English law, even if committed abroad (as where he encourages P, a UK national, to commit murder in Canada).

If para 1 does not apply, para 2 may be considered. This applies in much the same way as the Criminal Law Act 1977, s 1A, applies to conspiracies, namely where D provides encouragement

---

64   A prosecution for complicity in this plot was brought in *R v Bernard* (1858) 1 F & F 240, but the defendant was acquitted, leaving arguments as to jurisdiction unresolved.

65   See the Court of Appeal's struggle to make sense of s 46 of the Act in *R v Sadique* [2011] EWCA Crim 2872, [2012] 1 Cr App R 257.

or assistance from England and Wales and what he proposes or anticipates would be an offence abroad under local law.[66]

Finally, para 3 applies where there is no proven territorial connection with England and Wales, but where D would himself liable to prosecution under English law if he were to commit the anticipated offence in the place or country in question. This covers cases in which D encourages or assists the commission of an offence of universal jurisdiction, such as hijacking or torture, and matches the approach adopted in respect of conspiracy cases by the House of Lords in *Pinochet*,[67] but also covers cases in which D's nationality or status would make him subject to English jurisdiction, were he to commit the offence he encourages P to commit. Significantly there is no requirement that P would be subject to that jurisdiction. So if we go back to our example of the British and American paedophiles in Bangkok, D will commit an offence under s 44 of the 2007 Act if he encourages or assists P to sexually abuse a child there, if D himself is a UK national or resident to whom s 72 of the Sexual Offences Act 2003 would have applied. In contrast, P's own status is unimportant and it is equally unimportant, for this purpose, whether P ever does what D proposes.

In the converse scenario, where P, a UK national, is assisted or encouraged by his American friend, D, there is nothing in sch 4 or elsewhere that could bring D within the ambit of the Act.

The New Offence of Assisting Suicide

As previously noted, the original offence of complicity in suicide, contrary to the Suicide Act 1961, s 2(1), no longer exists in that form. The Coroners and Justice Act 1998 substituted a new offence of doing 'an act capable of encouraging or assisting the suicide or attempted suicide of another' with intent to encourage or assist it – an offence which the new s 2(1B) makes clear can be committed, 'whether or not a suicide, or an attempt at suicide, occurs'.

This creates the very offence that Lord Hope in *Purdy* thought had existed before. On facts such as those postulated in *Purdy* it removes any jurisdictional issues, because once D provides encouragement or assistance, with the requisite intent, the offence is at once complete. Booking P's ticket to Switzerland would suffice.

So is the law now clearer? Perhaps not in cases where D is abroad and the prospective suicide, P, is in England, because although the new s 2 is modelled on the Serious Crime Act 2007, s 44, it is not supported by any provision resembling s 52(1) of that Act. If D, in Canada, encourages P, in England, to kill herself, the courts would in all probability invoke something akin to the principle stated by Lord Griffiths in *Liangsiriprasert v United States*,[68] and assert jurisdiction on that basis. If D were to post a message on a 'suicide website' accessed by P in England, the courts might even reason that D acted (albeit remotely) in England,[69] but it is still a pity that the question was not directly addressed in the new legislation.[70]

---

66 If D wishes to argue that this offence would *not* have been punishable under local law, he must raise this issue for determination by the judge in accordance with a procedure set out in sch 4, para 2(2) to (4).

67 See p. 306 and (n 56), above.

68 [1991] AC 225. See (n 55), above.

69 *R v Perrin* [2002] EWCA Crim 747.

70 See Hirst (n 38).

Conclusions

Any reader who has struggled to this point will doubtless have come to at least one conclusion as to the state of the current law, namely that it is excessively complicated. But identifying this problem is a good deal easier than resolving it, especially when the jurisdictional issues affecting complicity and inchoate forms of participation are but one part of a wider picture involving criminal jurisdiction over crime generally. The law in respect of that wider picture has never been planned or codified as a coherent whole, but has simply developed or evolved, in much the same unplanned way that a shanty town develops or evolves: hence the multiplicity of rules and principles. And yet the rules we have do seem to work, in most cases at least.

If we were to ask what the law in respect of participation or complicity should be attempting to achieve, one might reply that it should above all seek to protect those within its borders from harm, whether that harm is threatened from within or without the territorial limits. By and large, the law does that. The *Robert Millar* and *Liangsiriprasert* principles together ensure that English criminal law applies to most 'cross-frontier' forms of complicity or conspiracy, and so on, aimed at England and Wales.

One might also reply that English law should do what it can to protect those abroad from those who are within the jurisdiction. England and Wales should not be a safe haven from whence harm can with impunity be caused elsewhere. The inchoate offences all address this need, so perhaps it does not greatly matter that the law relating to complicity in completed offences probably does not. There is of course a case for integrating the law on complicity more closely with the inchoate offences, as the Law Commission has proposed, but there is no grievous legal lacuna for ruthless criminals to exploit.

As for extraterritorial offences, the law relating to complicity is not as clear as it should be, perhaps because it rarely falls to be considered, but a logical approach to such cases (such as has been proposed above) will usually yield acceptable results. D's potential inchoate liability as a conspirator, and so on in such cases should broadly coincide with his potential liability as a perpetrator and that indeed is what the law provides.[71] The more difficult question is whether the law should allow a UK national to be charged as a secondary party to an extraterritorial offence when the alleged perpetrator is a foreigner who is not subject to our law. Here logic and policy considerations may conflict. Logic tells us that if P commits no offence under English law than D cannot be complicit in one. Policy considerations might, however, suggest that a UK national should not be allowed to evade extraterritorial law by getting a foreigner to do his dirty work for him. But the practical importance of that question is slight. Once again the inchoate offences may plug the gap, but in any case crimes committed in foreign countries are usually best left to local law and are rarely prosecuted in England and Wales, even where English law could properly be applied. Extradition may thus provide the better solution.

---

71   I say 'broadly' because there are (for example) some offences which only a man can commit, but in which a woman may conspire or be complicit. That must be true in extraterritorial cases as it is in domestic ones.

Chapter 13

Participation in Crime under Scots Law: The Doctrine of Art and Part

Fiona Leverick[1]

Introduction

There are two main ways in which the criminal law can recognise and punish indirect participation in crime. The first is via 'secondary offences', whereby a specific freestanding contribution to an actual or envisaged crime is punished in its own right as, for example, incitement or a conspiracy. In textbooks, such offences are usually discussed under the heading of inchoate liability[2] and this is an important distinction because the accused convicted of, say, incitement to murder is not labelled in the same way as the accused who is convicted of the primary offence. The second is via derivative liability, whereby an accused is deemed liable for a crime committed by another on the basis of a contribution he made to it prior to or during its commission. Unlike the secondary offences approach (which punishes the precise contribution made), the accused is liable for a crime which he did not personally commit. This presents considerable challenges to orthodox criminal doctrine, grounded as it is in notions of personal autonomy and accountability, and therefore normally requiring that an accused, for conviction, fulfil the *actus reus* and *mens rea* of the crime in question. Although it is possible to envisage a system of liability in which derivative liability plays no role,[3] no major common law system takes this approach.[4] As this volume demonstrates,[5] however, differences do exist between jurisdictions in terms of the rules governing derivative liability.

In Scotland, both forms of indirect participation are provided for. The law recognises the secondary offences of conspiracy and incitement, alongside other secondary offences recently introduced in relation to organised crime. It also recognises a form of derivative liability, termed art and part liability. The main focus of this chapter will be upon art and part liability, as it is here that useful comparisons can be made between Scotland and England and Wales.

---

1   In setting out the various forms of participatory liability in Scots law, the author has been greatly assisted by an unpublished paper prepared by Alistair Devlin, 'Art and Part: Complicity in Scots Law' (2006) (held by Fiona Leverick at Glasgow University). The author would also like to thank James Chalmers for his helpful comments on an earlier draft.

2   See for example Andrew Ashworth, *Principles of Criminal Law* (6th edn, Oxford University Press 2009) 10-11.

3   See the proposals floated by the Law Commission in its Consultation Paper *Assisting and Encouraging Crime* (Law Com CP 131, 1993) 4.24. These were abandoned in the subsequent report following strong academic criticism: Law Commission, *Inchoate Liability for Assisting and Encouraging Crime* (Law Com No 300, 2006) part 2.

4   See Chapter 1 of this volume.

5   See Chapters 15–26.

Before commencing, a brief note on terminology is in order. Under the doctrine of art and part, there is no formal distinction between the parties involved in an enterprise,[6] but it will often be helpful to distinguish between those accused who incur liability on the basis of the own actions (that is, through carrying out the *actus reus* of the offence with the requisite *mens rea*) and those whose liability is dependent on the art and part doctrine. The former will be referred to as a 'primary actor' (or A1), while the latter will be referred to as a 'secondary actor' (or A2).

Liability via Secondary Offences: Conspiracy, Incitement and the Organised Crime Provisions

Scots law recognises two main secondary offences: conspiracy and incitement. Both are governed by the common law. At the time of writing, there were no proposals to place these on a statutory footing,[7] aside, that is, from the provisions relating to serious organised crime discussed below.[8]

Conspiracy is defined as 'the agreement of two or more persons to further or achieve a criminal purpose'.[9] A criminal purpose is 'one which if attempted or achieved by action on the part of an individual would itself constitute a crime by the law of Scotland'.[10] The accused, if convicted, is convicted of 'a conspiracy to X' rather than of the substantive offence of X. The offence of conspiracy is of most use to the prosecution where no primary offence is ever committed or, perhaps more importantly, where the prosecution is unable to prove that a primary offence has been committed. If the primary offence was committed and could be proved, the accused could almost certainly be convicted of it art and part, given the broad nature of this doctrine. The rationale for punishing conspiracy generally focuses on either crime prevention or the enhanced danger posed by groups compared to individuals. Neither is particularly convincing,[11] especially when weighed against the counter-argument that it fails to respect personal autonomy to punish an accused who has taken no active steps whatsoever to perpetrate a criminal offence and who could still change his mind. Gordon notes that it has become increasingly common for the prosecution to charge conspiracy alongside the completed criminal offence[12] and describes this as 'arguably prejudicial' and 'certainly confusing'.[13] Incitement is committed where the accused 'reaches and seeks to influence the mind of another to the commission of a crime'.[14] There is no requirement that the accused actually instructed another person to commit the crime,[15] providing that the accused

---

6   See text accompanying (n 37).

7   As has been done in England and Wales under Part 2 of the Serious Crime Act 2007.

8   For completeness, mention should be made of s 1 of the Terrorism Act 2006, which criminalises the direct or indirect encouragement of terrorism, but which will not be covered here. For discussion, see Adrian Hunt, 'Criminal Prohibitions on Direct and Indirect Encouragement of Terrorism' [2007] Criminal Law Review 441.

9   *Maxwell v HM Advocate* 1980 JC 40 (HCJ) 43 (Lord Cameron), approved by a Full Bench in *Howitt v HM Advocate* 2000 JC 287 (HCJ).

10   Ibid.

11   Space precludes discussion here, but see Ian Dennis, 'The Rationale of Criminal Conspiracy' (1977) 93 Law Quarterly Review 39.

12   Gerald Gordon and Michael Christie, *The Criminal Law of Scotland Volume 1* (3rd edn, Sweet and Maxwell 2000) 6.59.

13   Ibid.

14   *Baxter v HM Advocate* 1998 JC 219 (HCJ) 221, quoting with approval the South African case of *S v Nkosiyana* 1966 (4) SA 655, 658-59.

15   Ibid. 221.

seriously intended the other party to commit the crime.[16] If prosecuted successfully, the accused is convicted of the offence of 'incitement to crime X'.

In addition to conspiracy and incitement, a complete account of Scots law must now consider the secondary liability provisions introduced in the Criminal Justice and Licensing (Scotland) Act 2010 in relation to serious organised crime, which came into force in December 2010. The two relevant provisions are sections 28 and 30.

Section 28 creates an offence of 'involvement in serious organised crime' and provides that 'a person who agrees with at least one other person to become involved in serious organised crime commits an offence'. Serious organised crime is defined in section 28(3) as 'crime involving two or more persons acting together for the principal purpose of committing or conspiring to commit a serious offence or a series of serious offences'. Section 28(3) goes on to define a serious offence as 'an indictable offence (a) committed with the intention of obtaining a material benefit for any person, or (b) which is an act of violence committed or a threat made with the intention of obtaining such a benefit in the future'. Conviction carries a maximum penalty of ten years imprisonment.

Section 30 creates an offence of 'directing serious organised crime', defined as 'directing another person ... to commit a serious offence'. The offence is committed where the accused '(a) does something, or a series of things, to direct the person to commit the offence, (b) intends that the thing or things done will persuade the person to commit the offence, and (c) intends that the thing or things done will (i) result in a person committing serious organised crime or (ii) enable a person to commit serious organised crime'.[17] The offence is freestanding and does not require that the primary offence takes place.[18] The maximum penalty available is 14 years imprisonment.

The stated objective of the Scottish Government in introducing these provisions was to 'tackle those involved in serious organised crime to help ensure Scotland is a safer and stronger place' and to 'send a message to those involved [in serious organised crime] that Scotland does not want their business'.[19] At the time of writing, the provisions had been in force only for a very short time and there had been no chance for any case law to develop.[20]

Sections 28 and 30 can be criticised on a number of fronts. The first is that they simply re-criminalise something which would already have been captured under the criminal law. The Scottish Government stated that section 28 was 'intended to capture those who become involved in criminal activity with at least one other person where their main purpose is to commit or conspire to commit serious offences for material gain'[21] and that section 30 would 'help capture those who do not engage directly in criminal conduct but who direct and incite others to commit serious offences'.[22] But this implies that such conduct would not already have been covered by the law, which is incorrect. Incitement and conspiracy can already be prosecuted under the common law, as discussed above, and the 2010 Act does not repeal these provisions. It is true that the penalties for breach of sections 28 and 30 are substantial, at ten and 14 years respectively, but given that

---

16 Ibid. 222.

17 Section 30(3).

18 Section 30(4).

19 Explanatory notes to the Criminal Justice and Licensing (Scotland) Bill, as introduced, 107.

20 In fact, at the time of writing, there was no evidence of any successful prosecutions under sections 28 or 30: see the Scottish Crime and Drug Enforcement Agency (SCDEA) website which, on its 'court results' page, reports numerous successful prosecutions under other legislation, most notably the Misuse of Drugs Act 1971, but none under sections 28 or 30 of the 2010 Act (<www.sdea.police.uk/News/court-results.html> accessed 4 January 2013).

21 Explanatory notes (n 19) 112.

22 Ibid. 116.

under the common law sentencing judges are not bound by any sentencing limits other than the powers of the court in which the Crown has chosen to prosecute the offence,[23] a conspiracy to commit a very serious offence could already have received a sentence of this magnitude. That said, there can be merit in reclassifying under a new heading behaviour that would already have been criminal. The publicity generated may help to send a message that such behaviour is particularly unacceptable which may, in turn, have a deterrent effect or help to reassure the public about their safety.[24] It might also be that there is something so distinctive about serious organised crime that those involved should be labelled in a way that communicates this, even if the sentence passed is no different to what it would have been under existing law.[25]

The labelling argument, even if it is accepted in principle, however, becomes less convincing given other criticisms that can be made of the legislation, most notably concerning the offence definitions. The definition in section 28(3) sets a very low threshold for what constitutes serious organised crime, given that any offence is potentially indictable in Scots law, with the exception of statutory offences where this possibility is specifically excluded. Thus it encompasses almost any 'normal' criminal activity that happens to have been organised in some way.[26]

Section 28 is also problematic in that it does not merely cover involvement, but also anyone who *agrees to become involved* in serious organised crime, which is not the same thing at all. As noted above in relation to conspiracy, punishing a mere agreement to enter into criminal activity is open to criticism, but given the weighty maximum penalty attached to section 28, this is of particular concern. Agreement sits very close to the beginning of the spectrum of participation in criminal activity, which runs from a mere guilty mind to that of actual perpetration. There is still plenty of time for the accused who agrees to become involved to change his mind and not become involved at all and a liberal system of criminal law should reflect this, both in terms of reduced culpability and the need to provide an incentive to the accused to recant.[27] A maximum penalty of ten years is worrying in this respect.

Derivative Liability: The Art and Part Doctrine

The main form of derivative liability that exists in Scots law is the common law doctrine of art and part. While England and Wales has (arguably) separate doctrines of 'aiding and abetting'[28] and of 'joint enterprise',[29] the concept of aiding and abetting is not one that plays a significant role in Scots law. The vast majority of cases of derivative liability are dealt with under the auspices of art and part, and thus the debates that have occurred in England over the relationship between 'aiding

---

23   Which ranges from life imprisonment in the High Court to 60 days imprisonment in the Justice of the Peace Courts. In Scotland the choice of court in which to prosecute lies entirely with the Crown (except in relation to those statutory offences which can only be prosecuted summarily or on indictment).

24   James Chalmers and Fiona Leverick, 'Fair Labelling in Criminal Law' (2008) 71 Modern Law Review 217, 243.

25   Ibid. For an argument that organised crime is distinctive and should be recognised as such, see L Campbell, *Organised Crime and the Law: A Comparative Analysis* (Hart 2013).

26   For a discussion of alternative ways of defining organised crime, see Campbell (n 25) chapter 2.

27   Antony Duff, *Criminal Attempts* (Clarendon Press 1996) 37.

28   Accessories and Abettors Act 1961 s 8 as amended by the Criminal Law Act 1977 s 65(7).

29   *R v Gnango* [2011] UKSC 59.

and abetting' and 'joint enterprise', or whether the two are separate concepts at all,[30] are unknown in Scots law.

That is not to say that aiding and abetting plays no role at all. On the recommendation of the Scottish Law Commission (SLC),[31] section 293(2) of the Criminal Procedure (Scotland) Act 1995 introduced a provision whereby any person who 'aids, abets, counsels, procures or incites' a person to commit a statutory offence 'shall be guilty of an offence' and shall be liable on conviction to the same punishment as might be imposed for the statutory offence in question. The provision is unnecessary, given that art and part liability for statutory offences already existed,[32] something that section 293(1) of the 1995 Act explicitly confirmed. That said, the main argument made by the SLC for introducing it was that it is sometimes more appropriate in labelling terms to convict an individual who has played a very minor role in an offence of aiding and abetting that offence, rather than of the substantive offence (which would be the result under the art and part doctrine).[33] The argument was one of labelling, rather than degree of punishment, as is clear from the recommendation that anyone convicted under the aiding and abetting provision should be liable for the same maximum penalty as for the substantive offence (and this was translated into the statute). This is a valid argument, as one of the main criticisms that can be made of the art and part doctrine is that it unfairly labels those who play only a minor role in a criminal offence. Notwithstanding, section 293(2) applies only to statutory offences and has been little used in Scots law,[34] where the dominant form of derivate liability is still the common law doctrine of art and part.[35]

Art and Part: The General Principle

The concept of art and part in Scots law has a long history and its origins can be traced back to the 1100s.[36] The basic principle is a simple one. All of those who contribute to the commission of a criminal offence are equally guilty of that offence, regardless of the nature or timing of their individual contribution.[37] As Lord Patrick put it in *HM Advocate v Lappen*:

> [I]f a number of men form a common plan whereby some are to commit the actual seizure of the
> property, and some according to the plan are to keep watch, and some according to the plan are

---

30   A difference of view is apparent even in the leading texts on criminal law. Ashworth (n 2) 420 describes joint enterprise as 'a separate doctrine' to aiding and abetting, but Ormerod describes it as an application of the ordinary principles of secondary liability (David Ormerod, *Smith and Hogan Criminal Law* (13th edn, Oxford University Press 2011) 229). The most recent cases support the latter view – see for example, *R v Stringer* [2011] EWCA Crim 1396; *R v Mendez* [2010] EWCA Crim 516; *R v A* [2010] EWCA Crim 1622.

31   Scottish Law Commission, *Art and Part Guilt of Statutory Offences* (Scot Law Com No 93, 1985).

32   It was first provided for in s 31 of the Criminal Justice (Scotland) Act 1949.

33   Gordon and Christie (n 12) 5.12. There was also an argument that it was necessary to deal with special capacity offences that restricted liability to persons within a particular class, but *Templeton v HM Advocate* 1988 JC 32 resolved this issue without the need for s 293(2).

34   While its existence was recognised in *H v Lord Advocate* [2011] HCJAC 77 [68] (in the context of an extradition appeal), charges under s 293(2) have never been the subject of a reported case.

35   Gordon and Christie (n 12) 5.15. The language of 'aiding and abetting' is sometimes used in common law charges in Scotland but this has 'no special meaning' and is used purely to avoid 'linguistic difficulty'.

36   See Alistair Devlin, 'The History of Art and Part', unpublished manuscript prepared in 2006 (held by Fiona Leverick at Glasgow University).

37   Unless their only contribution is to provide assistance after the event – see text accompanying (n 47).

to help to carry away the loot, and some according to the plan are to help to dispose of the loot, then, although the actual robbery may only have been committed by one or two of them, every one is guilty of the robbery, because they joined together in a common plan to commit the robbery.[38]

Thus under the doctrine of art and part, an accused can be liable for murder (or attempted murder), even if he inflicted no injuries on the deceased or was not present when the deceased was killed.[39]

For an accused to be convicted art and part of a criminal offence two requirements need to be satisfied: (1) he participated in some way in the offence and (2) he shared a 'common purpose' with the primary actor(s). Assuming the offence (or an attempted form of it) transpires,[40] he is fully liable for it, unless he successfully disassociates from the enterprise.[41]

Participation

Participation covers both the provision of some sort of assistance to a principal offender and a more equal contribution made to a joint enterprise. It is here where Scots law departs from that of England and Wales, where the provision of assistance to a principal offender would generally fall under the aiding and abetting provisions in the Accessories and Abettors Act 1961. Participation may be via material assistance but psychological assistance, such as encouragement, would also suffice. Mere presence at the scene, without either of these, would not suffice,[42] unless the accused contributed in some way by, for example, preventing assistance from reaching the victim[43] or instigating the offence.

In terms of timing, three possibilities exist and any one (or more) of these will suffice to establish participation for the purposes of art and part liability. First, the contribution may be instigatory,[44] covering, for example, the accused who issues an order that the offence be committed or through encouragement provides the initial impetus for the offence.[45] Second, the contribution may occur prior to the criminal act, perhaps through the supply of materials or by driving the primary actor to

---

38   1956 SLT 109 (IICJ) 110.

39   See for example *Vogan v HM Advocate* 2003 SCCR 564 (HCJ); *Poole v HM Advocate* 2009 SCCR 577 (HCJ).

40   Gordon and Christie (n 12) 5.02. It is not necessary that the principal offender is convicted of the offence for the secondary party to be liable art and part. It would for example be possible to convict A2 art and part of assault if he instructed a child to attack the victim or coerced another adult into doing so.

41   The law on disassociation in Scotland is under-developed but on the basis of the obiter remarks in *MacNeil v HM Advocate* 1986 JC 146 it can probably be concluded that an accused who withdraws from a joint enterprise before it is completed will not occur art and part liability 'if he clearly intimates to [the perpetrators] that he is withdrawing, and seeks to discourage them from proceeding with the plan, at a stage when, if his advice were followed, the crime would not be committed' (HCJ) 158 (Lord Justice-General Emslie).

42   *HM Advocate v Kerr* (1871) 2 Coup 334 (HCJ).

43   In *Gorman v HM Advocate* [2011] HCJAC 9 [9] it was held that participation in an attempted murder could be inferred on the basis of preventing assistance from reaching the complainer and shouting 'fucking hurry up' to the other participants in the attack.

44   Which could, of course, also be prosecuted as conspiracy or incitement.

45   Gordon and Christie (n 12) 5.21. It may even be that in some circumstances advice would suffice: see *Martin v Hamilton* 1989 JC 101 (HCJ).

the locus.[46] Third, it may occur during the criminal act itself, for example where a group of people spontaneously participate in a fight.

If the *only* contribution made by the accused took place after the primary offence had been committed, he should not be art and part liable as Scots law does not recognise accession after the fact. Thus, in *HM Advocate v Igoe*, evidence that the appellant knew that the deceased had been shot with a handgun, had moved the deceased's body and had removed the handgun from beside the body was insufficient to constitute participation in the killing.[47] That does not, however, preclude art and part liability where it can be demonstrated that the accused agreed in advance to provide assistance after the event, as in *Cameron v HM Advocate*,[48] where the contribution made by the appellant was to provide a garage where the proceeds of a robbery were hidden.

'A Common Purpose'

The second requirement of art and part liability is that there must be a 'common purpose' between the participants in the criminal enterprise. As the court put it in the leading case of *McKinnon v HM Advocate*:

> It is, of course, well established that, where a number of persons act together in pursuance of a common criminal purpose, each of them is criminally responsible for a crime which is committed in pursuance of that purpose, regardless of the part which he or she played, provided that the crime is within the scope of that common criminal purpose.[49]

This need not be a formal agreement and indeed it may arise spontaneously without any tacit agreement at all, as where a fight breaks out and several parties join in.[50] The concept is particularly useful where the perpetrator must have come from a limited group of persons but it is not possible to prove which one carried out the *actus reus*.[51]

It is when it comes to the application of the common purpose test that things become more complex. A distinction has developed between what has been termed antecedent concert and spontaneous concert.[52] Antecedent concert refers to the situation whereby two or more accused agree in advance that a crime is to be committed. So where A1 and A2 agree that a robbery is to take place and, in the course of that robbery, A1 produces a knife and kills the victim, the case would be analysed as one of antecedent concert. But if A1 and A2 chance upon the same individual and A1 spontaneously attacks her with a knife, while, for example, A2 prevents the victim from escaping, the case would be treated as one of spontaneous concert and A2's liability assessed on this basis. In real life, given the difficulties of proving the existence of a pre-agreed plan, the distinction is not always easily applied and the courts have recognised that what starts off as a case

---

46 As occurred in *Gorman* (n 43).

47 2010 SCCR 759 (HCJ) [14].

48 2008 SCCR 669 (HCJ).

49 2003 JC 29 (HCJ) [27].

50 For example *Scott v HM Advocate* [2011] HCJAC 27.

51 For example *Kidd v HM Advocate* [2010] HCJAC 98; *Docherty v HM Advocate* [2010] HCJAC 31.

52 The distinction can be traced back to Hume (Commentaries, i, 265-70). The first use of the term 'antecedent concert' appears to have been in *Spiers v HM Advocate* 1980 JC 36 at 38. The distinction between this and 'spontaneous concert' was cemented in *McKinnon* (n 49) [22].

of antecedent concert can develop spontaneously[53] and also that cases can be brought by the Crown using antecedent and spontaneous concert as alternate bases for conviction.[54]

While the basic test to be applied in cases of antecedent concert and spontaneous concert is the same – participation and a common purpose – different principles have developed to guide the application of the test. That said, the courts have not always specified whether a case is being determined on the basis of antecedent or spontaneous concert and thus there is some uncertainty as to whether particular principles are confined to one or other type of concert or have general application.[55]

Antecedent Concert

Where it can be proved that the accused were party to a prior agreement to commit an offence, the basis upon which liability will be assessed is that of antecedent concert. Where events stick to the common plan agreed, the assessment of liability is a simple one – any accused who participated in a common purpose to commit an offence will be fully liable for that offence, regardless of the particular role played. It is when events go beyond what was agreed that the assessment of liability becomes more complex. In England and Wales, where two parties agree to commit an offence, D2 can be convicted on the basis of joint enterprise liability for any additional offence committed by D1, providing that he foresaw that D1 might commit this offence during the course of the criminal enterprise.[56] The test is a subjective one, requiring actual foresight on the part of the defendant, albeit only of a possibility.

In Scotland, by contrast, liability is discerned on an objective basis. The question to be determined is not what was actually foreseen by the accused, but 'what was foreseeable as liable to happen, and hence what was or was not obvious in this respect'.[57] Thus:

> … an accused is guilty of murder art and part where, first, by his conduct, for example his words or actions, he actively associates himself with a common criminal purpose which is or includes the taking of human life or carries the obvious risk that human life will be taken, and, secondly, in the carrying out of that purpose murder is committed by someone else.[58]

The question of which, if any, personal characteristics of A2 would be taken into account in the application of the objective test has not been canvassed by the courts, although reference to other areas of the law suggests that these would be limited to age and sex.[59]

There is no requirement – or at least not in antecedent concert cases – for A2 to share the same *mens rea* as A1 or to have in his contemplation that A1 would act with the requisite *mens rea*. In *Brown v HM Advocate*,[60] where the victim was killed by a single deep stab wound, it was suggested

---

53   *Gorman* (n 43) [9].

54   *Crawford v HM Advocate* [2012] HCJAC 40 [3].

55   See for example *Docherty* (n 51); *Vogan* (n 39).

56   *R v A* [2010] EWCA Crim 1622 [37] as endorsed by the Supreme Court in *Gnango* (n 29) [14] (Lord Phillips of Worth Matravers PSC and Lord Judge CJ).

57   *McKinnon* (n 49) [29].

58   Ibid. [32]. For recent cases where this test has been applied, see *Poole* (n 39); *Docherty* (n 51); *Gorman* (n 43).

59   See for example the discussion in the context of criminal defences in James Chalmers and Fiona Leverick, *Criminal Defences and Pleas in Bar of Trial* (W. Green/SULI 2006) chapter 5.

60   1993 SCCR 382 (HCJ).

that this *was* a requirement and that a participant in a joint attack should not be found guilty of murder unless he 'had in contemplation, as part of [the] joint purpose, an act of the necessary degree of wicked recklessness such as that the deceased would be stabbed by plunging a knife into his heart'.[61] But in *McKinnon*, where a Full Bench was assembled to allow for the possibility of over-ruling earlier authorities, it was made clear that if *Brown* was suggesting that 'in a case of antecedent concert it is necessary for the jury to be satisfied as to what was contemplated by each accused at the time of the attack ... this approach was unwarranted'.[62] The correct approach in cases of antecedent concert is that:

> ... if the relevant concert is established, there is no separate question as to whether the individual accused had the necessary criminal intent which is required for the finding of guilt of that crime. In short, he or she is responsible for that crime in the same way as if he or she had personally committed it.[63]

This was confirmed in *Poole v HM Advocate*,[64] where the court stressed that the question was 'not ... whether there was evidence from which it could be said that the appellant had the *mens rea* necessary for murder' but rather whether it was 'objectively foreseeable to the appellant that such violence was liable to be used as carried an obvious risk of life being taken'.[65] In *Poole*, A1 and A2 were involved in a planned attack on two men, one of whom died (V1) and one of whom did not (V2). CCTV evidence showed A1 to be primarily attacking V1 (with an unidentified weapon) and A2 to be attacking V2 (with a snooker cue). V2 was severely injured but there does not appear to have been any question that his life was in danger. Despite not inflicting any life threatening injury on either V1 or V2, A2 was convicted art and part of V1's murder. A more exacting requirement that A2 share the same *mens rea* as A1 would almost certainly have led to a different result.[66]

Thus if there is evidence that A1 and A2 agreed to carry out a robbery, but A1 produced a knife and stabbed V through the heart, A2 could be convicted of murder even though he did not intend to kill V or inflict any violence upon V, nor did he display wicked recklessness towards V (or any other person),[67] nor did he foresee that A1 might kill V, providing it was reasonably foreseeable that A1 would do so.

The same objective test applies to cases involving non-fatal violence, as is evident from *Cameron v HM Advocate*.[68] Here, the accused formed a common plan to steal valuable cargo from a lorry[69] and in the course of events A1 threatened the driver of the lorry with a shotgun. A2's conviction for robbery was upheld, the *McKinnon* test of 'what was foreseeable as liable to

---

61   Ibid. 393. Wicked recklessness is one of two alternative forms of *mens rea* for murder in Scotland: see (n 67) below.

62   *McKinnon* (n 49) [22].

63   Ibid. [27].

64   *Poole* (n 39).

65   Ibid. [11].

66   See Andrew Choo, 'Joint Unlawful Enterprises and Murder' (1992) 55 Modern Law Review 870, 875 for an argument that A2 should be required to share the same *mens rea* as A1 in order to be convicted of murder.

67   The *mens rea* for murder is (wicked) intention to kill or wicked recklessness (which must be accompanied by an intention to inflict at least some physical injury: *HM Advocate v Purcell* 2008 JC 131).

68   *Cameron* (n 48).

69   Unusually there was direct evidence of the plan as A1 gave evidence against A2 who, on the basis of the Crown case, was the more culpable of the two, having instigated events.

happen' being applied and the court stressing that 'it need not be confined to what was in the actual knowledge or appreciation of the particular accused'.[70]

In *Black and Sneddon v HM Advocate*,[71] it was made clear that it is a matter for the jury to determine what was and what was not foreseeable in a particular case. Where it has been agreed that only weapons of a certain kind will be used and A1 unexpectedly produces a different type of weapon, it is open to the jury to convict on an art and part basis if the weapon is of a similar type to that which had already been agreed. Whether or not a weapon is of a similar type is a jury matter ('a knife is not as a matter of law different from a baseball bat'[72]) subject only to the qualification that there may be cases 'the nature of the weapon unexpectedly produced and used [by A1] and the manner of its use are such that no jury could properly conclude that its use in that manner was within the contemplation (in the sense of what is foreseeable) of the other participants in the particular criminal enterprise'.[73]

That said, the courts have set out some circumstances in which the reasonable foreseeability test will normally be satisfied. In *Shepherd v HM Advocate*,[74] the court held that it is always reasonably foreseeable that when domestic premises are broken into in the middle of the night, this may involve violence.[75] Likewise, in *Cameron*, the court held that where the plan of the parties is to steal valuable items (here, a particularly large cargo of tobacco held in a lorry), it is 'readily foreseeable, having regard to the security measures likely to be taken with so valuable a load, that violence in one form or another was liable to be used to take it'.[76]

In cases of homicide, it is open to the jury to convict A2 of murder where he knows that as part of the common criminal purpose weapons of a nature 'that can readily be used to kill' are being carried on the basis that 'it was foreseeable that such weapons were liable to be used with lethal effect'.[77] But a murder conviction need not necessarily result. As the court stated in *McKinnon*, this will depend on the circumstances:

> ... including the way in which it was envisaged that the weapons were to be or might be used. There is no rule of law that the jury must convict [of murder] ... The jury may conclude that they are not satisfied, in regard to an individual accused, that it was obvious that weapons were being carried or at any rate that such weapons might be used to kill the victim. If, for example, one of two accused is carrying a stick or even a penknife which, so far as the other accused is concerned, is intended to frighten a shopkeeper whom they intend to rob, the latter might well not be guilty of murder perpetrated by the former even though he had reason to anticipate that such a weapon would or might be used for that limited purpose.[78]

If a conviction for murder is not considered appropriate, the jury have another option, which is to return a verdict of culpable homicide,[79] as the court in *McKinnon* made clear:

---

70   *Cameron* (n 48) [15].
71   2006 SLT 685.
72   Ibid. [33]. See also *O'Connell v HM Advocate* 1987 SCCR 459 (HCJ).
73   *Black and Sneddon* (n 72) [33].
74   2010 SCCR 55 (HCJ).
75   Ibid. [5].
76   *Cameron* (n 48) [16].
77   *McKinnon* (n 49) [31].
78   Ibid.
79   Culpable homicide is the Scottish equivalent of manslaughter. Cf. England and Wales, where the jury would face an 'all or nothing' choice between convicting D2 of murder or convicting him solely on the basis of

Where [A2] is not proved to have associated himself with [a common purpose that includes the taking of human life] or is proved to have participated in some less serious common criminal purpose in the course of which the victim dies, the accused may be guilty art and part of culpable homicide, whether or not any other person is proved guilty of murder.[80]

Some guidance on this issue was provided in *Hopkinson v HM Advocate*,[81] where A1 and A2 had planned a robbery and both parties armed themselves with knives. It was established that A1 had inflicted the fatal wound.[82] A2 claimed he had carried a knife only to scare the deceased during the robbery and that, although he was aware that A1 had a knife, it was unforeseeable to him that A1 would use it to inflict violence and in fact he remonstrated with her when she did so.[83] The trial judge did not leave the possibility of a culpable homicide verdict to the jury and A2 appealed against his conviction for murder on the basis that the trial judge should have done so. The court upheld the appeal on this basis:

if it had been proved that the appellant and the co-accused had embarked upon a common criminal purpose to assault and rob the deceased with the use of knives, but that it had not been proved to their satisfaction either that the common criminal purpose had included the taking of human life or had carried with it the foreseeable risk that fatal injury might be inflicted, it would have been necessary for them to consider whether to acquit the appellant of any responsibility for the killing of the deceased, (which was the verdict the appellant sought), or to convict him of culpable homicide.[84]

The court continued:

The directions to the jury should have made clear that they would require to consider whether any agreement between the appellant and his co-accused, relating to the use of knives, (a) had been restricted to the limited purpose of scaring the deceased, without there having been any foreseeable risk of injury being inflicted; or (b) had involved the foreseeable risk that a knife might be used to inflict some form of non-fatal injury to the deceased; or (c) had involved the foreseeable risk of the infliction of life threatening injury to the deceased. The jury should have been directed that if the first of these alternatives applied the appellant could not have been convicted of culpable homicide; and that if the second or third alternative applied, such a verdict was available to the jury, provided they intended to convict the co-accused of murder or culpable homicide.[85]

Thus it seems that where there is evidence of an agreement between accused that a weapon be used only for the limited purpose of scaring the victim (and where it was not reasonably foreseeable that it would be used for any other purpose), neither a murder verdict nor a culpable homicide verdict is appropriate and the accused should be held responsible only for his own contribution (which in

---

his own acts; see Matthew Dyson, 'More Appealing Joint Enterprise' (2010) 69 Cambridge Law Journal 425.

80   *McKinnon* (n 49) [32]. A discriminating verdict of this nature would also be possible where A2 had a partial defence of diminished responsibility or provocation but A1 did not.

81   2009 HCJAC 9.

82   Ibid. [3].

83   Ibid. [3].

84   Ibid. [21]. The Crown did not seek a re-trial and the court substituted a verdict of culpable homicide for A2.

85   Ibid. [22].

Hopkinson was a robbery). But where it was reasonably foreseeable that a weapon would be used to inflict at least some injury on the victim, a culpable homicide verdict can be returned. A murder verdict, it would seem, should be limited to instances where there was a reasonably foreseeable risk of fatal injury.

The availability of a 'half-way house' verdict might be seen as a positive feature of Scots law compared to its counterpart south of the border, but the difficulty here is that it is not clear when such a verdict is appropriate. A culpable homicide verdict appears to be open to the jury under both option (b) (where it was reasonably foreseeable that non-fatal injury would result) and option (c) (where it was reasonably foreseeable that life threatening injury would result). But under option (c) a verdict of murder would also be legitimate and the jury is given no guidance as to how to decide between murder and culpable homicide in these circumstances. This has its advantages – it does leave a certain amount of flexibility in the law – but the danger is that, without more concrete guidelines, inconsistent jury verdicts will result.

Spontaneous Concert

Various principles have also developed to assist in the application of the common purpose test when a case is brought on the basis of spontaneous concert – that is, where there was no prior agreement between the parties to commit an offence (or where such an agreement cannot be proved). First, where A2 becomes aware during the course of an attack that A1 has used a weapon and A2 continues to participate in that attack regardless of this knowledge, he will be art and part liable for A1's acts.[86] Actual knowledge of the weapon is required – a finding that A2 ought to have known about the weapon is not sufficient. This was made clear in *Peden v HM Advocate*,[87] where the trial judge's direction that the jury would be entitled to find A2 guilty of assault to severe injury on the basis that she 'saw, knew, ought to have seen or known that a knife was being wielded by her man and she persisted in her own attack' was held to be a misdirection.[88] In *Dempsey v HM Advocate*,[89] it was held that the same principle applied to murder and that A2 could be convicted of murder 'if the jury were satisfied that it could be inferred from the evidence that [A2] knew that [A1] had a knife and was using it on the deceased, and that with that knowledge he continued with the joint attack on the deceased'.[90]

It is not entirely clear whether awareness on the part of A2 that A1 possesses a lethal weapon is sufficient for conviction or whether A2 must also have seen the weapon being used on the victim. In *Peden* and *Kidd*, the test set out was simply whether A2 knew that A1 had a weapon.[91] In *Dempsey*, however, the test was whether A2 'knew that A1 had a knife *and was using it on the deceased*'.[92] In *Crawford*, the test was different yet again: whether A2 'had known a knife *was going to be used*'.[93] *Herity* used similar language: 'in the knowledge that [a weapon] was being,

---

86   *Kidd* (n 51) [36].

87   2003 SLT 1047 (HCJ), confirmed in *Herity v HM Advocate* 2009 SCCR 590 (HCJ) [17] (also a case of assault to severe injury).

88   *Peden* (n 87) 1048. See also *Herity* (n 87) [17] and *Kidd* (n 51) [36].

89   *Dempsey v HM Advocate* 2005 JC 252 (HCJ).

90   Ibid. [11].

91   *Peden* (n 87) 1058; *Kidd* (n 51) [36].

92   *Dempsey* (n 89) [11] (emphasis added).

93   *Crawford* (n 54) [6] (emphasis added).

or was liable to be used.[94] In both *Crawford* and *Herity* the court made it clear that they were referring to spontaneous concert, but the language of 'liable/going to be used' is reminiscent of *McKinnon*,[95] an authority on antecedent concert, and seems more appropriate to that type of case.

Second, A2 can be art and part liable for the acts of A1 if he participates with A1 in a joint attack and uses a similar type of weapon or the same degree of violence as A1.[96] If a fatal injury is inflicted, A2 can be convicted of murder[97] (or in the case of a potentially fatal injury attempted murder)[98] on this basis. This is legitimate even if he was unaware of A1's weapon[99] and did not inflict the fatal injury himself (or – in the scenario where this principle is probably of most use – where it cannot be proved which of A1 or A2 inflicted the fatal injury). The question then becomes what constitutes a similar type of weapon in this context. In *Donnelly v HM Advocate*, an attempted murder case, the appeal court took the view that a jury would be entitled to consider a baseball bat sufficiently similar to a knife,[100] although the issue was not properly canvassed. In *Crawford v HM Advocate*, the appeal court was of the view that the jury was 'entitled to hold that participation in a knife assault by, for example, using a bottle to strike the victim on the head'[101] would suffice.

What is not entirely clear is whether the test set out in *Brown* is still good law in spontaneous concert cases, that is whether, in order to be convicted of murder on an art and part basis, A2 must have 'had in his contemplation' that A1 would act with the requisite *mens rea* for murder. In *McKinnon*, it was explicitly stated that it did not apply to antecedent concert but the possibility of it continuing to apply to spontaneous concert was left open. In *Crawford*, something close to the *Brown* test was approved by the appeal court. The trial judge directed the jury that if A2 knew that a knife was being used or was going to be used by A1 and nevertheless carried on participating in the attack, he could be found guilty of murder despite not having inflicted the lethal wound. The trial judge continued, however: 'if you thought [A2] did not appreciate fully the use of a knife and thought it was only going to be used to inflict a less serious injury then [A2] would lack the intent necessary for murder, but could be convicted of culpable homicide'.[102] The appeal court approved this direction, describing it as 'readily understandable to the jury' and 'sufficiently clear'.[103]

The reference to '*the* intent necessary for murder' is puzzling, as there are two alternate *mens rea* states for murder in Scots law, one of which is a (wicked)[104] intention to kill and the other of which is wicked recklessness (which must now also be accompanied by an intent to inflict at least some bodily harm on the victim).[105] But that aside, *Crawford* seems to suggest that a simple awareness that A1 had a lethal weapon is not enough to support a murder conviction in spontaneous concert cases. Rather A2 must have appreciated the manner in which the weapon would be used and if he did not then a culpable homicide verdict is appropriate. It could also be taken to imply that a more individualistic approach to *mens rea* is taken in spontaneous concert cases. In antecedent concert

---

94   *Herity* (n 87) [17] (emphasis added).
95   *McKinnon* (n 49).
96   *Donnelly v HM Advocate* 2007 SCCR 577 (HCJ) [31]; *Scott* (n 50) [22]; *Crawford* (n 54) [5].
97   *Crawford* (n 54) [5].
98   *Donnelly* (n 96) [30].
99   As was the case in ibid.
100   Ibid. [31].
101   *Crawford* (n 54) [5].
102   Ibid. [6].
103   Ibid. [6].
104   The term 'wicked' was added by the court in *Drury v HM Advocate* 2001 SLT 1013 (HCJ) to signify the requirement that the accused had no applicable defence, such as self-defence.
105   *Purcell* (n 67).

cases, *McKinnon* made it clear that there is no need for A2 to possess the *mens rea* for murder in order to be convicted of murder on an art and part basis. But if this was also true in spontaneous concert cases there would be no need to prove or infer *mens rea* on A2's part and thus 'lacking the intent necessary for murder' would not be a bar to conviction.

Not all homicide cases, of course, will involve the use of a weapon and the courts have set out a more general account of when it will be legitimate to return discriminating verdicts of murder and culpable homicide in respect of two participants in a fight which resulted in death. In *Melvin v HM Advocate*,[106] the court held that where two or more accused are charged with murder it is open to the jury to convict one of murder and one of culpable homicide where there was 'a disparity in the degree of participation' in the crime.[107] This option should not be taken where there are 'minute or unimportant differences between the actings' of the accused, but only in 'situations in which there might be demonstrated striking differences of relevant conduct'.[108]

Summary/Discussion

To summarise, there are three main differences between Scots law and the law of England and Wales: (1) the use of a single doctrine of art and part; (2) the use of an objective test to determine the liability of A2 where A1 commits an offence more serious than that agreed; and (3) the availability of discriminating verdicts of murder and culpable homicide where A1 and A2 both participate in a killing.

There is no doubt that Scots law is – at least in terms of the range of provisions – less complex than that of England and Wales. The main procedural mechanism for dealing with participation is the common law doctrine of art and part (alongside the provisions on incitement and conspiracy). There is no separate doctrine of aiding and abetting.[109] An accused who assists in a criminal venture is dealt with in exactly the same way as one who engages in a joint enterprise. That said, there are an increasing number of statutory provisions which have complicated the law. Section 293(2) of the Criminal Procedure (Scotland) Act 1995 introduced an aiding and abetting provision in relation to statutory offences. Sections 28 and 30 of the Criminal Justice and Licensing (Scotland) Act 2010 introduced offences of 'involvement in serious organised crime' and 'directing serious organised crime' respectively. None of these provisions criminalised conduct that would not already have been criminal under existing common law doctrine. Thus they are open to criticism on the basis that they were unnecessary, although, as has already been discussed, there may be arguments of labelling that can be made in their favour.[110]

Regardless of their merits, however, the statutory provisions are little used and the common law art and part doctrine is still the primary mechanism for dealing with participation in crime. This has the advantage of simplicity. The lengthy discussions that have dogged English law over the terminology of aiding and abetting versus that of joint enterprise (and the different tests applicable)[111] have not arisen in Scotland. But the main criticism that can be made of art and part

---

106   1984 SLT 365 (HCJ).

107   Ibid. 367 (Lord Cameron).

108   Ibid. 367 (Lord Avonside). *Melvin* was approved in *Docherty v HM Advocate* 2003 SCCR 772 (HCJ) 777.

109   Aside from in the very limited statutory context of section 293(2) discussed below.

110   Ibid. Text accompanying (n 24).

111   See Ormerod (n 30) 213, who identifies five different ways in which the term 'joint enterprise' has been used in the English case law.

as a general doctrine is that it fails to distinguish sufficiently between the culpability of multiple accused and that someone who provides minor assistance in a common plan to commit murder should not be labelled as a murderer in the same way as someone who afflicts the fatal blow. Different levels of culpability can, of course, be taken into account in sentencing, even in murder cases where the punishment part of the life sentence can be adjusted accordingly. But this does leave much in the hands of the vast discretion of the Scottish sentencing judge and would surely be looked upon in horror by, for example, legal observers in Germany, where not only is there a clear distinction between principals and solicitors as opposed to facilitators, but there are also mandatory sentencing provisions whereby facilitators must receive a discounted sentence.[112] It also sits uncomfortably with the notion that 'aiding/abetting' and 'participating in a joint enterprise' are conceptually distinct and should be treated as such, both for reasons of the structural coherence of the law and in terms of fairness to the accused who deserves to be labelled according to the exact nature of his involvement and contribution.[113]

The tests that are used to determine whether A2 should be convicted art and part can be subjected to similar criticism. The overall guiding principle is a simple one – A2 can be legitimately convicted of a criminal offence committed by A1 when there is a shared common purpose – but, as we have seen, certain principles guide the manner in which this should be applied in different factual situations. In cases of antecedent concert, where a common plan has been formed between A1 and A2 to commit a particular offence (say, robbery) but A1 commits a more serious offence (say murder), A2 will be art and part liable if it was reasonably foreseeable that A1 would use lethal violence. There is no requirement for actual foresight on the part of A2, which would be required under English law in similar circumstances, and there is no requirement that A2 possesses the *mens rea* for the more serious offence.[114] Convicting A2 of murder on the basis that it was reasonably foreseeable that A1 might use lethal violence in the course of a planned robbery can be criticised on a number of grounds. It over-criminalises A2[115] because he is convicted of a more serious offence than his moral culpability merits.[116] In this context, Krebs has argued for a more stringent test of 'acquiescence' in order for A2 to be convicted of any offence that A1 commits beyond what has been agreed between them.[117] It violates the principle of fair warning, which requires that a citizen is entitled to know in clear terms when criminal liability for a particular offence will be incurred so that she may adjust her conduct accordingly.[118] It also carries the risk that the test will simply fail to be applied by juries. Because a death *has* occurred, a jury may conclude without reflection that it must have been reasonably foreseeable that it would.

All of these are criticisms that have been made in the context of English law (where the test is that the defendant must have foreseen the possibility of the more serious offence being

---

112   See Markus Dubber, 'Criminalizing Complicity: A Comparative Analysis' (2007) 5 Journal of International Criminal Justice 977, 984.

113   Beatrice Krebs, 'Joint Criminal Enterprise' (2010) 73 Modern Law Review 578.

114   At least not in cases of antecedent concert. The issue is less clear in relation to spontaneous concert; see (nn 102-105) and accompanying text.

115   On which see for example Andrew Ashworth and Lucia Zedner, 'Defending the Criminal Law: Reflections on the Changing Character of Crime, Procedure and Sanctions' [2008] Criminal Law and Philosophy 2; Douglas Husak, *Overcriminalization: The Limits of the Criminal Law* (Oxford University Press 2007).

116   Bob Sullivan, 'First Degree Murder and Complicity: Conditions for Parity of Culpability Between Principal and Accomplice' (2007) 1 Criminal Law and Philosophy 271, 286.

117   Krebs (n 113) 604.

118   See Ashworth (n 2) 3.5.

committed).[119] But they resonate even more strongly in the Scottish context, where A2 can be convicted of murder even if he genuinely did not foresee the possibility that A1 would kill. One of the most scathing criticisms of English law has been made by Krebs, who warns that '[t]here is a real danger ... that the *foresight* test, not very demanding in and of itself, is in practice further diluted to one of *foreseeability*'[120] and criticises this on the basis that it 'can have devastating consequences for individuals [and] threatens the coherence and structure of the criminal law'.[121] This is precisely the test that we *do* have in Scotland and thus is open to exactly these criticisms.[122]

Some of the criticism of Scots law might be mitigated by the fact that, in the context of homicide, the liability of A1 and A2 can be differentiated. Thus, if A1 stabs and kills during the course of a planned robbery in which it was agreed by A1 and A2 that weapons would be used only to inflict a more minor injury, A1 can be legitimately convicted of murder and A2 of culpable homicide, something that would not be possible in England and Wales. This seems a just outcome. By actively associating himself with a venture in which knives were being carried, A2 surely bears some responsibility for the resulting death,[123] and the lack of a 'half way house' verdict of this nature has been criticised in the English context.[124] Likewise, in the context of spontaneous concert, a culpable homicide verdict can legitimately be returned where A1 and A2 both participate in a fight resulting in death, but where 'striking differences'[125] can be discerned between the conduct of the two. Once again, liability for culpable homicide seems a just compromise in these circumstances. Those who willingly participate in a joint attack should bear some responsibility beyond their individual contribution for doing so, whether this is justified[126] on an assumption of risk basis[127] or on the basis that A2's participation increases the likelihood that A1 will use lethal violence[128] or makes it easier for him to do so.

The difficulty is that no clear guidelines have been set out to assist Scottish juries in distinguishing between murder and culpable homicide in cases where A2's liability is founded upon art and part. This is particularly true of antecedent concert cases where, if *Hopkinson* is correct, a culpable homicide verdict is available both where the common plan 'had involved the foreseeable risk that [a weapon] might be used to inflict some form of non-fatal injury to the deceased' and where it 'had involved the foreseeable risk of the infliction of life threatening injury to the deceased'[129] and a jury need be given no further guidance as to how to discriminate. This is not uncommon in Scots law, where traditionally the courts have avoided spelling out detailed guidelines and have instead relied

---

119   See for example Ian Dennis, 'Adjusting the Boundaries of Murder: Complicity' [2008] Criminal Law Review 923, 924; Sullivan (n 116) 286.

120   Krebs (n 113) 583-84.

121   Ibid. 603.

122   Although in practice, it may be that the two tests are unlikely to generate different results, as it is never going to be possible to tell for sure what a particular accused actually foresaw.

123   Sullivan (n 116) 286.

124   Ibid. 286; Krebs (n 113) 596; Dyson (n 79) 427.

125   *Melvin* (n 106) 367 (Lord Avonside); *Docherty* (n 108) 777.

126   Detailed examination of the rationale for art and part liability lies beyond the scope of this chapter, but see Krebs (n 113) for an excellent critical discussion.

127   See the discussion in Krebs (n 113) 594-97. Krebs ultimately rejects this rationale, but in a different context.

128   There is an extensive body of research that suggests that groups are more inherently dangerous than individuals and that joint criminal ventures can take on a momentum of their own that makes the commission of further crimes more likely: see the sources cited by Krebs (n 113) 602.

129   *Hopkinson* (n 81) [22].

upon juries to apply a collective morality to the determination of liability.[130] The most obvious example is wicked recklessness as a *mens rea* state for murder, which allows juries to convict of murder those who they consider morally deserving of this label.[131] This could be regarded as a strength of the law, but it carries the obvious danger of inconsistency and requires us to place great faith in juries to somehow 'know', by pooling their collective experience and judgment, when an accused deserves to be labelled as a murderer and when he does not.[132] The jury, faced with the choice of whether to convict an accused art and part of murder or culpable homicide, a decision that can have an enormous significance for that individual, is being asked to engage in precisely this sort of exercise and that is something we should regard with unease. The label of 'murderer' is one that should be reserved only for the most culpable of accused. In allowing for a culpable homicide verdict where the accused played a minor role in a joint enterprise resulting in homicide, Scots law may have something to offer to other jurisdictions. But it is suggested here that an absence of clear guidelines as to when a culpable homicide verdict is appropriate is not something to be recommended as a model for law reform.

---

130   Lindsay Farmer, 'Scots Criminal Law' in Mark Mulhern (ed.), *Law: A Compendium of Scottish Ethnography* (Tuckwell Press/European Ethnological Research Centre 2012).

131   Gordon and Christie (n 12) 23.21. The flexibility has been limited by the addition of a requirement that the accused must intend to cause at least some physical injury in order to be convicted under the wicked recklessness limb; see *Purcell* (n 67).

132   See the critical comments of Lord Justice-Clerk Gill in *Petto v HM Advocate* 2012 JC 105 (HCJ) [21].

Chapter 14

Bishops in the Dock: Child Abuse and the Irish Law of Complicity

John Stannard[1]

On Friday 22 June 2012, as this chapter was being written, an elderly priest was remanded in custody to await sentence before a court in Philadelphia, USA after being convicted of child endangerment.[2] Monsignor William Lynn, an official in the Archdiocese of Philadelphia, was responsible for dealing with complaints of child abuse, and the essence of the case was that he had allowed priests known to be guilty of such conduct to continue in post or had transferred them elsewhere rather than reporting them to the civil authorities. The verdict was welcomed by victim support groups. One spokesman called it a 'watershed moment in the Catholic abuse crisis', saying that it stood as a warning to other church officials that they were no longer immune from judgment and punishment.[3] In the words of another, it sent 'a strong and clear message that shielding and enabling predator priests is a heinous crime that threatens families, communities and children, and must be punished as such'.[4] Calling for the revocation of Monsignor Lynn's bail, the head prosecutor said 'he deserves to go to prison like the criminal he is'.[5]

These events will not have gone unnoticed in Ireland, where the issue of child abuse in the church continues to make the headlines. This has two aspects, both of which came to prominence in the 1990s but related to events covering most of the twentieth century. The first aspect concerned the parish clergy, and was triggered by several notorious cases involving the conviction of priests with a history of abuse who had seemingly been allowed to carry on their activities over long periods despite the authorities being aware of their proclivities.[6] A series of official reports into

---

1   I am grateful to Jonathan Doak, Tom Obokata and Eimear Spain for their comments on the first draft of this chapter.
2   David Gibson, 'Monsignor William Lynn Convicted in Landmark Catholic Sex Abuse Case' (*Washington Post*, 22 June 2012) <http://www.washingtonpost.com/national/on-faith/monsignor-william-lynn-convicted-in-landmark-catholic-sex-abuse-case/2012/06/22/gJQAIcJsvV_story.html>; 'Monsignor William Lynn Becomes First US Priest Convicted for Abuse Cover Up' (*Telegraph*, 23 June 2012) <http://www.telegraph.co.uk/news/worldnews/northamerica/usa/9350689/Monsignor-William-Lynn-becomes-first-US-priest-convicted-for-abuse-cover-up.html>; Matt Williams, 'Monsignor William Lynn Seeks Release from Prison Over Cover-up Conviction' (*Guardian*, 30 June 2012) <http://www.guardian.co.uk/world/2012/jun/30/monsignor-william-lynn-seeks-release-prison?>; all accessed 2 July 2012.
3   See (n 1). Barbara Dorris of the Survivors Network of those Abused by Priests: *Washington Post*, 22 June 2012.
4   See (n 1). Terence McKiernan, head of BishopAccountability.org.
5   See (n 1).
6   The most notorious of these were Fr Brendan Smyth, Fr Ivan Payne, Fr Eugene Greene and Fr Sean Fortune; see Chris Moore, *Betrayal of Trust: The Father Brendan Smyth Affair and the Catholic Church* (Marino 1995); Martin Ridge and Gerald Cunningham, *Breaking the Silence* (Gill and Macmillan 2008); Tom Mooney, *All the Bishop's Men: Clerical Abuse in an Irish Diocese* (Collins Press 2011).

various dioceses[7] concluded that the response of the authorities had often been woefully inadequate, priests being allowed to continue in post or being moved from parish to parish with little or no consideration being given to the safety and welfare of children with whom they might come into contact.[8] Though better procedures were now in place,[9] their implementation had sometimes been tardy,[10] and in some areas there was still a long way to go.[11]

Even more disturbing were the revelations concerning the conduct of the church authorities in relation to children in institutions, many of which were run by religious orders. As in the case of the secular clergy, these came to light in the 1990s with a series of disclosures by former inmates of such institutions, most notably the Industrial Schools[12] and the Magdalen Laundries.[13] Following this, a Commission of Inquiry was set up[14] which concluded that physical and emotional abuse and neglect were features of these institutions,[15] and that in the case of institutions for boys the sexual abuse of inmates by members of staff was endemic.[16] Perpetrators of abuse were able to operate undetected for long periods,[17] and cases were managed with a view to minimising the risk of public disclosure and consequent damage to the reputation of the institution and the religious order concerned.[18] In many cases the authorities, despite being aware of the recidivist nature of sexual

---

7   *Ferns Report* (Department of Health and Children) (Stationery Office 2005) ('*Ferns Report*'); *Report into the Catholic Archdiocese of Dublin* (Commission of Investigation) (Stationery Office 2009) ('*Murphy Report*'); *Report by Commission of Investigation into Catholic Diocese of Cloyne* (Stationery Office 2010) ('*Cloyne Report*'). In November 2011, a similar series of reports was published by the National Board for Safeguarding Children in the Catholic Church (NBSCCC): <http://www.irishtimes.com/newspaper/breaking/2011/1130/breaking32.html> accessed 2 July 2012.

8   *Murphy Report* (n 6) 1.15; *Ferns Report* (n 6) 250-51.

9   A set of new procedures, the so-called 'Framework Document' (*Child Sexual Abuse: Framework for a Church Response*) was put in place by the Irish Bishops' Conference in 1996. See *Ferns Report* (n 6) 251-52; *Murphy Report* (n 6) 1.16; *Cloyne Report* (n 6) 1.16.

10   *Murphy Report* (n 6) 1.16.

11   See in particular *Cloyne Report* (n 6) 1.17, 1.18, 1.21.

12   These were set up under the Industrial Schools (Ireland) Act of 1868 to take care of 'neglected, abandoned and orphaned' children, and at their peak contained over 5,000 inmates. Conditions in the Industrial Schools came under scrutiny in the RTE documentary 'States of Fear', first broadcast in 1999; see also James M Smith, 'Remembering Ireland's Architecture of Containment: "Telling" Stories in The Butcher Boy and States of Fear' (2001) 36 Eire-Ireland: A Journal of Irish Studies <http://findarticles.com/p/articles/mi_m0FKX/is_2001_Fall-Winter/ai_83447251/?tag=content;col1> accessed 2 July 2012.

13   These were institutions for 'fallen women' set up in the nineteenth century. Originally Protestant in origin, most of them in Ireland were taken over by orders of Sisters. The issue of the Magdalen Laundries burst into the public eye in 1993 when over 150 dead bodies were discovered in the grounds of an old convent. This was followed up by various TV documentaries, including the 1997 Channel 4 documentary 'Sex in a Cold Climate' and the 1999 RTE documentary 'States of Fear'; see generally James M Smith, *Ireland's Magdalen Laundries and the Nation's Architecture of Containment* (University of Notre Dame Press 2007).

14   *Report of the Commission to Inquire into Child Abuse* (Stationery Office 2009) ('*Ryan Report*'). Provisions have recently been made for a similar inquiry in Northern Ireland, in the shape of the Inquiry into Historical Institutional Abuse Bill (NIA Bill 7/11-15), introduced into the Assembly on 12 June 2012; see note at [2012] 5 BNIL 62.

15   *Ryan Report*, Executive Summary, Conclusion 1.

16   Ibid. Conclusion [18].

17   Ibid. Conclusion [19].

18   Ibid. Conclusion [20].

abuse,[19] would transfer the offender to another location where he was free to abuse again.[20] All of this led to an angry reaction from commentators. One described the conditions for children held in church institutions for much of the twentieth century as 'the stuff of nightmares';[21] another called it 'the map of an Irish hell'.[22] Another even accused the church authorities of having effectively turned the island of Ireland into a concentration camp in which everything was controlled by the Church; it was not so much a scandal as a complete culture.[23]

One of the key issues for victims was the lack of criminal prosecutions against those responsible, including not only the actual perpetrators but also those in authority who had failed to act against them. In the words of one commentator: 'It is time that some of the priests who saw no evil in these evil men themselves feel the application of the law. Covering up paedophilia, transferring a notorious child rapist from parish to parish, denying access to Irish police to records, are surely crimes worth prosecuting'.[24]

The aim of this chapter is to explore this suggestion further. We have already seen how Monsignor William Lynn was convicted in Philadelphia for his neglect in dealing with child abuse in the diocese. To what extent might similar sanctions apply in the Irish context? We shall begin by looking at the present legal framework before considering the desirability of criminal prosecutions in this sort of case.

The Legal Framework

There are two possibilities here, one being the liability of individual persons in authority, and the other the liability of the church authorities as a body.

Individual Liability

There are four ways in which an individual person in authority might be liable for crimes of this nature, these being: (1) as an accomplice to the main crime; (2) for assisting an offender; (3) for concealment; and (4) other possible heads of liability.

Accomplice Liability

The general law here is the same throughout Ireland, namely that one who aids, abets, counsels or procures the commission of an offence is liable to be tried, convicted and punished as a principal

---

19   Ibid. Conclusion [21].

20   Ibid. Conclusion [22].

21   Madeline Bunting, 'An Abuse too Far by the Catholic Church' (*The Guardian*, 21 May 2009) <http://www.guardian.co.uk/commentisfree/belief/2009/may/21/catholic-abuse-ireland-ryan> accessed 14 June 2012.

22   'Ryan Report Commission to Inquire into Child Abuse' (*Dialogue Ireland*, 26 November 2009) <http://dialogueireland.wordpress.com/2009/11/26/ryan-report-commission-to-inquire-into-child-abuse/> accessed 14 June 2012.

23   Dom Mark Hederman OSB as quoted in Russell Shorto, 'The Irish Affliction' (*New York Times*, 9 February 2011) <http://www.nytimes.com/2011/02/13/magazine/13Irish-t.html?pagewanted=1&hpw> accessed 13 June 2012.

24   'Time to Prosecute Abuse Cover-ups in the Catholic Church' (*IrishCentral.com*, 23 December 2010) <http://www.irishcentral.com/news/Time-to-prosecute-abuse-cover-ups-in-the-Catholic-Church-112370014. html#ixzz1xmgyEfCH> accessed 14 June 2012.

offender.[25] The requirements for this are: (1) the commission of the main offence by the perpetrator ('P'); (2) D (the defendant) must have aided, abetted, counselled or procured the commission of that offence; (3) D must have had an intention to aid and abet; and (4) D must have known the type of crime that P was going to commit. There is also the problem of coincidence.

Commission of Main Offence

Since secondary liability is by its very nature derivative,[26] D cannot be convicted as an accomplice to an offence without proof that it has been committed,[27] at least by someone.[28] In some cases of this sort it is clear that P was given access to children by D, and that P then committed various offences in that capacity and was convicted of them.[29] However, in many other cases there was no record of a conviction against P;[30] indeed, sometimes there was no evidence of any crime at all having been committed by P in the wake of D's impugned conduct.[31]

Aiding, Abetting, Counselling or Procuring

Assuming that the principal crime can be proved, it will then have to be shown that D did something to assist or encourage it.[32] This is known as 'aiding, abetting, counselling or procuring', though it is not necessary to specify which of these D did provided that it can be shown that D did at least one of them.[33] Most cases of the sort we are discussing would have involved aiding, in that D facilitated P's criminal conduct by putting P in a position where P had easy access to children, either in a parish or in an institutional setting. In some cases this involved a positive action on D's part, as where P was appointed to a position of responsibility in full knowledge of P's proclivities.[34] In

---

25   Criminal Law Act 1997, s 7(1) (Republic of Ireland); Accessories and Abettors Act 1861, s 8 (Northern Ireland).

26   Barry McAuley and Paul McCutcheon, *Criminal Liability: A Grammar* (Round Hall, Sweet & Maxwell 2000) 490; *Vaux* (1591) Co Rep 44a, 44b.

27   *Morris v Tolman* [1923] 1 KB 166; *Thornton v Mitchell* [1940] 1 All ER 339. Apparent exceptions to this, as in *Bourne* (1952) 36 Cr App R 125 and *Cogan and Leak* [1976] QB 217, are best explained on the ground that the main perpetrator was protected by an excusatory defence which was personal to him or her; see *Taylor* [1983] Crim LR 656.

28   There is no need to prove that the perpetrator was *convicted*; indeed, it may not be possible in some cases to identify who the perpetrator was in the first place.

29   As in the case of Fr Donal Collins, *Ferns Report* (n 6) 124-34.

30   As in the cases of Br 'Adrien', *Ryan Report* (n 6) 7.405-7.432; Fr Sean Fortune, *Ferns Report* (n 6) 153-73; Fr Noel Reynolds, *Cloyne Report* (n 6) chapter 35. Names in quotation marks indicate pseudonyms. This of course does not prevent D being held liable, but it is certainly more difficult for D to be prosecuted in such cases.

31   As in the cases of Fr 'Cicero', *Murphy Report* (n 6) chapter 30; Br 'Gaillard', *Ryan Report* (n 6) 7.378-7.382; Fr 'Omega', *Ferns Report* (n 6) 204-205; Fr 'Tyrus', *Murphy Report* (n 6) chapter 18.

32   Andrew Simester, John Spencer, Bob Sullivan and Graham Virgo, *Simester and Sullivan's Criminal Law: Theory and Doctrine* (4th edn, Hart 2010) 7.4. David Ormerod, *Smith and Hogan: Criminal Law* (13th edn, Oxford University Press 2011) 8.4.1.1.

33   *Ferguson v Weaving* [1951] KB 814.

34   As in the cases of Br 'Perryn', *Ryan Report* (n 6) 8.69-8.74 and 8.292-8.304; Br 'Maslin', *Ryan Report* (n 6) 8.79-8.90; 'John Brander', *Ryan Report* (n 6) chapter 14; Fr Donal Gallagher, *Murphy Report* (n 6) chapter 22; Fr 'Sergius', *Cloyne Report* (n 6) chapter 42. In the case of Br 'Herve', *Ryan Report* (n 6)

other cases there was an omission by D to take appropriate action to prevent P's activities despite having a clear power to do so.[35]

Intention to Aid and Abet

Another key requirement of secondary liability is an 'intention to aid and abet'.[36] At first sight this might seem to rule out liability in this type of case; given the strict rules of Canon Law on the subject,[37] it would hardly have been the *intention* of the church authorities to assist the perpetrator in the commission of conduct of this kind. However, there is no requirement of *direct* intent in this context, in the sense that it was D's desire or purpose that the offence be committed;[38] D may indeed have been horrified at the prospect.[39] Rather, it is enough that D knew that P would be assisted.[40] This requirement relates to D's own conduct rather than to that of P;[41] there is no need to show that D realised that P was definitely going to commit the crime in question. This is an important point to which we must now turn.

Knowledge of Type of Crime

In some of the earlier cases the church authorities do not seem to have appreciated the recidivist nature of child abuse;[42] those responsible would often be removed from the scene on a temporary basis or reassigned elsewhere in the hope that they had now 'learned their lesson' and would not misbehave again.[43] To what extent would this be a defence in cases of this sort? Though the law is traditionally said to require knowledge of the essential elements of the principal offence,[44] this does not require proof of knowledge that that offence would definitely be committed; it is sufficient if D

7.329-7.350, the conclusion was that 'sending a Brother with this history to a residential school for boys was reckless and dangerous, and showed a disregard for the safety of children in care' (7.350).

35   As in the cases of Br 'Percival', *Ryan Report* (n 6) 8.91-8.104; 'Mr Russel', *Ryan Report* (n 6), 8.282-8.291; Fr James McNamee, *Murphy Report* (n 6) chapter 12; Fr 'Ronat', *Cloyne Report* (n 6) chapter 9. The essence of liability here seems to be not D's duty to the victims as such (which would make D liable as perpetrator, not merely as an accomplice), but the fact that D has the ability to make P refrain from the relevant conduct: Simester et al. (n 31) 216; *Du Cros v Lambourne* [1907] 1 KB 40; *Webster* [2006] EWCA Crim 415, [2006] 2 Cr App R 6. In cases such as the present this would arise from P's duty of obedience to his ecclesiastical superiors, either under the Canon Law or under the rules of his religious order.

36   Ian H Dennis, 'The Mental Element for Accessories' in Peter Smith (ed.), *Criminal Law: Essays in Honour of J C Smith* (Butterworths 1987) 44-55, Simester et al. (n 31) 220-26; Ormerod (n 31) 8.4.2.1.

37   This is discussed in chapter 4 of the *Murphy Report* (n 6).

38   Ormerod (n 31); Simester et al. (n 31) 220.

39   As in *DPP for Northern Ireland v Lynch* [1975] AC 653 at 678 (Lord Morris).

40   *National Coal Board v Gamble* [1959] 1 QB 11; *Cafferata v Wilson* [1936] 3 All ER 149; *Bryce* [2004] EWCA Crim 1231, [2004] 2 Cr App R 35. Perhaps it might be better to say, in line with *Woollin* [1999] AC 62 that the jury or magistrates are entitled to find intent in these cases but are not bound to do so; this would take care of cases such as *Gillick v West Norfolk and Wisbech Area Health Authority* [1986] AC 112, which seem to suggest a requirement of direct intent. See further Dennis (n 35).

41   Simester et al. (n 31).

42   *Murphy Report* (n 6) 7.312. See further below at (nn 106-109) and accompanying text.

43   As in the cases of Fr Donal Collins, *Ferns Report* (n 6) 124-34; Fr 'Corin', *Cloyne Report* (n 6) chapter 10; Fr Donal Gallagher, *Murphy Report* (n 6) chapter 22; Fr 'Ioannes', *Murphy Report* (n 6) chapter 17; Fr 'Iota', *Ferns Report* (n 6) 196-98; Fr James McNamee, *Murphy Report* (n 6) chapter 12.

44   *Johnson v Youden* [1950] 1 KB 544; Ormerod (n 31) 8.4.2.2.

foresees it as a possibility[45] or wilfully turns a blind eye to it.[46] Nor need it be shown that D knew of the exact crime that P was likely to commit; it is enough if a crime of that type is proved to have been within D's contemplation at the relevant time.[47] The test in cases of this sort would seem to be basically one of recklessness; D must have been aware of the risk, and the risk must be one which it was unreasonable to take in the circumstances known to D.[48]

The Problem of Coincidence

However, the biggest obstacle to a conviction in the present context is what might be called the problem of coincidence, that is to say the need to prove all the different elements outlined above in relation to *the same person*.[49] This will not be easy in cases of this type. Indeed, a theme that recurs over and over again in the reports is the lack of proper communication between the various different persons involved, be they heads of institutions and their successors,[50] religious orders and the secular clergy,[51] priors of religious houses and their overall superiors,[52] parish priests and bishops,[53] assistant bishops and the bishop in charge of the diocese,[54] or the bishops of different dioceses.[55] As in other contexts, this difficulty in bringing individuals within a large organisation to book gives rise to the question of corporate liability, to which we shall shortly turn.[56]

---

45   *Carter v Richardson* [1974] RTR 314; *Webster* [2006] EWCA Crim 415, [2006] RTR 19; Simester et al. (n 31) 226-27; Ormerod (n 31).

46   *Antonelli* (1905) 70 JP 4; Simester et al. (n 31) 226.

47   *Bainbridge* [1960] 1 KB 129; *DPP for NI v Maxwell* [1978] 1 WLR 1350. Authorities from the Republic on this issue are *People (DPP) v Madden* [1977] IR 336 and *People (DPP) v Egan* [1989] IR 681. Irish law requires knowledge of a 'crime of a similar nature' which seems to be without substantive difference to knowledge of the 'type of crime' required in *Maxwell*. In theory this could give rise to an enormous range of liability in cases of this sort, as with Br 'Perryn' (n 33) where P, who was known to the authorities for his brutality, was allowed to take up a post in a residential institution for boys and then embarked on what was described as a 'reign of terror' lasting for some 14 years. Fr Sean Fortune (n 29) and Fr James Doyle (below, n 49) both came to the attention of the authorities whilst still at the seminary, but were allowed to go forward for ordination and then abused children for most of their careers.

48   Ormerod (n 31) 8.3.3.2; *G* [2003] UKHL 50, [2004] 1 AC 1034 at [41] (Lord Bingham).

49   Hence the claim made by the Christian Brothers to the Ryan Commission that though in many cases members of the order had been transferred to residential institutions despite prior allegations of sexual abuse, there was no proof that the files had been consulted at the relevant time: *Ryan Report* (n 6) 8.450. Compare the cases of Fr 'Benito', *Murphy Report* (n 6) chapter 48; Br 'Leandre', *Ryan Report* (n 6) 8.305-8.309; Fr Patrick Maguire, *Murphy Report* (n 6) chapter 16.

50   As in the case of Fr James Doyle, *Ferns Report* (n 6) 134-40.

51   As in the cases of Fr Boland OFM, *Murphy Report* (n 6) chapter 32; Fr Donal Gallagher, *Murphy Report* (n 6) chapter 22; Fr 'Klaudius', *Murphy Report* (n 6) chapter 40; and Fr 'Terentius', *Murphy Report* (n 6) chapter 37.

52   As in the case of Br 'Perryn', *Ryan Report* (n 6) 8.302.

53   . As in the cases of Fr Carney, *Murphy Report* (n 6) chapter 28; and Fr 'Sergius', *Murphy Report* (n 6) chapter 42.

54   As in the cases of Fr Ivan Payne, *Murphy Report* (n 6) chapter 24; and Fr 'Septimus', *Murphy Report* (n 6) chapter 27.

55   As in the case of Fr Sean Fortune, *Ferns Report* (n 6) 153-73.

56   See text accompanying (nn 97-108).

Assisting an Offender

The second possibility is that D may be liable for assisting an offender – what used to be called being an accessory after the fact. In both Irish jurisdictions,[57] this requires proof: (1) that an offence of the appropriate type[58] has been committed by P, (2) knowledge or belief by P that D is guilty of that offence or some other offence of that type, and (3) that D has without lawful excuse done something with intent to impede the apprehension or prosecution of P. There appear to have been at least some cases where the church authorities have come close to this,[59] but there are no less than six problems in establishing liability in this kind of case.

First of all, it has to be shown that the offence in question has been committed, and committed by P.[60] We have already discussed this.[61]

Second, D must have known or at the very least believed that P was guilty of the offence.[62] Wilful blindness is not enough, though it can be evidence to support a finding of knowledge or belief.[63]

Third, there must be some act done by D.[64] It seems that any act will do,[65] though it has been said that bringing persuasion to bear is not enough.[66] However, D must have done *something*; a mere omission will not do.[67] This is an important limitation in the present context. In particular, failing to report P to the police or other authorities is not enough, though this may give rise to liability on another ground.

Fourth, the act must be done with the necessary ulterior intent, that is to impede the apprehension or prosecution of the perpetrator.[68] This is said to denote direct intent, in the sense that it was D's aim or purpose to do this.[69] Again, this is an important limitation. Under the old law, a person could not be an accessory after the fact merely on the basis of knowledge that his or her acts *might* be of assistance,[70] and there is no indication that the drafters of the statutory offence meant to change the position in this regard.[71]

---

57   Criminal Law Act 1997, s 7(2) (Republic of Ireland). Criminal Law Act (NI) 1967, s 4(1) (Northern Ireland).

58   That is to say, an 'arrestable' offence in the Irish Republic, and a 'relevant' offence in Northern Ireland.

59   As in the cases of Br 'Ricard', *Ryan Report* (n 6) 7.392; Fr Carney, *Murphy Report* (n 6) 28.87; and Fr '—', *Murphy Report* (n 6) 20.154 (the name is blanked out in the report). In other cases – for instance that of Fr 'Klaudius', *Murphy Report* (n 6) 40.34 – no evidence of obstruction could be found.

60   Ormerod (n 31) 9.1.1.1.

61   See text accompanying (nn 25-30).

62   Ormerod (n 31) 9.1.2.1.

63   Ibid.; *Sherif* [2008] EWCA Crim 2653, [2009] Cr App R (S) 33 at [27].

64   Ormerod (n 31) 9.1.1.2.

65   Ibid. Certainly sending P out of the jurisdiction, as in the cases of Br 'Ricard' and Fr '—' (n 58) would be enough.

66   As in the case of Fr Carney (n 52); Criminal Law Revision Committee, *Seventh Report, Felonies and Misdemeanours* (Cmnd 2659), para 28; Ormerod (n 31).

67   Ormerod (n 31) 9.1.1.2.

68   Ibid. 9.1.2.4.

69   Ibid.

70   *Jones* [1949] 1 KB 194; *Andrews and Craig* [1962] 3 All ER 961; John Smith and Brian Hogan, *Criminal Law* (Butterworths 1965) 86.

71   Cmnd 2659 (n 65) 30. But if D knew for certain that his or her actions would have this effect, it might be possible to find intent under the principle in *Woollin* [1999] AC 82.

Fifth, D must have had no lawful excuse or authority for the actions in question.[72] No guidance is given in the legislation as to what amounts to a lawful excuse in this context, but it is clear that there are some situations where it would be proper for actions of this sort to be taken at least by the victim of the offence,[73] if not by others.[74]

Finally, we have once again the problem of trying to find a single individual on whom to pin liability. We have already discussed the difficulties to which this may give rise,[75] and there is no need to repeat them here.

Concealment

Mere failure to report a crime to the police cannot amount to assisting an offender, but in the case of a felony it could amount to the old common law misdemeanour of 'misprision'. This was abolished in the Republic of Ireland in 1997, and in 1967 in the case of Northern Ireland, but such conduct can still amount to an offence in both jurisdictions. In the Republic, concealment is only an offence where done for reward,[76] but north of the border no such restriction applies. For D to be convicted of 'withholding information', as it is often called, it must be shown: (1) that a relevant offence has been committed; (2) that D knows or believes: (a) that the offence or some other relevant offence has been committed; and (b) that he or she has information which is likely to secure, or to be of material assistance in securing, the apprehension, prosecution or conviction of any person for that offence; and (3) that D has failed without reasonable excuse to give that information to a constable within a reasonable time.[77] Only the more serious offences are covered,[78] but even so the offence is extremely wide in its potential ambit.[79] Nor is it by any means a dead letter; on the contrary, it often crops up in the courts.[80] So what is there to prevent bishops and others in authority being convicted of withholding information in this sort of case? Once again there are a number of issues which might give rise to difficulty.

The first is the need to show that a relevant offence has actually been committed. This we have already discussed.[81]

The second is the requirement that D must either know or believe that he or she has information which might be of assistance. What is required is information; mere rumour or gossip will not do.[82]

Thirdly, D must have no reasonable excuse for the failure to disclose. It is unclear what would amount to a reasonable excuse in the present context, but it was held by the Northern Ireland Court

---

72   Ormerod (n 31) 9.1.2.5.

73   Cmnd 2659 (n 65) 28.

74   Andrew Ashworth, 'Prosecution, Police and Public: A Guide to Good Gatekeeping' (1984) 23 Howard Journal of Criminal Justice 65.

75   See text accompanying (nn 48-55).

76   Criminal Law Act 1997, s 8(2).

77   Criminal Law Act (NI) 1967, s 5(1).

78   The provision only applies to 'relevant' offences, that is to say those which carry a sentence of five years' imprisonment or more in the case of an adult: Criminal Law Act (NI) 1967, s 4(1A).

79   To adapt an example given by Glanville Williams, it could in theory cover someone who fails to report their ten-year-old child to the police for raiding the larder: *Criminal Law: The General Part* (Stevens 1961) para 141.

80   See for instance *Hill and Ors* [2005] NICC 8, [2008] 5 BNIL 73; *McHugh and Hilditch* [2009] NICC 42, [2009] 8 BNIL 77; *Kernohan and Ors* [2011] NICC 19, [2011] 4 BNIL 73.

81   See text accompanying (nn 25-30).

82   *Sykes v DPP* [1962] AC 528, 569 (Lord Goddard).

of Appeal in *McLean* that the phrase plainly admitted of excuses not otherwise recognised by law.[83] Reference may also be made to *DPP v Sykes*,[84] the leading authority on the old law of misprision, where Lord Denning set out a number of situations where in his opinion withholding information would not amount to an offence, including doctor and patient, solicitor and client, and clergyman and parishioner.[85]

Despite these possible restrictions, bishops and others might well have been liable for this offence in some of the cases we have been discussing,[86] though no prosecutions were ever brought.[87]

Other Possibilities

Though our focus is on the law of secondary liability, there are other ways in which a person in authority might be held liable in cases of this sort. These include the imposition of direct liability for harm in cases involving death[88] or serious injury,[89] child neglect,[90] obstructing the police[91] and (at least as far as Northern Ireland is concerned) liability under the Serious Crime Act 2007.[92] However, there are problems associated with all these approaches,[93] and for that reason it was recommended that an offence of 'reckless endangerment' be introduced into Irish law so

---

83   [1992] NI 68 at 72 (Kelly LJ).

84   [1962] AC 528.

85   Ibid. at 564. It was said by Smith and Hogan (n 69) that there was no authority for this list (541), but *some* limitation there must be; as the Criminal Law Commissioners said as long ago as 1840, the law cannot compel everyone to be an accuser, and it may sometimes be more convenient that offences should be passed over than that all should be made indiscriminately the subject of prosecution: 5th Report (1840) *Parliamentary Papers*, vol. xx, 36, as cited by Glanville Williams (n 78) 141.

86   As in the cases of Fr Sean Fortune and Fr Brendan Smyth (n 5), both of whom served in Northern Ireland.

87   According to the *Irish News* ('Cardinal Had "Meaningful Conversation" with PSNI', Saturday 23 June 2012), the police interviewed Cardinal Sean Brady, formerly Archbishop of Armagh, in connection with his failure to disclose the crimes committed by Fr Brendan Smyth (above, n 5). The Cardinal had admitted being present, albeit in a junior capacity, at a meeting in 1975 in which an oath of secrecy was administered to certain victims of Fr Smyth. At the end of the day it was decided that there could be no prosecution under section 5(1), as the relevant abuse had not taken place in Northern Ireland.

88   The reports make no findings as to how often this happened, but one witness claimed that out of his class of 39, no less than 17 had committed suicide: *Ryan Report* (n 6) 11.77.

89   See (n 6). This, of course, can include psychiatric injury: *Ireland: Burstow* [1998] AC 147. According to Volume 2 of the *Ryan Report*, effects reported by victims included suicide attempts, depression, nightmares, alcohol abuse and poor social functioning: see Tables 53 (industrial schools and reformatories), 65 (special needs schools and residential services), 84 (children's homes), 98 (hospitals), 111 (ordinary schools) and 120 (laundries, novitiates and other institutions). See also *Ferns Report* (n 6) 259-60; *Murphy Report* (n 6) 58.5-58.7; *Cloyne Report* (n 6) 27.7-27.22.

90   Children Act 2001, s 246(1) (Republic of Ireland), Children and Young Persons Act (NI) 1968, s 20(1) as amended by paragraph 18(a) of Schedule 9 of the Children (NI) Order 1995 (Northern Ireland).

91   Criminal Justice (Public Order) Act 1994, s 19(3) (Republic of Ireland), Police (NI) Act 1998, s 66 (Northern Ireland).

92   Serious Crime Act 2007, ss 44, 45 and 46.

93   In the first two cases (direct liability and child neglect) the main problem is showing a causal link between the defendant's conduct and the harm suffered, given the general rule that the chain of causation is broken by the voluntary acts of a third party: *Kennedy (No 2)* [2007] UKHL 38, [2008] 1 AC 269. A mere failure to report a crime could hardly amount to obstructing the police in the light of *Rice v Connolly* [1966] 2 QB 414, and the inchoate offences under sections 44 to 46 of the Serious Crime Act 2007 require either a

as to cover offences of this sort.[94] The result was section 176 of the Criminal Justice Act 2006, which makes it an offence for a person who has authority or control over a child or an abuser[95] to intentionally or recklessly endanger the child by causing him or her to be left in a situation which creates a substantial risk to the child of being a victim of serious harm or sexual abuse, or to fail to take reasonable steps to protect a child from such a risk while knowing that the child is in such a situation. Clearly this provision came too late to be of any use in many of the cases we have been describing,[96] but would be of great significance if such facts were to recur in the future.[97]

Corporate Liability

One problem with the lack of communication between different officials in a diocese or religious order is that it is not possible to identify a particular individual who is to blame.[98] The obvious answer to this problem is some form of corporate liability, whereby the diocese or order in question is prosecuted as a whole. As the law stands there is no problem imposing liability *in tort* on the church authorities in this sort of case,[99] but the question of *criminal* liability is a lot more tricky. Celia Wells identifies two main 'models of attribution' used in this context, the 'extensive vicarious' model and the 'restrictive identification' model.[100] Under the first model the organisation is liable for all its staff, but this approach is generally confined to regulatory offences,[101] and has in any event been held not to apply to secondary liability.[102] The second, which certainly applies in Northern Ireland at any rate,[103] covers all offences, and makes use of the doctrine of 'identification', whereby the state of mind of a person involved in the management of the organisation is attributed to the organisation as a whole. For this to happen, however, the person concerned must generally be senior enough to be regarded as the 'directing mind' of the organisation.[104] No doubt this might apply to the bishop of a diocese or

---

direct intent to encourage the commission of the relevant offence or knowledge or belief that it will (not may) be committed: see ss 44(2), 45(b)(i) and 46(1)(b)(i).

94   See (n 6). *Ferns Report* (n 6) Recommendation 14, 266.

95   Defined in section 176(1) as 'an individual believed by a person who has authority or control over that individual to have seriously harmed or sexually abused a child or more than one child'.

96   See (n 6). According to the *Cloyne Report* (n 6) 21.97 a complaint was brought under the Act against Bishop John Magee, who was in post from 1987 to 2009, but it was thrown out on the grounds that the abuse in question may all have taken place before the Act came into force.

97   See Laura Russell, 'Pursuing Criminal Liability for the Church and Its Decision Makers for Their Role in Priest Sexual Abuse' (2003) 81 Washington University Law Quarterly 885, 902-904.

98   See (nn 48-55) and accompanying text.

99   *Maga v Birmingham Roman Catholic Archdiocese Trustees* [2010] EWCA Civ 256, [2010] 1 WLR 1441; *E v English Province of Our Lady of Charity* [2011] EWHC 2871, [2012] 2 WLR 709; *JGE v Trustees of the Portsmouth Roman Catholic Diocesan Trust* [2012] EWCA Civ 938, [2012] PIQR P19.

100   Celia Wells, *Corporations and Criminal Responsibility* (2nd edn, Oxford University Press 2001) 101.

101   Simester et al. (n 31) 279.

102   *Ferguson v Weaving* [1951] 1 KB 814 at 194 (Lord Goddard CJ); *John Henshall (Quarries) Ltd v Harvey* [1965] 2 QB 233. At first sight *National Coal Board v Gamble* [1959] 1 QB 11 seems to go against this, but the point was deliberately not taken by the defence in that case; [1959] 1 QB at 25 (Devlin J).

103   In the Republic of Ireland the doctrine has not been applied to date in a criminal context, although it has been applied in a civil context: see Liz Campbell, Shane Kilcommins and Catherine O'Sullivan, *Criminal Law in Ireland; Cases and Commentary* (Clarus Press 2010) 188.

104   *Tesco Supermarkets Ltd v Nattrass* [1972] AC 153. A wider approach to the question was suggested by the Privy Council in *Meridian Global Funds Management Asia Ltd v Securities Commission* [1995] 2 AC

to the head of a religious order, but this rather defeats the whole point of invoking corporate liability in the first place, which is to get round the difficulty in allocating blame to a particular individual.[105] Certainly there are ways the law could and perhaps should be changed so as to escape this impasse,[106] but these are beyond the scope of the present chapter.

Why Prosecute?

All of this goes to show that obtaining a conviction in this sort of case is not as straightforward as it may seem. However, given that it is certainly not impossible, we need to ask whether and to what extent it is worth trying to do so. Various reasons can be given for the neglect of the church authorities in these cases, including the fear of false accusations,[107] the sense of loyalty to brother priests and religious,[108] and the feeling that such matters should be dealt with internally by the Church rather than left in the hands of the secular authorities.[109] However, the most striking factor in the equation is undoubtedly the historic attitude of the Church to accusations of child abuse. This has been recognised as a major problem since early times,[110] but until recently the focus was essentially on the punishment of the perpetrator rather than the protection of the victim;[111] hence the historic importance of 'due process' in Canon Law and the reluctance to impose sanctions save in the clearest of cases. In sum, the problem was not that the Church did not take child abuse seriously, but that it took it seriously in the wrong way.

One of the problems in punishing secondary liability is that it makes someone liable for a crime which he or she did not commit.[112] There are several justifications put forward for this. One is that offences involving more than one person are particularly serious;[113] this rationale applies well to cases

---

500, but it has been said that this relates very much to the statutory context of the relevant offence, and would in any event be unlikely to be applied to offences involving serious moral obloquy: Simester et al. (n 31) 279.

105   Hence the comment of James Gobert that the theory works best in cases where it is needed least and works least in cases where it is needed most: 'Corporate Criminality: Four Models of Fault' (1994) 14 Legal Studies 393, 401, quoted by Wells (n 99) 100.

106   Simester et al. (n 31) 279-83; Wells (n 99) ch 8.

107   Or, indeed, of true ones; according to the *Catholic Encyclopedia* the sin of 'detraction' involves the unjust damaging of another's good name by the revelation of some fault or crime even if the other is really guilty or at any rate is seriously believed to be guilty by the defamer; see <http://www.newadvent.org/cathen/04757a.htm> accessed 10 January 2013.

108   As in the *Ryan Report* (n 6) 8.412. The tendency of members of a group to modify their values, conduct and even perceptions in accordance with the norms and attitudes of that group is a sociological commonplace: see Solomon Asch, 'Effects of Group Pressure upon the Modification and Distortion of Judgments' in Harold S Guetzkow (ed.), *Groups, Leadership and Men* (Carnegie Press 1951) 177-90; Fred Luthans, *Organisational Behavior* (McGraw-Hill 1985); Rodney W Napier and Matti K Gershenfeld, *Groups: Theory and Experience* (6th edn, Houghton Mifflin 1999) ch 3; David O Moberg, *The Church as a Social Institution* (Prentice-Hall 1962).

109   This attitude goes back to New Testament times: see 1 Corinthians 6:1-6. The Apostolic Letter *Sacramentorum Sanctitas Tutela*, issued *motu proprio* by Pope John Paul II in 2001, reserves cases involving the sexual conduct of priests with minors to the Congregation for the Doctrine of the Faith, but it has been stressed since that this does not purport to replace the ordinary jurisdiction of the secular courts.

110   *Cloyne Report* (n 6) 1.18.

111   *Ferns Report* (n 6) 11-17.

112   Simester et al. (n 31) 204.

113   Andrew Ashworth, *Principles of Criminal Law* (6th edn, Oxford University Press 2009) 403.

involving joint perpetrators, and to cases falling under the 'joint enterprise' rule, but is less convincing in relation to other accomplices, whose contribution may have been more marginal. Another is that by his or her actions the accomplice 'joins in' the criminal enterprise or 'associates' himself or herself with the perpetrator in pursuing it;[114] this applies well to the accomplice who deliberately sets out with the purpose of lending assistance to the enterprise, but less well to the one who is basically indifferent as to its success.[115] Another is that the accomplice is responsible for causing the crime to take place;[116] this applies well in cases of procuring,[117] but less so in cases where it cannot be shown that the crime would not have taken place anyway without his or her contribution.[118] Clearly there are a variety of rationales at work here, some of which are more appropriate to one case and some to another. In cases of the sort we have been dealing with, the conduct of the church authorities will at least have *facilitated* the commission of the crime, or even actually caused it, in the sense that it would not have taken place had the perpetrator not been put in that position.

This being so, what punitive rationales would be served by mounting a prosecution in these cases? Clearly some punishment would be justified here on the basis of retribution or just desert,[119] bearing in mind such matters as the extent of the harm done, the role played by the authorities in that harm, and their culpability in allowing it to occur.[120] Another relevant rationale would be deterrence,[121] the aim being to try and ensure that the authorities took the problem more seriously in the future.[122] More importantly, conviction and punishment in cases of this sort can act, in the words of Lord Denning, as 'the emphatic denunciation by the community of a crime',[123] so providing

114   McAuley and McCutcheon (n 25) 456.

115   See text accompanying (nn 35-40).

116   FB Sayre, 'Criminal Responsibility for the Acts of Another' (1930) 43 Harvard Law Review 689; Keith Smith, *A Modern Treatise on the Law of Criminal Complicity* (Oxford University Press, 1991); Michael Moore, *Causation and Responsibility: An Essay in Law, Morals and Metaphysics* (Oxford University Press 2009); Simester et al. (n 31) 260-62.

117   Though even here there is a problem with the general principle that the voluntary acts of a third party break the chain of causation; see (n 92).

118   McAuley and McCutcheon (n 25) 456. In this connection George Fletcher refers to a 'problematic causal link' between D's conduct and the resulting harm: *Rethinking Criminal Law* (Little, Brown & Co 1978) 582.

119   Andrew Ashworth, *Sentencing and Criminal Justice* (4th edn, Cambridge University Press 2005) 3.3.5.

120   Ibid. 4.3; Andrew von Hirsch and Andrew Ashworth, *Proportionate Sentencing* (Oxford University Press 2005) Appendix 3. Obviously these factors could pull in different directions. Thus the harm involved in these cases is very high indeed, given the number of victims involved and the time over which it took place, but the authorities were not directly responsible for causing it and their state of mind with regard to its occurrence was negligent or at best reckless rather than intentional. If some form of corporate liability could be established, a far greater penalty would be justified than in the case of a particular individual, but devising the form that penalty ought to take would not be so easy; see Wells (n 99) 31-39.

121   Ashworth (n 119) 3.3.2. Given that the actual bishops or superiors involved would be unlikely to be in a position to offend again in cases of this sort, we would be talking about general deterrence here, at least in relation to individual liability.

122   One standard objection to theories of deterrence, namely that many crimes are committed on impulse, would not apply to bishops or superiors in this sort of case, though it might apply to the actual perpetrators. Similarly, given that bishops or superiors, and indeed church bodies as a whole, will generally have a lot more to lose than the normal run of offenders, deterrence is more likely to work in this sort of case; see generally Wells (n 99) 18-20.

123   Evidence given to the Home Office, *Report of the Royal Commission on Capital Punishment* (Cmnd 8932, 1953) 53, cited in Michael Cavadino and James Dignan, *The Penal System: An Introduction* (4th edn,

some degree of closure to the victims,[124] and also reinforcing the collective conscience of society by marking out the actions of the offender as wrong.[125] Thus for Anthony Duff state punishment can be seen in terms of *censure* (communicating to the offender the error of his or her actions), and *penance* (forcing the offender to confront the fact of his or her wrongdoing and to mend his or her ways).[126] The significance of this in the present context can hardly be missed.[127]

There are of course dangers in pursuing prosecutions of this sort, especially when directed against individuals as opposed to church institutions as a whole. One is the temptation to use individual defendants as scapegoats,[128] so that they have to bear the blame not only for their own misdeeds but for those of others who may be equally culpable, if not more so.[129] Another is the process of demonisation, whereby the complex problem of child abuse is seen in terms of the 'pervert priest' and the wider context is totally ignored.[130] Incidents such as the Kincora scandal in Northern Ireland[131] and similar scandals surrounding children's homes on the British mainland,[132]

Sage 2007) 46-47.

124   Thus Nicola Lacey speaks of the need to appease and satisfy what she terms the 'grievance-desires' of victims, not only so as to reduce their suffering and to forestall self-help, but also to demonstrate that the community takes seriously the harm done to the victim and takes upon itself the responsibility for upholding the standards breached, which it hopes to vindicate through the process of conviction and punishment: *State Punishment* (Routledge 1988) 184. In the same way, the rights guaranteed under ECHR Article 2 (right to life) and Article 3 (freedom from torture and inhuman and degrading treatment) impose a positive obligation on the state to protect those rights, if necessary by the imposition of criminal sanctions: see *LCB v UK* 23413/94 (1998) 27 EHRR 212 (Article 2); *Öneryildiz v Turkey* (48939/99) (2005) 41 EHRR 38; *MC v Bulgaria* (39272/98) (2005) 40 EHRR 20 (Article 3); Joanne Conaghan, 'Extending the Reach of Human Rights to Encompass Victims of Rape' (2005) 13 Feminist Legal Studies 145.

125   Émile Durkheim, *The Division of Labour in Society* (Free Press 1960) ch 2, cited by Cavadino and Dignan (n 122).

126   'Desert and Penance' in Andrew von Hirsch and Andrew Ashworth (eds), *Principled Sentencing: Readings on Theory and Policy* (2nd edn, Hart 1998) 161-67.

127   Miroslav Wolf, *Exclusion and Embrace: A Theological Exploration of Identity, Otherness and Reconciliation* (Abingdon Press 1994).

128   The very fact that it is so difficult to obtain convictions in this sort of case only serves to exacerbate this danger.

129   Thus in the case of Mgr William Lynn the main culprit (leaving aside the actual perpetrators of the abuse) seems to have been the Cardinal Archbishop of the Diocese, Antony Bevilacqua, but he had died before the trial took place (n 1).

130   For a fuller discussion of this phenomenon in the present context see Anne-Marie McAlinden, *The Shaming of Sexual Offenders: Risk, Retribution and Reintegration* (Hart 2007) 18-23.

131   In 1980, following media reports, three members of staff at this home, including a leading member of the Orange Order with links to loyalist paramilitary groups, were convicted in Belfast of numerous sexual offences committed against the inmates, including buggery and gross indecency; *Report of the Committee into Children's Homes and Hostels* (HMSO 1986) (*'Hughes Report'*).

132   These include the 'pindown' scandal in Staffordshire, the Ty Mawr inquiry and the case of the Hackney social worker Mark Trotter: see Allan Levy and Barbara Kahan, *The Pindown Experience and the Protection of Children: The Report of the Staffordshire Child Care Inquiry 1991* (Staffordshire County Council 1991); Gareth Williams and John McCreadie, *Ty Mawr Community Home Inquiry* (Gwent County Council 1992); JK Barratt, *The Report of the 1997 Inquiry into the 'Trotter Affair'* (London Borough of Hackney 1998). The very day on which this chapter was being submitted for publication was marked by the publication of the damning report into Winterbourne View, a care home for vulnerable adults in the Bristol area; 'Winterbourne View Abuse Report Calls for Changes to Care' (*BBC*, 7 August 2012) <http://www.bbc.co.uk/news/uk-england-bristol-19162516> accessed 7 August 2012.

together with the ongoing problem of clerical child abuse in other denominations,[133] serve to demonstrate that the issue of institutional abuse by persons in authority is not confined to the Roman Catholic Church. Even if it were, such abuse only accounts for a small part of the total problem.[134]

Conclusion

Before a criminal prosecution can be brought either in Northern Ireland or in the Republic, there are two tests that must be satisfied; there must be a reasonable prospect of obtaining a conviction,[135] and prosecution must be in the public interest.[136] On the basis of the present law, the first test would be hard to satisfy in cases of this type, mainly because of the difficulty in locating a particular guilty individual. The second test would cause less problems, though the prosecution of individuals is less easy to justify. The arguments for prosecution on a corporate basis are much stronger, but as in other cases the law is not well adapted to this. Such prosecutions could serve a valuable denunciatory role, but at the end of the day their value would be mainly symbolic. The reputation of the Roman Catholic Church in Ireland and elsewhere has suffered greatly as a result of these cases, and there have even been calls for it to be dissolved.[137] But this will not happen, and even if it did the ongoing scandal of child abuse in Ireland would still remain.

---

133   In May 2007, following three high-profile cases involving the convictions of respectively a vicar, a choirmaster and a churchwarden, the Archbishop of Canterbury admitted that mistakes had been made and that the Church of England had let people down; Jonathan Petre, 'Williams Admits CofE Failed to Protect Children' (*Telegraph*, 25 May 2007) <http://www.telegraph.co.uk/news/uknews/1552552/Williams-admits-CofE-failed-to-protect-children.html> accessed 12 July 2012. This was followed by the setting up of a special safeguarding liaison group chaired by the Bishop of Hereford and an exhaustive review of the procedures for dealing with complaints of child abuse in each diocese by an Independent Reviewer specially appointed for the purpose; Jonathan Wynne-Jones, 'C of E Child Abuse Was Ignored for Decades' (*Telegraph*, 21 October 2007) <http://www.telegraph.co.uk/news/uknews/1566826/C-of-E-child-abuse-was-ignored-for-decades.html> accessed 12 July 2012.

134   As McAlinden (n 129) points out, most child sexual abuse takes place in the family context (11). Thus according to Rape Crisis Network Ireland, 48.8 per cent of such claims in one year involved members of the family, 30.4 per cent friends and acquaintances, and only 12.2 per cent persons in authority: *2010 Rape Crisis Statistics and Annual Report*, Graph 21 <http://www.rcni.ie/uploads/RCNINationalRapeCrisisStatisticsAndAnnualReport2010.pdf> accessed 12 July 2012.

135   Director of Public Prosecutions, *Guidelines for Prosecutors* (2010), para 4.11 (Republic of Ireland) <http://www.dppireland.ie/filestore/documents/GUIDELINES_-_Revised_NOV_2010_eng.pdf>;   Public Prosecution Service NI, *Code for Prosecutors* (2008), para 4.2 (Northern Ireland) <http://www.ppsni.gov.uk/Branches/PPSNI/PPSNI/Files/Documents/Code%20for%20Prosecutors/Code%20for%20Prosecutors%20Revised%202008%20FINAL.pdf> all accessed 16 July 2012.

136   *Guidelines for Prosecutors* (n 134), para 4.4 (Republic of Ireland); *Code for Prosecutors* (n 134), para 4.3 (Northern Ireland).

137   See for instance Andrew Riggio, 'The Catholic Church Is Dangerous, Outdated and Should Dissolve' (*Yahoo!*, n.d.) <http://news.yahoo.com/catholic-church-dangerous-outdated-dissolve-204000761.html>; Ranty McRant, 'Should the Catholic Church Be Dissolved?' (*Godlike Productions*, 18 March 2010) <http://www.godlikeproductions.com/forum1/message1016047/pg1>; 'Question: Should the Catholic Church Be Dissolved? In Light of the Recent Revelations about the Nature of the Organisation, Organised Pedophilia etc'. (*answerbag*, 22 April 2010) <http://www.answerbag.com/q_view/2024025> all accessed 16 July 2012.

Chapter 15

France

Catherine Elliott

The Liability of Accomplices in French Criminal Law: Introduction

There are many similarities between the law on accomplice liability in France and that in England. Both systems have the same starting point, what the French would describe as *l'emprunt de la responsabilité*, which can literally be translated as 'the borrowing of liability'. This is a way of explaining that the liability of the accomplice is dependent on the liability of the principal offender: without a principal offence there can be no liability for complicity. While the terminology is different the law in both systems essentially covers help or encouragement provided before or at the time of the principal offence. Once found liable accomplices are punished as if they were the principal offender.[1] Thus, the French Criminal Code states:

> Art. 121-6. The accomplice of the offence ... will be punished as a principal offender.[2]

The differences between the two systems rest more in the finer details of the law on complicity. Of particular interest is the fact that in France, the rules on the existence of joint enterprise have not received the same level of attention from the courts as in England, though there are certainly similarities in the solutions reached.

General Principles

French crimes are divided into minor,[3] major[4] and serious offences.[5] Article 121-1 of the French Criminal Code lays down that a person is only criminally responsible for their own acts.[6] The principal offender is known as *l'auteur matériel* and is defined in article 121-4:

> The principal offender is the person who:
>
> 1. Commits the criminal conduct;

---

1   Art 121-6 of the French Criminal Code.
2   'Sera puni comme auteur le complice de l'infraction, au sens de l'article 121-7'.
3   *Une contravention.*
4   *Un délit.*
5   *Un crime.*
6   Art. 121-1: 'Nul n'est responsable pénalement que de son propre fait'.

2. Attempts to commit a serious offence, or, in the cases provided for by the legislation, a major offence.[7]

An equivalent provision that applies to minor crimes is contained in article R. 610-2. Thus, the principal offender usually commits or attempts to commit the prohibited act itself causing any relevant result.

Accomplices are called *les complices* and the key legislative provisions are articles 121-6 and 121-7:

> Art. 121-6. The accomplice of the offence, as defined in article 121-7, will be punished as a principal offender.

> Art. 121-7. An accomplice to a serious or major offence is the person who knowingly, by help or assistance, facilitated its preparation or commission.

> A person is also an accomplice who by gift, promise, threat, order, abuse of authority or power has incited an offence or given instructions to commit it.[8]

In English law the Accessories and Abettors Act 1861 refers to aiding, abetting, counselling and procuring. Interpretations in French law of the concepts of help and encouragement are very similar to aiding and abetting.[9] The other forms of accomplice participation in France are incitement[10] or the giving of instructions (through a gift, promise, threat, order or abuse of authority). In practice these concepts of incitement and the giving of instructions overlap significantly with counselling and procuring in English criminal law.

Before looking at the detailed rules on secondary party liability in France, we will look at the concept of innocent agents, the liability of masterminds and the concept of joint principals.

Innocent Agents

French law occasionally treats people who cause the commission of a principal offence, but do not actually personally carry out the *actus reus* of that offence, as the principal offender, known in these circumstances as *l'auteur intellectuel* (or sometimes *l'auteur moral* or *l'auteur média*).[11] This analysis of legal responsibility has similarities with the English notion of an innocent agent but its application is broader than this. Like the doctrine of innocent agency, liability can be imposed

---

7   'Est auteur de l'infraction la personne qui: 1. Commet les faits incriminés; 2. Tente de commettre un crime ou, dans les cas prévus par la loi, un délit'.

8   'Est complice d'un crime ou d'un délit la personne qui sciemment, par aide ou assistance, en a facilité la préparation ou la consommation. Est également complice la personne qui par don, promesse, menace, ordre, abus d'autorité ou de pouvoir aura provoqué à une infraction ou donné des instructions pour la commettre'.

9   Flavia Giustiniani, 'The Responsibility of Accomplices in the Case-Law of the Ad Hoc Tribunals' (2009) 20 Criminal Law Forum 417.

10   *La provocation*.

11   Cass crim 24 oct 1972, GP, 1973.I.218; Cass crim 4 déc 1974, GP, 1974.I, som 93; Laguier, 'La notion d'auteur moral', obs RSC, 1976, 409; Elies van Sliedregt, 'First published online: November 22, 2006 Joint Criminal Enterprise as a Pathway to Convicting Individuals for Genocide' (2007) 5 Journal of International Criminal Justice 184.

on the instigator of the crime where the actual person who carried out the crime is not criminally liable because they lack *mens rea* or they have a defence.[12] Therefore, the Criminal Division of the *Cour de cassation* has held in cases involving the illegal importation of drugs, that the acquittal of the principal offender on the basis that the *mens rea* of the crime did not exist in his case did not exclude the guilt of the person who had given him the drugs.[13] The man who physically carried the drugs, *l'auteur matériel*, was an innocent agent used as the tool of the instigator who was treated as a principal offender.

But in France, the concept of *l'auteur intellectuel* can also apply when the person who actually carried out the crime did have *mens rea* and is equally liable as a principal offender. In English law, where there is an innocent agent there is only one principal offender, the person who instigated the crime, the innocent agent dropping out of the picture. By contrast, in French criminal law, the doctrine of *l'auteur intellectuel* can extend to where both the instigator and the person who physically carried out the crime are both criminally liable and will together be treated as joint principals.[14] In this situation the instigator really has done no more than help or encourage another, but is still found liable as a principal offender. The *Cour de cassation* has observed that 'the person who helps the principal offender in carrying out the offence necessarily cooperates in the performance of the offence as a joint principal'.[15] This analysis, which goes against the letter and the spirit of article 121-7, can be explained by two practical considerations that were relevant in the past. Firstly, by labelling an accomplice as a joint principal the courts could sentence the defendants on the basis that there was an aggravating circumstance of gang involvement. So, the lookout for a theft committed by one individual was held to be a joint principal in order to allow both individuals to be prosecuted under the heading of theft committed in a group.[16] This manipulation of the law is no longer necessary now that the circumstance of a group is defined as the commission of the offence 'by several people acting as principal offenders or accomplices'.[17]

Secondly, the transformation of the accomplice into a joint principal allows the imposition of liability on the person who helps or assists the commission of an offence but whose conduct does not satisfy the rules on accomplice liability. For example, the principal offender may have only committed a minor offence that was not sufficient to be treated as the principal offence for the purposes of imposing liability on an accomplice. In one case the *Cour de cassation* declared as joint principals individuals who had accompanied a person carrying a flag judged to be subversive and forbidden by a local by-law.[18] In the same way, in order to punish people who had helped to prepare the commission of an offence, which was not punishable because the potential principal offender voluntarily stopped before the full offence was committed, the Criminal Division decided that they were joint principals to the attempt.[19] An accomplice was labelled as a joint principal to an offence of negligence (involuntary homicide), where he had lent his car to a friend who did not have a driving licence, and who almost immediately afterwards caused a fatal accident.[20]

---

12 Cass crim 19 avr 1945, S, 1945.I.82.
13 Cass crim 8 janv 2003, B no. 5; JCP 2003.II.10159, note Jeandidier.
14 Cass crim 7 mars 1972, B, no. 84.
15 'Celui qui assiste l'auteur dans les faits de consommation coopère nécessairement à la perpétration de l'infraction en qualité de coauteur'; Cass crim 24 aôut 1827, B no. 224.
16 Cass crim 25 janv 1973, Gaz Pal, 1973.I, som 94, note Doucet.
17 'Par plusieurs personnes agissant en qualité d'auteur ou de complice'.
18 Cass crim 24 juin 1922, S 1923.1.41, note Roux.
19 Cass crim 19 avr 1945, S 1945.1.82, concerning an abortion.
20 Cass crim 12 avr 1930, GP, 1930.II.95.

The impact of this transformation of the potential accomplice into a joint principal is less significant in practice today. Whilst under the old French Criminal Code, the punishment of the accomplice could be different from that of the principal offender; under the new Criminal Code which came into force in 1994, the accomplices should be punished as if they were the principal offenders.

Liability of Masterminds

Masterminds behind the crime will normally incur liability as accomplices though we have seen that sometimes the courts are prepared to treat them as joint principals on the basis that they are *l'auteur intellectuel*. Paragraph 2 of article 121-7 makes express reference to the fact that accomplices include people who have incited an offence or given instructions for its commission. Both these forms of the offence must be directed at a particular individual. A person who writes in a newspaper or on the internet encouraging the public at large to commit an offence or giving practical instructions on how to do so is not, therefore, an accomplice if a reader commits an offence after reading these publications.[21]

Incitement on its own is not enough, it must be accompanied by a gift, promise, threat, order or abuse of authority (which could be legal or moral authority).[22] The promise might be, for example, a promise to pay a hitman if he kills the victim. In one case, the owner of a restaurant promised to pay money to a woman if she agreed to play table tennis in a topless swimsuit.[23] General advice on how to commit a crime is not sufficient.[24] If the advice is detailed it can amount to instructions for the purposes of article 121-7.[25] A case where a threat gave rise to criminal liability involved an employer who obtained false statements from some of his employees by threatening to sack them.[26]

The giving of instructions is different to provocation because there is no need for pressure to have been placed on the principal offender. The wording of article 121-7 is slightly ambiguous about whether the instructions, like incitement, need to be accompanied by one of the circumstances listed. This comes down to an issue of statutory interpretation. Academic opinion is divided on this point and the matter has not yet been clarified by the courts. Precise instructions are required, the provision of vague information is not sufficient.[27] Providing a person with an address which could be burgled while the occupants are away would be sufficient and giving details of the future victim's movements has given rise to liability.[28] By contrast, when a man simply advised his mistress she could have an illegal abortion by means of injections, he was not liable as an accomplice because this information was too vague.[29] The instructions may be given directly or through the intermediary of a third person.[30] Liability will still be imposed even if the principal offender did not carry out the offence according to the instructions given by the accomplice. Thus,

---

21   Though sometimes this type of conduct can fall within the specific statutory offence laid down in article 24 of the Act of 29 July 1881 on Freedom of the Press.
22   Art 121-7 para 2.
23   Trib corr, Grasse, 23 sept 1964, JCP, 1965.II.13974, note A Rieg.
24   Cass crim 24 déc 1942, JCP, 1944.II.2651.
25   Cass crim 25 fév 1959.
26   Cass crim 24 juillet 1958, B, 573.
27   Cass crim 24 mars 1960.
28   Cass crim 21 juillet 1943, S, 1943.I.115.
29   Cass crim 24 déc 1942, S, 1944.I.7.
30   Cass crim 30 mai 1989, B, no. 222.

in one case, the accomplice had given the principal offender instructions on how to strangle the victim, but the victim was actually murdered using a gun.[31]

These two forms of complicity, incitement and instruction, must satisfy the normal requirements for accomplice liability discussed in the context of help and assistance below.

Joint Principals

Joint principals are known in French as *coauteurs*.[32] The law on joint principals is very similar in English and French criminal law. Joint principals are considered to have performed the acts which constitute the offence, whereas the accomplice has performed mere ancillary acts with a view to assisting or encouraging the offence. We have already noted that occasionally the French courts are prepared, for technical reasons, to treat individuals who would appear to have acted as accomplices, as joint principals.

In the reverse scenario, sometimes joint principals are treated as accomplices. Thus, in a judgment of 1848, it was stated that 'the joint principal of an offence necessarily helps the other guilty person in the commission of the offence and thereby automatically becomes his accomplice'.[33] This analysis is known as *complicité corespective* and it enables the court to sentence a person as an accomplice where this means they will receive a higher sentence. Thus, under the old Criminal Code there was a separate offence of parricide[34] and until 1981 this bore the death penalty, while the ordinary offence of murder incurred life imprisonment. Where two individuals killed the father of one of them, the son committed parricide. By treating the second individual as an accomplice, he too could be subjected to the death penalty.

The concept of *complicité corespective* is discussed further under the subheading 'Joint Criminal Enterprise', below.

Secondary Participation

There are many similarities between the general rules on secondary party liability in France and in England. In France (as in England) there are three key requirements to impose criminal liability on an accomplice. Firstly, a crime must have been committed by a principal offender; secondly, there must have been an act of complicity; and thirdly the accomplice must have the requisite *mens rea*. While these three requirements are the same in both systems, there are some fine differences in how these have been interpreted.

A Principal Offence

A crime must have been committed by the principal offender in order for liability to be imposed on the accomplice. The principal offence committed should normally be either a serious or a major offence. As regards minor offences, the new Criminal Code distinguishes according to the form of

---

31   Cass crim 31 janv 1974, JCP, 1975.II.17984, note Mayer-Jack, RSC, 1975.679, obs J. Larguier.

32   See Dominique Allix, *Essai sur la coaction* (LGDJ 1976); John Stewart Bell, Sophie Boyron and Simon Whittaker, *Principles of French Law* (Oxford University Press, 1998) 238.

33   'le coauteur d'un crime aide nécessairement l'auteur coupable dans les faits qui consomment l'action et devient, par la force des choses, son complice'; Cass crim 9 juillet 1848, S, 1848.I.527.

34   Arts 299 and 302 para 1 of the old Criminal Code.

complicity. Where the complicity took the form of the accomplice inciting or giving instructions (referred to together as instigating),[35] liability can be imposed.[36] By contrast, if the complicity takes the form simply of help or assistance, no liability can be imposed.[37]

Occasionally, help or assistance given for the commission of a minor offence will be separately punished as an offence in its own right. For example, the new Code punishes those who help or assist the commission of a breach of the peace,[38] or a minor offence against the person.[39] An Act of 5 March 2007 concerning the prevention of delinquent behaviour, created a new offence of recording and disseminating violent images. The aim of the offence was to deal with the problem of 'happy slapping'. This offence is contained in article 222-33-3 of the Criminal Code and effectively extends the scope of accomplice liability.

Accomplices are not liable where potential principal offenders have a defence that justifies their conduct. This includes the legitimate defence, an order of law and the order of a legitimate authority. They will also avoid liability where the potential principal offender benefits from an immunity; for example, Article 311-12 offers an immunity between spouses for the offence of theft. Complicity is not punishable where the acts of the principal offender can no longer be punished due to the expiry of the limitation period, or due to a general amnesty on offences of that type.

However, an accomplice can be punished, even though the principal offender has been acquitted if the acquittal is for subjective reasons of non-responsibility (such as the existence of the defence of constraint or insanity).[40] In other words, the accomplice can be punished, even if the principal offender escapes punishment provided a criminal act has still been committed. This can be viewed as an exception to the general principle that the accomplice's liability is 'borrowed' from the principal offender.

The principal offence can be an attempt, though a person cannot be liable for attempting to be an accomplice.[41] The *Cour de cassation* therefore decided, in a well-known case decided in 1962, that a doctor was not liable as an accomplice when he paid a hit-man to kill his wife and the hit-man kept the money but failed to carry out the offence. The doctor was not liable as an accomplice because there had been no criminal attempt.[42]

The case law has partly got round this potential gap in criminal liability by imposing instead liability for the inchoate offence of conspiracy.[43] In one case a man was found in possession of notes concerning the movements of a woman described at the trial as 'blond and attractive'. He admitted to the police that he had been contacted by a third party who had been rejected by the woman and wanted revenge. The third party had paid him money to attack her and driven him to the place where he was to carry out the attack. He had taken the money and spent it, but had subsequently changed his mind and not carried out the attack. The two men were both convicted of conspiracy.[44]

---

35 *Complicité par instigation.*
36 Art 121-7 para 2 and R 610-2.
37 Art 121-7 para 1.
38 Art R 623-2.
39 Art R 625-1.
40 Cass crim 21 mai 1990, B no. 205.
41 Cass crim 4 janv 1975, GP, 1343, note J-PD, obs Larguier, RSC, 1976, 707.
42 Cass crim 25 oct 1962, *Affaires Lacour et Schieb-Benamar*, JCP, 1963.II.12985, note R Vouin.
43 *Une association de malfaiteurs.*
44 Cass crim 30 avril 1996, B no. 176, RSC, 1977.100, obs Bernard Bouloc.

There must exist a sufficiently clear causal link between the conduct of the supposed accomplice and the commission (or the attempted commission) of the principal offence.[45] The principal offence need not have been the subject of a conviction. The absence of a conviction may be due to the fact that, for example, the principal offender has escaped detection or died.[46]

If the principal offence has been committed in France, it does not matter that the act of complicity has been committed in another country, it is punishable in France. In the reverse hypothesis of an offence committed outside France, the person who has been the accomplice in France can be convicted by the French courts, even if the principal offender has not been convicted by a foreign court, as long as a foreign court has confirmed that the offence was committed.[47]

An Act of Complicity

Under article 121-7, the act of complicity can be either an act of encouragement, assistance, incitement or instruction. We have already looked at incitement and instruction so the emphasis of this discussion will be on the most common forms of complicity – encouragement or assistance – though the same general rules apply to all these forms of conduct. The various acts of complicity which the legislation lists are not in themselves criminal, for example, borrowing a car[48] or handing-over a key.[49] A person who lends a car becomes punishable if the loan is done with a view to committing an offence.

The concept of assistance presupposes the presence of the accomplice at the scene of the crime. Presence at the scene is not required for 'helping'. In one case the director of a driving school was found to be an accomplice when he allowed a person who lacked the requisite professional qualification to give driving lessons.[50]

Article 121-7 specifies that the help or assistance must take place in order to facilitate the preparation or completion of the offence. The instigation, help or assistance must have been provided prior to or at the time of the principal offence.[51] Thus, acts carried out after the principal offence has been committed do not give rise to secondary party liability. There is an exception where help was provided after the commission of the offence but had been promised before the crime was committed. What matters therefore is the timing of the agreement between the accomplice and the principal offender. In one case an individual was found guilty as an accomplice where he had been paid by two women to wait at the wheel of a car ready for them to make their escape, while they went shoplifting.[52]

The act of complicity must have been accomplished and not merely attempted. You cannot have attempted complicity, for example if a person offered to lend a principal offender a weapon to commit a crime but their offer was rejected, or where a person intended to drive the principal offender to the scene of the crime, but their car broke down.

---

45   Philippe Salvage, 'Le lien de causalité en matière de complicité' [1981] Revue de science criminelle 25; Cass crim 3 nov 1981, B no. 289.

46   Cass crim 12 mai 1970, B no. 158, where the accomplice was convicted even though the principal offender remained unidentified.

47   Art 113-5.

48   Cass crim 6 déc 1967, B no. 311.

49   Cass crim 13 juin 1811, S, chr, 1809-1811.I.360.

50   *Montbéliard*, 22 nov 1963, D 1964, 78, note Pelier.

51   Cass crim 23 juillet 1927, S, 1929.I.73, note J Roux.

52   Cass crim 30 avr 1963, B no. 157, RSC, 1964.134, obs A Légal; Cass crim 8 nov 1972, B no. 329, D 1973, som 17.

The assistance rendered need not be effective.[53] Accordingly, it does not matter that the principal offender did not actually take advantage of the help or assistance provided.[54] Thus, it does not matter whether the tools provided to the thief were actually used.[55]

The help or assistance can be indirect. This occurs where the defendant assists the accomplice and not the principal offender. So an accomplice to an accomplice can be punished.[56] In one case, a housekeeper gave information to an acquaintance about the layout of her employer's house, and her acquaintance then passed this information on to a burglar.[57]

A positive act is usually required, an omission will not normally be enough. As in English law,[58] mere presence at the scene of a crime is not sufficient to constitute complicity.[59] Simply abstaining from acting is not sufficient. In a past one case a defendant was not considered liable for complicity when he found several individuals in the process of committing a crime and agreed to remain silent on the payment of a sum of money.[60] It is arguable that this conduct would amount to a criminal offence under English law.[61] In both France and England,[62] liability as an accomplice will be imposed on an individual who did not carry out a positive act if this abstention was blameworthy because he had a special duty to act, for example, a professional duty, and his mere presence effectively encouraged the principal offender. The French appear to have applied this principle to a wider range of scenarios than in England. Thus, in a French case the defendant was liable as an accomplice when he was present when his mistress had an illegal abortion.[63] The duty can arise from a prior agreement with the principal offender. This was the position in a case where an inspector of taxes agreed to turn a blind eye to the dishonest acts of the principal offender.[64] Or the accused may have had an obligation to act due to his or her profession. Thus, a club owner was liable as an accomplice when he failed to stop his clientele from causing excessive noise at night which prevented his neighbours from sleeping.[65] A police officer was found to be a secondary party to a theft when he failed to stop his colleague from committing the theft while they were on duty together.[66]

In addition, certain omissions, such as a failure to rescue, are criminalised *per se*, as autonomous crimes, so there is no need to fall back on the law of complicity.[67] Article 223-6 of the Criminal Code criminalises the failure to prevent 'by immediate action, without risk to himself or a third

---

53   Cass crim 17 mai 1962, D, 1962, 473.

54   Cass crim 17 mai 1962, D, 1962.4731; Cass crim 31 janv 1974, JCP, 1975.II.17984, note Mayer-Jack.

55   Cass crim 17 mai 1962, D, 1962, 473.

56   Cass crim 15 déc 2004, B no. 322.

57   Cass crim 1 sept 1987, B no. 308; 10 oct 1988 GP, 1989.1.189, note Doucet; Cass crim 30 mai 1989, B no. 222; obs Vitu, RSC, 1990, 325.

58   *R v Clarkson* [1971] 1 WLR 1402.

59   Cass crim 30 nov 1810, B no. 154; Cass crim 27 mars 1846, B no. 82; Cass crim 26 oct 1912, S, 1914.I.225, note J Roux.

60   Cass crim 15 janv 1948, S, 1949.I.81, note A Légal; Cass Ass Pl 20 janv 1964, JCP 1965.II.13.983, note Bouzat.

61   *Wilcox v Jeffrey* [1951] 1 All ER 464.

62   *Tuck v Robson* [1970] 1 All ER 1171.

63   Cass crim 5 nov 1941, S, 1942.I.89, note Bouzat.

64   Cass crim 27 oct 1971, B no. 284, RSC, 1972.376, obs J Larguier.

65   Cass crim 8 juillet 1949, JCP, 1949.II.5128, note Colombini.

66   Trib corr Aix, 14 janv 1947, JCP, 1947.II.3465, note Béraud.

67   Cf. Art 223(6) of the new Criminal Code.

party, either a serious or major offence against the bodily integrity of a person'.[68] This offence is aimed at preventing crimes against the person,[69] and so would not be committed if a person failed to prevent the commission of a theft or an act of corruption. The defendant must have voluntarily failed to prevent the offence. So, if a person thought that an offence could not be prevented, liability would not be imposed.

Article 223-6 also criminalises a person who wilfully fails 'to offer assistance to a person in danger which he could himself provide without risk to himself or to third parties, or by initiating rescue operations'.[70] This offence has potentially a broader application. The possible forms of action could involve the defendant personally trying to rescue the victim, or simply warning the police or fire service that a person is in danger. Because people are not expected to put themselves at risk, they would not normally be expected to intervene physically. A danger is defined as 'a critical situation that causes fear of grave consequences for the person exposed and risks either serious physical injury or loss of life'.[71] The prosecution must prove that the victim faced a real risk, not just a hypothetical risk.[72] The cause of the danger does not matter: it could be caused by the victim, the defendant, a third party or a natural occurrence. The offence can exist even if it was not possible to avert the peril, so no defence will arise from proving that any help that could have been given would have been ineffective.[73]

Mens Rea

The accomplice must know the criminal nature of the principal offender's conduct and have voluntarily participated in its commission. Article 121-7 specifies that the help or assistance must have been given 'knowingly'.[74] It also states that the instructions must be given 'in order to commit' the crime. Thus, the person who lends his car to a third party without knowing that the car was going to be used to commit an armed robbery is not an accomplice.

The *mens rea* of the accomplice must not be confused with that of the principal offender. The intention of the accomplice is simply knowledge of the criminal intent of the principal offender. It is not in any way necessary for the accomplice to share the intent of the principal offender. This point is illustrated by the case of Maurice Papon, a former government minister who was prosecuted for his involvement in the deportation of French Jews to extermination camps during the Second World War. The *Cour de cassation* found that he had been an accomplice to a crime against humanity and it was not necessary that he personally shared the same political ideology as the principal offenders.[75] It was sufficient that he knew that the principal offender wanted to exterminate the victims.

---

68 'par son action immédiate, sans risque pour lui ou pour les tiers, soit un crime, soit un délit contre l'intégrité corporelle de la personne'.

69 Cass crim 16 nov 1955, B no. 489.

70 'porter à une personne en péril l'assistance que, sans risque pour lui ou pour les tiers, il pouvait lui prêter soit par son action personnelle, soit en provoquant un secours'.

71 TC Rouen 9 aôut 1975 Dalloz 1975, 531.

72 Cass crim 13 nov 2005 JCP 1956.II.8560.

73 Cass crim 23 mars 1953, Bull Crim no. 104.

74 *Sciemment.*

75 Cass crim 23 janv 1997, D, 1997.147, note J Pradel.

The intention of the accomplice must exist at the time of the help, encouragement or provision of instructions. A person who realises afterwards that he or she has said too much does not thereby become an accomplice.

An individual can be found liable as a secondary party to an offence of carelessness. This could be committed, for example, where a passenger encourages a driver to speed and this causes an accident.[76] In one case, a bobsleigh was launched at excessive speed down a slope and killed a child. The driver was convicted as the principal offender, and the other occupants were convicted as his accomplices because 'bobsleighing constitutes a team sport in which all the participants have a role to play in driving the device'.[77]

Unlike in England where you can be an accomplice to even a strict liability offence,[78] in France you cannot help or encourage an offence of negligence. Instead, the perpetrator might sometimes be found in such a case to have been an innocent agent and the person who provided the help or encouragement a principal offender, or both the perpetrator and the assister could be treated as joint principals. In *Paemelabre*, the court failed to infer complicity in the unlawful slaughter of animals solely based on the fact that a man drove a truck containing pigs to a place where they were slaughtered and, afterwards, drove the carcases of the dead pigs away.[79]

Sometimes, the accomplices have not foreseen the commission of a specific type of offence, instead they have given an open hand to the principal offender. For example, where people are seeking revenge they might simply give some money to a person with a bad reputation and tell them to take revenge. In such circumstances the courts take the view that the accomplice accepts all the risks and is liable as a secondary party to whatever offence is subsequently committed.[80]

Joint Criminal Enterprise

'*La complicité corespective*' can be loosely translated as a 'joint enterprise'. The approaches taken under French and English law to this issue are remarkably similar. As with English law, the concept of a joint enterprise in French law is particularly useful to justify the conviction of a group of people who have violently attacked and killed their victim. When it is clear that all the members of the group hit the victim but it is not clear which one gave the fatal blow, criminal liability for the homicide can be imposed on all of them. Established case law considers that a joint principal is automatically an accomplice. It follows that 'the joint principal to a crime automatically helps the other party committing other crimes in the course of the enterprise and becomes automatically his accomplice'.[81] Each offender being an accomplice to any violence carried out by the other participant incurs liability and punishment for the most serious offence committed, as if he/she had personally carried out the crime. This is very similar to the approach taken in the English courts that there is no legal significance in the distinction between an accomplice and a principal offender

---

76   Cass crim 17 nov 1887, B no. 392; Cass crim 15 févr 1982, D, 1983.275, note D Mayer et JP Pizzio.

77   'la pratique du bobsleigh constitue un sport d'équipe dans lequel tous les participants ont un rôle à remplir dans la conduite de l'engin'; Chambéry, 8 mars 1956, JCP 1956.II.9224, note Vouin.

78   *Callow v Tillstone* (1900) 83 LT 411; *R v Webster* [2006] EWCA Crim 415, [2006] 2 Cr App R 6.

79   Cass crim 1 déc 1944, D, 1945.162 as cited in Bell, Sophie Boyron and Simon Whittaker, *Principles of French Law* (Oxford University Press, 1998) 232.

80   Cass crim 28 oct 1965, JCP, 1966.II.14524.

81   'Le coauteur d'un crime aide nécessairement l'autre coupable dans les faits qui consomment l'action et devient nécessairement son complice'; Cass crim 15 juin 1860, S, 1861.I.398.

where they are acting in a joint enterprise because the Accessories and Abettors Act 1861 states that accomplices will be convicted and punished as principal offenders.

French law has also had to grapple with the issue of 'parasitic accessory liability' which was the subject of discussion in the Supreme Court's decision in England in *Gnango* (see 'Errors and Transferred Malice' below). When the offence actually committed by the principal offender is different from the offence originally planned, under both systems if the actual offence committed is less serious and of the same nature as the planned one then the accomplice is still liable for the offence that is actually committed. For example, if the accomplice thought a murder would be committed in the course of the joint enterprise, but a non-fatal offence is actually committed by the principal offender, the accomplice will be liable for this.

If the crime committed is more serious than the one envisaged by the accomplice, the French cases distinguish between two scenarios. If the offence committed has no relationship with that planned (a person gives a principal offender a weapon to carry out a theft, and he uses it to carry out a murder) there is no accomplice liability.[82] Thus, if the offence committed has a different *actus reus* or *mens rea* than that foreseen by the potential accomplice, the latter is not liable. For example, where a person lent another a gun so that the other person could go hunting, but that person actually used the gun to kill someone, the owner of the gun could not be treated as an accomplice to the murder.[83] The creditor who gave a third party two revolvers to intimidate a debtor into paying back the money owed, could not be convicted as an accomplice to the murder of the caretaker of the building by the third party following an argument.[84] Thus, under both systems, the key issue is one of foresight: defendants will be liable for every consequence that they foresee might arise.

In one respect the French criminal law appears to go one step further than English criminal law and this is partly because of the way the criminal law offences are sometimes defined, with a core offence and then different potential aggravating factors which can have an impact on the maximum sentence. The crime committed by the principal offender may be the one envisaged during the joint enterprise, but was carried out in different circumstances from those that had initially been foreseen (for example, the theft envisaged turns out to be an aggravated theft). If the only difference between the offence foreseen and the offence committed is a secondary circumstance this will not prevent the accomplice from being liable provided he caused the offence to be committed. According to the *Cour de cassation*, the accomplice 'must foresee every form that this act might take, all the circumstances that could accompany it' and 'the accomplice incurs responsibility for every circumstance which forms part of the act pursued without necessarily having known of it'.[85]

Where a person provided information to help the commission of an ordinary theft, and the principal offender committed this offence at night with a group of people, the person will be liable as an accomplice to the aggravated form of theft. The courts take the view that 'he should have foreseen all these forms of the offence which the conduct was susceptible of giving rise to'.[86]

In a case known as *l'affaire du SAC* the instigator had wanted one member of the Service d'Action Civique (SAC) to be murdered and compromising documents removed. When the

---

82   Cass crim 13 janv 1955, D, 291, note Chavanne.

83   Orléans, 28 janv 1896, D, 97.2.5.

84   Cass crim 13 janv 1955, D, 291, note Chavanne.

85   'le complice devait prévoir toutes les qualifications dont le fait était susceptible, toutes les circonstances dont il pouvait être accompagnées .... Le complice encourt la responsabilité de toutes les circonstances qui qualifient l'acte poursuivi sans qu'il soit nécessaire qu'elle aient été connues de lui'; Cass crim 21 mai 1996, B no. 206.

86   'il devait prévoir toutes les qualifications dont le fait était susceptible'; Cass crim 31 déc 1947, B no. 270; 21 mai 1996, B no. 206, Dr pén, 1996, comm 213 et obs M Véron.

principal offenders went to the house of the intended victim, he was out, but they killed five members of the SAC who were there and could have been potential witnesses of their criminal plot. The instigator argued in his defence that he should not be liable as an accomplice because the crimes that were carried out were not foreseeable when he planned the original murder. This argument was rejected and he was found to be an accomplice to these killings. The *Cour de cassation* held that the object of each of the five murders was either to prepare, facilitate and execute the theft ordered by the instigator, or to avoid criminal liability of the principal offenders and their accomplices. The Court reaffirmed the principle that the accomplice bears responsibility for all the aggravating circumstances, even if he did not know them; it also ruled that on the facts of the case, the link between the instructions given by the instigator and the murder of the victims required for the purpose of accomplice liability had been satisfied.[87] By contrast, in another case the potential accomplice was not liable when he gave instructions for the killing of one individual, but the principal offender decided not to kill this person but killed another instead.[88]

Errors and Transferred Malice

Mistakes and transferred malice are of particular interest in the context of secondary party liability following the case of *R v Gnango*[89] in England. The principal offender and Gnango were shooting at each other in a car park. The principal offender missed Gnango but shot and killed by accident an innocent passer-by. The Supreme Court considered whether Gnango could be a secondary party to this murder, even though he was the intended victim. Ultimately, the court held that he should be liable as an accomplice to the murder relying on the doctrine of transferred malice. The reasoning of the majority was that he had knowingly encouraged the principal offender to attempt to kill him, and when the principal offender missed and hit the victim, the doctrine of transferred malice should apply not just to the principal offender but also to the secondary party.

As regards the law in France, no special rules have been developed with regard to the doctrine of transferred malice, instead the ordinary principles on mistake apply. These are very similar to the rules on mistake in England in that the impact of a mistake will generally depend on the type of *mens rea* required for a particular offence. Serious and major offences normally require general intention, but despite this reference to intention, this is actually quite a low level of intention which would frequently not be undermined by the existence of a mistake. The classic definition of general intention is provided by the eminent nineteenth-century French criminal lawyer, Emile Garçon:

> Intention, in its legal sense, is the desire to commit a crime as defined by the law; it is the accused's awareness that he is breaking a law.[90]

Thus, according to its classic definition, there are two mental elements that make up general intention: desire and awareness. The concept of awareness simply requires the accused to be aware

---

87   Cass crim 19 juin 1984, B no. 231.

88   Cass crim 10 mars 1977, D, 1977, IR 237, obs Larguier; Rev sc crim, 1979, 75.

89   [2011] UKSC 59.

90   'L'intention, dans son sens juridique, est la volonté de commettre le délit tel qu'il est déterminé par la loi; c'est la conscience, chez le coupable, d'enfreindre les prohibitions légales …' (Emile Garçon, *Code Pénal Annoté* (1st edn, Sirey 1901) art 1, no. 77).

that he or she is breaking the law. Because of the principle *nemo censetur ignorare legem* there is a presumption in French law that people know the law, so the existence of this element of general intention will normally be assumed. A legislative exception to this presumption was added by the new Criminal Code under article 122-3. This states that:

> A person is not criminally liable if they prove that they believed, due to an error of law that they were not in a position to avoid, to be allowed to legally carry out the act.[91]

This defence is limited to where the mistake as to the law was induced by a misrepresentation emanating from the civil service.[92]

As to the requirement of desire, this is traditionally interpreted as simply referring to a desire to commit the wrongful act and not a desire to commit the result of that act. Thus, if one takes the factual situation of a person throwing a stone at a victim and the victim dying as a result, to prove that the person has a general intention for the offence of murder it would merely need to be proved that they desired to throw the stone. For the purposes of general intention there would be no requirement to show the person desired the result of killing that person.[93]

Alongside general intention, the more serious crimes also require the existence of specific intent, which would be an intention to cause a relevant result. The offence of murder, for example, requires both general and specific intention. A mistake as to the identity of the victim would still not undermine the existence of a specific intent.

Some mistakes of fact may, however, mean that the *mens rea* of an intentional offence is absent. Thus, if individuals take objects belonging to someone else thinking that they are the owners, the offence of theft has not been committed. In one case, the head of a business that employed a foreign worker without a work permit believing he was French was not liable.[94] If the intention remains because the mistake related to a secondary element of the offence, then the defendant will still be liable. For example, if a person takes jewels thinking they were made with precious stones when in fact they were made of plastic they will still be liable for theft; or if the defendant kills one person thinking that they are killing another they have no defence.[95]

The doctrine of transferred malice in English law is essentially concerned with a mistake over the intended victim, which is in effect a mistake of fact. As French criminal law has not developed a specific doctrine of transferred malice, the general rules on mistake apply: that is, mistakes of fact will undermine the existence of an offence if they mean that there is no *mens rea*. Thus, where one victim is injured who was not the intended victim, the courts can impose liability either by treating this mistake as factually irrelevant (which is the same conclusion as is reached when the doctrine of transferred malice applies under English law) or by finding the defendant to have been reckless as to the infliction of harm on the ultimate victim.

---

91   'N'est pas pénalement responsable la personne qui justifie avoir cru, par une erreur sur le droit qu'elle n'était pas en mesure d'éviter, pouvoir légitimement accomplir l'acte'.

92   Cass crim 15 nov 1995, Dr pén 1996, comm 56; JCP 1996, éd G, IV, 440; JCP 1996, éd G, I, 3950, M Véron.

93   Note that the French offence of murder requires both general and specific intention.

94   Cass crim 1er oct 1987, B no. 327.

95   Cass crim 31 janv 1835, S I.564.

Withdrawal from Participation

Where accomplices, having incited, helped or assisted the commission of a principal offence, subsequently change their mind and wish to abandon the criminal enterprise, they can avoid liability if they take positive action to prevent the commission of the offence. So, if a potential accomplice lends a weapon to an individual to commit a robbery, he or she might avoid criminal liability by informing the police, taking back the weapon or warning the potential victim. Merely refusing to provide further assistance to the principal offender is not sufficient.[96] These rules, can be compared to the defence of withdrawal under English law, though the French have not drawn a distinction between withdrawal from a planned criminal enterprise and withdrawal from a spontaneous crime.[97]

Corporate Liability[98]

Before the French Revolution criminal liability could be imposed on legal entities under a Royal Ordinance of 1670. However, with the Revolution, corporations were abolished and along with this, corporate liability. Under the old Criminal Code, legal entities could only incur civil, disciplinary or administrative liability.[99] The *Cour de cassation* traditionally justified this position on the basis that a fine was a personal sanction that could only be imposed on individuals, not organisations.[100] The issue of corporate irresponsibility came to the public's attention when there was a national scandal involving the sale by state agencies of blood contaminated with the HIV virus.[101] A major reform introduced by the new Criminal Code which came into force in 1994, was the introduction of corporate liability. This is provided for by article 121-2, which states:

> Legal entities, with the exception of the State, are criminally liable for the offences committed on their account by their organs or representatives, according to the detailed rules set out in articles 121-4 and 121-7.

> However, local authorities and their associations incur criminal liability only for offences committed in the course of their activities which may be exercised through public service delegation conventions.

---

96   Cass crim 6 févr 1812, S, chr.

97   *R v Becerra* [1975] 62 Cr App R 212; *R v Mitchell and King* [1999] Crim LR 496.

98   Guy Stessens, 'Corporate Criminal Liability: A Comparative Perspective' [1994] International and Comparative Law Quarterly 493; Stephen Walt and William Laufer, 'Why Personhood Doesn't Matter: Corporate Criminal Liability and Sanctions' [1991] American Journal of Criminal Law 263; Sara Beale and Adam Safwat, 'What Developments in Western Europe Tell Us about American Critiques of Corporate Criminal Liability' [2004] Buffalo Criminal Law Review 89; Leonard Orland and Charles Cachera, 'Essay and Translation: Corporate Crime and Punishment in France: Criminal Responsibility of Legal Entities (Personnes Morales) Under the New French Criminal Code (Nouveau Code Penal)' (1995) 11 Conn J Int'l L 111, 114.

99   Mireille Delmas-Marty and Klaus Tiedemann, 'La criminalité, le droit pénal et les multinationales', 1979 JCP II no. 53, 2935.

100   Cass crim 8 mars 1883, DP, 1884, 1 p. 428; 27 fév 1968, B, no. 69.

101   Cass crim 22 juin 1994, B no. 93-83.900.

The criminal liability of legal entities does not exclude that of any natural persons who are perpetrators or accomplices to the same act, subject to the provisions of the fourth paragraph of article 121-3.[102]

The scope of corporate criminal liability remains quite limited in France, partly because of the restrictions expressly laid down in the legislation and partly because of the narrow interpretation given to this legislation by the courts.

Article 121-2 states that liability will be imposed on legal entities for offences committed on their account by their organs or representatives. An 'organ' of a legal entity consists of one or more private individuals on whom the law or articles of association have given a particular function in the organisation of the legal entity with regard to its administration or management, for example, a company director, a company secretary, shareholders, a manager and the mayor and general assembly of a local authority. There is some debate over whether an organ can consist of individuals who as a matter of fact have taken on a leadership role, even though they have not been formally appointed by law or company articles of association.[103]

As we will see below, the *Cour de cassation* will normally only impose corporate liability where the prosecution can identify one or more culpable individuals within the corporate organ. Under this narrow approach, even where a board of directors is collectively responsible for the commission of an offencee, liability will not be imputed to the corporation unless one of the board's members is found to be personally responsible for the commission of the offencee.[104] This interpretation renders the concept of 'organ' nearly coextensive with the concept of 'representative'.[105]

The term 'representative' means a high ranking officer, agent or (most importantly) a salaried employee with delegated authority from a corporate officer or organ of the company. The idea of a representative overlaps with the idea of an 'organ' of a legal entity, but extends to include representatives who have not been appointed under the law. For example, a consultant appointed by a company to represent it.

While generally public bodies can be criminally responsible for the exercise of any of their powers, paragraph 2 provides that local authorities can only be criminally liable for the exercise of delegated powers, but benefit from a type of immunity from criminal liability when they are exercising their own powers. The logic behind this provision is that local authorities should be treated in the same way as private individuals when they are carrying out their delegated responsibilities as these are similar types of activities to those that might be carried out by a private individual. In practice, this distinction between delegated and non-delegated powers is difficult to draw.[106] An Act of 11 December 2001 has provided the following definition:

---

102 'Les personnes morales, à l'exception de l'Etat, sont responsables pénalement, selon les distinctions des articles 121-4 à 121-7, des infractions commises pour leur compte, par leurs organes ou représentants.

Toutefois, les collectivités territoriales et leurs groupements ne sont responsables pénalement que des infractions commises dans l'exercice d'activités susceptibles de faire l'objet de conventions de délégation de service public.

La responsabilité pénale des personnes morales n'exclut pas celle des personnes physiques auteurs ou complices des mêmes faits, sous réserve des dispositions du quatrième alinéa de l'article 121-3'.

103 Quest. no. 5635, JO AN Q 22 nov 1993, 4170.

104 Cass crim 11 mai 1999, Dr pén, comm no. 140.

105 Sara Beale and Adam Safwat, 'What Developments in Western Europe Tell Us about American Critiques of Corporate Criminal Liability' [2004] Buffalo Criminal Law Review 89, 110.

106 Jean-François Auby, 'La délégation de service public: premier bilan et perspectives' (1996) RCP 1095.

A delegation of public service, is a contract under which a public body confers the management of a public service for which it has responsibility to a state or private delegate, for which payment is substantially linked to the provision of the service. The delegate can be required to undertake building works or acquire property necessary for the service.[107]

Powers that can be delegated include the provision of public transport, school dinners and the rubbish collection service.[108] Powers that cannot be delegated are those powers which can only be carried out by the state, such as the awarding of driving licences and the organisation of elections.

Initially, when the new Criminal Code came into force in 2004, corporate liability was only imposed when it was expressly provided for by the offence. This was known as the *principe de spécialité* but was heavily criticised and the rule was repealed by the Act of 9 March 2004.[109]

The criminal liability of legal entities is both indirect and personal. It is an indirect responsibility in that it can only arise as a result of the conduct of a physical person – the legislator has not provided a means of directly imputing blameworthy conduct on a legal entity. The need to establish the existence of an offence committed by a physical person results from the wording of article 121-2 of the Criminal Code which states that legal entities 'are responsible for the offences committed … by their organs or representatives'.[110] It is not the company itself which must satisfy the requirements of the criminal offence, but the physical person who is the 'organ or representative' of the company. No private individual needs to have actually been convicted of the offence, nor is it necessary to identify the relevant individual, though from an evidential point of view, this will often be useful.

A court will first establish whether one or more individuals have committed a criminal offence and then if the circumstances in which this offence has been committed allow it to be imputed to the legal entity under article 121-2 of the Criminal Code. The Criminal Division of the *Cour de cassation* has allowed an appeal on the basis that it is up to the court 'to decide whether the director of the company, the organ of the legal entity, had personal knowledge of the facts laid down in the statements and if the element of intention of the major offence had been satisfied'.[111]

Upper level managers have the legal capacity to represent their employer and thus engage the company's penal responsibility. In contrast, lower level employees do not have the capacity to represent their employer and therefore cannot engage its penal responsibility. This requirement bears some similarity to the idea of a 'directing mind' which is often required for the imposition of corporate liability in English law.[112]

A July 2000 amendment to article 121-3 of the new penal code effectively expanded the scope of liability for criminal negligence under article 121-2. Criminal negligence may now be imputed

---

107 'une délégation de service public est un contrat par lequel une personne morale de droit public confie la gestion d'un service public dont elle a la responsabilité à un délégataire public ou privé, dont la rémunération est substantiellement liée au résultat de l'exploitation du service. Le délégataire peut être chargé de construire des ouvrages ou d'acquérir des biens nécessaire au service'. See also *Préfet des Bouches du Rhône*, CE 15 avril 1996, Rec, 137. This definition was applied in a criminal court in *Commune de Saint-Maur*, 3 avril 2002, B no. 265, RJCA, 2002.

108 Rép Min no. 32824; JOAN Q 4 mars 1996, 1194.

109 Loi no. 2004-204 du 9 mars 2004.

110 'sont responsables des infractions commises … par leurs organes ou représentants'.

111 'de rechercher si le directeur général de la société, organe de la personne morale, avait eu personnellement connaissance des faits relatés dans les attestations et si l'élément intentionnel du délit était ainsi caractérisé'; Cass crim 2 déc 1997, B no. 420.

112 *Tesco Supermarkets v Nattrass* [1972] AC 153.

to a corporation because of the negligence of one of its officers, even when that person was not personally involved in the offence. The *Cour de cassation*, however, still appears to require that actual negligence on the part of a corporate representative is established.[113]

The *Cour de cassation* has rejected the suggestion that, as well as finding an individual linked to the company who has committed the relevant offence, the courts should also identify fault on the part of the company itself. It has stated:

> In the cases laid down by the law, the criminal fault of the organ or the representative suffices, when it is committed on behalf of the legal entity, in order to give rise to criminal liability of the latter, without it being necessary to establish a separate fault on the part of the legal entity.[114]

Corporate liability is only imposed under article 121-2 if the organ or the representative acted on its behalf.[115] Thus corporate liability will not arise when representatives of the company have acted in their own interests, for example, where employees during the course of their employment have made an illicit profit on the side.

Sentencing

The old Criminal Code (which applied until 1994) had based criminal liability on the principle of '*l'emprunt de la pénalité*'[116] under which the accomplice would be given the same punishment as the principal offender.[117] Article 121-6 of the new Criminal Code states that the accomplice to the offence 'will be punished as a principal offender'.[118] So liability is now based on the principle of '*l'emprunt de la criminalité*', in other words the act of the accomplice borrows the criminality from the wrongful act of the principal. In summary, under the old Code the accomplice was punished as if he were *the* principal offender, whereas under the new Code the accomplice is punished as if he were *a* principal offender. So under the new Code, the accomplice will be punished as if he were a principal offender, but will not necessarily receive the same penalty as the principal offender actually received.

Under the old Code the aggravating circumstances identified with respect to the principal would increase the accomplice's penalty, but this is not the case under the current law.[119] Part of the reason for this change was that with the introduction of corporate liability, some of the punishments that could be imposed on a company as a principal offender (such as dissolution of the company) would not be appropriate for an accomplice.[120] In fact, this change in philosophy has made little difference

---

113   Cass crim 24 oct 2000, B no. 308.

114   'Dans les cas prévus par la loi, la faute pénale de l'organe ou du représentant suffit, lorsqu'elle est commise pour le compte de la personne morale, à engager la responsabilité pénale de celle-ci, sans que doive être établie une faute distincte à la charge de la personne morale' ; Cass crim 26 juin 2001, B no. 161; Dr pén 2002, comm no. 8.

115   *pour le compte.*

116   Frédéric Desportes and Francis Le Gunehec, *Le Nouveau droit pénal* (14th edn, Economic 2007) 512.

117   Henri Bosly, 'Responsabilité et sanctions en matière de criminalité des affaires' [1982] Rev Int de Dr Pénal 126.

118   'sera puni comme auteur le complice de l'infraction'.

119   Giustiniani (n 9) 425.

120   JO Sénat, 12 mai 1989, 647.

in practice since the courts tend to impose lighter sentences on accomplices than on principal offenders.[121]

Where principal offenders are liable to have their sentence increased due to the existence of aggravating circumstances, the imposition of the aggravated sentence on an accomplice will depend on whether these circumstances are categorised as personal, impersonal[122] or mixed. Aggravating circumstances which are personal to the principal offender do not affect the accomplice. Such is the case of the repeat offender. But, for the same reason, the secondary party cannot benefit from reductions in the sentence due to the personal characteristics of the principal offender, such as that he or she is a minor.

Where the aggravating circumstances are impersonal, that is to say they relate to the offence rather than the individual, they can be applied to the accomplice. For example, the offence of theft is aggravated where it was committed in a group, involved breaking into a building or the use of a weapon. The increased sentence will be imposed on accomplices even if they did not know or approve of this mode of committing the offence.[123] In one case[124] the accused was convicted of complicity in theft for instigating the theft and waiting in the car while other individuals stole valuable jewellery from a woman, with the aggravating circumstance of pretending to be a policeman. The accused did not pretend to be a policeman but was nevertheless convicted of aggravated theft. The *Cour de cassation* held that the accomplice was liable for all the aggravating circumstances committed by the principal perpetrators, even if he was not aware of them. It was sufficient that the accomplice knew the facts that led to or encouraged the offence; it was not necessary that he be aware of the aggravating circumstances that accompanied the offence.

Aggravating circumstances which are linked both to the offender and to the offence (because they affect the way it was carried out) are known as *les circonstances aggravées mixtes*. An example is premeditation. Under the old Code these were treated like impersonal aggravated circumstances and were therefore applied to the accomplice as well as the principal offender. Thus, the accomplice of the son who killed his father incurred the aggravated sentence for parricide.[125] Whereas the son who was the accomplice of a man who killed the accomplice's father did not incur the aggravated sentence for parricide. This approach continues to be followed by the *Cour de cassation* despite the change in the wording of the legislation.[126]

Conclusion

There are many similarities between English and French law on the criminal liability of accomplices. This is partly because both systems have the same starting point: that liability of the accomplice is dependent on the existence of a principal offence and the accomplice is equally liable as the principal offender. No real difference stems from the pure fact that the French offence forms part of their Criminal Code whereas the English offence stems from an 1861 Act of Parliament, the level of detail provided by the legislation on the scope of liability is much the same in the two systems. Where there is some difference is in the level of guidance provided by the court judgments as

---

121 Cass crim 7 sept 2005, B no. 219, Dr pén 2005, comm 167.

122 *Les circonstances aggravantes réelles*.

123 Cass crim 26 janv 1957, B no. 32; Cass crim 21 mai 1996, B no. 206, Dr pén, 1996, comm 216, obs Véron.

124 Cass crim 31 déc 1947, B no. 270.

125 Cass crim 24 mars 1853, D, 1853.I.115.

126 Cass crim 7 sept 2005, Bull no. 219, 779.

to how these rules will be interpreted. This lack of detailed analysis is particularly noticeable in the context of the law on joint enterprise liability. In England there has been a plethora of senior court judgments interpreting and reinterpreting this area of law with a particular focus on the *mens rea* required in this context. The French legal system has a very different approach to court judgments, taking as its starting point since the French Revolution that the courts are not allowed to make law. The judgments only start to have weight when there is a consistent thread of decisions demonstrating a pattern in the way the courts will decide a certain issue. The Code itself makes no reference to the concept of a joint enterprise and the case law is not placing the same emphasis on this issue as can be seen in England. It is arguable that whereas the English law is uncertain because there have been too many contradictory judgments on this subject, any uncertainties in the French law exist because there has not been enough judicial guidance on the issue.

Chapter 16
Australia

Mirko Bagaric

Overview of Sources of Australian Criminal Law

Australia does not have uniform criminal law. Each of the six states (New South Wales, Queensland, South Australia, Tasmania, Victoria and Western Australia), the two territories (the Australian Capital Territory and Northern Territory) and the federal jurisdiction has its own criminal law.

In Victoria, New South Wales and South Australia the primary source of criminal law is the common law (which is derived from the common law of England). The criminal law in each of these jurisdictions is supplemented by various statutory provisions, with the main statutes being the *Crimes Act 1900* (NSW), *Criminal Law Consolidation Act 1935* (SA) and the *Crimes Act 1958* (Vic). Complicity is governed by the common law in New South Wales. It has a statutory basis in South Australia and Victoria. The statutory provisions in South Australia and Victoria are modelled on the common law.

The other jurisdictions (the federal jurisdiction, the Australian Capital Territory, Northern Territory, Queensland, Tasmania and Western Australia) are referred to as the 'Code jurisdictions'. The Codes are statutes which contain a comprehensive statement of the criminal law. The legislative schemes containing these codes are the *Criminal Code Act 1995* (Cth), *Criminal Code 2002* (ACT), *Criminal Code Act 1983* (NT), *Criminal Code Act 1899* (Qld), *Criminal Code Act 1924* (Tas) and the *Criminal Code Act Compilation Act 1913* (WA). The Codes in Queensland and Western Australia are very similar. The Code in the Australian Capital Territory is modelled on the Commonwealth Code, and the Northern Territory Code also contains aspects of the Commonwealth Code. In each of the Code jurisdictions the law on complicity is found in the relevant code.

In the Code jurisdictions the courts are not obliged to construe legislation in accordance with common law principles. However, pragmatically, the courts in the Code jurisdictions look to the common law for guidance in cases where the legislation is unclear or the relevant terminology has a particular meaning at common law.[1]

There is, in fact, considerable convergence throughout Australia regarding the substantive criminal laws and the principles governing participation in crime, and the general basis for attributing criminal liability for the acts of others.

General Principles: Types of Participation and Relevant Terminology

In Australia, liability for criminal conduct extends beyond the person who directly performs the act that constitutes a crime, to other people who in certain ways are involved in the commission of the offence. This area of the law is regarded as complex, often invoking loose and open-ended terminology.

---

1   See *R v Barlow* (1997) 188 CLR 1, 32 (Kirby J).

The main reason for the complexity of this area of the law stems from the competing considerations regarding the type of involvement that should attract criminal liability. A criminal act is often the end product of numerous acts by different individuals. Principles of causation, personal responsibility and blame command that often it is not only the person who committed the physical act constituting the offence who should be punished. On the other hand, the criminal law is the strongest form of condemnation in the legal system; hence, liability should not extend to acts which are only remotely connected with criminal behaviour. There is no clear manner in which to strike the balance between these considerations. Further, the almost infinite number of ways in which people can collectively contribute to the commission of a crime, and the impossibility of foreseeing all relevant future scenarios, militates against liability being couched in clear-cut rules.

The key distinction in this area is between principal parties (or principal offenders – sometimes also referred to as 'principals in the first degree') and secondary parties (or accessories).[2] The doctrine which results in accessories being liable is known as 'complicity'.

The term 'principal' encompasses those who are both present at the scene and those 'acting in concert' as part of a pre-conceived agreement, express or implied, to commit a crime. In these instances, each of the parties 'acting in concert' is regarded as a joint principal. Thus, in order to be a principal, it is not necessary that a party commits the physical act of the crime.

A person who has a remoter connection to the crime than a principal offender is called an 'accessory' – although this terminology is not consistent throughout the Australian jurisdictions.[3] An accessory is a party who promotes or encourages a crime *before* it occurs, or promotes or assists a crime and is present *during* the commission of the offence.

Being an accessory is not a distinct offence. The concept of accessory is merely a procedural mechanism for extending the range of parties that may incur liability as principal offenders. Thus, a person who is an accessory to a crime is triable as a principal offender. Nevertheless, the distinction between an offender who committed the offence and an accessory is relevant. The basis for ascribing liability is different and, at the sentencing stage, accessories are sometimes regarded as being less culpable than the person who perpetrated the offence.[4]

The only type of accessorial liability that is a discrete offence is 'accessory after the fact'. In order to be liable as an accessory after the fact, the accused must perform an act that assists, or has the potential to assist, the principal offender to evade justice as, for example, by assisting the offender to escape apprehension, prosecution, conviction or punishment.[5]

An accessory after the fact is a lesser form of culpability than an accessory or a principal offender because, at this point, the offence has already been completed. At common law, a person could only be guilty as an accessory after the fact if he or she had knowledge of all the relevant

---

2   The term 'principal offender' is employed in South Australia, Queensland, Western Australia and Victoria: *Criminal Law Consolidation Act 1935* (SA) s 267; *Criminal Code* (Qld) s 7; *Criminal Code* (WA) s 7; *Crimes Act 1958* (Vic) ss 323, 324. In some jurisdictions the term used is 'principal in the first degree': *Crimes Act 1900* (NSW) ss 345, 346; *Criminal Code* (Tas) s 3. In the ACT, Northern Territory and Commonwealth jurisdictions, no specific term is used to describe parties who actually commit the offence: see *Criminal Code* (Cth) s 11.2; *Criminal Code* (ACT) s 45.

3   Throughout Australia there are (generally minor) differences in the terms used to describe accessories and the tests used to ascribe accessorial liability. The relevant statutory provisions are as follows: *Criminal Code* (Cth) s 11.2; *Criminal Code* (ACT) s 45; *Crimes Act 1900* (NSW) ss 345, 346; *Criminal Code* (NT) ss 12(1)(a)-(c); *Criminal Code* (Qld) ss 7(1)(b), (c); *Criminal Law Consolidation Act 1935* (SA) s 267; *Criminal Code* (Tas) ss 3(1)(c), (d); *Crimes Act 1958* (Vic) ss 323, 324; *Criminal Code* (WA) ss 7(b), (c).

4   See further the discussion at the end of this chapter.

5   *R v Dawson* [1961] VR 773; *R v Barlow* (1962) 79 WN (NSW) 756.

facts that established the precise offence committed by the principal offender.[6] Thus, the accused would avoid liability if the principal offender was guilty of a slightly different offence than the one that s/he contemplated. Liability as an accessory after the fact now has a statutory foundation in most Australian jurisdictions.[7] This is a discrete offence, which is conceptually different from the principles which relate to complicity and, hence, is not considered further in this chapter. Thus, for the remainder of this chapter the term accessory does not extend to parties who are liable for assisting an offender *after* a crime has been completed.

Principals by Proxy: Use of Innocent Agents

A person can be guilty of a crime as the principal offender if he or she uses another person to carry out part of the crime, even when that other person is not guilty of any offence. This does not necessarily require resorting to the principle of accessorial liability. Instead, culpability arises from the doctrine of innocent agency.[8] The paradigm situation in which this occurs is where the instigator of the crime arranges for another individual to carry out the physical act of the offence. The person who directly commits the offence is termed an innocent agent because he or she does not possess the requisite mental state for the offence, whether because of general incompetence to commit a crime (for example, due to unsoundness of mind or being very young), or because of a specific defence that is available in the circumstances (for example, where a cargo attendant carries a suitcase through an airport not being aware that it contains drugs).[9]

The doctrine of innocent agency is best understood by treating the party who directly commits the crime as the inanimate object. The fact that an object cannot be convicted of a crime cannot be used as the basis for obviating the liability of the principal offender.

A seminal case in which the doctrine of innocent agent was applied was *R v Cogan*[10] where it was held that even rape could be committed through an innocent agent, where the person who had sex with the complainant did so at the instigation of the principal offender (in this case the husband of the complainant) believing the sex was consensual, in circumstances where the principal was aware that the complainant would not be consenting.[11]

The concept of innocent agency is not adequate to describe all cases where a person commits a crime through another person. Therefore, the concept that is also sometimes used is 'non-responsible agent'. The distinction between these two concepts is not clear. But non-responsible agent is typically used where the person who commits the crime has awareness that the action is wrong, but (wrongly) believes that a state of affairs exists such that a defence applies in the

---

6   *R v Stone* [1981] VR 737.

7   *Crimes Act* 1914 (Cth) s 6; *Criminal Code* (ACT) s 717; *Criminal Code* (NT) s 13; *Criminal Code* (Qld) s 10; *Criminal Law Consolidation Act* 1935 (SA) s 241; *Criminal Code* (Tas) ss 6, 161, 300; *Crimes Act* 1958 (Vic) s 325; *Criminal Code* (WA) s 10. In New South Wales, the common law continues to apply. Sections 347-50 of the *Crimes Act* 1900 (NSW) deal solely with matters of procedure and punishment concerning accessories after the fact. In Victoria and South Australia, the scope of the liability has been broadened by statute so that it is not necessary to establish that the accused was aware of the precise offence committed by the principal offender.

8   This doctrine has a statutory basis in a number of jurisdictions: *Criminal Code* (Qld) s 7(4); *Criminal Code* (Tas) s 3(2); *Criminal Code* (WA) s 7.

9   See, for example, *White v Ridley* (1978) 140 CLR 342; 52 ALJR 724.

10   [1976] QB 217.

11   The case was approved in *R v Demirian* [1989] VR 97 and *R v Matusevich* [1976] VR 470.

circumstances. An example is the case of *Osland v The Queen*[12] where a son was acquitted of murdering his father, despite the fact that he struck him to the head while he was sleeping. The mother, who told the son to kill the husband, was convicted of murder and it was held that her conviction should stand. In discussing the doctrinal basis for this McHugh J made clear that in some circumstances the notion of non-responsible agent is more apt than innocent agent:

> In cases where the person who performed the act the subject of the arrangement or understanding escapes liability, it is often said that that person has been the 'innocent agent' of the other participant or participants. But that description merely records the result that the person who performed those acts is not criminally liable. It is more accurate to describe the person, who escapes liability in a concert case where the other person is convicted, as a non-responsible agent. No doubt there are cases where the person who does the harm-causing act is innocent in a moral sense. For example, the accused may have induced a child of tender years to do the act which constitutes the *actus reus* of the crime, or imported drugs via an airline carrier. In that case, the agent is innocent of any wrongdoing and the accused is regarded as a principal in the first degree. The acts of the innocent person are attributed to the accused who is guilty of the crime because the latter has the necessary *mens rea*. The fact that the innocent agent is not guilty of the crime is of no relevance.

> But, in other cases, it is more accurate to describe the actual perpetrator as a non-responsible agent, rather than an innocent agent. Thus, in *R v Bourne* a husband was held guilty of bestiality after compelling his wife to have sexual intercourse with a dog. The husband was guilty even though his wife was never charged, presumably because the duress meant that she was not guilty of the offence.[13]

Perpetrator behind the Perpetrator: Liability of Masterminds/'Hintermen' for Acts of Otherwise Criminally Liable Agents?

The mastermind of an offence is liable for acts performed by criminally liable agents. They can be either liable as principals or accessories, pursuant to the principles discussed in this chapter. The classic 'scenario' is where a person pays a 'hit man' to kill a person. In such a case, both the mastermind and hit man are guilty of murder. Thus, they are guilty of the same substantive offence and any difference in culpability is reflected in the sentence.[14]

Joint Principals

Two or more people can be principal offenders, even where only one person directly commits the physical act constituting the crime. This is the case where the act was performed in accordance with a joint plan and the act was performed in the presence of the other party. In such circumstances, each of the accused is acting in concert. The principle is more fully set out by McHugh J in *Osland v R*[15] as follows:

---

12   (1998) 197 CLR 316.
13   Ibid. [85]-[86].
14   See discussion below.
15   (1998) 159 ALR 170.

... where a person was not only present at the scene with the person who committed the acts alleged to constitute the crime, but was there by reason of a pre-concert or agreement with that person to commit the crime. In that category, the liability of each person present as the result of the concert is not derivative but primary. He or she is a principal in the first degree. In that category each of the persons acting in concert is equally responsible for the acts of the other or others.

The general principle was clearly stated in *R v Lowery & King* (No 2) by Smith J who directed the jury in the following terms:

The law says that if two or more persons reach an understanding or arrangement that together they will commit a crime and then, while that understanding or arrangement is still on foot and has not been called off, they are both present at the scene of the crime and one or other of them does, or they do between them, in accordance with their understanding or arrangement, all the things that are necessary to constitute the crime, they are all equally guilty of that crime regardless of what part each played in its commission. In such cases they are said to have been acting in concert in committing the crime.

So far as is presently relevant, these principles were accurately and more fully stated by the New South Wales Court of Criminal Appeal in *Tangye*. The Court said:

(1) The law is that, where two or more persons carry out a joint criminal enterprise, each is responsible for the acts of the other or others in carrying out that enterprise. The Crown must establish both the existence of that joint criminal enterprise and the participation in it by the accused. (2) A joint criminal enterprise exists where two or more persons reach an understanding or arrangement amounting to an agreement between them that they will commit a crime. The understanding or arrangement need not be express, and its existence may be inferred from all the circumstances. It need not have been reached at any time before the crime is committed. The circumstances in which two or more persons are participating together in the commission of a particular crime may themselves establish an unspoken understanding or arrangement amounting to an agreement formed between them then and there to commit that crime. (3) A person participates in that joint criminal enterprise either by committing the agreed crime itself or simply by being present at the time when the crime is committed.

McHugh J also noted that because it is the acts, and not the crime, of the actual perpetrator that are attributed to the person acting in concert, if the person acting in concert has the relevant *mens rea*, her or she is guilty of the principal offence because the *actus reus* is attributed to him or her by reason of the agreement and presence at the scene. This means that an accused can be guilty of murder, although he/she did not commit the act that directly caused the death, and the person who committed that murder is guilty of a lesser offence, such as manslaughter, or even acquitted. This is doctrinally the correct position. The fact that the party who directly commits the physical act constituting a crime has a defence that is peculiar to him or her (such as insanity or self-defence) should not be transferrable to other parties.

Secondary Participation: Liability as an Accessory

At common law a person is liable as an accessory if he or she 'aids, abets, counsels or procures' the commission of an offence.[16] While each word has a different meaning, it is important to emphasise that 'all the words ... are ... instances of one general idea, that the person charged ... is in some way linked in purpose with the person actually committing the crime, and is by his words or conduct doing something to bring about, or rendering more likely, such commission'.[17]

The terms 'aiders' and 'abettors' are usually used to describe the conduct of parties that are present at the scene of the offence, while 'counsellors' and 'procurers' are normally absent when the offence is committed. The courts have held that these words should be given their ordinary meaning.[18]

'Aid' means to help, support or assist the principal offender.[19] An example is acting as a look-out while the principal offender robs a bank. There is no requirement that the secondary party actually aids the principal offender; it is sufficient that this was the purpose of the secondary offender. An 'abettor' is someone who encourages or incites the commission of the offence.[20] 'Counselling' involves advising or encouraging the offender prior to the commission of the offence.[21] 'Procuring' means to cause the offence to be committed[22] – it is the strongest form of assistance. To procure 'means to produce by endeavour'. You procure a thing by setting out to see that it happens and taking the appropriate steps to produce that happening.[23] Apart from procuring, to be liable as an accessory pursuant to one of the other limbs, it is not necessary to establish a causal connection between the acts of the secondary party and the principal offender.

In rare circumstances omissions are sufficient to ground secondary liability. In *R v Beck*[24] the Court stated:

> The fortuitous and passive presence of a mere spectator can be an irrelevance so far as an active offender is concerned. But, on the other hand, a calculated presence or a presence from which opportunity is taken can project positive encouragement and support to a principal offender.[25]

In *Croxford v The Queen*[26] it was noted that the acts of an accessory need not necessarily contribute to the offence:

---

16   This phrase is expressly adopted in South Australia and Victoria: *Criminal Law Consolidation Act* 1935 (SA) s 267; *Crimes Act* 1958 (Vic) ss 323, 324. The phrase encapsulates the common law position: *Giorgianni v R* (1985) 156 CLR 473, 492. Hence, this represents the current law in New South Wales. Similar terminology is used in the other jurisdictions: Criminal Code (Cth) s 11.2(2); Criminal Code (AC) s 11.2(2); *Criminal Code* (NT) ss 12(1)(a)-(c); *Criminal Code* (Qld) ss 7(1)(b), (c); *Criminal Code* (Tas) ss 3(1)(c), (d); *Criminal Code* (WA) ss 7(b), (c).

17   *R v Russell* [1933] VLR 59, 66-67.

18   *Attorney-General's Reference (No 1 of 1975) v R* [1975] QB 773.

19   *Thambiah v R* [1966] AC 37.

20   *Wilcox v Jeffrey* [1951] 1 All ER 464.

21   *Stuart v R* (1974) 134 CLR 426, 445.

22   *R v Beck* [1985] 1 All ER 571.

23   *Attorney-General's Reference (No 1 of 1975) v R* [1975] QB 773, 779.

24   [1985] 1 All ER 571.

25   Ibid. [38].

26   [2011] VSCA 433.

We return to counsel's submissions. The first of them appears to have proceeded on the assumption that to be liable as an aider and abettor, a person must cause the actions of the principal. That is an erroneous assumption. The prosecution need not prove that a principal was in fact encouraged or assisted by the conduct alleged to constitute aiding and abetting. So much is clear from the judgment of this Court in *R v Lam*. In *Lam* the Court of Appeal agreed with the ruling given by the trial judge, Redlich J (as his Honour then was), respecting the principles of law relating to aiding and abetting that the jury were to apply to the evidence before them.[27]

For present purposes the relevant part of his Honour's ruling was as follows:

> The prosecution is not required to establish that the acts said to constitute aiding and abetting in fact assisted or encouraged the principal in the first degree ... Such a direction to a jury would be too favourable. It would impose an impossible burden on the prosecution, who would rarely be in a position to place evidence before a jury as to the effect of the secondary participant's conduct on the principal offender's state of mind.

In *Giorgianni v The Queen*[28] the High Court held that for strict liability offences, a party cannot be liable as an accessory unless he or she is aware of the essential elements constituting the offence and intends for his or her conduct to facilitate the commission of the offence. Thus, the High Court took a narrow view of the *mens rea* that is necessary for an accused to be liable as an accessory. Liability only arises where the accused (a) knows that the principal will commit the physical element of the offence; (b) intends that his or her conduct will facilitate the commission of the offence; and (c) believes that the physical element of the offence will be committed with the requisite *mens rea* for the offence. It is not sufficient that the accused is merely reckless to the fact that the principal might commit the physical act constituting the offence.[29] Actual knowledge of all the essential facts of the offence is required and it is not sufficient that they be imputed or presumed.[30] Wilful blindness can amount to knowledge, but not negligence or recklessness.[31]

Warren[32] argues that the High Court of Australia[33] and other Australian courts[34] have broadened the *mens rea* required of the accessory to now include recklessness by the accessory. Hemming[35] holds similar views to those of Warren.

---

27 Ibid. [71].

28 (1985) 156 CLR 473.

29 See also, *R v Hartwick* [2005] VSCA 264.

30 *Giorgianni* (1985) 58 ALR 641, 664 (Gibbs CJ).

31 'Wilful blindness, in the sense that I have described, is treated as equivalent to knowledge but neither negligence nor recklessness is sufficient' (ibid. 651 (Gibbs CJ)).

32 IM Warren, 9.2 'Ancillary Liability' [9.2.41] Laws of Australia.

33 *Johns v The Queen* (1980) 143 CLR 108; (HCA, offence of murder: 'an act contemplated as a possible incident of the originally planned venture': [1980] HCA 3 at [24] citing Street CJ in earlier NSW CCA judgment); *Miller v The Queen* (1980) 32 ALR 321 (HCA; offence of murder; wording of Street CJ applied by HCA, 325).

34 *R v Le Broc* [2000] 2 VLR 43 (offence of aiding and abetting recklessly causing serious injury: 'It was not necessary to prove that the accomplice knew or believed that, by his actions, serious injury would be caused' [44]; plus 'the applicant knew that Egan at the very least foresaw that serious injury would result from his conduct' [63] at 65).

35 Hemming also alludes to *Gillard* [2003] 219 CLR 1 [117] as another case in which the HCA has at least recognised the possibility of recklessness as being part of the *mens rea* of the accessory. Andrew

Furthermore, it has been argued[36] that the accessory's criminal liability need not be based on his/her knowledge and intention that the principal offender was going to engage in a particular specific offence, as such knowledge and intention in relation to a similar type of offence is sufficient.

There have been other decisions which have placed doubt on *Giorgianni*'s necessity for the accessory's knowledge of the essential matters of the principal offence, such as *R v Annakin*[37] and *R v Stokes*.[38] However, because *Giorgianni* is a High Court decision, it impliedly overrules these other decisions in inferior courts. Academics have called for reforms to the intention and knowledge ruling in *Giorgianni*.[39]

The weight of authority suggests that while an accessory can obviously be liable for a less serious offence than the principal offender, he or she can also be liable for a more serious offence than that of the principal offender. The relevant principles regarding multiple participants in the same unlawful conduct were recently summarised by the Victorian Court of Criminal Appeal in *Croxford v The Queen*,[40] where the Court stated that it is possible that:

> (i) the participants can each be found guilty of different offences,[41] e.g., one of murder and another of manslaughter,[42]

> (ii) one participant can be found guilty and another found not guilty,[43] particularly where the mental state differs between parties,[44] for example, an aider and abettor can be convicted even though the principal offender has been acquitted,[45] particularly where the former has the requisite *mens rea* and the latter's wrongful conduct was excusable (e.g., due to duress, insanity or reasonable mistaken belief)[46] and

> (iii) different verdicts are possible for a joint offender and an accessory.[47]

Hemming, 'In Search of a Model Code Provision for Complicity and Common Purpose in Australia' (2011) 30(1) University of Tasmania Law Review 53.

36   IM Warren, 9.2 'Ancillary Liability' [9.2.47] Laws of Australia, citing various authorities such as *Bruce v Williams* (1990) 46 Australia Crim R 122.

37   (1988) 37 A Crim R 131.

38   (1990) 51 A Crim R 25.

39   S Bronitt, 'Defending *Giorgianni* – Part One: The Fault Required for Complicity' (1993) 17 Criminal Law Journal 242 argues for a restrictive fault element for common purpose based on intent in excluding both knowledge and recklessness; Stephen Odgers, 'Criminal Cases in the High Court of Australia: *McAuliffe and McAuliffe*' (1996) 20 Criminal Law Journal 43 suggests that the High Court has introduced a new doctrine of 'reckless accessoryship' akin to a new felony murder rule for accessories; Stephen Gray, 'I Didn't Know, I Wasn't There: Common Purpose and the Liability of Accessories to Crime' (1999) 23 Criminal Law Journal 201 argues for the abolition of the doctrine of common purpose in suggesting that this would simplify the law without altering the balance between the Crown and the defendant. Hemming (n 35) fn 4. Hemming also cites David Lanham, Bronwyn Bartal, Robert Evans and David Wood, *Criminal Laws in Australia* (Federation Press 2006) 500, for the same purpose.

40   [2011] VSCA 433.

41   *Croxford v The Queen* [2011] VSCA 433 [73] citing *R v Vollmer*.

42   Ibid. [75] citing *Likiardopolous v R* and [86] citing *Nguyen v R*.

43   Ibid. [122] citing *Hui Chi-ming v R*.

44   Ibid. [127].

45   Ibid. [80], citing *R v Cogan and Leak, Matusevich and Thompson; Giorgianni v R* and *Schultz v Petit*.

46   Ibid. [81]-[84], citing *Matusevich and Thompson*.

47   Ibid. [77] citing *R v Cogan and Leak*.

Specific Issue: Joint Criminal Enterprise

As noted above, where two or more persons are parties to a joint criminal enterprise, each person is liable, either as an accessory or as a principal offender, for the acts of the other or others that are performed in furtherance of that criminal enterprise. A key issue is the scope of a criminal enterprise.

At common law this is determined by the doctrine of common purpose. This focuses on an agreement (express or implied) between or among the parties concerning the scope of the criminal enterprise. The starting point in this regard is following a principle which was endorsed by Lord Parker in *R v Anderson; R v Morris*:[48]

> Where two persons embark on a joint enterprise, each is liable for the acts done in pursuance of that joint enterprise that includes liability for unusual consequences if they arise from the execution of the agreed joint enterprise but ... if one of the adventurers goes beyond what has been tacitly agreed as part of the common enterprise, his co-adventurer is not liable for the consequences of that unauthorised act ... It is for the jury in every case to decide whether what was done was part of the joint enterprise, or went beyond it and was in fact an act unauthorised by that joint enterprise.[49]

Each party is, therefore, liable for unusual or unforeseen consequences of an agreed criminal enterprise, so long as they occur during the implementation of the common design. This principle does not extend, however, to consequences that are part of a different enterprise. This is often a vague distinction.

In *McAuliffe v R*[50] the High Court considered a situation where the two appellants went with a third person to a park for the purpose of bashing or robbing someone. They attacked two people, killing one. The appellants submitted that the trial judge erred in directing the jury that they were guilty of murder if they contemplated the intentional infliction of grievous bodily harm by one of the other parties as a possible consequence of carrying out the joint enterprise and continued to participate in that enterprise. Brennan CJ, Deane, Dawson, Toohey and Gummow JJ stated:

> The doctrine of common purpose applies where a venture is undertaken by more than one person acting in concert in pursuit of a common criminal design. Such a venture may be described as a joint criminal enterprise. Those terms – common purpose, common design, concert, joint criminal enterprise – are used more or less interchangeably to invoke the doctrine which provides a means, often an additional means, of establishing the complicity of a secondary party in the commission of a crime. The liability which attaches to the traditional classifications of accessory before the fact and principal in the second degree may be enough to establish the guilt of a secondary party: in the case of an accessory before the fact where that party counsels or procures the commission of the crime, and in the case of a principal in the second degree where that party, being present at the scene, aids or abets its commission. But the complicity of a secondary party may also be established by reason of a common purpose shared with the principal offender or with that offender and others. Such a common purpose arises where a person reaches an understanding or arrangement amounting to an agreement between that person and another or others that they will

---

48   [1966] 2 QB 110.

49   This has been endorsed in numerous Australian decisions, including: *Smith, Garcia & Andreevski v The Queen* [2012] VSCA 5; *Varley v The Queen* (1976) 12 ALR 347.

50   (1995) 130 ALR 26.

commit a crime. The understanding or arrangement need not be express and may be inferred from all the circumstances. If one or other of the parties to the understanding or arrangement does, or they do between them, in accordance with the continuing understanding or arrangement, all those things which are necessary to constitute the crime, they are all equally guilty of the crime regardless of the part played by each in its commission.

Not only that, but each of the parties to the arrangement or understanding is guilty of any other crime falling within the scope of the common purpose which is committed in carrying out that purpose. Initially, the test of what fell within the scope of the common purpose was determined objectively so that liability was imposed for other crimes committed as a consequence of the commission of the crime which was the primary object of the criminal venture, whether or not those other crimes were contemplated by the parties to that venture. However, in accordance with the emphasis which the law now places upon the actual state of mind of an accused person, the test has become a subjective one and the scope of the common purpose is to be determined by what was contemplated by the parties sharing that purpose.[51]

In *McAuliffe*, the High Court of Australia appears to be extending the meaning of common purpose to the *possible*[52] consequences of the intended act in the agreement between parties. It has been argued[53] that *McAuliffe* also extends the *Giorgianni* intention rule to that of recklessness. *Miller v The Queen*[54] also stands for the same proposition in that the accessory was held criminally liable for murder where, though murder did not occur in many of the previous incidents involving the offenders, it did occur often enough to make that crime foreseeable.[55]

Effect of Errors and Transferred Malice of One Participant on the Liability of the Other Participants

There is little authority on the above issue, but the doctrine of transferred malice seems to apply to complicity scenarios, in a similar way to where a single offender commits a crime. Thus, where the principal offender accidentally kills an innocent bystander whilst unsuccessfully attempting to kill the nominated victim, both the principal and accessory will be guilty of murdering the bystander.[56]

The centuries old decision of *R v Saunders*[57] is sometimes regarded as supporting the proposition that transferred malice does not apply in the accessorial context. In this case, the husband counselled the principal to use a poisoned apple to kill his wife. The principal gave the poison apple to the wife, but she passed it to her daughter. The principal offender did not want to kill the daughter but did not alert her to the fact that the apple was poisoned. She died after eating the apple and the principal was found guilty of murder on the basis of transferred malice. The Court held that the

---

51   *Clayton v R* [2006] HCA 58.

52   *McAuliffe v R* (1995) 183 CLR 108 at [10], [11], [15], [17]-[20], relying on quotes from Street CJ in *R v Johns* (1978) 1 NSWLR 282 at 287-90 that were cited in *Johns v R* (1980) 143 CLR 108.

53   Hemming (n 35) [158].

54   (1980) 32 ALR 321.

55   The Code jurisdictions deal with the doctrine of common purpose in a similar manner: see section 11.2(2) of the *Criminal Code* (Cth); s 45 of the *Criminal Code* (ACT); s 8 of the *Criminal Code* (NT); s 8 of the *Criminal Code* (Qld); s 8 of the *Criminal Code* (WA); and s 4 of the *Criminal Code* (Tas).

56   *Mansell and Herbert's Case* (1558) 73 ER 279.

57   (1576) 2 Plowd 473.

principal was not guilty. However, this is not a case of transferred malice because the principal, by not alerting the daughter to the poison, then formed an intention or was reckless to the fact that she would be killed – this state of mind related to her as a specific identifiable victim, and was not one shared by the accessory.

Legislation in most Australian jurisdictions expressly deals with these scenarios by making the accessory liable for mistakes, accidents or different outcomes caused by a principal if it was intended that an offence of the type committed was possible or likely.[58]

Withdrawal from Participation

There is often a temporal gap between the involvement of an accessory in an offence and when the physical act is actually performed by the principal. Accordingly, it is often possible for an accessory to cease his or her involvement in the offence. The circumstances in which an accessory can effectively withdraw from a plan such as to exclude liability are unclear. The matter was considered by the High Court in *White v Ridley*.[59] Gibbs CJ stated that for withdrawal to operate as an effective defence:

> Where the accused has requested a person who is of sound and mature mind to do an act which the accused knows, but the agent does not know, is illegal, the accused will not be liable if he has given timely countermand of his request. The countermand must have been manifested by words or conduct sufficiently clear to bring it home to the mind of the agent that the accused no longer desires the agent to do what he was previously asked to do; a vague, ambiguous or perfunctory countermand would not be enough. And the accused must have done or said whatever was reasonably possible to counteract the effect of his earlier request. The countermand will not have been timely if it was given when it was too late to stop the train of events which was started by his request.[60]

Stephen and Aickin JJ, on the other hand, did not regard withdrawal as a defence *per se*, but rather stated that it can only exculpate the accessory where the conduct of the accessory breaks the chain of causation.

The possibility of effective withdrawal without communication with the other parties was recognised by the Full Court of Victoria in *R v Jensen*.[61] Informing the police was given as one example, but the Court accepted that other positive steps might also be enough. As the Victorian decision in *R v Jensen* was decided in 1975[62] before the High Court decision in *White v Ridley* was given in 1978, the dictum in *Jensen* recognising withdrawal without countermand might be regarded as impliedly overruled by the more restrictive approach taken by the majority judges in the later case of *White v Ridley*. However, neither *R v Jensen* nor the possibility of withdrawal by

---

58   See, *Criminal Code* (Cth) s 11.2(3)(a); *Criminal Code* (ACT) s 45; *Criminal Code* (NT) ss 8, 9; *Criminal Code* (Qld) ss 4, 8; *Criminal Code* (Tas) ss 4, 5; *Criminal Code* (WA) s 8.

59   (1978) 21 ALR 661.

60   The position adopted by Gibbs CJ is consistent with the position in s 8(2) of the *Criminal Code* (WA) and that endorsed in *R v Menniti* [1985] 1 Qd R 520 by Thomas and Derrington JJ.

61   [1980] VR 194.

62   The judgment in *Jensen* was given on the 6 November 1975, long before the case was actually reported in 1980. The judgment in *White v Ridley* was given on 5 October 1978.

reporting to the police was considered by the High Court in *White v Ridley*. It is, accordingly, open to Australian courts to recognise withdrawal without countermand.

In principle, there is no need for a counter demand for withdrawal to be effective. The focus should be on the effectiveness of the steps taken by a party to prevent the offence. Accordingly, informing police of the upcoming crime should be sufficient. This was expressly recognised in *R v Jensen*.[63]

Corporations

In Australia, corporations are separate legal entities.[64] They can be criminally liable for the full ambit of criminal offences (with the exception of rape) pursuant to the operation of the normal substantive criminal law rules and principles, and have the full ambit of criminal defences available to them.

Broadly, a corporation is responsible for the acts of the 'directing mind and will' acting on behalf of the corporation.[65] To this end, the courts have taken a substantive approach and accepted that the 'directing mind and will' of a corporation can extend beyond the board of directors.[66] As Lord Denning stated in *H L Bolton (Engineering) v T J Graham and Sons Ltd*:[67]

> A company may in many ways be likened to a human body. It has a brain and a nerve centre that controls what it does. It also has hands which hold the tools and act in accordance with directions from the centre. Some of the people in the company are mere servants and agents who are nothing more than the hands to do the work and cannot be said to represent the mind or will. Others are directors and managers who represent the directing mind and will of the company, and control what it does. The state of mind of these managers is the state of mind of the company and is treated by the law as such.

In some circumstances even employees or other individuals closely linked to the company could be the 'directing mind and will' of the company.[68] Whether the intentions of such person or persons are, in fact, imputed to the company will 'depend on the nature of the matter under consideration, the relative position of the officer or agent and other relevant factors and the circumstances of the case'.[69]

---

63   [1980] VR 194.

64   The main statute governing the workings and operations of corporations is the *Corporations Act 2001* (Cth), which applies uniformly throughout Australia.

65   *HL Bolton (Engineering) v TJ Graham and Sons Ltd* [1956] 3 All ER 624; *Hamilton v Whitehead* (1988) 166 CLR 121.

66   *Lennard's Carrying Company Limited v Asiatic Petroleum Company Ltd* [1915] AC 705 (HL) at 713, [1914-15] All ER Rep 280; and *Tesco Supermarkets Ltd v Nattras* [1972] AC 153 (HL) at 170, [1971] 2 All ER 127; *Hamilton v Whitehead* (1988) 166 CLR 121 at 127-28, 82 ALR 626, 629-30.

67   [1956] 3 All ER 624.

68   The shadow directors' phenomenon clearly illustrates this. A shadow director is a person not validly appointed as a director, but considered a director if 'the directors of the company or body are accustomed to act in accordance with the person's instructions or wishes': see s 9(b)(ii) of the *Corporations Act*.

69   *HL Bolton (Engineering) Co Ltd v TJ Graham & Sons Ltd* [1957] 1 QB 159 at 173, [1956] 3 All ER 624.

As a result of the distinctiveness of corporations from the individuals that run the corporation, if a corporation is guilty of a crime, its officers may not be liable. The opposite is also the case – if a company officer commits a crime in the context of corporate activities, this will not necessarily result in corporate liability.[70]

The distinctiveness of the corporation from its officers is underlined by the fact that a company officer can, in fact, even be guilty of defrauding the company, even where he or she is the directing mind and will of the company. This was illustrated by the High Court in the case of *Macleod v R*,[71] where it was held that a company director cannot give valid consent on the company's behalf to a fraudulent application of company property for the director's personal use – this is even if the company is in essence a one-person business.[72] Callinan J stated:

> A director or officer acting in breach of his obligations under statute law relating to companies, or in breach of its memorandum and articles of association, by using the money of the company for his own purpose is no more the voice or the amanuensis of the company, as between himself and the company, than a thief who gains access to its treasury and steals money from it, or a forger who forges a company cheque in his own favour.[73]

Given the distinctiveness of companies and their officers, the complicity doctrine can operate to ascribe criminal responsibility to company officers. In the corporate environment there are often many individuals who have some role in the conduct leading to corporate criminal activity. Often their role is not central or instrumental to the commission of the offence. Also, it is often the case that an individual may not be aware of the exact circumstances in which the offence will be committed. However, as we have seen, such considerations do not frustrate the operation of the complicity doctrine. Even the mere presence of a company officer at the meeting where a decision is made for the corporation to engage in criminal conduct can result in individual criminal culpability where the officer's presence provides positive encouragement and support for the principal offender (the company).[74]

Sentencing Regime for Participants

Sentencing in each of the nine Australian jurisdictions is governed by a combination of legislation and the common law.[75] There are differences between sentencing regimes throughout Australia but they share many commonalities, both in form and substance. Most importantly, in each jurisdiction,

---

70   *Hamilton v Whitehead* (n 65).

71   [2003] 214 CLR 230.

72   For a further discussion of this case, see Mirko Bagaric and James McConvill, 'Macleod and the Offence of Defrauding the Company in One Person Business: The Divergence between Legal Principle and Logic Widens' (2003) 16 Australian Journal of Corporate Law 39.

73   *Macleod* (n 71).

74   Mirko Bagaric and Jean DuPlessis, 'Expanding Criminal Sanctions for Corporate Crimes: Deprivation of Right to Work and Cancellation of Education Qualifications' (2003) 21 Companies and Securities Law Journal 7.

75   The main statutes that deal with sentencing in each jurisdiction are *Crimes Act 1900* (Cth) Part 1B (ss 16-22A); *Crimes (Sentencing) Act 2005* (ACT); *Crimes (Sentencing Procedure) Act 1999* (NSW); *Sentencing Act* (NT); *Penalties and Sentences Act 1992* (Qld); *Criminal Law (Sentencing) Act 1988* (SA); *Sentencing Act 1997* (Tas); *Sentencing Act 1991* (Vic); *Sentencing Act 1995* (WA).

the main objectives of sentencing are community protection, deterrence, denunciation and rehabilitation.[76] The main determinant which governs the severity of the sanction is the principle of proportionality,[77] which is the view that the harshness of the sanction should be commensurate with the seriousness of the offence.

There are no statutory provisions that expressly deal with the sentencing of principal parties as opposed to accessories. The distinction between principals and accessories in the sentencing calculus is reflected in the broader proportionality principle and, in particular, the harm limb. The seriousness of an offence is determined by two main variables. The first is the harm caused by the offence. The second is the culpability of the offender.

Offenders who have a greater role in an offence, have a higher degree of blameworthiness and, hence, are sentenced more severely. Offenders who plan and initiate an offence are regarded as being more culpable than those who merely have a role in carrying out some aspect of the crime.[78] Thus, in effect, accessories are generally punished less severely than principal offenders.

---

76 See Mirko Bagaric and Richard Edeny, *Australian Sentencing* (LexisNexis 2011) ch 1.

77 Ibid.

78 *Lowe v R* (1984) 154 CLR 606; *R v Willard* [2005] NSWSC 402; *R v Van Loi Nguyen* [2010] NSWCCA 226; *Chen v The Queen* [2010] NSWCCA 224. See also, *Crimes (Sentencing) Act 2005* (ACT) s 33(1)(i); *Penalties and Sentences Act 1992* (Qld) s 9(2)(d); and *Sentencing Act 1991* (Vic) s 5(2)(d).

Chapter 17

Canada

Kent Roach

Participation in Crime in Canada

The rules governing liability for participation in crime are found in the Canadian Criminal Code which provides the sole source for criminal offences in Canada. These rules are defined broadly to include traditional aspects of participation in crime such as aiding, abetting and procuring and to make all those involved in such forms of participation guilty of the same offence as the principal offender. The Supreme Court of Canada has held that the prosecutor need not chose between a theory that an accused was a principal offender or that he or she aided or abetted a crime because both satisfy the statutory definition of being guilty of an offence. The Court has also interpreted the concept of co-principal offenders broadly. The effect of these rulings is to create broad theories of liability where distinctions between degrees of culpable participation in crime are generally not relevant to determinations of criminal liability. At the same time, courts will generally consider different levels of participation in crime as an important factor in sentencing, but such considerations are precluded when offences such as murder have a mandatory penalty.

Canada has also codified a broad common enterprise rule that makes a person liable for all crimes that they knew or ought to have known would be a probable consequence of carrying out a common unlawful purpose. This rule has, however, been partially qualified for a limited number of offences, notably murder and attempted murder, by the courts under Canada's constitutional bill of rights. The Code's broad rules governing participation in crime are also central to organisational and corporate criminal liability rules added to the Canadian Criminal Code in 2003.

General Principles

With the exception of the crime of contempt of court, common law crimes in Canada have been abolished. Thus the starting point for considering participation in crime must be the relevant provisions of the Criminal Code which are as follows:

> 21. (1) Every one is a party to an offence who
> > (*a*) actually commits it;
> > (*b*) does or omits to do anything for the purpose of aiding any person to commit it; or
> > (*c*) abets any person in committing it.

> Common intention

> (2) Where two or more persons form an intention in common to carry out an unlawful purpose and to assist each other therein and any one of them, in carrying out the common purpose, commits an

offence, each of them who knew or ought to have known that the commission of the offence would be a probable consequence of carrying out the common purpose is a party to that offence.

Person counselling offence

22. (1) Where a person counsels another person to be a party to an offence and that other person is afterwards a party to that offence, the person who counselled is a party to that offence, notwithstanding that the offence was committed in a way different from that which was counselled.

(2) Every one who counsels another person to be a party to an offence is a party to every offence that the other commits in consequence of the counselling that the person who counselled knew or ought to have known was likely to be committed in consequence of the counselling.

(3) For the purposes of this Act, 'counsel' includes procure, solicit or incite.

23.1 For greater certainty, sections 21 to 23 apply in respect of an accused notwithstanding the fact that the person whom the accused aids or abets, counsels or procures or receives, comforts or assists cannot be convicted of the offence.[1]

A number of important principles follow from the above statutory structure. The first is that ss 21(1)(b) and (c), s 21(2) and s 22 effectively eliminate distinctions between principal and secondary liability found in the common law and other jurisdictions. They do so by deeming that a person who aids, abets, solicits a crime, or is in a common criminal enterprise under s 21(2) is a party to and guilty of the same offence as the principal offender.

This broad statutory approach has the potential to relieve the prosecutor of having to establish whether an accused is a principal offender who actually committed a crime or is a person who assisted or counselled the commission of the crime. The breadth of this approach was made clear in the leading case of *R v Thatcher*[2] decided by the Supreme Court of Canada in 1987.

Colin Thatcher, a prominent politician, was charged with killing his ex-wife Joanne Wilson under s 21(1) of the Criminal Code. The prosecution in its indictment did not differentiate between a charge under s 21(1)(a) on the basis that Thatcher actually committed the murder and charges under ss 21(1)(b) or (c) of aiding and abetting the commission of the murder. The prosecution's theory of the case was that either Thatcher killed Wilson himself or he hired another person to do so. The trial judge instructed the jury as follows:

At the outset I should explain to you that there are two ways in which the offence of murder could have been committed by this accused. If you find on the evidence and are satisfied beyond a reasonable doubt that Colin Thatcher did that act or actions himself that caused the death of JoAnn Wilson, it is open to you to find him guilty of murder. Alternatively, if you find that acts done or performed by the accused resulted in the death of JoAnn Wilson and were done with the intent that they cause her death, even though the actual killing was done by another or others, it is open to you to find this accused guilty of murder … Colin Thatcher is charged with committing the offence of

---

1   Criminal Code of Canada RSC 1985 c C-34 (as amended).
2   [1987] 1 SCR 652.

murder. If you do not find that he did the act of murder himself, he is equally guilty if you find and are satisfied that he either aided or abetted another or others in its commission.[3]

The defence called several witnesses to testify that Thatcher was in another city at the time of the murder and argued that the jury should acquit him because the prosecution had not established that Thatcher had assisted another person in the killing. (The prosecution had, however, called witnesses and electronic surveillance to the effect that Thatcher had given a third party a substantial sum of money to kill his wife.) The trial judge then instructed the jury that he could not agree with the defence argument and that 'as a matter of law that the fact that the Crown cannot adduce evidence that another individual or individuals actually did the act, does not preclude you from finding that the killing was done on behalf of Colin Thatcher and it is still open to you to return a finding of guilty of murder if you so find'.[4] The jury convicted Thatcher of planned and deliberate murder after four days of deliberation. Thatcher has always maintained his innocence but was unsuccessful in having his conviction overturned and a new trial ordered.[5] He is free on parole.

The Supreme Court upheld the conviction on appeal with Chief Justice Dickson concluding that the trial judge had 'accurately stated the law' under s 21 to the jury both with respect to the fact that 'the actual perpetrator need not be identified'[6] and that 'the whole point of s 21(1) is to put an aider or abettor on the same footing as the principal'.[7] He noted that the statutory provisions were designed to eliminate distinctions in the common law between principals in the second degree and accessories and to 'alleviate the necessity for the Crown choosing between two different forms of participation in a criminal offence. The law stipulates that both forms of participation are not only equally culpable, but should be treated as one single mode of incurring criminal liability'.[8] He added that the prosecutor did not have to distinguish between liability as an aider and abettor or liability as a principal offender in crafting the indictment. He adverted to the danger of acquitting the accused because the jury was divided about the appropriate theory of liability 'notwithstanding that each and every juror was certain beyond a reasonable doubt either that Thatcher personally killed his ex-wife or that he aided and abetted someone else who killed his ex-wife. This is precisely what s. 21 is designed to prevent'.[9]

Principals by Proxy: The Use of Innocent Agents

It follows from the broad general structure of s 21 of the Canadian Criminal Code, that a person would be guilty of an offence if he or she used an innocent agent as a proxy to commit a crime. One example would be a person who used an 11-year-old to sell drugs. Because the age of criminal

---

3   Ibid. [53]-[54].
4   Ibid. [54].
5   *Thatcher v Canada (Attorney General)* [1997] 1 FC 289.
6   *R v Thatcher* [1987] 1 SCR 652 [64].
7   Ibid. [66].
8   Ibid. [72].
9   Ibid. [72]. He elaborated: 'Suppose the evidence in a case is absolutely crystal clear that when X and Y entered Z's house, Z was alive, and when X and Y left, Z was dead. Suppose that in their evidence each of X and Y says that the other of them murdered Z but each admits to having aided and abetted. Are X and Y each to be acquitted if some of the jurors differ as to which of X and Y actually committed the offence? I can see absolutely no reason in policy or law to uphold such an egregious conclusion' (ibid. [82]).

responsibility in Canada is 12,[10] the child who sold the drugs could not be convicted of the crime. Nevertheless, an adult who got the child to sell the drugs would be guilty of trafficking in narcotics.

In the above scenario, the adult could be charged under various provisions of the Criminal Code and an examination of the possibilities provides a good overview of the breadth and variety of ways in which a person can be held culpable for participating in a crime. Depending on the facts, an adult who obtained illegal drugs and handled the money arising from the transactions might be liable as a joint principal offender. As will be discussed in greater detail below, the Supreme Court of Canada has recently upheld a jury instruction that a person charged with a murder could be guilty as a principal offender if he was 'otherwise an active participant' even though he did not actually shoot the victims.[11] This case raises the possibility that a person who used an innocent agent to commit the crime but was an 'active participant' in the enterprise might be held to be a co-principal offender.

At the same time, it would not be necessary for the prosecutor to charge a person who had an innocent agent commit the actual crime with being a co-principal offender. If the person aided or abetted the commission of the crime by the innocent agent this would make them a party to an offence under s 21(1)(b) or (c) of the Criminal Code. The Supreme Court has recently indicated that '[t]o aid under s. 21(1) (*b*) means to assist or help the actor. ... To abet within the meaning of s. 21(1) (*c*) includes encouraging, instigating, promoting or procuring the crime to be committed'.[12] An adult who supplied drugs for a child to sell would aid or assist in the trafficking of the narcotics. An adult who played a less active role, but nevertheless encouraged a child to sell drugs could be found guilty as an abettor under s 21(1)(c).

In addition, an adult could also be found guilty of being a party to trafficking in narcotics if he or she counselled a child to commit such an offence. Counselling is defined in s 22(3) to include procuring, soliciting or inciting the commission of an offence. An adult charged as a party to an offence by counselling an innocent agent to commit an offence would have to perform some act that falls within the broad definition of counselling and would also have to have the intent that the crime be committed.

Taken by itself, the scenario of a person using an innocent agent to commit a crime underlines that liability under the broad terms of ss 21 and 22 of the Criminal Code is not derivative to the liability of the person who actually commits the crime. Such a person may be an innocent agent who is unaware that they are delivering the drugs or a person who might have a valid defence to the commission of the crime such as a mental disorder sufficient to render the accused not responsible. Such a result is driven by the broad statutory nature of liability for participation in the crime.

Any doubt about the liability of a person who uses an innocent agent to commit a crime was dispelled in 1985 when Parliament enacted s 23.1 of the Criminal Code. It provides:

> For greater certainty, sections 21 to 23 apply in respect of an accused notwithstanding the fact that the person whom the accused aids or abets, counsels or procures or receives, comforts or assists cannot be convicted of the offence.

---

10   Criminal Code s 13.

11   *R v Pickton* [2010] 2 SCR 198 [33] (Charron J) for the majority indicated that it would have been preferable had the jury been instructed specifically about aiding and abetting but that the omission of such an instruction could only have benefited the accused (ibid. [12]). The dissenters in the case agreed that the alternatives of aiding and abetting could be put to the jury, but stated that 'the phrases "active participation", "acting in concert", or "joint venture" do not in and of themselves adequately convey the law of party liability to a trier of fact' (ibid. [38]).

12   *R v Briscoe* [2010] 1 SCR, 411 [14] citing *R v Greyeyes* [1997] 2 SCR 825 [26].

The genesis of this amendment was a decision by the Manitoba Court of Appeal that an accused could not be found guilty under s 464 of the offence of counselling an offence that was not committed when an adult counselled a child to commit an indecent act. The Court of Appeal ruled that because the child could not be convicted of the completed offence because he was less than 12 years of age that the adult should not be convicted.[13] This decision was in error because it disregarded the nature of the distinct offence of counselling a crime that is not committed. Even if the offence had involved the commission of a complete offence, for the reasons articulated above, an accused could be convicted under s 22 even if the person who actually committed the offence was an innocent agent.

In any event, Parliament eliminated any possible danger of a person using an innocent agent being found not guilty under either s 21 or s 22 by enacting s 23.1 of the Code. The new s 23.1 provides that a person who aids or abets, counsels or procures is guilty, and can be found guilty notwithstanding that the person so assisted 'cannot be convicted of the offence'. Commentators are agreed that even without the addition of s 23.1 that 'these sections would be interpreted in the same way'.[14]

In addition to the above statutory principles, the British Columbia Court of Appeal has held that the common law doctrine of innocent agency should be included in the interpretation of s 21. The case involved a passport office clerk who approved passport applications even though she knew that the applicants were using fake identification. She was charged among other offences with forging a false passport. She argued in her defence that she was not guilty because she did not actually produce the passport and the person who did produce the passport was innocent because that person relied upon the accused's approval of the passport application. The courts had little trouble rejecting such an argument. It noted that '[i]n English common law, the person who caused a felony to be committed, by means of the act of an innocent agent, was considered to be a principal in the first degree'.[15] The Court after noting the common law cases on innocent agency then concluded that 'a person who commits an offence by means of an instrument "whose movements are regulated" by him, actually commits the offence himself'.[16] The Court added that '21(1) (a) of the Criminal Code can and should be construed so as to give effect to the doctrine of innocent agency'.[17] This case suggests that an accused that uses an innocent agent to commit an offence should be found guilty as a principal offender. In addition, s 23.1 makes clear that such a person could also be found guilty as an aider, abettor or counsellor under ss 21(1)(b), (c) and 22.

Liability of Masterminds

As is the case with liability for crimes committed with innocent agents, the liability of masterminds is primarily an issue of the interpretation of the broad statutory provisions that provide for party liability. Canadian criminal law does not recognise a mastermind as a legal concept, though the classification of a person as a mastermind could be relevant at sentencing under s 718.1 which provides that the fundamental principle of sentencing is that a sentence must be proportionate to

---

13   *R v Richard* (1985) 30 CCC (3d) 127 (Man CA).

14   Kent Roach, *Criminal Law* (5th edn, Irwin Law 2012) 144-45; Eric Colvin and Sanjeev Anand, *Principles of Criminal Law* (3rd edn, Thomson 2007) 561; Morris Manning and Peter Sankoff, *Criminal Law* (4th edn, Butterworths 2009) 250.

15   *R v Berryman* (1990) 57 CCC (3d) 375, 380 (BCCA).

16   Ibid. 385.

17   Ibid. 86.

the gravity of the offence and the degree of responsibility of the offender. A conclusion that an accused was a mastermind could be an important aggravating factor in sentencing.[18]

As suggested above in relation to those who commit crimes through an innocent agent, a mastermind depending on their actual conduct might be found guilty as a principal or co-principal offender, an aider or abettor or a person who counselled an offence. The exact classification would not matter for the purposes of criminal liability because all of these forms of participation are treated the same in making the accused a party to the offence.

Joint Principals

The leading but not totally satisfactory case on joint principals is the Supreme Court of Canada's recent decision in *R v Pickton*.[19] In that case, involving a man accused of being a serial murderer, the jury was initially instructed according to the Crown's theory of the case that Pickton personally shot his multiple victims. The Supreme Court, however, upheld a subsequent jury instruction that left open the possibility that Pickton would be guilty if he was 'otherwise an active participant' in the killings and indicated that it was not necessary that he be the actual shooter to be guilty of murder. Charron J for the majority of the Supreme Court indicated that it would have been preferable had the jury been instructed specifically about aiding and abetting but that the omission of such an instruction could only have benefited the accused given that Pickton could have been guilty of aiding or abetting without necessarily having been an active participant in the killing.[20] The dissenters in the case agreed that the alternatives of aiding and abetting could be put to the jury, but stated that 'the phrases "active participation", "acting in concert", or "joint venture" do not in and of themselves adequately convey the law of party liability to a trier of fact'.[21]

Even before *Pickton*, a number of accused could be convicted of murder if they all knowingly assisted in the victim's death even though it was unclear which one of the accused actually killed the victim.[22] The court's decision in *Pickton* has been applied in a subsequent case where the courts found two drivers to be co-principal offenders in causing death by criminal negligence in an automobile accident.[23] The somewhat casual expansion of the concept of being co-principals in *Pickton* could be criticised, but in large part does not matter because a more restrictive approach to co-principal liability would still in almost every case result in a person labelled as a co-principal under *Pickton* being found guilty of the same offence under ss 21(1)(b) or (c) or 22.

---

18   See for example *R v Amara* 2010 ONCA 858 [19] justifying a life sentence because the accused was the mastermind of a terrorist plot involving many people.

19   [2010] 2 SCR 98.

20   Ibid. [12].

21   Ibid. [38].

22   *Chow Bew v The Queen* [1956] SCR 124; *R v Isaac* [1984] 1 SCR 74 [80]-[81]; *R v McMaster* [1996] 1 SCR 740 [33]; *R v McQuaid* [1998] 1 SCR 244; *R v Biniaris* [2000] 1 SCR 381; *R v Suzack* (2000) 141 CCC (3d) 449 (Ont CA); *R v H (LI)* (2003) 17 CR (6th) 338 [60] (Man CA); *R v Portillo* (2003) 17 CR (6th) 362 [71] (Ont CA); *R v JFD* (2005) 196 CCC (3d) 316 [14] (BCCA); *R v Rojos* (2006) 208 CCC (3d) 13 (BCCA).

23   *R v Hughes* 2011 BCCA 220.

Secondary Participation

Aiding and Abetting

A person who either aids or abets an offence is under s 21(1)(b) and (c) a party to that offence and guilty of the same offence as the person who actually commits the offence. It is common to speak of aiding and abetting together, but 'the two concepts are distinct, and liability can flow from either one. Broadly speaking, "[t]o aid under s. 21(1) (*b*) means to assist or help the actor. ... To abet within the meaning of s. 21(1) (*c*) includes encouraging, instigating, promoting or procuring the crime to be committed."'[24] Abetting has been held to include intentional encouragement whether by acts or words.[25] A person who distracts a security guard so that his or her friend can shoplift may aid a theft, whereas a sales clerk who encourages or allows a customer to shoplift would abet the theft. Both people would be guilty of theft, even though they did not themselves steal the merchandise. The terms 'aiding' and 'abetting' are generally used together, but they remain distinct forms of liability for being a party to an offence.

Consistent with the general trend in party liability in Canadian criminal law, aiding and abetting are generally interpreted in a broad fashion that includes many forms of assistance in crime. That said, a failure to act will not generally constitute aiding and abetting. In *Dunlop v R*,[26] Dickson J stated that a person is not guilty of aiding or abetting a rape:

> merely because he is present at the scene of a crime and does nothing to prevent it ... If there is no evidence of encouragement by him, a man's presence at the scene of the crime will not suffice to render him liable as aider and abettor. A person who, aware of a rape taking place in his presence, looks on and does nothing is not, as a matter of law, an accomplice. The classic case is the hardened urbanite who stands around in a subway station when an individual is murdered.

In the case, the accused were acquitted of rape on the basis that there was no evidence that they 'rendered aid, assistance, or encouragement' to the gang rape of a young woman.

The Court in that case did indicate, however, that presence at the commission of an offence can be evidence of aiding and abetting if accompanied by other factors such as prior knowledge that the crime was going to be committed. Similarly, presence at a crime that prevents the victim's escape or prevents the victim receiving assistance is a sufficient *actus reus*.[27] Some members of the Supreme Court have disapproved of a case in which an accused was found not to be a party to a rape, despite having witnessed the crime with his pants down.[28] At the same time, the Court has recently affirmed as sound the proposition in *Dunlop* that 'an accused's mere presence at the scene of a crime in circumstances consistent with innocence will not support a conviction'.[29] In that case it upheld the conviction of a man producing marijuana, on the basis that there was evidence beyond his mere presence to convict him because he was found sleeping in a camouflaged tent with

---

24   *Briscoe* (n 12) [14] citing *R v Greyeyes* (n 12) [26].

25   *R v Wobbes* 2008 ONCA 567 (CanLII) 2008 ONCA 567, 242 OAC 7, 235 CCC (3d) 561; *R v Hennessey* 2010 ABCA 274 para [39].

26   (1979) 47 CCC (2d) 93 at 111 (SCC) [*Dunlop*].

27   *R v Black* [1970] 4 CCC 251 (BCCA); *R v Stevenson* (1984) 11 CCC (3d) 443 (NSCA).

28   *R v Salajko* [1970] 1 CCC 352 (Ont CA) disapproved of in *R v Kirkness* (1990) 60 CCC (3d) 97, 106 (SCC) Wilson J (L'Heureux-Dubé J concurring).

29   *R v Jackson* 2007 SCC 52 [3] and [9].

fertiliser at a remote marijuana plantation. Two judges dissented, however, on the basis that there was no evidence of anything beyond the accused's presence at the site.

The position that mere presence and passive acquiescence in a crime is not sufficient to make a person an aider or abettor mirrors the criminal law's traditional reluctance to penalise omissions. As with omissions, however, courts recognise exceptions to this principle in cases where the person who stands by is under a specific legal duty to act. Owners of cars who do nothing while others engage in dangerous driving have been held to have abetted the dangerous driving because they did not exercise their power to control the use of their vehicle.[30] A senior officer in charge of a police lock-up has also been found to have aided and abetted an assault on a prisoner by failing to exercise his statutory duty to protect a prisoner in his charge.[31] The conclusion in these cases that a failure to act can amount to aiding and abetting is strengthened by the fact that section 21(1)(b) provides that one who *omits* to do anything for the purpose of aiding any person to commit an offence may be charged as a party to that offence. The broad definition of the *actus reus* of aiding and abetting is balanced with a requirement that the act or omission of assistance be committed for the purpose of assisting in the commission of the offence.

To be convicted as an aider or abettor, the accused must not only knowingly assist the principal, but also intend to assist the principal.[32] There are thus two different *mens rea* requirements for aiding and abetting: the intent to assist the principal offender; and, knowledge of the type but not the exact nature of the crime committed. Section 21(1)(b) requires that the accused act or omit to do anything for the purpose of aiding any person to commit an offence. A person who unwittingly delivers a bomb or administers a poison would not be guilty as a party to an offence, even though he or she may have committed the *actus reus* of assisting the commission of the offence.[33] Such a person would not have acted for the purpose or with the intent of aiding the offence.

The requirement that the accused act with the purpose of aiding the offence does not mean that the accused must desire that the offence be committed or even share the exact same *mens rea* as the principal offender. A person who assists in a robbery by driving the getaway car will have acted with the purpose of aiding the offence, even though he or she participated only because of death threats. Chief Justice Lamer has concluded that 'the expression "for the purpose of aiding" in section 21(1) (b), properly understood, does not require that the accused actively view the commission of the offence he or she is aiding as desirable in and of itself. As a result, the *mens rea* for aiding under section 21(1)(b) is not susceptible of being "negated" by duress'.[34]

The Ontario Court of Appeal has concluded with respect to section 21(1)(b) that 'purpose is synonymous with intent and does not include recklessness'.[35] It has also indicated that the high level of *mens rea* for section 21(1)(b) is justified not only by the specific purpose requirement in the section, but also by the need to ensure that a person who assists in the commission of an offence has a sufficient level of fault to justify convicting that person of the same offence as the person who actually committed the offence. Recklessness is not a sufficient form of fault to convict a person as a party to an offence under section 21(1)(b).[36] This is appropriate because an aider and abettor's involvement with the crime will be more peripheral than that of the principal offender(s) and the enlarged scope of criminal liability should be counter-balanced by higher fault requirements.

---

30   *R v Halmo* (1941) 76 CCC 116 (Ont CA); *R v Kulbacki* [1966] 1 CCC 167 (Man CA).

31   *R v Nixon* (1990) 57 CCC (3d) 97 (BCCA).

32   *R v Morgan* (1993) 80 CCC (3d) 16 [21] (Ont CA).

33   *Berryman* (n 15).

34   *Hibbert* (1995) 99 CCC (3d) 193, 214 (SCC).

35   *R v Roach* (2004) 192 CCC (3d) 557 [36] (Ont CA).

36   *Hibbert* (n 34) [26]; *R v L* (2003) 172 CCC (3d) 44 [48] (BCCA).

In addition to the intent or purpose to assist the principal offender, an aider or abettor must also know that the principal offender will commit the crime, but not necessarily precisely how the crime will be committed.[37] In other words, it is not necessary that the aider or abettor know all the details of the crime committed; it is sufficient that he or she was 'aware of the type of crime to be committed'[38] and knew 'the circumstances necessary to constitute the offence he is accused of aiding'.[39] In *R v Briscoe*,[40] the Supreme Court held that wilful blindness could be substituted for this knowledge requirement. It defined wilful blindness as a form of 'deliberate ignorance' that is distinct from recklessness. This suggests that the *mens rea* requirements for s 21(1)(b) are quite high and that recklessness will not suffice either for the intent to assist requirement or the knowledge of the crime that is being assisted.

A tricky issue is how this knowledge requirement for aiding and abetting plays out in the case of offences based on criminal negligence. In *R v Jackson*,[41] the Supreme Court held that it was an error to hold that a person who assisted in a killing could only be found guilty of manslaughter if he had a subjective knowledge that the victim would die. Such a requirement would be appropriate for murder but not manslaughter which only requires an objective foresight of non-trivial bodily harm. This approach has been followed in other cases of aiding and abetting crimes of negligence, but subject to the proper requirement that the accused have the subjective intent to assist in the dangerous acts that created the objective foresight of bodily harm.[42]

Counselling or Incitement

Section 22(1) provides that a person who counsels a crime that is committed becomes a party to that offence and, as such, is subject to the same punishment as if he or she had actually committed the offence. This provision applies 'notwithstanding that the offence was committed in a way different from that which was counselled'. An accused who counsels a person to kill another with a bomb would still be guilty of murder if the person counselled used a gun instead. In addition, section 22(2) expands liability further by providing that a counsellor becomes a party 'to every offence that the other commits in consequence of the counselling that the person who counselled knew or ought to have known was likely to be committed in consequence of the counselling'.

The *actus reus* of counselling remains the act of procuring, soliciting or inciting a crime. In addition, a crime must then be committed by the person counselled. The crime need not be committed in the same way as was counselled or even be the same crime that was counselled. It must, however, be a crime that was reasonably foreseeable from the counselling.

The accused must intentionally counsel a criminal offence under section 22(1). It would not be fair to hold that an accused is a party to an offence for comments that were not intended to solicit or incite a crime, but which had that effect. The Supreme Court has, however, suggested that the intent for the separate offence of counselling a crime that is not committed can be satisfied by knowingly counselling an offence while aware of an unjustified risk that the offence will likely be committed.[43] Most commentators have interpreted this as requiring that the accused only be reckless. Such an approach, however, threatens to undercut the high level of subjective intent

37 *Hibbert* (n 34) [17].
38 *R v Yanover* (1985) 20 CCC (3d) 300, 329 (Ont CA).
39 *R v FW Woolworth Co* (1974) 18 CCC (2d) 23, 32 (Ont CA).
40 *Briscoe* (n 12) [22]-[25].
41 [1993] 4 SCR 573.
42 *R v MR*, 2011 ONCA 190.
43 *R v Hamilton* [2005] 2 SCR 432 [29].

that normally accompanies party liability. For example, recklessness in the form of subjective advertence to the risk has not been a sufficient form of fault to make a counsellor of a crime guilty under s 22(1) of being a party to a crime. It remains to be seen whether this will change and recklessness will suffice under s 22(1) in light of the Court's seeming acceptance of recklessness for the separate offence of counselling a crime that is not committed.

Under section 22(2), an accused who intentionally counsels an offence is also a party 'to every offence that the other commits in consequence of the counselling that the person who counselled knew or ought to have known was likely to be committed in consequence of the counselling'. This extends liability not only to the offence intentionally counselled, but to any other offence that the person knew or ought to have known would be committed as a result of the counselling. The latter fault element of objective foreseeability would violate section 7 of the *Charter* when applied to murder or attempted murder, which the Court has held requires a minimum fault element of subjective foresight of death.[44] Nevertheless, objective foreseeability would be a constitutionally sufficient fault element for most other crimes. For example, an accused who counselled a severe beating could be convicted of manslaughter because he or she ought to have known that manslaughter could result.[45] The accused would, however, only be guilty of murder if he or she actually knew that death was likely to result.

Joint Criminal Enterprise

Joint criminal enterprise liability is determined under s 21(2) of the Code. This provision provides that those who 'form an intention in common to carry out an unlawful purpose and to assist each other therein' are parties to any consequential offence committed by one of them provided that the accused 'knew or ought to have known that the commission of the offence would be a probable consequence of carrying out the common purpose'. Thus, a person who agrees to a joint criminal enterprise to commit a robbery will also be guilty of any other offences that he or she knew or ought to know would probably occur as a result of committing a robbery. This is a fairly expansive rule, but one that has been somewhat narrowed by the courts.

Under section 21(2) there must be a formation of a common intent to assist each other in carrying out an unlawful purpose, but not necessarily any act of assistance.[46] It could be argued that this requires an agreement akin to conspiracy, although most cases do not dwell on the issue. In addition, it is assumed that the unlawful purpose means a purpose contrary to the Criminal Code. The subsequent offence committed has to be one that the accused either knows or ought to have known would be a probable consequence of carrying out the common purpose. In *Jackson*,[47] the Supreme Court held that the offence is not confined to that of which the principal offender was convicted, but encompasses any included offence. For example, a party to an unlawful purpose could be convicted of manslaughter, even though the principal was convicted of murder. This would happen when the party did not have the subjective foresight of death required for a murder conviction, but did have objective foresight of bodily harm necessary for a manslaughter conviction. Less clear is whether a party with the *mens rea* for murder can be convicted of murder

---

44   *R v Martineau* [1990] 2 SCR 633; *R v Logan* [1990] 2 SCR 731; *R v Chenier* (2006) 205 CCC (3d) 333 [62] (Ont CA).

45   Because of the fault element required for manslaughter, this conviction requires only objective foreseeability that bodily harm would result. *R v Jackson* (1993) 86 CCC (3d) 385 at 391 (SCC).

46   *R v Moore* (1984) 15 CCC (3d) 541, 555 (Ont CA).

47   (1993) 86 CCC (3d) 385.

even though the principal offender was only convicted of manslaughter. There is some authority that the party could only be convicted of the same offence as the principal offender,[48] but general principles suggest that a party with the required *mens rea* could be convicted of a more serious offence than a principal offender. For example, a sober or unprovoked accomplice might have the *mens rea* for murder even though the actual drunken or provoked killer might only have the *mens rea* for manslaughter.[49]

There are two distinct mental or fault elements for section 21(2): the first is the formation of the common unlawful purpose and the second is either subjective knowledge or objective foresight that the actual offence would be a probable consequence of carrying out the unlawful purpose. In *R v Paquette*,[50] the Supreme Court held that a person who drove others to a robbery had not formed a common unlawful purpose to assist them in the robbery because he had been forced at gun point to co-operate. Martland J stated:

> A person whose actions have been dictated by fear of death or of grievous bodily injury cannot be said to have formed a genuine common intent to carry out an unlawful purpose with the person who has threatened him with those consequences if he fails to co-operate.[51]

In *Hibbert*, the Supreme Court subsequently rejected this interpretation on the basis that section 21(2) requires only a common intent to commit the offence and not 'a mutuality of motives and desires between the party and the principal'.[52] On this reasoning, Paquette would have had the required mental element because he intended to commit a robbery even though he did not truly desire to commit the robbery. The fact that he wanted to commit a robbery only because his life was threatened would be a matter of motive that is not relevant to the mental element. It would, however, be relevant to whether Paquette had a common law defence of duress that would prevent his conviction. As with section 21(1)(b), the Court has rejected the idea that intent requires proof of desire even though section 21(2) requires the formation of an intention in common to assist in the commission of an offence. It was concerned that cases such as *Paquette* would complicate the task of the jury by considering duress as both a matter relevant to *mens rea* and as a separate defence and that it would not fulfil Parliament's purpose in widening the net of criminal liability to catch those who assist in the commission of crimes.

In most cases the accused will be liable if he or she either knew or ought to have known that the commission of the offence was a probable consequence of the common unlawful purpose. In *Logan*,[53] however, the Supreme Court declared the phrase 'ought to have known' to be an unjustified violation of the *Charter* when the accused is charged with murder or attempted murder. Section 7 of the *Charter* requires subjective as opposed to objective foresight of death for a conviction of murder or attempted murder. As Lamer CJ explained:

> When the principles of fundamental justice require subjective foresight in order to convict a principal of attempted murder, that same minimum degree of *mens rea* is constitutionally required to convict a party to the offence of attempted murder. Any conviction for attempted murder,

---

48   *R v Hébert* (1986) 51 CR (3d) 264 (NB CA).

49   *R v Remillard* [1921] SCR 21.

50   (1976) 30 CCC (2d) 417 (SCC).

51   Ibid. 423.

52   *Hibbert* (n 34) 216. See *Dunbar v R* (1936) 67 CCC 20 (SCC), also drawing a distinction between intention and motive when an accused was threatened if he did not assist in a robbery.

53   (1990) 58 CCC (3d) 391.

whether of the principal directly or of a party pursuant to s. 21(2), will carry enough stigma to trigger the constitutional requirement. To the extent that s. 21(2) would allow for the conviction of a party to the offence of attempted murder on the basis of objective foresight, its operation restricts s. 7 of the *Charter*.[54]

In cases of murder and attempted murder, the objective arm of section 21(2) should not be left to the jury and the jury should only convict if a party has actual foresight or knowledge that the principal offender would attempt to kill a person while carrying out their common unlawful purpose.[55]

Logan is a case of limited application. The Court stated that 'because of the importance of the legislative purpose, the objective component of section 21(2) can be justified with respect to most offenses'.[56] Lamer CJ concluded that it was not a principle of fundamental justice that a person convicted as a party to an offence has as high a *mens rea* as the principal offender. This means that a party could be convicted under the objective arm of section 21(2) even though subjective *mens rea* was required to convict the principal. For example, an accused who formed an unlawful purpose to rob a bank could be convicted of assault on the basis that he or she ought to have known an assault would occur, whereas the person who actually assaulted one of the guards or tellers would be convicted on the basis of a subjective intent to apply force. In upholding the objective arm of section 21(2) as constitutional in most cases, the Court emphasised the importance of recognising different degrees of involvement when exercising sentencing discretion.[57] A fundamental principle of sentencing is that the punishment be proportionate to the degree of the offender's responsibility.

The Effects of Errors/Transferred Malice by One Participant

What is the relevance of errors or impossibility to a charge of aiding and abetting? In *R v Chan*,[58] the Ontario Court of Appeal upheld a conviction for aiding a drug offence even though the drugs had been previously intercepted by the police and only contained a very small amount of heroin. The Court of Appeal held that what mattered in determining the *mens rea* was the accused's belief that he was dealing with heroin and not the truth of the matter. This suggests that the accused might have had the *mens rea* even if there were no drugs in the package that was received. The question then would be whether the accused had the necessary *actus reus* to be guilty of aiding or abetting the offence. If there were no drugs present, then it would be difficult to conclude that the accused had aided and abetted a drug offence. The accused would not necessarily be acquitted because he or she could be guilty of the separate offence of attempting to possess the heroin.

---

54   Ibid. 401.

55   *R v Rodney* (1990) 58 CCC (3d) 408 (SCC); *R v Laliberty* (1997) 117 CCC (3d) 97, 108 (Ont CA); *R v Portillo* (2004) 17 CR (6th) 362 [72]-[73] (Ont CA).

56   *Logan* (n 44) 403.

57   Lamer CJ stated: 'It must be remembered that within many offences there are varying degrees of guilt and it remains the function of the sentencing process to adjust the punishment for each individual offender accordingly. The argument that the principles of fundamental justice prohibit the conviction of a party to an offence on the basis of a lesser degree of *mens rea* than that required to convict the principal could only be supported, if at all, in a situation where the sentence for a particular offence is fixed. However, currently in Canada, the sentencing scheme is flexible enough to accommodate the varying degrees of culpability resulting from the operation of ss 21 and 22' (ibid. 398).

58   *R v Chan* (2003) 178 CCC (3d) 269 (Ont CA).

Another difficult issue is whether the *mens rea* of one party affects the *mens rea* of another. For example, where one offender has a firearm and another threatens to use it, both offenders can be guilty of the offence of using a firearm.[59] At the same time, Canadian courts have generally held that a purchaser of drugs is not guilty by reason of the purchase alone of aiding the more serious trafficking offence.[60] The courts are concerned that purchasers do not deserve the stigma of a trafficking conviction and are more appropriately convicted of possession of narcotics or possession with the intent to traffic, either as a principal offender or an aider or abettor. Assisting a person to purchase drugs is another matter. In *Greyeyes*, the Supreme Court upheld the trafficking conviction of a person who located a seller for a purchaser, negotiated the purchase price, and accepted $10 for his efforts.[61] The Court reasoned that these were not the acts of a mere purchaser, but rather the acts of one who offered crucial assistance to the trafficking. The accused had the dual *mens rea* of intending to assist the trafficking and knowledge that trafficking was being assisted. The accused, who acted as a go-between between the purchaser and the seller and assisted the trafficking transaction, was convicted and sentenced as a drug trafficker. Hopefully, his rather peripheral involvement in the trafficking enterprise would be considered at sentencing.

Withdrawal from Participation

Withdrawal from participation in a common enterprise is generally not seen as a distinct defence or doctrine in Canada. Nevertheless, an accused's actions in abandoning a crime may in some cases be evidence of a lack of intent as is the case with respect to attempts. The Supreme Court has, for example, upheld the acquittal of a man for murder who participated in a break-in in a home but who told the principal offender to stop strangling the victim because he was going to kill her. The Court held that the accused had given 'timely notice' to the accused that he was acting on his own.[62]

It is possible that an accused might abandon the common unlawful purpose under s 21(2) through timely notice. The Court's decision in *Hibbert*, however, suggests that reluctance to engage in the common unlawful purpose will not be inconsistent with the *mens rea*. Furthermore abandonment including surrender to the authorities or remorse after the commission of the relevant *actus reus* and *mens rea* will not relieve an accused of responsibility for having committed the crime. That said, an accused who forms a common unlawful purpose is not automatically responsible for all the crimes that his or her accomplice commits while pursuing that purpose. The accused is only liable for crimes that he or she knows or in most cases ought to have known would be a probable consequence of carrying out the common unlawful purpose.

The idea that there must be timely notice to ground a defence of abandonment of an intent to aid or abet is well-established in Canadian law, but in principle the matter is best viewed as a matter that can raise a reasonable doubt about specific *mens rea*.[63] In any event, abandonment will inevitably depend on the quality of any particular withdrawal or abandonment and the accused's

---

59   *R v Steele* 2007 SCC 36 [33].

60   *R v Poitras* (1974) 12 CCC (3d) 337 (SCC); *R v Meston* (1975) 28 CCC (2d) 497 (Ont CA). As Justice L'Heureux-Dubé has stated, 'despite his or her crucial assistance in helping to complete the sale of narcotics, the purchaser cannot *by this action alone* be found guilty of the offence of aiding and abetting the offence of trafficking' (*R v Greyeyes* (1997) 116 CCC (3d) 334, 340 [emphasis in original]).

61   *Greyeyes* (n 60).

62   *R v Kirkness* [1990] 3 SCR 74 citing *R v Whitehouse* [1941] 1 DLR 683 (BCCA), quoted with approval in *Miller v The Queen* [1977] 2 SCR 680.

63   Manning and Sankoff (n 14) 269.

particular form and degree of participation. For example, the notice must be 'timely' because if it occurs too late, the accused will already have committed the relevant *actus reus* and *mens rea*. An accused's remorse after the commission of a crime is not an act of abandonment relevant to criminal liability.

Corporate Liability

Although enacted primarily to replace and expand the common law concept of directing mind, new organisational liability provisions added to the Criminal Code of Canada in 2003 incorporate the provisions for party liability discussed above. The new provisions provide as follows:

> 22.1 In respect of an offence that requires the prosecution to prove negligence, an organization is a party to the offence if
>> (*a*) acting within the scope of their authority
>>> (i) one of its representatives is a party to the offence, or
>>> (ii) two or more of its representatives engage in conduct, whether by act or omission, such that, if it had been the conduct of only one representative, that representative would have been a party to the offence; and
>> (*b*) the senior officer who is responsible for the aspect of the organization's activities that is relevant to the offence departs – or the senior officers, collectively, depart – markedly from the standard of care that, in the circumstances, could reasonably be expected to prevent a representative of the organization from being a party to the offence.

> 22.2 In respect of an offence that requires the prosecution to prove fault – other than negligence – an organization is a party to the offence if, with the intent at least in part to benefit the organization, one of its senior officers:
>> (*a*) acting within the scope of their authority, is a party to the offence;
>> (*b*) having the mental state required to be a party to the offence and acting within the scope of their authority, directs the work of other representatives of the organization so that they do the act or make the omission specified in the offence; or
>> (*c*) knowing that a representative of the organization is or is about to be a party to the offence, does not take all reasonable measures to stop them from being a party to the offence.

The overall effects of the incorporation of the party provisions in the above organisational liability provisions is to expand the criminal liability of organisations.

Under s 22.1 which applies to negligence offences in the Criminal Code, representatives of an organisation either as individuals or collectively have to be found to be party to an offence such as criminal negligence causing death. The incorporation of the party provisions of ss 21 and 22 of the Code means that the representative does not necessarily have to have committed the negligence offence but may have aided or abetted another person to do so contrary to s 21(1)(b) or (c) or have counselled another person to do so under s 22(1). Although 'representative' is defined broadly to include agents and contractors of the organisation,[64] the incorporation of the party provisions

---

64   Criminal Code s 2.

means that a corporation could by means of the party provisions be held liable even if none of its representatives actually committed the offence. The incorporation of the parties provisions both expands liability and integrates the established jurisprudence of party liability, but at some price of making organisational liability rather complex.

Party liability also plays a critical role under s 22.2 which applies to subjective intent offences. Under s 22.2(a), a corporation is liable for such an offence if one of its senior officers is a party to an offence such as fraud under ss 21 or 22. As discussed above, this means that the corporation could be guilty of a subjective intent offence even though its senior officer did not commit the crime. The person who actually committed the offence may be connected to the corporation, but not senior enough within the corporation to have the policy making or managing responsibilities to be classified as a senior officer.[65] The person who actually commits the offence may, however, have no connection with the corporation, but rather be aided and abetted by the senior officer or counselled by the senior officer to commit the offence.

Under s 22.2(b), a corporation is liable if a senior officer with the mental state required to be a party directs the work of representatives 'so that they do the act or make the omission specified in the offence'. It is not exactly clear what this provision adds to party liability because it is arguable that a senior officer who directs a representative to commit an offence would in any event be guilty as a party to an offence under s 22.2(a) on the basis of having counselled the commission of an offence. On the other hand, courts may interpret s 22.2(b) as adding something to what already would be captured in s 22.2(a) and this would suggest that they would interpret direction in s 22.2 (b) to include something broader than counselling an offence under s 22. This provision has not yet been subject to judicial interpretation.

Finally, s 22.2(c) makes the corporation liable if a senior officer knows that a representative of the corporation is or is about to be party to the offence under ss 21 and 22 but fails to take all reasonable measures to stop them from being a party to the offence. This raises interesting issues about the combination of subjective and objective fault, but not issues specific to participation. In conclusion, the party provisions play a pivotal role in Canadian organisational liability and have the effect of expanding the criminal liability of corporations.

Sentencing

As mentioned above, judges are directed to examine an offender's degree of responsibility when sentencing an offender under s 718.1 which provides that proportionality is the fundamental principle of sentencing. Courts will have ability in sentencing to distinguish between different levels of participation that would otherwise be grouped together under ss 21 and 22 of the Criminal Code. It is important to note, however, that the classification of an offender's degree of responsibility in sentencing is done for the purposes of sentencing and is not bound in any way by the juristic distinctions in ss 21 and 22 between principal offenders and aiders and abetters and counsellors. It is thus possible for a court to find that a person who aided, abetted or counselled an offence is a mastermind or directing force that is deserving of more punishment than a person who actually committed the offence, but may not have done so without the mastermind's instigation.[66]

The ability of judges at sentencing to draw distinctions between different forms of involvement in crimes is limited when Parliament has imposed a mandatory sentence. Murder in Canada has

---

65 Again this term is defined in s 2 of the Criminal Code.
66 *Amara* (n 18) [19].

always had a mandatory sentence of life imprisonment and this was a consideration when the courts limited Canada's joint criminal enterprise rule to require that a person could only be convicted of murder if they knew (as opposed to ought to have known) that a murder would be the probable consequence of carrying out a common unlawful purpose.

Conclusion

This chapter has examined the broadly defined provisions within the Canadian Criminal Code with respect to participation in crime. These provisions have been interpreted to make no distinction between a person who actually commits an offence and a person who aids, abets or counsels the commission of the offence. Canada also has a broad joint criminal enterprise rule that makes a person liable for crimes that they know or ought to have known will be committed in carrying out a common unlawful purpose. The Canadian courts have interpreted these long standing provisions in the Canadian Criminal Code as designed to remedy the technicality of the English common law and to escape the mischief of a person being acquitted because the jury could not agree on whether he or she actually committed the offence or assisted another. The broad party provisions are also incorporated in the organisational liability provisions of the Canadian Criminal Code and have the effect of expanding corporate criminal liability. Finally, they have also influenced the Courts to define joint principal liability in a similarly broad fashion and to hold that a person can be guilty as a party even if the person who actually commits the offence is innocent.

The broad definition of participation in Canadian criminal law presents some dangers. An important restraint is that those who assist or counsel the commission of a crime should have a clear intent to do so if their more peripheral conduct is to make them a party to the same offence as the principal offenders. Canadian courts have restrained the broad joint criminal enterprise rule by holding that accused can only be guilty of murder and attempted murder if they subjectively knew that such high stigma and penalty crimes were a probable occurrence of the joint enterprise. That said, the courts now accept wilful blindness as an equivalent of knowledge. A person can be held liable of all crimes other than murder or attempted murder emerging from the joint criminal enterprise on the basis that he or she ought to have known that they would occur as a probable consequence of the common unlawful purpose. A person can also be held guilty of aiding and abetting crimes of negligence on the basis of intentional assistance in acts that are themselves negligent. Finally, the increasing use of mandatory minimum sentences in Canada will deprive judges of the power to use the full range of sentencing discretion as a safety valve to compensate for Canada's broad approach to the liability of those who participate in criminal conduct.

Chapter 18

Germany

Kai Ambos and Stefanie Bock

General Principles: Types of Participation and General Basis of Attributing Criminal Liability for Acts of Others

The main rules on participation are laid down in §§ 25-27 of the German Criminal Code ('*Strafgesetzbuch*' – StGB):[1]

§ 25: Principals

(1) Any person who commits the offence himself or through another shall be liable as a principal.
(2) If more than one person commit the offence jointly, each shall be liable as a principal (joint principals).

§ 26: Abetting

Any person who intentionally induces another to intentionally commit an unlawful act (abettor) shall be liable to be sentenced as if he were a principal.

§ 27: Aiding

(1) Any person who intentionally assists another in the intentional commission of an unlawful act shall be convicted and sentenced as an aider.
(2) The sentence for the aider shall be based on the penalty for a principal. It shall be mitigated pursuant to section 49 (1).

Thus, German criminal law distinguishes three levels or modes of participation in a crime: perpetration as a principal (§ 25 StGB), abetting/instigation (§ 26 StGB) and aiding (§ 27 StGB) as forms of secondary participation.[2] The first category can be subdivided further into single, direct perpetration (§ 25(1), alternative 1 StGB: 'any person who commits the offence himself'), (indirect) perpetration by proxy (§ 25(1), alternative 2 StGB: 'any person who commits the offence ... through another') and joint or co-perpetration (§ 25(2) StGB). While these kinds of involvement in crime give rise to principal liability, instigation and aiding are regarded as accessory (secondary or derivative) forms of participation. This differentiated approach applies only to intentionally committed crimes; there is no participation in negligence offences. With regard to

---

1   Translation according to Michael Bohlander, *The German Criminal Code: A Modern English Translation* (Hart 2008) 43.

2   Claus Roxin, *Strafrecht Allgemeiner Teil, Band II, Besondere Erscheinungsformen der Straftat* (C.H. Beck 2003) § 25 marginal note (hereinafter: mn) 1; Claus Roxin, 'Crimes as Part of Organized Power Structures' (2011) 9 Journal of International Criminal Justice (hereinafter: JICJ) 193, 195.

purely administrative offences ('*Ordnungswidrigkeiten*'), German law has opted for a unified concept of perpetration ('*Einheitstäterschaft*') and accordingly considers anyone as a perpetrator who has causally contributed to the fulfilment of the relevant *actus reus* regardless of the level or intensity of his or her actual involvement.[3] The same holds true for crimes of negligence.[4] In the normal case of intentional crimes, however, the very structure of §§ 25-27 StGB calls for a careful distinction between principals and secondary participants, in particular between joint perpetrators and aiders respectively perpetrators by proxy and instigators.[5] In this regard, German doctrine is heavily influenced by the 'control over' or 'domination of the act' theory ('*Tatherrschaftslehre*') developed by Claus Roxin in his fundamental work *Täterschaft und Tatherrschaft*.[6] According to this approach, '[a] person is a perpetrator if he controls the course of events; one who, in contrast, merely stimulates in someone else the decision to act or helps him to do so, but leaves the execution of the attributable act to the other person' is a mere accomplice.[7] In other words, the decisive criterion of all forms of perpetration is 'domination of' or 'control over the act'.[8] The courts, however, had originally favoured a more subjective approach relying (primarily or solely) on the actor's state of mind and not on the weight of his factual contribution. Accordingly, a person was considered a perpetrator if he wanted the offence as his own, that is, acted with an *animus auctoris*; if, in contrast, the participant just wished to support another person, he acted as an accomplice, that is, with *animus socii*.[9] Over the years the case law has increasingly introduced additional objective criteria and nowadays tends to distinguish principals from secondary participants on the basis of an overall assessment of the whole situation taking into account the actor's state of mind but also the objective importance of his contribution and his control over the act.[10] At the end of the day, the objective–subjective approach of the courts and the control over the act theory will in most cases lead to identical results.[11]

---

3   See only Michael Bohlander, *Principles of German Criminal Law* (Hart 2009) 153; Johannes Wessels and Werner Beulke, *Strafrecht Allgemeiner Teil, Die Straftat und ihr Aufbau* (42nd edn, C.F. Müller 2012) mn 506; Bernd Heinrich, *Strafrecht – Allgemeiner Teil* (3rd edn, Kohlhammer 2012) mn 1177; in detail Thomas Rotsch, *'Einheitstäterschaft' statt Tatherrschaft* (Mohr Siebeck 2009) 11, with regard to '*Ordnungswidrigkeiten*' 192.

4   Wessels and Beulke (n 3) mn 507; Karl Lackner and Kristian Kühl, *Strafgesetzbuch* (27th edn, C.H. Beck 2011) Vor § 25 mn 2; Rotsch (n 3) 197.

5   See also Thomas Weigend, 'Germany' in Kevin Jon Heller and Markus D. Dubber (eds), *The Handbook of Comparative Criminal Law* (Stanford University Press 2011) 252, 265.

6   Claus Roxin, *Täterschaft und Tatherrschaft* (de Gruyter 1963/6th edn, 2003) 60.

7   Roxin, 'Crimes' (n 2) 196.

8   Gerhard Werle and Boris Burghardt, 'Introductory Note' (2011) 9 JICJ 191.

9   With regard to the application of this subjective approach in an extreme form, RGSt (Entscheidungen des Reichsgerichts in Strafsachen) 74, 84 (bathtub case); BGHSt (Entscheidungen des Bundesgerichtshofes in Strafsachen) 18, 87 (*Staschynskij* case); see also the case law analysis by Volker Krey and Robert Esser, *Deutsches Strafrecht Allgemeiner Teil* (5th edn, Kohlhammer 2012) mn 817-24. It is, however, important to note the historical context of these decisions. In the case decided by the Supreme Court of the German Reich, the judges wanted to avoid the death penalty which was mandatory for principals of murder, but not for secondary participants; Fritz Hartung, 'Der "Badewannenfall"' [1954] Juristenzeitung (hereinafter: JZ) 430, 431; the *Staschynskij* decision of the Federal Supreme Court must be seen against the background of the Cold War, Bohlander (n 3) 162.

10   See only BGHSt 33, 50 (53); BGHSt 37, 289 (292); BGHSt 51, 219 (221); the case law is, however, not always consistent, see thereto Urs Kindhäuser, *Strafrecht Allgemeiner Teil* (5th edn, Nomos Verlag 2011) § 38 mn 40-41.

11   Weigend (n 5) 266; Bohlander (n 3) 163; Lackner and Kühl (n 4) Vor 25 mn 6.

Principals by Proxy: Use of Innocent Agents

According to § 25(1), alternative 2 StGB a person is a principal if he commits the offence through another person. In its classical form, this form of perpetration by means of another person presupposes that the person who commits the crime ('intermediary', '*Tatmittler*') is used as an instrument or tool by the indirect perpetrator as the 'man in the background' or mastermind ('*Hintermann*', hinterman). The intermediary is normally an innocent agent, and not responsible for the act (for exceptions see below). His corresponding factually subordinate position enables the indirect perpetrator to control the commission of the crime although he does not execute the crime with his own hands.[12] The indirect control exercised by the hinterman is typically based either on a mistake by the agent ('*Irrtumsherrschaft*', control based on superior information) or duress/coercion ('*Nötigungsherrschaft*', psychological control).[13] However, § 25(1), alternative 2 StGB is inapplicable if the relevant offence can only be committed by persons with a special status and special duties ('*Sonderdelikte*'), for example public officials, and the hinterman does not belong to this group of persons but is simply a private person. The same holds true if – as for example in the case of perjury – the respective offence must or can only be committed by the offender himself ('*eigenhändige Delikte*').[14]

German doctrine and the case law distinguish the following categories of perpetration by proxy:[15]

1. The agent A does not fulfil the *actus reus* of the offence. Example: D has received a confidential note in his capacity as civil servant. He asks his friend A, who is not a public official, to take this note from his desk and to forward it to the local newspaper for publication. A is not capable to fulfil the objective elements of the offence, that is, he cannot breach 'official secrets' (§ 353b StGB) because he is not a public official. According to one view, D, due to his official status, exercises a kind of normative control over the crime and can therefore be regarded as a principal by proxy committing the crime through innocent A.[16] Critics of this view, however, stress that D lacks any factual control over the act so that both D and A must go unpunished.[17]

In this context, doctrine also discusses cases in which the victim is made to harm himself, that is, agent and victim are the same person.[18] In the famous *Sirius* case, decided by the Federal Supreme Court in 1983,[19] D had persuaded A, an emotionally deeply disturbed woman, that he was

12   Wessels and Beulke (n 3) mn 535-36; Rudolf Rengier, *Strafrecht Allgemeiner Teil* (4th edn, C.H. Beck 2012) § 43 mn 1-2.

13   Roxin 'Crimes' (n 2) 196-97; Weigend (n 5) 266; Wolfgang Joecks, '§ 25' in Bernd von Heintschel-Heinegg (ed), *Münchener Kommentar zum Strafgesetzbuch, Band 1, §§ 1-37 StGB* (2nd edn, C.H. Beck 2011) mn 55.

14   Wessels and Beulke (n 3) mn 543; see also Günter Stratenwerth and Lothar Kuhlen, *Strafrecht Allgemeiner Teil* (6th edn, Verlag Franz Vahlen 2011) § 12 mn 73-76.

15   See in more detail Hans-Heinrich Jescheck and Thomas Weigend, *Lehrbuch des Strafrechts – Allgemeiner Teil* (5th edn, Duncker & Humblot 1996) 665-70; Heinrich (n 3) mn 1247-52a; Rengier (n 12) § 43 mn 6-37; Stratenwerth and Kuhlen (n 14) § 12 mn 31-72.

16   Case based on Heinrich (n 3) mn 1248; see also Rengier (n 12) § 43 mn 14-19.

17   Roxin (n 2) Strafrecht § 25 mn 275-80. D cannot be punished as an instigator since A – as a private person – does not fulfil the *actus reus* of the special offence of § 353b StGB and thus an intentional and unlawful main act is lacking (so-called '*limitierte Akzessorietät*', see in more detail (n 77) and accompanying text).

18   Krey and Esser (n 9) mn 904-19; Wessels and Beulke (n 3) mn 537.

19   BGHSt 32, 38.

an alien from the planet Sirius who had the task to select some especially worthy human beings for a life on Sirius. He convinced her that she – if she killed herself – could travel to Sirius where she would receive a new body. However, as life on Sirius was costly, A should take out a life insurance and nominate D as beneficiary before killing herself. D promised her to hold the money in trust and to transfer it for her to Sirius. A did as she was told but finally failed to kill herself.[20] A's attempted suicide is not a punishable act since § 212 StGB (murder) requires that the perpetrator kills another person.[21] Given, as we will show in more detail below, that secondary participation is accessorial to the act of a principal (*Akzessorietät*), the lack of liability of the victim A entails the same for D, that is, any participation in the (attempted) suicide of another person does not entail criminal responsibility.[22] The situation is, however, different, if the participant can be said to control the act and use the victim as an instrument against herself.[23] In the *Sirius* case, the Supreme Court held that A misled D to believe that she would not die but only change her body. Due to this misconception, D was not able to understand the meaning and consequences of her conduct, that is, that she was about to end her own life. A was found guilty of attempted murder by proxy because he had controlled D's actions based on his intellectual superiority and her extreme gullibility.[24]

Closely related to the *Sirius* case are situations in which the hinterman creates a mistaken motive in the agent. Take the following example: D tells A that she suffers from a severe disease which will soon become very painful; therefore A kills herself. One view would qualify D in this case also as a perpetrator by proxy because he makes A believe that committing suicide is her only option.[25] One must, however, not overlook that A knows that she kills herself and decides freely – albeit on mistaken grounds, that is, based on a false motive – to do so. D can only be said to control the situation if his lie causes a serious mental abnormality which would exclude A's ability to act in full self-determination.[26]

2. The agent lacks the necessary *mens rea*. Example: Doctor D asks nurse A to give patient V some medicine which he has secretly replaced with a deadly poison. If A – acting in good faith – administers the poison to V she lacks the intent to kill V. D, however, controls the situation because of his superior knowledge and is thus liable as a principle by proxy.[27]

3. The agent is justified. Example: D tells police officer A that V has committed serious crimes and wants to flee the country. A arrests V. A fulfils the objective and subjective elements of the crime of unlawful imprisonment (§ 239 StGB) but had a right to arrest the suspect V because of the alleged flight risk (which is sufficient under § 127 of the German Code of Criminal Procedure – '*Strafprozessordnung*', StPO). A's acts are justified, yet D has control over his act pursuant to his superior knowledge.[28]

---

20 For more detail on the facts of the case see Bohlander (n 3) 157-58.

21 Heinrich (n 3) mn 1248; Rengier (n 12) § 13 mn 77.

22 Kristian Kühl, *Strafrecht Allgemeiner Teil* (6th edn, Franz Vahlen Verlag 2008) § 20 mn 46; Wessels and Beulke (n 3) mn 539.

23 In more detail Heinrich (n 3) mn 1262-63; Krey and Esser (n 9) mn 904-19; Claus Roxin, 'Selbstmord durch Einschaltung eines vorsatzlosen Tatmittlers' in Gerhard Dannecker et al. (eds), *Festschrift für Harro Otto* (Carl Heymanns Verlag 2007) 441.

24 BGHSt 32, 38 (42).

25 Günther Heine, '§ 25' in Adolf Schönke and Horst Schröder (eds), *Strafgesetzbuch* (28th edn, C.H. Beck 2010) mn 11; in a similar vein BGH Goltdammer's Archiv für Strafrecht (hereinafter: GA) 1986, 508; Helmut Frister, *Strafrecht Allgemeiner Teil* (5th edn, C.H. Beck 2011) 390-91.

26 Roxin, *Strafrecht* (n 2) § 25 mn 72.

27 Weigend (n 5) 266; Rengier (n 12) § 43 mn 13; Frister (n 25) 385-86.

28 BGHSt 3, 4 (6); BGHSt 10, 306 (307).

4. The agent acts without guilt. Example: D persuades A, who is either insane or below the minimum age of criminal capacity,[29] to kill V. A is unable to appreciate the unlawfulness of his conduct or to behave accordingly and thus lacks criminal responsibility (§§ 19, 20 StGB). Under the German tripartite structure of offences (distinguishing between offence definition, general unlawfulness and guilt[30]) A lacks the necessary guilt. D may be said to have committed the crime of murder (§ 212 StGB) through A. However, as A has intentionally committed an unlawful act – the German law distinguishes strictly between the intent (as the psychological subjective side of the offence) and the normatively understood guilt or blameworthiness[31] – D's conduct may also be qualified as instigation in terms of § 26 StGB (see under 'Secondary Participation' below). According to the majority view, a defendant using a criminally incapable agent always controls the commission of the crime due to his psychological superiority and is therefore liable as principal by proxy.[32] The contrary view prefers in such instances to distinguish perpetration by proxy from instigation on a case by case basis, taking into account in particular the *factual* capacity of the agent to understand the quality of the conduct and to act freely.[33]

In this context, doctrine discusses also cases in which the agent is forced to commit the crime. Imagine, for example, that in our hospital case[34] doctor D holds a gun at nurse A's head and threatens to shoot her if she refuses to administer the poison to patient V. If A does as she is told she acts under duress (§ 35 StGB)[35] and cannot be blamed for having killed V. On the other hand, D, by inflicting such coercive pressure on A, has '*Nötigungsherrschaft*', that is, he exercises control over the act and thus commits the crime of murder through the innocent A in terms of § 25(1), alternative 2 StGB.[36]

Perpetrator behind the Perpetrator: Liability of Masterminds/'Hintermen' for Acts of Otherwise Criminally Liable Agents

As explained above the concept of perpetration through another person is predicated on some 'defect' in the person of the direct agent which enables the hinterman to exercise control over the agent, and this triggers his responsibility ('*Verantwortungsprinzip*'). Accordingly, § 25(1), alternative 2 StGB presupposes, as a rule, that the intermediary is not punishable.[37] However, exceptionally, German courts and doctrine recognise indirect perpetration even in case of a fully

---

29 According to § 19 StGB, children under 14 years of age lack criminal capacity.

30 George P. Fletcher, *Basic Concepts of Criminal Law* (Oxford University Press, 1998) 101; Claus Roxin, *Strafrecht Allgemeiner Teil, Band I, Grundlagen. Der Aufbau der Verbrechenslehre* (4th edn, C.H. Beck 2006) § 10 mn 13-26; Ambos (n 31) 2650-52; in a similar vein Bohlander (n 3) 16-18.

31 For an explanation see Kai Ambos, 'Toward a Universal System of Crime: Comments on George Fletcher's *Grammar of Criminal Law*' (2007) 28 Cardozo Law Review 2647, 2649-53, 2656-57.

32 See in particular Roxin, *Strafrecht* (n 2) § 25 mn 139-48; also Wessels and Beulke (n 3) mn 540; Jescheck and Weigend (n 15) 669.

33 RGSt 61, 265 (267); Reinhart Maurach, Karl Heinz Gössel and Heinz Zipf, *Strafrecht Allgemeiner Teil – Teilband 2, Erscheinungsformen des Verbrechens und Rechtsfolgen der Tat* (7th edn, C.F. Müller 1989) § 48 mn 79.

34 See (n 27) and accompanying text.

35 In German criminal law, the defence of duress may under certain limited circumstances exclude the actor's responsibility even if he kills one or more innocent persons, see only BGH Neue Juristische Wochenschrift (hereinafter: NJW) 1964, 255 (259); Kühl (n 22) § 12 mn 89.

36 Weigend (n 5) 266; see also Frister (n 25) 392.

37 BGHSt 30, 363 (364); Weigend (n 5) 266; Krey and Esser (n 9) mn 923.

responsible or culpable direct agent, that is, in the *special* case of an 'indirect perpetrator behind the direct perpetrator' ('*Täter hinter dem Täter*').

The concept goes back to the 'Lord of the Cats' case decided by the Federal Supreme Court in 1988:[38] D persuaded the gullible A to believe in the existence of the 'Lord of the Cats', an ancient, evil creature which has threatened the world for ages. A, who was emotionally totally dependent on D, was finally convinced to be a chosen warrior in the fight against the 'Lord of the Cats'. When D learned that her former lover had married V, she told A that the 'Lord of the Cats' would destroy mankind or kill at least millions of people if A did not sacrifice V to him. Despite pangs of conscience, A eventually decided to kill V in order to save mankind. He attacked her with a knife but V survived. The court found that A – regardless of his delusion – was not legally insane and that his mistaken belief in the existence of the 'Lord of the Cats' was avoidable, that is, his misconception regarding the existence of a threat to mankind could not spare him from punishment. Nevertheless, D was considered a perpetrator by proxy since she had caused and controlled A's delusion based on which he honestly believed that killing V was the only option to avoid greater harm, that is, he was not able to realise fully that he was doing something wrong. The fact that A could have avoided his mistake does not, in the court's view, diminish D's domination over him.[39]

In the same vein, the prevailing view in the literature regards a person who misleads the direct actor about the identity of the victim as a principal by proxy. Imagine, for example, that D knows that A wants to kill V_1 and falsely points out V_2 who is at the moment passing by, and tells A that this is V_1 although D is fully aware that this is not the case. As expected, A shoots and kills V_2 assuming that he is V_1. A has committed the crime of murder as a principal. His mistake concerning the identity of his victim (*error in persona*) does not affect his intent to kill the person in front of him and is thus irrelevant.[40] Despite the fact that A is fully criminally liable, it is D who has 'transferred' A's intent from V_1 to V_2. Thus, D has killed V_2 through the 'blind' A.[41]

Apart from such mistakes which do not exclude the criminal responsibility of the agent, the concept of the perpetrator behind the perpetrator became particularly relevant in the cases against civil and military leaders of the former German Democratic Republic (GDR), who had to answer for the killing of GDR citizens who wanted to cross the East German border. Although the border guards were fully criminally responsible for the shooting of these persons,[42] the Federal Supreme Court held the ruling GDR elite (*in casu* the members of the National Defence Council and the

---

38   BGHSt 35, 347.

39   In more detail on this case Joecks (n 13) mn 93-9; Friedrich Schaffstein, 'Der Täter hinter dem Täter bei vermeidbarem Verbotsirrtum und verminderter Schuldfähigkeit des Tatmittlers – Zugleich eine Besprechung von BGH – 4 StR 352/88' [1989] Neue Zeitschrift für Strafrecht (hereinafter: NStZ) 153; Wilfried Küper, 'Die dämonische Macht des "Katzenkönigs" oder: Probleme des Verbotsirrtums und Putativnotstandes an den Grenzen strafrechtlicher Begriffe' [1989] JZ 617 all with further references; see also the critical assessment of the Court's decision by Krey and Esser (n 9) mn 924-31; Stratenwerth and Kuhlen (n 14) § 12 mn 53-55.

40   Jescheck and Weigend (n 15) 311; Wessels and Beulke (n 3) mn 249; Mohamed Elewa Badar, '*Mens rea*: Mistake of Law and Mistake of Fact in German Criminal Law: A Survey for International Criminal Tribunals' (2005) 5 International Criminal Law Review (hereinafter: ICLR) 203, 238-39.

41   Roxin, *Strafrecht* (n 2) § 25 mn 102-103; Heine (n 25) mn 23; see, however, also the opposing views of Joecks (n 13) mn 114 (D as aider); Rolf Dietrich Herzberg, 'Grundfälle zur Lehre von Täterschaft und Teilnahme' [1974] Juristische Schulung (hereinafter: JuS) 574, 576-77 (D as an independent multiple principal, see thereto (n 54) and accompanying text); Stratenwerth and Kuhlen (n 14) § 12 mn 63 (D as instigator).

42   Most notably, the courts declared null and void § 27 of the East German Border Law which allowed for a shoot-to-kill policy *vis-à-vis* refugees under certain circumstances and as a means of last resort; see only the German Federal Constitutional Court in BVerfGE (Entscheidungen des Bundesverfassungsgerichts)

generals of the National People's Army) responsible as indirect perpetrators for having established the murderous border regime in the first place and being sure in the knowledge that the border guards would follow their instructions. As the Court explained elaborately:

> As members of the NDC the accused belonged to a body whose decisions formed the *mandatory* requirements for the fundamental orders, on which the border regime ... was based. They *knew* that the orders based on the decisions of the NDC were carried out. They had been notified of the victims of the border mines and the order to shoot ('*Schießbefehl*'). The executors of the acts which directly led to the killings acted as part of a *military hierarchy* in which their role was *specifically* set down. Neither did the accused have a completely subordinated role in relation to Honecker.[43]

Further, a commander of a border patrol – that is, a member of the mid-level command – was sentenced as an indirect perpetrator because of his *domination by command* ('*Befehlsherrschaft*') for ordering a subordinate to kill a refugee.[44] The courts invoked Roxin's theory of indirect perpetration by virtue of domination through and within an organisation ('*mittelbare Täterschaft kraft Organisationsherrschaft*').[45] According to this approach, the limited control of the hinterman over the fully responsible direct perpetrator – the latter may, at any time, decide to abandon the criminal plan – is compensated for by the control of the (criminal) organisation, which produces an unlimited number of potential willing executors. In other words: direct perpetrators acting with full criminal responsibility may be considered mere 'interchangeable intermediaries/proxies' ('fungible *Tatmittler*') since the system provides for a practically unlimited number of replacements and thereby for a high degree of flexibility as far as the personnel necessary to commit the crimes is concerned.[46] For this 'system'- or organisation-based argument one can also adduce the fact that the individual perpetrator has less autonomy than somebody acting *outside* a system or organisation. While the individual perpetrator possesses the direct *power* to carry out the act (*Tatmacht*),[47] the leaders of an organisation *dominate* the act by way of their control over the organisation and hence over him as one of its members.[48] Thus, ultimately, the control rests less on the interchangeable position of the individual actor but rather on the hierarchical control over the organisational apparatus, the criminal system, of which he is a part.[49]

This concept of hierarchical control may be applied *mutatis mutandis* to criminal corporations provided that they have – like the Mafia – sufficient organisational power structures.[50] The Federal

---

95, 96 (130); for more details and references see Kai Ambos, *Internationales Strafrecht* (3rd edn, C.H. Beck 2011) § 10 mn 86-87.

43   BGHSt 40, 218 (237-38) translation by Kai Ambos and Susan Padman Reich (emphasis added). This view has been confirmed by the subsequent case law: BGHSt 45, 270 (296); BGHSt 48, 77 (91).

44   BGH NJW 1996, 2043.

45   Roxin (n 6) 242-52, 653-54; Roxin, 'Crimes' (n 2) 197.

46   See in more detail Kai Ambos, *Der Allgemeine Teil* des *Völkerstrafrechts* (2nd edn, Duncker & Humblot 2004) 594, 597-98, 614 with further references; and Claus Roxin, 'Organisationsherrschaft als eigenständige Form mittelbarer Täterschaft' (2007) 125 Schweizerische Zeitschrift für Strafrecht (hereinafter: ZStR) 1, 13.

47   On this concept with regard to the direct perpetrator – as opposed to the leaders and organisers – Hans Vest, *Völkerrechtsverbrecher verfolgen: ein abgestuftes Mehrebenenmodell systematischer Tatherrschaft* (Stämpfli 2011) 358-60.

48   Ibid. 363.

49   ibid. 186.

50   Rengier (n 12) § 43 mn 63; Bohlander (n 3) 159; Wessels and Beulke (n 3) mn 541.

Supreme Court even went one step further and extended this doctrine to commercial companies and their directors.[51] This opinion is, however, far from being uncontested: critics argue in particular that an employee working for a company which acts (in principle) in accordance with the law can and must be expected not to comply with illegal orders. If he – due to an autonomous decision – declines to do so, he alone controls the commission of the crime. The hinterman can only be held responsible as an instigator.[52]

Joint Principals

According to § 25(2) StGB, persons who commit the offence jointly are liable as principals. This joint commission is characterised by a functional division of the criminal tasks between the different (at least two) co-perpetrators, which are linked by a common plan or agreement. Every co-perpetrator fulfils a certain task which contributes to the commission of the crime as a whole and without which its commission would not be possible. The common plan or agreement forms the basis of the reciprocal or mutual attribution – a key element of co-perpetration – of the different contributions, making every co-perpetrator responsible for the whole offence.[53]

The requirement of a common plan distinguishes joint principals from independent multiple principals (*Nebentäter*):[54] these act entirely independent from each other but nevertheless fulfil both the same elements of an offence *vis-à-vis* the same victim.[55] Independent multiple principals are responsible solely for their own conduct and are thus only liable if and insofar as their own individual actions fulfil the elements of an offence.[56] In other words: independent multiple principals are treated like single perpetrators.[57] Examples of independent multiple principals are rare, in particular with regard to intentional crimes. In the classic textbook example, A and B, independently from each other, put poison in V's tea. V drinks the tea and dies. Each dose of poison would have been sufficient to kill V. Both A and B are liable as principals for murder.[58] When it comes to negligence or recklessness, the concept of independent multiple principals may be used to illustrate that more than one person causally contributed to the commission of the crime. Take for example the killing spree of Winnenden, a small town near Stuttgart, in 2009: a 17-year-old boy killed 15 people with a gun he had taken from his father. The shooter has committed the crime of intentional murder. Since the father had failed to keep his weapon in safe custody and in doing so

---

51   BGHSt 48, 331 (342); BGHSt 49, 148 (163-64).

52   See only Rengier (n 12) § 43 mn 69; Roxin, *Strafrecht* (n 2) § 25 mn 130; Heine (n 25) mn 25b, all with further references.

53   See Roxin (n 6) 242-52, 653-54.

54   BGH NStZ 1996, 226; Heinrich (n 3) mn 1186; Krey and Esser (n 9) mn 944.

55   Bohlander (n 3) 160-61; Wessels and Beulke (n 3) mn 525.

56   Rengier (n 12) § 42 mn 3; Stratenwerth and Kuhlen (n 14) § 12 mn 99-100.

57   Heinrich (n 3) mn 1187; see also Bohlander (n 3) 161; Roxin, *Strafrecht* (n 2) § 25 mn 266.

58   Rengier (n 12) § 42 mn 4 in conjunction with § 13 mn 27; Heinrich (n 3) mn 1186; Krey and Esser (n 9) mn 943. This so-called cumulative causation presupposes that the two acts take effect at the same time. If it cannot be excluded that the one dose of poison has a lethal effect before the other, both A and B are – *in dubio pro reo* – guilty of only attempted murder; see Bohlander (n 3) 49; Rengier (n 12) § 13 mn 30-31.

had facilitated the killings, he may be liable for negligent manslaughter (§ 222 StGB).[59] Thus, son and father may be considered independent multiple principals.[60]

Turning back to § 25(2) StGB, co-perpetration requires the existence of a common plan between two or more persons and a substantial contribution by each co-perpetrator with regard to the realisation of the objective elements of the offence.[61] The latter element is crucial for distinguishing co-perpetration from aiding. Persons who are assigned subordinate roles – such as keeping watch or driving the getaway car – and have therefore no (functional) control over the act, are, as a rule, only liable as aiders.[62] It is highly controversial, however, whether the contribution must be made at the stage when the offence is actually being executed. The question gains particular relevance with regard to the responsibility of gang leaders. Take the classical case of the head of a criminal organisation, D, who plans in detail a bank robbery and allocates each individual task to different members of his gang but is himself not engaged in the actual execution of the plan. According to one view, a person who leaves the actual performance of the crime to the other gang members, refrains from exercising control over the act and thus does not make a *substantial* contribution to the commission of the crime.[63] D is therefore regarded as an instigator or – if his gang amounts to an organised power structure within the meaning of the *Organisationsherrschaftslehre*[64] – as a perpetrator by proxy.[65] In contrast, the German courts[66] and the prevailing literature assume that D is liable as a co-perpetrator, in particular because his lack of control in the execution stage is compensated by his dominant, decisive role in the planning stage.[67] In any event, § 25(2) StGB does not necessarily require the physical presence of all co-perpetrators at the scene of the crime. If the gang leader, for example, stays in direct contact with the other gang members via mobile phone, he controls the execution of his plan and is thus unanimously classified as a joint perpetrator.[68]

The other requirement, that is, the existence of a common plan, is at the same time the basis for the reciprocal attribution of the co-perpetrators' actions and limits their attribution. This means, in particular, that a co-perpetrator cannot be held responsible if his partner deviates from the common plan ('*Mittäterexzess*'). If, for example, A and B have agreed to beat up V without using weapons and if during the commission of the offence B draws his knife and kills V, the killing cannot be attributed to A because this was not part of the common plan. A is only responsible for causing

---

59   In the actual Winnenden case, the teenager committed suicide after the killing spree. Therefore, the criminal responsibility of his father became the focal point of interest. The District Court of Stuttgart (18 Kls 112 Js 21 916/09, 10 February 2011) found him guilty of negligent manslaughter and causing bodily harm by negligence and sentenced him to a suspended sentence of one year and nine months of imprisonment. The Federal Supreme Court, however, quashed the judgment for procedural reasons (1 StR 359/11, 22 March 2012), so that the case has to be retried. See in more detail on this case Wolfgang Mitsch, 'Fahrlässige Tötung oder fahrlässige Beihilfe zum Totschlag?' [2011] Zeitschrift für das Juristische Studium (ZJS) 126.

60   Rengier (n 12) § 42 mn 5.

61   Heinrich (n 3) mn 1222; see also Joecks (n 13) mn 190, mn 229.

62   Weigend (n 5) 266; Rengier (n 12) § 44 mn 45.

63   Roxin, *Strafrecht* (n 2) § 25 mn 189; Bernd Schünemann, '§ 25' in Heinrich Wilhelm Laufhütte, Ruth Rissing-van Saan and Klaus Tiedemann (eds), *Strafgesetzbuch – Leipziger Kommentar*, i (12th edn, de Gruyter Verlag 2007) mn 182; Krey and Esser (n 9) mn 978.

64   See (n 50) and accompanying text.

65   Roxin, *Strafrecht* (n 2) § 25 mn 210; Schünemann (n 63) mn 185.

66   BGHSt 33, 50 (53); BGHSt 37, 289 (292-93); BGH NStZ 2009, 25 (26).

67   See only Wessels and Beulke (n 3) mn 529; Stratenwerth and Kuhlen (n 14) § 12 mn 92-94; Heinrich (n 3) mn 1227-29 all with further references.

68   Roxin, *Strafrecht* (n 2) § 25 mn 200; Krey and Esser (n 9) mn 979; Wessels and Beulke (n 3) mn 529.

bodily harm by acting jointly with another (§ 224(1) no 4 StGB).[69] This holds true even if B is known to be impulsive and aggressive so that his excessive reaction was foreseeable. If A, however, is actually aware of the risk of an excess and nevertheless decides to carry out the criminal plan, essentially ignoring the risk (conditional intent – *dolus eventualis*), he can be held responsible for the murder of V pursuant to § 25(2) StGB.[70]

Most notably, the common plan may be developed further or spontaneously changed, even implicitly, and – in temporal terms – even during the commission of the offence.[71] This gives rise to the (highly controversial) question whether a person joining the collective commission of a crime at a later stage is liable for acts committed previously (so called successive co-perpetration, *sukzessive Mittäterschaft*).[72] Example: A breaks into the house of V, knocks him down and starts searching for valuables. After a while, he calls B for help. B sees the unconscious V but decides nevertheless to join A. Together they find some jewellery which they divide among themselves. While B was not even present when V was knocked down, that is, could not have had the respective intent, he has arguably approved this use of force subsequently with his joining A's search for valuables and is therefore liable as a joint principal for the robbery (§ 249 StGB).[73] Against this result, one may argue that A's use of violence was already completely terminated[74] when B appeared on the crime scene, it could therefore not be encompassed by a common plan. Thus, while A is criminally responsible for robbery (§ 249 StGB), B has only committed the crime of theft (§ 242 StGB).[75]

Secondary Participation

Abetting/Instigation

As already indicated above,[76] German criminal law distinguishes two forms of secondary participation: abetting/instigating (§ 26 StGB) and aiding (§ 27 StGB). Both are accessory in nature, that is, criminal responsibility depends on the principal offence;[77] more specifically an intentional and unlawful act by the principal is required. From this it follows, on the one hand, that accessory liability is excluded for negligent and justified and thus lawful acts by the main offender.[78] On the other hand, secondary participation is possible if the principal, although he has

---

69   BGH Neue Zeitschrift für Strafrecht – Rechtsprechungsreport (hereinafter: NStZ-RR) 2006, 37; Rengier (n 12) § 44 mn 23-27; see also the examples given by Bohlander (n 3) 165-66.

70   See BGH NStZ-RR 2005, 71 (72); BGHSt 53, 145 (155); Wessels and Beulke (n 3) mn 531.

71   Weigend (n 5) 266; Bohlander (n 3) 164; Rengier (n 12) § 44 mn 11; Heinrich (n 3) mn 1223.

72   See in more detail and with further references Uwe Murmann, 'Zu den Voraussetzungen der sukzessiven Beteiligung – zugleich Anmerkung zu BGH, Urt. v. 18.12.2007 – 1 StR 301/07, NStZ 2008, 280' [2008] ZJS 456.

73   This is apparently the approach favoured by the courts; cf. BGHSt 2, 344 (346 f.); BGH JZ 1981, 596; BGH NStZ 2008, 280.

74   The situation is different if A threatens V with a gun. In this case, A still employs means of coercion when B joins him (that is, the action which B joins is not yet terminated), so that co-perpetration is more readily possible; see Heinrich (n 3) mn 1239.

75   In the same vein Heinrich (n 3) mn 1238-39; Stratenwerth and Kuhlen (n 14) § 12 mn 88-89; Murmann (n 72) 459.

76   See (n 2) and accompanying text.

77   Bohlander (n 3) 168; Rengier (n 12) § 45 mn 1.

78   Insofar, the unified concept of perpetration (*Einheitstäterschaft*) applies; see (n 4) and accompanying text; critically Roxin, *Strafrecht* (n 2) § 26 mn 35-40.

committed an unlawful act, is not to blame for having done so, for example, because he is insane or acted under duress in terms of § 35 StGB.[79] This so-called principle of '*limitierte Akzessorität*' (limited dependence of secondary participation)[80] is closely linked to the German tripartite structure of offences (distinguishing between offence definition, general unlawfulness and guilt).[81] If the principal is not criminally liable because he cannot be blamed for his conduct, the hinterman could also be considered an instigator, so that perpetration by proxy and instigation must be carefully distinguished.[82]

The *actus reus* of instigation (§ 26 StGB) consists, apart from the already mentioned main (intentional and unlawful) act of the principal, of the actual instigating conduct of the accessory. Insofar it is contested whether instigation presupposes some kind of communication between the instigator and the perpetrator, or if the creation of a situation which causes another person to commit a crime is sufficient. Imagine, for example, that A leaves open a window hoping that someone breaks into the house. If D uses this opportunity and commits a crime of burglary, A shall – according to one view – be liable as an instigator pursuant to § 26 StGB because he has triggered the unlawful act.[83] The problem with this view is that one sometimes creates everyday situations or risks which may be used by others to commit criminal acts. To qualify this as punishable instigation would broaden liability too much.[84] This holds all the more true since instigators are punished like principals (see below).[85] Thus, the majority view requires some kind of communication, that is mental contact, between the instigator and the principal.[86]

In any event, the instigator must cause another person to commit the unlawful act.[87] Thus, a person who has already taken the decision to commit an offence, the so-called *omnimodo facturus*, cannot be instigated any more.[88] The communication with such a person with a view to convince him to commit an offence may either be qualified as attempted instigation or – in the sense of a reinforcement of the already existing criminal intention – as psychological assistance punishable pursuant to § 27 StGB.[89] The situation is different, if someone persuades the *omnimodo facturus* to commit another ('*Umstiftung*') or a more serious offence ('*Aufstiftung*'). Example: in order to take revenge on V, D wants to beat him up using only his fists. A may be liable as an instigator if he (a) convinces D to damage V's car instead[90] or (b) to use a baseball bat when beating him up.[91] If,

---

79 See also Wessels and Beulke (n 3) mn 553-54; Rengier (n 12) § 45 mn 13-16.

80 Bohlander (n 3) 168; in more detail Wolfgang Joecks, 'Vor §§ 26, 27' in Bernd von Heintschel-Heinegg (ed.), *Münchener Kommentar zum Strafgesetzbuch, Band 1, §§ 1-37 StGB* (2nd edn, C.H. Beck 2011) mn 18-27; Roxin, *Strafrecht* (n 2) § 25 mn 2-7, 32-40.

81 See (n 30) and accompanying text.

82 See already (nn 32-33) and accompanying text.

83 Kindhäuser (n 10) § 41 mn 10; Lackner and Kühl (n 4) § 26 mn 2; Jürgen Baumann, Ulrich Weber and Wolfgang Mitsch, *Strafrecht Allgemeiner Teil* (11th edn, Gieseking Verlag 2003) § 30 Rn. 63.

84 Roxin, *Strafrecht* (n 2) § 26 mn 76; in a similar vein Krey and Esser (n 9) mn 1038.

85 Rengier (n 12) § 45 mn 30; Krey and Esser (n 9) mn 1038.

86 Rengier (n 12) § 45 mn 30; Roxin, *Strafrecht* (n 2) § 26 mn 76; Wessels and Beulke (n 3) mn 568; Krey and Esser (n 9) mn 1038.

87 BGHSt 45, 373 (374); Bohlander (n 3) 168.

88 BGHSt 45, 373 (374); BGH NStZ-RR1996, 1; Bohlander (n 3) 168; Rengier (n 12) § 45 mn 33; Weigend (n 5) 267.

89 BGH NStZ-RR 1996, 1; Heinrich (n 3) mn 1295.

90 See also BGH NStZ-RR 1996, 1; Wessels and Beulke (n 3) mn 571; in more detail Roxin, *Strafrecht* (n 2) § 26 mn 91-101.

91 In this case, D – due to A's influence – commits the more serious offence of causing bodily harm by dangerous means (§ 224 StGB) instead of the basic offence (causing bodily harm, § 223 StGB); BGHSt 19,

in contrast, A talks D into a lesser offence (*'Abstifung'*), for example causing serious bodily harm instead of murder, A is not liable for instigating the lesser offence because he has in fact diminished the risk for the victim.[92]

On the subjective level, the instigator's intent must be twofold, that is, it must extend both to the principal offence and to the actual instigating conduct (*Doppelvorsatz*).[93] From the former it follows that the instigator must possess a sufficient notion of the offence and the general course of events, without, however, having to have knowledge of all the details.[94] As a rule, the instigator is only liable if and insofar as the principal's offence conforms to his intent. While minor discrepancies are irrelevant, the instigator is not responsible if the principal deviates excessively from the intent of the instigator.[95] Moreover, instigation is excluded if the 'instigator' does not want the offence to be completed. For this reason, the dominant view rejects the criminal responsibility of an *agent provocateur* since he only provokes criminal acts in order to obtain incriminating evidence.[96]

Aiding

Liability for aiding (§ 27 StGB) requires that the aider intentionally assists another person in the intentional commission of an unlawful act. Assisting means every conduct which enables, facilitates, expedites or intensifies the principal offence.[97] Whether there must be a causal link between the aider's conduct and the principal offence is highly controversial;[98] it is, however, generally assumed that the former need not be a *conditio sine qua non* for the latter.[99] The *mens rea* required for aiding is, as in the case of instigation, twofold: The aider must have sufficient knowledge of the principal offence and assist the principal intentionally. Generally, the considerations[100] on the subjective elements of instigation apply *mutatis mutandis*.[101] The aider's knowledge of the principal offence may, however, be less detailed than that of the instigator. It suffices if he is aware of the essential elements of the offence.[102]

§ 27 StGB typically also covers forms of mental or psychological support (*'psychische Beihilfe'*); in particular assistance by providing useful information about the victim or the crime scene.[103] The situation is more difficult if the aider merely encourages the principal in his criminal intentions.[104] According to the contested[105] jurisprudence of the Federal Supreme Court, the promise

---

339 (340); Roxin, *Strafrecht* (n 2) § 26 mn 104-105; Rengier (n 12) § 45 mn 37-38. These cases are, however, not uncontested. According to the opposing view, A is liable only as aider; Heinrich (n 3) mn 1302 with further references.
92   Wessels and Beulke (n 3) mn 571; Rengier (n 12) § 45 mn 43.
93   Weigend (n 5) 267; Bohlander (n 3) 168.
94   BGHSt 40, 218 (231); Weigend (n 5) 267.
95   Wessels and Beulke (n 3) mn 575; Heinrich (n 3) mn 1306; Krey and Esser (n 9) mn 1054.
96   BGH NStZ 2008, 41; OLG Stuttgart NJW 1999, 2751; in more detail Roxin, *Strafrecht* (n 2) § 26 mn 151-56; Krey and Esser (n 9) mn 1055-68.
97   Rengier (n 12) § 45 mn 82.
98   See Krey and Esser (n 9) mn 1078-81; Uwe Murmann, *Grundkurs Strafrecht* (C.H. Beck 2011) § 27 mn 121-28.
99   Weigend (n 5) 267; Rengier (n 12) § 45 mn 94.
100   See (n 93) and accompanying text.
101   Roxin, *Strafrecht* (n 2) § 26 mn 267.
102   BGHSt 42, 135 (138); Wessels and Beulke (n 3) mn 584; Bohlander (n 3) 173.
103   Kindhäuser (n 10) § 42 mn 5; Roxin, *Strafrecht* (n 2) § 26 mn 198.
104   For an example see (n 89) and accompanying text.
105   See in detail Roxin, *Strafrecht* (n 2) § 26 mn 197-209.

of an alibi[106] and even the plain approval of the unlawful act[107] can be considered aiding in terms of § 27 StGB, but not the mere presence at the crime scene.[108] Another controversy relates to the treatment of so-called neutral contributions to the crime ('*neutrale Handlung*'), that is, the criminal liability of professionals who – in exercising their everyday professional functions – objectively assist criminals: A sells a screwdriver to D who later uses it to burgle homes. Can A be held responsible as an aider to D's crimes? Should there be an objective minimum threshold in order not to criminalise socially desirable and legitimate conduct, but only a significant deviation from standard social or commercial behaviour?[109] Or shall criminal responsibility exclusively depend on the assistant's mental state? The Federal Supreme Court recognises criminal liability for neutral contributions in two cases: first, the professional *knows* that the principal will commit a wrong, which means that a mere *dolus eventualis* is not sufficient; secondly, the professional considers it merely possible that the principal will commit a wrongful act, but there exists concrete, objective evidence which clearly points to the principal's criminal intentions.[110]

Specific Issue: Joint Criminal Enterprise

German Criminal Law does not recognise the concept of joint criminal enterprise (JCE) as a discrete category of individual criminal responsibility. Insofar as JCE presupposes the existence of a common plan and the contribution of each JCE member to the realisation of the plan, it can, in a functional sense, be equated with co-perpetration in terms of § 25, paragraph 2 StGB.[111] The focus of the JCE doctrine on the collective or systemic commission of offences, however, marks a structural difference to the individualistic concept of co-perpetration which focuses on the joint commission by single perpetrators[112] and requires a clear distinction between joint principals and mere aiders.[113]

Effect of Errors and Transferred Malice/Aberratio Ictus Scenarios in the Person of One Participant on the Liability of the Other Participants

The effect of errors in the person of one participant on the liability of the other participants depends on the nature of the mistake and the mode of participation. In case of *perpetration through another person* the question arises whether and how errors of the innocent agent can be attributed to the principal. Take the following modification of our hospital cases:[114] doctor D asks nurse A, who is unaware of the true facts, to administer the poison to patient V_1 in room 1. Due to her short-

---

106   BGH NJW 1951, 451.

107   BGH NStZ 2002, 139.

108   BGH NStZ 1995, 490; BGH NStZ 2010, 224; for the even more extensive original jurisprudence, see Roxin, *Strafrecht* (n 2) § 26 mn 204.

109   See in more detail on the discussion Roxin, *Strafrecht* (n 2) § 26 mn 218-54; Peter Rackow, *Neutrale Handlungen als Problem des Strafrechts* (Peter Lang 2007) 129; Kai Ambos, 'Beihilfe durch Alltagshandlungen' [2000] Juristische Arbeitsblätter (hereinafter: JA) 721; all with further references.

110   BGHSt 46, 107 (112).

111   See Bohlander (n 3) 161; also Vest (n 47) 305, 386.

112   Vest (n 47) 305, 386.

113   Bohlander (n 3) 161; see also (nn 5, 62) and accompanying text.

114   See (nn 27, 35) and accompanying text.

sightedness, A goes into room 7 and gives the injection to patient V_2 who dies. A acted without knowledge with regard to the nature of the injection and thus without intent. If A had acted in bad faith, that is, if she had been aware that the injection was poisoned, her mistake concerning the identity of the victim would not affect her criminal liability, since she had the intent to kill a human being (irrelevant *error in persona*).[115] It is, however, questionable if the same holds true for D, since what is an irrelevant *error in persona* for A is a so-called *aberratio ictus*, that is, a situation where the 'act goes amiss', for D.[116] In the classical textbook example, D shoots at V_1 but the bullet unexpectedly hits and kills V_2.[117] In contrast to the *error in persona* scenario where D is in error about the identity of a factually selected target, D misses the selected and targeted object by accident. Therefore, the prevailing opinion in German case law and doctrine takes the view that D had no intention to kill V_2. He is therefore (only) liable for the attempted murder of V_1 and for the negligent manslaughter of V_2.[118] Turning back to the hospital case, one view holds that D has used A as a weapon so that her (for her irrelevant) *error in persona* is a (for him relevant) *aberratio ictus*.[119] Another view argues that it was D who had identified the victim by advising D exactly to which person in which room she should administer the injection, so that his mistake should be treated as an (irrelevant) *error in persona*, too. Yet, if the identification of the target is completely left to the direct agent, for example, by providing him merely with the victim's name, his mistake should result in an *aberratio ictus* for the indirect perpetrator.[120]

A similar discussion takes place in the context of *instigation*.[121] In the *Farm Heir Case* ('*Hoferbenfall*')[122] decided by the Federal Supreme Court in 1990, farmer D decided to kill his son and the heir to his farm, V_1, because of his brutality and ingratitude. Since he did not want to kill his son himself, he paid A to do so and gave him a photo of V_1. One night, A waited with his gun ready in the stable. When neighbour V_2 entered the barn, A took him to be V_1 and shot him dead. The court took the view that A's error had no effect on D's criminal responsibility and thus convicted him for instigating murder. In doing so, the Court clearly rejected the approach according to which an *error in persona* of the principal perpetrator always gives rise to an *aberratio ictus* of the instigator.[123] Most notably, however, the Court emphasised that D was conscious of the risk that A might confuse V_1 with somebody else but nevertheless left the identification of the actual target to him.[124] Thus, the court seems to favour a differentiated approach as explained above in the context of perpetration through another person.[125]

In the context of *joint perpetration*, an (irrelevant) *error in persona* of one co-perpetrator does not normally affect the criminal liability of the other co-perpetrators as long as the relevant act is

---

115   See (n 40) and accompanying text.

116   Badar (n 40) 239.

117   Kindhäuser (n 10) § 27 mn 52; Badar (n 40) 239; Murmann (n 98) § 24 mn 54.

118   BGHSt 34, 53 (55); Rengier (n 12) § 15 mn 34-38; Kindhäuser (n 10) § 27 mn 55-58; see also Badar (n 40) 239-40 and the critique by Bohlander (n 3) 73-74. According to the minority view, however, the *aberratio ictus* has no impact on the actor's *mens rea* if the targeted and the affected object are of equal value (for example, both are human beings); Frister (n 25) 148-50.

119   Baumann, Weber and Mitsch (n 83) § 21 mn 15; Jescheck and Weigend (n 15) 672.

120   Rengier (n 12) § 43 mn 74; Wessels and Beulke (n 3) mn 550; see also Bohlander (n 3) 160.

121   See the overview on the discussion by Heinrich (n 3) mn 1307-11 with further references.

122   BGHSt 37, 214. For the similar *Rose-Rosahl* case of the *Preußisches Obertribunal* (GA1859, 322), see Bohlander (n 3) 171.

123   This approach is nevertheless favoured *inter alia* by Heinrich (n 3) mn 1311 with further references.

124   BGHSt 37, 214 (218); in a similar vein BGH NStZ 1997, 294 (295).

125   See (n 120) and accompanying text.

part of the common plan: A and B burgle homes and have agreed beforehand to shoot at possible pursuers if this were necessary to avoid detection. The next time A and B have to flee from a crime scene, A notices a man following them. He believes him to be the house owner trying to arrest them, so he shoots him dead. In fact, the person was just a jogger who had not noticed the burglary. A's *error in persona* does not affect his intent to kill the person behind them. As he acted in accordance with their common plan, his conduct can be attributed to B so that both are liable as joint principals for murder.[126] The case becomes more complex in the following modified version: while on the run, A and B get separated. A again shoots at an alleged pursuer but this time it is B who, although badly injured, survives.[127] With respect to A, the result remains the same: despite the mistaken identity he has committed the crime of attempted murder (of B). For B, the situation is more complex since German law does not criminalise suicide or self-injury.[128] Thus, if B had shot himself, he would not have been criminally liable. Nevertheless, the Federal Supreme Court emphasised that A has committed the relevant act (which means that – technically speaking – B has not harmed himself), attributed this act to B and thus convicted him for attempted murder of himself.[129] Of course, this decision received a lot of criticism. It was argued that A and B had at least implicitly agreed not to shoot each other. A's shooting at B is therefore said to be beyond the common plan ('*Mittäterexzess*'),[130] so that a mutual attribution is excluded.[131]

Withdrawal from Participation

The question if and under which circumstances a participant may avoid punishment by withdrawing from participation depends on the point in time in which he abandons the effort to commit the offence. In the so-called preparation stage of a crime ('*Vorbereitungsphase*') – in which normally no criminal responsibility arises[132] – it is sufficient if the participant completely neutralises his preparatory contribution; it is not necessary that he prevents the commission of the crime by the other parties:[133] A lends a lock pick to D who wants to burgle V's house. Before D puts his plan into practise A changes his mind and gets his lock pick back. If D nevertheless manages to burgle V's house, A cannot be responsible for aiding because his contribution had no effect on the actual commission of the crime.[134] If, however, the participant is not able to neutralise his contribution and the offence is completed, his intention to abandon his involvement does not relieve him from criminal responsibility.[135] Imagine for example that A demands his lock pick back but D refuses and

---

126 Example based on Rengier (n 12) § 44 mn 30-31; see also Wessels and Beulke (n 3) mn 533.

127 BGHSt 11, 268.

128 See (n 21) and accompanying text.

129 BGHSt 11, 268 (271); concurring Rengier (n 12) § 44 mn 32-33; Heinrich (n 3) mn 1240.

130 See (n 69) and accompanying text.

131 Roxin, *Strafrecht* (n 2) § 25 mn 195; in detail on this case Jan Dehne-Niemann, 'Zum fünfzigjährigen Jubiläum des "Verfolgerfalls" (BGHSt 11, 268) – Beteiligung des Tatopfers an einem gegen das Tatopfer gerichteten Mordversuch?' [2008] ZJS 351.

132 Krey and Esser (n 9) mn 1193; Stratenwerth and Kuhlen (n 14) § 11 mn 6-9.

133 Wessels and Beulke (n 3) mn 650; Roxin, *Strafrecht* (n 2) § 30 mn 309-13; Kai Ambos, '§ 24 StGB' in Dieter Dölling, Gunnar Duttge and Dieter Rössner (eds), *Gesamtes Strafrecht – StGB, StPO, Nebengesetze, Handkommentar* (2nd edn, Nomos Verlag 2011) mn 24; see also BGHSt 4, 200 (201).

134 Example based on Roxin, *Strafrecht* (n 2) § 30 mn 301; Rengier (n 12) § 38 mn 11.

135 Roxin, *Strafrecht* (n 2) § 30 mn 314-30; Ambos (n 133) mn 24.

instead uses it to burgle V's house. A would be punishable for aiding;[136] his futile effort to prevent the commission by D can only be taken into account as a mitigating factor.

In case of attempts,[137] the requirements for withdrawal are set out in § 24 StGB which provides:

> (1) A person who of his own volition gives up the further execution of the offence or prevents its completion shall not be liable for the attempt. If the offence is not completed regardless of his actions, that person shall not be liable if he has made a voluntary and earnest effort to prevent the completion of the offence.

> (2) If more than one person participate in the offence, the person who voluntarily prevents its completion shall not be liable for the attempt. His voluntary and earnest effort to prevent the completion of the offence shall suffice for exemption from liability, if the offence is not completed regardless of his actions or is committed independently of his earlier contribution to the offence.[138]

Thus, § 24 StGB distinguishes between offences committed by a single perpetrator (paragraph 1) and offences committed by more than one person (paragraph 2). In the latter case, the requirements for abandonment are stricter because the involvement of several persons increases the risk, danger and likelihood of criminal conduct occurring because of the group dynamics.[139] § 24(2) StGB thus applies to principals by proxy, joint principals, instigators and aiders. Conversely, the main perpetrator who acts pursuant to an abetment or is assisted by other(s) has full control of the act so that § 24(1) StGB applies to a withdrawal. The same holds true for the fully responsible direct perpetrator who is dominated by an indirect perpetrator.[140]

Corporate Liability: Basic Rules

Germany is one of the few jurisdictions which does not provide for corporate criminal liability but rather limits the personal scope of criminal norms (and sanctions) to natural persons. The *ratio* for Germany's adherence to the ancient *societas delinquere non potest* rule[141] is that collective entities can neither act nor be blamed in a moral sense.[142] As a consequence, corporate liability does not sit well with the traditional German concept of crime which is predicated upon the personal blameworthiness of the actor.[143] Germany's restrictive approach is, however, by no means uncontested within the German academic community.[144] Thus, it remains to be seen whether it

---

136   Roxin, *Strafrecht* (n 2) § 30 mn 302; for a more complex case see BGHSt 28, 346.

137   According to § 22 StGB, an attempt occurs if a person 'takes steps that will immediately lead to the completion of the offence as envisaged by him', translation according to Bohlander (n 1) 42.

138   Translation according to Bohlander (n 1) 43.

139   Rengier (n 12) § 38 mn 5; Ambos (n 133) mn 22.

140   Ambos (n 133) mn 23 with further references. On the perpetrator behind the perpetrator, see already (nn 37 *et seq.*) and accompanying text.

141   Wolfgang Joecks 'Vor § 25' in Bernd von Heintschel-Heinegg (ed.), *Münchener Kommentar zum Strafgesetzbuch, Band 1, §§ 1-37 StGB* (2nd edn, C.H. Beck 2011) mn 17.

142   Ibid. mn 17; Weigend (n 5) 267.

143   Bohlander (n 3) 23; Thomas Weigend, 'Societas delinquere non potest?: A German Perspective' (2008) 6 JICJ 927, 936.

144   See the detailed overview on the German discussion by Weigend (n 143) 930-42 with further references.

will be changed in the near future, given in particular the increasing influence of the European law which seems to favour the concept of corporate liability.[145]

In any case, although there is no criminal responsibility of legal persons *stricto sensu*, the court may at least order the confiscation of corporate profits derived from unlawful acts committed by persons acting on their behalf.[146] In addition, German law provides for an administrative sanction of up to 1 million euros if a representative or other high-level employee of a corporation 'committed a criminal offence by which a duty of the corporation was violated or the corporation was enriched' (§ 30 *Gesetz über Ordnungswidrigkeiten* – law on administrative offences).[147]

Sentencing Regime for Participants

With regard to sentencing, all principals – be they single perpetrators, perpetrators by proxy or co-perpetrators – are treated equally in so far as their sentence is determined in accordance with the statutory sentencing frames as set out in the special part of the Criminal Code or in special criminal statutes. Thus, for example, in the case of murder, principals are liable to imprisonment of not less than five years (§ 212 StGB), the maximum term of imprisonment being 15 years (§ 38 StGB), unless the law provides for life imprisonment (as indeed it does for especially serious cases of murder under § 212(2) and § 211 StGB). Instigators in terms of § 26 StGB – although classified as secondary participants – are sentenced as if they were principals. Aiders, however, are granted a mandatory statutory discount (§§ 26, 49 StGB). For aiding murder, the statutory sentencing frame would, for example, be reduced to imprisonment from two years to 11 years and three months.

---

145   See only Article 4 on 'sanctions for legal persons' of the Second Protocol drawn up on the Basis of Article K.3 of the treaty on European Union, to the Convention on the Protection of the European Communities' Financial Interests.

146   § 73 StGB provides in its relevant parts:

1.) If an unlawful act has been committed and the principal or a secondary participant has acquired proceeds from it or obtained anything in order to commit it, the court shall order the confiscation of what was obtained …

2.) The order of confiscation shall extend to benefits derived from what was obtained. It may also extend to objects which the principal or secondary participant has acquired by way of sale of the acquired object, as a replacement for its destruction, damage to or forcible loss of it or on the basis of a surrogate right.

3.) If the principal or secondary participant acted for another and that person acquired anything thereby, the order of confiscation under subsections (1) and (2) above shall be made against him.

(Translation according to Bohlander (n 1) 75-76.)

147   Translation of the relevant parts of this norm according to Weigend (n 5) 267.

Chapter 19

Islamic Law

Mohammad Hedeyati-Kakhki

Introduction

The law concerning participation in criminal offences is a key measure of a legal system's fairness as it involves difficult balancing of moral culpability with the extent of punishment in cases with multiple offenders, who may have played vastly different roles in the criminal endeavour. This challenge is made more difficult in the context of Islamic Criminal Law, as there is no united, coherent set of rules to which one could refer when defining the rules as to liability and sentencing of participants. While common law systems may have to juggle and reconcile precedents which diverge on some legal point, a scholar of Islamic Law must look not only at traditional legal sources that are over a thousand years old, but also at legislation and practice within many Islamic countries (with varying degrees of adherence to Islamic law). A further complication is introduced by the influence of Western legal systems via the mechanisms of European colonial expansion; whilst many Islamic countries have reformed their colonial legal systems to conform with Islamic sources of law, some significant traces remain, including in the area of participation. Furthermore, some of the doctrines in question (for example the use of an innocent agent for a criminal offence) may appear esoteric and do not come before the courts very frequently. At the opposite end of the spectrum, the doctrine of joint criminal enterprise is of great practical significance in hundreds of cases before courts in Islamic countries every year. Accordingly, this chapter seeks to set out the more general position within 'Islamic Law' as based on traditional sources and then provide examples from particular jurisdictions. Needless to say, this digest is not and cannot be exhaustive, and the laws of particular Islamic countries merit individual study.

General Principles

> And no bearer of burdens shall bear another's burden, and if one heavily laden calls another to (bear) his load, nothing of it will be lifted even though he be near of kin.[1]

This is the principle that governs accountability of those involved in crime under Islamic law, with the view that individuals are only responsible for their own actions. This is in essence the same principle that is applied in English law where it is held that 'in general, criminal liability only results from personal fault. We do not punish people in criminal courts for the misdeeds of others',[2] and is indeed a widely upheld principle under international human rights law. The application is most clearly shown by the following *hadith*:

---

1 *Qu'ran* [35:18].
2 *Tesco Supermarkets Limited v Nattrass* [1972] AC 153, 179.

One of the daughters of 'Uthman died at Mecca. We went to attend her funeral procession. Ibn 'Umar and Ibn Abbas were also present. I sat in between them (or said, I sat beside one of them. Then a man came and sat beside me.) 'Abdullah bin 'Umar said to 'Amr bin 'Uthman, "Will you not prohibit crying as Allah's Apostle has said, 'The dead person is tortured by the crying of his relatives'.?" Ibn Abbas said, "Umar used to say so." Then he added narrating, "I accompanied Umar on a journey from Mecca till we reached Al-Baida. There he saw some travelers in the shade of a Samura (A kind of forest tree). He said (to me), 'Go and see who those travelers are'. So I went and saw that one of them was Suhaib. I told this to 'Umar who then asked me to call him. So I went back to Suhaib and said to him, 'Depart and follow the chief of the faithful believers'. Later, when 'Umar was stabbed, Suhaib came in weeping and saying, 'O my brother, O my friend!' (on this 'Umar said to him, 'O Suhaib! Are you weeping for me while the Prophet said, "The dead person is punished by some of the weeping of his relatives?"'" Ibn Abbas added, "When 'Umar died I told all this to Aisha and she said, 'May Allah be merciful to Umar. By Allah, Allah's Apostle did not say that a believer is punished by the weeping of his relatives. But he said, Allah increases the punishment of a non-believer because of the weeping of his relatives'. Aisha further added, 'The Quran is sufficient for you (to clear up this point) as Allah has stated: "No burdened soul will bear another's burden." (35.18)'." Ibn Abbas then said, "Only Allah makes one laugh or cry." Ibn Umar did not say anything after that.[3]

Furthermore, the following verse provides that each individual is liable for their contribution towards a sin/crime[4] and will therefore be treated accordingly:

And to all are (assigned) degrees according to the deeds which they (have done), and in order that (Allah) may recompense their deeds, and no injustice be done to them.[5]

Therefore, where more than one individual has been involved in the commission of a crime, it is essential to isolate the acts of each defendant so as to determine their level of culpability and the precise crimes of which they are guilty, if any. There are different modes, or assigned degrees, of participation with different levels of culpability and sentencing attached to the acts committed by each individual. However, as is the case in Western jurisdictions, it is not always possible to ascertain clearly who is the 'bearer of burdens', particularly when trying to assess the exact acts and the mental state of those involved.

Moreover, in some situations it is necessary to consider the consequences of an individual's acts, which may further complicate matters when deciding on the mode of participation, assessing culpability and assigning a sentence accordingly. The following verse makes it clear that where an individual does participate in an evil cause they share in its burden, 'Whoever recommends and helps a good cause becomes a partner therein; and whoever recommends and helps an evil cause, shares in its burden; and Allah has power over all things'.[6]

However, the extent to which this burden is shared is still dependent on an individual's own actions. To clarify this further, it was narrated by Abu Hurayrah[7] that the Prophet Muhammad said: 'He who called (people) to righteousness, there would be reward (assured) for him like the rewards of those who adhered to it, without their rewards being diminished in any respect. And he who

---

3   Sahih Bukhari, Book 2, Volume 23, Number 375.
4   'Sin' and 'crime' are interchangeable to the extent that all crimes are sins, but not vice versa.
5   *Qu'ran* [46:19].
6   *Qu'ran* [4:85].
7   Sahih Muslim 6470; as narrated by Abu Hurayrah.

called (people) to error, he shall have to carry (the burden) of its sin, like those who committed it, without their sins being diminished in any respect'. This *hadith* is predominantly used to advocate against any forms of *bi'dah*[8] and it is similarly relevant to circumstances relating to the degrees of participation and subsequent culpability. The *hadith* was recently used in terms of debating the authenticity of Shab-e-Baraat, which some consider to be an innovation rather than an authentic night of worship. In accordance with the *Qu'ran* and *hadith* it is stated that the inventors of this night will be punished for the sin of *bi'dah* just as the worshippers will be for observing the night. However, it must be emphasised that the focus continues to remain on individual culpability and the consequences that arise from the individual actions. In terms of performing the night of Shab-e-Baraat, the worshippers are carrying the burdens of their own sin in terms of observing *bi'dah*; that is their share of the burden. The inventor of the night will be carrying the burden of having introduced a *bi'dah* that is being followed. Applying this *hadith* to a different scenario, where an individual instigates a riot, the rioters will be liable for their actions and the individual will be liable for instigating this riot. Thus, where the Surah states '… and whoever recommends and helps an evil cause, shares in its burden', this sharing is dependent on each individual contribution to the overall burden.

Furthermore, it was narrated by Abdullah that the Prophet Muhammad said, 'None is killed unjustly, but the first son of Adam will have a part of its burden'.[9] Sufyan said, '… a part of its blood because he was first to establish the tradition of murdering'.[10] This may seem to be in contradiction to the principle that no bearer of burdens shall bear the burdens of another. However, the explanation behind this *hadith* is that the first son of Adam bears the burden because he introduced murder as a phenomenon. In any event it can be said that its application is limited as it refers to the first son of Adam only.

It must be highlighted that the principles found in the *Qu'ran* and *Sunnah* have formed the basis for establishing criminal laws in different Islamic countries and the application in each country varies according to its history, its society and its own interpretation. In some situations there may have been a transplantation of Western law from previous occupiers or influences from neighbouring countries.[11] The variations and the reasons behind the variations are outside the scope of this discussion. However, Islamic principles derived from the *Qu'ran* and *Sunnah* retain their importance in Islamic countries.

At this stage it may be useful to consider the following case that came before an Egyptian Court in 1879:

> Two men had entered the cattle pen of Muhammad Bey 'Abd Allat at night [probably to steal cattle, although this is not mentioned in the record] and killed a certain Ramadan Musa, who was sleeping there. The first defendant had hit him on the head with a big stone and the second one, when the victim still showed signs of life, had stabbed him in the belly with his knife. Ramadan died two days after the attack. During the trial the first defendant confessed that he, together with

---

8   *Bi'dah* is the concept of innovation; if one adds, amends, invents or innovates in any way any act or deed of worship in Islam which has not been specifically endorsed by Allah or the Prophet Muhammad then it is said to be *bi'dah* which is abhorred in Islam.

9   Sahih Bukhari, Volume 9, Book 92, Number 423.

10   Ibid.

11   While the influences of colonial law have often been mitigated by the efforts of Islamic legislators to ensure conformity between remaining Western laws and Islamic principles/sources, Western influences on the law of participation may account for the many similarities between Islamic and Western legal concepts in this respect.

the second defendant, had murdered Ramadan. Further it was established that both acts would have been lethal if they had been carried out separately. Against the second defendant, who did not confess, nothing was proven. Asked for his opinion, the Grand Mufti argued that the first defendant could not be sentenced to retaliation. Since the hitting with a stone and the stabbing with the knife had been consecutive acts and the victim had lived for more than one day after the attack, the cause of his death was to be ascribed to the second defendant, against whom nothing was proven legally. The first defendant, the Mufti explained, was to be punished by the state authorities on the strength of ta'zir[12,13]

In the above *fatwa* the principle applied was that whilst the acts of both individuals had been lethal in itself, as the victim had survived more than one day, liability will be placed upon the second defendant. This principle that the last person to strike is to be attributed with blame is not necessarily followed in every Islamic country and moreover it must be highlighted that this is a *fatwa* rather than a legal rule.[14] However, it does highlight the importance of undertaking a fact-finding exercise and isolating the circumstances of each individual involved in each case. This is precisely in order to understand who the bearer of the burden is in line with Islamic principles. With modern day technology it is now possible to establish more precisely what the cause of death was. Thus, if the situation arose today and medical evidence could prove that the first defendant's actions caused the death then liability will be apportioned to him. Similarly, if evidence proves that it was the second defendant's actions then blame is accordingly placed upon him. This is akin to the principles of intervening acts in English law as the second defendant's acts may be considered to have broken the chain of causation. In any event, it is not the case that the second party is completely exonerated. As the *fatwa* above shows, each will be apportioned a punishment under *ta'zir* dependent upon their criminal culpability, which in this scenario may be attempted murder.

Some Islamic countries have codified the legal position in relation to cases such as the Egyptian murder described above. Iran's Penal Code in Article 214 dictates that where injuries are inflicted by multiple assailants on the same person, with a lethal result attributable to all those injuries separately, then the assailants will be joint principals (thus primarily guilty of murder). On the other hand, Article 215 sets out the position where an assailant would be guilty of being an accessory instead; the difference between the two appears to be the extent of the causal link between the injury inflicted by that person and the lethal outcome for the victim.

Joint Principals

Under English criminal law, the principal is the individual whose actions can be considered to have caused the crime or who was at least the most immediate cause for its commission.[15] Thus, where a victim is shot dead, the individual who pulls the trigger is considered the principal offender and

---

12   *Ta'zir* is a discretionary punishment determined and meted out by a *qadi* (Islamic judge) such as imprisonment, fine and lashes. However, in some jurisdictions offences subject to *ta'zir*, such as heresy or espionage, may also attract the death penalty.

13   Rudolph Peters, *Crime and Punishment in Islamic Law: Theory and Practice from the Sixteenth to the Twenty-First Century* (Cambridge University Press 2006) 29.

14   A *fatwa* is a ruling on a point of Islamic law given by a recognised authority, for example the Supreme Leader of Iran. A legal rule on the other hand is a principle found in the statutes of Islamic countries or within the historical sources of Islam such as the *Qu'ran* and *Sunnah*.

15   David Ormerod, *Smith and Hogan's Criminal Law* (12th edn, Oxford University Press 2009) 180.

the one who, for example, buys the gun for the principal will be considered a secondary participant. However, in situations where more than one individual is directly responsible, they can both be classed as joint principals. This would be the situation where both individuals had stabbed the victim but it cannot be ascertained which of the two dealt the fatal blow. This does not necessarily mean the other will be completely exempt from all liability.

Islamic Law operates similar concepts of primary and secondary participant as required in accordance with the *Qu'ran*, which discusses the assigning of degrees of culpability.[16] In terms of assessing modes of participation there is no distinction between the differing terms of, for example, an abettor or accomplice, as all would be placed under the general umbrella term of secondary participants. However, given the need to establish each individual's contribution towards the crime the laws must remain *actus reus* focused. Thus, whilst there is no specific distinction between different types of secondary participants the level of culpability and the sentence which should be imposed will be dependent on what contribution was made. Thus, someone who provided encouragement to the principal offender to burgle a house would be sentenced differently to another who provided the equipment to carry out the burglary.

As Islamic jurisprudence seeks to punish in accordance with an individual's moral culpability and the harm caused by their actions, utilising factors not dissimilar to those influencing English law, there are significant similarities between the two in how joint principals are dealt with. Accordingly, the starting point is the type of aid rendered to the principal offender and whether the extent of involvement results in shared status as principal offenders. In straightforward cases, such as a robbery carried out by several persons, each of whom was responsible for an application of force against the victim and took some share of his property, the classification of the criminals as joint principals is uncontroversial in Islamic law generally. However, as one offender becomes more removed from the physical act of the offence, greater classification difficulties arise. What if, for example, the other robber remained outside the premises as a look-out and thus did not actually take any property or apply any force to the victim? The response of Islamic jurisprudence is to allow discretion for Islamic judges to assess the precise role of each participant and evaluate the effectiveness of their contribution to the final outcome and consider this at the sentencing stage. This would come into effect through the concept of *ta'zir* which makes provision for minimum and maximum measures, with a judge having discretion to prescribe appropriate punishment for each participant. In order to better equip judges in making such decisions, national legislatures can assist by providing precise provisions to determine the varying levels of criminal liability in the complex, modern legal world of the twenty-first century.

Whilst it is necessary to ascertain as far as possible who the principal offender is, where this is not possible the rules of Islamic jurisprudence allow that both offenders be sentenced as principals. This, however, depends on whether they could be considered to be principals in their own right. The reasoning behind this is that the alternative would be to exonerate both individuals of liability which would be unfair to the victim and moreover it would create a loophole open to abuse. Thus, the rules of joint principals are necessary in order to uphold law and order.

The difference between the rules relating to joint principals and joint criminal enterprise must be clarified at this stage. The differences depend not only on knowledge and intention of the offence to be committed, as well as what is foreseeable, but also on the contribution of each individual. With joint principals, both parties contribute to the *actus reus* of the offence whilst with joint criminal enterprise it is not always clear what contribution was made by all. The focus is on contribution towards the commission of the offence when trying to differentiate between a

---

16   *Qu'ran* [46:19].

principal, joint principal or secondary participant. This is complicated because each individual Islamic country has approached the matter differently.

It is important to note that in order to invoke the rules of joint principals both the *actus reus* and *mens rea* of the crimes need to be completed under Islamic law. Thus, where one person stabbed and the other person shot the victim, and both did so with the intention of committing a murder, then it is apparent that each individual's acts could have led to the death of the victim and it is not a defence to then state that the acts may not have actually caused the death of the person because another individual was involved. In this way the principle that no bearer of burden shall bear the burdens of another is upheld because each offender does have the burden upon them.

Pakistan's Penal Code (which is one of the more comprehensive legislative frameworks in Islamic criminal law) makes the rules relating to joint principals clear in Section 34 and further in Section 37, which states that 'when an offence is committed by means of several acts, whoever intentionally cooperates in the commission of that offence by doing any one of those acts, either singly or jointly with any other person, commits that offence'. This can be by act or omission but it is important that it is committed jointly albeit not necessarily at the same time. Thus, where two individuals agree to gradually poison the victim at different occasions and both administer the poison at different times then they are both guilty as joint principals. However, if two individuals happen to kill the victim independently of each other then they cannot be regarded as joint principals. Depending on the circumstances one would be guilty of murder and the other guilty of attempted murder.

In Afghanistan, whilst Article 36 of the Penal Code defines a principal offender and Article 39 defines an accomplice, there is no further definition within the Penal Code about joint principals. However, it is apparent that the concepts do exist when reading Article 14 which refers to principal offenders in the plural. It is also noteworthy that Article 39(2) states that a person is considered an accomplice 'when he enters in to an agreement with another person to commit a crime and the crime takes place as a result of this agreement'. Depending on the facts of the case and the evidence provided, this will allow discretion to the Courts as to whether an individual can be considered to be a principal offender or secondary participant.

Another well-developed system of law concerning such doctrines is the Egyptian Penal Code. The Code, in this respect, is based on the theory of 'Borrowed Criminality' adopted by the Egyptian legislature.[17] It treats the criminal act of a secondary participant as a distinct crime, such as in instigating a crime, thus allowing that offence to take place even if it had not been followed by an actual commission of the crime. The Code places emphasis on the multiplicity of offenders and the unity of the offence. Both elements should be present to enable secondary/joint principal liability. Accordingly, Article 39 of the Code defines the '*Principal*' as follows:

> A person is concerned as a principal in the commission of an offence: (1) Who commits such offence whether alone or in conjunction with others, or (2) Who in the case of an offence consisting of two or more acts, knowingly participates in such offence by doing one or more such acts.[18]

---

17   Mohamed A Arafa, 'Criminal Complicity: Accomplice Criminal Liability to the Criminal Offences. A Comparative Analysis Between the Egyptian Criminal Law System and the Criminal Law System of the United States of America' (1 February 2008) <http://papers.ssrn.com/sol3/papers.cfm?abstract_id=1933635> accessed 2 August 2012.

18   ME Badar, '"Just Convict Everyone!": Joint Perpetration: From Tadic to Statik and Back Again' (2006) 6 International Criminal Law Review 293-302, 298.

Joint principals are penalised equally in all circumstances, however, accomplices may incur a punishment equivalent to that of the principal offender, but not in all cases. Indeed in some circumstances an accomplice may be punished more harshly, for example where the accomplice was perceived to be the mastermind behind the crime. Particular examples in the Egyptian Penal Code are offences related to an escape from custody – the person helping the arrestee to escape is punished more harshly than the escapee himself.[19] In spite of the comparatively similar punishments for joint principals and secondary participants, the two concepts remain distinct. Thus for example, when considering criminal conspiracy, even though all the participants can be considered joint principals the courts will undertake a fact-finding exercise in order to identify the integral members of the conspiracy. In other words, the Courts are willing to consider whether an individual was a joint principal or a secondary participant to the conspiracy, such as if they suggested the conspiracy and had no further input.

Accordingly, the position in Islamic penal legislation as regards joint principals appears to be not unlike that in English law – that the objective nature of the shared criminal act coupled with sufficient proximity by the joint principals renders them similarly liable, leading to the same level of punishment. Their position is less advantageous than that of accomplices, whose liability/sentence may sometimes be lesser than that of the principal.

Joint Criminal Enterprise

The topic of joint criminal enterprise has been a cause for concern in Islamic law as it undermines the principle of individual responsibility. Nonetheless, its application can be seen in various Islamic countries. 'Whoever recommends and helps a good cause becomes a partner therein; and whoever recommends and helps an evil cause, shares in its burden; and Allah has power over all things'.[20] Previous discussion of the above verse has established that the sharing of burden relates to the individual contribution to the overall consequences of the offence. In joint criminal enterprise the individual contribution of each participant cannot in fact be dissected and thus it may be argued that the concept of joint criminal enterprise is contrary to Islamic principles. However, it has to be understood that the requirement is that all parties were collectively involved in the commission and it is apparent that all intended to commit the crime or at the very least could foresee that the crime will be committed. Thus the line of thought is that any of these individuals could have been the bearer of the burden. It must be stressed, however, that this is dependent on the interpretations by each individual legal system which may or may not allow the concept of joint criminal enterprise to be invoked. Furthermore, as will be seen below, the approach to sentencing in such situations will differ between different countries.

All participants in a joint criminal enterprise are considered principal offenders where they are all acting together with a common purpose, and thus each individual assumes responsibility for the actions of the other members of the group, provided that there was no departure from the agreed plan by any of the individuals involved. Rudolph Peters asserts:

---

19 Articles 138, 140 and 142 of the Egyptian Penal Code.

20 *Qu'ran* [4:85].

the only form of collective criminal liability in the law of *hadd*[21] is to be found in the doctrine of banditry, where the aggravating circumstances causing an increase in the punishment are not individualised. This means that if one of the persons participating in an incident of banditry seizes the property of one of the victims, all participants will be sentenced to amputation of the right hand and left foot, the punishment for banditry with misappropriation.[22]

Pakistan covers this in terms of *dacoity*, which is defined in Article 391 of the Penal Code as:

> When five or more persons conjointly commit or attempt to commit a robbery, or where the whole number of persons conjointly committing or attempting to commit a robbery and persons present and aiding such commission or attempt, amount to five or more, every person so committing, attempting or aiding is said to commit 'dacoity'.

More importantly, Article 400 of the Pakistan Penal Code states:

> Whoever, at any time after the passing of this Act, shall belong to a gang of persons associated for the purpose of habitually committing dacoity, shall be punished with imprisonment for life, or with rigorous imprisonment for a term which may extend to ten years, and shall also be liable to fine

Article 401 states:

> Whoever, at any time after the passing of this Act, shall belong to any wandering or other gang of persons associated for the purpose of habitually committing theft or robbery, and not being of thugs or dacoits, shall be punished with rigorous imprisonment for a term which may extend to seven years, and shall also be liable to fine.

Thus association with a gang and presence at the point of a crime may be sufficient to create criminal liability.

The extent of this collective criminal responsibility is dependent upon what was agreed between the parties and what occurred in fact. Thus where a group of individuals agree to rob a bank they will be liable for events that were agreed and those that could be foreseen as part of the agreement to rob a bank. If a member of the group goes beyond what was agreed or could be foreseen as a possible occurrence as a consequence of the agreement then only he or she is held liable for the additional crimes.

It is up for discussion whether banditry is the only situation in which collective criminal responsibility is involved. Rudolph Peters accepts that the Maliki school of thought allows its application to other criminal acts. Thus:

> they hold liable not only the person who by his acts has directly caused the victim's death, but all other persons who were involved in the crime, e.g. through abetting and offering assistance. Therefore, under Malikite law, both the person who prepared poison, knowing that it would be used to kill someone, and the person who actually administered it can be sentenced to death by

---

21   *Hadd/hudud* is a category of crime with fixed punishment, without any discretionary component. These offences are seen as acts against God, and the corresponding punishment has also been prescribed by Allah. Examples include fornication and consumption of alcohol.

22   Peters (n 13) 28.

way of retaliation. The same is true if, for instance, three men drag a person to an isolated place and only one of them actually shoots him.[23]

Of course it is dependent upon each individual country whether in the former scenario both the individual who prepared the poison and the one who administered it would be classed as principals, but generally under the Maliki school of thought such a possibility exists. Certainly it seems to be the case that many Islamic regimes extend the principle further than banditry. For example, Article 21 of the Sudanese Penal Code of 1991 states, 'if two or more commit an offence in execution of a criminal agreement between them, each shall be liable for that offence in the same manner as if it were committed by him alone and shall be punished with the punishment prescribed for it'.

Concerns about the application of joint criminal enterprise are heightened from a human rights perspective in relation to Islamic law when considering the sentencing of individuals in relation to the crime collectively committed, in particular the principle of *qisas* which allows retaliation and corporal punishment as a form of sanction. Human rights activists were greatly concerned by the execution of eight Bangladeshi nationals in Saudi Arabia who were found guilty of the death of an Egyptian man.[24] However, closer analysis of the circumstances of the case suggests deeper cultural issues which are not necessarily related to Islamic principles. It is noteworthy that the Hanbali school of thought is applied in Saudi Arabia, which requires strict equality between the number of people murdered and the number of people executed under the principle of *qisas*. Therefore, in general terms the courts will undertake a fact finding exercise in order to distinguish between the individual members of the collective group as far as possible in a bid to adhere to the Hanbali practices. The fact that this does not seem to have occurred in this case and that the eight men executed were foreign nationals from the Asian continent suggests that factors such as xenophobia may have impacted this decision.

Secondary Participation

The need to establish the different degrees of participation in crime under Islamic law is found within the following: 'And if anyone earns sin, he earns it against his own soul; For Allah is full of knowledge and wisdom'.[25]

In line with the principle that no bearer of burden shall bear the burdens of another, each individual is to be held accountable for the crimes, or sins, that they have committed. Thus, where an individual contributes towards the commissioning of an offence, they must be penalised in accordance with their contribution (its impact and extent).

As a practical example of how such laws are applied, a useful provision is contained in Pakistan's Penal Code, Article 114, which distinguishes accomplices and principal offenders:

> Whenever any person, who if absent would be liable to be punished as an abettor, is present when the act or offence for which he would be punishable in consequence of the abetment is committed, he shall be deemed to have committed such act or offence.

---

23 Ibid. 29.

24 Glen Carey, 'Saudi Arabia Beheads 8 Bangladeshis for Murder' (*Seattle Times*, 8 October 2011) <http://seattletimes.nwsource.com/html/nationworld/2016447767_beheadings09.html> accessed 3 August 2012.

25 *Surah An-Nisaa* 4:111.

Such a distinction has the benefit of simplicity – the person is either there or not, allowing for easy determination of joint principal status or secondary status. This is subject, of course, to the issue of how far from the offence can he physically be for Article 114 to still apply – would, as in the example above, standing outside the house while a robbery takes place be enough? However, this distinction arguably sacrifices equity for clarity, because presence alone (with no other requirement for further personal involvement for example assisting with restraint of a victim) does not necessarily make the 'principal offender' more culpable than an abettor who had stayed away from the scene of the crime.

Another example of such distinctions is the Egyptian Penal Code, which sets out secondary participation implications in some detail. Article (40) of the Code defines the 'Accomplice' as follows:

> A person is concerned as an accessory in the commission of an offence: (1) Who instigates to the commission of the act constituting the offence, provided that the act is the consequence of such instigation, or (2) Who is a party to an arrangement having for its object the commission of the offence, provided that the offence is the consequence of such arrangement, or (3) Who knowingly supplies weapons or other implements or means employed in the commission of the offence, or in any manner aids the principal or principals concerned in the offence in the preparation, facilitation, or commission thereof.

The Egyptian appellate courts have determined that it is the nature of the act carried out by the co-participant that determines his status, rather than the subjective perceptions of the participants.[26] For the *actus reus* of complicity to exist, the act of the accomplice must necessarily take the form of one of the three means enumerated by Article 40, namely instigation, preconceived arrangement and aid or assistance. Thus accomplice liability is not open-ended.

There is also a *mens rea* element required for accomplice liability to be established. The accomplice must have knowledge of all essential elements and facts constituting the offence. Particularly, he must be aware of the dangerousness that his act represents to the criminally protected interest. Furthermore, he should have knowledge of the result of his act. It is also a requisite that his 'will be directed at his act' as well as at the crime committed by the principal with all its legal elements and construction.[27]

In contrast with Egypt's more limited and targeted use of the 'accomplice' label (limited to just three types of *actus reus*), the approach of Iran's Penal Code to accomplice liability enumerates over a dozen potential kinds of *actus reus* in Articles 42 and 43.

Article 42 states:

> Any person who knowingly and intentionally associates with other or others in an offence punishable according to *Ta'zir* or deterrent punishments, and the offence is committed by their collective actions, whether the action of each one would be sufficient for committing the offence, whether the result of their actions are equal or not, is regarded as an accomplice to the offences. His/her punishment will be as though that of the person who had committed the offence ....

---

26   Sadiq Reza, 'Egypt' in K Heller and M Dubber (eds), *The Handbook of Comparative Criminal Law* (Stanford University Press 2011) 190.

27   Arafa (n 17) 19.

Article 43 dictates the types of actions that can lead to accomplice liability, such as inciting, encouraging, plotting, tricking or deceiving into criminal offences; or otherwise facilitating the offence. It specifies further that the court will punish the accomplice according to their circumstances and means and previous records.

Similarly Pakistan has a wide approach to accomplices, as set out in Sections 34 and 149 of the Pakistan Penal Code.[28] Anyone encouraging, advising, provoking or committing a crime will be liable, as will be anyone involved behind the scene.

It is arguable that Egypt's approach is preferable in that providing a small number of clearly defined modes of *actus reus* eliminates the type of vague liability that may be created due to Iran's and Pakistan's far wider interpretation of 'accomplice'.

Furthermore, Iran's Penal Code's classification of 'accomplices' with regard to political/national security offences is open to criticism on human rights grounds. Article 183 provides that 'whoever resorts to arms to wage terror and panic and perturb peace and security shall be considered as [an] enemy combatant' and 'enemy combatant' incorporates the very broad definition of 'accomplice' in Articles 42 and 43. In effect, this may mean that an individual associated with an illegal organisation in some fairly loose manner (such as by supplying them with water or food) may become as liable for a subsequent terrorist act as the principal offender, by being classified as an 'enemy combatant' without ever having used violence or providing any weapons to that end.

The Egyptian Penal Code's provisions are illustrative of Islamic Law's preferred approach to the issue of secondary participation and show how this role differs from that of the principal offender (although the punishment often is the same). By applying a relatively narrow definition of 'accomplice' (as contrasted with Iran's definition), the concept is of greater utility to the courts in applying these doctrines.

Perpetrator behind the Perpetrator

The 'mastermind' scenario, as the name implies, typically arises where the person committing the actual physical act that constitutes a criminal offence is acting under the direction and in accordance to the plan of another person planning the offence. This situation is particularly relevant to organised crime, with a murder-for-hire scenario being an archetypical one (involving a 'trigger man' and a hirer).

Under Islamic principles, the hit man will be regarded as the principal offender of the murder whilst the commissioner will be found guilty for assisting or inciting the crime. In other words the mastermind will be regarded as a secondary participant only. However, the position in Islamic Law is controversial in light of the fact that the offence of murder attracts the death penalty with retaliation as a form of retribution. It may therefore seem unfair that the hit man is the one to face the death penalty whilst the mastermind is only an accessory to the crime. On the one hand it may be argued that had it not been for the hit man the crime would not have been committed at all. On the other hand, it allows the party with the true intent, who primarily stood to benefit from the death, to avoid the primary penalty of retaliation. In the absence of the defence of duress for the crime of murder in Islamic Law, this result may be particularly unjust where the 'trigger man'

---

28 Section 149: 'If an offence is committed by any member of an unlawful assembly in prosecution of the common object of that assembly, or such as the members of that assembly knew to be likely to be committed in prosecution of that object, every person who, at the time of the committing of that offence, is a member of the same assembly, is guilty of that offence'.

was forced to kill the intended victim and is penalised in full whereas the source of the duress, the mastermind, receives a lighter punishment.

As an example of the statutory application of these principles and the distinction drawn between mastermind and 'trigger man' in Islamic Law, Section 114 of the Pakistan Penal Code states that where an abettor is present when the offence is committed, the abettor is deemed to have committed the act or offence. Therefore, should the hirer be present during the murder then the hirer can be considered as the principal and punished accordingly; however, in most cases the very reason why the hirer retains the services of a 'trigger man' is to avoid being at the scene of the crime.

Insofar as the criminal law should reflect the moral culpability and the harm done by an act, there is no apparent reason why a mastermind who chooses to 'play it safe' by staying away from the scene should be guilty of a lesser offence than a mastermind who chose to attend the scene. Section 114 of the Pakistan Penal Code does not require that the abettor assist in the crime once on the scene, merely to be present there. Thus there is no obvious distinction in the level of culpability to justify the status of principal offender versus secondary offender.

In this author's opinion, the position whereby the mastermind is guilty of the same offence and is sentenced to an equivalent punishment as the 'trigger man' should be the default position. This better reflects the moral culpability of the parties, and the fact that the hit man would not have killed the person in question if not prompted by the mastermind and based on the hierarchical group structure in organised crime scenarios. There appear to be two routes toward this legal end: either changing the position regarding 'masterminds' to reflect the regime found in many Western systems (which may involve some jurisprudential difficulties in terms of Islamic sources) or justifying a *de facto* change with reference to existing legal principles. For example, it is arguable that Islamic law may penalise the mastermind with retaliation because he caused the hit man to incur the punishment of death, in other words causing his death. Alternatively the mastermind may be held responsible for the blood money to be paid by the hit man to the victim's family (with the hit man still having to suffer the state-imposed punishment for murder).

Use of Innocent Agents

Innocent agents recognised by Islamic Law, in addition to children, are persons without mental capacity, persons who did not have the requisite *mens rea* and persons acting involuntarily.

As a matter of common sense and equity, the (moral) culprit should not be allowed to escape punishment simply because he used a child under the age of criminal responsibility. Islamic Law takes a commonsensical approach to the issue. Where the principal formed the requisite *mens rea* and procured an act that, once completed, resulted in the *actus reus* of the offence (for example ordering a child to carry out an assassination or to be a courier for stolen items), then the *actus reus* will essentially transfer to the principal offender even if his agent cannot be held criminally liable for the act due to incapacity, age and so on. The 'innocent agent' is but a vehicle for the principal offender. In most Islamic jurisdictions this position is applied via judicial reasoning and public policy rather than express statutory provisions or primary Islamic sources. However in Egypt's Penal Code, Article 42 stipulates:

> An accessory shall be liable to the penalties prescribed by law, even though the principal may be exempt from all penalty by reason of some ground of justification or by reason of the absence of criminal intent on his part or by reason of any other circumstances personal to himself.

Similarly, Afghan Penal Code, Article 41 makes clear that an accomplice is not excused from liability if the principal offender escapes punishment 'for any legal reason'.

Iran's Penal Code specifically deals with the situation where a child or a mentally incompetent person is used as a tool in a murder. Article 211 states that where this is the case (and, in the case of the child, he/she is young enough not to understand the consequences of the action), then only the person that compels, forces or persuades that person to commit the murder will be retaliated against. If the child is old enough to understand the consequences ('discerning') then the child will be protected but its relatives will need to pay compensation (blood money) to the victim's family, and the person who commissioned the killing will be sentenced to life imprisonment. This is an example of how some Islamic jurisdictions also recognise the possibility of 'innocent agents' receiving some form of sanction in spite of them not having committed a crime. This position sits more easily with the transfer of liability to the principal offender than those scenarios where no sanction whatsoever is possible for the innocent agent. For example Article 8 of the Sudan Penal Code 1991 states that (1) no responsibility lies on persons except who are sane in mind and act voluntarily; (2) there is no responsibility except for illegal acts committed with intent or an act committed negligently.

In a case in Pakistan where a mother used her daughter to give her father cough medicine, which unknown to the daughter turned out to be poison, and the father died, it was held 'in a Court of justice that mother is a guilty of murder since the daughter lacked *mens rea*'.[29] If an agent has sufficient knowledge then he may be held guilty by way of abetting. The case of Nawaz Sharif and Bhutto may be a good example of this kind.[30]

The codification of the above principles within Islamic countries' penal codes may deter crimes using innocent agents (however infrequent) by making it clear that the principal culprit cannot escape liability through such a setup. The author suggests that the adoption of wording similar to s 7(4) of the Queensland Criminal Code, which is quite clear and comprehensive, would be a foolproof means of codifying this desirable legal position.

Withdrawal from Participation

This doctrine addresses the situation where there is an interval between the act of the accessory and the completion of the offence by the principal offender. In Islamic jurisdictions the issue of withdrawal is addressed neither through legislation nor in primary Islamic sources, leaving jurists to make deductions from general principles. One such principle is that punishment corresponds to moral culpability and harm caused. The culpability of a person who chooses to withdraw from a crime is clearly lesser than that of someone who had not withdrawn. The harm will generally be lesser also, depending on the stage at which the person withdraws and how he attempts to mitigate the damage caused by his initial contribution. Accordingly an Islamic court considering a case of a person who had withdrawn will give credit for not going through with the offence in full, and ultimately determine whether he remains guilty of the offence by considering the stage at which he had withdrawn and whether he did anything to mitigate the harm.

Precisely what is required for an effective withdrawal will vary from case to case. It may depend on how imminent the completed offence is at the time of the attempted withdrawal by

---

29 Parties to a Crime or Law of Complicity <http://www.nasirlawsite.com/llb1/criminal.htm> accessed 15 August 2012.

30 Ibid.

the accomplice and also on the nature and assistance and encouragement already given by the accessory. Once assistance has been provided (for example the handing over of a firearm for a killing), an accessory can only avoid liability if he withdraws from the enterprise altogether; this should include steps to neutralise any involvement, in the above example by trying to take away the gun or reporting it to the police. Case law in England and Wales established that running away from the scene of a burglary whilst it is being committed by others does not constitute sufficient withdrawal, for instance. It is likely that an Islamic court would come to a similar conclusion on those facts.

There is some ambiguity as to this doctrine as it is not addressed in Islamic countries' legislation. For example, the Egyptian Penal Code makes no mention of this situation. However, judicial practice in Egypt created two main principles. First, the accomplice does not benefit from his abandonment if it comes at such a late stage that all the elements of complicity have crystallised into an actual offence and nothing can be done to backtrack on the complicity actions (for example if person A sells person B a handgun knowing he is likely to kill his wife with it, but is unable subsequently to do anything to retrieve the gun or inform the police of the culprit's identity). Thus, if the accessory desists and the principal pursues the criminal project until completion, the accomplice will nonetheless be punishable. Secondly, if the abandoning accomplice manages to neutralise the effects of his intervention, thus causing one of the elements of complicity to collapse, he will escape punishment for that reason. Removing the complicity is easier where the accomplice provided a knife or a gun (which can be taken away) and more difficult where it was intangible assistance (such as encouragement or information).[31]

As with other doctrines discussed in this article, withdrawal would benefit from greater attention from legislators in the Islamic jurisdictions.

Transferred Malice

The doctrine of transferred malice governs the establishment of chains of legal liability arising from acts that have been committed intentionally but have had an unintended consequence, such as an unintended victim (for example a bystander) being killed in the course of a fire fight. The Islamic variations of transferred malice are incorporated in various statutes and precedents with slight differences of interpretation across the many adherents to Islamic jurisprudence. The key factor in determining culpability is whether the intended target was a human being or an object. If the shooter's original intent was to harm a person, then he will be treated to have acted intentionally if the bullet/arrow/stone strikes and hurts unintended Victim 2 instead of the intended Victim 1. If on the other hand a non-human object was the target (for example a gunman only trying to fire at the vase to intimidate and not to hurt the individual), but the bullet then hit Victim 2, then this killing would be classified as a mistaken killing. This will still be punished, but attracts the lowest *diyah* (blood money) of the various types of homicide. When generally assessing the Shari'a position in relation to creating culpability for actions that may have elements of transferred malice, there appears to be three outcomes that can be expected (per the Reliance of the Traveller[32]). The act is classified either as resulting from honest mistake, committed by mistake but occurring when inflicting a deliberate injury or established to have been the intended consequence.

---

31   Arafa (n 17) 16.

32   *The Reliance of the Traveller* (*Umdat al-salik wa 'uddat al-nasik* [The Reliance of the Traveller and Tools of the Worshipper]), Translated by Nuh Ha Mim Keller (revised edn, Amana Publications 1994) 584.

As is often the case, various Islamic jurisdictions have interpreted this general approach differently, depending on the school of thought propounding the framework for that particular country's law. Homicide by mistake is never legally classified as such across all schools of Islamic jurisprudence. For example, Nigeria adopts a slightly altered legal position by virtue of its Maliki jurisprudence which allows it to integrate elements of intent and emotional state to establish the *mens rea* when certain conditions are satisfied. According to this doctrine, intent is assumed by inference if a person attacks another with a weapon or instrument that in general can be considered lethal or if he attacks another in anger and the other person dies. There is no intervening link present detailing the influence another party's involvement (for example the intended versus non-intended victim) may have on the perpetrator's legal liability. The court applying the law is likely to have regard to the general principle of who (or what) the intended target was, as described above, and make their judgment accordingly.

Iran's Penal Code addresses transferred malice with some elaboration. Generally, the position is consistent with the overarching Islamic Law position set out above. Article 295(a) of the Iranian Islamic Penal Code states that the crime would not be that of premeditated murder if the death or injury or loss of limb were caused by accident, that is to say, the offender neither intended to commit the crime nor intended to perform the action which caused the crime, as in the case where a person intends to shoot an animal, but hits the victim. Even in more complex situations where the original target was, in fact, a person (thus the act itself was intended, but not the result of killing the unintended victim), full liability for premeditated murder is not imposed. Article 296 of the Penal Code is particularly relevant to these scenarios:

> In cases where a person intends to shoot an object or an animal or another person but the bullet hits another person, his/her action will be considered to be a simple mistake.

This provision is available to allow for exemptions to liability in cases, for instance, where a police officer intends to shoot an armed individual whom he has the legal right to shoot, yet the bullet hits another individual, who then dies. The law would not wish to classify such an individual as a murderer, for public policy reasons.

Corporate Liability

The law recognises the view that an enterprise can be a legal person. Mahmood Sanusi states,

> it is well established that Islamic Law too recognizes the concept of juristic person. The juristic person is a presumed person, a legal entity with separate form from the individuals who establish them. It has some human features but not the human qualities. It is a presumed person but not a human being. It is therefore untrue that Islamic law does not recognize the concept of juristic person although admittedly the term juristic person is not mentioned explicitly by classical Muslim jurists (fuqaha).[33]

---

33   Mahmood M Sanusi, 'The Concept of Artificial Legal Entity and Limited Liability in Islamic Law', *Critical Issues on Islamic Banking, Finance and Takaful* <*www.kantakji.com/fiqh/files/fatawa/w228.doc*> *accessed 28 August 2012.*

The concept of a 'corporation' as a particular subspecies of a legal person does not have recognition in traditional Islamic law, however, with the *waqf* (a large unincorporated trust) having played the role of large commercial entities in place of Western-style corporations.[34] This means that corporate criminal liability is not a concept that is at the forefront of Islamic jurisprudence to the extent that it is in other legal systems around the world.

Nonetheless, it follows from the existence of liability for legal persons generally that criminal liability may also be so prescribed. Indeed Islamic Law, with its emphasis on the practice of holding people close to the perpetrator of the crime collectively responsible for paying the blood money (*diyya*) for that person's crime, is no stranger to the concept of collective criminal liability. Indeed the Pakistan Penal Code recognises that a 'person' can include a Company or Association or body of persons whether incorporated or not. Having established this separate legal personality under Islamic law, it is apparent that this legal person should also be held liable for its actions and obligations.

What is complicated, however, is the extent to which corporate liability can be attached to criminal offences when committed by the employees or agents of a company. This is complicated not only because it depends on the facts of each case and the relevant intention held by the individuals that committed the offence but also because it depends on the issue of sentencing as the usual punishments such as *qisas* or imprisonment cannot be used on a company. However, this does not exonerate company directors, employees and agents entirely of their actions. In Pakistan for example, section 194 of the Companies Ordinance 1984 states that

> save as provided in this section, any provision, for exempting any director, chief executive or officer of the company or any person, whether an officer of the company or not, employed by the company as auditor, from, or indemnifying him against, any liability which by virtue of any law would otherwise attach to him in respect of any negligence, default, breach of duty or breach of trust of which he may be guilty in relation to the company, shall be void ….

This therefore makes it clear that being a part of a company does not exonerate such individuals of their own liabilities under the law. Thus, it is possible to pursue actions against both the company and individuals within the company for their respective criminal liabilities, in the criminal courts. Furthermore, the Companies Ordinance 1984 provides its own set of penalties in order to deal with different types of criminal behaviour. For example, where it transpires that company directors or other individuals within the company have behaved fraudulently, section 413 holds them personally responsible.

There is a disparity between various Islamic countries' statutory bases for corporate criminal liability. Whereas Pakistan has legislated to make such liability express, the majority of national legislatures (or other governing bodies) have not devoted much attention to this issue. This is perhaps explained by the lack of emphasis on 'corporations' in the traditional sources of Islamic Law. Such an omission ought to be remedied in line with the developments in the business world and the prevalence of corporate bodies in the modern world. In the twenty-first century, corporations increasingly rival governments in size and reach, conducting vast operations abroad (in particular natural resource exploration/exploitation in the Middle East), there ought to be clearly understood regulations for criminal corporate liability throughout the Islamic jurisdictions.

---

34   Timur Kuran, 'The Absence of the Corporation in Islamic Law: Origins and Persistence' (*Dukespace*, 28 February 2006) <http://dukespace.lib.duke.edu/dspace/bitstream/handle/10161/2546/Kuran_The_Absence_of.pdf%3Fsequence%3D1> accessed 17 July 2012.

Sentencing Regimes for Participants

> On no soul Allah places a burden greater than it can bear. It gets every good that it earns, and it suffers every ill that it earns ...[35]

In accordance with the above principle, the sentencing regime for participants should be commensurate with each participant's level of involvement and the resulting harm. Nonetheless, some flexibility in Islamic jurisdictions' sentencing is sacrificed for the sake of deterrence, namely by equating the punishments for principal offenders with those of accomplices. This is done to deter accomplices from providing assistance that will enable a future serious offence taking place; in many situations, the much more serious offence in which the assistance results (for example murder) would not be possible at all without the less serious act of the accomplice (for example providing a gun).

Naturally, some distinctions have to be drawn between accomplices and principal offenders in sentencing in order to avoid manifest injustice. In Islamic countries, this results in some variable sentencing. As set out above, one such example is the distinction between a mastermind and a 'trigger man', as they are treated as a secondary and a primary participant respectively.

A useful example is Egypt's Penal Code, as it enumerates a range of penalties for accomplices – some harsher and some more lenient than the penalties applicable to principal offenders. As mentioned, the starting point for accomplice liability is set out in Article 41, which states, 'Except in cases where the law specially provides otherwise, an accessory to an offence shall incur the penalty prescribed by law for the offence'. A distinction must be drawn between such equality in principle and in practice. While no definitive statistics are available on this point, it is likely that an accomplice actually receives a relatively lighter punishment for the same offence because he is able to provide better mitigation at the sentencing stage (for example, 'it was not my idea'). The principle behind equating the starting points for the two categories of criminal is legally sound, however. For example in Egypt's Penal Code, where accomplice liability is based on the idea of 'borrowed criminality' from the principal offender to the accomplice, part of the 'borrowing' is the sentence for that offence.

An example of an offence where the accomplice can in effect receive a more lenient punishment is murder – Article 235 of the Egyptian Penal Code allows an accomplice to a murder to be punished either via the death penalty or detention for life. This allows the court flexibility to penalise the accomplice, using its case-by-case discretion, at a lower level than the principal (who is more likely to be sentenced to death).

It is important that the sentencing regime creates exceptions that enable a court to avoid genuine injustice. In Egypt's case, this is created by Article 41 of the Code, which states that if:

> ... (1) the effect of circumstance personal to the principal, which is such as to modify the character of the offence, shall not extend to an accessory who had no knowledge of such circumstances and,

> (2) that when the character of the crime varies according to the knowledge or intent with which it had been committed, an accessory shall be punished by the penalty which he would have incurred if the principal had acted with the same knowledge or intent as that of the accessory ...

---

35   *Qu'ran* [2:286].

Consequently the lesser *mens rea* of the accomplice can dictate his punishment, instead of the court having to base that punishment on the *mens rea* of the principal offender. This can avoid injustice where the principal offender had the particular intention to commit murder, whereas the accomplice only intended harm falling short of murder.

An example of a comparable approach to sentencing of accomplices is found in the Afghan Penal Code. The general position is that the accomplices 'shall be sentenced to the punishment of the crime in which he has taken part unless the law stipulates otherwise' and is not excused from liability if the principal offender escapes punishment 'for any legal reason' (Afghan Penal Code Article 41). Harsher still is Article 42 which stipulates that the accomplice assumes the criminal responsibility of the crime committed by the principal perpetrator, even if it is not the crime that had been previously agreed upon (that is, an offence outside the contemplation of the parties but still subject to a foreseeability test). However, the fact that the Afghan Penal Code allows for judicial discretion in terms of minimums and maximums does mitigate the potential harshness, by allowing the judge to determine relative culpability and sentence accordingly.[36]

In sum, the sentencing regime appears to find a reasonable compromise between the aims of the criminal justice system including providing retribution for victims/their families, deterrence and reforming the offender (by equating the principal/accomplice sentences as the starting point), and flexibility by allowing the judge some discretion within minimums/maximums. It appears prudent for Islamic jurisdictions to include the equivalent of Article 41 of the Egyptian Penal Code to enable the courts to have greater clarity as to how accomplice sentences may be mitigated.

Conclusion

One surprising result of this analysis is the likely degree of similarity between Islamic law concerning doctrines of participation (in general and as set out in the various Penal Codes of Islamic countries) and Western law. Significant parallels can be drawn between the legal position regarding sentencing, for example, which follows the same basic principles of equating accomplice and principal sentences as in certain Western jurisdictions, such as English and Wales. Similarly, the definition and elements of accomplice liability are largely similar between the jurisdictions; for example Egypt's enumeration of *actus reus* for accomplice liability will not surprise lawyers within Commonwealth jurisdictions.

Some distinctions remain, for example in the treatment of masterminds and 'trigger men', within the context of assigning primary and secondary participant roles in murder trials. It is also apparent that some Islamic jurisdictions could benefit from greater codification of 'participation' doctrines, especially for more nuanced issues such as crimes committed via innocent agents, transferred malice and corporate liability. Those countries that could benefit from such codification could adopt statutory wording from other Islamic countries or even borrow from common law jurisdictions, whose precedent-based systems allow for even fairly obscure 'participation' scenarios to have been addressed. The very fact that the analysed jurisdictions' legal principles regarding accomplice/participant liability are broadly similar allows for effective sharing of legal experience and concepts between them in this respect.

---

36   'An Introduction to the Criminal Law of Afghanistan' (*Afghanistan Legal Education Project (ALEP)*) <http://alep.stanford.edu/wp-content/uploads/2011/02/ALEP-CRIMINAL-1ST-EDITION.pdf> accessed 25 July 2012.

Chapter 20

The Netherlands

Hein D. Wolswijk

General Principles

Core Provisions

Dutch criminal law regulates participation in offences in Title V of the First Book ('General provisions'[1]) of the Dutch Penal Code. The core provisions of this regulation are to be found in articles 47 and 48:[2]

Art. 47

1. The following persons shall be liable as principals:

> 1° those who commit the offence, either personally or jointly with another, or through another person;
> 2° those who, by means of gifts, promises, abuse of authority, use of violence, threat or deception or through providing an opportunity, means or information, intentionally instigate the commission of the offence.

2. ...

Art. 48

The following persons shall be liable as aiders:

> 1° those who intentionally assist in the commission of the felony;
> 2° those who intentionally provide the opportunity, means or information to commit the felony.

These provisions have remained largely unamended since the introduction of the Penal Code in 1886. The most important amendment to Title V was not about participation, but about the recognition of corporate entities as persons with legal capacity. Since 1976, art. 51.1 has provided that offences can be committed by both natural persons and corporate entities. The criminal liability of corporate entities will be discussed at the end of this contribution. At that point I will also briefly discuss the criminal liability of those who directed the offence committed by the corporate entity.

---

1   All quotations and articles are translations into English by the author.
2   All articles refer to the Dutch Penal Code.

Perpetrators and Participants; Principals and Aiders

Art. 47.1.1° starts with the person who commits the offence 'personally'. He is the perpetrator ('*pleger*') of the offence. The perpetrator fulfils all the material and subjective elements (*actus reus* and *mens rea*) of the offence. Apart from perpetration, the law – as is made clear by arts 47 and 48 – distinguishes four forms of participation:

- perpetration-by-proxy ('*doen plegen*', art. 47.1.1°)
- co-perpetration ('*medeplegen*', art. 47.1.1°)
- instigation ('*uitlokking*', art. 47.1.2°)
- aiding ('*medeplichtigheid*', art. 48.1° and art. 48.2°)

The criminal liability of these participants is based on the fact that they have contributed – each in their own way – to the commission of an offence. The law also distinguishes between principals and aiders. Perpetrators-by-proxy, co-perpetrators and instigators are not only participants, but also principals (art. 47.1). An aider is a participant, but not a principal (art. 48). The fact that a co-perpetrator, a perpetrator-by-proxy and an instigator are all called principals merely means that they are regarded as equal to perpetrators in the sense that they can be punished as severely as the perpetrator. The lesser degree of liability of an aider is reflected in the maximum sentence, which is one third lower than the maximum sentence for principals (art. 49.1). Moreover, only an aider to a felony is punishable; an aider to a misdemeanour is not.

Direct and Indirect Participation

Doctrinally, a distinction is also made between 'direct' and 'indirect' forms of participation. This distinction is roughly the same as the distinction made in many other countries between principals and secondary participants. Co-perpetration and perpetration-by-proxy are regarded as direct forms of participation; instigation and aiding are indirect forms of participation. Although the co-perpetrator and the perpetrator-by-proxy are not perpetrators themselves, these direct forms of participation are closely related to perpetration. Direct participants take the place of the perpetrator, so to speak. This applies most strongly to co-perpetration. The co-perpetrators' actions are attributed to each other and it is their joint actions which meet the elements of the offence.

   One of the characteristics of direct participation is that the elements of the offence can be 'distributed' across the participants. To illustrate this, we will take an example involving theft preceded by forcible entry (art. 311): A breaks the window of a house (forcible entry), B steals an item from the house (theft). Depending on the circumstances (for example if A and B jointly planned the offence), A and B may be co-perpetrators of theft preceded by forcible entry. With indirect forms of participation it is not possible to 'share' the offence in this way; the perpetrator has to have committed all the elements of the offence. If A were to be regarded not as a co-perpetrator but only as an aider, then B would only be liable as the perpetrator of simple theft (art. 310) and A for assisting in the commission of this felony. As we shall see later, several other characteristics are related to this distinction between direct and indirect participation.

Dependence Principle

Under Dutch law the so-called 'principle of dependence' ('*accessoriteitsbeginsel*') applies to all forms of participation, namely that participation is only punishable if an offence – the principal offence – has in fact been committed. The principal offence may of course be a 'completed' offence, but it may also be an inchoate offence, that is, punishable attempt (art. 45.1) or even punishable preparation (art. 46.1).[3] Furthermore, participation in an offence can in itself function as a principal offence; 'participation in participation', for example instigating someone to assist in a crime, is therefore punishable. The extent of liability also depends on the principal offence. If A is willing to assist in a murder committed by B, and B decides to go no further than assault (art. 300.1), A cannot be an aider to murder (art. 289), since that offence has not been committed. However, A is an aider to assault. If B acted with intent to kill, but only inflicted bodily harm, A is liable for aiding attempted murder.

It follows from the dependence principle that an 'attempt to participate' does not constitute punishable participation. For example: A wants to instigate B to commit an offence, but B is not willing to do so ('attempted instigation', that is, incitement, see below). Or A tries to help in a felony committed by B, and B commits the felony, but without taking advantage of A's help ('attempted aiding').

Intent

All forms of participation are characterised by intentional action. For example, co-perpetrators work together deliberately and an instigator deliberately sets out to persuade another person to perform an action. Of course, it is also possible to contribute to an offence by negligence, but this does not constitute criminal participation. The extent to which a participant must also have intent to bring about all the elements of the principal offence will be discussed separately below in relation to each form of participation.

Some comments should be made about the general concept of intent. Dutch criminal law recognises several gradations of intent, including not only 'wilful intent' (*dolus directus*) and 'awareness of a high degree of probability' (*dolus indirectus*), but also 'conditional intent' (*dolus eventualis*, '*bedingter Vorsatz*'), which is considered the lower limit of intent. Conditional intent means that the perpetrator is aware of the considerable risk that a certain result will occur, yet nevertheless accepts that risk.[4] Under this definition, conditional intent includes not only a cognitive element (awareness of the risk), but also an element, albeit slight, of volition (accepting the risk). As regards the latter point, intention is distinguished from *culpa* in the form of 'advertent negligence'. With advertent (or 'conscious') negligence, the perpetrator is likewise aware of the considerable risk that the result will take place, but instead of accepting this risk, trusts that the result will not occur.

This broad concept of intent is used not only in relation to perpetration, but also to participation. If A instigates B to injure C seriously by stabbing C with a knife and B deliberately stabs C to death, A has intent to kill C if, even though C's death was not his purpose, he knowingly accepted the considerable risk that B might kill C (which may be the case when, for example, A told B to stab C in the stomach).

Intent may be 'general', that is, the participant does not have to intend the exact details of the principal offence.[5] If A tells B where C is staying, in the belief that this will help B to stab C to

---

3   An attempt is only punishable in the case of a felony, not of a misdemeanour; preparation is only punishable in the case of felonies with a maximum prison sentence of no less than eight years.

4   See, for example, HR 25 March 2003, *NJ* 2003, 552.

5   J de Hullu, *Materieel strafrecht: Over algemene leerstukken van strafrechtelijke aansprakelijkheid naar Nederlands recht* (5th edn, Deventer 2012) 428.

death with a knife, he is an aider to murder, even if perpetrator B does not stab the victim to death, but shoots him to death.

Other Kinds of Liability for Participatory Acts

Dutch law contains several provisions which make 'participation-like' acts punishable outside the general provisions about participation. A few of these provisions will be discussed briefly.

Quite soon after the Code came into effect, the consequence of the dependence principle (see above) was no longer deemed acceptable as far as *instigation* was concerned. Incitement ('attempted instigation') is now made punishable, not as a form of participation, but as an inchoate offence in art. 46a: 'An attempt to induce another to commit a felony by employing one of the means listed in art. 47.1.2° …'. The maximum sentence is one third lower than for 'ordinary' instigation under art. 47. If A wants to instigate B to commit murder, but B does nothing, A is liable for incitement to murder. If B goes along with the plan, but ultimately does not go as far as A wanted and commits aggravated assault instead of murder, then A is liable for both incitement to murder (art. 46a) and instigation of aggravated assault (art. 47).[6]

Another example concerns the concept of participation *after* the fact. The general forms of participation (arts 47 and 48) all refer to actions performed before or at the same time as the principal offence. A number of provisions make a certain form of being an aider after the fact punishable as a separate offence. In everyday practice, the broad provisions relating to handling stolen goods and money laundering are particularly important (art. 416-420c).

Developments after 1886: From Physical to Functional Perpetration

Although the legal provisions relating to participation have scarcely changed since the introduction of the Code in 1886, the law that applies today is different from that of over a century ago. Changed views about criminal liability have been manifested mainly within the framework of the existing provisions through case law.

In the late nineteenth century, the legislator, influenced by the exact sciences, approached reality very much in terms of cause and effect.[7] Their point of departure was a restricted, physical concept of perpetration:[8] the perpetrator is the direct physical cause of the offence; his or her personal action, effected by means of an 'intentional muscle movement', matches the elements of the offence. Someone who contributes to the effectuation of the offence in any other way can only be liable as a participant. When drafting the provisions regarding participation, the legislator attached importance to various distinctions: between a contribution which could be regarded as a *causa* of the offence and a contribution which constituted only a *conditio*, between 'physical' and 'mental' causes, and between a contribution made at the same time the felony was committed (*causa* or *conditio proxima*) and a contribution which preceded the felony (*causa* or *conditio remota*).

The legal provisions regarding participation still bear traces of this cause-and-effect approach, as we shall see below, but the way of thinking of the legislator of 1886 has long since been replaced by a broader 'functional' concept, and much less importance is nowadays attached to the distinctions referred to above. In the first place, this development has widened the concept

---

6   The regulation of concurrent sentences means that the maximum sentence in that case is the maximum sentence for incitement to murder.
7   See GAM Strijards, *Aansprakelijkheidsgronden* (Zwolle 1988) 20.
8   Felonies of omission did exist, but were regarded as exceptions.

of perpetration itself. One can be a perpetrator not only by fulfilling the elements of an offence 'physically' (for example transporting of illegal weapons by the truck driver), but also by fulfilling them 'functionally' (transporting by the owner of the company or the company itself). This is referred to as 'functional perpetration'. Because of this, to a certain extent there is less need for forms of participation. Secondly, this development has also influenced the scope of the forms of participation. Co-perpetration in particular is interpreted much more broadly than it used to be.

In the following sections the various forms of participation will be discussed in greater detail. A concept which is the odd one out is that of 'functional perpetration', referred to above. Although a functional perpetrator is not a participant, in order to understand fully the concept of functional perpetration, it will be helpful to take a closer look at perpetration-by-proxy first.

Perpetration-by-Proxy

Actus Reus

A perpetrator-by-proxy is someone who causes another person to commit an offence without that other person being liable for that offence. The absence of liability of the other person – the 'immediate perpetrator' – is a requirement which was introduced in the case law just a few years after the Code came into effect in the late nineteenth century.[9] This requirement is derived from the distinction between a perpetrator-by-proxy and another kind of participator – an instigator. An instigator also deliberately persuades another person to commit an offence. However, for instigation this persuasion must be accomplished through one of a limited number of means of instigation listed in art. 47.1.2°. No such limitation applies to perpetration-by-proxy. If perpetration-by-proxy could also be established even when the direct perpetrator is liable, then the restriction that applies to instigation would be pointless.

The situation the legislator of 1886 had in mind with perpetration-by-proxy was that the immediate perpetrator would be acting without intent, fault or responsibility: he is an 'unresisting tool' in the hands of the principal offender.[10] For example: A tells B to shoot at C with a fake pistol. However, A does not give B a fake pistol, but a real one. A knows this, but B does not. Then B shoots C dead. B is not liable for murder, because he had no intention to kill C. A is liable as a perpetrator-by-proxy of this offence. The fact that the immediate perpetrator is liable for a different offence – B may have committed manslaughter (causing death through criminal negligence, art. 307) – does not change anything as far as perpetration-by-proxy is concerned.

Particularly the existence of perpetration-by-proxy as a form of participation shows that the legislator of 1886 had a limited, physical conception of perpetration. Even if another person was used as a tool, there was no question of the person initiating the offence being the perpetrator.[11] Over time, perpetration-by-proxy became wider in scope. It now became also possible when the immediate perpetrator was not liable for some other reason. Specifically, this applies to cases where the immediate perpetrator lacks a certain quality, so that it is impossible for him or her to commit the offence. If the offence is 'excavation of a mound by the owner, without a permit', then only the owner of a mound can commit this offence. If the owner gets some other person to excavate his

---

9   HR 27 June 1898, *Weekblad van het recht*, 7146.

10   De Hullu (n 5) 454.

11   The only exception was if the other person could not be said to have performed an action – that is, an 'intentional muscle movement'. If A deliberately pushes B through a window pane causing it to break, B has not performed an action. A is then the perpetrator of criminal damage.

mound without a permit, then the owner is liable as a perpetrator-by-proxy of this offence, even if the other person knows there is no permit.[12] Because of this development, perpetration-by-proxy has largely lost the character of a form of direct participation and has become more like instigation.

Mens Rea

As we have seen, perpetration-by-proxy implies deliberately causing another person to perform an act. The perpetrator-by-proxy does not have to have intent in relation to the lack of criminal liability of the other person. Because perpetration-by-proxy – at least in origin – is a direct form of participation, related to perpetration, the perpetrator-by-proxy only has to intend those elements of the principal offence which a perpetrator would also have to intend. Perpetration-by-proxy of murder requires intent to kill the victim. Perpetration-by-proxy of an offence of negligence is possible – as in manslaughter. It is possible for a person deliberately to cause another person to perform an act which he knows is dangerous, without intending the consequences. For example, A jumps into a taxi and forces driver B, by pointing a gun to his head, to drive in an irresponsible way, leading to a traffic accident in which C dies. B is probably not liable (duress); A is, if he trusted that the dangerous driving would not lead to a fatal accident, liable as a perpetrator-by-proxy of manslaughter.[13] This 'construct' actually has little practical relevance in the case of an offence such as manslaughter; as a rule the perpetrator-by-proxy can also simply be regarded as the perpetrator of this offence of negligence. It is in the case of misdemeanours – for which proof of neither intent nor negligence is required – that it is particularly important that a perpetrator-by-proxy only has to intend those elements of the offence which a perpetrator would also have to intend. To perpetrate the offence of 'selling spoilt meat', knowledge that the meat is spoilt is not required. Nor is it required for perpetration-by-proxy of this offence; intent to instigate the other person's actual deed – selling the meat – suffices.

Functional Perpetration

Actus Reus

In the early twentieth century, courts began to acknowledge that human action is not restricted to what people do with their hands and to attribute the results of the physical actions of a certain individual to a different individual because of the functional relationship between them. In legal doctrine this became known as functional perpetration. It has been described as follows: 'The core element of functional perpetration is that an individual who has not perpetrated the offence personally in the physical sense can nevertheless be regarded as the perpetrator, because that person is responsible for the action. This person is deemed to have perpetrated the offence personally'.[14] The *actus reus* of the offence is interpreted in such a way as to include 'allowing commission by another' (functional interpretation). Examples that spring to mind are the owner of a business who 'sells', 'transports' or 'delivers' goods, or the 'excavation' of a mound by its owner (see the example above). Not only the person behind the counter sells spoilt meat; the owner of the shop

---

12   HR 19 December 1910, *Weekblad van het recht*, 9122.

13   J Remmelink, *Mr. D. Hazewinkel-Suringa's Inleiding tot de studie van het Nederlandse strafrecht* (15th edn, Deventer 1996) 434.

14   De Hullu (n 5) 153. See also E Gritter, 'Functioneel daderschap: dogmatische inbedding en praktische uitwerking' in *Opstellen Materieel strafrecht* (Nijmegen 2009) 13.

may also be considered to 'sell'. In fact, it is irrelevant to the owner's functional perpetratorship whether or not the 'physical seller' is liable.

This development led to a need for criteria to determine when a person can be regarded as the functional perpetrator of an offence. Although the case law is not always clear and there is ongoing discussion among scholars,[15] a judgment by the Supreme Court in 1954 still seems to represent the dominant view.[16] This case dealt with the question whether the owner of a business could be held liable for offences committed 'physically' by an employee, his export manager. The offences in question were the illegal export of iron wire and making false declarations to the customs authorities about the country where the goods were produced. The Supreme Court ruled:

> acts, such like these, as completing forms in violation of the law, sending those forms to the Import and Export office and the export of merchandise, could only then be qualified as 'acts of the accused', if he had the power of decision whether those acts occurred or not, and if those acts belonged to the realm of activities which the accused, as appearing from the general course of daily events, accepted or used to accept.

These criteria – in short, 'power to decision' and 'acceptance' – have gained wide acceptance in legal practice. 'Power to decision' means that a person had actual control over the execution of the illegal actions; the functional perpetrator is in a position to prevent the physical perpetrator from performing the criminal acts. This may for instance stem from their hierarchical relationship. The exact meaning of 'acceptance' has long been the subject of controversy.[17] Several authors have argued that 'acceptance' is a subjective criterion implying a form of intent. However, as recent case law has made clear, 'accepting' includes 'failure to take reasonable care to prevent the action being performed'.[18] Mere proof of failure to take appropriate steps to prevent criminal harm, for example when employees are inadequately supervised, suffices to establish 'acceptance'[19] – and this does not necessarily equate to some form of intent.

Mens Rea

The criteria of power and acceptance only relate to the *actus reus* of the offence; they are about attributing the actions of one person to another person. The *mens rea* element – if required – cannot be attributed from one person to another; the (functional) perpetrator himself must have the required form of *mens rea*.[20]

Relationship to Participation

The development of functional perpetration has broadened the scope of perpetration (that is, committing the offence personally, see above) and made perpetration-by-proxy virtually redundant. This is particularly true in relation to commercial offences, in which functional

---

15   See E Sikkema, *De strafrechtelijke aansprakelijkheid van leidinggevenden in Nederland* (Nijmegen 2010).
16   HR 23 February 1954, *NJ* 1954, 378.
17   See E Gritter, 'Functioneel plegen door een natuurlijke persoon' in *Plegen en deelnemen* (Deventer 2007) 25.
18   HR 21 October 2003, *NJ* 2006, 328.
19   Gritter (n 17) 21.
20   HR 23 February 1954, *NJ* 1954, 378.

perpetration plays a major role. But classic offences can also have functional perpetrators, as the following case shows: a gynaecologist had requested an abortion for a woman who was more than 24 weeks pregnant. Because in principle the aborted foetus would have been viable outside the mother's body, this abortion was regarded as murder (art. 82a). A special detail in this case was that the doctor had had the abortion carried out by a trainee doctor, who – unlike the doctor – was unaware of the duration of the pregnancy and therefore did not have intent to kill a human being capable of living outside the womb (and was therefore not liable for murder). This is actually a classic example of perpetration-by-proxy of murder. However, the doctor was found guilty as a perpetrator – without any further explanation;[21] it was the doctor himself who (functionally) had taken another person's life.

Co-Perpetration

Actus Reus

Co-perpetration arises when two or more individuals collaborate to commit an offence. It is not required that each of the collaborating individuals carry out every element of the offence. The elements can be 'distributed' across the various individuals. This is also possible with offences which require a certain quality; a person who is not a public officer can be a co-perpetrator of an offence involving abuse of public office, provided that person knows that the other co-perpetrator is a public officer.

As far as the legislator of 1886 was concerned, a co-perpetrator, like a perpetrator, was an *auctor fysicus*; a co-perpetrator 'physically' caused the offence. The situation the legislator had in mind was that two or more individuals executed the offence together; the co-perpetrator performs an 'implementing act', thus carrying out one or more elements of the offence. For example: together A and B lift up a heavy rock and together they throw the rock from a bridge with the intention of killing C. Any involvement which is less direct resulted only in one of them being an aider (or an instigator). According to this view keeping watch during the commission of a theft is not co-perpetration but assistance, since keeping watch is not in itself an implementing act of theft, but only assistance in such an act. However, over time co-perpetration became much wider in scope. This began with a wider interpretation of the concept of an implementing act.[22] If A breaks a window and B removes an item of property from the house, only B has perpetrated the *central* implementing act of the felony of theft preceded by forcible entry. Nevertheless, A can be a co-perpetrator of this felony because he has carried out part of the execution; A broke the window, which matches the 'forcible entry' element of the felony.[23] But the case law, influenced by the transition from the limited physical concept of an act to a functional concept, went much further. Just as a perpetrator no longer has to perform the physical act implementing the offence, the co-perpetrator no longer

---

21   HR 29 May 1990, *NJ* 1991, 217. Obviously, since the doctor *requested* the abortion *knowing* the foetus would have been viable outside the mother's body, in this case the functional perpetrator did much more than 'control' and 'accept' the trainee's actions.

22   Remmelink (n 13) 437.

23   This widening of the concept of an 'implementing act' was in keeping with the concept of an implementing act in relation to an attempted felony. An attempted felony must involve the beginning of the execution of the felony in question. However, actions preceding the principal action of an offence can also be regarded as the 'beginning of execution'; breaking a window may be seen as attempted theft preceded by forcible entry, even if the principal act – the removal of property – has not yet begun.

has to participate directly in the physical implementation. According to settled case law, people are co-perpetrators if they have knowingly and *sufficiently closely* cooperated in committing the offence.[24] Presence at the scene of the offence is not required, and the co-perpetrator's contribution may have preceded the actual execution of the offence. An example is the case of a shooting at a school, in which a Turkish father was prosecuted for his close involvement in the attempted honour killing by his son of a youth called Hassan. The father had stirred up his son's emotions, taken him to the school where Hassan was and let him go into the school with a loaded pistol. The father himself had waited outside the school in his car. Because of the steering and organising role he had played, the father was found guilty of co-perpetration of attempted murder.[25]

Because of this broader interpretation, in practice co-perpetration has become the most important form of participation. Individuals behind the scenes who could formerly only be regarded as instigators or perpetrators-by-proxy can now often also be regarded as co-perpetrators. Prosecution for co-perpetration has several advantages. The limitations associated with instigating and perpetration-by-proxy – certain means to be used or the non-liability of the immediate offender – do not apply to co-perpetration. Moreover, the charge does not have to specify in detail who the other co-perpetrators were or which actions were performed by which co-perpetrator.

The broader interpretation of co-perpetration is particularly important in connection with aiding, since the maximum sentence for aiders is a third lower than for co-perpetrators and aiding a misdemeanour is not punishable. Actions which were formerly regarded only as assistance may now qualify as co-perpetration. However, one problem with this is that the 'sufficiently close cooperation' criterion is rather vague. The same applies to 'making a substantial contribution' as an explanation of this criterion, whereas for assistance a less substantial contribution is enough.[26] This means that it is not always easy to distinguish between mere assistance and co-perpetration. Nonetheless, the case law reveals some factors that may indicate 'sufficiently close cooperation':[27] joint planning of the offence;[28] a clear distribution of tasks, especially if the same distribution has been used before in previous offences;[29] fulfilling an important role in the preparation and/or execution;[30] failing to distance oneself and/or being present at crucial points.[31] So, for instance, a person who is on the lookout during a theft is a co-perpetrator if this person shared in the planning of the theft or was involved with the same person or persons in previous offences using the same method. Co-perpetration was interpreted very broadly in another case involving an honour killing: a daughter in an Afghan family had allegedly disgraced the family. The girl's father, after consulting with the male members of the family, had killed the girl. The mother was accused of co-perpetration of the murder. She had not participated in the decision-making, but she did know about it and she accompanied her husband and daughter in the car to a house to which she had a key and where the girl was to be strangled. The Court found that in this case there was 'sufficiently close cooperation'. According to the Supreme Court, the Court was able to take into account the fact that when the mother heard about the plans to murder the girl, she failed to distance herself from these

---

24 See De Hullu (n 5) 437.

25 HR 17 September 2002, *LJN* AE6118.

26 This explanation of the 'sufficiently close cooperation' criterion is not used in case law, only in literature. See, for example, De Hullu (n 5) 439.

27 See De Hullu (n 5) 443; JM van Bemmelen and ThW van Veen, *Het materiële strafrecht, Algemeen deel* (14th edn, revision by DH de Jong and G Knigge, Deventer 2003) 229.

28 HR 12 February 2002, *NJ* 2002, 351.

29 HR 12 November 1996, *NJ* 1997, 190.

30 HR 24 January 1995, *NJ* 1995, 352.

31 HR 12 April 2005, *NJ* 2005, 577.

plans. Whether the mother made a '*substantial* contribution' to the felony is questionable. At any rate, the case shows clearly that 'sufficiently close cooperation' certainly does not mean that the contributions of the co-perpetrators must be equal.

The aforementioned factors of presence and failing to distance oneself – also referred to by the Supreme Court in the judgment on honour killing discussed above – should be used with caution. Failing to distance oneself in that case was probably relevant in the sense of *continuing* to collaborate. If previous positive involvement is lacking, being present and failing to distance oneself may not constitute co-perpetration. In connection with co-perpetration of vandalism, the Supreme Court ruled that 'merely being present and not distancing oneself from vandalism carried out by another person, and merely consenting to that vandalism, both individually and taken together, are insufficient'.[32] The reason for this is that being present, failing to distance oneself and consenting (in the sense of not objecting noticeably) do not in themselves necessarily imply a contribution to the commission of the offence, let alone a contribution that can be regarded as sufficiently close cooperation. Furthermore, the 'indicative strength' of these factors depends on the offence in question. For example, with unlawful depriving a person of his freedom (art. 282), being present or failing to distance oneself may in itself come down to a (substantial) contribution to the offence, since it can hinder the victim to go where he wants.[33]

Knowing Collaboration

Co-perpetration assumes deliberate, therefore knowing, collaboration. For co-perpetration of more than one offence – for instance, the victim is first raped and then murdered – this knowing (and sufficiently close) collaboration must extend to all of these offences. However, in the case law the requirements for meeting this collaboration criterion are not very high. Previous planning or extensive prior consultation is not necessary. An example is a case in which the defendant was found guilty of two counts of co-perpetration of murder.[34] The first murder had been planned in advance. The defendant's role was to make sure the intended victim did not run away. However, the intended victim unexpectedly appeared in the company of another individual. First the intended victim was killed and then the other person, who had tried to get away. Although no consultation had taken place about the fate of the second person, the defendant was found guilty of co-perpetration because he continued to play his part in the offence when the intended victim came out in the company of the other person and even when the second victim tried to run away and was then stabbed with a knife by one of the defendant's co-perpetrators.

Mens Rea

Because co-perpetration is a direct form of participation and therefore closely related to perpetration, the same conditions regarding intent to commit the offence apply as for perpetration (and perpetration-by-proxy); this means that the co-perpetrator's intent only has to relate to the elements of the offence to which the ordinary perpetrator's intent would also have to relate. Co-perpetration of an offence of negligence is also possible; two individuals deliberately perform an action together which they should both have realised in advance was a dangerous action:[35] A and

---

32   HR 22 December 2009, *NJ* 2010, 193.
33   HR 11 January 2000, *NJ* 2000, 228; HR 26 September 2006, *LJN* AX9405; see also De Hullu (n 5) 444.
34   HR 14 October 2003, *NJ* 2004, 103.
35   See, for example, HR 9 July 2009, *NJ* 2009, 482.

B lift up a heavy rock and together they throw the rock from a bridge, without noticing that at that moment C is passing by.

Unlike with instigating and aiding (see below), the legislator made no provisions for a case in which co-perpetrators have different intentions.[36] A and B attack C together; A strikes C with the intention of killing him; B strikes C with the intention for assault; C dies as a result of the joint effects of the blows inflicted by A and B. B cannot be a co-perpetrator of murder, because his intention was not to kill C. A and B are certainly co-perpetrators of assault. But can A also be regarded as a co-perpetrator of murder (while B is a co-perpetrator of assault)? Can just one co-perpetrator be implicated in an offence? This point of view has been defended in the literature.[37] The reasoning is that with co-perpetration, because of the knowing collaboration, the actions of each perpetrator can be attributed to the other, while ultimately the intentions of each individual determine their liability. This may mean that co-perpetrators are liable for different offences (as in our example) or even that there is only one co-perpetrator, because the other person with whom he or she collaborated had no intention at all of committing an offence. An example: two individuals collaborate to induce a third individual to hand over an item; one of the two has the intention to defraud the third person, the other does not have any criminal intention at all. However, the Supreme Court has a different view; it relates the knowing collaboration not only to the actions carried out, but to the offence; co-perpetrators collaborate in order to commit an offence. This is not the case when someone is prosecuted for co-perpetration of an intentional offence and it turns out in the course of the proceedings against this person that the other person did not have the intention to commit that offence.[38] In certain circumstances – the person who did have the intention has used the unknowing other individual to implement his criminal plan – this might be a case of perpetration-by-proxy or functional perpetration.

In practice, problems relating to differences in intent are often 'solved' by assuming conditional intent. This often happens with co-perpetration of robbery (art. 312), as in the following case:[39] two burglars were caught by the police. The defendant D1 immediately obeyed the command to raise his hands and stand against the window. His co-defendant D2 on the other hand turned around and started to shoot, wounding one of the police officers. The defendant D1 stated that he did not intend any violence. However, according to the Supreme Court the fact that D1 knew that D2 carried a gun and that he had gone with him nevertheless showed that the defendant had conditional intent in relation to the violence committed by D2. It is open to question how compelling this reasoning is. Of course, it is possible that the defendant did in fact realise that there was a very real risk of violence and that he had accepted that risk. But it is also possible that it did not occur to him at all that the weapon might be used, for instance, because his partner always carried a weapon, or that the possibility did occur to him, but that he thought it was very unlikely (advertent negligence). In this case, one might wonder if the Court, when setting out to prove intent, was still interested in the defendant's state of mind – in what the defendant really knew and wanted. Did the Court not simply 'attribute' intent to the defendant?

---

36 Probably the legislator did not even think of such a situation; their point of departure was that co-perpetrators execute a felony jointly, and that in that case it is not very likely that they will have different intentions.

37 Van Bemmelen and Van Veen (n 27) 232; G Knigge, 'Het opzet van de deelnemer' in *Glijdende schalen* (Nijmegen 2003) 319.

38 HR 6 December 2005, *NJ* 2007, 455.

39 HR 20 January 1998, *NJ* 1998, 426.

Because of the importance of this issue, we will examine another judgment.[40] In this case the defendant D1, accompanied by his brother D2 and his brother's brother-in-law D3, had gone to get a pistol to settle a fight with some Albanians which had arisen in a disco. However, D2, who was known as a sensible person, had taken the pistol away from D1 because – as D2 said himself – he was 'afraid of the consequences'. D1 had then rushed back towards the disco, followed by D2 and D3. When the doorman refused to let him in, there was a scuffle at the door. At some point D2 pulled out the pistol, which he still had with him, and shot at the door. Three girls standing behind it were wounded – two of them fatally. It was assumed that D1 had intent to kill the victims and he was found guilty of two counts of co-perpetration of murder and one count of co-perpetration of attempt thereto. The Court found that D1 must have realised when they arrived at the disco for the second time that D2 would still have the pistol with him. The Court also found that by participating in the violent struggle at the door of the disco D1 had accepted the considerable risk that D2 would try to enforce their desire to enter the disco by shooting at the doorman he could see through the glass pane in the door. According to the Supreme Court, in this case the Court could have ruled that D1 did in fact have conditional intent to kill. This judgment has been questioned in the literature.[41] Would it not have come as a surprise for D1 that his brother used the pistol, in view of his otherwise sensible nature and his motivation for taking the pistol away from him? Surely D1, now that his pistol had been taken away from him to prevent him using it, would have thought the chance that their joint attempt to enter the disco would end in murder was extremely small – if such a possibility had occurred to him at all? Once again, one might wonder whether in proving intent the Court was actually interested in D1's exact state of mind. To make matters clearer, the Supreme Court drew attention to the 'course of events preceding the shooting and the defendant's active role in those events'. Indeed, some may consider that that active role makes it acceptable to hold the defendant liable for co-perpetration of murder. However unexpected D2's use of the pistol was, the defendant probably did not experience it as an act that went beyond the framework of their joint attempt to enter the disco. The defendant might have done it himself, so to speak. On this basis the ultimate result – liability for co-perpetration of murder – may be found satisfactory. But it has little to do with the classic interpretation of (conditional) intent, which is all about what the defendant actually knew and wanted. The reasoning seems to go beyond evidential inference from facts. When intent is established, other factors also seem to play a role. Seen from this point of view, establishing intent is to some extent not only a factual issue, but also a normative issue, involving an element of 'attribution'.

Indirect Participation: Instigation and Aiding

Instigating – Actus Reus

The instigator is the *auctor intellectualis* of the offence – a person who causes another person to decide that he will commit an offence (psychological causality). This is why the legislator considered that instigators, like perpetrators-by-proxy and co-perpetrators (*auctores physici*), cause an offence to take place. An instigator is therefore also regarded as a 'principal' (art. 47.1). Unlike with perpetration-by-proxy, in the case of instigation the person instigated – the actual perpetrator – is criminally liable. As a result, in the view of the legislator of 1886, and the 'physical causality'

---

40   HR 8 May 2001, *NJ* 2001, 480.
41   Knigge (n 37) 318.

frame of reference, this form of participation was a little problematic. The actual ('physical') perpetrator is the 'real' cause of the offence – the *causa proxima*; the instigator is a *causa remota*. For this reason, the legislator did not want to make instigation punishable without any restrictions; instigation is punishable only if the other person has been incited by one of the statutory means (art. 47.1). Initially there were six of these: gifts, promises, abuse of authority, use of violence, threat and deception. Later three more 'neutral' means were added: providing opportunity, means and information.

In practice, this exhaustive list is not really felt to be a restriction. The means – and there are quite a large number of them – are interpreted broadly in the case law.[42] This is especially true of 'providing information'. In the case law this is taken to mean 'information of a factual nature which is important in connection with the intended felony in the sense that in the circumstances of the case this information will help to bring about the felony'.[43] This definition does not only cover information which makes it *intellectually* easier for the perpetrator to commit a particular offence, such as passing on the code of a safe, but also information which makes it *morally* easier to commit the offence. The only restriction in this definition of 'providing information' is that the information must be *factual*.[44] For example, A tells B that C wants to murder B, which is information that may induce B to decide to murder C 'pre-emptively'. However, simple encouragement to commit an offence ('go on, just do it!') – although this certainly may cause a decision to kill – does not constitute providing information of a factual nature and is therefore not regarded as instigating.

Aiding – Actus Reus

An aider is the only type of participant who is not also a principal. In the view of the legislator of 1886, an aider's contribution to a felony was not a *causa*, but only a *conditio*, a favourable condition. Art. 48 distinguishes two kinds of aiding. By intentionally assisting with the commission of a felony (art. 48.1°) the legislator meant being an aider *during* the perpetration of the felony, for instance keeping watch while a theft is taking place. This type of aiding is not defined more closely. It covers every kind of aid provided during the perpetration of the felony. The second type of aider (art. 48.2°) makes his contribution *before* the fact. This is more closely circumscribed; by virtue of art. 48.2°, an aider before the fact provides only opportunity, means or information to facilitate the felony. These three means (in a broad sense) can also function as means of instigation (see above). The difference is that with instigation the result must be to cause the perpetrator to want to commit the felony, whereas in the case of an aider the perpetrator already wants to commit the felony and the provision of opportunity, means or information at most reinforces that desire.

The limitations in the definition of aiding before the fact can be traced back, again, to the views of the legislator of 1886 regarding liability in general (see above), and in particular the temporal factor. Being an aider at the fact is a *conditio proxima*, being an aider before the fact a *conditio remota*. And the further the aider's contribution is removed from the principal offence, the more reservations the legislator had about holding that aider liable. But just as with instigation, these limitations do not amount to much. The three elements that can be provided – opportunity, means and information – are interpreted broadly. Only purely 'moral support' in the form of encouragement or a plea does not seem to be included (see also with instigation, above).[45] Moreover, the Supreme

---

42 De Hullu (n 5) 466.

43 HR 27 February 2001, *NJ* 2001, 308.

44 HD Wolswijk, 'Inlichtingen versus aansporingen' in *Constante waarden* (Den Haag 2008) 266. See also De Hullu (n 5) 464.

45 HD Wolswijk, 'Voorafgaande en gelijktijdige medeplichtigheid' [2011] Delikt en Delinkwent 1127.

Court recently ruled that the boundaries between the two types of aiding cannot be strictly defined and that the distinction between the two should be relativised. Once again, changes in the concept of an 'action' play a role. The Supreme Court states that 'over time, the physical aspect of actions – and therefore the temporal element of those actions – has become less prominent in the case law regarding perpetration of and participation in punishable offences'.[46] The consequence of this ruling is probably that the phrase 'assisting with the felony' in art. 48.1° can also be taken to include assistance before the felony, which in turn would mean that being an aider before the fact is no longer limited to the actions listed in art. 48.2°. This would in fact make art. 48.2° redundant.

Mens Rea

Both instigators and aiders are assumed to have intent, firstly in relation to the act of participation and secondly in relation to the offence. The instigator does not have to intend the person instigated to be liable. With regard to intent in relation to the principal offence, these indirect forms of participation are different from the direct forms of participation (perpetration-by-proxy and co-perpetration). In principle, the indirect participant's intent must relate to all the objective elements of the punishable offence, even if this does not apply to the perpetrator. This is particularly important in the case of instigation of misdemeanours (aiding a misdemeanour is not punishable), which usually do not include an element of intent or *culpa*. To use an example well known in the literature: a person who instigates another person to commit the offence of riding a bicycle without a bell has to know that the bicycle has no bell, whereas this is not necessary to commit the actual offence. The justification of this difference is that the instigator is in a different position from the perpetrator and therefore does not have the same responsibility.[47] Because it is the cyclist's responsibility to check that there is a bell on his or her bicycle, it is reasonable to hold the instigator liable only if he or she knew the bicycle had no bell. Instigation of and assisting with an offence of negligence is also possible, just as with the direct forms of participation. In that case, intent only has to relate to the negligent action, not its consequence. However, an instigator in particular will then usually be regarded as the perpetrator of the offence (unless he or she lacks a quality required for the offence in question).

With the indirect forms of participation in particular it is quite likely that the offence committed is different – to a greater or lesser extent – from the offence intended by the participant. Sometimes these differences can be 'ironed out' by a broad interpretation of conditional intent, as can also happen with co-perpetration (see above). For instance, a person who instigates someone to grab a handbag will in many cases be considered to have accepted a considerable risk that the violence generally required to perform this action would be used (conditional intent). In this case, the person has instigated not theft (art. 310), but robbery (art. 312).

For cases in which it cannot be ascertained that the instigator or aider intended the offence actually committed to take place, the law has special provisions. With regard to instigation, pursuant to art. 47.2 only 'actions intentionally incited[48] are to be taken into consideration'. If A instigates B to inflict grievous bodily harm (art. 302.1), but B decides to go further and commits a murder, A is not an instigator of murder, since he did not intend the victim's death; A is liable

---

46   HR 22 March 2011, *NJ* 2011, 341.

47   Knigge (n 37) 298.

48   Plus the consequences of such actions, meaning objective, aggravating consequences, such as inflicting grievous bodily harm resulting in death. A perpetrator is liable for a consequence like this even if he or she did not intend it to happen, and the same applies to an instigator. If inflicting grievous bodily harm (art. 302.1) results in death, the person who instigated to inflict grievous bodily harm is liable for instigation to inflict grievous bodily harm resulting in death (art. 302.2).

for instigating grievous bodily harm (since murder 'includes' inflicting grievous bodily harm). A slightly different provision applies to aiders. Pursuant to art. 49.4, only 'those actions that were intentionally facilitated or promoted[49] by the aider are to be taken into consideration *in sentencing*'. This means that the aider is *found guilty* of being an aider to the felony that was *committed*, but that the *severity* of the sentence depends on the felony he or she *intended*. In the case where A commits robbery, whereas aider B only intended to commit theft, B is nevertheless found guilty of being an aider to robbery; however, he is sentenced as though he were an aider to theft.

An important issue is the relationship between the offence committed and the offence the instigator or aider intended.[50] In the examples referred to above it seems obvious that the instigator and aider are liable for – at least – the offence they intended to take place. If the instigator intended theft, but robbery was in fact committed, then the intended theft *also* took place. If the aider intended grievous bodily harm and murder eventuated, then the intended grievous bodily harm *also* took place. The interesting question is whether or not these participants can be liable if they intended an offence which ultimately did *not* take place. In a fairly recent judgment the Dutch Supreme Court answered this question in the affirmative as regards aiders. The felony committed and the felony the aider intended to help commit must be 'sufficiently closely connected'.[51] This connection can also be present even if the felony the aider had in mind is not committed, as in this particular case: A gives B a knife, intending B to threaten the victim (art. 285), but B uses the knife to stab the victim to death immediately, without any preceding threat. A is still an aider to murder because, under the circumstances, the committed murder and the intended threat were sufficiently closely connected (but A is sentenced as though he were an aider to threat). If a false key given to someone to commit theft is not used for that purpose but to set the house on fire, there will not be a sufficiently close connection and the person providing the key would not be an aider to arson (although he did contribute to the commission of this offence). Nor is this person an aider to theft, because that offence did not take place (dependence principle). A tried to be an aider to that felony, but 'attempted assistance' is not punishable as a form of participation.

It is unclear whether the approach chosen in the case of aiders also applies to instigators.

Error in Persona (Mistaken Identity) and Aberratio Ictus (Transferred Malice Scenarios)

As already noted, the participant does not have to intend the exact details of the principal offence; there may be 'general intent'. But the offence the participant intended must correspond sufficiently closely to the offence actually perpetrated. It is not clear when exactly this is the case; there is very little case law on this point. In the literature, which also pays little attention to this, it is assumed without further explanation – that there is insufficient correspondence if the difference lies in the identity of the victim.[52] A instigates B to kill C, but B kills D instead, in the mistaken belief he is killing C. For B this mistaken identity is irrelevant; he commits a murder. As for A: although his action was the cause of the murder that was committed, he did not intend *this* felony and therefore did not deliberately instigate it. A is liable for incitement to murder C (art. 46a).

Sometimes an error can still be 'compensated for' if conditional intent is taken broadly enough. If A took the possibility that B might make a mistake into account and accepted this possibility,

---

49   Again, plus the consequences of such actions. See (n 48).
50   See Knigge (n 37); HD Wolswijk, 'Medeplichtigheid en opzet' [2010] Delikt en Delinkwent 858.
51   HR 22 March 2011, *NJ* 2011, 342.
52   Remmelink (n 13) 461.

then A had conditional intent in relation to the killing of D. A certain case involving instigating the theft of a photocopier goes quite a long way in this regard.[53] The defendant, who wanted to make counterfeit money, had hired two men to steal a colour photocopier. He had given them exact instructions about the machine he wanted them to steal. However, the two men came back with a black and white photocopier. The defendant was found guilty of instigating them to steal the black and white photocopier, because he had knowingly accepted the considerable chance that the thieves would steal a different item from the one he had intended.

Aberratio ictus is a different story: A incites B to kill C; B aims at C, but hits D. In this case it is assumed that B is liable for attempted murder of C (and possibly for involuntary manslaughter of D). A is liable for instigating attempted murder of C.[54]

Withdrawal

Art. 46b provides: 'Neither preparation nor an attempt to commit a crime obtains where the felony is not completed due to circumstances which depend on the volition of the perpetrator'. This provision on voluntary withdrawal focuses primarily on the perpetrator. A person who personally performs actions in preparation of a felony or attempts to commit a felony is not liable if he or she withdraws voluntarily. The law does not say anything about the consequences of this for a participant in the attempt or preparation,[55] yet recently the Supreme Court provided some clarity regarding this issue.[56] A co-perpetrator who voluntarily prevents a felony from being completed (for example by stopping the other co-perpetrator from going any further) will be in the clear by virtue of art. 46b, but this does not affect the liability of the other co-perpetrator who was not involved in the 'non-completion' of the felony. This is different in the case of the indirect forms of participation, instigating and aiding; unlike in most other countries, voluntary withdrawal on the part of the perpetrator means that the instigator and the aider are not liable either. Regarding the position of instigators and aiders, the Supreme Court invokes legislative history; however, no compelling evidence can be found in legal doctrine to support this position. For an instigator, ultimately it makes little difference. In this situation even though an instigator would not be liable as a participant, his or her actions would be covered by art. 46a, incitement. There is no special provision for aiders in such cases; they are not liable, unless their actions constitute a separate felony in themselves.

The provision about voluntary withdrawal also applies to incitement. Incitement is deemed to exist so long as the intended principal has not reached the stage of attempting the principal offence. A promises B a reward if he kills C, but B has not yet done anything. If A now prevents B from reaching the stage of a punishable attempt, for instance by immediately talking him out of it again or by stopping B before he can begin to carry out the felony, then A will not be liable by virtue of art. 46b.[57]

---

53   HR 29 April 1997, *NJ* 1997, 654.

54   Remmelink (n 13) 462. Other scenarios are not dealt with in case law or literature.

55   Moreover, under Dutch law, the exact nature of voluntary withdrawal is unclear. Does it mean that there is no longer a principal offence? Or does the principal offence still 'exist', but is the perpetrator no longer liable? See De Hullu (n 5) 406.

56   HR 12 April 2011, *NJ* 2011, 358.

57   HR 5 December 2000, *NJ* 2001, 139; HD Wolswijk, 'Poging een ander te bewegen een misdrijf te begaan' in *Plegen en deelnemen* (Deventer 2007) 236.

Finally, can a participant also achieve impunity by means of 'voluntary withdrawal'? This is about the situation where the perpetrator has already reached the stage of a punishable attempt whereupon the participant prevents the felony from being completed. With regard to co-perpetration, this question has already been answered above: a co-perpetrator is free of liability if he or she personally prevents the felony from being completed. But what about instigators and aiders? A instigates B to murder C; just as B shoots C, A pulls C away so that B misses him. B is certainly liable for attempted murder. A incited B to this attempted murder, but is A now also liable? Dutch law is unclear on this point.[58] The provisions about voluntary withdrawal in art. 46b do not apply – at least not directly – to forms of indirect participation (instigation and aiding). The legislator did not think of a case like this at all and so far the Supreme Court has not had to consider such a case. One possibility is that art. 46b might be applied by way of analogy to an instigator or an aider. However, an argument against this is that in this scenario there is a liable perpetrator: Shouldn't the instigator or the aider be liable for contributing to this state of affairs? On the other hand, the perpetrator himself has the opportunity, under law (art. 46b), to achieve impunity by withdrawing voluntarily (but in the case in question failed to take that opportunity). Why should that opportunity not also be granted to instigators and aiders?[59] This is also in keeping with what is seen in Dutch law as the reasoning behind the impunity granted as a consequence of voluntary withdrawal: it is the most certain way to stop the felony in its tracks and prevent a violation of legal interests.[60]

Corporate Liability

Corporate Entities

Actus reus Under Dutch criminal law, a corporate entity can be liable both as a perpetrator and as a participant. In principle, a corporate entity can commit any kind of offence – an intentional felony, a felony of negligence or a misdemeanour.[61]

The law does not determine in what circumstances a corporate entity can commit an offence. In 2003 the Supreme Court gave a general ruling on this issue.[62] The basic premise is that a corporation can be liable if an illegal act has taken place that can be 'reasonably attributed' to that corporation. The Court formulates the guiding principle that it 'may' be reasonable to attribute the illegal action to the corporation if it took place 'within the scope' of the corporation. The Court then non-exhaustively sums up 'circumstances' in which actions 'may' be said to have been carried out within the scope of a corporation: the offence in question involves an action of an employee of the corporation; the action fits in with the corporation's normal business; the corporation profited from the action; the corporation had control over the actions and accepted them (acceptance in this context includes failure to take reasonable care to prevent the actions from being performed, for example when employees are inadequately supervised; see also above).

---

58 See HD Wolswijk, 'Enkele opmerkingen over vrijwillig terugtreden bij deelneming' in *Pet af* (Nijmegen 2007) 537.

59 As is also the case in many other systems of law, for example the German system (see § 24.2 Strafgesetzbuch).

60 Remmelink (n 13) 408.

61 See BF Keulen and E Gritter, 'Corporate Criminal Liability in the Netherlands' (*Electronic Journal of Comparative Law*, December 2010) <http://www.ejcl.org/143/art143-9.pdf> accessed 12 January 2013.

62 HR 21 October 2003, *NJ* 2006, 328.

Whether or not it is reasonable to attribute the actions of natural persons to the corporate entity therefore very much depends on the circumstances; there are no general, clear-cut criteria.[63] However, it is clear that certain criteria are *not* applied. For instance, to attribute such actions to a corporation it is not necessary for the corporation's executive management to be aware that an employee is performing unlawful acts, let alone that the management has ordered the employee to do so.

Mens rea   The 2003 judgment is only about the attribution of actions to the corporate entity. A different question is in what circumstances a corporate entity can be considered to have acted with intent or negligently. Again, there are no clear rules.[64] Sometimes a natural person's intention can be attributed to the corporate entity. However, knowledge at management level is not always required. One can only say, in general, that the higher the position in the corporation a person holds, the more likely it is that person's intent will be attributed to the corporation. Another way of establishing the *mens rea* of a corporation is to derive the *mens rea* from other circumstances related to the corporation itself, such as the corporation's policy and decisions.

Liability of Persons 'in Control'

If an offence has been committed by a corporate entity, then pursuant to art. 51.2 not only the corporate entity itself, but also 'those who ordered that offence to be committed and those under whose actual direction the offence was committed' are liable. This liability can be seen as a form of indirect participation, with the special feature that the offence has to have been committed by a corporate entity. Liability is not limited to the formal executive officers or employees of the corporation. Under this provision a person can be liable who was in no way officially connected to the corporation but did in fact pull the strings, while the actual executive officer was a mere puppet acting under this person's directions.[65]

Unlike 'ordering', 'actual direction' does not require any *active* involvement in the offence committed by the corporation. On the other hand, holding a formal executive position in the corporation does not in itself result in liability.[66] According to the Supreme Court, the illegal actions may be considered to have been performed under the actual direction of a certain executive 'if this executive failed to take measures to prevent such actions, although in a position and reasonably required to do so, and knowingly accepted the considerable risk that such actions would take place'.[67] Just as with 'ordinary' forms of participation, 'actual direction' requires conditional intent with regard to the offence committed by the corporate entity.

Concluding Remarks

In general the Dutch legislation regarding participation in an offence is not regarded as problematic. The provisions were first drawn up in the nineteenth century, but have been kept up to date through

---

63   E Gritter, 'De strafbaarheid van de rechtspersoon' in *Plegen en deelnemen* (Deventer 2007) 59. See also, De Hullu (n 5) 169.

64   Gritter (n 63) 66; De Hullu (n 5) 267.

65   HR 16 June 1981, *NJ* 1981, 586.

66   HR 24 August 2004, *LJN* Andrew1508.

67   HR 16 December 1986, *NJ* 1987, 321. See also WH Vellinga and F Vellinga-Schootstra, 'Eenheid in daderschap?' in *Systeem in ontwikkeling* (Nijmegen 2005). See also, Sikkema (n 15).

case law, so that a drastic review of the law does not seem necessary. It is only in relation to fairly minor points that adaptation is recommended.[68] The exhaustive enumeration of means of instigation could be dropped, as could the limitations in the definition of an aider before the fact. It has also been suggested that perpetration-by-proxy could be dropped as a separate form of participation and included under instigation; following on from this, it should be irrelevant whether the perpetrator himself or herself is liable.[69] These adaptations would not lead to essential changes to the law as it now applies.

A more interesting question, which has drawn less attention, is whether or not the dependence principle should be retained. The principle is already being relativised. The offence does not have to be a completed felony, but can also be a punishable attempt or even punishable preparatory actions. Moreover, the principle has also become less important because certain actions have been made punishable outside the provisions on participation. As well as the general offence of incitement (art. 46a), various other actions which essentially can be regarded as forms of participation have been made offences in themselves. For example, recently – in 2010 – providing the opportunity, means or information to commit violence against persons or property was made punishable as a separate offence (art. 141a), even if this violence did not actually take place. This is actually a variation on 'attempted aiding'. These punishable offences outside the provisions on participation may lead to a certain imbalance and are a reason to question the dependence principle itself.

The fact that by and large the provisions about participation work satisfactorily does not mean that there are no areas of concern. There are two issues that are important in practical terms. The first relates to the distinction between perpetration and various forms of participation. Perpetration and co-perpetration in particular have gained a much wider scope as a result of the transition from the concept of an act as being essentially physical to the concept of functional action. Due to this change, over time the distinctions between perpetration and participation have become less clear-cut. There is some overlap, for instance between perpetration and instigating, between instigating and co-perpetration and between co-perpetration and aiding. On the whole, overlaps like these are not seen as being particularly problematic.[70] Nevertheless, the distinction between co-perpetration and aiding in particular deserves attention, because consequences are attached to this distinction – especially the maximum sentence, which is one third lower for aiders than for co-perpetrators – and because the distinction between these two forms of participation is the most difficult one to make. It has been suggested that aiding could be included in co-perpetration or that an aider could be upgraded to a principal.[71] This would mean heading towards a kind of 'unified perpetrator' concept (*'Einheitstäterbegriff'*), in which differences in the contributions to the offence are only expressed in sentencing.[72] However, there does not seem to be much support for this idea among legal practitioners or in the literature; aiding, as a separate and less serious form of participation, associated with a lower maximum sentence, still has a right to exist.[73]

Another area requiring attention is the concept of intent. In practice, Dutch courts quite readily assume that a participant, particularly a co-perpetrator, had conditional intent to commit the principal offence in question. When a court ascertains this intent, sometimes it seems the court is

---

68   See, for example, De Hullu (n 5) 498; BF Keulen, F Vellinga-Schootstra, AA van Dijk, K Lindenberg and HD Wolswijk, *Daderschap en deelneming doorgelicht* (Zutphen 2010) 120.

69   In that case a provision would have to be made for offences for which the perpetrator must have a certain quality.

70   See, for example, De Hullu (n 5) 493.

71   W Wedzinga, 'Boekbespreking' [1999] Delikt en Delinkwent 545.

72   An advocate of this concept is MM van Toorenburg, *Medeplegen* (Deventer 1998).

73   De Hullu (n 5) 498; Keulen et al. (n 68) 114.

not only concerned with what the defendant actually knew and wanted, but that other factors also play a role. This means that establishing intent has become a partly normative issue – an issue of attribution. This does not necessarily lead to unreasonable results, nor is there necessarily any objection to a less factual and more normative concept of intent from a theoretical perspective. The problem is that those other factors – criteria which help to determine whether or not intent can be proved – have not yet been made sufficiently explicit in the case law and in the literature. As a result it remains unclear when intent can be proved.

Chapter 21

New Zealand

Julia Tolmie

General Principles: Types of Participation and General Basis of Attributing Criminal Liability for Acts of Others

Section 66 of the Crimes Act 1961 (NZ) is the general provision that governs modes of participatory liability in New Zealand. Section 66(1)(a) provides for the principal offenders liability, with glosses added by the common law doctrines of innocent agency and joint offending for situations where the offender acts through or in concert with another. A recent development is the expansion of the criminal duties to act, and the development of the law on causation, so that a person can be liable as a principal offender in respect of the consequences that flow on from simply being aware of the risk of, and yet not taking reasonable steps to interfere with, another person's offending against a victim that they have a duty to protect.

Section 66 sets out two pathways to liability as a secondary party. Under s 66(1)(b)-(d) a person is liable for their intentional assistance or encouragement of another's offending. Under s 66(2) where two or more people embark on a crime together and one commits incidental crimes, which were not agreed upon but were foreseen by their co-accused as occurring in the execution of the main offence, they are 'parties' to these other crimes under the 'common purpose doctrine'.

There is a debate about the proper relationship between these two forms of party liability. Beatrice Krebs suggests that the common purpose doctrine as it evolved at common law was originally designed to be exculpatory.[1] Anything which fell within the scope of the joint enterprise was already covered by the law on aiding and abetting, so the doctrine of common purpose was designed to limit the liability of the party for any incidental crimes committed by their associates which went beyond the common plan to those which they were able to predict as being a probable outcome of executing the plan. The doctrine codified in section 66(2) on this view would function to piggy back on s 66(1) in instances where there were joint principals, or a principal and a party, and where the principal committed additional crimes beyond the scope of what was agreed upon. The alternative view is that the common purpose doctrine is an independent form of secondary liability and is primarily inculpatory. For example, Simester clearly views joint enterprise as a distinct and broader form of accessorial liability that flows on the wrongfulness of groups of people embarking on criminal endeavours.[2] In New Zealand the debate appears to have been resolved in favour of s 66(2) constituting a distinct and broader form of accessorial liability, but this position has been arrived at as a matter of unconsidered assumption rather than reasoned argument.[3] The theoretical basis for the common purpose doctrine has never been fully engaged with in the New Zealand case law, much of which involves the articulation and application of

---

1 Beatrice Krebs, 'Joint Criminal Enterprise' (2010) 73(4) Modern Law Review 578. See also John Smith, 'Criminal Liability of Accessories: Law and Law Reform' (1997) 113 Law Quarterly Review 453, 462-63.

2 Andrew Simester, 'The Mental Element in Complicity' (2006) 122 Law Quarterly Review 578, 599.

3 *R v Waho* (NZCA, 27 April 2005).

principles at a vague degree of generality, with many discussions morphing the different legal requirements into each other.

In addition to the general provisions contained in s 66 there are a number of provisions criminalising particular variations of criminal participation. Some of these offences represent instances where gaps in accessorial liability are filled.[4] Other offences provide for those involved in offending by association to be understood as joint principals. For example, s 98A contains the recently enacted offence of 'participation in an organised criminal group'.[5]

The basis for holding companies criminally liable is also touched upon in this chapter. The issue here is not the need to hold one person accountable, either as a principal or as a party, for their participation in, and support of, another person's offending. Instead the issue is whose actions and state of mind can be attributed to the company so that they *are* the actions and state of mind of the company itself. An overlap between these bodies of principle occurs in cases such as *Evans v Commissioner of Inland Revenue*,[6] where both forms of liability existed on the same set of facts. There it was held that the same actions and state of mind on the part of the director which constituted the company's offending as a principal could simultaneously satisfy the requirements for party liability in respect of him in his capacity as director.

Principals by Proxy: Use of Innocent Agents

The English Law Commission has recommended enacting the common law doctrine of innocent agency to require that the accused meet three criteria.[7] First, they intend the innocent agent to commit the *actus reus* of the crime, second they cause the innocent agent to commit the *actus reus* of the crime and third, they personally have the *mens rea* for the crime. In addition, the victim should be innocent of the offence because of age, mental incapacity or lack of *mens rea*. The law then treats the accused as the principal, acting through the agent who is not regarded as a participant in the crime. The New Zealand courts have not been this precise about the criteria which must be satisfied to activate the doctrine of innocent agency but the few cases in which the doctrine has been successfully applied generally demonstrate, at a minimum, the last three of these requirements.[8]

Some crimes may, however, be impossible to commit through an innocent agent.[9] For example, crimes that by definition can only be committed by a person with a particular status. It is also hard to imagine a scenario where a failure to act, in breach of a duty to act, can be performed by someone who does not actually bear the duty themselves. Into this category might also fall crimes that it is difficult to imagine an agent committing *innocently* on behalf of someone else. For example rape, and strict liability offences. And in *R v Thompson*,[10] the court made it clear that, unless the victim

---

4   See Crimes Act 1961 (NZ) s 71(1) (being an accessory after the fact); s 179 (aiding and abetting a suicide); s 174 (counselling or attempting to procure a murder when the murder is not committed).

5   See also Crimes Act 1961 (NZ) s 235(b) (aggravated robbery); s 86 (unlawful assembly); s 87 (riot).

6   (NZCA, 17 June 2009).

7   The Law Commission, *Participating in Crime* (Law Com No 305, 2007) 4.27.

8   It is not always clear that the New Zealand cases require that the accused *intend* the innocent agent to commit the *actus reus*, so much as they cause them to commit the *actus reus* whilst in possession themselves of the necessary *mens rea* for criminality: *Narayan v Police* [2010] NZAR 36 (HC). But see *R v Paterson* [1976] 2 NZLR 494; *Police v B* [1990] 2 NZLR 504.

9   *Paterson* (n 8); *Police* (n 8).

10 [2005] 3 NZLR 577.

is independently acting as the legal agent of the accused, they cannot be considered in criminal law as the principal's 'innocent agent' for the purpose of committing a crime in which they are also the victim. However, as *Narayan v Police*[11] demonstrates, a person can be both the victim of a crime and, simultaneously, an innocent agent in respect of a second crime against another victim.

Joint Principals

Several people will be 'joint principals' when each person separately satisfies some part of the *actus reus* for the offence, together their actions make up the complete *actus reus*, and each of them has the full *mens rea* for the offence. This is a common law doctrine in New Zealand, which has been applied in a small number of cases involving complex fraud transactions or group attacks and where the courts have considered it a 'forced and unnatural' analysis of the facts to proceed as though only one person was the principal, helped by the others.[12]

Secondary Participation

A person will be liable as a party to someone else's offending under s 66(1)(b)-(d) if four requirements are satisfied on the facts:

- they aid, abet, incite, counsel or procure the principal to commit an offence;
- they do this prior to or contemporaneously with the offence being committed;[13]
- they have knowledge, at that time, of the essential matters that constitute the offence;[14] and
- they intend to help or encourage the principal to commit the offence.

Actus Reus: Aiding, Abetting, Inciting, Counselling or Procuring

The terms 'aiding, abetting, inciting, counselling or procuring' have been given the meanings in New Zealand that they have acquired elsewhere. Essentially they are all variations of behaviour that assists,[15] encourages[16] or influences[17] the principal in the offending.

One of the interesting issues in this area is whether simply witnessing another person's offending can attract criminal liability. It is said that presence alone, even if deliberate, will not amount to the encouragement or assistance of the principal's offending without some additional factor which lends it the necessary additional ingredient of support or help.[18] This could be prior behaviour that

---

11 *Narayan* (n 8).

12 *Ngamu v R* [2010] 3 NZLR 547. See also *The Queen v Tukaki* (NZCA, 14 June 2006); *R v Harawira* [1989] 2 NZLR 714.

13 *R v Fa'apusa* (NZCA, 13 December 2006) [25]; *Larkins v Police* [1987] 2 NZLR 282.

14 *Singh Adab v R* (NZCA, 10 December 2003).

15 *Larkins v Police* (n 13) 287, 290; *R v Afa, Luamanu and Tasilimu* (NZ HC, Auckland, 2 June 2000) [11], [13]; *R v Morgan* (NZ HC, Auckland, 10 February 2006).

16 *R v Tamatea* (2003) 20 CRNZ 363; *R v Schriek* [1997] 2 NZLR 139; *R v Briggs, Tafutu and Tafutu* (NZCA, 29 November 2001).

17 *Cardin Laurant Ltd v Commerce Commission* [1990] 3 NZLR 563.

18 *Schriek* (n 16); *R v Misitea* [1987] 2 NZLR 257; *R v Loper* (NZCA, 22 May 2000); *Briggs* (n 16); *Evans* (n 6).

assists the offender to get into the position to offend,[19] or it could be control or ownership of the vehicle or premises in which the offending takes place, such that there is the power to intervene and the deliberate non-exercise of that power.[20] Deliberate presence can, of course, directly contribute to the offending if it is proved to provide the principal with an audience,[21] signify to them that they have backup should the need arise, coerce them in their offending[22] or intimidate the victim so that they do not resist.

In *R v Witika*,[23] it was held that if there is a duty to act – for example, the duty on a parent or caregiver of a vulnerable adult to protect their charge from harm – then a failure to do anything to stop another person's offending might amount to encouragement of that person's offending. It has since been suggested that, without more, it 'aids' the perpetrator in committing an assault if the failure to act permits the assault to take place.[24] Recent case law goes further and has started to attribute primary liability in these circumstances on the basis that the breach of a duty to intervene to prevent an assault on the victim can be said to have directly caused any consequence (such as death) that results from that assault.[25] This expansion of criminality is likely to be assisted by the statutory enactment in 2011 of a duty on a parent or caregiver to protect a child or vulnerable adult in their care from 'harm',[26] and of an obligation to take reasonable steps to protect a child or vulnerable adult in a person's household from the threat of serious violence posed by someone else.[27]

Mens Rea

There must be an *intention* to assist or encourage the offender in committing the offence, simply knowing that it is probable that support or encouragement will be provided is not enough.[28] On the other hand, it is the assistance or encouragement that must be intended. There is no requirement that the accused desire that the principal commit the offence itself.[29]

The party must, at the same time as intentionally providing help and encouragement, 'know the essential matters that constitute the offence'.[30] *Cooper v Ministry of Transport*[31] suggested that recklessness rather than knowledge might be sufficient in respect of 'unknowable facts', such as the exact blood alcohol level of someone else.[32] However, *Cooper* was decided in 1991 and does not sit well with the opinion, recently expressed by the New Zealand Supreme Court in *R v Edmonds*,[33]

---

19 *R v Junior Inoke* [2008] NZCA 403 [26]; *R v Duncan* [2008] NZCA 365; *Makita Tere Junior v R* (NZCA, 27 June 2005) [15].

20 *Cooper v Ministry of Transport* [1991] 2 NZLR 693; *Police v A* [2006] DCR 141; *Police v Warburton* [2004] DCR 848; *Evans* (n 6).

21 *Shriek* (n 16); *R v McCausland* (NZCA, 5 December 2005) [15].

22 *R v Zizov; Reusen* (NZ HC, Auckland, 12 November 2003).

23 [1993] 2 NZLR 424, 430-31.

24 Andrew Simester and Warren Brookbanks, *Principles of Criminal Law* (3rd edn, Brookers 2007) 172. See also *R v Brough* (NZCA, 27 February 1997) 10; *R v Crossan* (NZ HC, Invercargill, 7 July 1998).

25 *The Queen v Kuka*. See also *R v Proude* (NZ HC, Auckland, 25 November 2009) [43] (Keane J).

26 Crimes Act 1961 (NZ) ss 151, 152, 195.

27 Crimes Act 1961 (NZ) s 195A. This duty extends to a staff member in a hospital or rest home.

28 *R v Wentworth* [1993] 2 NZLR 450; *R v Snelleksz* (NZ HC, Timaru, 16 December 2009) [19]; *R v Pene* (NZCA, 1 July 1980).

29 *Singh* (n 14) [41]; *R v Pulman* (NZ HC, Auckland, 30 October 2009); *Wentworth* (n 28).

30 *R v Edmonds* [2011] NZSC 159, [22]; *Singh* (n 14) [39]; *R v Kimura* (1992) 9 CRNZ 115, 117.

31 *Cooper* (n 20).

32 Simester (n 2) 585.

33 *Edmonds* (n 30).

that the *mens rea* standards are stricter in respect of party liability by aiding and abetting under s 66(1)(b)-(d) than they are under the common purpose doctrine in s 66(2) (where recklessness as to the principal's offending is expressly sufficient).[34] The rationale for higher standards of *mens rea* in s 66(1)(b)-(d) is that there is nothing inherently wrongful in many of the actions which might comprise the *actus reus* of assistance or encouragement and, unlike under the common purpose doctrine, the parties have not already demonstrated moral culpability by committing to a joint criminal venture.[35]

It must be established that the secondary party knew that the principal intended doing actions that constitute the *actus reus* of an offence, with the level of *mens rea* required for that offence.[36] The need for knowledge of the essential matters of the principals offending, however, does not mean that it is necessary to prove the accused had 'knowledge of the precise crime', in the sense of, for example, knowing the 'particular date and particular premises' in which it would occur.[37] Similarly, if the party contemplates the offence but its execution differs in a materially insignificant way they cannot escape liability on that basis.[38]

There is authority to the effect that uncertainty about which of a range of known offences was to be committed, and which of a number of contemplated means was to be adopted, does not imply ignorance of the essential ingredients of the alternative actually chosen.[39] It is worth noting that this comes close to diluting the *mens rea* standard required from 'knowledge' of the essential matters to 'recklessness' – in other words, awareness of a risk that the essential matters will take place. These authorities are older and coincident with those raising the possibility of a reduced *mens rea* standard in respect of this form of party liability.[40]

The crucial issue may be whether the secondary party knew that facts which satisfied all the legal requirements of the offence that actually took place would occur. Thus in *R v Kimura*,[41] it was held that aggravated burglary involving a weapon was not the same 'type of offence' as simple burglary. The weapon was therefore an 'essential element' of aggravated burglary for the purposes of s 66(1) and, because the party did not know that the principal had a knife, a conviction of simple burglary was substituted instead.[42]

Having said this, it has been suggested that consequences to which the fault requirement does not extend (that is, which do not require *mens rea* in respect of the principal offence) are not 'essential matters' of the offence, although it is not clear in principle why these particular types of *actus reus* elements should be treated differently for the purposes of party liability under s 66(1)(b)-(d). It is now settled, for example, that death is not an 'essential element' for the purposes of s 66(1)(b)-(d) party liability for manslaughter[43] or felony murder under s 168.[44] Nonetheless, as was

---

34 Ibid. [25].

35 Law Commission (n 7) 67-69.

36 *Cooper* (n 20); *R v Crooks* [1981] 2 NZLR 53; *Miller v MOT* [1986] 1 NZLR 660, 674.

37 *R v Waikato and Tawera* (NZ HC, Hamilton, 28 March 2001) [18]. See also *R v Rider* [1995] 2 NZLR 271, 273; *Witika* (n 23) 432.

38 See s 70. This does not cover aiding, although equivalent common law principles do; see *Cooper* (n 20).

39 *Cooper* (n 20); *R v Baker* (1909) 28 NZLR 536; *Kimura* (n 30); *Wentworth* (n 28); *Witika* (n 23).

40 As noted above, they do not sit well with the recent Supreme Court decision *Edmonds* (n 30).

41 *Kimura* (n 30).

42 The court said that different considerations might have applied if the case was put under s 66(2). See also *R v Morland* (NZCA, 6 September 1999); *R v King* [2010] NZCA 236.

43 *R v Renata* (1991) 7 CRNZ 616.

44 *R v Rapira* [2003] 3 NZLR 794; *R v Hardiman* [1995] 2 NZLR 650.

made clear by the Court of Appeal in *R v Hartley*,[45] to be guilty of manslaughter the secondary party must still have aided and abetted the 'type of offending', in other words the kind of assault, that caused the death in fact. In *Hartley*,[46] because what was contemplated was an assault with fists and what actually caused the death was an assault with a weapon that the accused was unaware that the principal had, they were not guilty of manslaughter as a party under s 66(1).[47] Furthermore, because intention or recklessness as to death on the part of the principal is necessary to establish a murder under s 167 of the Crimes Act 1961 (NZ), a party to such a murder under s 66(1)(b)-(d) must know that the principal will commit the unlawful act that results in death with either intention or recklessness as to death.[48]

Specific Issue: Joint Criminal Enterprise

A person will be a party under the 'doctrine of common intention' as set out in s 66(2) when the following elements are satisfied on the facts:

- the principal and the secondary party form a 'common intention to prosecute any unlawful purpose and to assist each other therein';
- the principal commits an incidental crime 'in the prosecution of the common purpose'; and
- the secondary party knows that committing the incidental crime was 'a probable consequence of the prosecution of the common purpose'.

The Common Unlawful Purpose

The significance of the common unlawful purpose is that joining this purpose may be the *only thing* that the accused actually does towards the commission of any crime, and the shared unlawful purpose may be for a crime that is far less serious than the incidental crime for which they are then held accountable because they foresaw that crime as at risk of occurring. It is also worth noting that foresight alone does not constitute a commitment to the crime taking place – it is human nature to hope for the best even when the worst is seen as perhaps occurring.[49] The rationale for allowing foresight to be enough to convict in this context, as opposed to the intention and knowledge required under s 66(1)(b)-(d), is that the person has already committed to the shared criminal venture that spins off into the additional offending and is therefore not morally innocent. Simester explains how liability is founded in affiliation in the following terms, suggesting the need for affiliation to be firmly established as a precursor to liability:

> By forming a joint enterprise, [D] signs up to its goal. In doing so, she accepts responsibility for the wrongs perpetuated in realizing that goal, even though they be done by someone else. Her joining with P in a common purpose means that she is no longer fully in command of how the purpose is

---

45 *R v Hartley* [2007] 3 NZLR 299.

46 Ibid.

47 See also *Rameka, Ahsin, McCallum and Rippon v R* (NZCA, 18 March 2011); *R v Aupouri* [2007] NZCA 86, [5]; *R v Atkins and Taylor* [2007] NZCA 103.

48 *Edmonds* (n 30).

49 Krebs (n 1) 594.

achieved ... Yet her commitment to the common purpose implies an acceptance of the choices and actions that are taken by P in the course of realizing that purpose.[50]

The need for an unequivocal and clear personal commitment to join with others in pursuing a criminal offence is also underscored by the fact that the accused's *mens rea* in respect of the incidental crime is usually inferred as a consequence of finding that they joined the common agreement.[51]

Evidence of a commitment to the common purpose   In New Zealand it is no longer possible to argue that liability under s 66(2) should be built on liability under s 66(1) in respect of the crime that forms the common purpose.[52] In *R v Waho*,[53] the New Zealand Court of Appeal simply referred to the need to establish an agreement between two or more people to commit a crime. The court did, however, make it clear that the agreement had to involve the parties to the agreement 'helping each other to carry it out', which implies a level of assistance or support from the secondary party in respect of the main offending that would be sufficient to constitute aiding or abetting under s 66(1)(b)-(c).[54]

The concern here is that an agreement to pursue jointly a crime will be inferred too readily from the actions of those who are young, working class and caught up in a dysfunctional culture of gangs, intoxicants and machismo because, with the benefit of hindsight, it is known that one of the group has engaged in an act of brutality. For example, in *Rameka, Ahsin, McCallum and Rippon v R*[55] the court, whilst expressing caution about inferring a common purpose to assault rival gang members simply because threats were yelled in public (these were possibly no more than evidence of a dysfunctional lifestyle and normal animosity between gangs), went on to infer the existence of a common purpose from the 'alarming parallels' (without spelling out these parallels or it being clear that the attack had any particularly distinctive features) between some of the threats and the later attack, as well as the brandishing of a butcher's knife by one of the occupants in the car prior to the attack which all the occupants in the car were aware of (although this weapon was not actually used in the attack).

What is an 'unlawful' purpose?   The 'unlawful purpose' referred to in s 66(2) has traditionally been understood to be a crime. Of course, the proliferation of overlapping criminal offences, and the advent of offences that criminalise participation in other people's offending (such as s 98A), increase the ability of the prosecution to characterise any set of facts as involving the commission of multiple offences in order to fit a case within s 66(2), as opposed to having to meet the stricter requirements of s 66(1).[56]

In a number of recent cases the New Zealand courts have allowed the Crown to be vague about the precise crime that is being pursued as the common purpose. For example, the Supreme Court in *R v Edmonds*[57] characterised the common unlawful purpose as being 'to pursue the group of

50   Simester (n 2) 580-600.
51   *R v Ma'u; Redman* [2008] NZCA 117, [69].
52   Krebs (n 1) 588-89, speaks of the 'danger that ... the existence of a joint enterprise is affirmed without much ado on the basis of an arrangement to commit a different offence than the one under consideration ...'.
53   *Waho* (n 3).
54   *Hartley* (n 45) [26], [32].
55   (NZCA, 18 March 2011).
56   *R v Curtis* [1988] 1 NZLR 734.
57   *Edmonds* (n 30).

scaffolders and to cause serious violence to somebody in the group'. This does not actually specify a crime – it is a vague statement of purpose which potentially encompasses any one of a number of crimes involving interpersonal violence, which could conceivably include the incidental crime of manslaughter that was in issue under s 66(2).[58]

Committing the Incidental Crime in 'the Prosecution of the Common Purpose'

Conceptualising 'the prosecution of the common purpose'   There are two overlapping issues here – whether the common purpose itself is what is being executed at the time (or whether the principal has embarked on their own independent offending), and whether the incidental crimes are in 'the prosecution' of that purpose or have departed from it. How the 'prosecution of the common purpose' is to be conceptualised in law – and therefore how one is to go about determining where its parameters lie on any given set of facts – is presently unclear.

One possible interpretation is that 'the prosecution of the common purpose' covers all crimes that fall within the *scope* or parameters of the express or tacit agreement between the parties ('authorisation').[59] The tacit agreement will include the authority to improvise around the occurrence of unpredicted circumstances in the execution of the common purpose.[60] Viewing the issue in this way opens the possibility for the accused to expressly contract out of criminal liability for foreseeable incidental crimes by closely defining what they will and will not authorise the principal to do. However, it does not sit with an understanding of the purpose of the 'common purpose doctrine' as being to limit liability in respect of those incidental crimes that go *beyond* the scope of what was agreed upon.

A second approach, and one which is to be found in the more recent New Zealand cases, is to assume that the common purpose doctrine covers those incidental crimes that depart from the common purpose (and are therefore not within its 'scope') but were foreseen by the party when s/he committed to the joint enterprise ('contemplation').[61] If the issue is what the accessory subjectively foresaw then this approach would conflate the *mens rea* for the common purpose doctrine with the requirement that the incidental crime occur in its 'prosecution' because the tests for the two requirements are identical. The alternative possibility is that the prosecution of the common purpose encompasses everything that is *objectively* predictable as a likely consequence of what was either expressly or tacitly agreed between the parties. The court in *R v Te Moni*[62] provided an example of what they considered would 'step right outside the boundaries of the common purpose': where the principal committed 'a rape while engaged in a routine robbery'. The rape is not in the prosecution of the common purpose because it is unpredictable as an event that could happen in the course of a robbery.

A third approach would be to interpret the rationale for this requirement as being to make sure that the common purpose doctrine encompasses only those crimes which have a connection in time and place to the main offending, whilst leaving it to the *mens rea* requirements of s 66(2) to limit the party's liability for such crimes to those which were also subjectively predicted. A 'rape whilst engaged in a routine robbery' under this approach (contrary to what was suggested in *R v Te*

---

58   See also *Waho* (n 3).

59   *R v Morrison* [1968] NZLR 156; *R v Greening and Mason* (1990) 6 CRNZ 191, 195 (Tipping J).

60   *R v Tomkins* [1985] 2 NZLR 253. See also Gerald Orchard, 'Joint and Several Murder and Manslaughter' [1986] New Zealand Law Journal 45.

61   *Rapira* (n 44); *R v Te Moni* (1997) 15 CRNZ 439.

62   *Te Moni* (n 61).

Moni[63]) is committed in the prosecution of the common purpose in the sense that it is committed during the execution of the common purpose by the principal.[64]

How narrowly/broadly should the common purpose be defined as being for these purposes? Crimes can exist in the *abstract* – as legal requirements that need to be met, or foresight/agreement that certain actions will occur that satisfy those requirements – and in *practice* – as sets of facts in which people actually behave in particular ways that satisfy the requirements for criminal liability. Because party liability involves agreements, predictions and performance in fact, there is constant slippage between these two planes. The issue is the degree of correspondence that has to occur between what was agreed or foreseen and what happened in fact for the requirements of party liability to be met. Clearly it would be silly to require what happened in practice to correspond closely with any agreement or prediction in all of the minute details of execution in order for secondary parties to be liable. There are many variables in the real world that it is impossible to predict or control for, and anyone executing an agreement will need to be able to improvise around these. However, there is a point where what happens in practice is so different from what was agreed upon or predicted that it is unfair to see the principal's associates as being party to it.

At issue is how broadly or narrowly the common purpose should be defined as being for the purpose of determining what constitutes its execution and what incidental offending goes beyond its prosecution. Is the common purpose to be defined as the general crime that is being pursued, for example, the crime of burglary? Or is it defined as encompassing all or part of the detail agreed upon between the parties when discussing the execution of the planned crime? For example, is the common purpose to commit the crime of burglary by entering particular premises on a particular date, carrying no weapons and with the intention to exit without force if surprised?

In *R v Tomkins*,[65] it was suggested that where the party foresaw the principal committing a murder in respect of a particular victim but the killing occurred at a time or in circumstances very different from anything the accused had ever contemplated – so different that he should not be fairly regarded as acting in the common purpose – the secondary party will not be liable for murder. This seems to suggest that the common purpose could include a certain amount of the agreed detail of its execution.[66] By way of contrast, in *Joseph v R*[67] Hammond J held that a secondary party could potentially be a party to the common purpose of aggravated burglary even though he had been misled by the principal in respect of specific details of the plan, in this instance the identity of the victim. It was held that what mattered was that the secondary party had entered the building with weapons and the intent to commit a crime therein. Thus, whilst the parties had a difference of understanding about some of the details of the execution, they had agreed on facts that satisfied the ultimate legal requirements of the offence they were executing.

How specific or general the common purpose will be defined as being may, in the end, depend on the particular facts. In *R v Edmonds*,[68] the issue arose in the guise of whether the common purpose was confined to, or was broader, than the use of known weapons. The Supreme Court said

---

63   *Te Moni* [1998] 1 NZLR 641.

64   *R v Edmonds* (n 30) [48].

65   *Tomkins* (n 60).

66   Orchard (n 60) has criticised this decision. It is doubtful there would be consensus today that a party's culpability is significantly reduced merely because the principal kills the person the party had in mind in very different circumstances from those he foresaw, especially if the significance of the difference is that there is an increased probability of apprehension.

67   (NZ HC, Hamilton, 12 December 2000).

68   *Edmonds* (n 30).

that sometimes evidence that the alleged party was carrying or knew about a weapon might be the only evidence that they shared an alleged common purpose. However:

> In other cases the common purpose may be best assessed by reference to the results the defendants intended to bring about. Thus the evidence may show that the defendant was a party to a common purpose to inflict serious, and potentially life threatening violence in whatever way was convenient, including, say, kicks to the head. In such a case, the alleged party could still be found guilty of murder even if the fatal injury was inflicted not by kicking but rather with a tyre lever which, unbeknown to that party, one of the other members of the group had brought to the fracas.[69]

Whilst the court acknowledged that there may be cases where the common purpose does not include weapons or is limited to the use of certain weapons,

> providing the Crown can establish a relevant and sufficient common purpose and a recognition that the offence ultimately committed was a probable consequence of its implementation, it is difficult to conceive of a situation where the nature of the weapon used would be of controlling significance in determining whether the offence occurred in the course of implementing the common purpose.[70]

The Secondary Party Must Foresee the Incidental Crime as a 'Probable Consequence'

The secondary party must subjectively foresee, as a 'probable consequence' of pursuing the common unlawful purpose, the accused committing the *actus reus* of the crime with the appropriate *mens rea* to constitute guilt.[71] The phrase 'probable consequence' has been defined as meaning awareness that an event 'could well happen',[72] or is a 'real and substantial risk'.[73] It does not mean 'more probable than not'.[74]

Consequences: homicide   One unresolved issue in New Zealand is whether death has to be foreseen by the defendant to be a party to a homicide under s 66(2).[75] Older New Zealand authority supports the position that the accused could not have 'known' that culpable homicide was a

---

69   Ibid. [50].

70   Ibid. [51].

71   *Hagen* (NZCA, 4 December 2002); *R v Kopelani* (NZCA, 23 November 2005); *R v Leuluaialii* (NZCA, 22 November 2006); *R v Chadwick*, HC, Napier, T13/99, 9 February 2000.

72   *R v Gush* [1980] 2 NZLR 92.

73   *Hagen* (n 71); *Te Moni* (n 61).

74   *Gush* (n 72); *R v Akuhara* (NZCA, 3 September 1986).

75   It has been settled that if the principal is convicted of murder, his associates can be convicted of manslaughter or murder, depending on whether they saw the principal committing the unlawful act that caused death with the *mens rea* for murder or not: *R v Hamilton* [1987] 2 NZLR 245; *Tomkins* (n 60); *Edmonds* (n 30); *Leuluaialii* (n 71). Although party liability is derivative the theoretical basis for allowing the secondary party to be guilty of manslaughter even though the primary party has committed murder is that both murder and manslaughter are variants of the one offence of culpable homicide.

probable consequence of pursuing the common purpose without foreseeing a death.[76]

Recent authority, however, has begun to retreat from this position. Thus the Court of Appeal in *R v Rapira*[77] distinguished the cases requiring foresight of death as dealing with murder under s 167, where it has always been accepted that it must be established that the secondary party had awareness that the principal possessed the *mens rea* required for s 167 murder: intention or recklessness as to death.[78] In *Rapira*, the issue was s 66(2) party liability in respect of a felony murder under s 168 and the court held that '[j]ust as intention to kill or knowledge that death is likely to ensue is not necessary for the liability of the principal under s 168, it is not necessary for a secondary party'.[79] It went on to suggest that it is also 'not necessary for the offence of manslaughter that death be intended or foreseen by a secondary party', so long as they foresee the unlawful act that 'attracts the operation of the law of manslaughter if death ensues'. Similarly, it is well established[80] that in a case under s 66(2) where the defendant knew that a weapon (or weapons) were on hand and might be used, even if only to threaten the victim, and the weapon is used to kill, a verdict of manslaughter will be open.[81]

The most recent Supreme Court decision which could have authoritatively determined whether death must be foreseen for party liability to a homicide under s 66(2) did not make a definitive ruling. In *R v Edmonds*[82] the court suggested that foreseeability of death by the secondary party was 'arguably' not necessary but left open the possibility that it might be necessary under s 66(2) for manslaughter and s 167 murder, but not s 168 felony murder. It suggested no sensible basis in principle, as opposed to an accident of precedent, as to why this distinction should be made.

What specificity of detail in the execution of the incidental offence has to be foreseen as probable?

Is the party required to foresee the precise manner in which the incidental offence plays out? Or is it enough that they foresaw the general offence that took place, even if they did not foresee the exact details of its occurrence? At issue is whether the party is required to foresee *actions* of the same type as those that comprised the *actus reus* as it played out in reality or whether it is sufficient that they simply foresaw the generic *offence* occurring, even if it occurred by means of different actions from those it was expected the principal would perform.

---

76 *R v Hirawani; Wilson and Henry* (NZCA, 30 November 1990); *R v Doctor* [1985] 1 CRNZ 627; Tipping J in *Greening and Mason* (n 59) 195; *R v Hamilton* (n 75); *Tomkins* (n 60) 255-56; *Te Moni* (n 61) 647; *Rapira* (n 44) [25].

77 *Rapira* (n 44).

78 *Edmonds* (n 30).

79 *Rapira* (n 44) 804 (relying on *R v Morrison* [1968] NZLR 156; *R v Hardiman* [1995] 2 NZLR 650, 652; *R v Tuhoro* [1998] 3 NZLR 568). The court thought its position on s 168 was justified by the 'legislative intent that persons prepared to inflict serious violence to facilitate the commission of grave crimes must take the consequences if death results' (804), noting 'the increasing number of persons prepared to combine for major criminal activity' (805).

80 *Hartley* (n 45); *Tomkins* (n 60) 254; *Hamilton* (n 75).

81 Of course if the party to an assault is aware (for the purposes of s 66(2)) that the death of the victim was a probable outcome then they may also be liable for manslaughter if they did not see it occurring in circumstances that amounted to murder; *Hartley* (n 45); *Tomkins* (n 60) 246; *Kopelani* (n 71); *Te Moni* (n 61).

82 *Edmonds* (n 30).

The approach taken in the English cases[83] (and some of the older New Zealand decisions[84]) seems to have focused on the nature of the actions that were foreseen. Therefore in England it is considered that if the principal's *specific conduct* which comprised the actual offending was of a 'fundamentally different' nature from the act which *was* predicted by the party, then the party cannot be held accountable for the offending on the basis that it is either a departure from the common purpose or that they fail the test for *mens rea* because the incidental crime was not foreseen.[85] According to the English Court of Appeal in *R v Mendez*,[86] the specific actions of the principal will be 'fundamentally different' if they are actions which are more violent or involve a different level of dangerousness than acts of the nature which the alleged party foresaw.

In New Zealand, on the other hand, the focus of the more recent cases is on whether the party foresaw the generic legal *offence* that actually took place, even if the factual details of how it manifested were quite different from what was foreseen, and even if what was actually done by the principal might be considered to, in its nature, carry a higher degree of risk than the specific behaviour which had been foreseen by the alleged party.

The issue has commonly arisen in both jurisdictions in the context of incidental crimes of interpersonal violence where the party did not know that the weapon or a weapon of similar lethality to that used in the assault was being carried by the principal and might be used in the attack. In contrast to the position taken in England, the New Zealand Supreme Court in *R v Edmonds*[87] has definitively held that there is no legal requirement that the secondary party foresee the use of the exact weapon that was wielded by the principal, or even a weapon of similar lethality, in order to be liable as a secondary party in respect of its use.[88] The court said that what was material for the purposes of s 66(2) was that the accused appreciated that the ultimate result (meaning the generic crime in issue) was probable rather than that he foresaw 'the exact concatenation of events' which, in the end, brought that result about. The court said that s 66(2):

> recognizes only one relevant level of risk, which is the probability of the offence in issue being committed. If the level of risk recognized by the secondary party is at that standard, it cannot matter that the actual level of risk was greater than recognized. It follows that there can be no stand-alone requirement that common purpose liability depends on the party's knowledge that one or more members of his group were armed or, if so, with what weapons. As well, given the wording of s 66(2), there is no scope for a liability test which rests on concepts of fundamental difference associated with the level of danger recognized by the party.[89]

The court thought there were a number of problems with elevating the requirement that the accused had knowledge of the specific weapon or its equivalent into legal principle. The first is that such

---

83　*R v Powell; R v English* [1999] 1 AC 1, [1997] 4 All ER 545 (HL); *R v Rahman* [2008] UKHL 45, [2009] 1 AC 129, [2008] 3 WLR 264, [2008] 3 All ER 351 (HL); *R v Mendez* [2010] EWCA Crim 516, [2011] QB 876, [2011] 3 WLR 1, [2010] 3 All ER 231 (CA); *R v Uddin* [1999] QB 431, [1998] 2 All ER 744 (CA).

84　*Hamilton* (n 75).

85　See *R v Mitchell* [2008] EWCA Crim 2552, [2009] 1 Cr App R 31. Note that the UK Law Commission (n 7) suggests that the 'fundamentally different act' rule only applies when the alleged party did not foresee that the principal would kill the victim with the intention of killing the victim (as opposed to causing grievous bodily harm). See *Rahman* (n 83).

86　*Mendez* (n 83) [48]; *Rahman* (n 83).

87　*Edmonds* (n 30).

88　See also *Waho* (n 3); *Vaihu* [2009] NZCA 111.

89　*Edmonds* (n 30) [47].

knowledge does not bear a precise correlation with the accuracy of the parties' foresight of the risk of death or serious injury. The likelihood of serious injury or death predominantly depends not on the type of weapon used in an assault but the personalities and intention of those engaged, their states of emotional arousal and whether they have consumed alcohol or drugs and so on. Secondly, tests as to whether the weapon that was foreseen was fundamentally different in lethality to that used are indeterminate both legally and factually. And even if there was stability in judicial approach to the factors that are material to the application of the test, each case in the end is a value judgment for the jury.

Even after *R v Edmonds*,[90] it remains a question of fact in New Zealand as to what the accused foresaw happening, and knowledge of the fact that there were weapons may be relevant to that issue.[91] Thus William Young P. in *R v Vaihu*[92] said that on some facts a member of a group might appreciate, for example, that the intentional infliction of grievous bodily harm was what was proposed without necessarily knowing that members of the group were armed, but sometimes: 'it will not be possible for a rational jury to infer the required knowledge in relation to a particular defendant unless sure that the defendant was aware that members of his party were armed'.[93]

Effect of Errors and Transferred Malice/Aberratio ictus Scenarios in the Person of One Participant on the Liability of the Other Participants

Transferred malice, although criticised in the academic literature as having 'insufficient theoretical underpinnings',[94] is established as a doctrine in the common law of New Zealand.[95] In *Narayan v Police*,[96] Justice French commented, '[t]he basis of the doctrine is that if a defendant with the *mens rea* of a particular crime causes the *actus reus* of the same crime, he is guilty even although the result is in some respects an unintended one'. In relation to murder the doctrine finds statutory expression in respect of intentional and one of the two forms of reckless murder set out in s 167 of the Crimes Act 1961 (NZ). Section 167(c) provides that an intention to kill, or to cause bodily injury known to be likely to cause death, directed at one person is sufficient to amount to the *mens rea* for murder in respect of another person mistakenly killed instead.[97]

---

90 *Edmonds* (n 30).

91 Those judgments of the New Zealand Court of Appeal that have required a knowledge of the weapon direction must, after *Edmonds* (n 30), be understood as instances where knowledge of the weapon on the part of the party was factually necessary in order to be able to infer that the incidental offence was foreseen: *Rameka* (n 55); *Hartley* (n 45); *Vaihu* (n 88).

92 *Vaihu* (n 88) [88]. See also *Ma'u* (n 51) [26]; *Hirawani* (n 76).

93 See also *Leuluaialii* (n 71).

94 See Michael Bohlander, 'Transferred Malice and Transferred Defenses: A Critique of the Traditional Doctrine and Arguments for a Change in Paradigm' (2010) 13(3) New Criminal Law Review 555; Andrew Ashworth, 'Transferred Malice and Punishment for Unforeseen Consequences' in Peter Glazebrook (ed.), *Reshaping the Criminal Law* (Stevens 1978).

95 *R v Emery* [2012] NZHC 391; *Police v Gill* (DC, Greymouth, 9 November 2009); *R v Clayton, Pearce and Edgarton* [2008] NZCA 523; *Narayan* (n 8); *Chandler v R* (NZ HC, Napier, 10 February 1993); *R v Challis and Box* [2008] NZCA 470.

96 *Narayan* (n 8).

97 Section 167(c) does not apply to the second form of reckless murder set out in s 167(d), where 'the offender for any unlawful object does an act that he knows to be likely to cause death, and thereby kills any person, though he may have desired that his object should be effected without hurting anyone'.

There is no New Zealand case law applying the doctrine of transferred malice to parties, leaving it unclear whether mistakes and, what kinds of mistakes, made by the principal will be transposed to the party. Elsewhere it is thought that, whilst mistakes made by the principal might be attributed to the party by applying the doctrine of transferred malice to the party as well as the principal, deliberate deviations from the plan by the principal will amount to departures from the common purpose with the result that the party could not be held liable.[98] It is worth pointing out that, as noted above, recent New Zealand cases have tended to focus less on the specific actions to be performed by the principal which were agreed upon or predicted by the parties and more on the end result – the legal requirements of the generic offence that they were pursuing or foresaw as occurring. The result is that many deviations by the principal, whether mistaken or deliberate – so long as they do not mean that the generic offence that is being pursued has fundamentally changed – will not be considered to be departures from the common purpose so as to alleviate the secondary party from liability. This can be illustrated by *Joseph v R*[99] in which, as noted above, the principal deceived the party as to the intended victim, but this was considered an irrelevant detail. They had agreed on the commission of a burglary, and a lack of mutuality around the identity of the victim did not prevent them from having formed a common plan. Of course it remains possible, even after *R v Edmonds*,[100] that the agreement between the parties can make it clear that certain details are part of the plan, so that a deviation in those details materially affects whether what is done can be considered to be an execution of the common plan. The problems attendant on the transferred malice doctrine, 'increased exponentially' when the doctrine is applied to 'multiple actor situations', have been well documented elsewhere and need not be revisited here.[101]

There is a similar lack of jurisprudence in New Zealand on the issue of whether defences available to the principal are transferred (along with the transferred *mens rea*) from their intended to their accidental victim[102] and, further, whether the secondary party can benefit from any defences (transferred or otherwise) that are available to the principal.[103] The little relevant case law on the operation of defences in the context of party liability suggests that the fact that the principal 'can avail themselves of a defence not available to the secondary party' does not necessarily mean that the prosecution cannot prove the commission of an offence by the principal that the accused can then be held to be a party to. There is no discussion in the New Zealand case law, for example, of the possibility that a justificatory defence may prevent the *actus reus* from occurring in the first place, meaning that no offending has taken place for the accused to be a party to. Indeed the basis

---

98   Michael Bohlander, 'Problems of Transferred Malice in Multiple-actor Scenarios' (2010) 74 Journal of Criminal Law 145.

99   *Joseph* (n 67).

100   *Edmonds* (n 30).

101   Bohlander (n 98) 150-55.

102   The defence of provocation, now repealed in New Zealand, was one of the few criminal defences to specify explicitly that it was transferred from a targeted to an unintended victim (see the former s 169(6), Crimes Act 1961 (NZ)).

103   For example, in *Sweetman v Industries and Commerce Development* [1970] NZLR 139 it was held that the fact that the principal offender had a defence did not mean that a party to their offending could not be convicted under s 18(1) of the Economic Stabilisation Act 1948. The court said that there is, 'a requirement that the prosecution be able to prove the commission of an offence by a principal offender, regardless of whether that person is known or charged. The same can apply if the principal offender has been acquitted, for example where that person can avail himself or herself of a defence not available to the secondary party'.

for holding that the party cannot be held liable if the only possible principal is acquitted is said to be 'unjust inconsistency', rather than a lack of any underlying offending to be privy to.[104]

Withdrawal from Participation

Because liability as a party is said to be derivative the party can undo their participation and withdraw from their involvement in the crime at any time before the crime is committed or seriously attempted. In *R v Pink*,[105] Hammond J set out the requirements for an effective withdrawal as follows:

- first, there must be notice of withdrawal by words or actions;
- secondly that withdrawal must be unequivocal;
- thirdly, the withdrawal must be communicated to the principal offenders; and
- fourthly the withdrawal may only be effected by taking all reasonable steps to undo the effect of the party's previous actions.

What are reasonable steps to undo the effects of previous participation will depend on the facts of the case and the extent of the accused's previous participation.[106] If the accused's acts were 'overt and influential', or actually materially assisted the crime, they might be required to take 'positive steps to intercede and prevent the crime from occurring'. If the accused's participation was counselling or encouraging the principal then attempts 'to dissuade the principal offenders from proceeding' or expressing discouragement might be enough.

Corporate Liability: Basic Rules

Section 2 of the Crimes Act 1961 (NZ) defines a 'person' to include a 'company',[107] and this has created the opportunity for companies to be liable either as a principal offender or as a party in respect of most criminal offences.[108] An interesting exception is homicide (murder or manslaughter). Homicide is defined in s 158 of the Crimes Act 1961 (NZ) to mean 'the killing of a human being by another', and it has been held that this prevents a company from being able to commit a homicide because, whilst such a body might be a legal person, it is not a human being.[109] Such a result has no basis in principle and appears to be the consequence of an inadvertence in drafting. Of course, it is still the case that a company can be held liable as a secondary party under s 66 in respect of a homicide committed by a human being.

---

104   *R v Pirret; Epapara; and Mihaka* (NZ HC, Rotorua, 17 March 2010); *Sweetman* (n 103); *R v Waaka* (NZ HC, Hamilton, 9 July 2001).

105   *R v Pink* [2001] 2 NZLR 860. These have subsequently been endorsed by the Court of Appeal in *R v Ngawaka* (NZCA, 6 October 2004) and *Rameka* (n 55).

106   *Rameka* (n 55).

107   Interestingly, 'person' is also defined to include a 'board, society' and 'any other body of persons, whether incorporated or not' in 'relation to such acts and things as it or they are capable of doing'.

108   Under s 361 of the Crimes Act 1961 (NZ) a company is able to enter a plea through an appointed representative.

109   *R v Murray Wright Ltd* [1970] NZLR 476.

Companies famously have 'no soul to damn and no body to kick'. How then is liability to be attributed to a body that acts through others but is essentially a legal fiction? Whose actions are the actions of the company? And whose state of mind is the mind of the company for the purpose of satisfying the *mens rea* requirements for criminal liability? In New Zealand the principles for attributing criminal liability to a company are to be found in the case law rather than statute, and these rules are still in a rudimentary stage of development.

Putting aside the narrow range of regulatory offences for which vicarious liability may be permitted,[110] the basic rule is that before an individual's actions and state of mind can be held to represent the company itself, that person must be in control of the company or a sphere of its activities.[111] This rule is, however, qualified in two ways. First, actual or de facto control may count as control for the purposes of attribution, even though nominal or formal control is in the hands of someone else.[112] Secondly, although traditionally the relevant person acting as the company was the 'directing mind and will of the company'[113] either generally or in the relevant sphere of activity, if applying that rule will defeat the clear legislative intention that a particular law should apply to companies then the courts will tailor the rule of attribution to the particular substantive crime that is to be enforced. The relevant question is 'whose act (or knowledge or state of mind) was *for this purpose* intended to count as the act etc. of the company?'[114] Thus in *Linework Limited v Department of Labour*,[115] the actions and omissions of a supervisor operating as a site foreman were held to be the actions and omissions of the company for the purposes of charges under the Health and Safety in Employment Act 1992 in respect of a failure to take all practicable steps to ensure the safety of its employees at work. Blanchard J remarked:

> The Act is concerned with the safety of the employees at work – for example, on the floor of the factory, on building sites, and while operating vehicles, plant and machinery. In practical terms, this is a world far removed from administrative offices which are the natural habitat of senior or middle level management. The statutory obligations upon an employer and, in particular, its obligation to provide on the job supervision of safety practices, must be viewed with this setting in mind. It is difficult to believe that Parliament would have intended that the relevant acts and omissions of the person in charge of a work site should not be attributable to the employer.[116]

What this means is that it is 'a question of construction in each case whether the enforcement of the particular statute or regulation requires that knowledge of an act, or the state of mind with which it is done, should be attributed to the company'.[117]

There are those who suggest that it may not always be appropriate to 'humanise' companies for the purposes of attributing criminal responsibility – that companies, unlike humans, are group entities, each with its own unique corporate culture.[118] Suggestions that it would be appropriate

---

110   Simester and Brookbanks (n 24) 205-206.

111   Ibid. 206, 212.

112   See *Meridan Global Funds Management Asia Ltd v Securities Commission* [1995] 3 NZLR 7.

113   *Tesco Supermarkets Ltd v Nattrass* [1972] AC 153, [1971] 2 All ER 127 (HL); *Nordik Industries Ltd v Regional Controller of Inland Revenue* [1976] 1 NZLR 194.

114   *Meridan* (n 112) 12.

115   [2001] 2 NZLR 639.

116   Ibid. [23].

117   Simester and Brookbanks (n 24) 209.

118   See, for example, Brent Fisse and John Braithwaite, *Corporations, Crime and Accountability* (Cambridge University Press 1993).

then to aggregate the actions and knowledge of a range of employees or to attribute criminal liability for fault as it manifests in a corporate 'culture' have, however, thus far not found favour with the New Zealand courts.[119]

Sentencing Regime for Participants

Although the legal requirements for establishing party liability are different from those necessary to establish the principal offender's liability, once these requirements are satisfied on the facts the result is that both the principal and any parties are convicted of the principal offence. There is, therefore, no formal differentiation in New Zealand sentencing law or process between principals and parties. Having said this, clearly any sentence will reflect (amongst other relevant factors) the defendant's degree of participation in the offending.

Although there is also no special provision for the sentencing of companies, s 39 of the Sentencing Act 2002 (NZ) has particular salience for these types of defendants. Where the offence in question mandates a penalty that is clearly inappropriate for a company, a company can still be prosecuted for that offence as long as at least one other penalty that is appropriate for a company is available.[120] Section 39 gives the court the general power to commute imprisonment, community based sentences and home detention (all sentences which are not appropriate for companies) to a fine instead.

Conclusion

This chapter has traversed the basic rules governing participatory liability in New Zealand. Such an exercise makes it apparent that the 'common purpose doctrine' in s 66(2) appears to be the form of participatory liability that has attracted the most recent judicial attention – perhaps because it is the form of party liability that is seen as being more easily satisfied and therefore more commonly charged, at least in cases involving group violence. It has perhaps also become clear that recent developments in respect of this form of liability risk over-reach, and that such developments have occurred without considered analysis of their implications. This area of criminal law in New Zealand, arguably more than any other, appears to be characterised by doctrinal vagueness.

---

119 *Progressive Enterprises Ltd v Commerce Commission* (2008) 12 TCLR 284 (HC); *Commerce Commission v Progressive Enterprises* [2010] NZCA 374 (CA).

120 *Police v Purser Asphalts & Contractors Ltd* [1990] 1 NZLR 693.

Chapter 22

Spain

Manuel Cancio Meliá and Ana Garrocho Salcedo

Introduction

General Principles: Types of Participation and General Basis
for Attributing Criminal Liability for Acts of Others

Spanish criminal law is among several systems devised around the *principle of legality*.[1] Consequently, no customary definition exists – via case law – of the various offences; these are established through legislation. However, general rules of criminal liability form a separate field of study, known as the 'General Part' of Criminal Law, an autonomous subject in university studies of law, and also a separate part in the Penal Code (articles 10-137).

Within the Continental sphere, Spanish Criminal Law has been largely influenced by German legal theory.[2] In this regard, since the 1920s (and particularly following the end of the dictatorship of General Franco in 1975) both the judicial approach to deciding cases and the principles informed by Spanish Criminal Law have been determined via the importation of German legal theory and doctrine.

Spanish law distinguishes between principals and participants. The Penal Code describes three forms of principal: direct individual principal, joint principals and *autoría mediata* (indirect principal or principal using another person as an instrument). In the field of participation, the Penal Code also differentiates between 'abetting', 'necessary cooperation' (*cooperación necesaria*) and complicity. The first two of these forms of participation fall within the category of principal whereby the defendant is liable as if he or she committed the offence.

The relevant provisions are articles 27, 28 and 29 PC:[3]

Article 27

Those criminally responsible for felonies and misdemeanors are the principals and their accessories.

Article 28

---

1   An excellent synthesis is found in Luis Chiesa and Carlos Gómez-Jara, 'Spanish Criminal Law' in Kevin Jon Heller and Markus Dirk Dubber (eds), *The Handbook of Comparative Criminal Law* (Stanford University Press 2009); available at SSRN: <http://ssrn.com/abstract=1317689> accessed 15 July 2012; see also the broader narrative by Lorena Bachmaier and Antonio del Moral García, *Criminal Law in Spain* (Wolters Kluwer 2010).

2   See the concise explanation of the German theoretical context by Markus Dirk Dubber, 'Theories of Crime and Punishment in German Criminal Law' (2005) 53 American Journal of Comparative Law 679.

3   Official translation by the Spanish Ministry of Justice, available at: <http://www.mjusticia.gob.es/cs/Satellite/es/1215198252168/DetalleInformacion.html> accessed 16 September 2012.

Principals are those who perpetrate the act themselves, alone, jointly, or by means of another used to aid and abet.

The following shall also be deemed principals:

a) Whoever directly induces another or others to commit a crime;
b) Whoever cooperates in the commission thereof by an act without which a crime could not have been committed.

Article 29

Accessories are those who are not included in the preceding Article, but cooperate in carrying out the offence with prior or simultaneous acts.

Apart from these basic rules, the Spanish law on intervention in a criminal offence contains special rules for crimes committed through the media (article 30 PC), a specific rule for the directors of a legal entity (article 31 PC) and, since the recent reform of the legal text in the 2010,[4] a system of criminal accountability for several legal entities with respect to a series of criminal violations committed from within those institutions (article 31 bis PC).

When attempting to distinguish between principals and participants, the first point of departure lies in the principle of legality: the conduct described in the Special Part is always tied to the figure of the principal, that is, the person who carries out the act, and, consequently, the forms of participation imply an *extension* of criminal liability through the rules of the General Part.[5]

The concept of the principal has been developed mainly by academic commentary, starting from the basis that the principle of legality does not constrain to such an extent the interpretation of the General Part as it does the Special Part. It is the principal who carries out the act and to whom such an act can be attributed as his own.[6] These principals, in a strict sense, are those mentioned in subsection (1) of article 28 PC: individual principals, joint principals and indirect principals (*autores mediatos*). In contrast, those 'deemed' principals for sentencing purposes are the participants mentioned in subsection (2) (abettors and those whose cooperation is for some reason necessary for the offence to be committed).

The notion of a principal offence is based on a *restrictive concept*.[7] Consequently, 'participation is intervention in someone else's act'.[8] Three conceptions of the role of principal have been posited:[9]

---

4   This entails the latest reform made to the PC, by Organic Law 5/2010 (entry into force: December 23, 2010), which affected an extensive part of the legal text.

5   Articles 27-29 PC. See, Santiago Mir Puig, *Derecho penal, Parte General* (9th edn, revision by Víctor Gómez Martín, Reppertor 2011) 14/1.

6   Mir Puig (n 5) 14/2.

7   See, for example, Enrique Gimbernat Ordeig, *Autor y cómplice en Derecho penal* (1st edn, Universidad de Madrid 1966) 217 ff; Gonzalo Rodríguez Mourullo, in Juan Córdoba Roda and Gonzalo Rodríguez Mourullo, *Comentarios al Código penal* (Ariel 1972) 801 f.

8   Mir Puig (n 5) 15/27.

9   Subjectivist theories resulted in the status of principal depending on the *voluntas auctoris*; see on doctrinal evolution only Eugenio Cuello Calón, *Derecho penal. Parte General*, vol. I, *Parte General* (3rd edn, Bosch 1935) 513 ff, 518; Mir Puig (n 5) 14/19 ff.; José Cerezo Mir, *Derecho penal. Parte General* (BdF 2008) 929 ff.

Objective-formal theory (since the nineteenth century)   Under objective-formal theory (since the nineteenth century),[10] the definition of principal depends on the objective description of the prohibited conduct in the offences of the Special Part. Someone who executes the offence will be a principal. Nevertheless, for some time now it has been observed that the objective-formal theory is inadequate – as a consequence of which it is already being abandoned in theoretical discourse – since it is incapable of correctly comprehending several circumstances, and at the same time is over-inclusive of others. Thus, for example, it is under-inclusive in the case of joint principals: with the objective-formal point of view it is not possible to explain several circumstances (those in which one of the joint principals does not carry out acts in a strict sense: for example, the head of a gang of thieves who limits himself to giving orders, but does not himself touch any goods that are to be stolen). Nor would it be capable of explaining the figure of the indirect principal (*autoría mediata*), since here the indirect principal does not carry out by himself any action prohibited by law. On the other hand, in many violations in which the legal description is poor (such as, for example, in homicide: 'to kill'), objective-formal theory could expand the notion of principal incorrectly to the point of including any causal agent. In this regard, if the conduct described is construed – as was done at the end of the nineteenth century – in purely causal terms (for example, to kill is to cause death), especially in offences involving negligence, any causation could be considered as principal participation (as in the case of causing a death through conduct within the permitted risk, such as facilitating that someone places himself in danger, for example, by lending him a dangerous instrument).

Objective-material theory   Objective-material theory aims[11] to overcome the deficiencies of the objective-formal theory by referencing the importance of the principal's objective contribution to the criminal offence. It has been argued, however, that the notion of 'importance' is rather vague, and that by placing emphasis on what is objective (external to the principal), one ceases to adequately take into consideration the relevant subjective elements (internal to the principal).

Theory of control or command over the act   The doctrine of theory of control or command over the act[12] (originally developed in Germany) arose in the middle of the twentieth century as a proposal of the group of authors led by Hans Welzel, which attempted to emphasise the importance of the subjective elements of the criminal offence. On the subject of defining the principal, this culminated in a mixed concept, the objective-subjective principal, in which the element of the objective contribution of the offender is given equal weight with his will to let it materialise. Thus, the notion of principal is made flexible and cases of joint principals and indirect principals (*autoría mediata*) can be explained without difficulty. Despite not being exempt from criticism,[13] the theory of dominion or control over the act is today dominant amongst commentators and throughout case law.[14]

As noted above, the Spanish dualism of the principal and participant implies that the contribution of the participant is that of an 'accessory', that is, it is construed as a contribution to the *act of the principal*. Hence, the *accessorial nature of the participation* becomes the central focus of

---

10   No longer upheld in present doctrine; see references in Rodríguez Mourullo (n 7) 801 f.

11   See, for example, the references in Gimbernat Ordeig (n 7) 116 ff.

12   The main work of reference (also in Spain) is Claus Roxin, *Täterschaft und Tatherrschaft* (8th edn, Walter de Gruyter 2006) 60 ff; Gómez-Jara and Chiesa (n 1) 22 translate the expression as 'control over the event' theory.

13   The most frequent of which is that of 'diffuse'; see, in this regard, for example, Fernando Molina Fernández, *Memento Penal* (Francis Lefebvre 2010) no 2921.

14   See only Cerezo Mir (n 9) 934; Molina Fernández (n 13) no 2951.

participation theory.[15] The specific effects of accessorial liability are customarily described in two ways:[16] 'quantitative accessoriness' and 'qualitative accessoriness'. In the former, liability is only generated for the participant when the attempt to stage the offence begins. Hence, if an individual has been abetted and/or received support from a third party but decides against committing the offence, neither party can be found liable.[17] Qualitative accessoriness, on the other hand, refers to the degree of accountability of the principal necessary to determine the accountability of the participant. The first approach to tackle this issue is referred to as 'minimum accessorial' liability, and implies that it is sufficient for the accountability of the participant that the conduct of the principal complies with the legal description (as far as objective and subjective matters are concerned) of the offence, even though a justificatory defence exists in the person of the principal and/or the principal is not personally culpable. A second view tends to be called 'limited accessorial' liability, and means that the participant is criminally liable only if the principal's conduct complies with the offence description and, in addition, no justification exists. The third opinion, called 'maximum accessorial' liability, requires that the principal commits the substantive offence (*tipicidad*: the conduct in question coincides with what the Law describes as an offence) in the absence of a defence (*antijuridicidad*: there is no cause for justification), that is, he or she is deemed personally culpable (*culpabilidad*: the event is personally reproachable to the agent). The majority of opinion in Spain leans towards the second view of limited accessoriness, both on the basis of arguments deriving from the wording of the law (since articles 28 and 29 speak of the 'event', and this tends to be construed as an unlawful event, that is, one which complies with the legal description and where any justification is absent) as well as the material argument that the justification of a given conduct has general, *erga omnes* effect.

Sentencing Regime for Participants

As noted above, the sentencing regime is somewhat peculiar. Despite entailing a restrictive definition of the term principal, of the three forms of participation, the two most relevant ones (abetting and necessary cooperation) lead to the same sentence as for a principal, and only complicity has a lesser sentencing frame, as established by articles 28,[18] 61 and 63 PC:

> Article 61
>
> When the Law establishes a sentence, it shall be deemed to be imposed on the principals of the consummated offence.
>
> Article 63
>
> Accomplices of a consummated or attempted crime shall be sentenced to a lower degree of sentence than that provided by law for the principals of the same offence.[19]

---

15   The decisive monograph is by Enrique Peñaranda Ramos, *La participación en el delito y el principio de accesoriedad* (Tecnos 1990).

16   See, for example, Cerezo Mir (n 9) 950; Mir Puig (n 5) 15/34; Molina Fernández (n 13) no 2976.

17   Unless we are dealing with one of the cases of preparatory acts exceptionally incriminated in the PC in specific offences, and defined in article 17 PC (conspiracy or proposition to commit a crime).

18   See above page 512.

19   According to article 70.1.2 PC, the lower scale of the sentence is determined by taking the minimum sentence provided by Law, deducting one-half of its amount, and thus setting the new minimum limit. Hence,

The above applies to 'normal' violations, that is, intentional, positive-act offences. The majority of commentators believe that the rules around principals and participation are also applicable to negligence offences – unlike in Germany. However, this is controversial and has virtually no relevance in practice where a unitary concept of negligent principal appears to exist.[20]

Principals

The '*direct principal*' is the basic form of principal and poses no problems in application.

Indirect Principals

Article 28 PC expressly recognises '*indirect principal*' ('*autoría mediata*') as a form of principalship and determines that it is an indirect principal (*autor mediato*) who carries out the criminal act 'by means of another used as an instrument' who acts without criminal liability. The indirect principal or *hinterman* does not take part directly in the execution of the offence.[21]

Doctrine and case law have identified three major groups of cases of indirect principals, *stricto sensu*, in intentional offences:

1. absence of unlawful conduct on the part of the instrument, either due to the atypical nature of his conduct, or the existence of a justificatory defence;
2. instances where the instrument has made an error; and,
3. circumstances where the instrument lacks capacity, for example, due to age, illness, mental disability, fear or coercion, etc.

Absence of unlawful conduct of the agent   Within this first group of cases fall those situations in which the indirect principal uses an agent who does not act within the meaning of the law, for example, as a consequence of being under a state of hypnosis or a reflex. In these cases there is no voluntary human action. Consequently, part of Spanish doctrine considers that these cases fall into the category of *direct principal*.[22] Furthermore, the instrument may act atypically due to absence of the 'objective imputation' (that is, despite the damage characteristic of a particular offence having been caused, this has been done within the risk permitted by law. For example, the instrument causes bodily harm to another during the course of a football match – within the rules of the game – or because a specific subjective element of the criminal offence in question is missing (thus, for example, if the instrument uncovers, in the frame of the offence of uncovering secrets [art. 197 PC], intimate data about the victim, but does so without the intent required by that offence

---

for example, the lower degree of sentence to that provided for homicide (ten to 15 years imprisonment, article 138 PC) would be five to ten years imprisonment.

20 See only Cerezo Mir (n 9) 955 ff; Mir Puig (n 5) 15/37 ff.

21 Carolina Bolea Bardón, *Autoría mediata en Derecho penal* (Tirant lo Blanch 2000) 148.

22 So, for example, Bolea Bardón (n 21) 149; Mir Puig (n 5) 14/55. Molina Fernández (n 13) no 2931. Conversely, Muñoz Conde considers cases of absence of action of the instrument as cases of indirect principals; see Francisco Muñoz Conde and Mercedes García Arán, *Derecho penal, Parte General* (8th edn, Tirant lo Blanch 2010) 485.

– to 'uncover secrets or violate the privacy' of the victim).[23]

Within these cases of absence of classification of the conduct of the instrument the cases of 'non-qualified wilful instrument' (cases in which the instrument acts with intent, but without meeting the necessary personal characteristics for the offence, such as, for example, being a judge for the offence of malfeasance) in special offences should also be mentioned and which, notwithstanding the above, will be addressed below.

Furthermore, within this first group of cases of indirect principals, we include those cases in which the agent's acts are fully justified, for example, when a superior orders a subordinate to perform an arrest for spurious reasons which are unknown to the subordinate.[24] In this case, the subordinate would act without liability, believing he is acting in the legitimate exercise of his position; in such case, his error is inevitable. Notwithstanding the above, the event would be fully attributable to the hierarchical superior who issued the order: one who causes the instrument to act in a cause of justification is accountable as indirect principal of the criminal offence committed.

Errors of the agent   The second group (errors of the agent) is formed by those cases in which the agent commits an act based on a criminally relevant error. One must thus distinguish between the occurrence of a *mistake of fact (de facto)* and *a mistake of law (de jure)*.

Generally speaking, in cases of mistake of fact, the indirect principal creates or provokes an error based on which the agent acts without knowledge of the elements of the offence, thus negating intent; an example is the drug courier who is unaware that he is carrying drugs in his luggage.[25] If, however, in such cases the agent could have avoided the error, he himself may remain liable for potential negligent offences.[26]

In cases of unavoidable mistakes of law, the agent acts with intent, but without guilt. However, problems arise if the mistake was avoidable and the agent thus acts with intent and merely reduced guilt.[27] In these cases, a part of the literature appears to advocate negating the use of the figure of indirect principals, and of classifying this as cases of abetting of the agent.[28]

Effect of errors in persona/aberratio ictus scenarios in the person of one participant on the liability of the other participants   One question that has generated a certain doctrinal polemic[29] – although not as much as, for example, in Germany – lies in how to resolve those cases of inducement in which the executer of the event makes an error *in persona vel objecto* (for example, intends to shoot A but shoots B in error) upon identifying the object of his action (an error that has always been considered irrelevant). The question lies in whether that error should also be irrelevant for the inducer, or whether, conversely, it should be deemed to decrease his liability. This can occur in two cases posed in doctrine: the first, if it is believed that the executer's error makes the event a scenario *aberation ictus* (the subject correctly identifies the material object, but errs in striking; in

---

23   *Inter alia*, Mir Puig (n 5) 14/62 ff.; Muñoz Conde and García Arán (n 22) 435.

24   Example taken from José Manuel Gómez Benítez, *Teoría jurídica del delito, Derecho penal Parte General* (Civitas 1984) 146.

25   Article 14 PC.

26   Spanish doctrine recognises the possibility of someone being an indirect principal when the agent acts in a culpable manner, for example, Bolea Bardón (n 21) 181-83.

27   Gómez Benítez (n 24) 144.

28   For example, Gómez Benítez (n 24) 144-45. On the treatment of circumstances in which an avoidable error occurs, see *in extenso* Bolea Bardón (n 21) 205, with abundant references on German doctrine.

29   See, Enrique Peñaranda Ramos, in Pablo Sánchez-Ostiz Gutiérrez (ed.), *Casos que hicieron doctrina en Derecho penal* (La Ley 2011) 61, 69-72.

this case, the majority solution is to hold that he be convicted of attempted wilful homicide – the attempt to kill another person at whom he aims with a firearm – plus a negligence-based offence (the death effectively occurring in the person hit by the deviated shot)), which implies a reduction of sentence. Other commentators hold that the inducement, in this case, is but attempted, since the executer carried out a different act from the one induced. This also means a reduction of sentence, or complete impunity, since attempted inducement is punishable under the Spanish PC only as a preparatory act.

Finally, case law and another group of commentators tend to hold that the executer's error should not affect the liability of the inducer. There have not been many occasions in which this constellation has reached the courts. The closest is the case of an author who executed his mandate to murder another man despite realising that the person before him was not the target.[30] Here it is clear that the inducer cannot be held liable for inducement to commit a consummated murder, since the executer deliberately changed his target, straying from the content of attempted inducement. Conversely, the Supreme Court indicates in its resolution, *obiter dicta*, that the solution should be different if an error *in persona* has occurred. The Supreme Court has also upheld this criterion, without further reasoning, in another case of murder for hire – which was held to be an attempt – and error *in persona*. The case entailed an attempted political murder of a political objector to the regime of Equatl New Guinea carried out in Madrid. The executer expecting him confused him with his brother – which, for the court, confirmed the irrelevance of the executer's error.[31] The option of proposing differentiating solutions which evaluate on a case-by-case basis whether the error *in persona* of the executer remains within the margin of what is induced is beginning to derive significant support from the courts. The essential criteria will therefore lie in verifying whether the executer has followed the plan of execution in its essential aspects – and identification of the material target – included in the inducement.[32]

Fear, coercion and so on   The final category encompasses those cases in which the *hinterman* uses persons under the age of capacity or insane persons, as well as people who act out of fear or coercion. In these cases, the agent acts with intent but without guilt or criminal capacity.

Notwithstanding the above, two potential exceptions exist: cases of a *an agent who acts with intent but lacks a certain quality to commit the offence*,[33] and cases of *hierarchically organised structures*. In both situations, the agent is a person who acts with intent and is himself fully accountable.

Absence of necessary quality in the agent   In certain circumstances an agent must have certain qualities before an offence can be committed (such as, for example, being a public civil servant). An example of this would be the private secretary of a public civil servant who destroys, at the request of the civil servant, papers entrusted to the civil servant by reason of his position.[34] In relation to the offence of abuse of trust in the custody of documents (article 413 PC) only the *civil servant* or the *authority* who carries out the conduct of destruction or making the document unusable commits the crime. Thus, the conduct of the civil servant goes unpunished, since the participation (in this case as abettor) in the agent's act does not create liability by virtue of the

---

30   Supreme Court Judgment 791/1998, of 13 November.

31   Supreme Court Judgment 256/2008, of 14 May.

32   See only Peñaranda Ramos (n 29) 73 ff., 78 f.

33   *Special offences* are considered to be those that require special qualities. See Víctor Gómez Martín, *Los delitos especiales* (Edisofer 2006).

34   Example taken from Mir Puig (n 5) 15/22.

principle of accessoriness of participation. Nevertheless, and starting from this context, in order to avoid the non-punishment of both subjects (agent and *hinterman*) the category of indirect principal was applied to a *non-qualified intentional agent*. Through this form of principal, the *hinterman* could be accountable as an indirect principal while the agent would be a participant. This does not pose any problem if the agent acts through error or coercion, that is, when the *hinterman* truly dominates the will of the executer instrument.[35] Nevertheless, this is much more questionable when the agent acts voluntarily,[36] since in these cases, the conduct of the agent is atypical and the conduct of the *hinterman* does not differ from a form of abetting as a form of secondary participation in an act which itself is no offence, which technically leads to both forms of conduct going unpunished.[37]

Hierarchically organised power structures The theory of organised apparatuses of power as a particular form of the use of the indirect principal was introduced for the first time in Germany by Claus Roxin in 1963.[38] In the context of the criminal proceedings in Jerusalem against Adolf Eichmann, Roxin raised the possibility of using the concept of indirect principals with respect to the commanders or heads of certain organisations or hierarchies of power whose purpose had to be the commission of criminal offences,[39] where persons exchangeable within the organisational structure interacted.[40] In these cases Roxin believed that the heads of the organisation or the commanders completely dominated the power apparatus and could expect that once an order was issued, it would be carried out by the members of the organisation.[41] Notwithstanding that the subordinate members of the organisation could be fully accountable subjects, there is no obstacle for the head or mastermind to dominate the criminal apparatus, thereby being the indirect principal of what is done by subordinates.

Nevertheless, the fact that the subordinates are themselves fully accountable caused part of the literature to oppose this *sui generis* indirect principal model, preferring to subsume these types of

---

35   *Inter alia*, Bolea Bardón (n 21) 408, 413 ff.

36   The following declare themselves openly opposed to applying this in cases of non-qualified intentional agents who act voluntarily: in Germany, Roxin (n 12) 695 ff. (this author relying on the application of the theory of the offences of violation of duty (*Pflichtdelikte*) in order to avoid the impunity of both intervening parties, vid. Roxin (n 12) 393 ff.); in Spain, Gimbernat Ordeig (n 7) 292-98; Miguel Díaz y García Conlledo, *La autoría en Derecho penal* (PPU 1991) 601-602.

37   In Spain, this solution which leads to impunity is advocated by Gimbernat Ordeig (n 7) 298; Gonzalo Rodríguez Mourullo, 'El autor mediato en Derecho español' (in Anuario de Derecho penal y Ciencias Penales 1969) 475; Gonzalo Quintero Olivares, *Los delitos especiales y la teoría de la participación en Derecho penal español* (Cymys 1974) 106; Díaz y García Conlledo (n 36) 730. Against this, for example, Gómez Benítez (n 24) 157-58, close to the approach of Roxin. In favour of the indirect principal model in cases of non-qualified intentional agents when neither error nor coercion occurs; Patricia Faraldo Cabana, *Responsabilidad penal del dirigente en estructuras jerárquicas. La autoría mediata con aparatos organizados de poder* (Tirant lo blanch 2003) 126-27. In some cases, the courts admit the punishment of the agent as a participant and of the *hinterman* as principal, on the basis of his specific duty, for example Supreme Court Judgment 539/2003, of 30 April; 1493/1999, of 21 December; 274/1996, of 2 May.

38   See Roxin (n 12) 242-52.

39   For this reason Roxin excluded similar circumstances that could be posed within the concept of criminal enterprise; Roxin (n 12) 249-51. The following also reject this possibility for Spain, for example Bolea Bardón (n 21) 400-401; Faraldo Cabana (n 37) 100.

40   See Roxin (n 12) 244-45.

41   Ibid.

circumstances under the concept of joint principals,[42] or of other forms of participation such as abetting.[43] Spanish courts have not applied the indirect principal model to organised apparatuses of power.[44] In proceedings for offences of terrorism or organised crime, it was preferred to have recourse to the general models of joint principals, abetting or necessary cooperation.[45]

Another alternative is to utilise the concept of *commission by omission*, regulated in article 11 PC.[46] Since the PC of 1995, Spanish Criminal Law has finally had an express provision about when the omission of preventing a criminal offence is equivalent to having committed it by positive act. Such liability is based on whether the offender has a duty to act or protect a certain legal interest.

Hence, in certain circumstances, liability may be based on the intentional or negligent non-prevention by superiors of crimes committed by their subordinates.[47]

Joint Principals

Article 28 PC covers *joint principals*. Spanish law does not require that each and every one of the elements of the offence are fulfilled by each of the joint principals, but it suffices that all of them contribute during the actual commission of the offence an essential element based on their common

---

42 In Spain, for example, Antonio González-Cuellar advocates – in the context of offences against the environment – considering executives as principals in omission offences albeit with lower sentences or liability in those cases in which their subordinates cannot be held liable. If they are liable, he advocates considering the commanders as joint principals, 'La responsabilidad penal de los órganos de dirección de la empresa en delitos contra el medio ambiente' in Libro Homenaje al Profesor Dr. Gonzalo Rodríguez Mourullo (Civitas 2005) 1499, 1500. Also Muñoz Conde and García Arán (n 22) 437, advocate that the bosses (and the members) of a band are all joint principals. In Germany some say that these cases should be considered as a case of joint principals, HJ Jescheck and T Weigend, Lehrbuch des Strafrechts, Allgemeiner Teil (5th edn, Duncker & Humblot 1996) 670; Günther Jakobs, *Strafrecht, Allgemeiner Teil: die Grundlagen und die Zurechnungslehre. Lehrbuch* (2nd edn, Walter de Gruyter 1991) 649.

43 See Gimbernat Ordeig (n 7) 189 ff., who states that 'the activity of Hitler and of those with whom the idea of genocide arose and the manner of carrying it out, convincing others to execute it and to establish the apparatus the offence required, should be classified as abetting'. In Germany, in the same sense, see Michael Köhler, *Strafrecht. Allgemeiner Teil* (Springer 1997) 510; Joachim Renzikowski, *Restriktiver Täterbegriff und fahrlässige Beteiligung* (Mohr Siebeck 1997) 87-90.

44 Supreme Court Judgment 708/2010, of 14 July (case of *Latin Kings*) in which the Supreme Court echoes the existence of indirect principals in the case of organised apparatuses of power, although it does not apply it directly in the case in question.

45 See Héctor Olásolo Alonso, *Ensayos de Derecho penal y procesal internacional* (Tirant lo Blanch 2011) 202, 204; as well as the detailed study of Alicia Gil Gil, 'El Caso Español' in *Imputación de Crímenes de los Subordinados al Dirigente: Un Estudio Comparado* (Temis 2008) 100.

46 The Special Part of the Spanish PC incorporates cases of commission by omission in specific offences, for example, in the case of article 176 PC, which reflects the liability of civil servants for torture committed by subordinate civil servants; and in article 615 bis PC, which regulates the so-called 'superior responsibility' in the context of violations of international criminal law. See the recent Supreme Court Judgment 1136/2001, of 2 November, convicting a sergeant of the Civil Guard for not preventing torture of members of ETA carried out by subordinates. See also, Supreme Court Judgment 257/2009, of 30 March, convicting the head of the top commanders of the terrorist organisation BobAndrewO for omission (article 11 PC) for attempted offence abduction. Furthermore, the concept of commission by omission is applicable to corporate crime; see also the separate opinion by Judge Bacigalupo Zapater to Supreme Court Judgment 234/2010, of 11 March.

47 See Enrique Peñaranda Ramos, 'Sobre la responsabilidad en comisión por omisión respecto a hechos cometidos delictivos cometidos en la empresa (y en otras organizaciones)' in *Derecho y justicia penal en el siglo XXI: Liber amicorum en homenaje al profesor Antonio González-Cuéllar García* (Colex 2006) 413, 423.

purpose.[48] In fact, the courts have held that when the contribution takes place in the preparatory phase, the actions of that participant are secondary in nature, namely 'necessary cooperation' punishable pursuant to article 28(b) PC.[49]

The Spanish courts mainly apply the theory of control over the act mentioned above, in this case as a *functional control over the event*, that is, 'a singular form of division of work for carrying out the shared criminal project', a 'bond between the parties in the form of common resolution', considering, with regard to the subjective aspect, that if conditional intent is given regarding the possibility of bodily harm in the common plan, every joint perpetrator is to be held responsible for the whole act, including injury or death.[50]

The concept of joint principals thus requires the existence of an 'agreement of intent or mutual agreement'.[51] Without this, there would be no basis for the main effect of the entire concept, namely that of the 'principle of reciprocal attribution' among all joint principals.[52] The mutual agreement marks the limit of mutual attribution of the acts of individual parties.[53] Conduct which deviates from that agreement is therefore not part of the core effect of mutual attribution.[54]

With respect to the *characteristics* of the agreement, literature and case law both agree that it may be express or implied, and prior or subsequent to the start of the execution of the criminal offence.[55] In the case of an *ad hoc* agreement during the commission phase, the courts require[56] that:

1) one person must have commenced the execution of the offence;

2) subsequently another joins the first in order to achieve the completion of the crime initiated by the former;

---

48   See, for example, Mir Puig (n 5) 15/13, who holds that joint principals are 'not only those who execute the elements of the offence in a formal sense, but rather all those who contribute an essential part of carrying out the plan during the execution phase' (italics in original); Molina Fernández (n 13) nos 2952-54; in Spain, Muñoz Conde admits, notwithstanding, non-executory joint principalship (n 22). That is, cases of joint principals in which not all joint principals come to execute materially and directly part of the offence; Muñoz Conde (n 22) 436-37. See also Supreme Court Judgments 77/2007 of 7 February; 529/2005, of 27 April; 1049/2005, of 20 September; 5.10.93; 2.7.94; 28.11.97; 903/98 of 2 July. On the quality of the joint principal's contribution in the execution phase, the courts require that it must be decisive for the execution of the criminal act, although not necessarily be part of the nucleus of the criminal offence (that is, that it not form part of the legal description of the offence). See, for example Supreme Court Judgment 529/2005, of 27 April (case of Maremágnum).

49   Supreme Court Judgments 708/2010, of 14 July; 434/2007, of 16 May; and 699/2005, of 6 June.

50   Supreme Court Judgment 434/2007, of 16 May; and 850/2007, of 18 October.

51   Gómez Benítez (n 24) 139; Díaz y García Conlledo (n 36) 653-54; Mir Puig (n 5) 15/15; Molina Fernández (n 13) no 2952, who considers the mutual agreement to be the 'true nucleus' of the concept.

52   Mir Puig (n 5) 15/16 ff. Similarly, Supreme Court Judgment 77/2007, of 7 February.

53   *Inter alia*, Mir Puig (n 5) 15/20.

54   As in the majority of case law, see Supreme Court Judgments 1032/2006, of 25 October; 1139/2005, of 11 October; 474/2005, of 17 March; and 417/1998, of 24 March.

55   Supreme Court Judgments 251/2004 of 26 February; 1339/2004 of 24 November; 474/2005 of 17 March; 529/2005 of 27 April; 1003/2006, of 19 October; and 601/2007, of 4 July. Mir Puig (n 5) 15/15; Molina Fernández (n 13) no 2952.

56   Supreme Court Judgments 1385/2011, of 22 December; 474/2005, of 17 March; 969/2001, of 28 May; 974/2000, of 26 July; 417/1998, of 24 March; and 742/1993, of 29 March.

3) the new person incorporates in his actions the previous act by the first party, taking advantage of the situation previously created; mere knowledge will not suffice;

4) the new party must join before the offence has been completed, as there can be no ex-post-facto participation.

One of the main problems in this context is that of potential *excesses* by one of the joint principals, resulting in the non-application of the principle of reciprocal attribution. Especially important here are situations in which the commission of a certain offence was not explicitly contemplated but where this presents itself as a natural consequence in the course of events, for example, in cases of theft with violence or intimidation, where one of the parties ends up killing the victim. In these cases, the courts tend to look to the *theory of foreseeable deviations* in order to distinguish between an excessive act and a foreseeable consequence:

> [T]he prior arrangement to carry out an offence of theft with violence or intimidation which does not *a priori* exclude any risk to life or the physical integrity of persons, makes liable for the theft all direct participants … even though only one of them causes that result.

In those cases, it is held that 'the participant who is not the material perpetrator of the act of homicide or injury may be considered acting with conditional intent if in the "course" of the predatory act bodily attacks may be reached'.[57] Spanish law does not exclude the use of the concept of joint principals in cases of deviations from the initial plan, provided that such deviations remain within the ordinary course of events to be expected for the intended conduct.[58]

Joint Criminal Enterprise

Spanish law addresses situations similar to those described under *joint criminal enterprise* (macro-criminality, organised crime) from two different levels.[59] On the one hand, it applies the general rules of participation set out above, on the other and mainly after the 2010 reforms, it provides for specific offences based on scenarios, such as, for example, membership in or management of an illegal association, organisation or group (articles 515 ff./570 bis ff. PC), irrespective of whether any crimes have been committed within the context of those criminal associations, which themselves would follow the general rules.[60] Spain thus for criminal policy reasons subscribes to a criminalisation of the preparatory phase in certain well-known and high-risk criminogenic

---

57 Supreme Court Judgments 1500/2002, of 18 September; 1147/1995, of 20 November; 1326/1995, of 21 December; 2159/1994, of 7 December; and 780/1993, of 31 March.

58 In the same sense, see the recent Supreme Court Judgment 1385/2011, of 22 December.

59 See for this dualist approach regarding the membership offence and the actual offence carried out by a member in the context of terrorism the Supreme Court Judgment 1140/2010, of 29 December, with references to further case law.

60 In the case of terrorist organisations, the crime of mere *abstract* collaboration with such organisations is also punished separately in article 576 PC.

contexts without the need for an actual offence or even an attempt to occur.[61] This may actually have acquired the same function as *conspiracy* in several common law systems.[62]

Secondary Participation

Three forms of secondary participation exist: two of them carry the same sentence as in the case of the principal (abetting and necessary cooperation) and one entails a considerable reduction (complicity).

Abetting

Abetting is not defined by the PC because article 28 II (a) PC only states that the following are abettors: '... those who directly abet[63] another or others to execute [the offence]'. The concept of abetting has been developed by the literature and case law, and essentially consists of causing in another, by means of psychological influence, the commission of a crime as a principal.[64]

Abetting has, therefore, an objective side (to cause the commission of the offence by another) and a subjective, intentional side. Causation must be a determining factor of the principal's action, in such a manner that there is no abetting in constellations of an *omnimodo facturus*. The influence can consist of any act of communication that incites another to commit the crime (in such a manner that it is not sufficient, for example, merely to create a situation that facilitates the commission of the act and thereby generates the principal's decision). Abetting must be 'direct', that is, both the event to be committed must be specified (a specific crime, albeit in legal detail) and the other person must be induced to commit it.[65] Despite some insular instances in case law to the contrary, the majority of the literature rejects the concept of 'chain abetting' unless it falls under necessary cooperaton). Both the complete offence as well as an attempt can be abetted. An attempt to abet may lead to punishment as a preparatory act of 'proposition' in accordance with article 17 PC related to offences for which mere preparatory acts are punishable in themselves. One tends to speak about a 'dual intent': intent to abet and intent to see the offence committed; this intent of the abettor 'constitutes the limit of his liability',[66] since he will not be accountable for any excesses of the principal, should the latter commit an offence different from or more serious than the one to which he was incited.

Necessary Cooperation and Complicity

Necessary cooperation (*cooperación necesaria*) and complicity are interdependent concepts, since article 29 PC defines the latter in negative terms. The delineation of both figures – with important

---

61   Manuel Cancio Meliá, 'The Wrongfulness of Crimes of Unlawful Association' (2008) 11 New Criminal Law Review 563.

62   See Cancio Meliá, 'Delitos de organización: criminalidad organizada *común* y delitos de terrorismo' in Julio Díaz-Maroto Villarejo (ed.), *Estudios sobre las reformas del Código penal operadas por las LO 5/2010, de 22 de junio, y 3/2011, de 28 de enero* (Civitas-Thomson 2011) 643.

63   The official translation uses the word 'induce', which is closer to the Spanish 'inducir'.

64   Mir Puig (n 5) 15/51.

65   Incitement aimed at multiple persons is deemed a preparatory act in article 18 PC.

66   Mir Puig (n 5) 15/74.

consequences as regards punishment – is the most important problem in judicial application,[67] and the absence of clarity of the legal provision has led several authors to propose the elimination of the distinction between the two concepts.[68] Essentially, there are two positions: on the one hand, the question is asked whether in the specific case, the cooperation was necessary for production of the result. On the other hand, Gimbernat Ordeig proposes to examine in each case how scarce the assistance provided is.[69] The courts use rather eclectic criteria:[70]

> According to the jurisprudence of this Court, the necessary cooperation provided by article 28 b) PC of 1995 exists, when one cooperates with the direct perpetrator by a contribution without which the crime would not have been committed (theory of *conditio sine qua non*), when one contributes something that is not easy to obtain otherwise (theory of scarce goods), or when the person who cooperates can prevent the commission of the crime by withdrawing his participation (theory of control over the act); complicity occurs when, if the circumstances stated above (characterizing necessary cooperation) do not exist, there is an accidental, non-conditional participation that is secondary in nature. In sum, the view today is that neither the accomplice nor the necessary cooperator have functional control over the act, because the event belongs to the material perpetrator, and as a consequence of withdrawal of his mandate from the inducer, as a consequence of which the relevance of his participation in the specific case is the best theory that can explain its dogmatic differences, notwithstanding the theory of scarce goods also being quite useful, in several circumstances, such as the case at hand. In other words, the accessory participant of either nature never dominates the event, inasmuch as his contribution generally occurs prior to the event's execution.[71]

Differences between Principals and Participants

The Spanish Penal Code has reached the following position as far as the question of differing qualities or aggravating and mitigating circumstances are concerned:

Article 65

1. Aggravating or mitigating circumstances consisting of any cause of a personal nature shall only aggravate or mitigate the accountability of those fulfilling those circumstances.

2. Those that involve the material execution of the act, or the means used to perpetrate it, shall only be used to aggravate or mitigate the accountability of those who have had knowledge thereof at the time of the act, or of their cooperation in the offence.

3. When the abettor or the necessary cooperator do not fulfill the conditions, qualities or personal criteria which are the basis for a finding of guilty, the court may impose a lower degree of punishment than that stated by law for the crime concerned.

---

67 Mir Puig (n 5) 15/77.
68 Cerezo Mir (n 9) 967.
69 Cerezo Mir (n 9) 152.
70 Mir Puig (n 5) 15/78.
71 Supreme Court Judgment 268/2012, of 12 March.

As may be observed, article 65 PC contemplates specific rules on *communicability*, the possibility that the others participate in a circumstance that is present in only one of the participants in the offence, of certain mitigating and aggravating circumstances in cases of joint delinquency.[72] Article 65.1 PC declares impossible the existence or recognition of an aggravating or mitigating circumstance, when that circumstance is of a personal nature and does not occur in the participant. Article 65.2 PC alludes to objective aggravating or mitigating circumstances, connected to the material execution or the means employed for commission of the offence, which can only be applied to those parties who *are aware* of their existence at the time of their intervention in the offence.[73]

Article 65.3 PC contains the most polemic and complex section of the entire rule.[74] It contains a rule of optional mitigation for abettors and necessary cooperators in *special offences*,[75] when none of the intervening parties possesses the conditions, qualities or personal criteria that the applicable offence requires in order to be the principal. It should be recalled that for Spanish law, abettors and necessary cooperators are subject to the same sentence as principals, and that generally in Spain the principle of accessoriness and, consequently, the unity of the criteria for attributing liability, govern with respect to secondary participation.

Hence, in *genuine special offences*, the legislator authorises the reduction of the sentence for abettors and necessary cooperators, because these persons do not have the essential qualities in order to be principals (and, consequently, to be sanctioned as such).

In the scope of *derivative special offences*, abetting or necessary cooperation can be punished by bifurcating the accusation, or maintaining the unity of accusation that pertains to the main principal by virtue of the principle of accessoriness. This latter option comes from an excessively formal understanding of the principle of accessoriness regarding the secondary participation, while the second option appears to safeguard more adequately the punishment of personal violations effectively carried out.

If bifurcation of the accusation of each intervening party in improper special offences is selected, the *extaneous* participant will be accountable for the common offence (theft), while the executer will be liable for the special offence committed (embezzlement), in such a manner that each person can be punished for the crime effectively committed.[76] Furthermore, when the inducer or the necessary cooperator in the event is an *intraneus* subject (a subject qualified to carry out the classified crime), the latter must be liable for the special offence in which he participates, while the non-qualified executer (*extraneus*) must be punished for the applicable common offence. Said

---

72   Mir Puig (n 5) 25/7 considers that the scheme of article 65 only applies with respect to the catalogue of *generic* aggravating and mitigating circumstances (articles 21-23 PC), since with respect to qualifying or privileged circumstances, present in the offence descriptions, the scheme of communicability taken from the classification of the offence in question as described in the Code should apply. Notwithstanding the above, Molina Fernández observes that article 65 is applicable to any mitigating or aggravating circumstance regardless of whether they are generic or are included in the specific offence descriptions which contain them; Molina Fernández (n 13) no 2999.

73   *Inter alia*, Mir Puig (n 5) 25/7.

74   See in this context Enrique Peñaranda Ramos, 'Sobre el alcance del art 65.3 CP. Al mismo tiempo: una contribución a la crítica de la teoría de los delitos de infracción de deber' in *Estudios penales en homenaje a Enrique Gimbernat* (Edisofer 2008). Ricardo Robles Planas, *Garantes y cómplices* (Atelier 2007); and Ricardo Robles and Eduardo Riggi, 'El extraño artículo 65.3 del Código penal' (2008) 4 Revista InDret.

75   See in such respect the brief explanation of special criminal offences (n 29) and related text.

76   The pertinence of such bifurcation is so upheld, for example, by Molina Fernández (n 13) no 3001.

solution is in perfect harmony with the approach contained in article 65.1 PC on the subject of communicability of circumstances in cases of joint delinquency.[77]

Notwithstanding the above, if it is chosen to maintain the unity of accusation in these cases, as case law chooses to do,[78] the non-qualified participant (*extraneus*) should be punished for the crime executed by the qualified subject (*intraneus*), which is often criticised as being disproportionate, in light of the fact that the *extraneus* participant does not have the special characteristics required by the classification of the offence. For this reason, prior to the 2003 reform,[79] case law operated through the analogical mitigating circumstance and, at present, the application of article 65.3 PC carries with it the *possibility* of reducing the sentence by one degree in the case of these participants.

Another one of the problems posed by the wording of article 65.3 PC is whether accomplices in special offences should have their sentence lowered, beyond the lower degree sentence to which they are already entitled pursuant to article 63 PC – a matter not yet resolved via case law.

Withdrawal from Participation

In cases of multiple participants in a criminal offence, the effective abandonment of one of the subjects not only carries with it the abandonment of that subject's personal intervention, but rather a '*serious, firm*' attempt to prevent the completion of the offence, as prescribed by article 16.3 PC. It is not necessary that the subject succeeds in preventing the commission of the offence but rather his attempt to do so is sufficient:

Article 16

1. An attempted offence takes place when a person begins to perpetrate an offence by direct action, perpetrating all or part of the acts that objectively should produce the intended result, and notwithstanding this, such is not attained due to causes beyond the control of the principal.

2. Whoever voluntarily avoids the offence being consummated, either by going no further with its commission when already commenced, or by preventing the result from taking place, shall be exempt from criminal accountability, without prejudice to the accountability he may have incurred for the acts perpetrated, should these already have constituted another felony or misdemeanor.

3. When various subjects intervene in an act, the one or those who desist from execution thereof once already commenced, and who prevent or attempt to prevent consummation, in a serious, firm manner, shall be exempt from criminal accountability, without prejudice to accountability they may have incurred for the acts perpetrated, should these already have constituted another felony or misdemeanor.

77　Hence, for example, Robles Planas (n 74) 117; Molina Fernández (n 13) no 3001.

78　See, for example, Supreme Court Judgment of 26 January 1994; Supreme Court Judgments 274/1996, of 20 May; 1493/1999, of 21 December; and 20/2002, of 28 March.

79　See the argument in the Supreme Court Judgment 1493/1999, of 21 December, establishing in such regard that 'the absence of violation of the special duty of principal entails, as a general rule, a lesser content of the illegality of the participant, but does not eliminate his cooperation in the violation of the duty of the principal in the damage of the legal asset', and then goes on to lower the participant's sentence, applying an analogical mitigating circumstance.

In comparison to the withdrawal of a sole principal, something more than the mere abandonment of the execution is necessary, although it is not required that he be successful in the attempt to neutralise what he put into play together with the other participants, but rather that he only show an unequivocal intent, manifested in his acts, to prevent the carrying out of his contribution.

Art. 31 bis PC: Corporate Liability – Basic Rules

In Spain, the addition of criminal liability for legal entities was introduced through the reform of the PC via Organic Law 5/2010, of June 22. Specifically, article 31 bis PC provides the following regulation:

> "1. In the cases provided by this Code, legal entities shall be held criminally accountable for the felonies committed in their name or on their behalf, and to their benefit, by their legal representatives and *de facto* or *de jure* administrators.
>
> In the same cases, legal entities shall also be criminally accountable for the felonies committed when perpetrating the corporate activities and on account and to the advantage thereof, who, these being committed by the natural persons mentioned in the preceding Section, were able to perpetrate the acts as due control was not exercised over them in view of the specific circumstances of the case.
>
> 2. The criminal accountability of legal entities shall be applicable whenever there is record of a felony being committed that must have been committed by the person who holds office or perpetrates the duties referred to in the preceding Section, even when the specific natural person responsible has not been individually identified, or it has not been possible to prosecute that person. When fines are handed down to both as a consequence of these acts, the courts shall modulate the respective amounts, so that the resulting sum is not disproportionate in relation to the seriousness of such acts.
>
> 3. Occurrence, in the persons who have materially perpetrated the acts or those who have made these possible due to not having exercised due control, of circumstances that affect the culpability of the accused or aggravate his responsibility, or the fact that those persons have died or have escaped the action of justice, shall not exclude or modify the criminal accountability of legal persons, without prejudice to what is set forth in the following Section.
>
> 4. Circumstances that mitigate criminal accountability of legal persons may only be deemed to concur when, after the offence is committed, they have carried out the following activities through their legal representatives:
>
>> a. Having proceeded, prior to having knowledge of judicial proceedings being brought against them, to confess the offences committed by them to the principalities;
>> b. Having collaborated in investigation of the events, providing evidence, at any moment of the proceedings, that is new and decisive to clarify the criminal liabilities arising from the events;
>> c. Having proceeded at any time during the proceedings, and prior to the trial itself, to repair or decrease the damage caused by the offence;

d. Having established, prior to the trial itself, measures that are effective to prevent and discover criminal offences that might be committed in the future using the means or under the coverage of the legal entity.

5. The provisions related to criminal accountability of legal persons shall not be applicable to the State, to the territorial and institutional Public Administrations, to the Regulatory Bodies, the Public Agencies and Corporate Entities, to political parties and Trade Unions, to organizations under Public International Law, or to others that exercise public powers of sovereignty, administration, or in the case of State Mercantile companies that implement public policies or provide services of general economic interest.

   In these cases, the courts may issue a declaration of criminal liability in the event that they perceive that it entails a legal form created by its promoters, founders, directors or representatives for the purpose of evading potential criminal liability".

In general, the newly proposed model attempts to prevent organisational defects in companies,[80] which favour the commission of certain offences for their own benefit.[81] The offence committed, attributable to the company, may have been committed either by the director or by a representative of the company, or by an employee. In both cases, it must entail offences committed to take advantage of the company, committed for or on its behalf, and which, to a certain extent, emanate from a lack of order in the entity's organisation.

Sentences provided by Spanish law are: fines, suspension of activities, closing down of premises, prohibition of certain activities, administrative disqualification, judicial receivership and dissolution of the legal entity.

---

80   For an overview of the model of criminal liability of legal entities, see Jacobo Dopico Gómez-Aller, *Memento Penal* (Francis Lefebvre 2010) nos 3150-235; Carlos Gómez-Jara Díez, 'La responsabilidad penal de las personas jurídicas en la reforma del Código Penal' (2010) 14962 La Ley.

81   NB: The PC provides for a *closed* catalogue of criminal offences (*numerus clausus*) for which the legislator has contemplated potential corporate liability.

Chapter 23

South Africa

Gerhard Kemp

General Principles: Types of Participation and General Basis
of Attributing Criminal Liability for Acts of Others

In South African criminal law a basic distinction is drawn between participation before the completion of the crime and participation after the completion of the crime. The former category consists of the two types of participants, namely perpetrators and accomplices. The latter refers to accessories after the fact.

In older South African cases (and certainly before 1980) terms such as *actual perpetrator* or *principal offender* were sometimes used by the courts. The courts also used the collective term *socius criminis* ('partner in crime') to refer to any participant in criminal conduct. It is pointed out below that this term is no longer appropriate in light of developments in South African criminal law theory and practice.[1]

Modern South African criminal law theory is the result of many influences, notably Roman-Dutch law, English law, German legal doctrine (to a lesser extent) and, of course, post-1994 constitutional jurisprudence.[2] One of the first pronouncements on the basis of attributing criminal liability for the acts of others can be found in the old case of *R v Peerkhan and Lalloo*.[3] Chief Justice Innes declared as follows:

> In the case of common law offences any person who knowingly aids and assists in the perpetration of a crime is punishable as if he had committed it. The English law calls such an one a principal in the second degree; and there is much curious learning as to when a man is a principal in the second, and when in the first degree. Our law knows no distinction between principals in the first and second degrees, or between principals in the second degree and accessories. It calls a person who aids, abets, counsels or assists in a crime a *socius criminis* – an accomplice or partner in the crime. And being so, he is under Roman-Dutch law as guilty, and liable to as much punishment, as if he had been the actual perpetrator of the deed.[4]

The above statement by Chief Justice Innes was criticised for its lack of appreciation for the more nuanced historical roots of the legal basis of criminal liability based on participation in crime. It

---

1 For an overview, see Gerhard Kemp (ed.) and others, *Criminal Law in South Africa* (Oxford University Press 2012) ch 24; Jonathan Burchell, *South African Criminal Law and Procedure* (Vol I, 4th edn, Juta 2011) ch 34; CR Snyman, *Strafreg* (6th edn, LexisNexis 2012) ch 7.

2 In 1994 South Africa became fully democratic after centuries of colonialism and apartheid. The post-apartheid democratic order is based on the rule of law and a supreme Constitution with an enforceable Bill of Rights. All common law and statutory law must be in conformity with the rights and values provided for and protected in the Constitution.

3 1906 TS 798.

4 Ibid. 802.

was pointed out that, although Roman-Dutch law did not recognise the same categories as were recognised in English law, it was not the position that all participants in crime were treated and punished the same under Roman-Dutch law. Indeed, the position in Roman-Dutch law was too vague and inconsistent as to state it as a general principle.[5]

In 1980 the Appellate Division of the High Court (now the Supreme Court of Appeal) delivered a much needed judgment that helped to clarify the doctrinal position in South African criminal law regarding participants in crime. In *State v Williams*,[6] Judge Joubert made the following distinction:

> An accomplice's liability is accessory in nature so that there can be no question of an accomplice without a perpetrator or co-perpetrator who commits the crime. A perpetrator complies with all the requirements of the definition of the relevant crime. Where co-perpetrators commit the crime in concert, each co-perpetrator complies with the requirements of the definition of the relevant crime. On the other hand, an accomplice is not a perpetrator or co-perpetrator, since he lacks the *actus reus* of the perpetrator. An accomplice associates himself wittingly with the commission of the crime by the perpetrator or co-perpetrator in that he knowingly affords the perpetrator or co-perpetrator the opportunity, the means or the information which furthers the commission of the crime .... [A]ccording to general principles there must be a causal connection between the accomplice's assistance and the commission of the crime by the perpetrator or co-perpetrator .... He is ... liable as an accomplice to murder on the ground of his own act, either a positive act or an omission, to further the commission of the murder, and his own fault, viz the intent that the victim must be killed, coupled with the act (*actus reus*) of the perpetrator or co-perpetrator to kill the victim unlawfully.[7]

The uncertain and rather murky Roman-Dutch positions on criminal liability for acts of others, as well as the unsatisfactory English law concept of *socius criminis*, were to a large extent put to rest by the Appellate Division's judgment in *Williams*. Thus, after the judgment in *Williams*, the three main categories[8] of participants in South African criminal law are:

- perpetrators (and co-perpetrators)
- accomplices
- accessories after the fact

Although the judgment in *Williams* brought doctrinal and terminological clarity to a large extent, some criticism was levelled against the court's methodology. South African commentators generally agree that, in order to determine liability under one of the three main categories of participation, it is essential first to determine whether the participant is a perpetrator. If an accused participant is not a perpetrator, the possibility of accomplice liability is triggered.[9] Burchell identifies three separate situations where an accused may be liable as a perpetrator:

---

5   For criticism of the judgment in *Peerkhan and Lalloo*, see JC de Wet and HC Swanepoel, *Strafreg* (4th edn by JC de Wet, Butterworth 1985) 189-90.

6   1980 (1) SA 60 (A).

7   Ibid. 63 (in the original Afrikaans). For the English translation, see Burchell (n 1) 515.

8   Kemp (n 1) 234; Snyman (n 1) 268-69.

9   Burchell (n 1) 489.

1. Where he or she personally satisfies the definitional elements of the crime and is, therefore, a perpetrator in his or her own right (liability is in no way accessory or dependent on the conduct of another person), or

2. Where he or she, although possessing the requisite capacity and the fault element (*mens rea*) for the crime in question, does not personally comply with all of the elements of the unlawful conduct in question, and the conduct of the perpetrator is 'attributed' or 'imputed' to him or her, by virtue of his or her prior agreement or active association in a common purpose to commit the crime in question, or

3. Where a person procures another person, who may be an innocent or unwilling agent, to commit a crime.[10]

The Appellate Division in *Williams* did not follow the method of first determining whether an accused is a perpetrator and only if the answer is negative, move on to determine whether the accused is perhaps an accomplice. As a result one of the accused persons was (wrongly) convicted as an accomplice (and not as a co-perpetrator). Indeed, this particular accused person shared (with two others) a common purpose to kill the deceased. The court *should* have convicted this accused as a co-perpetrator – especially given the exposition (per Judge Joubert) of the relevant criminal law theory, as quoted above.[11]

Principals by Proxy: Use of Innocent Agents

It was noted above that one of the possible scenarios where liability as a perpetrator will be appropriate is where the accused procured another person (the innocent agent) to commit a crime. A typical situation may be where the accused employed a young child, or an animal, or a mentally impaired person, to commit the crime. In this context it is important to note that under South African law children under the age of ten do not have criminal capacity.[12] Thus, the question is if, for instance, a man asks his nine-year-old son to steal something from a shop, on what legal basis the man could be held criminally liable.

The Roman-Dutch authorities (which informed the development of the South African common law) were not always very clear on this subject, as mentioned above. However, some, like the Dutch author Johannes Voet, were better in approaching the matter from a principled and dogmatically sound basis. Voet rejected the notion that a person could be held criminally liable *ex mandato*. Where a man asked another man to commit a crime, and the latter adhered to the request, both would be liable as perpetrators. If, however, the second man acted innocently (lacking the necessary *mens rea*, for instance) then only the first man (the principal) would be

10 Ibid. 487.

11 For academic commentary on the implications of the judgment in *Williams*, see Burchell (n 1) 518; F van Oosten, 'Discussion of *Claassen* 1979 (4) SA 460 (ZRA); *Penton* 1979 (2) PH H 175 (A); *Williams* 1980 (1) SA 60 (A)' [1980] De Jure 156-63; JMT Labuschagne, 'Discussion of *Williams* 1980 (1) SA 60 (A)' [1980] De Jure 163-64; CR Snyman, 'Discussion of *Williams*' [1980] Tydskrif vir die Suid-Afrikaanse Reg/ Journal of South African Law 188-91; JCW van Rooyen, 'Discussion of *Williams* 1980 (1) SA 60 (A)' [1983] De Jure 198-200.

12 Child Justice Act 75 of 2008, s 7(1); discussion in Kemp (n 1) 156-57.

criminally liable as perpetrator.[13] South African courts held in a number of cases that the conduct of the innocent agent (for instance the young child) can indeed be attributed to the principal. In some cases reference was made to the rule *qui facit per alium facit per se* ('he who does an act through another, does it himself').[14] It is not necessary to rely on the *qui facit* principle if the principal offender personally satisfies the definitional elements of the crime. He would then simply be a co-perpetrator (or the sole perpetrator, if the agent is innocent).[15]

Perpetrator behind the Perpetrator: Liability of Masterminds/'Hintermen' for Acts of Otherwise Criminally Liable Agents

In *State v Nkosiyana* it was held that an inciter is 'one who reaches and seeks to influence the mind of another to the commission of a crime'.[16] In terms of legal theory and principle, it is correct to say that the inciter is guilty of *incitement* only up to the point where the incitee commits the crime thus incited. The incitee (the criminally liable agent) is then a perpetrator in his own right. When the incited crime is indeed committed, the inciter becomes either a *perpetrator* or an *accomplice* to the crime in question.[17]

South African statutory law is less nuanced than the above mentioned theoretical position would suggest. Section 18(2)(b) of the Riotous Assemblies Act 17 of 1956 provides as follows:

> [a]ny person who ... incites, instigates, commands, or procures any other person to commit any offence, whether at common law or against a statute or statutory regulation, shall be guilty of an offence and liable on conviction to the punishment to which a person convicted of actually committing that offence would be liable.

If the *agent* is thus criminally liable (in other words the crime as envisaged or instigated by the inciter indeed materialised) the Riotous Assemblies Act should, in principle, not apply.[18] The 'mastermind' is then more than an inciter; he becomes perpetrator (or accomplice) – depending on the facts and his contribution.[19]

Joint Principals

The clear theoretical distinction between perpetrators and accomplices does not imply that in cases where there are multiple participants, only *one* can be the principal perpetrator, and the others have

13   Voet 17 1 6, as discussed in De Wet (n 5) 181-82.
14   *State v Cupido* 1975 (1) SA 537; *State v Jadwat Bros (Pty) Ltd* 1977 (4) SA 815 (D). See also discussion in Burchell (n 1) 487-88.
15   Burchell (n 1) 488.
16   *State v Nkosiyana* 1966 (4) SA 655 (A) at 658 (Holmes JA).
17   Burchell (n 1) 541; Snyman (n 1) 309.
18   *Rex v Milne and Erleigh* (7) 1951 (1) SA 791 (A).
19   *State v Khoza* 1973 (4) SA 23 (O); *State v Smith* 1984 (1) SA 583 (A).

to be (by implication) lesser perpetrators or accomplices.[20] A survey of case law suggests that there can indeed be *joint principals* if their conduct and state of mind satisfy the elements of the crime.[21]

Secondary Participation

After the judgment in *State v Williams* (as was noted above), the theoretical boundary between perpetrator liability and accomplice liability was firmly established. Judge of Appeal Joubert described the essential contribution of an accomplice as 'furthering' or 'assisting' the commission of the crime.[22] Of course, conduct constituting 'furthering' or 'assisting' are open ended and will depend on what is needed in terms of the primary criminal conduct. From Judge Joubert's seemingly simple and straightforward characterisation of conduct constituting accomplice liability a number of dogmatic questions flow. These are briefly noted below.

Causality is the key element in consequence crimes. On a murder charge, the prosecution must show that the accused *intentionally and unlawfully caused the death of another human*. It is clear that if someone satisfies these elements, then he or she will be the perpetrator. If more than one person intentionally and unlawfully caused the death of another human being, those individuals can be held criminally liable as co-perpetrators. A group of individuals can also be held liable as perpetrators in terms of the common purpose doctrine, which is considered below. The question is whether an individual can 'further' or 'assist' in the commission of a consequence crime, thus causing the result (for instance, death, in the case of murder) and not be held liable as perpetrator but as an accomplice?

A number of South African authors pointed out that 'further' (as meant by Judge Joubert in *State v Williams*) in the context of consequence crimes can only mean 'causally further'.[23] These authors found that the Appellate Division in *State v Williams* wrongly convicted an accused as an 'accessory to murder' – he was simply a co-perpetrator since he (also) *caused* the death of the deceased. Although he was not the primary perpetrator, his conduct (of assisting the primary perpetrator) facilitated the murder. Thus, in terms of this view, an individual who, by his conduct, (causally) furthers a certain result should, in the case of consequence crimes, simply be regarded as a co-perpetrator.

There is also a second theoretical position: Burchell noted that the above point of view in terms of which there can be no accomplice liability for consequence crimes, does not take into account the distinction between *factual causation*[24] and *legal causation*. The latter involves the question of policy limits on the extent of liability.[25] In terms of South African jurisprudence, it seems to be clear that for consequence crimes, both factual and legal causation are required. Burchell confirms that both factual and legal causation are required for perpetrator liability (as is indeed the case in terms of South African jurisprudence), but only factual causation in the sense of 'furthering'

---

20   Snyman (n 1) 271; De Wet (n 5) 191.

21   *Rex v Mhlongo* 1948 (1) SA 1109 (T); *State v Maxaba* 1981 (1) SA 1148 (A); *State v Maelangwe* 1999 (1) SACR 133 (NC); *State v Kimberley* 2004 (2) SACR 38 (EC); *State v Buda* 2004 (1) SACR 9 (T).

22   *Williams* (n 6) [63] (Joubert JA).

23   De Wet and Swanepoel (n 5) 187, 201; RC Whiting, 'Principals and Accessories in Crime' (1980) 97 South African Law Journal 199; Snyman (n 1) 287-89.

24   Usually expressed as the *conditio sine qua non* test. 'An act is a cause of a consequence if the act cannot be notionally eliminated from the sequence of events, without the consequence also disappearing' (Burchell (n 1) 96).

25   Ibid. 97-98.

or 'assisting' in the commission of the crime for *accomplice* liability. The result would be a meaningful differentiation between perpetrator liability and accomplice liability in consequence crimes. Thus, the accomplice, according to Burchell's view, commits a crime in his or her own right. The determination of liability (either as perpetrator or accomplice) will be informed by the degree of participation before the completion of the crime.[26]

Although Burchell's view is theoretically appealing, the reality is that 'degrees of participation' in consequence crimes are often very difficult to determine. From a practical point of view, participants in consequence crimes are perhaps better classified as either perpetrators or co-perpetrators (based on factual and legal causation or common purpose).

For other crimes the theoretical distinction between an accomplice and a perpetrator not only makes dogmatic sense, but also seems to be clear and practical.

Specific Issue: Joint Criminal Enterprise

The term 'joint criminal enterprise' is not generally used in South African criminal law literature or case law. However the Constitutional Court used the term when deciding on the constitutionality of the *doctrine of common purpose*. The court (per Judge Moseneke) reasoned that the common purpose doctrine in South African criminal law is not unconstitutional since it is 'rationally connected to the legitimate objective of limiting and controlling joint criminal enterprise'.[27] Some authors also define the doctrine of common purpose with reference to joint criminal enterprise. Burchell defines it as follows:

> Where two or more people agree to commit a crime or actively associate in a joint unlawful enterprise, each will be responsible for specific criminal conduct committed by one of their number which falls within their common design. Liability arises from their 'common purpose' to commit the crime.[28]

Thus, for purposes of this discussion, the terms 'common purpose' or 'doctrine of common purpose' are employed. It should at any rate be distinguished from the doctrine of 'joint criminal enterprise' under *international criminal law*.[29] Joint criminal enterprise (or JCE) under international criminal law can be described with reference to three forms or manifestations:[30]

- The basic form 'applies whenever several persons agree to commit a crime and execute it, with corresponding intent according to their common design'. This basic form of JCE is comparable to the doctrine of common purpose under South African law, as defined above.
- The second form of JCE stems from the so-called 'concentration camp cases' and has a

---

26   Ibid. 519.

27   *State v Thebus* 2003 (2) SACR 319 (CC) [18] (Moseneke J).

28   Burchell (n 1) 489.

29   In modern international criminal law first applied in *Prosecutor v Tadić*, ICTY (Appeals Chamber) 15 Jul 1999 [194]. See also Elies van Sliedregt, 'Joint Criminal Enterprise as a Pathway to Convicting Individuals for Genocide' (2007) 5 Journal of International Criminal Justice 184; Verena Haan, 'The Development of the Concept of Joint Criminal Enterprise at the International Criminal Tribunal for the Former Yugoslavia' (2005) 5 International Criminal Law Review 167; Gerhard Werle, *Principles of International Criminal Law* (2nd edn, TMC Asser Press 2009) 174-75.

30   Werle (n 29) 174-75; Kemp (n 1) 243-44.

clear link with the history and development of international criminal law. The focus in this category is on structures or systems aimed at the ill-treatment of people, often resulting in or specifically aimed at the commission of crimes under international law, such as crimes against humanity. The perpetrators share and act with the intent to further the system of mistreatment. There is not a specific form of the common purpose doctrine in South Africa that would be comparable to this form of JCE.

- The third form of JCE is where participants in a JCE commit 'excesses that go beyond the framework of the common plan'.[31] International jurisprudence seems to suggest that participants in a JCE can be held responsible even for the excesses that went beyond the (original) plan or framework of the common plan. This is, however, qualified in that the consequences of the acts were natural and foreseeable, and the participants willingly took the risk of their occurrence.[32] Extended forms of common purpose are controversial, and this aspect is explored below with reference to the development of the common purpose doctrine in South Africa, the controversial application of 'expanded forms' of the doctrine during the apartheid years, and jurisprudential limitations on the application of the common purpose doctrine in modern South African criminal law.

The common purpose doctrine, as applied in South Africa, means that the state does not have to prove that each participant contributed towards causing the prohibited consequence: the conduct of each participant is attributed to the others who share in the common purpose. During the apartheid years and the (often violent) struggle against the apartheid-regime, the state often relied on the common purpose doctrine in order to prosecute large groups of people who had participated in (violent) public demonstrations and acts of protest which sometimes resulted in the death of individuals.[33]

One of the most notorious cases was that of *State v Safatsa*[34] – the case of the so-called Sharpeville Six. The salient facts were as follows: the deputy mayor of a black township near Johannesburg was murdered by a group of people. The group (about a hundred persons) first attacked the deputy mayor's house. They threw stones and petrol bombs at the house and the house was set alight. When the deputy mayor fled his house he was caught by members of the crowd of people. Some members of the group started to throw stones at the deputy mayor while others bashed him on the head with stones. While he was unconscious he was put on top of his car, doused in petrol, and then

---

31   Werle (n 29) 175.

32   Ibid. 175.

33   For a vivid and gripping narrative history of one of the most notorious cases – that of the so-called Upington 25 – see Andrea Durbach, *Upington* (David Philip 1999). A crowd of people (including young persons) were taking part in a meeting to express their opposition and dissatisfaction with members of the discredited local town council (seen as nothing more than an extension of the apartheid structures). In this case a local policeman (employed by the said town council) was murdered by a group of people. The trial court convicted 25 persons for murder. The doctrine of common purpose informed the judge's findings. Rather controversially, and implicit in the trial court's reasoning on the common purpose, 'was the belief that the crowd in front [of the deceased's] house was essentially made up of the same people who chased and assaulted him at the post office houses some distance away. The findings that there existed a common purpose to kill [the deceased] and that all the accused were party to this common purpose from its inception were the basis upon which the court found 25 of the 26 accused guilty of murder' (Durbach 36). This imputation of intent to a large group of people (who were not part of a static crowd or identifiable gang) had serious consequences: at that stage in South African legal history the death sentence was still mandatory for murder convictions.

34   *State v Safatsa and others* 1988 (1) SA 868 (A).

set alight. The deputy mayor burned to death. Importantly, a post mortem indicated that he would have died as a result of the wounds to his head (caused by the stoning), even if he was not burned. The police subsequently identified eight members of the group of people and they were arrested and tried for murder. The trial court convicted six of the eight of murder and they were sentenced to death.[35] They appealed against the convictions and sentences.

One of the grounds of appeal was that the State failed to prove a *causal connection* between the conduct of each individual accused and the death of the deputy mayor. The Appellate Division (now the Supreme Court of Appeal) rejected the legal grounds upon which the appeal was built. The Appellate Division held that the six appellants shared a common purpose to kill the deputy mayor. This common purpose was shared with the crowd as a whole. Furthermore, the appellants – by their conduct – actively associated themselves with achieving the common purpose. Finally, the appellants all had the necessary intention to commit murder. Of course, the missing element was that of causation. But with reference to that element the Appellate Division rejected the argument that the State had to prove a causal connection between the conduct of each participant and the death of the murder victim. Indeed, where the State relies on the doctrine of common purpose, the element of causation does not play the same role as in ordinary matters where the criminal liability of a perpetrator or co-perpetrators needs to be determined.

In post-apartheid South Africa, the constitutionality of the doctrine of common purpose was put before the Constitutional Court in the case of *State v Thebus*.[36] The main arguments against the constitutionality of the common purpose doctrine were as follows:

• By failing to distinguish between individual participants, the doctrine de-individualised and de-humanised these persons, thus infringing on their right to human dignity.
• The doctrine of common purpose bases criminal liability on the most tenuous link with individual conduct, thus violating the right not to be deprived of freedom in an arbitrary way.
• The doctrine of common purpose reduces the requirements of proof for certain elements of a crime to suit the convenience of the state, thus violating the presumption of innocence and a fair criminal process.[37]

The Constitutional Court was, however, not persuaded by the above arguments and found that the doctrine of common purpose as such is not unconstitutional. The court reasoned as follows:

> Common purpose does not amount to an arbitrary deprivation of freedom. The doctrine is rationally connected to the legitimate objective of limiting and controlling joint criminal enterprise. It serves vital purposes in our criminal justice system. Absent the rule of common purpose, all but actual perpetrators of a crime and their accomplices will be beyond the reach of our criminal justice system, despite their unlawful and intentional participation in the commission of the crime. Such an outcome would not accord with the considerable societal distaste for crimes by common design. Group, organised or collaborative misdeeds strike more harshly at the fabric of society and the rights of victims than crimes perpetrated by individuals. Effective prosecution of crime is a legitimate, 'pressing social need'. The need for 'a strong deterrent to violent crime' is well acknowledged

---

35   The death penalty was at the time still imposed for crimes like murder and rape. The death penalty was declared unconstitutional and abolished after the introduction of democracy under a new Constitution with a justiciable Bill of Rights; see *State v Makwanyane* 1995 (3) SA 391 (CC).

36   *State v Thebus* 2003 (2) SACR 319 (CC).

37   Kemp (n 1) 242.

because 'widespread violent crime is deeply destructive of the fabric of our society'. There is a real and pressing social concern about the high levels of crime. In practice, joint criminal conduct often poses peculiar difficulties of proof of the result of the conduct of each accused, a problem which hardly arises in the case of an individual accused person. Thus there is no objection to this norm of culpability even though it bypasses the requirement of causation.[38]

The continued existence and application of the common purpose doctrine in South African criminal law was to a large extent justified by the Constitutional Court on policy and pragmatic grounds, as is clear from the judgment in *State v Thebus*.[39] However, it remains a problematic doctrine from a theoretical point of view. Since it is mostly[40] (although not exclusively[41]) applied in murder cases, the implications for an individual accused can be serious. In this regard it is also necessary to point out that South African law does not distinguish between different degrees of murder – murder is murder.[42]

In terms of sentencing,[43] courts do not always draw sufficient distinction between the individual participants on the basis of their actual roles in and contribution towards the commission of the crime in question.[44]

In addition to the observations above, one can also note that because of the way intent in the form of *dolus eventualis* is normally established (by way of inferential reasoning) it can, in some cases, amount to the (now theoretically defunct) '*versari in re illicita* rule in disguise'.[45] The notion that an individual could be held liable for the *unintended consequences* of an illegal activity was rejected in South Africa five decades ago.[46] But it seems that a robust application of the common purpose doctrine can bring the *versari* rule back to life in certain contexts – which is obviously not in line with the development and application of modern criminal law theory in South Africa.

Effect of Errors and Transferred Malice/Aberratio ictus Scenarios

Aberratio ictus ('going astray of the blow') scenarios do not involve mistakes. The South African Appellate Division accepted that 'where a person commits an act intending to murder one person

---

38 *Thebus* (n 36) [40].

39 For criticism of the rather 'weak' policy and pragmatic reasons advanced by the Constitutional Court, see Snyman (n 1) 281.

40 Snyman (n 1) 276.

41 For the application of the common purpose doctrine in cases other than murder, see *State v Maelangwe* 1999 (10 SACR 133 (NC) (housebreaking with intent to commit a crime); *R v Wilkens* 1941 TPD 276 and *State v Mashotonga* 1962 (2) SA 321 (R) (public violence); *State v Peraic* 1965 (2) PH H201 (A) and *State v Khambule* 2001 (1) SACR 501 (SCA) (robbery); *State v A* 1993 (1) SACR 600 (A) and *State v Mitchell* 1992 (1) SACR 17 (A) (assault); *State v Mongalo* 1978 (1) SA 414 (O) and *State v Windvogel* 1998 (1) SACR 125 (C) (theft); *State v Del Ré* 1990 (1) SACR 392 (W) (fraud); *State v Banda* 1990 (3) SA 466 (B) (treason); *State v Mambo* 2006 (2) SACR 563 (SCA) (escape from custody).

42 Kemp (n 1) 240.

43 See also discussion on 'Sentencing Regime for Participants' below.

44 Jonathan Burchell, *Principles of Criminal law* (3rd edn, Juta 2005) 575.

45 Kemp (n 1) para 240. See also comments below (on *aberratio ictus* rule, the doctrine of *versari in re illicita*, and the modern subjective approach to *mens rea*).

46 *State v Van der Mescht* 1962 (1) SA 521 (A).

and kills another he is guilty of murdering that other person'.[47] However, later cases suggest that the *aberratio ictus* rule has no place in South African criminal law theory.

It is interesting to note that those judgments that were critical of the continued application of the *aberratio ictus* rule also linked their criticism to the movement away from the doctrine *versari in re illicita* (liability for the unintended consequences of unlawful conduct). With the emphasis on *mens rea* as an essential element of criminal liability, the Appellate Division rejected the notion that intent can be transferred, thus abolishing the *versari* doctrine.[48] The notion of transferred intent (or 'transferred malice') forms the basis of the *aberratio ictus* rule. But this notion is in conflict with a proper understanding of *dolus*, including *dolus eventualis*. Indeed, Snyman correctly argues that the 'transferred malice' approach does not take into account the (very real) possibility that an accused would abandon his action if he knew that someone other than his intended target was going to be harmed.[49]

The policy rationale often put forward as justification for the retention of the *aberratio ictus* rule, namely that in true *aberratio ictus* scenarios (the accused wanted to kill A but hit Z) the accused would go free if it was not for the *aberratio ictus* rule, falls away because the accused can still be held liable for (a) attempt (if he did not foresee the eventual turn of events but nevertheless wanted to achieve some specific outcome that did not in reality materialise), or, if he had the necessary intent in the form of at least *dolus eventualis*, for the original intended crime itself. In *State v Mtshiza*[50] a minority opinion was delivered that eventually resulted in an acceptance by the Appellate Division of the subjective approach to *mens rea* and the rejection of the *aberratio ictus* rule.[51] In an elegant exposition of the approach in modern South African criminal law doctrine, Judge of Appeal Holmes stated:

> [C]riminal liability is not regarded as attaching to an act or a consequence unless it was attended by *mens rea* ... Accordingly, if A assaults B and in consequence B dies, A is not criminally responsible for his death unless – (a) he foresaw the possibility of resultant death, yet persisted in his deed, reckless whether death ensured or not; or (b) he ought to have foreseen the reasonable possibility of resultant death. In (a) the *mens rea* is the type of intent known as *dolus eventualis*, and the crime is murder; in (b) the *mens rea* is *culpa*, and the crime is culpable homicide.[52]

It is clear that there is no place in modern South African criminal law theory for the *aberratio ictus* rule. A proper application of the principles relating to *dolus* and *culpa*, as well as liability based on attempt, makes this rule obsolete and at odds with criminal law doctrine.

---

47   *R v Koza* 1949 (4) SA 555 (A) [557] (Centlivres JA).
48   *State v Bernardus* 1965 (3) SA 287 (A).
49   Snyman (n 1) 206.
50   *State v Mtshiza* 1970 (3) SA 747 (A).
51   *State v Mavhungu* 1981 (1) SA 56 (A). In a number of high court judgments the *aberratio ictus* rule was rejected on the basis that *mens rea* for the crime charged is required (and 'transferred malice' or 'transferred intent' cannot be substitutes for the element of *mens rea* in subjective form). See *State v Tissen* 1979 (4) SA 293 (T); *State v Raisa* 1979 (4) SA 541 (O); *State v Mkansi* 2004 (1) SACR 281 (T).
52   *Mtshiza* [752A-C] (Holmes JA).

Withdrawal from Participation

Generally speaking, and as an evidential matter, it was held that the 'more advanced an accused person's participation in the commission of the crime, the more pertinent and pronounced his conduct will have to be to convince a court, after the event, that he genuinely meant to dissociate himself from it at the time'.[53] In *State v Musingadi*, Acting Judge of Appeal Comrie noted that there is not an exhaustive list of factors that would be relevant to the question whether a participant has effectively withdrawn from participation. The judge stated:

> [M]uch will depend on the circumstances: On the manner and degree of the accused's participation; on how far the commission of the crime has proceeded; on the manner and timing of disengagement; and, in some instances, on what steps the accused took or could have taken to prevent the commission or completion of the crime.[54]

Indeed, it seems that an accused who participated in the commission of a crime can change his or her mind and withdraw from the commission of the crime, but still be held criminally liable if the commission of the crime was so far advanced that the accused's withdrawal was no longer enough; something positive (a preventative act) was required.[55] The basis for criminal liability here is arguably based on legal policy (essentially a value judgment taking account of all the facts).[56] It flows from an application of the accused's intention in the form of *dolus eventualis*: he or she has foreseen the possibility that a certain chain of events would be triggered by his or her conduct and participation in the commission of a crime, but carried on regardless. At some point withdrawal will quite literally be too late and then something positive is required to stop or at least change the chain of events.

Corporate Criminal Liability: Basic Rules

As a preliminary point it must be noted that the notion that juristic persons have an existence in law independently from the natural persons or other entities that form their members, is well-established in South African law.[57] The question of corporate criminal liability was a bit more contentious – at least from an academic point of view.

English common law had a major impact on the development of corporate criminal liability in South African law. This form of criminal liability was based on a form of vicarious liability. Indeed, early South African cases recognised this as the basis for holding corporations criminally liable.[58] With the adoption of the Criminal Procedure Act of 1917, and its successors – the Criminal Procedure Act of 1939 and now the current Criminal Procedure Act of 1977 – the criminal liability of corporations is dealt with in terms of statute, not the common law. While the courts (and most

---

53   *State v Nduli and others* 1993 (2) SACR 501 (A) [504F].

54   *State v Musingadi* 2005 (1) SACR 395 (SCA) [35].

55   Ibid. [39].

56   Andrew Paizes and Matthew Chakalson, 'Criminal Law' [1992] Annual Survey of South African Law 491, 511.

57   *Salomon v Salomon & Co Ltd* [1897] AC 22; *Dadoo v Krugersdorp Municipal Council* 1920 AD 530. See also Kemp (n 1) ch 22; Dennis Davis and Farouk Cassim (eds) *Companies and Other Business Structures in South Africa* (2nd edn, Oxford University Press 2010) 23-27.

58   For instance in *R v Dundee Coal Mining Co* 1904 NDP 23.

academic commentators) accepted the notion of corporate criminal liability (whether based on the English common law form of vicarious liability, or in terms of the relevant statutory framework) those commentators of purist inclination objected to the idea that abstract entities like corporations can be held criminally liable.

De Wet, for instance, argued that the emphasis in criminal law is on the personal nature of criminal liability. The author, with reference to Von Savigny's statement that criminal law concerns itself with human conduct, and with reference to the general principles of criminal law, rejected the notion of corporate criminal liability. From a legal-historical perspective, De Wet further objected to the acceptance of corporate criminal liability in South African law, because the important Roman law and Roman-Dutch law sources did not provide authority for the theory that corporate criminal liability was part of South African common law. De Wet at any rate rejected the (old) English common law notion of corporate criminal liability based on vicarious liability as well as the statutory forms of corporate criminal liability later adopted in South Africa as unsound and prone to unintended and even absurd consequences.[59]

It has to be said that some of De Wet's concerns (in terms of procedure) were to some extent addressed in the current Criminal Procedure Act. But of course De Wet's objections were in the first place fundamentally against the notion of corporate criminal liability as such.

Although De Wet was an influential author who has made a considerable contribution to the development of South African criminal law theory,[60] his misgivings about the notion of corporate criminal liability never impacted a great deal (if at all) on case law or, for that matter, the statutory forms of corporate criminal liability.

Corporate criminal liability is currently provided for in the Criminal Procedure Act of 1977. Section 332 of the Act provides for the substantive and procedural matters as follows:

> 332. Prosecution of corporations and members of associations. –
>
> (1) For the purpose of imposing upon a corporate body criminal liability for any offence, whether under any law or at common law –
>> (*a*) any act performed, with or without a particular intent, by or on instructions or with permission, express or implied, given by a director or servant of that corporate body; and
>> (*b*) the omission, with or without a particular intent, of any act which ought to have been but was not performed by or on instructions given by a director or servant of that corporate body, in the exercise of his powers or in the performance of his duties as such director or servant or in furthering or endeavouring to further the interests of that corporate body, shall be deemed to have been performed (and with

---

59   De Wet (n 5) 53-62. For instance, the author refers to some of the unfair procedural consequences of the acceptance of corporate criminal liability. In earlier South African cases, the company was never criminally charged in its own name, and was, of course, represented by a director or employee. The problem was that the director or employee could resign, and then the whole process had to start over again. The obvious solution – to charge the company in its own name – never occurred to the authorities. See for instance *Herold NO v Johannesburg City Council* 1947 (2) SA 1257 (A); *R v Reyrink* 1947 (4) SA 312 (C); *R v Barry* 1950 (1) SA 317 (N).

60   See evaluation by CR Snyman, 'The Tension between Legal Theory and Policy Considerations in the General Principles of Criminal Law' in Jonathan Burchell and Adele Erasmus (eds), *Criminal Justice in a New Society: Essays in Honour of Solly Leeman* (Juta 2003) 2-4.

the same intent, if any) by that corporate body or, as the case may be, to have been an omission (and with the same intent, if any) on the part of that corporate body.

(2) In any prosecution against a corporate body, a director or servant of that corporate body shall be cited, as representative of that corporate body, as the offender, and thereupon the person so cited may, as such representative, be dealt with as if he were the person accused of having committed the offence in question: Provided that –

> (*a*) if the said person pleads guilty, other than by way of admitting guilt under section 57, the plea shall not be valid unless the corporate body authorized him to plead guilty;
>
> (*b*) if at any stage of the proceedings the said person ceases to be a director or servant of that corporate body or absconds or is unable to attend, the court in question may, at the request of the prosecutor, from time to time substitute for the said person any other person who is a director or servant of the said corporate body at the time of the said substitution, and thereupon the proceedings shall continue as if no substitution had taken place;

(*c*) if the said person, as representing the corporate body, is convicted, the court convicting him shall not impose upon him in his representative capacity any punishment, whether direct or as an alternative, other than a fine, even if the relevant law makes no provision for the imposition of a fine in respect of the offence in question, and such fine shall be payable by the corporate body and may be recovered by attachment and sale of property of the corporate body in terms of *section 288*;

> (*d*) the citation of a director or servant of a corporate body as aforesaid, to represent that corporate body in any prosecution instituted against it, shall not exempt that director or servant from prosecution for that offence in terms of subsection (5).

(3) In criminal proceedings against a corporate body, any record which was made or kept by a director, servant or agent of the corporate body within the scope of his activities as such director, servant or agent, or any document which was at any time in the custody or under the control of any such director, servant or agent within the scope of his activities as such director, servant or agent, shall be admissible in evidence against the accused.

(4) For the purposes of subsection (3) any record made or kept by a director, servant or agent of a corporate body or any document which was at any time in his custody or under his control, shall be presumed to have been made or kept by him or to have been in his custody or under his control within the scope of his activities as such director, servant or agent, unless the contrary is proved.

(5) When an offence has been committed, whether by the performance of any act or by the failure to perform any act, for which any corporate body is or was liable to prosecution, any person who was, at the time of the commission of the offence, a director or servant of the corporate body shall be deemed to be guilty of the said offence, unless it is proved that he did not take part in the commission of the offence and that he could not have prevented it, and shall be liable to prosecution therefor, either jointly with the corporate body or apart therefrom, and shall on conviction be personally liable to punishment therefor.

(6) In criminal proceedings against a director or servant of a corporate body in respect of an offence –

        (*a*) any evidence which would be or was admissible against that corporate body in a prosecution for that offence, shall be admissible against the accused;

        (*b*) whether or not such corporate body is or was liable to prosecution for the said offence, any document, memorandum, book or record which was drawn up, entered up or kept in the ordinary course of business of that corporate body or which was at any time in the custody or under the control of any director, servant or agent, of such corporate body, in his capacity as director, servant or agent, shall be *prima facie* proof of its contents and admissible in evidence against the accused, unless he is able to prove that at all material times he had no knowledge of the said document, memorandum, book or record, in so far as its contents are relevant to the offence charged, and was in no way party to the drawing up of such document or memorandum or the making of any relevant entries in such book or record.

(7) When a member of an association of persons, other than a corporate body, has, in carrying on the business or affairs of that association or in furthering or in endeavouring to further its interests, committed an offence, whether by the performance of any act or by the failure to perform any act, any person who was, at the time of the commission of the offence, a member of that association, shall be deemed to be guilty of the said offence, unless it is proved that he did not take part in the commission of the offence and that he could not have prevented it: Provided that if the business or affairs of the association are governed or controlled by a committee or other similar governing body, the provisions of this subsection shall not apply to any person who was not at the time of the commission of the offence a member of that committee or other body.

(8) In any proceedings against a member of an association of persons in respect of an offence mentioned in subsection (7) any record which was made or kept by any member or servant or agent of the association within the scope of his activities as such member, servant or agent, or any document which was at any time in the custody or under the control of any such member, servant or agent within the scope of his activities as such member, servant or agent, shall be admissible in evidence against the accused.

(9) For the purposes of subsection (8) any record made or kept by a member or servant or agent of an association, or any document which was at any time in his custody or under his control, shall be presumed to have been made or kept by him or to have been in his custody or under his control within the scope of his activities as such member or servant or agent, unless the contrary is proved.

(10) In this section the word 'director' in relation to a corporate body means any person who controls or governs that corporate body or who is a member of a body or group of persons which controls or governs that corporate body or, where there is no such body or group, who is a member of that corporate body.

(11) The provisions of this section shall be additional to and not in substitution for any other law which provides for a prosecution against corporate bodies or their directors or servants or against associations of persons or their members.

(12) Where a summons under this Act is to be served on a corporate body, it shall be served on the director or servant referred to *in subsection (2)* and in the manner referred to in *section 54(2).*

Acts of the directors or employees are deemed to be the acts of the corporation. Obviously such acts must be acts relating to the business – not private acts of the director or employee in his or her own capacity. Fault is also attributed to the corporation in this way.[61] In theory, if not always in practice, the effect of section 332 is that corporations can be held criminally liable for almost all offences.[62]

Section 332 corporate criminal liability is not based on vicarious liability. The corporation is *deemed* to have fault; the fault of the director/employee that is attributed to the corporate body.[63] Thus, the corporation is *committing* the crime by fulfilling all the elements necessary for liability. From a practical point of view, and as a matter of principle, it was held that a corporation cannot be convicted when the employee or director on whose conduct the prosecution relied was acquitted. The Supreme Court of Appeal reasoned that the elements of the crime are attributed to the corporation via the director or employee, who are indeed the acting and thinking 'organs' of the corporate body.[64]

It is important to note that section 332(5) (quoted above) was declared unconstitutional and invalid by the Constitutional Court.[65] The effect of section 332(5) was to place a reverse onus on the accused (the director or employee of the corporation) in instances where the corporation was guilty of a crime. The director/employee then had to show that he or she did not take part in the commission of the crime, or was somehow not at fault. Clearly this provision put quite a burden on directors and employees to prove their own innocence and was therefore in violation of the constitutionally protected presumption of innocence. It is obvious from the wording of section 332(7) – concerning unincorporated associations – that the same constitutional problems might arise.[66] However, this section has yet to be challenged in court on constitutional grounds.[67]

While authors like De Wet (discussed above) were opposed to the very notion of corporate criminal liability (mainly, in the case of De Wet, because of legal-historical and dogmatic reasons), more recently commentators have started to question the constitutionality and scope of the liability created via section 332(1). As the venerable Professor Ellison Kahn noted, section 332(1) can very well be described as 'a legal straitjacket from which even a Houdini of the law could not escape'.[68]

---

61   *State v Peer* 1968 (4) SA 460 (N).

62   *State v Joseph Mtshumayeli (Pty) Ltd* 1971 (1) SA 33 (RA); *Ex parte Minister van Justisie: In re S v Suid-Afrikaanse Uitsaaikorporasie* 1992 (4) SA 804 (A); *State v Dersley* 1997 (2) SACR 253 (C); A Rycroft, 'Corporate Homicide' [2004] South African Journal of Criminal Justice 141-57; Burchell (n 1) 477.

63   Criminal Procedure Act 1977, s 332(2).

64   *State v SA Metal & Machinery Co (Pty) Ltd* 2010 (2) SACR 413 (SCA).

65   *State v Coetzee* 1997 (3) SA 527 (CC).

66   See comments by Burchell (n 1) 479.

67   Legislation adopted after the judgment in *Coetzee* seems to confirm the view that s 332(7) might be constitutionally problematic. See for instance s 15(1)(b) Implementation of the Geneva Conventions Act 8 of 2012 (non-applicability of s 332(7) of the Criminal Procedure Act in terms of corporate criminal liability for offences under the Implementation of the Geneva Conventions Act).

68   As quoted by Louise Jordaan, 'New Perspectives on the Criminal Liability of Corporate Bodies' in Burchell and Erasmus (n 60) 50.

Other commentators objected to the 'irrebuttable deeming provision' as per section 332(1) and the severe consequences for the morally blameless corporation (and its innocent members).[69]

The scope of section 332(1) is indeed very wide. As long as the director or employee was acting to further the interests of the corporation (even if such conduct was strictly speaking not part of the job description or terms of employment) the conduct may be attributed to the corporation. It is largely irrelevant whether the corporation had knowledge of the criminal conduct by the director or employee.[70] Furthermore, as Jordaan pointed out, the unlawful conduct of third persons, acting on the instruction of or with the permission of a director or employee, 'may be imputed to the corporate body'.[71] There is, however, some limitation on the scope of corporate liability based on the conduct of a third party: some degree of control by the corporation over the action of the third party is namely required.[72]

With reference to the basic structure of corporate criminal liability in terms of section 332(1) of the Criminal Procedure Act, one can say that it is indeed akin to vicarious liability, although the comparison is not perfect. But from a policy and constitutional perspective the same objection that one would raise against vicarious (and strict) liability, can certainly also be raised against the very wide scope of corporate criminal liability under South African law.[73]

Sentencing Regime for Participants

South African criminal law is not codified, and neither is sentencing. Specific sentences are normally provided for in specific legislation, or under the common law. Sentencing in South Africa is structured around a general enabling statutory provision, namely section 276 of the Criminal Procedure Act of 1977. However, this section is complementary to the specific legislative provisions and the common law. An important addition to the sentencing regime is the so-called 'discretionary minimum sentences' for certain serious offences, provided for in the Criminal Law Amendment Act 105 of 1997, as amended by the Criminal Law (Sentencing) Amendment Act 38 of 2007. This regime of minimum sentences (in respect of certain serious offences, including murder) applies unless the relevant court finds that 'substantial and compelling circumstances' exist. Thus, for instance, an accused convicted of having raped his victim multiple times must be sentenced to life imprisonment,[74] unless, of course, the court is satisfied that a lesser sentence is justified based on substantial and compelling circumstances.[75]

The general position in South African criminal law is that perpetrators and accomplices face the same sentencing regime. This means that, in terms of the general principles of sentencing, there

---

69   H Van Eeden, K Hopkins and C Adendorff, 'Criminal Liability of Morally Blameless Corporations' (2011) September De Rebus 27.

70   *State v African Bank of South Africa Ltd* 1990 (2) SACR 585; *State v Film Fun Holdings (Pty) Ltd* 1977 (2) SA 377.

71   Jordaan (n 68) 51.

72   Ibid. 51; *R v Murray and Steward* 1950 (1) SA 104 (C).

73   See Jordaan's argument based on the Constitution. Jordaan (n 68) 53. For further critical commentary, see V Borg-Jorgensen and K Van der Linde, 'Corporate Criminal Liability in South Africa: Time for Change? (part 1)' (2011) 3 Journal of South African Law 452; (part 2) (2011) 4 Journal of South African Law 684.

74   General Law Amendment Act 105 of 1997 (as amended), s 51(1) (as read with Part I of Schedule 2).

75   General Law Amendment Act 105 of 1997 (as amended), s 51(3)(a). In the context of rape, factors such as the low intellect of the accused, and sexual abuse of the accused, were held to be substantial and compelling factors. See for instance *S v RO & another* 2010 (2) SACR 248 (SCA).

is no formalised regime of differentiation between the categories of participants. The appropriate sentence will be determined by the extent of participation.[76]

The above comment regarding sentencing must be qualified with reference to minimum prescribed sentences for certain serious crimes like murder, rape and other serious crimes of violence. These minimum sentences are applicable to participants who were part of a common purpose (for instance, to commit murder). The minimum sentences are also, in principle, applicable to accomplices.[77] Of course, it was argued above that, in strict dogmatic terms, it is not really possible to speak of an 'accomplice to murder'. For this crime the sentencing regime for multiple participants will simply refer to the *perpetrators* who were responsible for the murder. One should also be careful not to conflate the *participation* of more than one participant in a given crime with the *seriousness* of the crime. Thus, for instance, where an accomplice held down a woman so that she can be raped by the perpetrator, it was held that minimum sentencing of life imprisonment (the prescribed minimum sentence where a victim is raped more than once by a perpetrator) is not applicable. The focus is on the single act of rape; not the number of participants.[78]

Concluding Remarks

The various doctrines associated with participation in crime in South Africa have Roman, Roman-Dutch and English law roots. These diverse historical roots often resulted in muddled theory and confusing jurisprudence. It was left to the Supreme Court of Appeal, and, more recently, the Constitutional Court, to bring clarity, consistency and fairness to the relevant doctrines. While comparative law (notably modern English law and German law) contributed to the development of South African criminal law theory, it has been the profound impact of the post-apartheid Constitution and Bill of Rights that stand out. Legislative reform (for instance on corporate criminal liability, conspiracy and sentencing, as discussed in this contribution) is, of course, the most *obvious* example of legal change. However, it is submitted that academic writing and, importantly, the jurisprudence of the Supreme Court of Appeal and the Constitutional Court, that has had the most beneficial impact on South African criminal law doctrine in the context of participation in crime. The complexities of participation in crime must, in a constitutional democracy like South Africa, be dealt with using a balanced approach. The abrogation of the *versari* doctrine and the constitutionalisation of the common purpose doctrine serve to illustrate the on-going development of South African criminal law theory in the context of participation in crime.

---

76   Burchell (n 1) 522; Snyman (n 1) 289; *State v X* 1974 (1) SA 344 (RA).
77   *State v N* 2000 (1) SACR 209 (W).
78   *S v Kimberley & another* 2005 (2) SACR 663 (SCA); *S v Senyolo* 2010 (2) SACR 571 (GSJ).

Chapter 24

Sweden

Petter Asp and Magnus Ulväng

General Principles: Types of Participation and General Basis of Attributing Criminal Liability for Acts of Others

Introduction

Swedish law recognises two types of participation in crime – acting as a principal and furthering of a crime through complicity. The law on complicity can be understood only in relation to the general rules and principles that define what it means to be a principal or a perpetrator.

Generally one can say that a principal is a person who fulfils the prerequisites of a certain offence (the one who kills when it comes to murder, the one who steals when it comes to theft and so on), while an accomplice is a person whose actions as such do not fall within the definition of the offence but whose acts have furthered the act of the principal in one way or the other.

It should be observed that a person may fulfil the prerequisites of a certain offence not merely by performing it him- or herself, but also by causing another person to perform it (making use of another person more or less as a tool).[1] It should also be observed that it is not a necessary requirement that the principal carries out the offence alone. According to Swedish law it is possible to be a principal by embarking on a crime together with others. Two or more persons can be principals (co-perpetrators) as long as every party carry out the act that fulfils the prerequisites of the offence. Two or more persons can also be considered to be principals in cases where they have performed the act as a common endeavour, but have had slightly different tasks. Consider, for example, a robbery, where A has threatened the victim, B has taken the victim's wallet and C has been acting as a lookout at the place of the robbery.[2]

The rules on complicity in Chapter 23 section 4 of the Swedish Criminal Code extend the possibilities to hold persons responsible by stating that not only the person that actually 'committed the act' (in any of the abovementioned ways) may be held responsible, but also 'anyone who furthered it by advice or act'. The provision reads as follows:

> 4 § Punishment as provided for an act in this Code shall be imposed not only on the person who committed the act but also on anyone who furthered it by advice or act. The same shall also apply to any other act punishable with imprisonment under another Law or statutory instrument.
>
> A person who is not regarded as the perpetrator shall, if he induced another to commit the act, be sentenced for instigation of the crime and otherwise for aiding the crime.

---

1   See page 562 ff.
2   See page 567 ff.

Each accomplice shall be judged according to the intent or the negligence attributable to him. Punishments defined in law for the act of a manager, debtor or other person in a special position shall also be imposed on anyone who was an accomplice to the act of such person.

The provisions of this paragraph do not apply if the law provides otherwise in special cases.[3]

Responsibility for complicity is generally applicable to any act fulfilling the requirements of an offence in the Swedish Criminal Code, as well as to any prohibited act outside the code for which the perpetrator can be sentenced to imprisonment (that is, the provision on complicity does not apply to offences outside the Criminal Code that can only be punished by a fine).

Basically there are three major themes which have to be considered within the complicity doctrine:

1. there has to be an act in which one can participate (a complicity object),
2. the accomplice must have 'furthered' the main act, and
3. the accomplice must have acted (that is, furthered the offence) with the required intent or negligence.

The Complicity Object

First, responsibility for complicity presupposes something in which the accomplice can participate. In Swedish legal doctrine this is normally referred to as a complicity object (or an offence in the objective sense). In order to understand how the complicity object is construed one must have a basic understanding of the concept of an offence under Swedish law.

Basically, the structure of an offence under Swedish law can be described as in Figure 24.1.

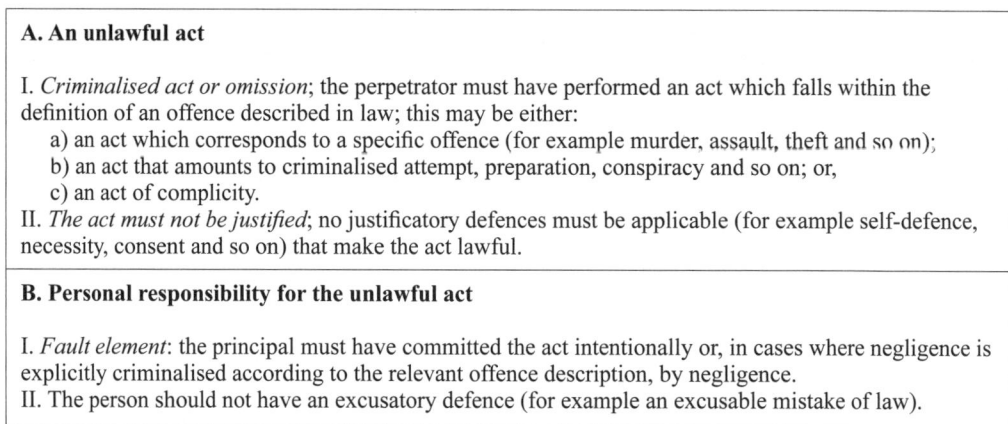

A. An unlawful act

I. *Criminalised act or omission*; the perpetrator must have performed an act which falls within the definition of an offence described in law; this may be either:
    a) an act which corresponds to a specific offence (for example murder, assault, theft and so on);
    b) an act that amounts to criminalised attempt, preparation, conspiracy and so on; or,
    c) an act of complicity.
II. *The act must not be justified*; no justificatory defences must be applicable (for example self-defence, necessity, consent and so on) that make the act lawful.

B. Personal responsibility for the unlawful act

I. *Fault element*: the principal must have committed the act intentionally or, in cases where negligence is explicitly criminalised according to the relevant offence description, by negligence.
II. The person should not have an excusatory defence (for example an excusable mistake of law).

Figure 24.1   The structure of an offence under Swedish law

---

3   The Ministry of Justice, Official translation of The Swedish Penal Code, Ds 1999:36. In the following text we will use the terminology used in this official translation (that is, we will refer to the two forms of secondary participation as *aiding* and *instigation*). This might not correspond to normal British language standards. That is, however, an advantage, since it underlines that we are referring not to a general understanding of aiding, abetting, encouraging and so on but to the specific Swedish concepts.

As a general rule one may say that complicity, that is, responsibility as an accomplice, does not presuppose that the principal has committed a full offence, but it requires at least an unlawful act, that is, an act that fulfils the requirements under A I and A II above.

The rule that the principal has to perform an unlawful act in order to create a complicity object is not entirely without exception. To a limited extent one is allowed to transfer or acquire certain circumstances from an aider or instigator when constructing the complicity object.[4]

For example if a freelance book-keeper is performing an act that could be subsumed under a book-keeping offence, this does not in and of itself amount to an offence as long as and because the book-keeper does not have a duty himself to keep books. If, however, the book-keeper performs his act on behalf of a person or company that has such a duty (that is, someone who has instigated the act), then the duty to keep books may be 'transferred' from this person. If one combines this duty with the act performed by the book-keeper then we get an act that fulfils the requirement of the book-keeping offence.[5] This possibility to transfer circumstances from an aider or instigator is seldom used in practice and it is of importance mainly when it comes to (a) crimes that can only be committed by someone who holds a specific position (if this position is held by an aider or instigator but not by the principal, this prerequisite may be transferred to the principal), and (b) crimes which in the offence description requires some form of ulterior intent (if this intent is held by an aider or instigator but not by the principal, this prerequisite may be transferred to the principal).

However, whether the principal also fulfils the requirements of personal liability (that is, the requirements under B) is immaterial for the liability of the accomplice. This means that the responsibility of the accomplice is not accessorial to the commission of the complete offence as such, but 'accessorial merely to the unlawful act' performed by the principal (the complicity object). Consider the following example:

> *Example 1.* A is attacked by B who uses serious violence against him. If a bystander (C), in these circumstances, hands a gun to A which A then uses against B in order to defend himself, then A's act might be justified according to the rules on self-defence. If so, A has not committed an unlawful act. Thus, there is no complicity object, that is, nothing to which C can be an accomplice. C cannot be held responsible for furthering any unlawful act. However, if A uses force to an unjustifiable extent, then the act will not be justified. Thus A has committed an unlawful act to which C can be an accomplice. This applies irrespective of whether A fulfils the requirements under B I and B II.

When the law talks about furthering an 'act', it refers not to an abstract offence description but to a concrete occurrence that has actually taken place. How this act is to be labelled is not conclusive for how the responsibility of a secondary party is to be construed. Very often an unlawful act can be subsumed under different offence descriptions, which is explained by the fact that many offence descriptions overlap each other (for example due to the fact that the legislator has, as separate offences, criminalised similar acts with different fault requirements and so on). As an example one can consider the abovementioned scenario. If A kills B (causes B's death) by shooting him, then he has committed several different unlawful acts, for example murder and involuntary manslaughter (both offences have a common *actus reus*, the causing of another person's death),

---

4   See the preparatory works to the Swedish Criminal Code, Official Investigations of the State (SOU) 1944:69, 97. See also, Carl Erik Herlitz, *Parties to a Crime and the Notion of a Complicity Object* (Iustus förlag 1992) 224; and Petter Asp, Magnus Ulväng and Nils Jareborg, *Kriminalrättens grunder* (Iustus förlag 2010) 473.

5   Swedish Criminal Code Chapter 11 section 5.

but also battery (by causing of bodily harm). At this stage, that is when constructing the complicity object, one disregards the rules and principles of multiple charges and duplicity, which means that the complicity object entails all offences under whose description the act can be subsumed (that is, murder as well as involuntary manslaughter and assault). Each party to the crime will be judged according to the fault attributable to them. The complicity object remains the same for all parties.

An act of complicity can in itself constitute a complicity object (if the act is not justified).[6] Thus, it is possible to create chains of complicity (for example, aiding someone who aids a murder, instigating the aiding of a forgery and so on). However, all chains have to start – or end (if viewed from the opposite perspective) – with a specific concrete offence or an inchoate offence in the first place (that is, the primary complicity object must be created by a principal).

'Furthering' the Complicity Object

The act of an accomplice can be described as 'furthering the complicity object'. This follows from Chapter 23 section 4 that states that punishment shall be imposed not only on the person who committed the act (that is, the complicity object) but also on anyone who furthered it by advice or action.

This can consist of virtually any type of assistance: physical assistance (for example help with carrying things) or psychological assistance (for example encouragement or advice). The assistance can be delivered in advance or at the time of the commission of the offence. One cannot, however, be liable for complicity if one has only contributed after the event.

Basically, there are two different types of responsibility for accomplices – responsibility for *instigation* and responsibility for otherwise *aiding* (encouraging or otherwise assisting) the crime. The law distinguishes between those who have 'induced' the principal to commit the act (instigators) and persons who have merely furthered the complicity object (aiders).

The furthering element is fulfilled when a person has induced another to commit the offence. Responsibility for instigation covers not only cases where a person explicitly gives another person the task of committing the crime, but also other cases where the person has otherwise caused the commission of the crime (for example by encouraging the principal in a situation where he or she is hesitating and has not decided whether to commit the crime). In cases of procurement without the knowledge of the principal, Swedish courts will probably be inclined to label the act as assistance even if it was causal in relation to the complicity object.

In the case of assisting, the requirement is fulfilled not only in cases in which the accomplice has actually made the commission of the crime easier but also in cases in which the accomplice has merely contributed by encouraging the principal or by strengthening him or her by engaging in the criminal project, for example by mere encouragement or by contributing with advise that turns out to be irrelevant or even misleading. It is, according to a commonly used expression, enough if the accomplice has 'strengthened the principal in his or her intent' to commit the offence. If such an act is causal in relation to the complicity object it might be labelled as instigation, but if this can not be shown (for example in cases where the support merely made the principal feel more comfortable) the correct label is aiding. Even people who assist in a clumsy way – and thus actually make it harder to commit the crime – are considered to have 'furthered' the act. In the same way a person who assists by doing something which turns out to be unnecessary (that is, watching out for passers-by in a situation where no one passes) will have 'furthered' the act. The minimum

---

6   See Figure 24.1 (A I. c).

requirements are set fairly low. In one Supreme Court decision, an accused was sentenced for aiding assault due to the fact that he held the perpetrators coat during the assault.[7]

If one adds the categories of instigators and aiders to the principals we end up with a system which contains three different categories:

- *Principals*: the ones who (after interpretation of the act and the requirements of the law) have actually performed the unlawful act thereby creating the complicity object (an unlawful act, that is, an act that falls under the relevant offence description and which is not justified).
- *Instigators*: persons who have induced – not merely contributed to – the commission of the complicity object.
- *Aiders*: any person who otherwise furthers the complicity object.

Mens rea

According to Chapter 23 section 4(3) of the Swedish Criminal Code '[e]ach accomplice shall be judged according to the intent or the negligence attributable to him'. This means that the outcome for the principal and the accomplice may be different depending on their level of fault.

Let us once more use example 1 above, but this time we shall assume that A's act is not justified. Thus we have a case where A (the principal) has killed B under circumstances which do not justify the killing and where someone has 'furthered' this act by handing the gun to the principal. In such a case the principal would have created a complicity object that includes, *inter alia*, murder,[8] causing another's death (negligent homicide)[9] and assault.[10]

The responsibility of the principal and the aider will now be dependent upon their individual *mens rea*. If the principal has intent in relation to the killing, but the aider is only negligent in this regard (C might have assumed that the principal would only injure B), then the principal (A) will be convicted of murder or causing another's death (negligent homicide), while the aider (C) will be convicted for aiding causing another's death and for aiding assault.[11] Another possible result is that A is acquitted (he might have thought that he and B were simply playing and that the gun was not real and this mistake might not even be considered negligent) while C, who was fully aware that he handed A a real gun, might be held responsible as an accomplice to murder. Thus, persons can be convicted of assisting or instigating an offence also in cases where nobody is convicted as a principal. In such cases it might at times be possible to convict C as a principal, but it is always possible (and formally correct) to use the law on complicity.

Re-labelling: Final Adjustment

As explained above Swedish law distinguishes between those who are principals on the one hand and instigators/aiders on the other hand. The basic difference between these categories is that the former can be held responsible on the basis of the specific offence (murder, theft and so on), that is, their acts fall within the scope of the offence description, while the latter cannot be held responsible without mediation of the section on complicity in Chapter 23 section 4 of the Criminal Code.

---

7 See Swedish Supreme Court Case NJA 1963, 574.
8 Swedish Criminal Code Chapter 3 section 1.
9 Ibid. section 7.
10 Ibid. section 5.
11 See, for example, NJA 1996, 27.

Swedish law, however, also allows for a re-labelling which could be described as an adjustment made at the very end of the process. Under this procedure persons who *are* principals (that is, who actually fulfil the requirements of a specific offence), may in the end be designated as instigators or aiders (depending on whether one or the other fits best) and persons who *are* 'only' instigators or aiders (that is, persons who do not fulfil the requirements of a specific offence, but are held responsible under Chapter 23 section 4) may in the end be designated as principals. A court can in this way extend (designate an aider or instigator as principal), reduce (designate a principal as an aider or instigator) or convert the role (do both things at the same time) of the parties. This possibility to re-designate the roles of the parties has been criticised in legal commentary and in 1996 a governmental legislative inquiry proposed that it should be abolished.[12] The legislator, however, chose not to alter the rules. The simple idea behind this possibility to re-label persons is to allow for flexibility in order to reach reasonable results that correspond to the general perception of a certain event. (See 'Special Issue: Re-labelling the Roles of Perpetrators' below, for more details on this possibility to re-label the parties.)

Joint Principals

Chapter 23 section 4 does not explicitly say that more than one person can commit the offence jointly, and the preparatory works of the law are rather silent on how and when it is possible to view several perpetrators as principals in a joint enterprise. Co-perpetration is nevertheless possible also in Swedish law and for some crimes it is a necessary requirement that more than one principal act in concert with other principles. Committing for example riot or mutiny presuppose 'a crowd of people' or 'a gathering of members' doing something together.[13] Anyone acting in such a common endeavour are denoted as a principal.

This does not mean that any party to a crime, acting in a joint unlawful enterprise can be labelled a principal.[14] The prerequisites for holding someone responsible as a co-perpetrator in a joint criminal project are rather strict.

When people act together and thereby fulfil the constituting elements of a crime, it is often unclear whether the involved parties have acted as principals or accomplices. This is because all parties to a crime are in a wide sense participating in the completion. Consider the following two scenarios:

> *Example 2*: Four persons (A, B, C and D) decide to rob a bank together. In advance, they distribute the tasks to be carried out at the scene of the crime. A will drive the car and stay outside the bank. B shall be at the entrance to help the others get into the bank and later secure the escape route after the money has been taken. C and D will enter the office, C will point the gun at the clerk and D will threaten him and demand money. C and D shall later carry the money out of the bank.

---

12   The preparatory works to the Swedish Criminal Code, Official Investigations of the State (SOU) 1996:185 and Government Bill to Parliament (proposition) 2000/01:85.

13   Swedish Criminal Code Chapter 16 section 1 (riot) and Swedish Criminal Code Chapter 16 section 6 (mutiny).

14   Swedish law does not have a distinct doctrine of joint enterprise similar to that found in English law; Andrew Simester and Bob Sullivan, *Criminal Law, Theory and Doctrine* (Hart 2007) 220. A person embarking on a crime together with others will either be labelled an accomplice (instigator or aider) or a co-perpetrator (principal). As indicated above, courts are allowed to re-label the roles of the participators at the very end of the process. See page 568 ff.

Example 3: Suppose further that A, B, C and D, after they have committed the robbery, are pursued by the police. All of them are armed with automatic guns. They decided before carrying out the robbery that if necessary they will fire upon the police in order to get away. After a while the vehicle is stopped and they all step out and open fire. Two policemen are killed. It is later established that the lethal gunshots came from the same weapon, but whose weapon it was is unclear.

These examples show that co-perpetration can sometimes concern situations where each party to a crime contributes only a part of what is necessary to fulfil the constituting elements of the offence (example 2) whereas in other cases all parties perform the typical acts necessary to fulfil the offence description (example 3) and it is thus often thought immaterial who actually caused effect.[15] Although not everybody has carried out all of the acts required to fulfil the constituting elements of the offences ('take the life of another' and 'steal from another by means of violence'),[16] it is nevertheless possible to convict all of the perpetrators (A–D) as principals for bank robbery as well as murder of the policemen.

According to the dominant view in doctrine, any co-perpetrator can be called a principal as long as the parties involved in the enterprise can be said to have fulfilled the elements in the offence descriptions *together*.[17] Acting 'together' is practically the same as doing something 'in cooperation' which presuppose some sort of reciprocal understanding or common purpose.[18] It is thus possible to interpret the offence descriptions as if more than one principal can fulfil the act requirements.

Logically 'doing something together' ought to be something more than '(only) furthering someone else's act'. Otherwise there would be no reason to separate principals from accomplices. To delineate the ambit of co-perpetration (principal) one must analyse the concept of 'together' and what it means to do something 'in cooperation'. There is in Swedish law no clear definition of either of these concepts. The law also allows the courts – at least in special circumstances – to express the legal characterisation of the parties' role in a rather free manner, thus seemingly making a strict separation between a principal and an accomplice unnecessary.[19] Nevertheless, according to Swedish doctrine, it is necessary to decide who (in a common endeavour) is to be seen as the principal and who as a mere accomplice by applying the material definitions in the first place. This is mainly because it is the principal who establishes the complicity object, thus determining the framework of responsibility for accomplices.

Furthermore, to do something 'in cooperation' implies that there must be some mutual understanding between the parties relating to the actions undertaken 'together'. It is not sufficient that one person commits half of the offence on his own whereas another commits the remaining part on his own (for example A strikes B down, leaving her unconscious, whereupon C later comes by and takes advantage of B's condition by sexually abusing her).[20] Thus, each co-perpetrator must mutually further the other perpetrator's act. On the other hand, such a description does not offer

---

15   See, for example, Swedish Supreme Court case NJA 2002, 489.
16   Swedish Criminal Code Chapter 3 section 1 (murder) and Chapter 8 section 5 (robbery).
17   Simester and Sullivan (n 14) 220.
18   Asp et al. (n 4) 463.
19   See page 568 ff.
20   Asp et al. (n 4) 463. Responsibility for rape in Swedish law presupposes that the victim has been *forced* into having sexual intercourse (or other comparable sexual act); Swedish Criminal Code Chapter 6 section 1. Thus, the violence or threats (or something negating the victim's consent) must have been present at the time of the sexual activity. When two persons together fulfil the act requirements of the offence description, a minimum requirement for liability would be that they could be said to further each others' acts.

much of a definition since 'furthering another principal's action' is also the definition of being an accomplice.

Some guidance of how co-perpetration can be distinguished is offered in criminal law doctrine and through the interpretation of precedents and case law:

1. As said above, characterising the degree of responsibility is always a matter of interpreting the offence descriptions. As a minimum requirement, the persons involved must do something that fulfils the act requirement in the offence description. Whether a person's actions can be said to fall within the ambit of the offence depends on what kind of act requirements the offence description entails. Co-perpetration requires that all the parties can be said to participate in the conduct that fulfils the elements of the offence description, but as said, not everyone has to do everything.

    In cases where the offence description is simple it can be rather easy to establish co-perpetration. If two persons for example assault someone together, it is usually immaterial exactly who delivered which blow to the victim as long as everyone involved can be said to have 'inflicted bodily injury, illness or pain upon another'.[21] The same is true for the situation in example 3 above. Whether it was the bullets of A, B, C or D that killed the policemen is of no real relevance as long as it can be established that they all were in on the common endeavour of 'killing the policemen'.[22]

    When it comes to the example with a bank robbery it is likewise obvious that perpetrators C and D have 'stolen ... by means of violence or by a threat implying ... an imminent danger'.[23] It is of no direct relevance whether it was C who threatened the bank clerk and D who took the money or the other way around. Whether A (in the car) or B (at the entrance door) can be said to have 'stolen by means of violence' is nevertheless open to question. Courts will have to decide whether it is justified to denote an accomplice as a perpetrator (principal) or not. What kind of influence on the chain of events each perpetrator has had – for example in the planning and later in the execution of the crime – as well as whether or not it was a coincidence or random who was doing what at the scene of the crime, will matter when roles are designated to the parties.

2. Responsibility for co-perpetration further requires that all agents involved fulfil the general fault-requirement. Thus, everyone participating in a common endeavour must have acted with the required intent (or – in cases where recklessness is criminalised according to the relevant offence description – recklessness).[24]

    Co-perpetration further requires that the parties have acted with a certain reciprocal understanding of the other agent's actions.[25] Committing a crime 'in cooperation', thus, presupposes that the involved have reached a common intention (consensus) on the matter of carrying out the act. It is not of importance whether the parties have made any pre-

---

This presupposes that the different parts of the act must be carried out, to some extent, simultaneously and that each actor must be aware of the acts of the other (common purpose or mutual understanding).

21   Swedish Criminal Code Chapter 3 section 5 (assault).
22   See page 563 ff.
23   Swedish Criminal Code Chapter 8 section 5 (robbery).
24   It is, however, unlikely that the idea of co-perpetration can be used when it comes to offences of negligence since it is difficult to see how the parties can fulfil the requirement of reciprocal understanding.
25   If two persons, simultaneously but irrespectively of each other, fulfil the constituting elements of an offence without any mutual understanding or common purpose and so on, they can both be denoted principals but not *co-perpetrators*.

arranged plan or if they have expressly and explicitly deliberated or consulted each other before or during their actions. Instead an implicit understanding of the mutual intention to act together is sufficient.

In addition to what has been said, Swedish law sometimes allows for judges to interpret the offence description in a manner according to which it possible to view a person behind a crime directly as the perpetrator (principal) even though he has not established the complicity object himself. The situation we have in mind occurs when A does something that fulfils the constituting elements of a crime, but B has instigated the act as well as controlled and planned the acts carried out by A in the background. If A sends B to a bank to cash an uncovered cheque and a bank clerk cashes it, then both A and B can sometimes be said to have fulfilled the elements in the offence description of fraud. Regardless of whether B has intentionally committed a crime (or only established a complicity object), they can both be said to have induced the clerk (through deception or causing of error) to cash the cheque. It is not necessary to employ the doctrinal concept of indirect participation via the use for example of innocent agents.[26] They can both (directly) be viewed as co-perpetrators.[27]

To what extent it is possible to engage the concept of direct perpetration on agents behind the actual act – who thus merely instigates the other agent – depends on the interpretation of the offence description and how far this can be stretched.

Principals by Proxy: Use of Innocent Agents and Perpetrator behind the Perpetrator

The notion of an 'innocent agent' derives its significance from the concept of indirect perpetration. The notion of innocent agents refers closely to what has been said above regarding common endeavours. Viewing a party to a crime as an 'innocent agent', even though his acts fall within the *actus reus* requirements of the crime, does not exclude the possibility that someone else may be responsible.

The basic idea behind the doctrine of innocent agents is that persons, even though they have carried out all the actions that fulfil the constituting *actus reus* elements of a crime, sometimes ought not to be labelled perpetrators – or punished at all – since they have only served as the tools or instruments of another person's crime.[28] A prerequisite for being an innocent agent is that the person in question is unaware of the significance of his actions or that he does not embark on the crime voluntarily (because of for example coercion, deceit, misuse of his youth or dependent status and so on). The result has been arranged by someone in the background, who used the other person to bring about the *actus reus*. In situations like these, it would obviously be unjustified to blame the one who has perpetrated the act personally, since he or she has acted within the control of another. In the same way it would be inappropriate to punish the *hinterman* only as an aider or instigator of the offence. This latter person is usually the one who controlled the other person.

---

26   See page 567 f.

27   See Asp et al. (n 4) 464. See also Supreme Court case NJA 1964, 197 I and Court of Appeal case RH 1993:82.

28   Observe that Swedish law does not recognise a rule requiring that an offender has criminal capacity. Thus, a child or a mentally incompetent person can commit a crime as well as establish a complicity object. Lack of capacity or diminished responsibility is taken into account at the sentencing stage.

Example 4: A parent who, trains his child to steal can be seen as the direct perpetrator even though it is the child who fulfils the *actus reus* (theft). The parent has fulfilled the elements of the *actus reus* by the instrument of the child. The latter is thus rendered innocent.

Example 5: If someone (B) deliberately pushes another (B) into C's bookshelf for the purpose of destroying C's collection of valuable porcelain, then A would be viewed as the principal. B has only been used as a tool by being forced into destroying the property.

It is irrelevant whether or not the child or the forced person in the examples have actually committed a crime or merely served to establish the complicity object. In both cases, the *hinterman* will be seen as the perpetrator and the agent will not be liable.

It is not required that the agent lacks criminal capacity. Adults can be 'innocent' if they do not know or understand that they are completing the *actus reus*:

Example 6: Suppose A places a parcel containing drugs in the unknowing B's pocket just before they are to go through customs. Later, after they have passed the customs officer, A slips his hand into B's pocket and takes the parcel back. In such circumstances A would be viewed as the direct perpetrator and B would be an innocent agent.[29]

If the agent lacks neither capacity nor understanding (intent), he can never be categorised as an *innocent* agent. The only exception would be cases of *concursus necessarius*, that is, situations where it, according to the offence description, is necessary with the participation of another party. This is usually the victim of the crime or the subject representing the protected interest behind criminalisation. For example a woman who agrees to an illegal abortion is in a way an accomplice to a crime carried out by the person performing the abortion. Nevertheless, the prohibition against illegal abortion is not to be construed to include such cases. According to Swedish law the woman is the victim whether she consents or even *de facto* instigates a person to carry out the unlawful act.[30] The same is true in situations where for example a person under 15 years of age instigates a grown up to have sexual intercourse with him- or herself. The offence of 'rape of a minor' has been created for the purpose of protecting children under 15 from sexual intercourse.[31] In the eyes of the law, a child is the victim regardless of whether he or she is willing to give up this protection; thus the child is always regarded as a victim and not as a co-offender.[32] The initiative of a child can thus never make the act justified.

Special Issue: Re-labelling the Roles of Perpetrators

In order to be labelled a principal, any participator of a crime must as a main rule – alone or together with a co-perpetrator – either carry out the act according to the offence description or use someone else as an instrument to undertake the criminalised behaviour. Other forms of contribution to the completion of a crime – for example assistance, aiding, abetting, procuring or even instigation – will be labelled secondary participation (instigation or aiding; see page 559 f).

---

29 Observe that Swedish law does not recognise strict liability offences.
30 See for example Government Bill to Parliament (proposition) 1974:70, 29.
31 Swedish Criminal Code Chapter 6 section 4 (rape of a minor).
32 See Government Bill to Parliament (proposition) 2004/05:45, 67 and Petter Asp, *Sex och samtycke* (Iustus förlag 2010) 66.

However, there is, as has been explained above, a possibility for a secondary participant to be sentenced as a principal and for principals to be sentenced as secondary parties. According to Chapter 23 section 4 paragraph 2 of the Swedish Criminal Code, anyone 'who is not regarded as the perpetrator' shall be sentenced for instigation of the crime and otherwise for aiding the crime.[33] The quoted phrase is interpreted as a warrant for courts subsequently to assign and designate appropriate roles to the perpetrators (in a wide sense) regardless of whether they have acted as principals or mere accomplices (in a strict sense).[34] Such an extended possibility to classify offenders according to what seems 'natural' gives judges a wide discretion to alter the roles of the perpetrators and accomplices. Re-labelling the roles of the perpetrators is done as a final stage in the process of assigning criminal liability. After a court has found parties to a crime liable as either principals or accomplices in the first place, alterations are made at another level in the process.

There exists several possibilities for a court to punish a party to the crime in accordance with what the court may 'feel' is the correct outcome (even though it is contrary to the general principles of complicity).

Firstly, a perpetrator who has done exactly that which fulfils the constituting elements of the offence may be denoted as an accomplice if there are reasons to adjust the designation of the parties. The class of principals is thus reduced.[35]

Secondly, it is possible to alter the roles in the opposite manner. An accomplice, who 'only' has instigated or otherwise aided the unlawful act, may in special circumstances be convicted as a principal. The class of principals is thus extended.[36]

Finally, it is possible to engage both modes simultaneously. By labelling the principal as an accomplice, and vice versa, the designation of roles is inversed.[37]

A textbook example of when a court might use the possibility of a re-labelling of responsibility would be the case where company executive (A) instructs his secretary (B) to commit embezzlement solely in favour of A.[38] If we assume that B understands the meaning of his actions, and for some reason carries out the deed, then he cannot be viewed an innocent agent even if he himself has no financial gains of the crime. B will instead, in the first place, be viewed as the principal committing embezzlement. A, on the other hand, can not be viewed as the perpetrator (principal), since he has not acted according to the offence description ('appropriated property' and so on); neither is he a co-perpetrator or someone who has used the secretary as an instrument. A is merely the instigator of the crime. However, if one scrutinises the scenario, it is obvious that A has acted in such a way that he ought to be regarded as a principal.

Theoretically the court can punish any party to a crime as a principal regardless of whether he or she took part in the commission of the offence or not. The far limit of this doctrine is unclear. The only thing that can be said to unite these situations, in which the possibility of a free denotation is used, is some sort of a need to adjust outcomes that are thought of as 'unreasonable'. Swedish law in this field is remarkably unclear as to how and when it is 'natural' to engage this adjustment. As a reference point it is said that it is usually required that the party in question 'took part in

---

33   The paragraph is quoted in full, see page 556.

34   In the preparatory works it was said that it was not necessary, or even suitable, to stipulate in detail what the notion of perpetration should entail. Instead it was thought better to leave it to case law to decide whether a party is thought to have acted in such a way that he ought to be regarded as a principal. See the preparatory works to the Swedish Criminal Code, Official Investigations of the State (SOU) 1944:69, 92.

35   See, for example, Supreme Court case NJA 1964, 255.

36   See, for example, Supreme Court cases NJA 1966, 299 and NJA 1992, 474.

37   See, Supreme Court cases NJA 1982, 525 and NJA 2006, 535.

38   See, Official Investigations of the State (SOU) 1996:185, 193.

the commission of the offence to such a degree that he *ought to be* regarded as a perpetrator'.[39] This would entail situations discussed above, namely those of co-perpetration and using innocent agents. But concerning these categories there is no need for a possibility of re-labelling the roles. 'Masterminds/hintermen', just as co-perpetrators, are usually denoted directly as principals.[40] A practice of re-labelling goes beyond such standard cases.

The typical cases where a practice of a free way re-labelling would be used are cases were courts need to establish the complicity object by acquiring a capacity of a special agent (*intraneus*)[41] from an accomplice.[42] This would be the case when the law requires the perpetrator to be for example a 'debtor'.[43] If the person who fulfils the prerequisites of an offence does not belong to this special class, but the person instigating the perpetrator does, then the capacity of being a 'debtor' can be acquired thus establishing the necessary complicity object. Thus, crimes against creditors may be committed by a (strict) perpetrator who is not a debtor. In situations where a certain capacity or such has been acquired from someone other than the perpetrator, it is often 'natural' also to denote the secondary participant (belonging to the special class of possible perpetrators) as a principal, thus extending the class of principals.[44]

Another typical case where the roles of the perpetrators are likely to be re-labelled is a situation where the complicity object has been established (or qualified) through acquisition of an excess *mens rea* element (ulterior intent) from the furtherer. If a perpetrator has unlawfully taken something that belongs to another, then he will be liable for *unlawful dispossession*.[45] In order to sentence a perpetrator for theft, Swedish law requires 'intent to acquire the goods'.[46] If the furtherer, but not the (strict) perpetrator, has this intention, then the complicity object may be qualified to entail theft (provided that the appropriation involves financial loss). If we assume that someone (A), with the intention of acquiring a car, instigates someone else (B), lacking intent to deprive, to appropriate a vehicle, then the established complicity object would entail unlawful dispossession as well as theft. In such a case, a court could sentence A as a principal for theft.[47] B, who lacked the intent to permanently deprive the owner of his car, could only be sentenced for unlawful dispossession. Whether B ought to be designated a principal or re-labelled a furtherer is open to question.

What makes a practice of re-labelling the roles of the perpetrators problematic is that it undermines the stringent principles of interpretation of offence descriptions. Someone not directly taking part in the outer commission of the offence nevertheless can be subsumed under the text in question. The practice of re-labelling thus clashes with the principle of legality. Although it may be possible to find reasons for a judicial re-characterisation power, there are several disadvantages.

---

39   See the preparatory works to the Swedish Criminal Code, Official Investigations of the State (SOU) 1944:69, 92. See also Supreme Court cases NJA 1960, 622; NJA 1997, 507; and NJA 2006, 535.

40   See above in the sections on Joint Principals and Principals by Proxy.

41   A lot of crimes are characterised by requiring that the perpetrator must belong to a special class of persons, involving the ownership of certain duties or a special capacity, for example 'debtor', 'trader', 'person liable to pay taxes' and so on These special agents are called *intraneus*. Herlitz (n 4) 225.

42   On the possibility in Swedish law to transfer or acquire certain circumstances from an aider or instigator when constructing the complicity object, see page 557.

43   See for example crimes against creditors, Swedish Criminal Code Chapter 11.

44   Whether or not the direct perpetrator should be re-labelled a secondary participant is open to question. The roles could be reversed if the participation of the (strict) principal was very minor compared to the secondary participants.

45   Swedish Criminal Code Chapter 8 section 8.

46   Ibid. Chapter 8 section 1.

47   Swedish Supreme Court case NJA 1964, 255.

Firstly, the courts are not obliged to give reasons.[48] Thus it often remains unclear whether an agent 'is' the principal or 'should be viewed as a perpetrator'. Secondly, and as a direct consequence, this practice sometimes makes it virtually impossible to know afterwards if a court actually has used the power and thus altered the roles of the parties or not. Since it is very difficult to know whom the court saw as the material principal, it becomes equally unclear how the complicity object was established. Since it is primarily the principal who does this by carrying out his unlawful act – and the complicity object sets the limits as to what an accomplice can be convicted for – it is of great importance to know who the court thinks has materially established the complicity object.[49]

Effect of Errors and Transferred Malice/Aberratio ictus Scenarios in the Person of One Participant on the Liability of the Other Participants

Swedish law has no clear position on *aberratio ictus*. Basically there are two different solutions that are discussed:

a). If A aims at B in order to kill her but (by accident) hits C, then A should be convicted of attempted murder in relation to B and negligent homicide in relation to C.

b). As under (a), but A should be convicted of the murder in relation to C because if A has the intent to kill a human being, it is immaterial whether B or C dies because both B and C are equal objects (humans) from the perspective of the criminal law.

As regards the choice between these two models there is no case law from the Supreme Court and in legal doctrine both alternatives have their proponents.[50] As a short summary of the arguments used in the legal doctrine one can say that alternative (b) seems to be most consistent if viewed from the general understanding of the intent-requirement (the law does not require intent to harm a specific person or a specific thing; the important thing is that the perpetrator's intent corresponds to the prerequisites of the offence and offences are framed in general terms; that is, they proscribe harming 'someone' – not harming 'B' or 'C'). Further, alternative (b) works also in cases where attempt and negligence are not criminalised (in such cases alternative (a) may lead to counterintuitive results). In addition alternative (b) is applied in cases of *error in persona* (if A hits a person which he or she thinks is B, but in reality is C, then A will be convicted of having committed the full offence against C irrespective of his mistake) and it has not been explained why these types of mistakes should be treated differently than the *aberratio ictus* type of mistakes. It could be argued, however, that alternative (a) – at least in some cases – represents the situation better than alternative (b), especially if one takes into account the relationships between the parties involved. For example, if A tries to

---

48   Courts are neither obliged to cite Chapter 23 section 4 paragraph in the decision nor to use any formula in the wording of the decision in order to indicate that the roles of the parties have been altered. Nevertheless, a certain way of writing decisions sometimes indicates that courts have used the extended possibility to state, for example, 'a party to the crime has participated in the commission of the offence to such a degree that he should be viewed as a perpetrator ...'. See for example Supreme Court cases NJA 1966, 299 and NJA 1992, 474.

49   For criticism of this practice, see for example Herlitz (n 4) 244 ff. and Asp et al. (n 4) 477 and the preparatory works to the Swedish Criminal Code, Official Investigations of the State (SOU) 1996:185, 219.

50   See for example Ivar Agge and Hans Thornstedt, *Straffrättens allmänna del* (Juristförlaget 1984) 113 (who advocates alternative a) and Nils Jareborg, *Allmän kriminalrätt* (Iustus förlag 2001) 345 f. (who advocates alternative b).

kill B but happens to kill C, it might seem strange to represent the act as completed murder, with the consequence that B will not be given the status of a victim or a party in the criminal process against A. It is furthermore clear that A has acted with the required intent for attempt (in relation to B) and (at least in typical cases) with negligence (in relation to C). As regards alternative (b), this is at times (wrongly) questioned: 'How can A be convicted of murder in relation to C? He did not intend to kill C'. Thus using alternative (a) means that one does not use the concept of intent in a way which conflicts with the general (public's) understanding of it.

The question has been dealt with in two fairly recent cases by the Court of Appeal. In the first one (a case of causing bodily harm, where A threw a can of beer against one person but hit another one) the Court of Appeal found that alternative (a) should be applied.[51] In a more recent case the Court of Appeal found that the Courts should have the freedom to choose between the different models depending on what is reasonable in the individual case.[52] The idea of the Court of Appeal in this second case seems to be that it is acceptable as a matter of principle to convict A according to the second model (that is, there is no impediment for 'transferring' the intent from one object to the other),[53] but that it might, at times, represent the act and the event better to convict A of attempt in combination with an offence of negligence.

Since the situation is unclear when it comes to principals it is, of course, unclear also with respect to accomplices. It seems likely, however, that the solution as regards accomplices will as a general rule follow the one for principals. Thus, if A is convicted according to alternative (a) for attempt and for an offence of negligence, a person who has aided or instigated the act will be convicted for aiding/instigating the attempt and the offence of negligence.[54] And if A is convicted of the full offence in line with alternative (b), the accomplice will be convicted for having aided/instigated this offence.[55]

---

51   See Court of Appeal case RH 2001:2.

52   See judgment of the Court of Appeal of Skåne and Blekinge in case no B 2193-09 (to be found only in commercial legal databases).

53   The word 'transferring' is perhaps a bit misleading since it is not a question of whether one can transfer the intent from one object to another; the question is rather whether one should focus on A's intent to kill B or on A's intent to kill another human being.

54   Under Swedish law it is, as indicated earlier in the text, possible to be convicted of aiding an offence of negligence. If there is a causal relation between the aiding and the effect one may, as a matter of principle, also be convicted of the negligent offence as a principal. However, Swedish courts actually use the possibility to label persons aiders of negligent offences. See, for example Swedish Supreme Court case NJA 1996, 27.

55   It seems quite clear that if alternative (b) is chosen as the solution for principals then this will apply also for any accomplices. One should perhaps not, however, exclude the possibility to use alternative (a) for the principal and alternative (b) for the accomplice(s). The distinction between *aberratio ictus* and *error in persona* becomes blurred as soon as one does not have a person who aims at something concrete (in time and space) and this is often the case when it comes to accomplices. For example, if A instigates B to kill C and B kills D in the belief that it was C, this can (from the point of view of A) be described either as a case of *error in persona* or as a case of *aberratio ictus*. Due to this one can argue that it is immaterial from the point of view of A, whether B kills D in an *aberratio ictus* situation or in an *error in persona* situation and that one should make use of the *aberratio ictus* solution (alternative (a)) only in relation to persons who actually have 'aimed' at a specific target in time and space. Thus, even if alternative (a) is chosen for the principal this does not seem to exclude the possibility to use alternative (b) in relation to accomplices. As regards Swedish law, such a differentiated solution may be justified by reference to Chapter 23 section 4 subsection 3 of the Criminal Code ('Each accomplice shall be judged according to the intent or the negligence attributable to him').

Withdrawal from Participation

As a general rule it is not possible to withdraw from participation, but this rule is not without exceptions.

Firstly, since assistance may be provided in advance (that is, before the complicity object is created by the principal) and since the creation of a complicity object is a necessary condition for liability as an accomplice, the presumptive accomplice can 'withdraw from participation' by making sure that the principal does not create any complicity object:

> *Example 7.* If B gives advice to A on how to commit a certain offence, B will be responsible for *aiding* from the moment that A carries out the offence or from the moment A makes herself guilty of preparation or attempt to commit it. If B, after having given the advice, changes his or her mind and then convinces A not to carry on with her plans, no complicity object will be created and, consequently, it will not be possible to hold B responsible for aiding. There is according to Swedish law no liability to attempted aiding (as opposed to aiding an attempt).

In these cases B withdraws from participation by preventing the creation of a complicity object. This is, of course, not really a case of withdrawal, but rather a possibility to withdraw from an act which (presumptively) could amount to complicity (aiding) if A fulfils her plans.

Secondly, according to Chapter 23 section 3 of the Swedish Criminal Code it is possible to withdraw from *preparation, conspiracy and attempt.*

Responsibility for attempting, preparing or conspiring to commit a crime shall not exist if a person voluntarily, by breaking off the execution of the crime or otherwise, has prevented its completion. Even if the crime was completed, a person who has unlawfully had to do with means to that end may not be held criminally responsible for that reason if he has voluntarily prevented the criminal use of the means.[56]

This provision applies not only to the principal but also to aiders and instigators. This means that an accomplice may withdraw from participation also in cases where a complicity object has been created by the principal. One example might be the following:

> *Example 8.* B gives advice to A on how to prepare and how to commit a certain offence (for example a murder). A prepares the offence in a way which makes A liable of preparation (preparing murder).[57] This means that A creates a complicity object and that the act of B (that is, to give advice) turns into an act of aiding (aiding preparation of murder). If B, at this stage, voluntarily prevents the completion of the murder, then B will not be liable for aiding the preparation of murder). The same applies if A commits conspiracy or attempt instead of preparation.

Such withdrawal does not affect the liability of other parties, that is, if B prevents the completion of the offence by telling the police about A's plans, B will not be held responsible, but A will still be responsible for his or her preparation (conversely the withdrawal of A will not exempt B from responsibility). It should be underlined that the provision applies only to cases of attempt, preparation and conspiracy (and to participation to such offences) and not to full offences.

---

56   The Ministry of Justice, Official translation of The Swedish Penal Code, Ds 1999:36.

57   Preparation is a specific inchoate offence which is committed if one, for example, with the intent to commit certain serious offences, concerns oneself with things that are especially adapted to use as means when committing an offence (for example guns, explosives and so on).

Corporate Liability: Basic Rules

Under Swedish law only natural persons can commit a crime and only natural persons can be punished. There is, however, a special sanction that can be imposed on legal persons and other 'entrepreneurs' for crimes committed in the business of the entrepreneur or the legal person. Such a corporate fine is not formally a form of punishment, but is instead defined as a 'special consequence' that can be imposed on the occasion of conviction.[58] The basic preconditions for imposing a corporate fine according to Chapter 36 section 7 of the Criminal Code are that:

1. an offence has been committed in the exercise of business activity of an entrepreneur (the entrepreneur can either be a legal person or natural person);
2. the offence committed is not one which can only be punished by a lump sum fine;[59]
3. (a) the entrepreneur has not done what could reasonably be required of him for preventing the crime or (b) the crime has been committed by either a person in a leading position or by a person who has had a special responsibility for control in the business; and,
4. the crime is not directed against the entrepreneur.

The imposition of a corporate fine takes, according to Chapter 36 section 10 of the Criminal Code, precedence before individual responsibility when it comes to minor offences committed by negligence. Thus, on the condition that the crime was committed by negligence and that it cannot be punished by more than a fine, the prosecutor may indict the individual – that is, the one who actually committed the offence – only if their prosecution is called for in the public interest. The idea behind this primacy of corporate responsibility when it comes to minor offences committed by negligence is that the responsibility for such crimes often rests upon the organisation, that is, the position and the task assigned to the position is often more important as such than the person actually holding the position and carrying out the task. Thus, it is often fairer to hold the organisation as such responsible for the occurrence of such offences.

Sentencing Regime for Participants

The overall sentencing rationale in Swedish law is just desert and the idea that the offender's punishment should be fairly proportionate in its severity with the seriousness of the criminal conduct for which he is convicted.[60] Sentencing is thus done in accordance with the principle of retrospective proportionality and measured according to the seriousness of the crime (*penal value*); in assessing this, consideration is given only to the harmfulness of the conduct and the personal culpability of the offender. Hence, sentencing for crimes of complicity can often be significantly more lenient than sentences for perpetration. The principal is usually the one who has caused most harm and he is also often the person who has shown that he is prepared to carry out the crime. An accomplice is normally, so to speak, further from the actual causing of harm; his intent focuses on furthering someone else's act rather than on causing the harm himself.

---

58   Another special consequence of a crime is forfeiture.
59   Lump sum fines are fines of a certain amount (for example 3,600 SEK for a certain type of speeding) as opposed to day fines.
60   See for example Andrew von Hirsch and Nils Jareborg in Andrew von Hirsch and Andrew Ashworth, *Principled Sentencing* (Hart 1998) 240.

The Criminal Code, however, makes no explicit distinction between perpetrators and accomplices when it comes to sentencing. According to Chapter 23 section 4 the same punishment parameters are applicable to all parties to a crime. Principals and accomplices are thus sentenced according to the same penalty scale. Furthermore, according to Chapter 23 section 5 the law further states that the punishment of *any of the parties* to the crime can be mitigated in those instances mentioned. The legislator did not make any difference between perpetration and complicity in this context, either. The provision reads as follows:

> If someone has been induced to be an accomplice to crime by coercion, deceit or misuse of his youth, innocence or dependent status or has been an accomplice only to a minor extent, the punishment imposed may be less than that otherwise provided for the crime. Punishment shall not be imposed in petty cases. This also applies where the issue is one of imposing a punishment provided for a person in a special position on an accomplice.[61]

Thus, being an accomplice does not automatically imply lesser responsibility or blameworthiness. As explained above, an instigator can sometimes be the 'mastermind' or the driving force behind a crime just as a principal can be a mere instrument in the hands of an accomplice.[62] As a consequence, both perpetrators and accomplices can have their sentences mitigated if they have been induced to the crime by 'strong influence from others' or if they are thought to have participated in the crime 'to a minor extent' (compared to the other parties of the crime). In practice, however, it is most common that accomplices get the benefit of mitigation.

The law clearly states that any party to crime who has participated after being subjected to strong influence by someone is thought less blameworthy. Correspondingly, inducing another person to take part in a crime by coercion, deceit or misuse of that person's youthfulness, lack of understanding or dependent status are circumstances that enhance the penal value.[63] Hence, any party to a crime who has been subjected to such influence can plead extenuating circumstances. Since someone – a principal or an accomplice – must been the one who has *exerted the influence* on the other(s), not all parties to a crime can have their sentence mitigated.

The second ground for mitigation, that is, 'minor participation', focuses on the relative importance that actions of the party had in comparison to other parties' actions. In this assessment both quantitative and qualitative aspects are relevant. Even though a perpetrator's participation was necessary for the completion of the crime, he can still be rendered less culpable, if his actions – on the whole – are thought to be less relevant than the others. On the other hand, the *mens rea* element can negate the insignificance of the actual behaviour itself. For example, if someone has invested heavily in the planning of the crime, courts are likely not to offer any mitigation although the actual act committed by the participator turns out to be of little importance or even superfluous for the completion of the crime.

---

61   The Ministry of Justice, Official translation of The Swedish Penal Code, Ds 1999:36.

62   See above in the sections on Joint Principals and Principals by Proxy. Swedish law thus contains two different ways of adjusting the result of the assessment of who is considered to be the principal and who is the accomplice in situations when the latter is the more blameworthy agent. Either courts use the possibility of re-characterising any party to the crime according to what seems to be most 'natural' or they adhere to their labelling, but later mitigate the sentence of the party thought to be less culpable. Both these alternatives constitute a clear expression of the relativity in the assessment of the blameworthiness with regard to the parties to a crime. It has been criticised that the law offers both these adjustment possibilities. See Herlitz (n 4) 248.

63   Swedish Criminal Code Chapter 29 section 2 [5].

In a case where an accomplice has *aided* the crime by offering mere physical help (for example supplying a tool or a weapon) or psychological encouragement, mitigation is usually offered to the secondary party on the basis that he has participated in the crime 'to a minor extent'.

Under exceptional circumstances a party to a crime can be discharged from criminal liability altogether, namely if his contribution to the crime (a) was induced by strong influence, or (b) was of minor importance, and (c) the circumstances in the case were such that the crime is judged to be a petty offence.[64] A textbook example would be someone furthering someone else's disorderly conduct (for example swimming nude in a fountain in a public place) by merely offering encouragement, although the perpetrator is already determined to go through with his offence regardless of the support from the accomplice. In such circumstances it is already doubtful whether the encouragement is unlawful at all; that is, the furthering of the complicity object does not suffice the general requirement of carelessness (in the direction of furthering a crime of disorderly conduct).[65] In any case, any such furthering of an offence would be rendered so insignificant that the acts of the accomplice are deemed lawful.

---

64   The criteria of a petty offence relates to the penal value. Any crime that would amount only to a fine would be rendered a 'petty' offence.

65   The culpa-requirement here takes the form of carelessness, being part of the *actus reus*-requirement. See Nils Jareborg, *Essays in Criminal Law* (Iustus förlag 1988) 30 ff.

Chapter 25
Turkey

R. Murat Önok

General Principles: Types of Participation and General Basis of Attributing Criminal Liability for Acts of Others

Introduction

Certain crimes require by virtue of their legal elements the participation of more than one perpetrator to their commission. Such crimes are called '*çok failli suçlar*', which may be translated as 'crimes requiring multiple perpetrators' (*concorso necessario* in Italian).[1] Examples are Art. 252 of the Turkish Penal Code (hereinafter 'TPC') concerning bribery, or Art. 220 regarding the establishment of criminal organisations.

On the other hand, the legal elements of most crimes can be fulfilled by a single perpetrator. When such crimes are committed with the contribution of various persons, rules regarding participation (*iştirak*) apply.[2] It is accepted in academic writings that the reason why participants to a crime are punished is the causal contribution offered to the commission of a crime.[3] Rules concerning the punishment of secondary participants expand the scope of criminal responsibility by punishing otherwise not typical conduct.[4] It is by virtue of the 'rule of dependence', based on the personal relationship between the secondary participant and the principal(s), that the former

---

1 Sulhi Dönmezer and Sahir Erman, *Nazari ve Tatbiki Ceza Hukuku, Genel Kısım, Cilt: II* (11th edn, Beta 1997) 437; Nevzat Toroslu, *Ceza Hukuku Genel Kısım* (16th edn, Savaş 2011) 329; Türkan Yalçın Sancar, *Çok Failli Suçlar* (Ankara 1998) 41 et seq.; Kayıhan İçel and A Hakan Evik, *İçel Ceza Hukuku Genel Hükümler – 2. Kitap* (4th edn, Beta 2007) 261; Bahri Öztürk and Mustafa Ruhan Erdem, *Uygulamalı Ceza Hukuku ve Güvenlik Tedbirleri Hukuku* (11th edn, Seçkin 2011) 323; Nur Centel, Hamide Zafer and Özlem Çakmut, *Türk Ceza Hukukuna Giriş* (7th edn, Beta 2011) 473; Timur Demirbaş, *Ceza Hukuku Genel Hükümler* (7th edn, Seçkin 2011) 453; Hakan Hakeri, *Ceza Hukuku Genel Hükümler* (13th edn, Adalet 2012) 435.

2 Dönmezer and Erman (n 1) 446; Faruk Erem, Ahmet Danışman and Mehmet Emin Artuk, *Ceza Hukuku Genel Hükümler* (14th edn, Seçkin 1997) 357; Toroslu (n 1) 295; Mehmet Emin Artuk, Ahmet Gökcen and A Caner Yenidünya, *Ceza Hukuku Genel Hükümler* (4th edn, Turhan 2009) 630; Öztürk and Erdem (n 1) 323; Doğan Soyaslan, *Ceza Hukuku Genel Hükümler* (3rd edn, Yetkin 2005) 471; Demirbaş (n 1) 456; Devrim Aydın, *Türk Ceza Hukukunda Suça İştirak* (Yetkin 2009) 25. For extensive information regarding the historical development and legal basis of participation refer to İzzet Özgenç, *Suça İştirakin Hukuki Esası ve Faillik* (Istanbul 1996) 23 et seq.

3 Öztürk and Erdem (n 1) 337; Mahmut Koca and İlhan Üzülmez, *Türk Ceza Hukuku Genel Hükümler* (4th edn, Seçkin 2011) 379. Such contribution renders the participant culpable himself. Compare İzzet Özgenç, *Türk Ceza Hukuku Genel Hükümler* (6th edn, Seçkin 2011) 444; Zeki Hafızoğulları and Muharrem Özen, *Türk Ceza Hukuku Genel Hükümler* (3rd edn, US-A Yayıncılık 2010) 349-51.

4 Toroslu (n 1) 299; İçel and Evik (n 1) 264; Artuk, Gökcen and Yenidünya (n 2) 637; Centel, Zafer and Çakmut (n 1) 475; Özgenç 'Criminal Law' (n 3) 481; Hafızoğulları and Özen (n 3) 346; Veli Özer Özbek, M Nihat Kanbur, Pınar Bacaksız, Koray Doğan and İlker Tepe, *Türk Ceza Hukuku Genel Hükümler* (2nd edn, Seçkin 2011) 486; Hamide Zafer, *Ceza Hukuku Genel Hükümler* (Beta 2010) 307.

is held responsible for the unjust behaviour amounting to a criminal offence committed by the latter.[5]

Types of Participation

It might be said that the provisions of the TPC concerning participation are highly influenced by the German Penal Code (*Strafgesetzbuch* – StGB).[6] The TPC adopts the system which is known as 'duality' (*ikilik sistemi*) with regard to the punishment of participants.[7] Their punishment is determined in view of the importance of their role in, and the causal contribution to, the commission of the crime.[8] Hence, the TPC adopts the understanding of the principal in the strict sense (*dar anlamda faillik*) whereby entering into a conduct which is causal for the realisation of the typical result does not suffice to be qualified as a principal.[9] It is through the 'rule of dependence' that aiders and abettors are also punished. Rules concerning participation only apply to intentional crimes (Art. 40 (1)). Therefore, there can be no participation to negligent crimes.[10]

As opposed to some other penal codes (such as the 1930 Italian Penal Code), the fact that a crime was committed in participation does not constitute a general aggravating circumstance.[11] Even so, with regard to certain crimes (for example, sexual assault, threat, deprivation of liberty, robbery) the fact that the offence was committed in joint participation constitutes a qualifying circumstance.

---

5   Özgenç 'Criminal Law' (n 3) 482.

6   Öztürk and Erdem (n 1) 323.

7   İçel and Evik (n 1) 265; Demirbaş (n 1) 459; Soyaslan (n 2) 500; Centel, Zafer and Çakmut (n 1) 477; Hakeri (n 1) 438; Koca and Üzülmez (n 3) 359; Hafızoğulları and Özen (n 3) 367-68. Compare Özbek et al. (n 4) 491 (the authors argue that a mixed system has been adopted). Interestingly, according to the official explanation of Art. 37, the understanding of the previous Penal Code (Law no. 765) based on the duality system has been abandoned. However, an analysis of the relevant provisions illustrates that the duality system has, in fact, been preserved, as the sentencing regime is determined according to the type of participation involved.

8   Ayhan Önder, *Ceza Hukuku Dersleri* (Filiz Kitabevi 1992) 417; İçel and Evik (n 1) 265; Centel, Zafer and Çakmut (n 1) 476; Öztürk and Erdem (n 1) 323; Aydın (n 2) 131; Özbek et al. (n 4) 488.

9   Centel, Zafer and Çakmut (n 1) 475; Öztürk and Erdem (n 1) 327; Özgenç 'Criminal Law' (n 3) 444.

10   However, where there is an intentional participation to a negligent crime, the rules concerning indirect perpetration may apply (in this direction, Öztürk and Erdem (n 1) 338). Further see Demirbaş (n 1) 456 (the author argues that there might be participation to crimes committed with advertent/conscious negligence).

11   Artuk, Gökcen and Yenidünya (n 2) 632.

Participation is divided into two categories:[12] principals (*faillik*) and complicity (*suç ortaklığı/ şeriklik* – secondary participants).[13]

Principals may be categorised under four categories:[14] sole perpetrators/principals, joint principals, indirect principals and multiple independent principals (MIPs). In its primary form (sole principal), the principal is the agent who realises the wrongful behaviour described in the legal definition of the crime.[15]

'Complicity' (secondary participation) includes abetting (*azmettirme*, *Anstiftung* in German) and, literally, assistance (*yardım etme*, aiding, *Beihilfe* in German). In the TPC, assistance refers to both 'material assistance' (*maddi yardım*) and 'moral/mental assistance' (*manevi yardım*).

In distinguishing between principals and secondary participants, the theory concerning 'control/ command over the act' is adopted by the TPC,[16] and supported in academic writings[17] and judicial decisions.[18]

In that sense, control over the act might occur in three ways.[19] The primary form is 'control over the conduct' (*harekete hâkimiyet*). The typical manifestation is 'direct/sole perpetration' (*doğrudan/ tek başına faillik*), where the perpetrator fulfils all the required objective and subjective legal

---

12 Court of Cassation (Grand Chamber) judgment of 02/02/2010, 1-239/14. The previous PC made a distinction between principal and secondary participation (*asli/fer'i faillik*), further dividing each category into material and moral (Dönmezer and Erman (n 1) 518 et seq.). In that vein, principal material participation (*asli maddi faillik*) included physical perpetration (*irtikap eden*) and direct joint perpetration (*doğrudan doğruya beraber işlemek*). Principal moral participation (*asli manevi faillik*) referred to abetting, whereas secondary material and moral participation (*fer'i maddi ve manevi faillik*) comprised the different types of conduct which are now categorised under 'assistance'. In addition, Art. 65 also provided for 'compulsory secondary participation' (*zorunlu fer'i iştirak*), which referred to acts which were, by nature, of secondary nature with regard to the perpetration of the crime in question, but without which the crime could not have been committed. In such cases, the compulsory secondary participant was treated as a principal. This provision no longer exists, and the new code would treat most such cases under 'joint perpetration' (*müşterek faillik*). However, the two categories do not correspond as joint perpetration requires to exercise 'command' over the criminal act, but does not, on the other hand, require the contribution to be indispensable in the causal sense for the completion of the crime (compare Centel, Zafer and Çakmut (n 1) 496; Hakeri (n 1) 469).

13 Özgenç 'Participation' (n 2) 139-43. See also Özgenç 'Criminal Law' (n 3) 472; Artuk, Gökcen and Yenidünya (n 2) 631, 640; Centel, Zafer and Çakmut (n 1) 484; Demirbaş (n 1) 460; Koca and Üzülmez (n 3) 360; Özbek et al. (n 4) 490. Compare Soyaslan (n 2) 476; İçel and Evik (n 1) 275; Aydın (n 2) 131 for a three-fold distinction between perpetration, abetting and assistance. Further compare Hakeri (n 1) 438 (the author makes a two-fold distinction between primary participation and assistance, and classifies abettors under the former category).

14 Öztürk and Erdem (n 1) 323; Zafer (n 4) 316 et seq. Most writers (for example Artuk, Gökcen and Yenidünya (n 2) 631; Demirbaş (n 1) 460; Hakeri (n 1) 462-63; Özbek et al. (n 4) 490) do not list MIPs amongst principals.

15 Özgenç 'Participation' (n 2) 139.

16 The official explanation of Art. 37 of the TPC clarifies that the types of participation shall be determined according to the measure of control established over the commission of the act.

17 Toroslu (n 1) 326; Artuk, Gökcen and Yenidünya (n 2) 642; Centel, Zafer and Çakmut (n 1) 478; Öztürk and Erdem (n 1) 324; Demirbaş (n 1) 462; Özgenç 'Criminal Law' (n 3) 446; Koca and Üzülmez (n 3) 362; Özbek et al. (n 4) 491.

18 Court of Cassation (Grand Chamber) judgment of 20/01/2009 (no. 1-232/2); Court of Cassation (1st Chamber) judgment of 16/12/2009 (no. 10577/7790); Court of Cassation (5th Chamber) judgment of 01/06/2009 (no. 3381/6645).

19 Öztürk and Erdem (n 1) 326; Özgenç 'Criminal Law' (n 3) 444; Koca and Üzülmez (n 3) 362.

elements of the crime with his own conduct.[20] To put it in different words, the direct perpetrator is the person who realises the material elements of the crime through his own conduct, or, the person who physically carries out the prohibited conduct in the legal definition of the crime, accompanied by the requisite mental element. As can be seen, the subjective theory which emphasises the offender's *mens rea* is totally discarded.[21] A second manifestation of control is 'control over the will' (*iradeye hâkimiyet*). This refers to the indirect perpetrator, who is the agent committing the criminal offence through another person. A third type is 'functional control'. We shall explain the latter two types of control further below, under 'principals by proxy' and 'joint criminal enterprise'.

In addition, certain authors[22] list '*yan faillik*' (*Nebentäterschaft* in German), which can be conceptualised as 'multiple independent principals' (MIPs), amongst principals. This is the case when different authors, neither sharing any common plan, nor using one another as agents or aiding and abetting each other, embark on the commission of a crime against the same victim entirely independently.[23] In Turkish academic writings the concept of MIP is used to explain negligent crimes where the independent acts of various authors cause a harmful result. In such cases, the responsibility of MIPs is determined according to TPC Art. 22(5), which states 'In crimes committed through negligence by more than one perpetrator, each one is responsible according to his own fault. The punishment of each perpetrator shall be determined independently according to his own fault'.[24] As can be seen, no distinction between principals and secondary participation is made with regard to negligent crimes. The fact that there are multiple perpetrators who are collectively guilty does not require the punishment to be reduced or divided between them according to the individual guilt of each one.[25] As in German law,[26] any person participating in the commission of a negligent offence, if not a principal offender, may only be held responsible under general rules relating to negligence. Exceptionally, it is argued that the concept of MIP can also be utilised for intentional crimes, where more than one perpetrator realises the typical result in the absence of a common criminal plan, as in the case of two agents shooting the same victim without knowing of each other's act and intention.[27] However, criminal law textbooks usually treat this example within the scope of the link of causality.[28]

On the other hand, some crimes demand a perpetrator's special status (*özgü suçlar* in Turkish, *Sonderdelikte* in German), for example, the crime of embezzlement (TPC Art. 247) may only be committed by a public officer.[29] Again, certain crimes are committed *manu propria* (*bizzat işlenebilen suç* in Turkish, *Eigenhändige Delikte* in German), in other words, the statutory definition requires a physical act to be personally committed by the perpetrator,[30] for example perjury. In such

---

20   Öztürk and Erdem (n 1) 327; Koca and Üzülmez (n 3) 363.
21   Koca and Üzülmez (n 3) 363.
22   Öztürk and Erdem (n 1) 336; Koca and Üzülmez (n 3) 362; Zafer (n 4) 319.
23   Michael Bohlander, *Principles of German Criminal Law* (Hart 2009) 160-61.
24   Unless otherwise noted, all translations are the author's.
25   Before the entry into force of the new PC, in such cases each perpetrator was assigned a degree of guilt judged over a *scale of eight*, and the punishment was 'distributed' accordingly. For example, if (A) was found 2/8 culpable, and (B) was found 6/8 culpable, the punishment was determined accordingly.
26   Bohlander (n 23) 155.
27   Öztürk and Erdem (n 1) 336.
28   For example, Koca and Üzülmez (n 3) 119; Hakeri (n 1) 454. Further see Özbek et al. (n 4) 492.
29   Özgenç 'Participation' (n 2) 165 et seq. See also Toroslu (n 1) 323; Soyaslan (n 2) 498-99; Centel, Zafer and Çakmut (n 1) 497; Demirbaş (n 1) 463; Koca and Üzülmez (n 3) 367.
30   Özgenç 'Participation' (n 2) 172-78; Demirbaş (n 1) 464; Koca and Üzülmez (n 3) 367; Aydın (n 2) 271.

crimes, only the subject holding such status, or the perpetrator committing the required act may be considered as the perpetrator, all other persons who have participated in the commission of the crime may only be held responsible either under abetting or assistance (TPC Art. 40(2)).[31]

Requirements for the Application of the Rules on Participation

For all participants, the basic condition for responsibility is that the act perpetrated by the principal must be unlawful and committed intentionally (TPC Art. 40). This is a result of the 'dependence rule' (*iştirakte bağlılık*, *Akzessorietät* in German).[32] The abettor and the aider are held responsible because of the contribution offered to the crime committed by the principal.[33] However, the principal does not need to be culpable, which shows that the Code adopts a 'limited dependence' rule (*sınırlı bağlılık kuralı*).[34] According to the second sentence of TPC Art. 40(1), each person participating in the commission of the crime shall be sentenced according to his own culpable act, irrespective of the personal circumstances which exclude the punishment of the others.

As for the basic conditions of participation, the first – and obvious – one is the existence of more than one act (including omissions) committed by more than one person.[35]

A second requirement is the existence of a causal link between the acts of the participants and the commission of the crime.[36] It is sufficient that the behaviour of the participant facilitates or supports the typical conduct of the principal.[37]

A third condition is that the execution of the crime in question must have commenced. Indeed, in order to be held responsible for participation, the crime in question must have been at least attempted (Art. 40(3)).[38] This is another result of the dependence rule, which links the responsibility of participants to the criminal act committed by the principals.

Fourth, as a moral element, the participants must possess the intent to participate in the commission of a specific crime.[39]

The implications of these conditions shall be elaborated further below.

Participation in Misdemeanours

The TPC followed the tendency to 'decriminalise' as far as possible certain acts which concern the protection of legal values of lesser importance by excluding misdemeanours (*kabahatler*) from its scope. In the previous Penal Code, crimes had been classified as either a felony (*cürüm*) or a

---

31 Öztürk and Erdem (n 1) 328.

32 Demirbaş (n 1) 475; Öztürk and Erdem (n 1) 337; Koca and Üzülmez (n 3) 379-84; Aydın (n 2) 108 et seq.

33 Öztürk and Erdem (n 1) 337; Demirbaş (n 1) 473.

34 Demirbaş (n 1) 474-75; Koca and Üzülmez (n 3) 381.

35 Dönmezer and Erman (n 1) 466; Toroslu (n 1) 304; Soyaslan (n 2) 478-80; İçel and Evik (n 1) 266; Centel, Zafer and Çakmut (n 1) 479; Hakeri (n 1) 440-45; Aydın (n 2) 87; Özbek et al. (n 4) 501.

36 Dönmezer and Erman (n 1) 473; Toroslu (n 1) 307 et seq.; Soyaslan (n 2) 481-83; İçel and Evik (n 1) 267-69; Artuk, Gökcen and Yenidünya (n 2) 651; Hakeri (n 1) 445; Aydın (n 2) 97 et seq.; Özbek et al. (n 4) 501.

37 Demirbaş (n 1) 477; in similar sense Hafızoğulları and Özen (n 3) 355; Zafer (n 4) 314.

38 Aydın (n 2) 106. Further see Toroslu (n 1) 306-307; İçel and Evik (n 1) 270-71; Artuk, Gökcen and Yenidünya (n 2) 651; Centel, Zafer and Çakmut (n 1) 481; Demirbaş (n 1) 475; Hakeri (n 1) 455.

39 Dönmezer and Erman (n 1) 478; Toroslu (n 1) 313; Soyaslan (n 2) 484-85; İçel and Evik (n 1) 269; Hakeri (n 1) 451; Aydın (n 2) 112; Özbek et al. (n 4) 501.

misdemeanour. Whereas the new TPC lays down some of the old misdemeanours as a criminal offence, most misdemeanours are now punished by a separate law (the Law on Misdemeanours (Law no. 5326)). Those committing misdemeanours are now subject to administrative sanctions.[40] Art. 14 of the Law no. 5326 provides a specific rule concerning participation: where more than one person participates in the commission of a misdemeanour, they shall each be subject to an administrative fine as a principal (para 1). Thus, the system of equality has been adopted, whereby all participants to a misdemeanour are held equally responsible.[41] When a special status is required to be the perpetrator of a misdemeanour, those participating to its commission but not holding the required status shall also be subject to an administrative fine as principals. This is a deviance from the understanding of the TPC Art. 40(2) whereby participants not holding the required special status may only be held responsible according to the rules on abetting or assistance. Finally, according to Art. 14(4) of the Law no. 5326, when an act committed in participation constitutes a criminal offence for one participant on account of the special status he holds, and a misdemeanour for the other participants who do not hold such special status, all participants shall be held responsible for the criminal offence in accordance with the provisions of the TPC concerning participation to a crime.[42]

Principals by Proxy: Use of Innocent Agents

A category of offender which is considered as a principal is that of 'indirect perpetration' (*dolaylı faillik*), where any person who uses another as an instrument in the commission of a crime shall be held responsible as a principal (TPC Art. 37(2)).[43] Indirect perpetration exists where the crime can be qualified as the creation of the person 'behind the scenes'. This requires the will of the person controlling the action to command, or direct the will of the physical perpetrator.[44] This is different from abetting where the physical perpetrator's will is not overridden, and the abettor does not have full control over the principal's actions.[45] The purpose is to hold responsible the person (referred to as *longa manus* in Latin) controlling the action of the physical perpetrator who, in most cases, lacks criminal capacity or acts without guilt.[46] TPC Art. 37(2) will also apply where the agent and the victim are one and the same person, as in the case of the agent being forced (or induced) to hurt or to kill himself.[47]

There are also special provisions concerning indirect perpetration. According to TPC Art. 84(4), 'Any person who directs, or compels through the use of force or threat, a person whose capacity to comprehend the meaning and consequences of the act is undeveloped or eliminated, to commit

---

40   Note that objections to administrative sanctions are dealt with by criminal courts (Zeynel T. Kangal, *Kabahatler Hukuku* (XII Levha 2011) 297 et seq.).

41   Kangal 'Misdemeanors' (n 40) 156; Koca and Üzülmez (n 3) 359.

42   Kangal 'Misdemeanors' (n 40) 166.

43   Özgenç 'Participation' (n 2) 197 et seq.

44   Hans-Heinrich Jescheck and Ulrich Sieber, *Alman Ceza Hukukuna Giriş – Alman Ceza Hukuku – Kusur İlkesi – Ceza Hukukunun Sınırları* (Feridun Yenisey tr, 2nd edn, Beta 2007) 44; İçel and Evik (n 1) 274.

45   Centel, Zafer and Çakmut (n 1) 488; Demirbaş (n 1) 473; Koca and Üzülmez (n 3) 369; Bohlander (n 23) 168.

46   Aydın (n 2) 142-43; Demirbaş (n 1) 472. It might also be that the instrumentalised agent is acting objectively lawfully or is not fulfilling either the material element or the mental element of the offence (Bohlander (n 23) 156; Jescheck and Sieber (n 44) 45 for examples; further see Hakeri (n 1) 469-75).

47   Demirbaş (n 1) 471; Hakeri (n 1) 471. In this case, the act of the instrumentalised agent would not be 'typical' as these crimes need to be committed against another person (Bohlander (n 23) 156).

suicide shall be held responsible for intentional killing'.[48] Similarly, according to Art. 267 concerning false accusation, where the person has been arrested or detained as a result of the accusation, and that person has been acquitted or a decision not to prosecute has been taken, the offender shall also be held responsible for deprivation of liberty (TPC Art. 109) as an indirect perpetrator. A provision to the same direction is also included in para 5 of Art. 272 concerning perjury.

In order to deter the use of innocent agents, Art. 37(2) provides that the punishment of a person who uses another agent who lacks criminal capacity as an instrument shall be increased by one-third to one-half.[49] Whereas this provision might be useful in order to deter the instrumentalisation of agents lacking free will, it is open to criticism in that the principal by proxy is punished even more severely than if he had physically committed the crime.[50]

Finally, where the innocent agent exceeds the intent of the principal by proxy (by committing a more serious or a different crime), the former may not be held responsible for the more serious or different crime.[51]

Perpetrator behind the Perpetrator: Liability of Masterminds/ Hintermen' for Acts of Otherwise Criminally Liable Agents

The responsibility of the 'perpetrator behind the perpetrator' would correspond to indirect perpetration under Turkish law. However, in the classic instance of indirect perpetration, as explained above, the direct perpetrator is not responsible for the crime, and the indirect perpetrator uses the executor (the direct perpetrator) as a tool or an instrument for the commission of the crime.

Whether someone can be a principal by proxy even though the agent himself is responsible for the crime, is a novel issue in Turkish practice. In principle, a person who is responsible for his own acts cannot be regarded as the instrument of another person (principle of responsibility). However, it is accepted in academic writings[52] that the perpetrator behind the perpetrator can exercise command over the direct perpetrator. This is the case when the person who is behind the direct perpetrators is in control of a criminal organisation in which agents are reduced to a mere cog in the wheel.[53] In such a case, it is argued that the 'hinterman' should be treated as a direct perpetrator.

In this regard, TPC Art. 220 concerning 'Establishing Organisations for the Purpose of Committing Crimes' incorporates very interesting provisions. Art. 220(5) provides for the following: 'Any leaders of such organisations shall also be sentenced as if they were the offenders in respect of any offence committed in the course of the organisation's activities'. This provision shows that a person, even where he has not taken part in the physical commission of the crime, can be treated as a joint principal in accordance with the theory of control over the act. This will be the case if he/she was decisive in its planning and organisation.[54] This is a reflection of the theory of indirect perpetration based on organised command mechanisms (*mittelbare Täterschaft kraft*

---

48   This provision is criticised in academic writings (Durmuş Tezcan, Mustafa Ruhan Erdem and R Murat Önok, *Teorik ve Pratik Ceza Özel Hukuku* (7th edn, Seçkin 2010) 183) for being redundant taken into account the existence of TPC Art. 37(2), and for failing to make reference to 'deceit', which is another means through which a person can be induced to commit suicide.

49   The increase only applies in case of conviction to imprisonment for a specific term.

50   For a similar criticism, Özgenç 'Criminal Law' (n 3) 471.

51   Hakeri (n 1) 460.

52   Öztürk and Erdem (n 1) 333.

53   Koca and Üzülmez (n 3) 373.

54   Öztürk and Erdem (n 1) 331.

organisatorischer Machtapparate) developed by Roxin.[55] The idea is that a person who, within the structure of the organisation, has been assigned a duty in committing a crime which falls within the criminal purpose of the organisation, is easily replaceable in case he fails to fulfil this duty.[56] In this system, orders are carried out automatically, independently from the personality of those carrying them out.[57] Hence, it is the creator or leader of the structure that has the central role in the mechanism, and he should be treated as a principal. Art. 220(5) does not require any enquiry into whether the leaders of the organisation participated in the planning and organisation of each single act committed in the course of the organisation's activities.[58] However, the provision is problematic in that it does not require the judge to enquire whether the leaders have played an important role in the execution of the crime,[59] or whether they were a factor in, or even aware of, the commission of such crimes.[60]

Secondary Participation

Introduction

Secondary participation includes abetting and assistance. In the TPC, assistance refers to both material assistance (*maddi yardım*, aiding), and encouragement, or 'moral/mental assistance' (*manevi yardım*) as it is termed in Turkish penal law. As explained before, to hold aiders or abettors

---

55   Osman İsfen, 'Yeni TCK'da Organize Hâkimiyet Mekanizmalarına Dayalı Dolaylı Faillik Kuramı (TCK m. 220/5)' (2006) 7 Hukuki Perspektifler Dergisi 53.

56   Vesile Sonay Daragenli Evik, 'Örgütlenme Suçları ve İştirak İlişkisi' in Eric Hilgendorf and Yener Ünver (eds), *Alman-Türk Karşılaştırmalı Ceza Hukuku, Cilt III – Prof. Dr. Köksal Bayraktar'a Armağan* (Yeditepe Üniversitesi Hukuk Fakültesi Yayını 2010) 165; Koca and Üzülmez (n 3) 373.

57   İsfen (n 55) 55.

58   Öztürk and Erdem (n 1) 331. Quite amazingly, one of the most influential academics taking part in the drafting of the new Penal Code revealed in his own book (İzzet Özgenç, *Türk Ceza Kanunu Gazi Şerhi Genel Hükümler* (Seçkin 2005) 509) that while proposing this formula his intention was to convince the members of the drafting commission to *eventually* accept the formulation that he really intended: 'Leaders of the organisation shall also be sentenced, as the case may be, as principals or participants in respect of all crimes committed in the course of the organisation's activities'. *Özgenç* explains that the purpose was to propose an extreme formula, and then, settle for less. However, the initial formulation was adopted by the members of the commission without any objection, and his later efforts to introduce the intended formulation proved fruitless! For a criticism of this provision (and also of its original intended version) based on the idea that it is an instance of strict liability see Cihan Kavlak, *Suç İşlemek Amacıyla Örgüt Kurma Suçu* (Seçkin 2011) 364-67. Further see Daragenli Evik (n 56) who argues (at 166-67) that, in line with the case law of the Italian *Corte di Cassazione*, only leaders who have a causal link with the commission of the crime through their own material or moral/mental contribution should be held responsible through the application of the rules on participation. Hence, their mere position within the organisation should not suffice to hold them responsible for all crimes committed in the course of the organisation's activities.

59   Koca and Üzülmez (n 3) 365. Further see Özgenç 'Criminal Law' (n 3) 457-58.

60   Kavlak (n 58) 366. Further see Koca and Üzülmez (n 3) 374 (the judge should enquire whether the leaders are in control, in accordance with the principle of being substitutable, of the act perpetrated by lower-ranked agents, otherwise Art. 220(5) would lead to strict liability); İsfen (n 55) 57 (the principle of being substitutable should be taken into account, but this is made impossible by the clear wording of the provision). The principle is mentioned in the official explanation of the Article, however, the explanation is not an integral part of the TPC, thus, it is not binding.

responsible, it suffices, by virtue of the rule of 'limited dependence', that the principal has acted unlawfully and intentionally.

Again by virtue of the rule of dependence, the execution of the crime in question must have commenced for the secondary participants to be punished. Contrary to, for example, German criminal law (StGB § 30),[61] attempted participation is not punished. So, if abetting has not produced any result (*neticesiz azmettirme* – literally, abetting without result), and the person has not even attempted to commit the crime to which he has been instigated, no responsibility arises for the abettor.[62] Certain authors criticise this understanding calling for the amendment of the TPC in order to penalise the abettors in such instances.[63]

Abetting

Although abettors are subject to the full punishment, they are regarded as secondary participants.[64] While Art. 38 does not define the term, it may be said that abetting is to arouse in another person the thought to commit an intentional and unlawful act constituting a criminal offence (TPC Art. 38).[65] However, the conduct of the abettor does not have to be the sole cause leading to the principal's decision to commit a crime.[66] It is argued that where the direct perpetrator has already taken the decision to commit a crime, but he is instigated to commit the qualified version of it, the abettor may only be held responsible for aiding, but not for instigating the crime in question.[67] There can be no abetting by omission.[68] It is argued that, since the intent of the abettor must be directed at the completion of the crime, *agent provocateur*s cannot be punished as abettors,[69] but the majority opinion is in the opposite direction.[70] Successive or 'chain' abetting (instigating a person to instigate

---

61 Jescheck and Sieber (n 44) 47; Bohlander (n 23) 175.

62 İçel and Evik (n 1) 277; Artuk, Gökcen and Yenidünya (n 2) 656; Öztürk and Erdem (n 1) 342; Soyaslan (n 2) 481; Centel, Zafer and Çakmut (n 1) 481; Demirbaş (n 1) 476; Ali Kemal Yıldız, *5237 Sayılı Türk Ceza Kanunu Seminer Notları* (İstanbul Barosu Yayınları 2007) 120; Aydın (n 2) 108, 171.

63 Özgenç 'Criminal Law' (n 3) 475; Özbek et al. (n 4) 504 .

64 Özgenç 'Criminal Law' (n 3) 472.

65 For different definitions you may refer to Önder (n 8) 437; Artuk, Gökcen and Yenidünya (n 2) 654; Soyaslan (n 2) 477; Centel, Zafer and Çakmut (n 1) 489; Öztürk and Erdem (n 1) 338-39; Demirbaş (n 1) 478; Hakeri (n 1) 475; Koca and Üzülmez (n 3) 384; Aydın (n 2) 166; Hafızoğulları and Özen (n 3) 371.

66 Öztürk and Erdem (n 1) 339; Koca and Üzülmez (n 3) 385.

67 Öztürk and Erdem (n 1) 340; Hakeri (n 1) 477; Koca and Üzülmez (n 3) 386. Where the person who has decided to commit a crime has been convinced to commit a lesser one instead (for example theft instead of robbery), the abettor cannot be punished as the lighter crime is comprised by the crime that was going to be committed by the perpetrator (Hakeri (n 1) 476). If the perpetrator was convinced to commit a *lighter* but altogether different crime (for example swindling instead of robbery), the abettor should be held responsible.

68 Öztürk and Erdem (n 1) 340; Demirbaş (n 1) 478; Özgenç 'Criminal Law' (n 3) 472; Koca and Üzülmez (n 3) 389. Not to be confused with abetting to commit an omissive crime, which is possible.

69 In this direction Court of Cassation (5th Chamber) judgment of 06/07/2006 (cited by Hakeri (n 1) 485). See also Öztürk and Erdem (n 1) 340; Koca and Üzülmez (n 3) 388.

70 İçel and Evik (n 1) 280; Artuk, Gökcen and Yenidünya (n 2) 664; Centel, Zafer and Çakmut (n 1) 499-500; Demirbaş (n 1) 490; Hafızoğulları and Özen (n 3) 358. Further see Özbek et al. (n 4) 509-11. According to these writers, the provisions on voluntary abandonment shall apply.

a third person) is possible.[71] Where the abettor also participates in the commission of the crime as a principal, he will only be held responsible as principal.[72]

The abettor will only be held responsible insofar as his intent and the act committed by the principal agent (including its consequence) coincide. Where the physical perpetrator qualitatively or quantitatively exceeds the intent of the abettor (by committing a different crime altogether, or a more serious crime), the abettor shall only be held responsible for the result that he intended.[73] However, where there is a 'result-qualified offence' (*netice sebebiyle ağırlaşan suçlar, erfolgsqualifizierte Delikte* in German), by virtue of TPC Art. 23,[74] the abettor will be held responsible if the extended result was foreseeable to him.[75]

When the agent commits a crime that is lighter than the one intended and instigated by the abettor, as in the case of the agent lightly wounding the victim who he was supposed to strangle to death, on account of the rule of dependence, the abettor can only be held responsible for the crime ultimately committed by the agent. However, when the lighter crime is qualitatively different from the one instigated (for example committing theft against the victim who was supposed to be murdered), the abettor will incur no criminal responsibility.[76] These remarks also apply to aiders.

There are two interesting provisions regarding abetting.[77] First, according to Art. 38(2), if a person is instigated to commit a crime by taking advantage of the influence of a direct descendent or direct antecedent relationship, the punishment of the abettor shall be increased by one-third to one-half. The same increase applies in case of abetting a minor, even if there is no such relationship.[78] In both cases, the provision only applies in case of conviction to a specific term of imprisonment.[79] Secondly, where the identity of the abettor is unknown, the principal or participant who ensures his identification will get a reduced sentence.[80] Mere naming of the abettor is insufficient; the revelation should be useful in discovering the material truth.[81]

---

71   Artuk, Gökcen and Yenidünya (n 2) 654; Öztürk and Erdem (n 1) 343; Demirbaş (n 1) 479; Hakeri (n 1) 476; Koca and Üzülmez (n 3) 385.

72   In this direction, Court of Cassation (Grand Chamber) judgment of 07/03/1998 (no. 590/72).

73   Centel, Zafer and Çakmut (n 1) 482; Özgenç 'Criminal Law' (n 3) 476; Demirbaş (n 1) 480; Koca and Üzülmez (n 3) 388. Compare Öztürk and Erdem (n 1) 341: what is decisive here is whether the deviation from the intention of the abettor is important or not.

74   'Where an act causes a more serious result, or a result other than that intended, a person will only be held responsible if he has acted, at least, with negligence in respect of such result'.

75   Court of Cassation (1st Chamber) judgment of 25/03/2010 (no. 6619/1544); Court of Cassation (1st Chamber) judgment of 08/10/2008 (no. 7061/6851).

76   Compare Toroslu (n 1) 321 (if the different crime is a foreseeable consequence of the conduct agreed upon, all participants shall be held responsible for the different crime); Hafızoğulları and Özen (n 3) 365 (if there is a causal link between the acts of the participants and the result that was not agreed upon, and the result is foreseeable, all participants will be held responsible). Further compare İçel and Evik (n 1) 277.

77   The previous PC provided for a reducement in the sentence of the abettor if the physical perpetrator had a 'personal advantage' in committing the crime. This provision no longer exists.

78   This provision has been criticised in academic writings as it is hard to understand why a joint principal committing the crime together with a minor will be given a lighter punishment than the abettor (Aydın (n 2) 151). Similarly, as the abettor is already subject to the full statutory punishment, it is hard to explain in terms of criminal policy the reason for the further aggravation of the punishment (Özgenç 'Criminal Law' (n 3) 474; Öztürk and Erdem (n 1) 343).

79   Özgenç 'Criminal Law' (n 3) 474; Koca and Üzülmez (n 3) 390.

80   This provision has been criticised for not being applicable to those who help identify the direct perpetrator (Hafızoğulları and Özen (n 3) 361).

81   In this direction Hafızoğulları and Özen (n 3) 361-62; Zafer (n 4) 323.

Aider

Material assistance (aiding) and moral/mental assistance (encouraging) not amounting to abetting are punished under TPC Art. 39. An aider is an accomplice who:

a. provides the means used for the commission of the crime, or facilitates the execution of a crime by providing assistance before or after its commission (material assistance);
b. encourages the commission of a crime,[82] or reinforces the decision to commit a crime,[83] or promises that he will assist after the commission of a crime,[84] or provides guidance as to how a crime is to be committed[85] (moral assistance).

Assistance must be intentional: the intent must comprise both the principal act and the act which constitutes assistance.[86] However, it is sufficient for the aider to know the important elements of the criminal offence; ignorance of the details is irrelevant.[87] When the principal exceeds the intent of the aider, the latter can only be held responsible for the intended result, except for result-qualified offences where any participants for which the qualified result was foreseeable will be held responsible for the extended consequence.[88] The majority opines that the assistance offered must have a causal link to the completion of the crime.[89]

Concerning the effect of qualifying circumstances of the crime on participants,[90] unlike the German Penal Code (§ 28 II) which lays down clear rules on the matter, there is no specific rule.[91] It can be said that personal circumstances which either result in the inapplicability or the mitigation of the punishment do not affect other participants.[92] However, circumstances for the exclusion or mitigation of punishment which are of an objective nature (for example the minimal value of the property with regard to theft) shall be applied to all participants.[93]

---

82 This is different from abetting in that the principal considers the commission of the crime, but has not yet reached a decision to that effect.

83 This is different from the above in that the decision to commit the crime has already been taken, and the aider merely supports this decision.

84 The promise has to be made before the commission of the crime, it is irrelevant if the promise is later not kept (Öztürk and Erdem (n 1) 346; Demirbaş (n 1) 483-84; Koca and Üzülmez (n 3) 394; Özbek et al. (n 4) 512).

85 This has to happen before the commission of the crime, otherwise there is joint perpetration (Öztürk and Erdem (n 1) 346; İçel and Evik (n 1) 283; Demirbaş (n 1) 485; Hakeri (n 1) 482; Koca and Üzülmez (n 3) 394).

86 Öztürk and Erdem (n 1) 345; Demirbaş (n 1) 481.

87 Öztürk and Erdem (n 1) 345; Demirbaş (n 1) 481.

88 İçel and Evik (n 1) 271.

89 Öztürk and Erdem (n 1) 345; Demirbaş (n 1) 478; Özgenç 'Criminal Law' (n 3) 478; Koca and Üzülmez (n 3) 392. However, the contribution need not be indispensable or even highly important for the completion of the crime, it is sufficient that the commission of the typical conduct is facilitated or merely supported.

90 'If the law provides that special personal characteristics aggravate, mitigate or exclude punishment, then this shall apply only to the participants (the perpetrator or the inciter or accessory) as to whom they exist' (<http://www.iuscomp.org/gla/statutes/StGB.htm#164> accessed 3 September 2012).

91 This is another matter which attracted serious criticism (Aydın (n 2) 232).

92 Öztürk and Erdem (n 1) 347; Soyaslan (n 2) 490; Demirbaş (n 1) 491-93; Hakeri (n 1) 484-85; Koca and Üzülmez (n 3) 381; Aydın (n 2) 232; Zafer (n 4) 324-25.

93 Öztürk and Erdem (n 1) 347; Soyaslan (n 2) 490; Hakeri (n 1) 484; Aydın (n 2) 233.

With regard to qualifying circumstances which aggravate the punishment, each participant shall be held responsible in light of his own culpable act (Art. 40(1)). Thus, the intent of the participants will be decisive, and such aggravating circumstances will only apply to those participants who have knowledge of their existence.[94] As a result of the dependence rule, it is argued that if husband (A) was to assist girlfriend (B) in murdering his own wife (C), (A) could not be held responsible for qualified murder (on account of the spousal relationship between him and (C)).[95] However, the case law on the issue is not settled.[96] On the other hand, if (A) and (B) were to act as joint principals, (A) would have committed qualified murder, whereas (B) would not be held responsible for the aggravating circumstance.[97]

Specific Issue: Joint Criminal Enterprise (JCE)

The closest concept in Turkish law to the English law concept of JCE is that of 'joint principals' (*birlikte/müşterek faillik*). According to Art. 37(1), each person who jointly commits the act laid down in the legal definition of the crime shall be held responsible as a principal.

As in any system where the punishment of the participants is determined in view of the importance of their role (and the causal contribution) in the commission of the crime, the TPC requires a distinction to be made between joint principals and secondary participants. The criterion adopted in Turkish academic writings and judicial decisions relies on whether the participant has 'control/command' (*hakimiyet*) over the execution of the crime.[98] In that sense, each joint principal must have a determining influence over the completion or not of the crime.[99] In case of joint principals, the key term is having 'functional control' over the act. This is taken as being able to exercise command over the development of the typical event, commanding the course of events, that is, being capable of exercising control over the process of materialisation of the crime.[100] If this is the case, the participant will be regarded as a joint principal. If the contribution of the participant to the crime does not fall into one of these three categories of control, he/she will be treated as a secondary participant ('assistant').

---

94   İçel and Evik (n 1) 271; Öztürk and Erdem (n 1) 347; Soyaslan (n 2) 490; Demirbaş (n 1) 493; Özbek et al. (n 4) 502; Zafer (n 4) 324. Compare Hafızoğulları and Özen (n 3) 362-63 (the writer draws a distinction between personal aggravating circumstances and objective/factual aggravating circumstances, and requires an additional condition for the reflection to the participants of the former category: that the circumstance in question facilitates the commission of the crime or is effective upon its commission). Further compare Aydın (n 2) 234 (the writer requires for both the reflection of personal and objective aggravating circumstances that the circumstance in question facilitates the commission of the crime or that it is effective upon its commission).

95   Demirbaş (n 1) 493; Koca and Üzülmez (n 3) 383. For an example in the opposite direction Hakeri (n 1) 484.

96   For a decision holding the other participants responsible for the qualifying circumstance, see Court of Cassation (1st Chamber) judgment of 01/02/2010 (no. 438/493); for decisions in the contrary direction, see Court of Cassation (1st Chamber) judgment of 10/02/2010 (no. 2844/758) and Court of Cassation (1st Chamber) judgment of 25/10/2007 (no. 4960/805) (cited by Demirbaş (n 1) 493).

97   In this direction Court of Cassation (1st Chamber) judgment of 12/06/2008 (no. 489/4996). See also Hakeri (n 1) 484; Koca and Üzülmez (n 3) 383.

98   Özgenç 'Participation' (n 2) 261 et seq. Also see Artuk, Gökcen and Yenidünya (n 2) 643-44; Centel, Zafer and Çakmut (n 1) 485; Öztürk and Erdem (n 1) 326; Koca and Üzülmez (n 3) 361-62; Hakeri (n 1) 462.

99   Özgenç 'Criminal Law' (n 3) 448; Özbek et al. (n 4) 496; Zafer (n 4) 317.

100   Öztürk and Erdem (n 1) 326; Özgenç 'Criminal Law' (n 3) 446 et seq.; Hakeri (n 1) 463; Koca and Üzülmez (n 3) 361.

Joint perpetration also includes those acts which are not typical (that is, they do not correspond to the act prohibited in the legal definition of the crime) but are important (but not necessarily indispensable) for the commission of the typical act indicated in the statutory definition of the crime.[101] An example would be the role of a lookout during a robbery where the lack of his presence would create the risk of failing to realise the typical act of the robbery. Whether the lookout is a principal or a secondary participant will be decided according to the 'control' criterion applicable to determining the status of principal.

There are two requirements for being qualified as a joint principal:[102]

a. The existence of a common decision concerning the commission of a criminal act on the basis of mutual co-operation (subjective element). In other words, joint principals act on the basis of a common, mutually communicated and agreed plan.[103]
b. Jointly committing the act, in the sense of each participant contributing to the commission of the act, and such contributions being mutually complementary (objective element). It is this division of labour that makes possible, or facilitates the commission of the crime, or significantly reduces the risk of failure.[104]

As opposed to secondary participants, the responsibility of joint principals is not based on the dependence rule, but on their personal direct contact with the unlawful behaviour which amounts to a crime.[105] Since the acts of joint principals are mutually attributable to one another, it is not necessary for each of them to fulfil all the material elements of the crime with their own conduct.[106] This is why, as opposed to the relationship between the aider and the principal, joint principals have to be aware of each other's contribution. However, when a crime requires the act to be committed pursuant to a specific intent, a participant that does not carry the requisite intent may not be treated as a joint principal.[107] Physical presence at the crime scene is not required in order to be held responsible as a joint principal, as long as the 'functional command' criterion is fulfilled.[108] In fact, in parallel with German practice,[109] a contribution made at the preparatory stage of the crime may lead to being held responsible as a joint principal.[110] A contribution offered after commencement of the execution of the crime may also qualify the agent as a joint principal,[111] as long as a subsequent

---

101   Öztürk and Erdem (n 1) 331; Aydın (n 2) 135; Özbek et al. (n 4) 493-94.

102   Jescheck and Sieber (n 44) 46; Artuk, Gökcen and Yenidünya (n 2) 643; Öztürk and Erdem (n 1) 329; Özbek et al. (n 4) 495-99.

103   Bohlander (n 23) 163.

104   Koca and Üzülmez (n 3) 363. On the other hand, it need not be determined that the contribution was indispensable in the causal sense for the commission of the crime (Özgenç 'Criminal Law' (n 3) 450).

105   Özgenç 'Criminal Law' (n 3) 447.

106   Artuk, Gökcen and Yenidünya (n 2) 644; Centel, Zafer and Çakmut (n 1) 486; Demirbaş (n 1) 467-68; Özgenç 'Criminal Law' (n 3) 447; Hakeri (n 1) 464.

107   Koca and Üzülmez (n 3) 367.

108   In this direction, Court of Cassation (1st Chamber) judgment of 25/07/2007 (no. 6133/4096).

109   BGH NStZ 1999 at 609; BGH NStZ 202 at 200; BGH NStZ 2003 at 253 (cited by Öztürk and Erdem (n 1) 331).

110   Öztürk and Erdem (n 1) 331; Özgenç 'Criminal Law' (n 3) 450; in the opposite direction Hakeri (n 1) 464. This is one of the differences with the 'direct joint perpetrator' category embodied in the previous penal code, as the acts of the direct joint perpetrator had to be committed simultaneously with the physical perpetrator's executory acts (Özgenç 'Criminal Law' (n 3) 446).

111   In this direction Court of Cassation (Grand Chamber) judgment of 13/10/2009 (no. 1-194/235) (cited by Özbek et al. (n 4) 498).

common decision exists, and the contribution suffices to accept that control has been established over the whole act.[112] Finally, it is argued that omission offences can also be committed jointly, where each participant is under a duty to act.[113]

Joint principals are only responsible for the acts of other joint principals when these acts fall within the scope of the common plan.[114] Thus, when one of the joint principals acts outside the common plan, other joint principals may not be held responsible if there is an 'important deviation' from that common decision. For example,[115] (A) and (B) decide to commit theft against (C), and agree that there will be absolutely no resort to violence. If (B) exercises violence against (C) during the commission of the act, (A) can only be punished for theft, whereas (B) can be punished for robbery. On the other hand, joint principals will all be held responsible in case of irrelevant deviations which do not have a bearing on the gravity and dangerousness of the act, in particular when they are foreseeable taking into account the circumstances of the specific case.[116] In case of result-qualified offences, by virtue of TPC Art. 23, joint principals for which the qualified result was foreseeable will be held responsible for the extended consequence.[117]

In the previous Penal Code, there was a special provision (Art. 463) reducing the punishment of joint principals in cases of intentional killing and wounding where the person actually causing the result was not identifiable. Having adopted the criterion of 'control over the act', the new TPC does not incorporate such a provision as all joint principals will be held responsible for the death or injury, regardless of which individual perpetrator actually caused the result.[118]

Effect of Errors and Transferred Malice/Aberratio ictus Scenarios in the Person of One Participant on the Liability of the Other Participants

These scenarios are usually debated from the viewpoint of the abettor. With regard to error and *aberratio ictus*, the issue is resolved in the framework of the provisions concerning error (TPC Art. 30) and so-called formal concurrence (TPC Art. 44, *fikri içtima* in Turkish, *concorso formale/ideale* in Italian).[119] Therefore, by virtue of the impersonality principle whereby the law only requires the

---

112   Demirbaş (n 1) 465; Özgenç 'Criminal Law' (n 3) 458; Koca and Üzülmez (n 3) 365.

113   Özgenç 'Criminal Law' (n 3) 469; Koca and Üzülmez (n 3) 368; Hakeri (n 1) 466. Further see Öztürk and Erdem (n 1) 332 (the authors also argue that joint perpetration may also apply between an agent's positive act and another agent's omission, as long as the typical result is a consequence of the co-operation between the positive act and the omission which is in violation of the duty to act. In the opposite direction, Özgenç 'Criminal Law' (n 3) 469).

114   Koca and Üzülmez (n 3) 367.

115   Öztürk and Erdem (n 1) 329.

116   Öztürk and Erdem (n 1) 330; compare Özgenç 'Criminal Law' (n 3) 461.

117   Öztürk and Erdem (n 1) 330; Demirbaş (n 1) 470; Koca and Üzülmez (n 3) 367. Compare *Özgenç* 'Criminal Law' (n 3) who argues (at 461) that if the extended result has been caused intentionally by one of the joint principals, the others can not be held liable for it.

118   In this direction, Court of Cassation (1st Chamber) judgment of 25/12/2006 (no. 5707/5963). Further see Öztürk and Erdem (n 1) 331; Tezcan, Erdem and Önok (n 48) 180; Özgenç 'Criminal Law' (n 3) 451-52. Compare Centel, Zafer and Çakmut (n 1) 486-87; Hafızoğulları and Özen (n 3) 370.

119   According to Art. 44, a person who commits more than one offence through a single act shall only be sentenced for the crime which requires the heaviest punishment. What is meant here is only the conduct (*hareket, Handlung* in German). So, if a single conduct causes more than one result of criminal importance, there is 'a single act' for the purpose of Art. 44 and its provisions shall apply (Artuk, Gökcen and Yenidünya (n 2) 688; Centel, Zafer and Çakmut (n 1) 505; Öztürk and Erdem (n 1) 318; Demirbaş (n 1) 509; Koca and

death of a human being, instances of error in the person of the victim are deemed irrelevant from the viewpoint of both the abettor and the principal agent, with the only exception being when the identity of the victim is an aggravating circumstance in the statutory definition of the crime (TPC Art. 30(2)).[120]

As for *aberratio ictus* (for example (A) convinces (B) to shoot (C) dead, however, (B) misses and shoots (D) instead) it is argued that the intent of the abettor is decisive and he will be held responsible for the result ultimately caused by the principal agent if he acted with *dolus directus* or *dolus eventualis* in respect of the actual result.[121] According to another view,[122] an error in the person or the object is irrelevant when it is within the boundaries of foreseeability according to general life experience; however, in case of *aberratio ictus*, the abettor shall be held responsible for the attempted intentional crime (against (C)), whereas he cannot be held responsible for the negligent completed crime (against (D)) because the rules concerning participation only apply to intentional crimes. Finally, a different view argues that, in case of *aberratio ictus*, since the abettor's intent is specifically directed at (C), he cannot be held responsible for the harm suffered by (D).[123]

In case of joint principals, it is argued that in both cases, where the error or *aberratio* is irrelevant, there is no effect from the viewpoint of criminal responsibility, and all joint participants shall be held responsible as if the intended result had materialised.[124]

In the case of principals by proxy, when the agent incurs an error in the object of the crime, such mistake shall be treated as an *aberratio ictus* from the perspective of the principal by proxy, hence, the indirect perpetrator should be held responsible for attempting the intended crime, and for a completed negligent crime with regard to the result caused by the innocent agent.[125]

It does not seem possible to speak about any established case law of the Court of Cassation on these aspects. Academic views are also inconclusive as each author seems to address the problem only from the viewpoint of a specific participant.

Withdrawal from Participation

Voluntary abandonment by one participant in crimes committed by multiple participants is regulated in TPC Art. 41. The first paragraph of this article provides that only the person who voluntarily abandons the attempt to commit an offence may benefit from the abandonment provisions.[126] This is

---

Üzülmez (n 3) 402; Özbek et al. (n 4) 534; in the opposite direction Toroslu (n 1) 344; İçel and Evik (n 1) 289-90; Hakeri (n 1) 523).

120 Koca and Üzülmez (n 3) 389, Özgenç 'Criminal Law' (n 3) 477.

121 Koca and Üzülmez (n 3) 389 (however, even in this case, TPC Art. 44 concerning formal concurrence shall apply).

122 Öztürk and Erdem (n 1) 342. The writers hold the same opinion (at 345) with regard to the responsibility of aiders, in case of error by the principal.

123 Hakeri (n 1) 461-62.

124 Öztürk and Erdem (n 1) 330; Demirbaş (n 1) 466. In the same direction, with regard to error, Koca and Üzülmez (n 3) 367.

125 Öztürk and Erdem (n 1) 335 (the rules on formal concurrence (TPC Art. 44) shall apply, so that the principal by proxy will only be punished for the crime requiring the harshest sentence). Compare Demirbaş (n 1) 473.

126 According to TPC Art. 36, an offender who voluntarily abandons the executory acts of the crime, or who prevents through his own effort the completion of the crime or the realisation of the result, shall not be punished for that attempt. However, where the acts already committed constitute an independent offence, the perpetrator shall be punished with regard to such offence.

because voluntary abandonment constitutes a personal ground for excluding punishment.[127] Hence, where the direct perpetrator abandons the commission of the crime at the attempt stage, this has no relevance for other participants.[128] Where an aider withdraws, academic writings argue that the crime should have been completed independently of the prior contribution of the participant who gave up supporting its commission.[129] Note, however, that Art. 41(2) provides that the voluntary abandonment provisions shall apply if: a) the offence was not committed for a reason outside the effort of the person voluntarily abandoning the commission of the crime, or b) the offence was committed despite the best effort by the person who voluntarily abandoned the commission of the crime, to prevent its commission. In the last option, contrary to the German Penal Code § 24 II, there is no explicit requirement that the crime is committed *independently* of the participant's earlier contribution.

In case of principals by proxy, it is argued that the agent must be prevented from completing the executory acts, or where they have been completed, the typical result must be stopped from materialising in order for the indirect perpetrator to benefit from the provision on voluntary abandonment.[130]

Corporate Liability: Basic Rules

TPC Art. 20 provides that criminal responsibility is personal, and no one shall be held responsible for the act of another. According to sub-section 2, criminal punishment shall not be imposed on legal entities. However, sanctions in the form of security measures[131] prescribed by law may be applied.

One of the results of the adoption of the principle of culpability is that a person who has not acted culpably may not be punished.[132] According to academic writings, guilt cannot be imputed to legal entities,[133] and they cannot 'act' in the criminal sense.[134] Hence, they cannot 'commit' criminal offences, and may only be subjected to security measures, but not criminal punishment.[135]

---

127   Özgenç 'Criminal Law' (n 3) 489.

128   Özgenç 'Criminal Law' (n 3) 491; Hakeri (n 1) 449; Koca and Üzülmez (n 3) 397; Özbek et al. (n 4) 514. Obviously, if the direct perpetrator has abandoned the crime at the preparatory phase, there will be no criminal responsibility for any of the participants (Demirbaş (n 1) 487; Hakeri (n 1) 448).

129   Aydın (n 2) 237-38. See also Soyaslan (n 2) 491; Demirbaş (n 1) 488; Hakeri (n 1) 450; Özbek et al. (n 4) 514; Hafızoğulları and Özen (n 3) 365.

130   Koca and Üzülmez (n 3) 398.

131   The TPC provides for two types of sanctions: punishments (*cezalar* – Arts. 45-52), and correctional/preventional/reformatory measures (which are called 'security measures' (*güvenlik tedbirleri*) – Arts. 53-60). Punishment is based on and determined according to culpability, whereas security measures are a response to, and must be proportional to the 'danger' posed by the criminal.

132   Öztürk and Erdem (n 1) 50; Centel, Zafer and Çakmut (n 1) 43; Demirbaş (n 1) 55; Koca and Üzülmez (n 3) 42; Özbek et al. (n 4) 76.

133   T Zeynel Kangal, *Tüzel Kişilerin Ceza Sorumluluğu* (Seçkin 2003) 134; İçel and Evik (n 1) 56.

134   Kangal 'Legal Persons' (n 133) 125-26. See also Önder (n 8) 163; Öztürk and Erdem (n 1) 172.

135   Önder (n 8) 164-65; Toroslu (n 1) 364; Artuk, Gökcen and Yenidünya (n 2) 298-99; Soyaslan (n 2) 504; Demirbaş (n 1) 219; Kangal 'Legal Persons' (n 133) 141-45, 208-9; Aydın (n 2) 83; Özbek et al. (n 4) 205. Compare Dönmezer and Erman (n 1) 413. Further see Haluk Toroslu, *Ceza Müeyyidesi* (Savaş 2010) 87 (the author argues that since this rule does not have constitutional value, laws enacted after the entry into force of the TPC may still provide for criminal sanctions against legal persons). Note that the draft TPC provided that, in cases explicitly provided for by the law, legal persons would be 'responsible' for crimes committed

Security measures applicable to legal entities are the revocation of the license to operate, and confiscation.[136] It may be disputed whether these measures constitute, in reality, security measures or punishment proper (in the criminal sense). In addition, legal entities may face administrative sanctions, such as administrative fines.

According to TPC Art. 60(1), the license to operate may be revoked under certain conditions:

- the legal entity must be subject to civil law[137] and operating under the license granted by a public institution;
- there must be a conviction for an intentional crime;
- the crime must have been committed for the benefit of the legal entity;
- the crime must have been committed by misusing the permission conferred by such license;
- the crime must have been committed through the participation of the organs or representatives of the legal entity.

The revocation is permanent.[138] However, the court cannot dissolve the legal entity in question.[139] According to Art. 60(2), the provisions relating to confiscation shall also apply to civil legal entities in relation to crimes committed for the benefit of such entities.

However, where the application of these provisions could lead to more serious consequences than the crime itself, as in the case of many workers facing unemployment in case of shutting down a factory,[140] the judge may decide not to impose such measures, Art 60(3). Finally, the provisions of Art. 60 shall only apply where specifically stated in the law, Art. 60(4).

Sentencing Regime for Participants

With regard to the sentencing regime, Turkey adopts the system whereby a normative distinction is drawn between different modes of participation, and a different tariff of penalties applicable to each category is provided by law.

The principals (sole perpetrators, joint principals, principals by proxy, MIPs) and the abettor will be sentenced to the full punishment determined by law for the crime in question.[141]

Aiders (assistants) will benefit from a statutory discount: a term of 15–20 years if the crime committed requires aggravated life imprisonment, a term of 10–15 years if the crime committed requires life imprisonment. The penalty shall be reduced by one-half in all other cases. However, in this case, the penalty to be imposed shall not exceed eight years. The judge does not have any discretion concerning the reduction, it is mandatory.

'to its benefit' by its organs or representatives. In addition, the Constitutional Court had previously held that attribution of criminal responsibility to legal entities was not in violation of the principle of personal criminal responsibility (see the judgments of 16/06/1964 (no. 101/49) and 19/09/1991 (no. 2/30)).

136   Confiscation of property (Art. 54) and confiscation of proceeds from the crime (Art. 55).
137   Therefore, public institutions (legal entities operating under public law) are excluded from the scope of this article.
138   Özbek et al. (n 4) 612.
139   Özgenç 'Criminal Law' (n 3) 738; Koca and Üzülmez (n 3) 526.
140   Özbek et al. (n 4) 612.
141   Note, however, the provisions in the second and third paragraph of Art. 38.

Chapter 26

United States

Luis E. Chiesa

General Principles

The special part of a criminal code defines the types of conduct that the state considers worthy of criminal punishment. As a general rule, these crimes are defined in a way that the only one who can commit the offence is the person who actually engages in the prohibited conduct. In contrast, those who help others engage in conduct that is constitutive of the crime are typically not subject to punishment if the definition of the offence in the special part of the criminal code is construed literally. Thus, for example, homicide was defined at common law as the 'unlawful killing of a human being with malice aforethought'.[1] Taken literally, only those who actually kill a human being would be punished for homicide. In contrast, those who help another kill a human being would *not* be liable for homicide, for the offence as defined at common law only criminalises the *killing* of a human being, not facilitating or aiding another to kill a human being. In sum, absent a doctrine that states otherwise, the one who shoots and kills the victim would be liable for homicide, whereas the one who gave the shooter the gun would not be liable for homicide because he did not kill the victim.

It would, of course, be intolerable for society if criminal laws punished only those who actually engage in the offence while not punishing those who help others commit it. As a result, the doctrine of criminal participation was developed and is now codified in the general part of criminal codes throughout the United States. The effect of this doctrine is to expand the scope of application of criminal offences defined in the special part of codes to encompass conduct that would otherwise remain unpunished. In practical terms, the general doctrine of participation allows the state to punish not only those who actually engage in conduct constitutive of the offence, but also those who help others consummate the crime.

As with most substantive criminal law doctrines in the United States, the issue of criminal participation may be approached from either the traditional common law perspective or from the (relatively) more recent Model Penal Code perspective. This section begins by focusing on the types of participation punishable in the United States at common law. Subsequently, the section will focus on the Model Penal Code approach to criminal participation.

Common Law Approach to Criminal Participation

At common law, parties were punished as either principals or accessories.[2] Principals were divided into principals in the first degree and principals in the second degree. Accessories, in turn, were

---

1 See, for example, California Penal Code §187.
2 These categories only applied in felony cases. As to misdemeanours, all parties to the crime were considered principals.

split into accessories before the fact and accessories after the fact.[3] It was originally believed that both first and second degree principals and accessories before and after the fact should be punished equally.[4] However, it was later determined that accessories after the fact were not true parties to crime, for their contribution took place after the offence was consummated.[5] As a result, accessories after the fact were eventually punished in a different way than principals and accessories before the fact.[6]

The main difference between principals and accessories is a temporal one. Principals contribute to the commission of the offence by engaging in conduct that is contemporaneous to the consummation of the offence. In contrast, the aid provided by accessories is the product of conduct that takes place either before the crime is committed or after the offence is completed.

A principal in the first degree is the person who engages in an act or an omission that brings about the commission of the offence.[7] She is the person who commits the crime with her own hands by, for example, shooting the gun that kills the victim in the case of homicide or engaging in non-consensual sexual intercourse in the case of rape. The principal in the first degree is, therefore, the actual perpetrator of the offence. She is the person, in other words, who controls both how the crime will be consummated and when it will be carried out.

In contrast, a principal in the second degree is one who helps others commit a crime by engaging in acts or omissions that are contemporaneous to the commission of the offence.[8] Strictly speaking, principals in the second degree are not the actual perpetrators of the crime, for they do not commit the crime themselves nor do they control how or when the offence will be completed. They merely provide help or encourage another to commit the offence. The principal in the second degree may contribute to the consummation of the offence by either helping the actual perpetrator commit the crime or by inducing, commanding or encouraging the perpetrator to engage in conduct constitutive of the offence. Examples of the former would be the person who gives a gun to the perpetrator for him to kill the victim or the person who is present at the scene of the crime to render aid if necessary. Examples of the latter include the person who encourages the perpetrator by cheering him on or the person who tells the perpetrator to shoot the victim. Because their contribution consists in either rendering aid to the perpetrator of the crime or in encouraging the perpetrator, principals in the second degree are frequently called 'aiders and abettors'.[9]

An accessory before the fact is a person who contributes to the commission of the crime by engaging in conduct that takes place before the crime is committed. Like principals in the second degree, accessories after the crime do not actually engage in the conduct that is constitutive of the offence. They are not, in other words, the true perpetrators of the offence. As a result – like principals in the second degree – accessories after the fact engage in acts or omissions that either aid or encourage another to commit an offence. Nevertheless, unlike principals in the second degree, accessories before the fact are not present when the perpetrator commits the offence. If the accessory is actually present when the offence is committed, he would be considered a principal in the second degree. The help provided by the accessory before the fact may consist in either providing goods or services that will help the perpetrator commit the future crime or encouraging or counselling the commission of the future offence. An example of the former is that of the person

---

3   Bl Comm 4(3) 34-39.
4   Wayne R LaFave, *Substantive Criminal Law* (2nd edn, West 2011) §13.1.
5   Ibid.
6   Ibid.
7   Bl Comm (n 3).
8   Ibid.
9   See for example, *United States v. Ambrose*, 740 F.2d 505 (7th Cir., 1985).

who provides the perpetrator with a key that she will need in order to break into an apartment to commit a burglary.[10] An example of the latter would be a person who meets with another in order to induce him to commit a crime in the future.

Finally, an accessory after the fact is a person who helps the perpetrator of a completed crime avoid apprehension.[11] While accessories after the fact were originally treated like accessories before the fact, today accessories after the fact are typically punished less severely than accessories before the fact.[12] The reason for this is that accessories after the fact do not really help the perpetrator complete the offence, given that the help provided in these cases takes place *after* the crime is consummated. In contrast, accessories before the fact are true accomplices of the perpetrator.[13] They, for example, help the perpetrator kill the victim. On the other hand, the accessory after the fact is not really an accomplice to the perpetrator. Thus, it cannot be said that the accessory after the fact of a homicide helped the perpetrator kill the victim. Consequently, whatever blameworthiness attaches in these cases is a product of covering up a past crime, not of contributing to bringing about a present or future crime.

Model Penal Code Approach to Criminal Participation

The common law distinction between principals and accessories was abandoned in most American jurisdictions, due at least in part to the fact that a person charged as a principal could not be convicted of being an accessory even if that is what the evidence presented during the trial established. Similarly, a person charged as an accessory could not be convicted if the evidence demonstrated that he was actually a principal. This procedural quirk produced manifestly unjust results. This problem was rectified in many jurisdictions by legislation that provided that accessories could be tried and convicted even if it was demonstrated that they were really principals and vice versa.

Eventually, the drafters of the Model Penal Code decided to abandon the principal/accessory distinction altogether.[14] More than half of American jurisdictions have followed suit.[15] In lieu of the common law categories, §2.06 of the Code distinguishes between perpetrators and accomplices. Perpetrators are those who either commit the offence 'by their own conduct' or 'by the conduct of another person for which they are legally accountable'.[16] On the other hand, a person is an accomplice if she solicits another to commit an offence, aids or agrees to aid another person in the

---

10   Again, if the key is provided when the perpetrator is engaging in the burglary, the contribution will be considered that of a principal in the second degree rather than that of an accessory before the fact.

11   Blackstone (n 3).

12   See, for example, Model Penal Code §242.

13   An interesting case arises if before the offence is committed an accessory promises to help someone avoid apprehension after the crime is committed. This, for example, of the person who – before the crime takes place – promises the perpetrator that he will perform surgery that will change his appearance so that he avoids detection. It would be tempting to consider this person an accessory after the fact because the promised help will take place after the crime is consummated. Nevertheless, it is appropriate to consider this person an accessory before the fact, for his promise to help the perpetrator amounts to an act of encouragement that strengthens the perpetrator's resolve. It communicates to the perpetrator that he should go ahead with the crime, for the accessory will be there to make sure everything turns out all right.

14   Model Penal Code §2.06.

15   Comments to Model Penal Code §2.06, 299.

16   Model Penal Code §2.06(1).

commission of a crime, or fails to make an effort to prevent a crime when she had a legal duty to do so.[17] The precise scope of these categories is fleshed out in the following sections.

Principals by Proxy: Use of Innocent Agents

As a general rule, the perpetrator is the person who actually engages in the conduct that is constitutive of the offence.[18] Obvious cases are those of the shooter who kills the victim or the thief who takes the money from the bank. In contrast, the person who helps another engage in conduct that is constitutive of the crime is typically considered an accomplice rather than a perpetrator. However, there are some instances in which a person is considered a perpetrator even though he did not personally engage in the conduct that constituted the offence. The most universally accepted instance is that of the person who causes an innocent or irresponsible agent to commit a crime. In such cases, as the drafters of the Model Penal Code point out, the person 'is accountable … as if the conduct were his own'.[19]

The irresponsible agent may be innocent for various reasons. The most common are either because his conduct is excused as a result of a defence of insanity or infancy, or because he fails to act with the degree of culpability that is necessary to satisfy the elements of the offence charged. An example of the former is the case of *Johnson v. State*, in which an Alabama court held that the person who incited an insane person to kill is guilty as a perpetrator in much the same way as if he had committed the crime himself.[20] Another example is *Rouse v. Commonwealth*, which involved a child who was forced to operate a vehicle recklessly.[21] An example of the latter is *United States v. Kenofskey*, in which a person was held to commit mail fraud by causing a person to mail a letter that unbeknownst to him contained a fraudulent life insurance death claim.[22]

With regard to the culpability with which the actor who causes an innocent person to commit a crime must act, the Model Penal Code holds that 'a defendant is accountable for the behavior of an innocent … person when he has caused such behavior to occur, provided that he caused it [with the form of culpability] that the law requires for commission of the crime with which he has been charged'.[23] The person who causes an innocent person to commit the crime is thus liable on the basis of his own culpability rather than on the basis of the culpability of the person that he used to commit the offence. Thus, for example, a person who recklessly causes a child to kill purposely (by giving the child a gun, for example) is liable for reckless homicide rather than for a purposeful homicide.[24] Similarly, a person who negligently causes an innocent person to make false statements in exchange for property is not liable for theft by false pretences because he does not act with the purpose to make false statements (or cause someone else to make false statements).[25]

---

17 Model Penal Code §2.06(3).
18 In common law terminology, these persons would be considered principals in the first degree.
19 Comments to Model Penal Code §2.06(2)(a), 300.
20 38 So. 182 (1904).
21 303 S.W.2d 265 (Ky. 1957).
22 243 U.S. 440 (1917).
23 Comments to Model Penal Code §2.06(2)(a), 302.
24 Ibid.
25 Ibid. 303.

Perpetrator Behind the Perpetrator

In civil law jurisdictions it is hotly debated whether someone who orchestrates, plans or authorises the commission of certain offences may be held liable as a perpetrator of such offences even when the individuals who actually commit the crimes satisfy the requirements to be held liable as perpetrators themselves.[26] The typical case is that of a person who exerts complete control over an organisation who is held liable as a perpetrator for the crimes that are committed by the organisation's members even if the members themselves may also be held liable as perpetrators. This is what happened in Germany with many Nazi leaders who planned the atrocities perpetrated during the Holocaust.[27] German scholars and courts eventually developed a doctrine called 'perpetrator behind the perpetrator' that authorised punishing those who planned the atrocities as perpetrators even though they were not the ones who actually engaged in the conduct constitutive of the offence.[28]

The theory of the perpetrator behind the perpetrator is of practical importance if the mastermind who controls the organisation cannot otherwise be held liable for the crimes committed by the organisation's members. It might also be important if the mastermind could be held criminally liable for the acts of the organisation's members but would be punished less than those who actually carried out the crimes. Punishing the mastermind less than the ones who carry out the crime might strike some as counterintuitive, since those who carry out the crimes are merely a cog in the organisational wheel and, as a result, they seem to behave in a less culpable way than the mastermind who actually controls the organisation. At the very least those who actually carry out the crimes do not appear to behave more culpably than the mastermind who is in charge of the organisation. Consequently, if the doctrine of criminal participation in a given jurisdiction left such masterminds unpunished or if it mandated that they be punished less than the ones who actually carried out the crimes, the arguments in favour of creating rules that treat the masterminds as actual perpetrators of the crime become more powerful.

This is not, however, the case in America. Masterminds that would in principle be treated as 'perpetrators behind the perpetrator' in Germany and other civil law countries can be held liable as accomplices in the United States if they either encouraged the members of the organisation to commit the crimes or otherwise facilitated the commission of the offences. This will be the case in the vast majority of instances. While technically not perpetrators, accomplices in the United States may be punished as severely as perpetrators, so the distinction between perpetrators and accomplices in this context is of little, if any, practical importance.[29] As a result, there has been no need to develop the doctrine of 'perpetrator behind the perpetrator' in America. Those who are in control of an organisation will be liable for the crimes committed by the members of the organisation as long as their acts amount to either encouragement or facilitation of the crimes. Furthermore, such masterminds may be punished as severely as the actual perpetrators even if they are technically considered accomplices.

---

26   See, for example, Hans Heinrich Jescheck and Thomas Weigend, *Tratado de Derecho Penal: Parte General* 722 (trans. Olmedo Cardenete, 5th edn, Comares 2002).

27   Ibid.

28   Ibid.

29   This is an issue that may be of importance in civil law countries, as some accomplices are punished considerably less than perpetrators in several civil law jurisdictions.

Joint Principals

Perpetrators can act either alone or with others. In civil law jurisdictions, a perpetrator who acts alone is simply a perpetrator. However, if the perpetrator commits the offence along with others, then all of the persons involved become 'co-perpetrators' or joint principals. As a general rule, a person is a joint principal in civil law jurisdictions if she acts with others pursuant to a common plan and the contribution of each one of the parties is essential to the commission of the offence. If the contribution of one of the parties is not essential to the commission of the offence, then that party should be treated as an accomplice rather than as a perpetrator.

The category of joint principals has no direct analogue in the United States. In America the main distinction is between perpetrators and accomplices. Both common law and Model Penal Code approaches to criminal participation make no formal distinction between perpetrators who carry out the crime alone and those who do so jointly with other co-perpetrators. This, of course, does not mean that cases that would be treated as instances of co-perpetration or joint perpetration are not punished in American jurisdictions. Actors who jointly engage in conduct that is constitutive of the crime would be treated as either principals in the first (if they were present at the scene of the crime) or second degree (if they were not present at the scene of the crime) at common law or as perpetrators or accomplices under the Model Penal Code.

It is often debated in civil law jurisdictions whether a person should be treated as a joint principal or as an accomplice. The determinative factor in such debates is often whether the actor's contribution was necessary or essential for the consummation of the offence. If the actor's contribution was essential, the law would treat the party as a joint principal. However, if the contribution was not essential, the law would usually treat the party as an accomplice. In such jurisdictions the debate may be of some practical import, given that in many civil law countries certain accomplices cannot be punished as severely as perpetrators.

In contrast, deciding whether someone ought to be punished as a (joint) perpetrator or as an accomplice is of little practical importance in the United States. Since American criminal law authorises punishing accomplices as severely as perpetrators, there is little need to develop fine distinctions between those that should be punished as joint perpetrators who actually commit the crime and those who should be punished as accomplices who merely help others carry out the conduct that is constitutive of the offence.

Secondary Participation

In the United States, secondary participants are called accomplices. An accomplice is a person who aids or abets another in the commission of an offence. At common law, such aiders and abettors were considered either principals in the second degree if they were present at the scene of the crime or accessories before the fact if they were not present. The Model Penal Code eliminated such distinctions. As a result, the Code considers that all those who encourage or help another in the commission of the offence are accomplices regardless of whether they were present when the perpetrator actually carried out the conduct constitutive of the offence.[30]

---

30   Model Penal Code §2.06(3).

Conduct Elements of Accomplice Liability

The conduct element of complicity is encouraging or rendering aid to the person who commits the offence. A person may encourage the perpetrator in many different ways. The person might, for example, promise to pay the perpetrator money if the offence is committed. The person may also advise the perpetrator as to how to commit the crime.[31] The person may also generally encourage the perpetrator by words or gestures designed to strengthen the perpetrator's resolve. Physical aid may also be rendered in different ways. The person may, for example, provide the perpetrator with the gun or the car that will be used during the commission of the offence.[32] Furthermore, it is usually held that any aid or encouragement provided is sufficient to satisfy the conduct requirement of complicity liability. It is therefore not necessary that the aid or encouragement be considered a 'but for' cause of the criminal result.[33]

One particularly thorny issue has to do with whether a person's mere presence at the scene of the crime is enough to hold him liable for accomplice liability. The general rule is that mere presence is not enough for imposition of accomplice liability. As a result, standing by while someone else abuses a child is not enough for liability if the person who stood by had no special duty to prevent the commission of the offence.[34] This does not mean, however, that mere presence is irrelevant to assessing accomplice liability. It is often held that presence coupled with some act or omission that in some way aids or encourages the commission of the offence is enough for accomplice liability. The British case of *Wilcox v. Jeffery* is frequently cited by American courts and commentators as illustrative of this matter.[35] In *Wilcox*, the defendant was charged with being an accomplice to the perpetrator's crime of staging an illegal concert. The perpetrator was a famous musician who held a concert although he knew that he had been denied the visa that was necessary for him to lawfully enter the country and perform. The defendant was aware of this fact, but nevertheless bought a ticket to assist the concert. He also applauded and cheered on the defendant while the performance was taking place. The court held that the defendant was liable as an accomplice.[36] Liability followed from his presence at the concert hall *plus* his various acts of encouragement such as buying the ticket for the concert and applauding and cheering on the defendant's performance.

Given that mere presence alone is typically not enough to establish accomplice liability, an actor's failure to prevent the commission of a crime by another is generally not enough to trigger complicity liability.[37] Nevertheless, liability may be imposed if the person who fails to prevent the offence had a legal duty to make a proper effort to do so.[38] A typical case is that of the parent who witnesses someone else abuse the parent's child and does nothing to prevent the abuse.[39]

A more complicated case arises when a police officer witnesses and fails to prevent the commission of a serious crime such as robbery, burglary or homicide. This is an important but undertheorised issue. According to the drafters of the Model Penal Code, a 'police officer or watchman who closes his eyes to a robbery or burglary [and] fails to present an obstacle to its commission' should be held liable as an accomplice as long as he acted with the purpose of

---

31 LaFave (n 4) §13.2(a).
32 Ibid.
33 *State ex rel. Martin v. Tally*, 15 So. 722 (1894).
34 See for example, *Pope v. State*, 396 A.2d 1054 (1979).
35 [1951] 1 All ER 464 (King's Bench Division).
36 Ibid.
37 *State v. Powell*, 83 S.E. 310 (1914).
38 Model Penal Code §2.06(3)(iii).
39 See for example, *State v. Walden*, 293 S.E.2d 780 (1982).

promoting or facilitating the perpetration of the crime.[40] While there is scant case law on this issue, the high court of Puerto Rico recently held that a police officer may be held liable as an accomplice to homicide if he failed to prevent the killing of an innocent human being and he had enough time to do so.[41]

Culpability Elements of Complicity

There is much debate as to what is the culpability element of accomplice liability. While there is general consensus that one who purposely aids or encourages another to commit an offence is liable as an accomplice, it is unclear whether providing aid with knowledge that such aid facilitates the commission of an offence is punishable as complicity. It is even more controversial whether recklessly or negligently engaging in acts that facilitate the commission of an offence may trigger accomplice liability.

According to the Model Penal Code, liability for complicity is appropriate only if the actor had the purpose of promoting or facilitating the commission of the offence.[42] The Code defines purpose as having the conscious objective of bringing about the prohibited conduct.[43] The Model Penal Code approach thus excludes knowing assistance or encouragement from the scope of complicity liability. Therefore, under the Code providing a knife to someone whom the actor knew was going to use the knife to kill another would not trigger complicity liability. The Code's solution is not accepted in all jurisdictions. A contrary view was forcefully defended by Judge Parker in *Backun v. United States*.[44] According to Judge Parker, 'one who sells a gun to another knowing that he is buying it to commit a murder, would hardly escape conviction as an accessory to the murder by showing that he received full price for the gun' and therefore did not have a stake in the consummation of the murder or the purpose of facilitating the commission of the offence.[45]

A similar position was initially defended by the drafters of the Model Penal Code. The original draft of the Code expanded the scope of accomplice liability to cover knowing assistance or encouragement as long as the aid or encouragement provided by the actor 'substantially facilitated' the commission of the offence.[46] Had the proposal been accepted, knowing assistance or encouragement would trigger accomplice liability regardless of whether the assistance rendered was substantial, whereas knowing assistance or encouragement would trigger accomplice liability *only* if the assistance or encouragement was substantial. The original proposal was ultimately rejected by the members of the American Law Institute. Nevertheless, several American jurisdictions followed the lead of the original draft of the Code and therefore do criminalise knowing assistance or encouragement. Perhaps the most salient example is New York, which provides that a person is criminally liable when 'believing it probable that he is rendering aid to a person who intends to commit a crime, he engages in conduct which provides such persons with means or opportunity for the commission thereof'.[47] Strictly speaking, engaging in this type of conduct is not considered a form of accomplice liability in New York.[48] Rather, it is considered a freestanding offence called

---

40   Comments to Model Penal Code §2.06(3)(a)(iii), 320.
41   *Pueblo v. Sustache*, 176 D.P.R. 250 (2009).
42   Model Penal Code §2.06(3)(a).
43   Model Penal Code §2.02.
44   112 F.2d 635, 637 (4th Cir., 1940).
45   Ibid.
46   Comments to Model Penal Code §2.06(3)(a), 314-15.
47   N.Y. Penal Law §115.00.
48   LaFave (n 4) §13.2(d).

'criminal facilitation' that is punished less severely than the standard forms of complicity liability. Note furthermore that the conduct element of knowing criminal facilitation is heightened in comparison to the conduct element of standard accomplice liability. While any assistance, however trivial, suffices to satisfy the conduct element of standard accomplice liability, New York's criminal facilitation statute requires that the aid rendered consist in either providing the means to commit the offence or the opportunity to do so.[49] Several states have enacted similar provisions.[50]

Another important issue regarding the culpability element of complicity liability has to do with the mental element that the accomplice must have when the crime committed by the perpetrator is a result crime. Assume, for example, that the passenger of a car purposely encourages the driver of the vehicle to drive recklessly at speeds considerably faster than what would be appropriate under the circumstances. As a result of his reckless conduct, the driver is involved in an accident which causes the death of a person. The driver is surely liable for reckless manslaughter. However, is the passenger liable as an accomplice to the driver's reckless killing?

American jurisdictions are split with regard to this issue. Some hold that a person may not be held liable as an accomplice to a crime requiring that a result be caused recklessly.[51] The underlying reasoning is that complicity liability requires that the accomplice purposely render aid or encourage the commission of the crime and that a person cannot purposely aid the commission of a reckless offence, for purpose and recklessness are mutually exclusive. It is either your conscious objective to cause the result (purpose) or it is not your conscious objective to cause the result although you are aware that there is a substantial likelihood that the result will take place (recklessness). Acceptance of the proposition that an actor can purposely aid a reckless act is tantamount, in other words, to accepting that a person can intend to aid an unintentional act. This strikes some courts as a contradiction.

In contrast, other jurisdictions hold that a person may be held liable as an accomplice to a reckless result crime. Furthermore, it has been held that an actor may be accountable as an accomplice to a negligent result crime. The rationale underlying this conclusion is that accomplice liability requires that the person purposely aid or encourage the perpetrator's *conduct*, but not that the person have the purpose of producing a certain *result*. In the driving example, the perpetrator's conduct was driving at reckless speeds. Note that the passenger did, in fact, *purposely* encourage such conduct. According to some courts, this is enough to satisfy the culpability element of accomplice liability. But what about the passenger's culpability with regard to the result? Those who defend imposing accomplice liability in cases such as these argue that the person may be held liable as an accomplice for the result crime as long as he had the purpose to aid or encourage the perpetrator's conduct *and* if 'he acts with the kind of culpability, if any, with respect to [the] result that is sufficient for the commission of the offense'.[52]

Returning to the driving example, the passenger would be liable as an accomplice to the reckless homicide as long as he had the purpose of encouraging the driver's reckless driving and he was reckless with regard to the possibility of someone dying as a result of the reckless driving. The same logic would apply to cases in which the actor is charged with being an accomplice to a negligent result crime such as negligent homicide. According to this approach, the person may be held liable as an accomplice to a negligent homicide as long as she had the purpose of encouraging the perpetrator's conduct *and* she acted negligently with regard to the possibility

---

49   Ibid.

50   See Kentucky Penal Code §506.080; Arizona Penal Code §13-1004; Tennessee Penal Code §39-11-403.

51   See for example, *People v. Marshall*, 106 N.W.2d 842 (1961).

52   Model Penal Code §2.06(4).

of death. This is the solution followed by the Model Penal Code. The Code drafters also make clear that this approach allows for the accomplice to be convicted of a different crime than the perpetrator. Ultimately, as the drafters of the Model Penal Code explain, while the perpetrator's conduct is attributed or imputed to the accomplice, 'the liability of each [is] measured by his own degree of culpability toward the result'.[53] Consequently, it is possible for the accomplice to be held liable for a crime that is the same, less or more aggravated than the crime that the perpetrator actually committed. If, for example, the accomplice purposely encouraged the reckless driving, it is possible for the accomplice to be held liable for reckless homicide if he was *aware* that the driver's conduct created a substantial and unjustifiable risk of death.[54] The driver, in turn, may be held liable for murder – a more serious crime than reckless homicide – if he was aware of the risk and acted with gross indifference to the value of human life.[55] However, the driver may be held liable for negligent homicide – a less serious crime than reckless homicide – if he was *not* aware that his conduct created a substantial risk of death.

Finally, a handful of American jurisdictions hold accomplices liable for all reasonably foreseeable crimes committed by the perpetrator regardless of whether the accomplice acted with the kind of culpability demanded by the definition of the crime with which he is charged. The leading case cited in support of this approach is *People v. Luparello*.[56] The defendant in the case asked several of his friends to extract information from a certain man 'at any cost'. The friends visited the man and killed him after unsuccessfully trying to extract the information from him. Although the defendant was not present when the friends visited the victim, he was charged with being an accomplice to the murder. The defendant claimed that his plan was merely to scare the victim. He further argued that he should not be held liable as an accomplice to murder because he did not have the purpose of killing the victim. Nevertheless, the California Court of Appeals convicted him as an accomplice to murder arguing that 'liability is extended to reach the actual crime committed, rather than the planned or "intended" crime, on the policy [that] aiders and abettors should be responsible for the criminal harms they have naturally, probably and foreseeably put in motion'.[57]

While the *Luparello* approach is followed in some states, a majority of jurisdictions reject it. The position is also rejected by the Model Penal Code. According to the drafters of the Code, accomplices should be liable only for crimes committed that were 'fairly envisaged in the purposes of the association'.[58] Consequently, the drafters believe that 'when a wholly different crime has been committed, thus involving conduct not within the conscious objectives of the accomplice, he is not liable for it' and that 'the liability of the accomplice ought not be extended beyond the purpose that he shares'.[59]

---

53   Comments to Model Penal Code §2.06, 321.

54   This is how the Model Penal Code defines recklessness. See Model Penal Code §2.02(2)(c).

55   Reckless homicide is considered murder under the Model Penal Code if, in addition to acting recklessly, the person acts with gross indifference to the value of human life. Model Penal Code §210.2(1)(b).

56   231 Cal. Rptr. 832 (1987).

57   Ibid.

58   Comments to Model Penal Code §2.06, 310-13.

59   Ibid.

Specific Issue: Joint Criminal Enterprise and *Pinkerton* Liability

The origins of the doctrine of joint criminal enterprise may be traced back to English common law. Nevertheless, the doctrine gained much international attention when various international tribunals invoked a variation of it in order to deal with the problems inherent in group criminality.[60] Pursuant to this doctrine, those who agree to commit a crime and engage in acts in furtherance of the agreement are jointly liable as perpetrators for the crimes committed by the group.[61] In its most extreme form, joint criminal enterprise authorises holding those who agree to commit a crime liable for reasonably foreseeable offences committed by the group regardless of whether they were envisaged in the original plan and of how trivial or insubstantial the individual member's contributions are.[62] This expansive version of the doctrine has received substantial criticism in the scholarly literature.[63] Nevertheless, it continues to play an important role in the jurisprudence of several international tribunals.[64]

Conspiracy in General

American criminal law punishes the 'conspiracy' to commit a crime as an autonomous offence. In its original formulation, conspiracy was viewed as a freestanding offence rather than as a form of accessorial liability. In essence, the crime of conspiracy consists in the agreement by two or more persons to commit an offence.[65] In its basic form, the conduct element of the crime of conspiracy is the mere agreement to commit a crime in the future.[66] Nothing else is needed to establish liability for conspiracy. More specifically, the standard form of conspiracy liability does not require that the actors perform any acts – substantial or not – in furtherance of the conspiracy. The crime is thus consummated at the time that the minds meet and an agreement to commit a future crime is reached.[67] It is also important to note that at common law there had to be an actual meeting of the minds in order for the agreement to be punished as conspiracy. Therefore, conspiracy liability would not attach if one of the parties was feigning agreement.[68] Nevertheless, the Model Penal Code rejects this approach. According to the Code, a person is liable for conspiracy as long as he believed that a real agreement had been reached. Whether or not the co-conspirator feigned agreement is thus irrelevant to liability for conspiracy under the Code.[69]

Some jurisdictions now require that one of the actors engage in an overt act in furtherance of the conspiracy in order for liability for conspiracy to be imposed.[70] Nevertheless, it is only

60   See, generally, *Prosecutor v. Vasiljevic*, ICTY (Appeals Chamber), judgment of 29 November 2002.

61   See, generally, Gerhard Werle, *Principles of International Criminal Law* (Asser Press 2009) 174.

62   *Prosecutor v. Kvocka*, ICTY (Appeals Chamber), judgment of 28 February 2005.

63   Werle (n 61) 175.

64   See for example, *Prosecutor v. Simba*, ICTR (Trial Chamber), judgment of 13 December 2005; *Prosecutor v. Brima*, SCSL (Trial Chamber), judgment of 20 June 2007.

65   For more on the nature of the agreement that gives rise to conspiracy liability see, generally, *United States v. James*, 528 F.2d 999 (5th Cir., 1976).

66   Ibid.

67   Ibid.

68   This is called the 'bilateral agreement' approach to conspiracy. See for example, *United States v. Delgado*, 631 F.3d 685 (5th Cir. 2011).

69   The Model Penal Code formulation is called the 'unilateral agreement' approach to conspiracy. See for example, *García v. State*, 394 N.E.2d 106 (1979).

70   See, for example, *Yates v. United States*, 354 U.S. 298, 334 (1957).

necessary that one party to the conspiracy engage in an overt act. Once this happens, the overt act is imputed to the rest of the members of the conspiracy and they can all be held liable for conspiracy regardless of who actually engaged in the overt act.

Rationale for Punishing Conspiracy and Merger Between Conspiracy and Consummated Offence

There is some debate as to what is the rationale for punishing conspiracy. Some argue that it is best to think of conspiracy as an inchoate offence that simply criminalises certain preparatory acts that might otherwise not be criminalised pursuant to the general doctrine of attempt liability.[71] On the other hand, some argue that conspiracy is an autonomous offence that is criminalised not as an inchoate crime, but rather as a distinct course of conduct that is more dangerous than a run of the mill inchoate crime. According to this theory, the risk inherent in the kind of group criminality that the offence of conspiracy is designed to curtail is qualitatively different than the risk inherent when someone who acts alone engages in acts that are criminalised as an attempt or some other inchoate crime.

Whether the offence of conspiracy is viewed as a type of inchoate crime or as an autonomous offence that is designed to curb the special danger inherent in group criminality is of substantial practical import. As a general rule, jurisdictions that view conspiracy as an inchoate crime typically hold that the offence of conspiracy merges with the completed offence if the conspirators successfully consummate the crime.[72] Therefore, in such jurisdictions a defendant cannot be punished both for a completed offence and a conspiracy to commit the offence in much the same manner as they cannot be convicted of a consummated offence and an attempt to commit the same offence. This is the position adopted in the Model Penal Code.[73] In contrast, jurisdictions that view conspiracy as an autonomous offence that seeks to inhibit the special dangers inherent in group criminality often hold that conspiracy does not merge with the completed offence and conspirators can thus be held liable both for the consummated offence and for conspiracy to commit the same offence.[74]

Conspiracy as a Form of Accessorial Liability: The Controversial Pinkerton Doctrine

Although there is no necessary connection between conspiracy liability and accomplice liability,[75] the United States Supreme Court held in the (in)famous *Pinkerton* case that co-conspirators are liable as *accomplices* for all reasonably foreseeable substantive crimes committed by fellow co-conspirators in furtherance of the conspiracy.[76] Imagine, for example, that A and B agree to kill C. The next day, the police arrest A for an unrelated crime. Six months later, while A is still in jail pursuant to pretrial detention, B finally kills C. According to the *Pinkerton* doctrine, A is liable not only for conspiracy to murder C, but also for C's murder as an accomplice to B. Liability for murder follows under *Pinkerton* regardless of whether A engaged in an act in furtherance of the conspiracy and regardless of whether it was physically impossible for A to help B kill the victim

71 This is how conspiracy is viewed in the Model Penal Code. See Model Penal Code §§1.07(1)(b) and 5.05(3).
72 See for example, *State v. Hardison*, 492 A.2d 1009 (1985).
73 Model Penal Code §5.05(3).
74 See for example, N.Y. Jur.2d, Crim Law §2604 nn 86-93.
75 Strictly speaking, conspiracy is *not* a type of accessorial liability that is imposed for aiding or encouraging the consummated crimes of others. Rather, it is either a kind of inchoate crime or an autonomous offence that is designed to inhibit the special danger inherent in group criminality.
76 *Pinkerton v. United States*, 328 U.S. 650 (1946).

given that A was in jail. The only limitation is that the crime committed by B must be reasonably foreseeable in light of the conspiratorial agreement. As a result, A could also be held liable under *Pinkerton* of a host of crimes that B might commit in furtherance of the original agreement, such as illegal gun possession, fleeing or evading police and even burglary (if A illegally entered C's home with the intent of killing C).

Many American jurisdictions reject *Pinkerton*, as does the Model Penal Code. According to the drafters of the Code, the *Pinkerton* approach ought to be rejected because 'law would lose all sense of just proportion if simply because of the conspiracy itself each [co-conspirator] were held accountable for thousands of additional offenses of which he was completely unaware and which he did not influence at all'.[77] According to the Model Penal Code, conspiracy is not an autonomous source of accessorial liability. Conspirators may be punished as accomplices only if the acts that they engage in are sufficient to satisfy the conduct and culpability elements of accomplice liability. That is, conspirators may be punished as accomplices of crimes committed by other conspirators only if they aid or encourage the commission of the offence and they act with the purpose of aiding or encouraging the offence and whatever culpability with respect to the result is sufficient for the commission of the crime.[78]

Effect of Errors and Transferred Malice/Aberratio ictus Scenarios in the Person of one Participant on the Liability of the Other Participants

At common law, accomplice liability was viewed as derivative from the liability of the perpetrator.[79] This explains why the early common law rule was that an accomplice could only be tried after the perpetrator was found criminally liable.[80] This view has implications for cases in which the perpetrator's state of mind is different from the accomplice's state of mind. Assume, for example, that A took an umbrella that belonged to someone else in the mistaken belief that it was his umbrella. Furthermore, assume that B helped the perpetrator take the umbrella. Finally, assume that B did not believe that the umbrella belonged to A and that B was unaware that A mistakenly believed that the umbrella belonged to him. In this case, A is not liable for theft because his mistake negates the culpability required for the commission of the offence.[81] May B nevertheless be held liable for complicity to theft? Given that at common law accomplice liability is viewed as derivative from the principal's liability, B may not be held liable for theft because the perpetrator did not satisfy the elements of the offence of theft. Since accomplice liability is derivative from the liability of the principal, B may not be held liable as an accomplice to theft if A did not engage in conduct that amounts to theft, *even if B did, in fact, believe that he was helping someone else engage in theft*.[82] Furthermore, viewing complicity liability as derivative from the perpetrator's liability leads to the conclusion that an accomplice may not be held liable for a more serious offence than the perpetrator. Since the traditional common law view is that the accomplice's liability is parasitic on

---

77 Comment to Model Penal Code §2.06(3), 307.
78 Ibid.
79 Paul H. Robinson, *Criminal Law* (Aspen 1997) 323.
80 See for example, *State v. Graham*, 182 So. 711 (1938).
81 The perpetrator must be at least reckless with regard to whether the umbrella belongs to him. Assuming that the perpetrator honestly believed that the umbrella belonged to him, such an honest belief would negate recklessness.
82 Nevertheless, B may be held liable for attempted complicity to theft.

the perpetrator's liability, it would make little sense to punish the accomplice for a graver offence than the one that the perpetrator actually committed.[83]

The Model Penal Code represents a departure from the traditional common law view that complicity liability is derivative from the liability of the perpetrator. According to the Code, the effect of complicity liability is to attribute the *conduct* of the principal to the accomplice. Therefore, the accomplice can be held liable for murder even if he did not actually kill the victim because the perpetrator's *conduct* (shooting the victim, for example) is imputed to the accomplice as a result of the rules that govern accomplice liability. Nevertheless, the drafters of the Code make clear that accomplice liability will ultimately depend on the accomplice's culpability with regard to the elements of the offence. That is, the perpetrator's culpable mental state is not imputed to the accomplice. As a result, 'the accomplice may be convicted of a different degree of crime than the principal actor', depending on whether the accomplice acted with a more or less culpable mental state than the perpetrator.[84]

This approach is best illustrated by the California case of *People v. McCoy*.[85] The perpetrator in *McCoy* shot and killed the victim in the good faith but unreasonable belief that he was doing so in self-defence. Consequently, the perpetrator could at most be held liable for manslaughter because in California an unreasonable but good faith belief that force is necessary pursuant to self-defence reduces what would otherwise be murder to manslaughter. Does this mean that the defendant charged as an accomplice to the perpetrator's killing in *McCoy* may not be convicted of a more serious offence than manslaughter? The *McCoy* court ruled that there was no such bar and that the accomplice could be convicted of a more serious offence than the perpetrator because 'when a person, with the mental state necessary for an aider and abettor, helps or induces another to kill, that person's guilt is determined by the combined acts of all the participants as well as that person's own *mens rea*'.[86] Consequently, the Court held that 'if that person's *mens rea* is more culpable than another's, that person's guilt may be greater even if the other might be deemed the actual perpetrator'.[87] The same is true the other way around. Under the Model Penal Code complicity rules, an accomplice may be liable for a less serious crime than the perpetrator. Once again, what is imputed to the accomplice is the conduct of the perpetrator, not his mental state. Therefore, perpetrator and accomplice are ultimately held liable for crimes that reflect their own culpable mental state. If the accomplice acted with a less culpable mental state than the perpetrator, the accomplice will be held liable for a less serious crime that reflects his lesser culpability. In *Moore v. Lowe*, for example, the defendant hired a killer to kill her husband. The court held that even if the perpetrator (the hired killer) is guilty of murder because he acted with malice, the accomplice (the spouse who hired the killer) may be liable for the lesser offence of manslaughter if she hired the killer while under the heat of passion.[88] In sum, under the Model Penal Code formulation of complicity the culpability of the different participants simply do not transfer to the rest. Each participant is held liable in accordance with his or her culpability, which may or may not be the same as the rest of the participants, including the perpetrator.

Another interesting scenario arises when the accomplice intends to help the perpetrator harm a certain person, but it turns out that the perpetrator accidentally harms a different individual. Assume, for example, that A gives a gun to B with the purpose of helping B shoot and kill C.

---

83 Robinson (n 79) 345-46.
84 Comments to Model Penal Code §2.06, 327.
85 24 P.3d 1210 (2001), 1216.
86 Ibid.
87 Ibid.
88 180 S.E. 1 (W. Va. 1935).

Although B shoots C with intent to kill, the shot misses its target and instead hits and kills D. Is A liable as an accomplice to B's killing of D in spite of the fact that A's intent was to help B kill C? While there is scant case law regarding this matter, courts seem to be willing to apply the common law doctrine of transferred intent in such cases.[89] As a result, the accomplice will likely be held liable as long as he had the purpose to bring about the general harm caused by the perpetrator (for example death in homicide cases) regardless of whether he intended to harm the victim who was actually harmed.[90]

Withdrawal from Participation

Even if an accomplice engages in acts that are sufficient to trigger accomplice liability, most American jurisdictions provide that an accomplice may avoid punishment by the timely termination of his participation in the crime.[91] In order for the accomplice's termination to defeat liability it must take place before the perpetrator consummates the crime. Furthermore, it must either 'wholly deprive [his complicity] of effectiveness in the commission of the offense or give timely warning to law enforcement authorities or otherwise make proper efforts to prevent the commission of the offense'.[92] What amounts to sufficient termination depends on the type of assistance given by the perpetrator. If the aid given by the perpetrator consists in providing goods or services, a statement of withdrawal from the criminal enterprise is not generally sufficient to constitute termination.[93] In such cases the accomplice must do what is necessary to get back the goods that he supplied or to deprive the services that he provided of effectiveness. In contrast, when the assistance provided by the accomplice was requesting that a crime be committed or encouraging the commission of an offence, 'countermanding disapproval may suffice to nullify its influence, provided it is heard in time to allow reconsideration by those planning to commit the crime'.[94] Sometimes the only thing that an accomplice can do to prevent the crime is to make independent efforts to stop the commission of the offence. In such cases, the accomplice may establish termination by alerting the police in a timely manner or by making other proper efforts to prevent the crime.[95]

Corporate Liability: Basic Rules

Although imposition of corporate criminal liability remains deeply controversial in many civil law countries, in America corporations have been held criminally liable since at least the beginning of the twentieth century.[96] The common law approach to corporate criminal liability in the United States is derived from the tort doctrine of *respondeat superior*. According to this view, a corporation may be held criminally liable for the acts of its agents if 'an agent (1) commits a crime, (2) within

---

89 See for example, *In Re T.K.*, 849 N.E.2d 286 (2006).
90 Ibid.
91 See for example, Model Penal Code §2.06(6)(c).
92 Ibid.
93 Comments to Model Penal Code §2.06(6)(c), 326.
94 Ibid. See, also, *State v. Peterson*, 4 N.W.2d 826 (1942).
95 Ibid.
96 See for example, *New York Central & Hudson River Railroad Co. v United States*, 212 U.S. 481 (1909).

the scope of employment, [and] (3) with the intent to benefit the corporation'.[97] The imposition of corporate liability under this approach is quite broad. It has been held, for example, that a corporation is liable for the acts of its employees made within the scope of their employment even if such acts are contrary to the corporation's policies as long as they were performed with the intent to benefit the corporation.[98]

As is so often the case, the Model Penal Code rejects the common law approach. The Model Penal Code distinguishes between imposition of corporate liability for violations and offences defined by a statute other than the Code and imposition of corporate liability for true crimes defined as such in the Code.[99] While the Model Penal Code tracks the common law *respondeat superior* approach when the offence charged is a violation or a non-code crime, it exonerates the corporation of liability if a 'high managerial agent having supervisory responsibility over the subject matter of the offense employed due diligence to prevent its commission'.[100]

Furthermore, although the Code adopts a version of *respondeat superior* when the offence charged is minor, it altogether rejects this theory as a basis for corporate liability when the offence charged is conduct defined in the Code as a crime rather than as a violation. According to the Code, when the offence charged is a crime corporate liability may be imposed only if 'the commission of the offense was authorized, requested, commanded, performed or recklessly tolerated by the board of directors or by a high managerial agent acting in behalf of the corporation within the scope of his office or employment'.[101] This approach is considerably more restrictive than the *respondeat superior* approach to corporate criminal liability.

A related issue has to do with the liability of corporate officials for the criminal acts of their employees. Some jurisdictions impose vicarious liability on corporate officials for the offences committed by their employees as long as the official had authority or responsibility over the activities that gave rise to the criminal act.[102] This has come to be known as the *responsible corporate officer* doctrine. Nevertheless, an official may escape liability if he can demonstrate that he was 'powerless to prevent' the violation.[103] It seems, however, that showing that the official exercised reasonable care is not enough to defeat liability.[104] Some courts have thus defined the duty of corporate officials in this context as one requiring that they exercise 'extraordinary care'.[105]

The Model Penal Code adopts a different approach. The Code rejects imposing vicarious liability on corporate officials for the acts of their employees. Instead, liability is imposed in such cases only if the official having responsibility over the activities that gave rise to the conduct constitutive of the offence was reckless in failing to prevent the crimes.[106]

---

97   Note, 'Developments in the Law: Corporate Crime: Regulating Corporate Behavior Through Criminal Sanctions' (1979) 92 Harvard Law Review 1227, 1247.

98   See for example, *United States v. Hilton Hotels Corp.*, 467 F.2d 1000 (1972).

99   Model Penal Code §2.07(1)(a).

100   Model Penal Code §2.07(5).

101   Model Penal Code §2.07(1)(c).

102   See, for example, *United States v. Park*, 421 U.S. 658 (1975).

103   Robinson (n 79) 358.

104   Ibid.

105   *United States v. New England Grocers Supply Co.*, 488 F. Supp. 230 (1980).

106   Model Penal Code §2.07(6)(b).

Sentencing Regime for Participants

American criminal law makes no formal distinction between accomplices and perpetrators in terms of the maximum amount of punishment that can be imposed on one or the other. Therefore, as a general rule, accomplices may be punished as severely as perpetrators. Nevertheless, the sentencing judge has discretion to punish accomplices less than perpetrators if she believes that the circumstances surrounding the criminal act warrant making such a determination. The sentencing judge also has discretion to punish some accomplices more or less depending on their personal blameworthiness and other relevant factors. Note, however, that whether to punish some accomplices less severely than others or to punish accomplices in general less severely than perpetrators is entirely up to the sentencing judge. There is no mitigation of punishment as a matter of right, even when the contributions of the participant are trivial.[107] The United States Sentencing Guidelines do provide for a 'downwards adjustment' in offence level if the defendant is a 'minimal participant' in the offence.[108] These guidelines, however, are merely advisory and are therefore not binding on the sentencing judge.[109] It thus continues to be the case that accomplices may be punished as severely as perpetrators, even when the conduct giving rise to accomplice liability is trivial.

---

107   Joshua Dressler, 'Reforming Complicity Law: Trivial Assistance as a Lesser Offense' (2008) 5 Ohio State Journal of Criminal Law 427. It bears mentioning that Professor Dressler favours punishing trivial assistance less than non-trivial assistance. Alas, Dressler's position does not reflect the current state of American law regarding this issue.

108   U.S. Sentencing Guidelines Manual §3B1.2 (2007).

109   *United States v. Booker*, 543 U.S. 220 (2005).

Index